Lecture Notes in Artificial Intelligence 8473

Subseries of Lecture Notes in Computer Science

LNAI Series Editors

Randy Goebel
 University of Alberta, Edmonton, Canada
Yuzuru Tanaka
 Hokkaido University, Sapporo, Japan
Wolfgang Wahlster
 DFKI and Saarland University, Saarbrücken, Germany

LNAI Founding Series Editor

Joerg Siekmann
 DFKI and Saarland University, Saarbrücken, Germany

Yves Demazeau   Franco Zambonelli
Juan M. Corchado   Javier Bajo (Eds.)

Advances in Practical Applications of Heterogeneous Multi-Agent Systems

The PAAMS Collection

12th International Conference, PAAMS 2014
Salamanca, Spain, June 4-6, 2014
Proceedings

Volume Editors

Yves Demazeau
Centre National de la Recherche Scientifique
Grenoble, France
E-mail: yves.demazeau@imag.fr

Franco Zambonelli
Università degli Studi di Modena e Reggio Emilia
Reggio Emilia, Italy
E-mail: franco.zambonelli@unimore.it

Juan M. Corchado
Universidad de Salamanca, Spain
E-mail: corchado@usal.es

Javier Bajo
Universidad Politécnica de Madrid, Spain
E-mail: javier.bajo@upm.es

ISSN 0302-9743   e-ISSN 1611-3349
ISBN 978-3-319-07550-1   e-ISBN 978-3-319-07551-8
DOI 10.1007/978-3-319-07551-8
Springer Cham Heidelberg New York Dordrecht London

Library of Congress Control Number: 2014939855

LNCS Sublibrary: SL 7 – Artificial Intelligence

© Springer International Publishing Switzerland 2014
This work is subject to copyright. All rights are reserved by the Publisher, whether the whole or part of the material is concerned, specifically the rights of translation, reprinting, reuse of illustrations, recitation, broadcasting, reproduction on microfilms or in any other physical way, and transmission or information storage and retrieval, electronic adaptation, computer software, or by similar or dissimilar methodology now known or hereafter developed. Exempted from this legal reservation are brief excerpts in connection with reviews or scholarly analysis or material supplied specifically for the purpose of being entered and executed on a computer system, for exclusive use by the purchaser of the work. Duplication of this publication or parts thereof is permitted only under the provisions of the Copyright Law of the Publisher's location, in ist current version, and permission for use must always be obtained from Springer. Permissions for use may be obtained through RightsLink at the Copyright Clearance Center. Violations are liable to prosecution under the respective Copyright Law.
The use of general descriptive names, registered names, trademarks, service marks, etc. in this publication does not imply, even in the absence of a specific statement, that such names are exempt from the relevant protective laws and regulations and therefore free for general use.
While the advice and information in this book are believed to be true and accurate at the date of publication, neither the authors nor the editors nor the publisher can accept any legal responsibility for any errors or omissions that may be made. The publisher makes no warranty, express or implied, with respect to the material contained herein.

Typesetting: Camera-ready by author, data conversion by Scientific Publishing Services, Chennai, India

Printed on acid-free paper

Springer is part of Springer Science+Business Media (www.springer.com)

Preface

Research on agents and multi-agent systems has matured during the last decade and many effective applications of this technology are now deployed. An international forum to present and discuss the latest scientific developments and their effective applications, to assess the impact of the approach, and to facilitate technology transfer, has become a necessity and was created a few years ago.

PAAMS, the International Conference on Practical Applications of Agents and Multi-Agent Systems, is the international yearly event for presenting, discussing, and disseminating the latest developments and the most important outcomes related to real-world applications. It provides a unique opportunity to bring multi-disciplinary experts, academics, and practitioners together to exchange their experience in the development and deployment of agents and multi-agent systems.

This volume presents the papers that were accepted for the 2014 edition of PAAMS. These articles report on the application and validation of agent-based models, methods, and technologies in a number of key application areas, including: agent-oriented software engineering, conversations, motion coordination and unmanned aerial vehicles, Web and service systems, robotics exploration, smart cities and infrastructures, and social systems. Each paper submitted to PAAMS 2014 went through a stringent peer review by three members of the international committee composed of 97 internationally renowned researchers from 26 countries. From the 52 submissions received, 12 were selected for full presentation at the conference; another 14 papers were accepted as short presentations. In addition, a demonstration track featuring innovative and emergent applications of agent and multi-agent systems and technologies in real-world domains was organized. There were 19 demonstrations shown and this volume contains a description of each of them.

We would like to thank all the contributing authors, the members of the Program Committee, the sponsors (IEEE SMC Spain, IBM, AEPIA, AFIA, University of Salamanca and CNRS), and the Organizing Committee for their hard and highly valuable work. Their work helped contribute to the success of the PAAMS 2014 event. Thanks for your help – PAAMS 2014 would not exist without your contribution.

Yves Demazeau
Franco Zambonelli
Juan Manuel Corchado
Javier Bajo

Organization

General Co-chairs

Yves Demazeau	Centre National de la Recherche Scientifique, France
Franco Zambonelli	University of Modena and Reggio Emilia, Italy
Juan M. Corchado	University of Salamanca, Spain
Javier Bajo	Polytechnic University of Madrid, Spain

Advisory Board

Frank Dignum	Utrecht University, The Netherlands
Toru Ishida	University of Kyoto, Japan
Jörg P. Müller	Technische Universität Clausthal, Germany
Juan Pavón	Universidad Complutense de Madrid, Spain
Michal Pěchouček	Czech Technical University in Prague, Czech Republic

Program Committee

Emmanuel Adam	University of Grenoble, France
Carole Adam	University of Grenoble, France
Frederic Amblard	University of Toulouse, France
Francesco Amigoni	Politecnico di Milano, Italy
Javier Bajo	Polytechnic University of Madrid, Spain
Jeremy Baxter	QinetiQ, USA
Michael Berger	Docuware AG, Germany
Olivier Boissier	Ecole Nationale Superieure des Mines de Saint Etienne, France
Vicente Botti	Polytechnic University of Valencia, Spain
Lars Braubach	Universität Hamburg, Germany
Stefano Bromuri	University of Applied Sciences Western Switzerland, Switzerland
Longbing Cao	University of Technology Sydney, Australia
Javier Carbo	University Carlos III of Madrid, Spain
Luis Fernando Castillo	University of Caldas, Colombia
Lawrence Cavedon	RMIT Melbourne, Australia
Pierre Chevaillier	University of Brest, France
Caroline Chopinaud	MASA Group, France
Helder Coelho	University of Lisbon, Portugal
Juan Manuel Corchado	University of Salamanca, Spain

Vincent Corruble   LIP6, Université Pierre et Marie Curie,
                            (Paris 6), France
Keith Decker   University of Delaware, USA
Alexis Drogoul   Institut de Recherche pour le Développement,
                            Vietnam
Julie Dugdale   University of Grenoble, France
Amal Elfallah Seghrouchni University of Paris 6, France
Johannes Fähndrich   Technische Universität Berlin / DAI Labor,
                            Germany
Jose Luis Fernandez
  Marquez   University of Geneva, Italy
Maksims Fiosins   Clausthal University of Technology, Germany
Klaus Fischer   DFKI, Germany
Rubén Fuentes   University Complutense de Madrid, Spain
Javier Gil Quijano   CEA, LIST, LIMA, France
Sylvain Giroux   University of Sherbrooke, Canada
Marie-Pierre Gleizes   University of Toulouse, France
Daniela Godoy   ISISTAN, Argentina
Jorge Gomez-Sanz   University Complutense de Madrid, Spain
Vladimir Gorodetski   University of Saint Petersburg, Russia
Charles Gouin-Vallerand   Télé-Université du Québec, Canada
Salima Hassas   Université Claude Bernard-Lyon1, France
Vincent Hilaire   UTBM, France
Koen Hindriks   University of Delft, The Netherlands
Benjamin Hirsch   Khalifa University, EBTIC,
                            United Arab Emirates
Martin Hofmann   Lockheed Martin, USA
Tom Holvoet   Catholic University of Leuven, Belgium
Shinichi Honiden   National Institute of Informatics Tokyo, Japan
Jomi Fred Hubner   Universidad Federale de Santa Catarina, Brazil
Toru Ishida   University of Kyoto, Japan
Takayuki Ito   Massachusetts Institute of Technology, USA
Michal Jakob   Czech Technical University in Prague,
                            Czech Republic
Vicente Julian   Polytechnic University of Valencia, Spain
Achilles Kameas   University of Patras, Greece
Takahiro Kawamura   Toshiba, Japan
Jeffrey Kephart   IBM T.J. Watson Research Center, USA
Stefan Kirn   Universität Hohenheim, Germany
Franziska Kluegl   University of Örebro, Sweden
Matthias Klusch   DFKI, Germany
Martin Kollingbaum   University of Aberdeen, UK
Ryszard Kowalczyk   Swinburne University of Technology, Australia
Jaroslaw Kozlak   University of Science and Technology
                            in Krakow, Poland
Rene Mandiau   University of Valenciennes, France

Philippe Mathieu	University of Lille, France
Eric Matson	Purdue University, USA
Felipe Meneguzzi	PUCRS, Brazil
Fabien Michel	University of Reims, France
José M. Molina	Universidad Carlos III de Madrid, Spain
Mirko Morandini	University of Trento, Italy
Jean-Pierre Muller	CIRAD, France
Jörg P. Müller	Clausthal University of Technology, Germany
Victor Noel	IRIT, France
Peter Novak	Czech Technical University in Prague, Czech Republic
Akhihiko Ohsuga	University of Electro-Communications, Japan
Eugenio Oliveira	University of Porto, Portugal
Andrea Omicini	University of Bologna, Italy
Sascha Ossowski	University of Rey Juan Carlos, Spain
Julian Padget	University of Bath, UK
Juan Pavon	University Complutense de Madrid, Spain
Paolo Petta	University of Vienna, Austria
Sebastien Picault	Equipe SMAC, (LIFL UMR 8022) - Université Lille 1, France
Alessandro Ricci	University of Bologna, Italy
Juan Antonio Rodriguez Aguilar	AI Research Institute, Spain
Jordi Sabater Mir	IIIA-CSIC, Spain
Silvia Schiaffino	ISISTAN, Argentina
Leonid Sheremetov	Mexican Petroleum Institute, Mexico
Jaime Sichman	University of Sao Paulo, Brazil
Viviane Silva	Universidade Federal Fluminense, Brazil
Elizabeth Sklar	Brooklyn College, City University of New York, USA
Graeme Stevenson	University of St. Andrews, UK
Sonia Suárez	University of A Coruña, Spain
Toshiharu Sugawara	Waseda University, Japan
Patrick Taillandier	UMR IDEES, MTG, France
Paolo Torroni	University of Bologna, Italy
Rainer Unland	University of Duisburg, Germany
Domenico Ursino	University of Reggio Calabria, Italy
László Zsolt Varga	MTA SZTAKI, Hungary
Jacques Verriet	Embedded Systems Institute, The Netherlands
José Villar	University of Oviedo, Spain
Gerhard Weiss	University of Maastricht, The Netherlands
Niek Wijngaards	Thales, D-CIS lab, The Netherlands
Gaku Yamamoto	IBM, Japan

Organizing Committee

Juan M. Corchado (Chair)	University of Salamanca, Spain
Javier Bajo (Co-chair)	Polytechnic University of Madrid, Spain
Juan F. De Paz	University of Salamanca, Spain
Sara Rodríguez	University of Salamanca, Spain
Dante I. Tapia	University of Salamanca, Spain
Fernando de la Prieta Pintado	University of Salamanca, Spain
Davinia Carolina Zato Domínguez	University of Salamanca, Spain
Gabriel Villarrubia González	University of Salamanca, Spain
Antonio Juan Sánchez Martín	University of Salamanca, Spain

PAAMS 2014 Sponsors

Table of Contents

Regular Papers

HPLAN: Facilitating the Implementation of Joint Human-Agent Activities 1
    Sebastian Ahrndt, Philipp Ebert, Johannes Fähndrich, and Sahin Albayrak

Reliable Multi-robot Map Merging of Inaccurate Maps 13
    Ilze Andersone and Agris Nikitenko

Task-Oriented Conversational Behavior of Agents for Collaboration in Human-Agent Teamwork 25
    Mukesh Barange, Alexandre Kabil, Camille De Keukelaere, and Pierre Chevaillier

Agent-Based Simulation of Complex Aviation Incidents by Integrating Different Cognitive Agent Models 38
    Tibor Bosse, Nataliya M. Mogles, and Jan Treur

A Multi-agent Based Optimised Server Selection Scheme for SOC in Pervasive Environment 50
    Bikash Choudhury, Piyali Dey, Animesh Dutta, and Subhrabrata Choudhury

Influence of Participation Rates and Service Level Differentiation on Community Driven Predictions 62
    Rutger Claes, Katrien Van den Berghe, and Tom Holvoet

Anticipatory Coordination of Electric Vehicle Allocation to Fast Charging Infrastructure 74
    Kristof Coninx, Rutger Claes, Stijn Vandael, Niels Leemput, Tom Holvoet, and Geert Deconinck

Bilateral Negotiation of a Meeting Point in a Maze 86
    Fabien Delecroix, Maxime Morge, and Jean-Christophe Routier

Agent Negotiation for Different Needs in Smart Parking Allocation 98
    Claudia Di Napoli, Dario Di Nocera, and Silvia Rossi

Design of Forces Driving Adaptation of Agent Organizations 110
    Sergio Esparcia, Olivier Boissier, and Estefanía Argente

Practical Multi-Agent System Application for Simulation of Tourists in Madrid Routes with INGENIAS 122
    Iván García-Magariño

Domain and Subtask-Adaptive Conversational Agents to Provide
an Enhanced Human-Agent Interaction 134
   David Griol, José Manuel Molina, and Araceli Sanchís de Miguel

Dynamic Scheduling of Ready Mixed Concrete Delivery Problem Using
Delegate MAS 146
   Shaza Hanif and Tom Holvoet

Handling Safety-Related Non-Functional Requirements in Embedded
Multi-Agent System Design 159
   Jean-Paul Jamont, Clément Raievsky, and Michel Occello

The Multi-agent Patrolling Problem Theoretical Results about Cyclic
Strategies 171
   Fabrice Lauri, Jean-Charles Créput, and Abderrafiaa Koukam

Representation of Interactions in a Multi-Level Multi-Agent Model
for Cartography Constraint Solving 183
   Adrien Maudet, Guillaume Touya, Cécile Duchêne, and
   Sébastien Picault

Practical Application of Matchmaking Problem: Trainee Allocation
for Teachers 195
   Maxime Morge and Eric Piette

A Control Architecture of Complex Systems Based on Multi-agent
Models 207
   Tomás Navarrete Gutiérrez, Laurent Ciarletta, and Vincent Chevrier

Monitoring Oil Pipeline Infrastructures with Multiple Unmanned
Aerial Vehicles 219
   Jakub Ondráček, Ondřej Vaněk, and Michal Pěchouček

Planning When Goals Change: A Moving Target Search Approach 231
   Damien Pellier, Humbert Fiorino, and Marc Métivier

Agent Clusters: The Usual vs. The Unusual 244
   Kavin Preethi Narasimhan and Graham White

An Agent-Based Architecture to Model and Manipulate Context
Knowledge 256
   Ludo Stellingwerff and Giovanni E. Pazienza

Practical Applications of the Web-Based Agent Platform 'Eve' 268
   Ludo Stellingwerff, Jos de Jong, and Giovanni E. Pazienza

Multi-Armed Bandit Policies for Reputation Systems 279
   Thibaut Vallée, Grégory Bonnet, and François Bourdon

MASSA: Multi-Agent System to Support Functional Annotation   291
    Daniela Xavier, Berta Crespo, Rubén Fuentes-Fernández, and
    Jorge J. Gómez-Sanz

A Multi-agent System for Nested Inquiry Dialogues   303
    Chunli Yan, Juan Carlos Nieves, and Helena Lindgren

Demo Papers

The C^2BDI Agent Architecture for Teamwork Coordination Using
Spoken Dialogues between Virtual Agents and Users   315
    Mukesh Barange, Alexandre Kabil, and Pierre Chevaillier

Agent Based Simulation for Creating Ambient Assisted Living
Solutions   319
    Pablo Campillo-Sanchez and Jorge J. Gómez-Sanz

A Microscopic Traffic Simulation Platform for Coordinated Charging
of Electric Vehicles   323
    Kristof Coninx and Tom Holvoet

Bilateral Negotiation of a Meeting Point in a Maze: Demonstration   327
    Fabien Delecroix, Maxime Morge, and Jean-Christophe Routier

Using Negotiation for Parking Selection in Smart Cities   331
    Claudia Di Napoli, Dario Di Nocera, and Silvia Rossi

Developing Multimodal Conversational Agents: From the Use
of VoiceXML to Android-Based Applications   335
    David Griol, José Manuel Molina, and Araceli Sanchís de Miguel

Addressing Large Scale and Dynamic Scheduling by Nature Inspired
Mechanism   339
    Shaza Hanif, Shahab Ud Din, and Tom Holvoet

Illustrating an Intuitive and Informative Learning Platform for Third
Level Education   343
    Olapeju Latifat Ayoola and Eleni Mangina

A Federation Layer for Query Processing over the Web of Linked
Data   347
    Xuejin Li, Zhendong Niu, Chunxia Zhang, and Junyue Cao

Market Garden: A Simulation Environment for Research and User
Experience in Smart Grids   351
    Bart Liefers, Felix N. Claessen, Eric Pauwels,
    Peter A.N. Bosman, and Han La Poutré

Multi-agent Multi-level Cartographic Generalisation in CartAGen 355
Adrien Maudet, Guillaume Touya, Cécile Duchêne, and Sébastien Picault

An Agent-Based Approach for the Design of the Future European Air Traffic Management System 359
Martin Molina, Jorge Martin, and Sergio Carrasco

Multi-robot System for Vacuum Cleaning Domain 363
Agris Nikitenko, Janis Grundspenkis, Aleksis Liekna, Martins Ekmanis, Guntis Kulikovskis, and Ilze Andersone

receteame.com: A Persuasive Social Recommendation System 367
Javier Palanca, Stella Heras, Vicente Botti, and Vicente Julián

Automatic Electricity Markets Data Extraction for Realistic Multi-agent Simulations 371
Ivo F. Pereira, Tiago M. Sousa, Isabel Praca, Ana Freitas, Tiago Pinto, Zita Vale, and Hugo Morais

Look, Who's Talking: Simulations of Agent Clusters 375
Kavin Preethi Narasimhan and Graham White

Developing Intelligent Virtual Environments Using MAM5 Meta-Model 379
J.A. Rincon, Carlos Carrascosa, and Emilia Garcia

Multi-agent Platform for Designing Real Time Adaptive Scheduling Systems 383
Petr Skobelev, Denis Budaev, Vladimir Laruhin, Evgeny Levin, and Igor Mayorov

An Agent-Managed Ad-hoc Social Network to Facilitate F2F Networking at PAAMS 2014 387
Ludo Stellingwerff and Giovanni E. Pazienza

Author Index 391

HPLAN: Facilitating the Implementation of Joint Human-Agent Activities

Sebastian Ahrndt*, Philipp Ebert, Johannes Fähndrich, and Sahin Albayrak

DAI-Laboratory, Technische Universität Berlin,
Faculty of Electrical Engineering and Computer Science,
Ernst-Reuter-Platz 7, 10587 Berlin, Germany
sebastian.ahrndt@dai-labor.de

Abstract. When it comes to planning for joint human-agent activities, one has to consider not only flexible plan execution and social constraints but also the dynamic nature of humans. This can be achieved by providing additional information about the characteristics of a human. As an example one need to take the physical and psychological condition of the elderly into consideration when developing collaborative applications like socially assistive robots. This work outlines HPLAN, an extension to the agent-framework JIAC V, that takes this requirement into account. HPLAN is strongly related to the conceptual model of dynamic planning components and integrates humans as avatars into a life cycle of planning, execution and learning.

1 Introduction

Following *H.H. Clark* [5, p. 3], joint human-agent activities can be defined as an extended set of actions that is executed by an ensemble of natural and artificial agents who are coordinating with each other [5, 16]. These agents coordinate to overcome their inherent limitations. As examples, consider agents with a sensory malfunction (perception level), humans with a disease like dementia (cognition level) or robots that are not able to overcome obstacles like stairs (execution level).

Planning procedures that account for joint human-agent activities are computed by Human-Aware Planning (HAP) components [4]. HAP is mainly required when the situation involves artificial and natural agents in the same environment, the actions of the artificial agents being planned and those of the natural agents being predicted only. One assumption of currently available human-aware planning components (e.g., [2–4, 14, 19]) is that whenever a human is predicted to fulfil a task, the human will provide results in a timely fashion. This assumption is questionable since the 'Quality of Behaviour' that a human is able to provide differs for each human. For instance, consider the activities of daily living [23] (ADL)—a measure for the self-sustainability of elderly people. Whether an elderly person is able to perform an ADL depends on the persons physical and psychological condition. Therefore it is necessary for planning agents to take such information into consideration. This work presents the

---
* Corresponding author.

first steps to use this kind of information and to relax the mentioned assumption to a more general one. That is, whenever a human is predicted to fulfil a task, the human may perform the task or not and provide results either in time or delayed [1]. We introduce an extension to the agent-framework JIAC V [13, 17] named HPLAN, which enables the development of joint human-agent activities by providing three capabilities: (1) a generic link to several AI planners, (2) the use of additional information to influence the action selection of a planning process and (3) the integration of reinforcement learning techniques to adapt the additional information to the individual [7].

Indeed, the main contribution of this work is the presentation of an implementation, as the related work mainly presents conceptual frameworks. For example, *Kirsch et al.* [14] proposes a combination of TRANER and RoLL. TRANER is a planning system providing a library of reactive plans for autonomous household robots. RoLL is a robot programming language with a strong focus on machine learning. The combination of both enables to transform the available plans based on experience made during the execution. The work states that the strength of the system are not applied planning/learning techniques but the concept of combining two frameworks to facilitate joint human-agent activities. *Alami et al.* [2] propose to adjust the planning process to different types of humans using InterActionAgents each one providing information about an individual. The concept lacks details about the use of such information during the actual planning. *Cirillo et al.* [4] presents a more advanced solution combining activity recognition and the conceptual model of planning components. Other existing approaches [3, 19] plan without providing additional information about the human agents. Nevertheless, several authors emphasise to take such information into account [15, 19].

The remainder of this work is structured as follows. First, we will outline the bigger picture of our study using the already mentioned example of planning ADL, e.g. when developing socially assistive robots [22] in Section 2. In Section 3 we describe the approach combining available techniques to create a development environment for joint human-agent activities. Section 4 presents a technical evaluation using the Blocks World [11], where humans as additional actors suffering from weakness are introduced and cooperate with a robot to solve Blocks World problems. This scenario is far away from a real-world scenario and simulates a cooperative setting. Nevertheless, it was chosen to technically evaluate whether the design-decisions done are applicable to cooperative settings and to gain first experiences developing applications with HPLAN. Eventually, we conclude the work and give an outlook on future work in Section 5.

2 Motivation

To outline the objective of the work, imagine a socially assistive robot helping elderly people to stay independent at home. Such a robot should support the elderlies in the activities of daily living. Here older adults and robots cooperate to maintain the personal autonomy of the elderly. Yet, the aim of the cooperation it not to leave all task to the artificial agents, but to help the human as much as

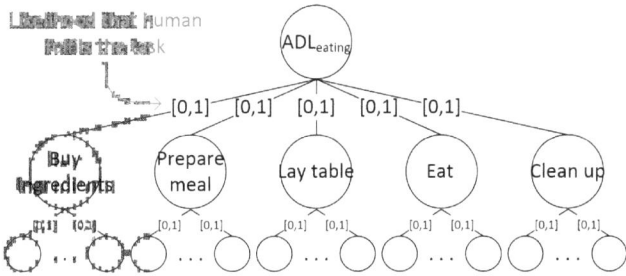

Fig. 1. Eating is one of the activities of daily living, visualised here as a hierarchical task network describing the decomposition of the complex task ADL_{eating} to atomic actions (e.g. a possible leaf named pay for ingredients). Whether an elderly person is able to perform the task depends on its physical and psychological condition making the availability of such information necessary for agents planning procedures. The goal of our approach is to provide an estimate of the likelihood that an action is successfully executed by the human.

necessary and as little as possible. Planning for this kind of joint human-agent activity requires knowledge about which agent—the artificial or the human—can perform which task and how likely the task is achieved. For this purpose the agent planning needs to predict the course of action of the human. Fig. 1 illustrates this objective for the ADL eating that comprises not only the actual consumption but also preparation and follow-up tasks.

The main objective of our work is to provide more information about the human—in terms of habits, abilities, personality and behaviour—and to use this information to sharpen the likelihood that the human can/will fulfil a task. For instance, the ability of a human to slice ingredients during the prepare meal task depends on the physical and psychological conditions of the human. These conditions can be influenced by diseases like Parkinson and its accompanying symptoms like tremble. As another example, weakness as a symptom of several diseases can diminish the ability to set up or clean up a table. To sharpen the estimated value of how good a human can fulfil a task, we want to investigate the use of additional information in combination with learning techniques. In particular, we do not aim to implement a new planning system but use existing ones as black boxes.

3 Approach

The goal of this work is to present a way to provide more information about humans to the planning process of joint human-agent activities. We want to accomplish this in terms of a more accurate cost estimate for specific capabilities. The costs are used to indicate the likelihood that a task will be performed, *i.e.* lower cost indicates a higher likelihood and vice versa. We do not aim to develop a new planner, but to use existing solutions as far as possible. In consequence, our approach is to use the cost estimates to influence the action selection of a planning process, where the actual planning procedure is a black box. The idea is to integrate the costs into the planning process providing a—roughly speaking—dynamic heuristic about the possible course of action of a human user. *Sisbot et al.* [20] already showed the usefulness of this idea in the adjacent research field of Human-Aware Navigation. The authors used the A* search algorithm [12] for the motion planning of robots. Such robots should avoid to approach humans from behind during the motion. To accomplish this the authors attached higher cost to actions in the back of humans and thus influenced the path-finding without changing the algorithm.

3.1 Agent-Model Construction

To transfer this idea to a collaborative setting, we represent each human as part of the agent-system similar to the concept of InterActionAgents presented by *Alami et al.* [2]. In this work avatars named actor agents each represent a human or an artificial agent. Each actor agent representing a human provides information about the capabilities and the personality of the human. In a formal way this can be expressed using the following agent-model for an actor agent a_h:

$$\{A_{a_h}, P_{a_h}, cost : A_{a_h} \times P_{a_h} \to \mathbb{R}\}.$$

Here, $A_{a_h} \subseteq A$ is the set of capabilities (actions) that a human is able to provide. In our example, A_{a_h} would include actions necessary for the activities of daily living. The behaviour of a human is represented by the set of personality $P_{a_h} \subseteq P$, where each $p \in P$ represents a personality trait with range $[0, 1]$. This abstraction serves as a wild-card for a specific type of information. For our example, this might be a psychological trait from a theory like the Five Factor Model [18] or information about a disease. The agent-model is completed with the relation *cost* between actions and personality. This relation is used to dynamically assign costs in terms of a real number to each action, which will later be used to generate plans with minimised costs.

3.2 Planning for Joint-Human Agent Activities

A system suitable for a planning process for joint human-agent activities needs to create a plan, execute it, learn from the execution and start over. Therefore it must be able to determine the current state of the environment, to detect failure and to replan if necessary. Furthermore, experiences generated from the execution of actions must be used to improve the task delegation process.

Concept. Fig. 2 illustrates the architecture of our approach and visualises the relationship to the conceptual model for dynamic planning systems introduced by *Ghallab et al.* [10, p. 9]. Here, the controller handles the execution of plans generated by the planner based on an initial state and a set of goals that are provided by an external source. The controller executes actions, processes observations from the environment and informs the planner about the plan execution

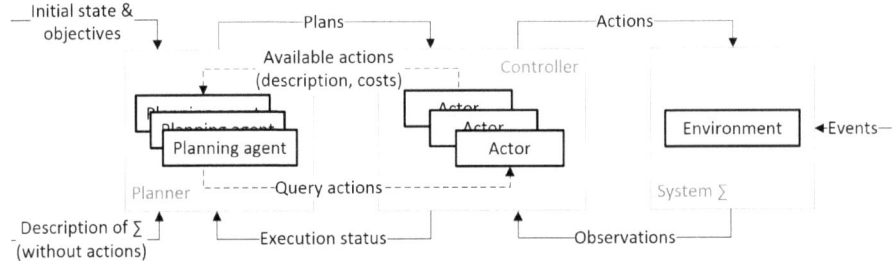

Fig. 2. High-level architecture of HPLAN visualised as part of the conceptual model for dynamic planning components (greyed out) [10, p. 9]. The planning capabilities are provided by planning agents, which can be actors as well. The initial domain description encloses no action descriptions as the available actions are only provided by the actors at runtime. The process starts with a new objective triggering an agent with planning capabilities to query all available actors. The actors then provide an action description and a cost estimate for each action that they want to offer for the planning process.

status. In our approach, a controller contains a set of actors, each representing a human or an artificial agent that is capable of manipulating the environment. The planning process for a new objective starts by querying all actor agents about their available actions and the associated cost predictions to generate a full domain description. The query is executed by an agent with planning capabilities, which can be an actor agent or an agent solely responsible for planning processes. The queried information is used to generate a plan in which each task is delegated to the most capable agent. During the execution, the observations generated in the environment are evaluated by the associated actor. If a failure occurs, it is reported back to the planner to trigger replanning. Furthermore, the actor agents representing a human learn from each execution experience and adapt their cost predictions accordingly, therefore completing the life cycle of planning, executing and learning.

Implementation. The described structure was implemented as an extension module for the agent-framework JIAC V [13, 17] (Java Intelligent Agent Componentware – Version V). We extended the action annotation process used in the agent-framework with the ability to annotate human-action descriptions. In JIAC V the expose annotation is used to declare an agent's actions. Listing 1.1 shows an annotation for an action named *sliceIngredients*. At runtime all relevant information is extracted from the annotation and its attributes. Here, the *name* of an action is used to register it in the dictionary of each agent platform (the dictionary is a yellow-page service). The *scope* of the action is used to control its visibility. It controls whether the action is visible to all existing agents, to the agents on a single platform or only to the agent owning such action. The *actor* defines if an action is provided by an artificial or natural agent. The *descr* provides the action description in the selected planning language. The *cost* attribute holds the current cost estimate for this action by this actor. This estimate is automatically embedded

```
@Expose(
  name  = ADL_EATING_PREPARE_SLICE,
  scope = ActionScope.GLOBAL,
  actor = ActorType.HUMAN,
  descr = ADL_EATING_PREPARE_SLICE_DESCR
  cost  = ADL_EATING_PREPARE_SLICE_COST
)
public void sliceIngredients(){
   // Implementation of user interaction
}
```

Listing 1.1. Example of annotating actions when developing actors that represent humans

into the action description when the planning agents queries the multi-agent system about the available actions.

As indicated in the listing, developers have to provide a description for an action and the way the actor interacts with the human user when the action is used. Developers are not required to implement the action's logic, as the action will be executed by humans. For the actual planning, we implemented a planning module using the planning library Planning4J.[1] This approach enables planning with various AI planners, even if they are written in other programming languages than Java. Actions are described using the planning language PDDL [9], which was objectified to ease the manipulation of the associated action costs and to support reusability. We use the concept of numerical fluents first introduced in PDDL2.1 [8] to assign costs to actions. Furthermore, we use the minimisation plan-metric—also first introduced with PDDL2.1—for the quantitative directive of plan creation.

3.3 Stateless Q-learning to estimate Costs

We apply stateless Q-learning [6] in order to estimate the expected costs of executing an action according to the personality traits of an agent. We drop the state dependency as the goal of this work is to learn the ability of an agent to fulfil a specific task, not to learn the utility of an action in a specific state of the environment, which will be done in the future.

By definition, a learning agent interacts with its environment by performing an action a at time t. In return, the agent receives a reward $r_t(a)$ and iteratively improves its estimate $Q_t(a)$ of the expected reward for each action a. In other words the agent builds an estimate of the expected costs of executing an action a. This estimate is iteratively updated using the following equation, known as the Q-learning update rule. Here, the parameter α with range $[0,1]$ denotes the learning rate, helping to control the influence of new experiences to the current cost estimate:

$$Q_{t+1}(a) \leftarrow Q_t(a) + \alpha \left(r_t(a) - Q_t(a) \right).$$

---

[1] For more information about Planning4J and the supported AI planning solutions the interested reader is refereed to https://code.google.com/p/planning4j.

We choose the Q-learning update rule because the sample-average method would not react fast enough to changing capabilities of humans in the long run (e.g., if a human gets tired of performing a repetitive task). To learn from feedback, the effects of actions have to be evaluated by some criteria according to the type of the reward signal. Such a reward signal can be of qualitative (e.g., in terms of 'failure' and 'success') or quantitative nature (e.g., in terms of time steps required to execute an action). As both signal types require different computation and the interpretation of the reward signal is domain dependent, we developed different interfaces to encapsulate the actual implementation. Fig. 3 shows a more detailed view of an actor agent and introduces some of the interfaces, which are provided for developers.

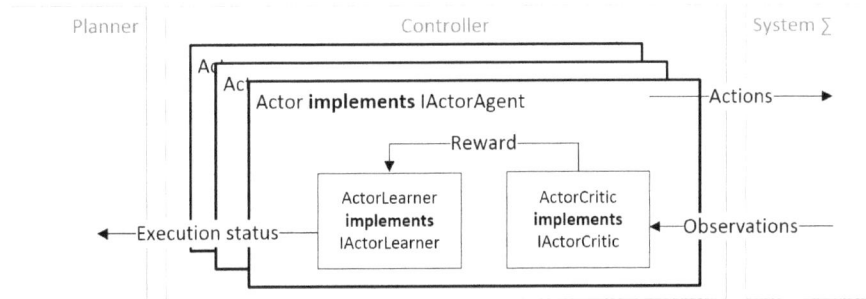

Fig. 3. A more detailed view of an actor agent. Each JIAC V agent consist of several components named AgentBeans which encapsulate functionalities. An actor representing a human is equipped with at least two AgentBeans, one named ActorCritic and one named ActorLearner. The ActorCritic evaluates the observations and is responsible for generating the reward signal. In other words, the ActorCritic preprocesses observations, which can for example be derived from sensor signals, to generate a computable reward signal such as 'failure' or 'success'. The ActorLearner then uses these reward signals to adjust the cost of the associated actions using machine learning techniques. In its current implementation the ActorLearner uses stateless Q-learning.

The above-mentioned learning procedure is applied by the available actors each time they manipulate the environment. Agents with planning capabilities then use this information to produce plans with minimal overall costs. To ensure that the approach is able to reach minimised plan costs, we applied the ϵ-greedy policy as the action selection strategy (if not otherwise stated we use an exploration rate of $\epsilon = 0.1$) [21]. This guarantees that $Q_t(a)$ converges to $Q^*(a)$ for $t \to \infty$, where $Q^*(a)$ is the mean reward received when a is executed [21].

4 Case Study

We used a classical planning problem—the Blocks World [11]—to evaluate the presented approach. The Blocks World in our evaluation scenario contains two types of effectors, namely robots and humans. Each can move blocks, but the efficiency of humans is higher on average. Humans suffer from weakness and in consequence have the potential to make errors for tasks that involve boxes that are more than one level of the ground. Related to our examples, this might be the task to carry dishes from the table to the wall cupboard or vice versa. We introduce two types of errors: Failure at moving a block (denoted as external factor ext_c) and the timely execution of moving a block (denoted as external factor ext_r). The external factors ($ext_{c,r}$) serve as hidden properties not accessible to the planning system and not known to the human-agent representing a human. In consequence, the human-agent must observe the environment during the action executions by its associated human. To represent this information, we use the hidden properties as personality traits for the actor agents representing the human. The goal is to determine the helpfulness of a human being to reach a given goal with $P_{HELP} = \{p_c, p_r\}$. Cooperation (p_c) measures a human's ability to fulfil a task. It indicates the likeliness that the human succeeds or fails to execute a given task. Reliability (p_r) measures a human's ability to provide results either in time or delayed. It indicates the likeliness that a task will be processed in time and the expected time delay.

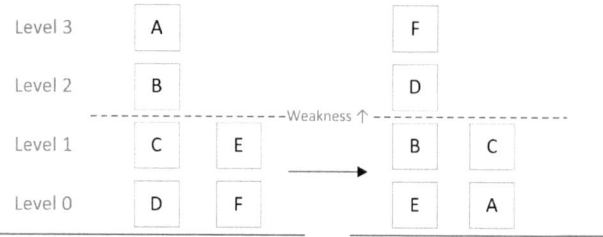

Fig. 4. Evaluation scenario visualising the initial state (left) and the goal state (right). Each action that is executed by a human actor more than one level of the table triggers weakness.

Fig. 4 shows one evaluation scenario. Given this scenario, we are able to manually calculate minimal plan costs for different cooperation and reliability values. To test whether the system adapts to dynamic external factors during runtime, we change the human behaviour after $n = 50$ solutions from $ext_c = 0.3, ext_r = 1.6$ to $ext_c = 0, ext_r = 1$, simulating a human that does not suffer from weakness and requires one time step to execute each action. After 50 experiences at $n = 101$ we restore the previously used external factors, simulating a human that fails in 30% of all weakness triggering tasks and requires 1.6 time steps to execute such actions. The change in behaviour enables us to observe the ability of the system to adapt a model that was already learned.

Given these requirements, we implemented an actor agent that is able to process observations to determine the helpfulness of a human. Here, the ActorCritic distinguish a qualitative reward signal in terms of 'failure' and 'success', which is used to learn p_c, and a quantitative reward signal in terms of time steps required to execute an action, which is used to learn p_r. As both require different computation, the reward signal is processed using the following twofold equation:

$$r_t(a) \leftarrow \begin{cases} \rho \times c(a) & \text{if 'failure'} \\ \Delta_t(a) & \text{otherwise} \end{cases}.$$

Here, the parameter ρ is a constant factor to punish the execution of an action a if the execution has failed, whereas $c(a) \leftarrow Q_{t_0}(a)$ is the initial cost estimate for action a provided by the developer. The execution time of an action a is denoted as $\Delta_t(a)$.

To determine whether the system improves the cost effectiveness of solving a problem, we use the average cost $C_n^m = \frac{\sum_{i=0}^{m} c_{i,n}}{m}$ to solve the problem after n previous experiences averaged over m rounds. Each experience solves one instance of the problem, including necessary replannings. The use of this average value removes statistical variations introduced by ext_c and ext_r for large numbers of m. If not explicitly stated, we will use $n = 1\ldots150, m = 100$ for the experiments. Furthermore—in a real world scenario—humans would expect the planner to produce legible behaviour and therefore consider if a human feels safe and comfortable [15]. Using the cost-progression is not suitable to show this, as a human has a different point of view on what an optimal plan is. Humans in our scenario would prefer a plan that delegates as few weakness affected tasks to them as possible if they are suffering from weakness. Humans suffering from weakness might also not want to be frequently asked to execute tasks they are not able to perform.

Fig. 5 illustrates the number of tasks inducing weakness that are assigned to the human agent and the robot. The number of weakness affected tasks that the human has to execute decreases significantly for the two stages in which the human suffers from weakness. The graph confirms that tasks that are not executed by the human are executed by the robot instead. At the beginning of $stage_1$ more weakness affected tasks are executed by the human than required to solve the problem. This is due to the fact that a number of failures occur and the tasks therefore have to be executed multiple times (underpinned by the number of replannings). As the planner delegates all tasks to the human at first, the human executes up to 5.4 tasks to solve a problem. Note that this behaviour was expected as in the initial action description the humans performance were assumed higher on average (2 : 1). This was done to ensure that the planner tries to assign actions to the human actor frequently. At the end of $stage_2$ the planner is correctly confident that the human is not suffering from weakness and the human is delegated all four weakness affected tasks that are required to solve the problem. At the transition point between $stage_2$ and $stage_3$ the planner is still confident that the human does not suffer from weakness. The human then changes its internal model and the system again has to replan multiple times until it adapts to the failure rate of the human agent. This creates a peak in the number of weakness affected tasks executed to solve the problem. Associated with this observation the costs drop to the near optimum during all three stages.

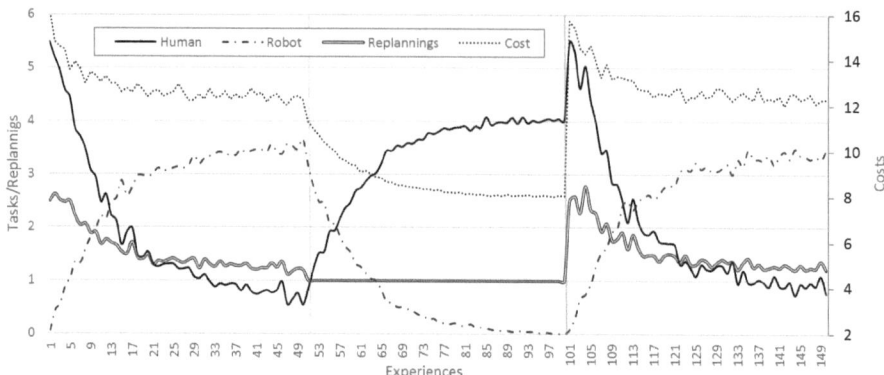

Fig. 5. Diagram shows the number of weakness triggering tasks executed by the human agent, number of task executed by the robot, number of replannings done during the simulation and the overall cost-progression ($\alpha = 0.1$). The optimal plan costs are $stage_{1,3} = 12$, $stage_2 = 8$. In $stage_2$ the human does not suffer from weakness, to test whether the system adapts to dynamically changing behaviour. For evaluation purposes we used scenarios small enough to enable cost calculation manually.

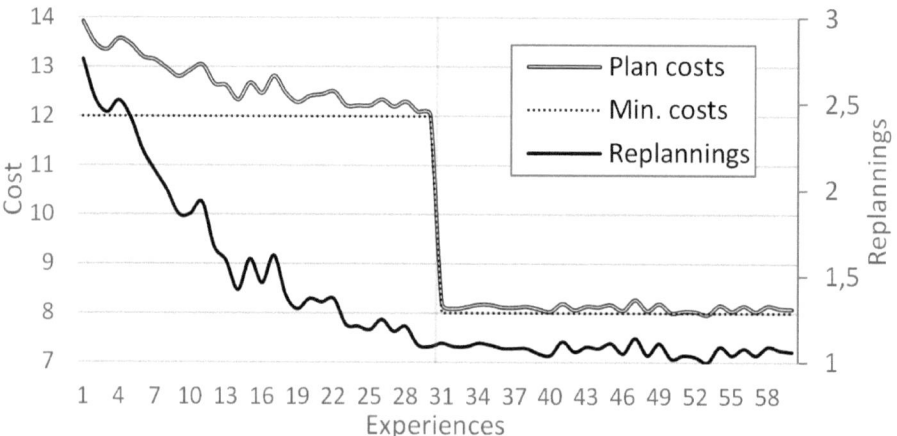

Fig. 6. Cost progression and number of replannings when changing the problem during runtime ($n = 1 \ldots 60, m = 100, \epsilon = 0.01$)

To show that the system learns problem independent, we tested the use of an already adapted model to solve other problems. To show this, we replace the problem with a different one after $n = 30$. The time-optimal solution plan for this problem takes 8 time steps. If the system does indeed learn problem independent behaviour, we would expect the system to perform efficiently on the second problem without adaptation. Fig. 6 shows, that the system reaches an near time-optimal solution on the second problem without additional adaptation (also underpinned by the number of replannings). We can therefore conclude that the system does not simply learn problem specific behaviour but indeed learns the hidden properties of the human agents. Furthermore, we can conclude that the additional information forwarded in terms of a more accurate cost estimate influence the action selection of the planning process in a positive manner.

5 Conclusion

We presented an agent-based architecture named HPLAN that facilitates the development of joint human-agent activities. HPLAN is strongly related to the conceptual model of planning and implements the life cycle of planning, executing and learning. The related work shows that contemporary solutions lack in terms of learning and adapting to humans and in consequence sacrifice potential in terms of planning efficiency and the generation of legible behaviour. The presented technical evaluation shows that our approach is able to reach near optimal plan cost after a short number of experiences. The approach also reduces the number of non-optimal action assignments to humans. The evaluation results indicate, that the concept of forwarding additional information to the planning component is promising in terms of a more accurate cost estimate. Nevertheless, the case-study is just a technical evaluation of the system emphasising that HPLAN facilitates the implementation of joint human-agent activities. In future work it will be interesting to see if using one Q-learner for each information is applicable for real-world applications. Furthermore, currently each additional information influences the cost of each action, leaving the actual context out of consideration. It might be necessary to find a more fine-granular way since the 'Quality of Behaviour' a human is able to provide not only differs for each human but also differs for several contexts.

References

1. Ahrndt, S.: Improving human-aware planning. In: Klusch, M., Thimm, M., Paprzycki, M. (eds.) MATES 2013. LNCS, vol. 8076, pp. 400–403. Springer, Heidelberg (2013)
2. Alami, R., Clodic, A., Montreuil, V., Sisbot, E.A., Chatila, R.: Task planning for human-robot interaction. In: Bailly, G., Crowley, J.L., Privat, G. (eds.) Proc. of the sOc-EUSAI 2005, pp. 81–85. ACM Press (2005)
3. Alili, S., Warnier, M., Ali, M., Alami, R.: Planning and plan-execution for human-robot cooperative task achievement. In: Proc. of the 19th ICAPS, pp. 1–6 (2009)
4. Cirillo, M., Karlsson, L., Saffiotti, A.: Human-aware task planning: An application to mobile robots. ACM Trans. Intell. Syst. Technol. 1(2), 1–26 (2010)
5. Clark, H.H.: Using Language. Cambridge Univ. Press (1996)
6. Claus, C., Boutilier, C.: Thy dynamics of reinforcement learning in cooperative multiagent systems. In: Proc. of the 15th AAAI, pp. 746–752 (1998)
7. Ebert, P.: Improving Human-Aware Planning through Reinforcement Learning – A Multi-Agent Based Approach. Master's thesis, TU Berlin (2013)
8. Fox, M., Long, D.: PDDL2.1: An extension to PDDL for expressing temporal planning domains. Artifical Intelligence Research 20, 61–124 (2003)

9. Ghallab, M., Howe, A., Knoblock, C., et al.: PDDL – The Planning Domain Definition Language. Yale Center for Computational Vision and Control (1998)
10. Ghallab, M., Nau, D., Traverso, P.: Automated Planning: Theory & Practice. Morgan Kaufmann (2004)
11. Gupta, N., Nau, D.S.: On the complexity of blocks-world planning. Artifical Intelligence 56(2-3), 223–254 (1992)
12. Hart, P., Nilsson, N., Raphael, B.: A formal basis for the heuristic determination of minimum cost paths. IEEE Transactions on Systems Science and Cybernetics 4(2), 100–107 (1968)
13. Hirsch, B., Konnerth, T., Heßler, A.: Merging agents and services – the JIAC agent platform. In: Bordini, R.H., Dastani, M., Dix, J., Amal, E.F.S. (eds.) Multi-Agent Programming: Languages, Tools and Applications, pp. 159–185. Springer (2009)
14. Kirsch, A., Kruse, T., Mösenlechner, L.: An integrated planning and learning framework for human-robot interaction. In: Proc. of the 19th ICAPS, pp. 1–6 (2009)
15. Kirsch, A., Kruse, T., Sisbot, E.A., et al.: Plan-based control of joint human-robot activities. KI – Künstliche Intelligenz 24(3), 223–231 (2010)
16. Klein, G., Woods, D.D., Bradshaw, J.M., Hoffmann, R.R., Feltovich, P.J.: Ten challenges for making automation a 'team player' in joint human-agent activity. Human-Centered Computing 19(6), 91–95 (2004)
17. Lützenberger, M., Küster, T., Konnerth, T., et al.: JIAC V –A MAS framework for industrial applications (extended abstract). In: Ito, T., Jonker, C., Gini, M., Shehory, O. (eds.) Proc. of the 12th AAMAS, pp. 1189–1190 (2013)
18. McCrea, R.R., John, O.P.: An introduction to the five-factor model and its applications. Personality 60(2), 175–215 (1992)
19. Montreuil, V., Clodic, A., Alami, R.: Planning human centered robot activities. In: IEEE SMC, pp. 2618–2623 (2007)
20. Sisbot, E.A., Marin-Urias, L.F., Alami, R., Simeon, T.: A human aware mobile robot motion planner. IEEE Transactions on Robotics 23(5), 874–883 (2007)
21. Sutton, R.S., Barto, A.G.: Reinforcement Learning: An Introduction. Adaptive Computation and Machine Learning. MIT Press (May 1998)
22. Tapus, A., Matarić, M.J., Scassellati, B.: The grand challenges in socially assistive robotics. IEEE Robotics and Automation Magazin 14(1), 35–42 (2007)
23. Wiener, J.M., Hanley, R.J., Clark, R., Nostrand, J.F.V.: Measuring the activities of daily living: Comparison across national surveys. Tech. rep., U.S. Department of Health and Human Services (1990), http://aspe.hhs.gov/daltcp/reports/meacmpes.pdf (last access: February 25, 2014)

Reliable Multi-robot Map Merging of Inaccurate Maps

Andersone Ilze and Nikitenko Agris

Riga Technical University, Latvia
1 Kalku Street,
LV-1658, Latvia
{ilze.andersone,agris.nikitenko}@rtu.lv

Abstract. The multi-robot teams have a potential to significantly speed up the mapping process of the environment, compared to the single robot mapping. However, in multi-robot case the problem of merging the information collected by individual robots must be addressed. There are many map merging approaches that allow the fusion of the maps, when the relative positions of the robots are known initially or are discovered during the mapping. The case, when relative positions of robots are unknown, is considered by relatively few researchers. This paper presents a novel method of map merging during multi-robot exploration, when the relative positions of the robots are not known.

Keywords: Map merging, Robotic mapping.

1 Introduction

One of the fundamental problems in mobile robotics is the environment mapping problem. Robots need to be able to construct a map of the environment and to use it for the navigation or other tasks. As the use of robot teams becomes more and more popular, the issue of robot coordination becomes important. If multiple robots are used for the exploration of the environment, their collected information has to be fused into one global map. The fusion of the map information from multiple robots into one global map is called map merging [1].

The existing map merging approaches offer various solutions for situations, when the relative locations of the robots and consequently the relations between the local maps are known [1-6]. In this case the order of merging is straightforward – either all maps are merged simultaneously [2, 3, 5] or the maps are merged, when overlaps are detected [1, 4, 6].

The problem that is still virtually untouched is the map merging during exploration and mapping, if the relative robot positions are not known. This problem so far has been mainly considered as a fusion of two local maps [7-12], and the optimal map merging order is usually assumed to be known. In reality, however, the merging result by unknown positions is a hypothesis about the actual transformation (rotation and translations) between the maps, and the result is never certain. The hypothesis may be incorrect, and therefore the merging process must incorporate the ability to cancel the map merging decision to avoid losing information acquired after the merging – this is a task, which is critically important, if the map merging is to take place during exploration without human expert support. The researchers in [7-12] evaluate the map merging results by applying some kind of acceptance metrics. Unfortunately the proposed metrics do not guarantee reliable results.

Only few researchers have addressed the problem of a reliable map merging [13, 14]. In [13] the problem of the reliable map merging is addressed as a decision, where both the absolute likelihood (the similarity of the two maps for a particular transformation) and the relative likelihood (the similarity of the two maps for a particular transformation compared with other transformations) are taken into account. This work, however, does not consider a particular case where the acquired result is wrong and has to be reverted. Instead, the emphasis is put on the avoidance of inaccurate results.

In [14] it is admitted that it is natural to make mistakes during map merging. Therefore the merged maps need to be stored in a way that allows a simple discarding of incorrect hypothesis without losing the whole map or information acquired after map merging. The authors of this approach propose to use layered storage, where each layer stores a map produced by a single robot along with merging results. The main problem with this approach is that all merged maps have to be updated with every sensor reading of all included maps, and it requires a significant CPU overhead.

This paper proposes a novel map merging method that supports map merging during multi-robot exploration, when the relative positions of the robots are unknown. The approach uses binary tree merging that is modified to deal with the fact that during the exploration the robot maps are continuously updated. To improve the recognition of correct hypotheses, a novel map merging evaluation metric developed by the authors is used for hypothesis evaluation. The method provides the following advantages over simple fusion of two maps:

— It provides the reversibility of map merging – at any mapping point it is possible to return to the point before the map merging without losing information acquired by individual robots after the merging.
— The decision to merge two local maps is only made, if the evaluation of the proposed map merging hypothesis exceeds previously empirically set threshold (the map merging hypothesis is believable).

2 Reliable Map Merging Method

The chapter describes the proposed method for reliable robot map merging. This method can be used for the proposal and rejection of map merging hypotheses without losing information that is acquired after the map merging.

The proposed method consists of two parts, each of which fulfils an important role (see Figure 1): (a) Global map merging and (b) Local map merging. The global map merging and hypothesis maintenance part oversees the creation of the global map and checks, whether the proposed hypotheses are correct. The local map merging searches for transformations between two maps by taking into account the previous experience of map mergings. The global and local map merging is discussed in more detail further in chapter.

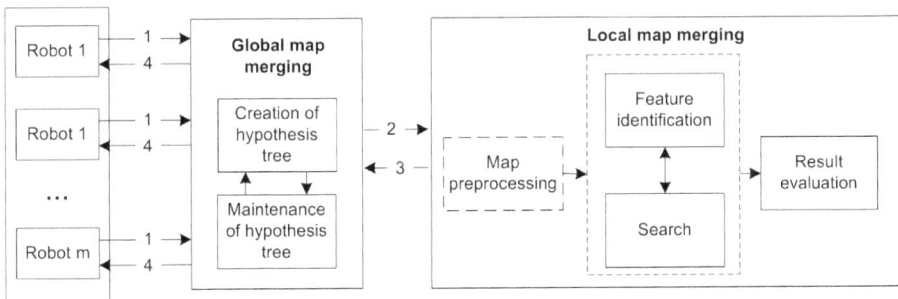

Fig. 1. The general structure of the proposed map merging method. Information flows: 1) robot local maps; 2) map pairs and the rejected hypothesis list; 3) map merging hypotheses and messages about the success/failure of map merging; 4) hypothesis tree and all local maps of the robots

The proposed map merging method is developed and evaluated for a particular map type – metric occupancy grid maps [15] – but it may be adapted and used for other map types with a condition that the relative positioning of the maps can be defined as a hypothesis and used for merging updated maps later. The method is intended for a centralised map merging.

2.1 Global Map Merging

To provide the reversibility of map merging, it is important to choose an appropriate data structure for storing local and global maps. Otherwise, if robots merge their local maps and continue mapping with a common global map, it can be complicated to separate maps without losing information that is acquired after the merging.

As stated before, the map merging has to be revertible action and therefore the map merging result is not a global map but a <u>map merging hypothesis</u>. In the context of this paper, the map merging hypothesis is defined as a triple in equation (1). The hypothesis contains information about the two merged maps and their transformation. The transformation is the positioning of the second map relative to the first map – the translations and the rotation.

$$\text{<map or hypothesis, map or hypothesis, transformation>} \quad (1)$$

Such representation of hypothesis allows to use the local maps in the creation of global map and to reject hypotheses at any time without the need to restore the maps of all proposed hypotheses.

One map merging hypothesis is not sufficient, if the environment is being explored by more than two robots. In case of larger robot groups the global map is created gradually by merging local maps sequentially. If all mergings are successful, the global map can be acquired by performing $n-1$ map mergings (where n is the count of local maps). In such case each map is used exactly once for the merging.

The authors propose to use a specific data structure to represent the dependencies between map merging hypotheses - the hypothesis tree. Formally the hypothesis tree is a set of full binary trees has the following properties:

- The leaf nodes of the tree are the local maps, and these nodes are unique in the whole tree set, i.e., every local map is represented as a leaf node in the tree set exactly once.
- Every tree node, that is not a leaf node, represents one map merging hypothesis, and the children of this node are local maps and/or hypotheses, the merging of which is the basis of hypothesis.
- Every tree root is the highest level map merging hypothesis.

The highest level map merging hypothesis is a hypothesis that is not involved in the creation of any other hypothesis, or its node is not a child of any other node. If the hypothesis tree set has only one binary tree, then its root or highest level map merging hypothesis is the global map hypothesis. Figure 2 shows examples of hypothesis trees that contain one and two trees.

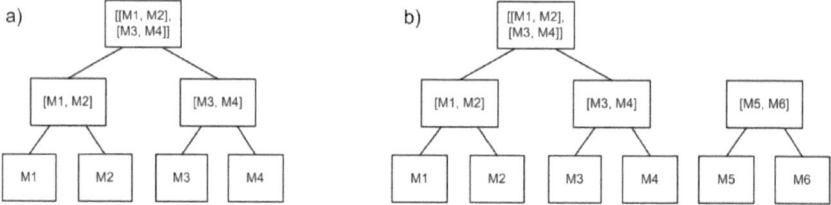

Fig. 2. Examples of hypothesis tree: a) one tree set, b) two tree set

The hypothesis tree is updated in two cases:

- Adding of hypothesis. A new hypothesis, that exceeds the hypothesis acceptance threshold, is proposed during the map merging. A hypothesis acceptance threshold is exceeded, if the similarity of maps computed by some similarity metric is higher than the preset threshold value. Usually this threshold represents the relative number of cells that must be similar in the common part of maps [8].
- Deletion of hypothesis. It is discovered during the evaluation of the hypothesis tree that the hypothesis is no longer believable, i.e. its evaluation is no longer higher than then hypothesis confirmation threshold. If the hypothesis is deleted, then it is added to rejected hypothesis list, so that it is not proposed repeatedly.

The highest level hypotheses are proposed by hierarchically merging the lower level maps and/or hypotheses. During the mapping the robots supplement their local maps and the mergings based on these maps are changing. The highest level maps are gradually created from the lower level maps, and every step in this process is evaluated. If it is discovered that the hypothesis is no longer credible, this hypothesis is deleted and all the higher level hypotheses that depend on it are also discarded. An example of this situation is depicted in Figure 3.

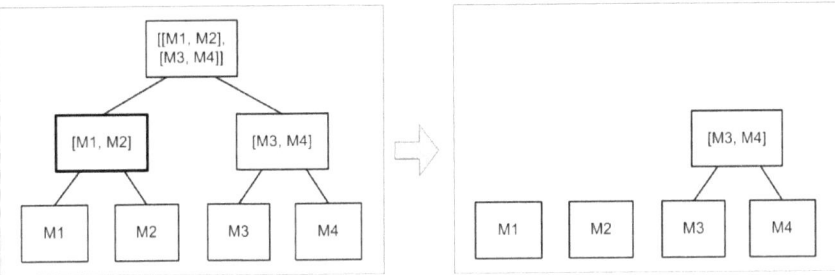

Fig. 3. An example of hypothesis rejection. A hypothesis [M1, M2] is rejected. It is discarded from the hypothesis list. The hypothesis [[M1, M2], [M3, M4]] is also discarded, because it is proposed by using the rejected hypothesis [M1, M2].

The global map merging algorithm after receiving local map can be summarized in pseudo-code as shown in Figure 4.

```
Procedure Global_map_merging (HT, RHL, LMS, Local_map):
Begin
LMS.Add_or_Replace(Local_map);
Foreach (Hypothesis in HT) do
  Hypothesis.Compute_Evaluation(LMS);
  If (Hypothesis.Evaluation < Eval_threshold) then
    HT.Discard(Hypothesis);
    RHL.Update(Hypothesis);
If (LMS.Count > HT.Map_count_in_largest_hypothesis)
then
  Map_pair ← Choose(LMS, HT);
  New_hypothesis ← Merging(Map_pair);
  If (New_hypothesis.Evaluation ≥ Eval_threshold) then
    HT.Add(New_hypothesis);
  Else
    RHL.Add(New_hypothesis);
End;
```

Fig. 4. A pseudo-code of global map merging algorithm. HT – hypothesis tree; RHL – rejected hypothesis list; LMS – local map set. At first, all hypotheses in HT are reevaluated. If HT does not contain a hypothesis that includes all maps in local set, then new merging/-s are performed. Based on the evaluation results the new hypothesis is added either to HT or RHL.

2.2 Local Map Merging

The local map merging part of the proposed method implements the aspect of local map merging – the search for transformation of two maps, map merging by using found transformation and the evaluation of the result. As a result a map merging hypothesis is proposed. The map pair to be merged and the rejected hypothesis list is received from the global map merging part. The result of local map merging is either map merging hypothesis or a message about the failure of map merging attempt.

The local map merging method must allow the merging of occupancy grid maps (or other map type, that depends on the used robot system) during mapping, when the relative positions are unknown, and it must be able to propose multiple map merging hypotheses. For local map merging the map merging by using Hough Transformation was chosen, that corresponds to these requirements [9]. Any other local map merging method can be used instead, if it complies to the requirements listed above.

2.3 Hypothesis Evaluation

Both global map merging and local map merging require a means to evaluate a map merging hypothesis to determine its validity. The map merging hypothesis can be evaluated by comparing the similarity of two maps, where one map is transformed accordingly to the hypothesis.

To evaluate the proposed map merging hypothesis, a numerical evaluation of map merging hypothesis must be introduced. Although the introduction of this evaluation does not guarantee correct map merging result, it helps to discard obviously incorrect transformations. An additional restriction is that the acceptance and rejection of the map merging hypotheses must be automatic without the involvement of human experts. To achieve this, two numerical values are required [8]:

— The evaluation of the map merging hypothesis – an evaluation that describes the similarity of the common area of two maps by the current transformation hypothesis.
— The map merging hypothesis acceptance threshold – if the evaluation of the map merging hypothesis exceeds this threshold, the two maps are considered acceptably merged and the map merging hypothesis is confirmed.

To assess similarity of maps for the given hypothesis the authors have developed an algorithm that takes into account map inaccuracies and allows changing the influence of particular cell types on the result [16]. The map similarity value is computed using Equation 2. The weight of 'occupied' cells varies from 0 to 1. If this value exceeds 0.5, the influence of 'occupied' cell similarity impacts the result more than 'free' cells, and vice versa.

$$MS_{m1,m2} = w_{occ} * s_{occ} + (1 - w_{occ}) * s_{free} \qquad (2)$$

w_{occ} – 'occupied' cell weight, s_{occ} – 'occupied' cell similarity evaluation, s_{free} – 'free' cell similarity evaluation.

To compute the similarity only one parameter is required – the distance threshold d_{max} that describes, how large the mapping error is allowed to be in the given mapping system. This threshold defines the Manhattan distance, in which two cells are considered to be 'within reach of each other' – sufficiently close to possibly represent the same obstacle.

Both the 'occupied' cell similarity and 'free' cell similarities are computed by creating and using distance grids of the maps (an example of a map and its distance grid is shown in Figure 5). The distance grid of a map represents each cell's Manhattan distance to the closest cell with previously defined target value.

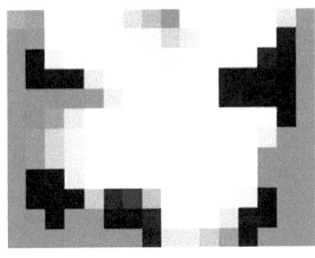

Fig. 5. Example of a map and its distance grid. Numbers in grid cells show the nearest Manhattan distance to 'occupied' (black) cells. Negative values ('-') depict 'unknown' areas in map.

Once the distance grids are computed, the algorithm uses two counters – 'sim' for similar cells and 'dis' for dissimilar cells – to compute the map similarity for each cell type. It must be noted, that the cell must be of the currently considered cell type at least in one map to initiate comparison:

— If a cell value is 'unknown' in either map, then no counters are increased.
— If a cell value is similar in both maps, then the cells are considered similar and the 'sim' counter is increased by one.
— If a cell value in the maps differs, then the distance grid is used to determine the Manhattan distance to the closest cell. If the distance falls within the distance threshold d_{max}, then the cells are considered similar and the 'sim' counter is increased by one. Otherwise, 'dis' counter is increased by one.

The cell similarity is the ratio between similar cell count and the total considered cell count. The map similarity for each cell type is computed twice (first map against the second, and vice versa), and the average value is used as cell similarity evaluations s_{occ} or s_{free}.

3 Experimental Environment and Results

For the evaluation of the map merging method robot maps created by the robot system developed in Riga Technical University were used (see Figure 6). The robots in this system rely on landmarks on ceilings and odometry for localization [17] and close range sensors for obstacle detection and mapping [18]. If the robot loses the sight of the landmark, it relies on its odometry and inner kinematic model for position evaluation, while the landmark configuration ensures that the robot cannot travel long without seeing at least one landmark. Therefore small position inaccuracies are common and the maps are rather noisy, but large position inaccuracies are very rare.

Fig. 6. The robot system used for map acquisition

The developed method was evaluated by performing experiments in three different environment configurations. In one case eight partial maps were created by robots. In the other two environment configurations nine partial maps were created. Each mapping run was recorded by saving partial maps sequentially in time. An example of one such map sequence is shown in Figure 7.

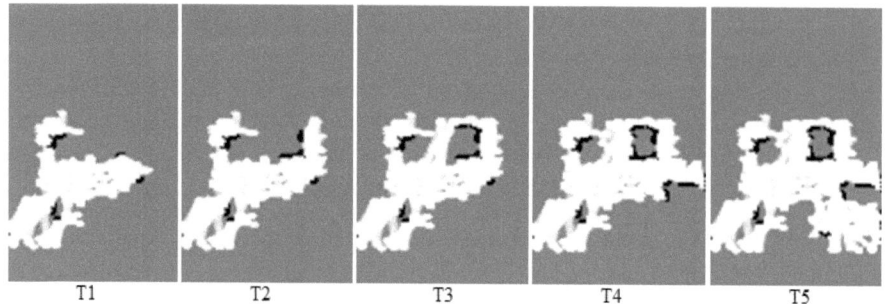

Fig. 7. An example of the evolution of one map in time T1-T5. Black cells – occupied, white cells – free, gray cells – unknown. Note: this is a map.

3.1 Experimental Setup

With each map set 36 global map creation attempts were made (in total 104 global map creation attempts) – each set was run with the combinations of three parameters:

- Three different hypothesis acceptance thresholds – [0.93, 0.95, 0.97]. The empirical tests show that locally inaccurate maps, like the ones used in further experiments, cannot be merged, if the threshold is too high.
- Four hypothesis evaluation distance thresholds d_{max} [0, 1, 2, 3]. The lowest distance threshold $d_{max}=0$ basically turns the hypothesis evaluation into comparison of cell values – no nearby cells are taken into account. Distance threshold $d_{max}=2$ is approximately the same as the actual error distance in maps – most inaccuracies fall within this range.
- Three local merging sets [8, 16, 24]. Local merging set shows how many transformations are computed by the local map merging approach. From these transformations the best is chosen as a new hypothesis. The more transformations are computed, the higher probability that the correct merging will be found. On the downside, more time will be necessary to compute all transformations.

In each map merging configuration 10 merging steps were recorded. The count of local mergings in each step was chosen to be [n - 1], where n is the current count of the higher level hypotheses. [n - 1] is the minimum count of mergings necessary to create the global map, if all mergings are successful. It was verified that more merging steps do not yield more proposed hypotheses in any configuration.

3.2 Experimental Result Summary

The results in Figure 8 show the average percentage of map count in each configuration's largest hypotheses (configuration being [distance threshold, acceptance threshold, local merging set]). The goal is to acquire a single global map hypothesis, therefore more maps included in the largest hypothesis indicate better results.

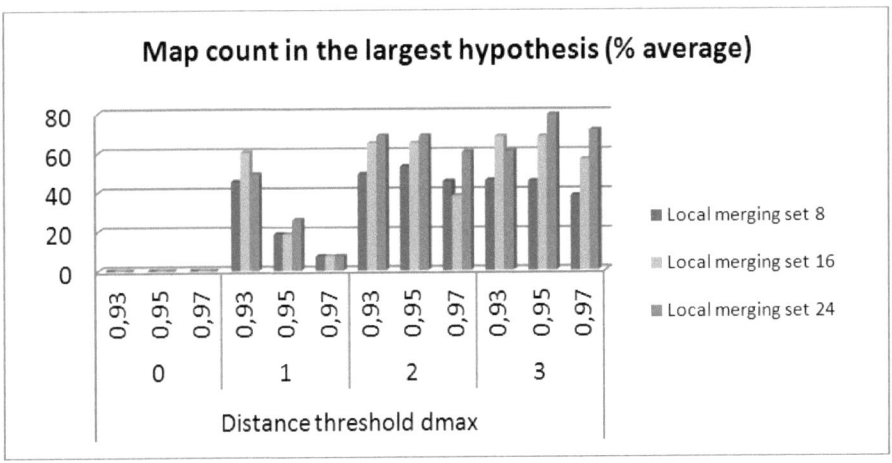

Fig. 8. The map count in the largest hypothesis (average percentage) for all configurations

In general larger local merging sets tend to increase the map count in the largest hypothesis, although there are some exceptions. These exceptions are caused because sometimes higher level maps cannot be merged by the used local map merging method while their lower level components can, and different merging sequence can significantly influence the result.

Higher acceptance thresholds reduce the set of hypotheses that are accepted as potentially valid. This trend can be best observed by the distance threshold $d_{max}=1$, where the map count in the largest hypothesis becomes very low by acceptance threshold 0.97.

The distance threshold $d_{max}=0$ yields no hypotheses in all configurations and map sets. All the other d_{max} values return at least partial global maps. The values $d_{max}=2$ and $d_{max}=3$ give the best results, with $d_{max}=3$ being slightly better at finding more complete global hypotheses (respectively 68.51% and 79.16% in best configurations).

However, Figure 9 shows that the distance threshold $d_{max}=3$ is unable to recognize incorrect mergings. In total 62.96% results with $d_{max}=3$ contain at least one incorrect hypothesis. It shows that the use of higher distance thresholds can produce larger global maps, but the risk of wrong mergings is also higher.

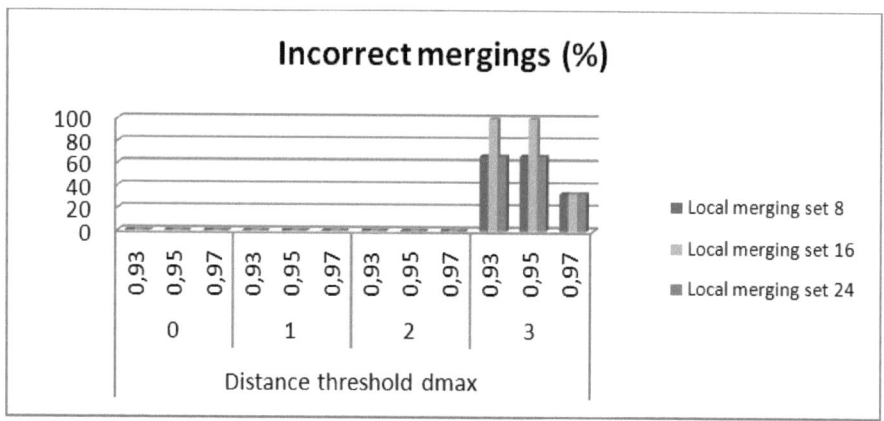

Fig. 9. The incorrect mergings (percentage from merging count) for all configurations

To set the distance threshold in a robot system, two values should be considered: a) the noise in maps in terms of arbitrary cell position on map and in reality and b) cell size. The d_{max} value should be approximately equal to the distance of most errors in terms of cell size. From several possible values the authors of this paper recommend to use the highest distance threshold that yields acceptable level of incorrect mergings. In this particular robot system the distance threshold $d_{max}=2$ should be used.

The Figure 10 shows the average count of rejected hypotheses. In almost all configurations some hypotheses were rejected (in most of the configurations with 0% rejected hypotheses no hypotheses were proposed). From 7.41% to as much as 50.43% hypotheses, which were proposed by using local maps from the earlier stages of mapping, were rejected, when additional information about the environment was

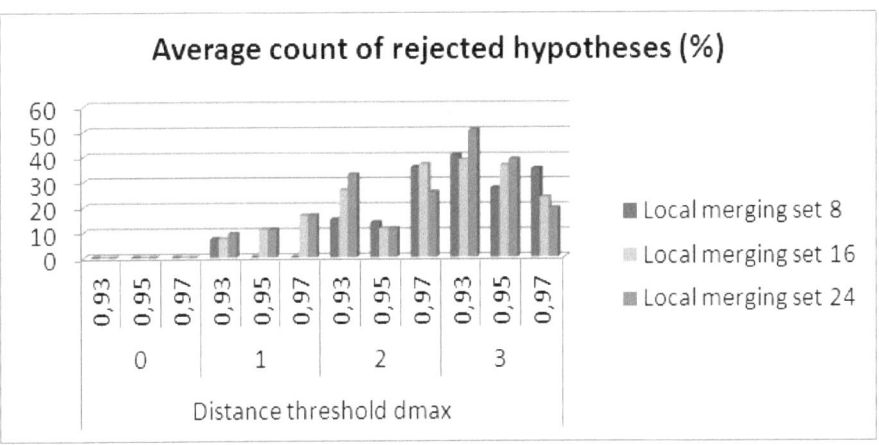

Fig. 10. Average count of the rejected hypotheses (percentage from all proposed hypotheses) for all configurations

acquired by the robots. These results demonstrate the necessity of map merging reversibility.

4 Conclusions

The experimental results show that the proposed global map merging method can create partial global maps and in some cases full global maps from multiple local maps, but the parameters must be chosen carefully for the best performance. The use of higher distance thresholds can achieve larger global maps, but the risk of wrong mergings is also higher. In general, there are two main obstacles that interfere with successful full global map creation:

— The limitations of local map merging methods. No local map merging method known by the authors detects the common areas of maps in all cases, even if they do exist.
— Naturally persistent noise in the maps. The map inaccuracies make it hard or in some cases even impossible to set the parameters of the proposed method (distance threshold d_{max} and hypothesis acceptance threshold) so that all the acceptable mergings were accepted and all the wrong mergings were rejected.

Some cases in experiments indicate that it is sometimes possible to merge lower level maps but not their highest level counterparts. This is especially true, if the sizes of the highest level maps to be merged are very different. The future work will be made to improve the method by allowing the merging attempts of not only highest level maps but also their components.

Acknowledgements. The paper is created within RTU funded project „Multi robot floor cleaning systems" ZI-2013/2.

References

1. Ko, J., Stewart, B., Fox, D., Konolige, K., Limketkai, B.: A practical, decision-theoretic approach to multi-robot mapping and exploration. In: IEEE/RSJ International Conference on Intelligent Robots and Systems (IROS 2003), vol. 4, pp. 3232–3238. IEEE (2003)
2. Thrun, S., Burgard, W., Fox, D.: A probabilistic approach to concurrent mapping and localization for mobile robots. Autonomous Robots 5, 253–271 (1998)
3. Simmons, R., Apfelbaum, D., Burgard, W., Fox, D., Moors, M., Thrun, S., Younes, H.: Coordination for multi-robot exploration and mapping. In: AAAI/IAAI, pp. 852–858 (2000)
4. Roy, N., Dudek, G.: Collaborative robot exploration and rendezvous: Algorithms, performance bounds and observations. Autonomous Robots 11, 117–136 (2001)
5. Burgard, W., Moors, M., Schneider, F.: Collaborative exploration of unknown environments with teams of mobile robots. In: Beetz, M., Hertzberg, J., Ghallab, M., Pollack, M.E. (eds.) Dagstuhl Seminar 2001. LNCS (LNAI), vol. 2466, pp. 52–70. Springer, Heidelberg (2002)
6. Roumeliotis, S.I., Bekey, G.A.: Distributed multirobot localization. IEEE Transactions on Robotics and Automation 18, 781–795 (2002)
7. Amigoni, F., Gasparini, S., Gini, M.: Merging partial maps without using odometry. Multi-Robot Systems. In: From Swarms to Intelligent Automata Volume III, pp. 133–144. Springer (2005)
8. Birk, A., Carpin, S.: Merging occupancy grid maps from multiple robots. Proceedings of the IEEE 94, 1384–1397 (2006)
9. Carpin, S.: Fast and accurate map merging for multi-robot systems. Autonomous Robots 25, 305–316 (2008)
10. Adluru, N., Latecki, L.J., Sobel, M., Lakaemper, R.: Merging maps of multiple robots. In: 19th International Conference on Pattern Recognition, ICPR 2008, pp. 1–4. IEEE (2008)
11. Topal, S., Erkmen, E., Erkmen, A.M.: A novel map merging methodology for multi-robot systems. In: Proceedings of the World Congress on Engineering and Computer Science, pp. 383–387 (2010)
12. Alnounou, Y., Paulik, M.J., Krishnan, M., Hudas, G., Overholt, J.: Occupancy Grid Map Merging Using Feature Maps. DTIC Document (2010)
13. Konolige, K., Fox, D., Limketkai, B., Ko, J., Stewart, B.: Map merging for distributed robot navigation. In: IEEE/RSJ International Conference on Intelligent Robots and Systems (IROS 2003), pp. 212–217. IEEE (2003)
14. Huang, W.H., Beevers, K.R.: Topological map merging. The International Journal of Robotics Research 24, 601–613 (2005)
15. Siegwart, R., Nourbakhsh, I.R.: Introduction to Autonomous Mobile Robots. The MIT press (2004)
16. Andersone, I., Liekna, A.: Robot Map Similarity Evaluation for Non-identical Maps. In: 12th International Scientific Conference on Engineering for Rural Development 2013, Jelgava, pp. 456–461 (2013)
17. Nikitenko, A., Liekna, A., Ekmanis, M., Kulikovskis, G., Andersone, I.: Single Robot Localisation Approach for Indoor Robotic Systems through Integration of Odometry and Artificial Landmarks. Applied Computer Systems 14, 50–58 (2013)
18. Andersone, I., Liekna, A., Nikitenko, A.: Mapping Implementation for Multi-robot System with Glyph Localisation. Applied Computer Systems 14, 67–72 (2013)

Task-Oriented Conversational Behavior of Agents for Collaboration in Human-Agent Teamwork

Mukesh Barange, Alexandre Kabil,
Camille De Keukelaere, and Pierre Chevaillier

ENIB–UEB; Lab-STICC, France

Abstract. Coordination is an essential ingredient for human-agent teamwork. It requires team members to share knowledge to establish common grounding and mutual awareness among them. This paper proposes a behavioral architecture C^2BDI that enhances the knowledge sharing using natural language communication between team members. Collaborative conversation protocols and resource allocation mechanism have been defined that provide proactive behavior to agents for coordination. This architecture has been applied to a real scenario in a collaborative virtual environment for learning. The solution enables users to coordinate with other team members.

Keywords: Human interaction with autonomous agents, Cooperation, Dialogue Management, Decision-Making, Resource Sharing.

1 Introduction

In collaborative virtual environments (VE) for training, users, namely learners, work together with autonomous agents to perform a collective activity. The educational objective is not only to learn the task, but also to acquire social skills in order to be efficient in the coordination of the activity with other team members [3]. The ability to coordinate with others relies on common grounding [9] and mutual awareness [17]. Common grounding leads team members to share a common point of view about their collective goals, plans, and resources they can use to achieve them [9]. Mutual awareness means that team members act to get information about others' activities by direct perception or information seeking, and to provide information about theirs' through dialogues [17].

Collaboration in a human-agent teamwork poses many important challenges. First, there exist no global resource that human team members and virtual agents can rely on to share their knowledge. Second, the structure of coordination between human-agent team members is open by nature: virtual agents need to adopt the flexibility of human behavior, as users may not necessarily strictly follow the rules of coordination. In contrast, in agent-agent interactions, agents follow the rigid structure of interaction protocols (e.g., contract net protocol). Thus, the ability to coordinate with human team members requires to reason about their shared actions, shared resources and, about the situations where team members need the coordination. Moreover, in human-human teamwork, team members pro-actively provide information needed by other team members based on the anticipation of other's need of information [12].

This paper focuses on the task-oriented collaborative conversational behavior of virtual agents in a mixed human-agent team. Other aspects of spoken interaction with embodied virtual agents, such as non-verbal behaviors, perception, auto speech recognition, and text to speech etc. are out of the scope of this study. As team members must have the shared understanding of skills, goals and intentions of other team members, we proposed a belief-desire-intention based (BDI-like) agent architecture named as *collaborative-Conversational BDI agent architecture* (C^2BDI). The contributions of this paper include: (1) definition of collaborative conversational protocols to establish mutual awareness and common grounding among team members; (2) resource allocation mechanism for effective coordination through the means of communication; and (3) decision-making mechanism where dialogues and beliefs about other agents are used to guide the action selection mechanism allowing agents to collaborate with their team members. The approach consists in formalizing the conversational behavior of the agent related to the coordination of the activity, which reduces the necessity to explicitly define communicative actions in the action plan.

In section 2, we present related work on human-agent teamwork. Section 3 presents different components of our architecture. The conversational behavior is detailed in section 4. The next section illustrates how the solution fulfils requirements of real educational scenarios. Finally, section 6 summaries our positioning.

2 Related Work

Both AI and dialogue literature agree that to coordinate their activities, agents must have the joint-intention towards achieving the group goal [10] and must have the common plan [13]. The joint-intention theory specifies that agents have common intentions towards the group goal [10], whereas the shared-plan theory [13] specifies that even agents share a common plan, it does not guarantee that agents have the commitment towards the group to achieve shared goal. The C^2BDI architecture takes advantage of these theories to establish common grounding and mutual awareness among human-agent team members.

Numbers of human-agent team models have been proposed. Collagen agent [16] is built upon the human discourse theory and collaborates with a user to solve domain problems such as planning a travel itinerary. In [5], collaboration in teams are governed by teamwork notification policies, where agents inform the user when an important event occurs. To achieve collaboration, [19] proposed a four stage model that includes (i) recognising potential for cooperation, (ii) team formation (iii) plan formation, and (iv) plan execution. Based on this model, [11] describes how collective intentions from the team formation stage are build-up using information-seeking speech act based dialogues. Moreover, [4] proposed an agent based dialogue system by providing dialogue acts for collaborative problem solving between a user and a system. In contrast, C²BDI agents coordinate with team members not only at the beginning, but also during the realisation of the shared task. Recently, [12] have proposed a theoretical framework on proactive information exchange in agent teamwork to establish shared mental model using shared-plan [13]. Furthermore, sharing common resources among team members requires coordination mechanism to manage resource usage. In [15], authors have proposed a negotiation based model, in which agents negotiate to maximise the resource utilisation. In contrast, C²BDI agent, based on the anticipation of others' needs, provides opportunities to other members to choose resources.

One of the prominent approaches for dialogue modelling is the information state (IS) approach [18]. The IS defined in [6] contains contextual information of dialogue that includes dialogue, semantic, cognitive, perceptual, and social context. This model includes major aspects to control natural language dialogues. However, it does not include contextual information about the shared task. This leads to an incoherence between dialogue context and shared task in progress. In [14], an IS based interaction model for *Max* agent has been proposed that considers coordination as an implicit characteristic of team members, Comparing with [14], C²BDI agents exhibit both reactive and proactive conversational behaviors, and explicitly handle cooperative situations between team members. Moreover, [6] proposed a taxonomy of dialogue acts (DIT++) based on the dialogue interpretation theory. Semantics of these dialogue acts are based on the IS based approach. We are motivated to use it to understand and interpret conversation between human-agent team due to its following characteristics: (i) it is mainly used for annotation and interpretation of dialogues in human-human conversation; (ii) it supports task oriented conversation; and (iii) it has become the ISO 24617-2 international standard for dialogue interpretation using dialogue acts.

3 C²BDI Agent Architecture

In this section, we describe components of C²BDI agent architecture that provide deliberative and conversational behaviours for collaboration (Fig. 1). The agent architecture is based on the theory of shared-plan [13] and joint-intention [10].

The C²BDI agent is considered to be situated in an informed VE [7]. It perceives VE through the perception module. The current perceived state of VE is an instantiation of concepts the agent holds in its semantic knowledge. The perception allows agents to enrich their knowledge, and to monitor the progress of the shared activity. Since, the state of VE can be changed due to interactions by team members, the belief revision function periodically updates knowledge base of the agent, and maintains its consistency. It ensures the coherence of the knowledge elements acquired from the perception of the VE and from the natural language dialogues. The dialogue manager allows an agent to share its knowledge with other team members using natural language communication. It supports both reactive and proactive conversation behavior, and ensures coordination of the activity. The decision-making uses private beliefs and beliefs about others to decide whether to elaborate the plan, to identify collaborative situations, to react in the current situation, or to exchange information with other

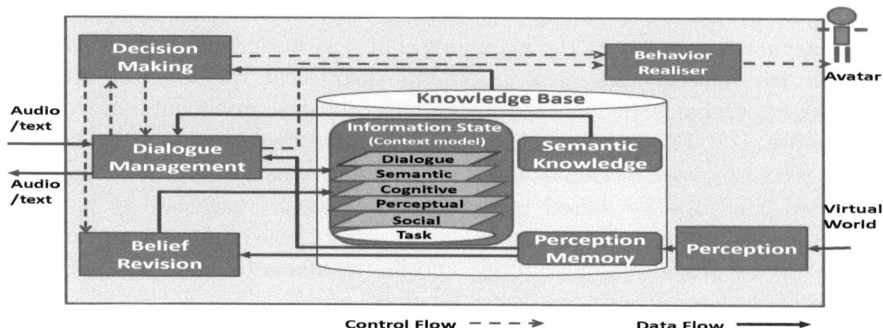

Fig. 1. Components of Agent architecture and data flow

team members. The behavior realiser module is responsible for the execution of actions and for the turn taking behavior of the agent.

3.1 Knowledge Organisation and Processing

The knowledge base consists of semantic knowledge, perception memory and IS (Fig. 1). The semantic modeling of VE [7] is used as semantic knowledge. It contains semantic information that is known a priori by the agent, such as knowledge concerning concepts, and individual and shared plans. Following the shared-plan theory [13], C^2BDI agents share the same semantic knowledge about VE and the group activity. This characteristic supports proactive conversation behavior of the agent, as first, it allows the decision-making process to identify collaborative situations and information needed by other team members, and second, it provides information about the action and resource interdependencies with other team members. The perception memory acquires information about the state of VE perceived by the perception module, whereas, the IS contains contextual information about the current activity and dialogues.

The natural language understanding (NLU) and generation (NLG) of spoken dialogues is based on the rule based approach [1]. When the agent receives an utterance, it uses NLU rules to determine the corresponding dialogue act [6]. It identifies dialogue contents using semantic knowledge and contextual information from IS. The dialogue manager processes these dialogue acts and updates IS based on update rules similar to [18]. When the agent has communicative intentions, it constructs dialogue act moves and adds to IS. NLG rules are used to generate utterance corresponding to these acts based on the current context from IS. The details of the dialogue management approach can be found in [2].

3.2 Information State

The IS is primarily used in literature [18,6] to control natural language dialogues. The semantic context of the IS is instantiated from concepts the agent holds in semantic knowledge, depending on the progress of the shared task. It includes the

Dialogue Context	agent-dialogue-acts, addressee-dialogue-acts, dialogue-act-history, next-moves	
Semantic Context	agenda, qud, communication-plan, beliefs, expected-dialogue-acts	
Cognitive Context	mutual-belief	
Social Context	communication-pressure	
Perception Context	object-in-focus, agent-in-focus, third-person-in-focus	
Task Context	cooperative-info	group-goal, group-desire, group-intention joint-goal, joint-desire, joint-intention, joint-commitment
	task	task-focus, goals, desires

Fig. 2. Extended Information State of [6] in C^2BDI architecture

agenda that contains dialogue goals. To cooperate with other team members, the agent needs not only the information about the current context of the collective activity, but also beliefs about team members to establish common grounding and mutual awareness. To acquire these information, we extend the IS based context model of [6] by adding the *task context* to it (Fig. 2). We extended its usage as the source of knowledge between decision-making and conversational behavior of the C^2BDI agent to establish coherence between these two processes. In C^2BDI agent, the IS works as an *active memory*.

The *task context* includes information about the *task*. It contains intentions in *task-focus*, goals, and desires of the agent. The C^2BDI agent follows the theory of joint-intention [10]. It ensures that each team member has common intention towards the team goal. Therefore, the *task context* also contains *cooperative-information* that includes beliefs about *group-goal, group-desire, group-intention, joint-goal, joint-desire, joint-intention,* and *joint-commitment*. We distinguish among individual, group and joint intentions of the agent.

The *group-goal* indicates that the agent knows that all team members want to achieve the goal at a time or another. Similarly, *group-desire* and *group-intention* can be defined analogously. For an agent a *group-intention* becomes a *joint-intention* when the agent knows that this intention is shared by other team members. To form a *joint-intention*, a necessary condition is that the agent must have individual intention to achieve this goal. Similarly, the semantics of joint-desire and joint-goal indicates that all team members have the same *group-desire* and *group-goal* respectively, and all team members know it. Thus, these shared mental attitudes towards the group, specify that each member holds beliefs about other team members, and each member mutually believes that every member has the same mental attitude.

The *joint-intention* only ensures that each member is individually committed to acting. The agent must also ensure the commitment of others to achieve this shared goal. Agents must communicate with other team members to obtain their *joint-commitments*. The agent has a *joint-commitment* towards the group, if and only if, each member of the group has the mutual belief about the same *group-goal*, the agent has the *joint-intention* about to achieve that goal, and each agent of the group is individually committed to achieve this goal. Hence, the IS not only contains information about the current context of the dialogue, but also that of the collaborative task, i.e., beliefs about other team members potentially useful for the agent for its decision-making.

4 Conversational Behavior

The conversational behavior allows C^2BDI agents to share their knowledge with other team members using natural language communication, and ensures the coordination of the team activity. The agent interprets and generates the dialogues based on semantics of dialogue acts proposed in [6]. To achieve coordination among team members, we propose *collaborative conversational protocols*, and resource allocation mechanism for the agent.

4.1 Collaborative Conversational Protocols

As we want the agent to be proactive and cooperative, we define three collaborative conversational protocols (CCP). They ensure the establishment of collaboration among team members to achieve a *group-goal*, and its end when the current goal is achieved. Every team member participating in a collaborative activity enters in collaboration at the same time, and remains committed towards the group until the activity is finished.

CCP-1: When the agent has a new *group-goal* to achieve, it communicates with other team members to establish *joint-commitment*, and to ensure that every team member use the same plan to achieve the *group-goal*.

When the agent has one or more *group-goals* to achieve, and if it has no mutual belief about them, it constructs *Set-Q(what-team-next-goal)* dialogue act addressing it to the group. By addressing this open question, the agent allows both users and other agents to actively participate in the conversation. If the agent receives the choice of the goal from another team member, it adds mutual belief about *group-goal* and *group-intention* to its *cognitive context*, and adds the belief about *joint-goal* to the *task context*. It then confirms this choice by sending positive acknowledgement (by constructing *Auto-feedback(positive-ack)*).

When the agent receives *Set-Q(what-team-next-goal)* and has no mutual belief about *group-goal*, i.e., no other team member has already replied to the question, it can decide to reply based on its response time. It chooses one of the available goals based on its own preference rules, and informs sender by constructing *Inform(team-next-goal)* dialogue act. When the agent receives positive acknowledgement from one of the team members, it modifies its IS by adding mutual belief about *group-goal* and *group-intention*, and belief about *joint-goal*.

If the agent has *joint-goal*, but not *joint-intention* to achieve this goal, the agent needs to ensure that every team member will follow the same plan to achieve *group-goal*. If the agent has more than one plan to achieve this goal, it constructs *Choice-Q(which-plan)* act and address it to the group, or if the agent has only one plan for the goal, it constructs *Check-Q(action-plan)* act addressing to the group. When the agent receives a choice of the plan, or the confirmation of the choice of a plan, it adds *joint-intention* to its *task context*. It confirms this by sending positive acknowledgement, and constructs the belief about *joint-commitment*. When the agent receives *Choice-Q(which-plan)* or *Check-Q(action-plan)*, and has no mutual belief about *group-intention*, it constructs

Inform(plan-choice) or *Confirm* dialogue act respectively to inform about its plan selection. When it receives positive acknowledgement from one of the team members, it adds individual- and joint-commitment to achieve the group-goal.

CCP-2: When the agent has performed all its planned actions of the shared activity, but the activity is not yet finished, agent requests other team members to inform him when the activity will be finished.

The agent generates *Directive-request(inform-goal-achieved)* to ask other members to inform it when the activity will be finished. When the agent receives this dialogue act, it adds communicative goal *Inform(goal-achieved)* to its agenda.

CCP-3: The agent who finished the last action of the shared activity, informs other team members that the activity is terminated.

The preconditions for CCP-3 are that the agent believes that it has performed the last action of the collaborative activity, and it has the *joint-commitment* to achieve *group-goal*. If preconditions are satisfied, it constructs *Inform(activity-finished)* dialogue act addressing it to the group. When the agent receives the information that the last action of the activity has been finished, and has the belief about *joint-commitment* in its *task context* and has a communicative goal *Inform(goal-achieved)* to achieve, it constructs *Inform(goal-achieved)* dialogue act to inform other team members that the goal has been achieved. It then adds the belief about the achievement of the goal, and removes the corresponding intention from the *task context*. When the agent receives the information about goal achievement, it removes the corresponding intention from the *task context*, and drops the communicative goal *Inform(goal-achieved)* if it has.

These protocols add expectations of information from other team members which need to be satisfied. In a human-agent team, the user's behavior is uncertain, i.e., user may not necessarily follow these protocols. As the agent updates their beliefs using perception information which can make the expectation to be true from the observation of actions of user perceived by the agent, or from the information provided by other team members.

4.2 Resource Allocation between Team Members

Agents must acquire resources necessary to carry out an action. It acquires a resource when needed, and releases it when it is no more required. The resource allocation mechanism for C^2BDI agent is described in Algo. 1. The resource can be allocated to an agent when the action to be executed contains explicit declaration of the resource, or when the resource is shareable and constraints on the resource (e.g., maximum number of users) are satisfied. The conflict situation arises when the action contains only the declaration of the type of resource, and there exist resource dependency with other agents. If no instance is available, it constructs *Directive-request(inform-resource-release)* to ask other team members about the availability of the resource. If at least one instance is available, it constructs *Set-Q(what-resource-choice)* dialogue act to ask the other agent about resource choice. Then, it chooses the available resource, and

Algorithm 1. Resource Allocation mechanism for C^2BDI agent

Require: $Plan(g), action_p, R_x$
1: let $r_k \in instances(R_x)$ ▷ r_k be an instance of R_k
2: **if** $action_p$ contains explicit declaration of a resource r_k **then**
3:    choose-available-resource(R_x, r_k) ▷ Agent acquires the resource r_k
4: **else if** $\|available - instances(R_x)\| = 0$ **then** ▷ no instance is currently free
5:    **if** $A_j = $ Bel(Resource-choice ? $R_x\ r_k$) **then** ▷ A_j has acquired the resource
6:      IS $\Leftarrow$ pushAgenda(Directive-request A_j inform-resource-release R_x)
7:    **else** ▷ agent don't know who acquired the resource
8:      IS $\Leftarrow$ pushAgenda(Directive-request ALL inform-resource-release R_x)
9: **else if** $\|available - instances(R_x)\| >= 1$ **then** ▷ at least one resource instance is available
10:    **if** there exist no inter dependency for R_x **then**
11:      choose-available-resource(R_x, r_k) ▷ Agent acquires the resource r_k
12:    **else**
13:      let there exist inter dependency of R_x with A_j
14:      **if** $\|instances(R_x)\| = 1$ **then** ▷ there exist only one instance of type R_x
15:        **if** the resource r_k is shareable and constraints on R_x are satisfied **then**
16:          choose-available-resource(R_x, r_k)
17:        **if** Bel(resource-choice $A_j\ r_k$) or Bel(resource-needed $A_j\ R_x$) **then**
18:          IS$\Leftarrow$pushAgenda(Directive-request A_j inform-resource-release R_x)
19:        **else**
20:          r_k=choose-available-resource(R_x), ▷ Agent acquires available instance of R_x
21:          IS$\Leftarrow$pushAgenda(inform-resource-choice $A_j\ r_k$)
22:      **else** ▷ More than one instance of resource is available
23:        IS $\Leftarrow$ pushAgenda(Set-Q(what-resource-choice $A_j\ R_x$))
24:        IS $\Leftarrow$ addExpected(resource-choice $A_j\ R_x$) ▷ expecting resource choice from A_j
25:        $r_k = $ choose-available-resource(R_x), IS $\Leftarrow$ pushAgenda(inform-resource-choice $A_j\ r_k$)
26: **else if** received(Set-Q(what-resource-choice $A_j\ R_x$)) **then** ▷ A_j requests for resource choice
27:    $r_k = $ choose-available-resource(R_x) ▷ Agent acquires available instance of R_x
28:    IS$\Leftarrow$pushAgenda(inform-resource-choice $A_j\ r_k$)

informs its choice to other team members by creating *Inform(resource-choice)* dialogue act. Similarly, an agent informs its choice to the sender if it has received *Set-Q(what-resource-choice)* request. In this mechanism, agents give chance to other team members to choose resources in the situation of resource conflict.

4.3 Decision Making

In C²BDI agent, decision-making is governed by information about current goals, shared activity plan, and knowledge of the agent (IS and semantic knowledge). The decision making algorithm is shown in Algo. 2. It verifies whether the agenda in IS is not empty or *task-focus* contains communicative intentions. If so, control is passed to the conversational behavior that supports natural language communication. Otherwise, it chooses the plan to be realised. It identifies cooperative situations in the collective activity where the agent can not progress without assistance. That is, if preconditions for one of the CCPs is satisfied, the control is passed to the conversational behavior. Otherwise, if the agent has an action to be performed that uses a resource, the control is passed to the resource allocation mechanism. These Cooperative situations generate communicative intentions in the agenda that cause the agent to interact with team members to share their knowledge. The agent updates its IS if the control is passed to the conversational behavior, and deliberate the plan to generate a new intention. Once the intention

Algorithm 2. Decision making algorithm

Require: *IS*
1: B = IS.SemanticContext.Belief, D = IS.Task-Context.Desire, I = IS.Task-Context.Intention
   agenda= IS.Semantic-context.Agenda
2: **while** true **do**
3:    update-perception(ρ) and Compute B, D, I
4:    $\Pi \Leftarrow$ Plan(P, I)
5:    **while** !$\Pi.empty()$ **do**
6:      **if** agenda is not empty or the agent has received an utterance **then**
7:         Process Conversation-Behavior()
8:         Compute new B, D, I , $\Pi \Leftarrow$ Plan(P, I)
9:      **if** the *task-focus* contains communicative intention **then**
10:         Process Conversation-Behavior()
11:      Identify-Cooperative-Situation in the current plan Π
12:      **if** Cooperative-Situation is matched **then**
13:         Process Conversation-behavior()
14:      $\alpha \Leftarrow$ Plan-action(Π), execute(α)

is generated, the agent selects actions to be realised and, updates its *task-focus* in IS to maintain knowledge about the current context of the task.

5 Application Scenario

Let us consider a motivational scenario where three agents (may include both virtual or real), named as Virginie, Sebastien, and Alexandre need to assemble a furniture. To do so, they need to choose tablets from the table (Fig. 3:left) and place them on shelves (Fig. 3:right). Following sequence of dialogues describe a typical interaction between them where a user plays the role of Alexandre.

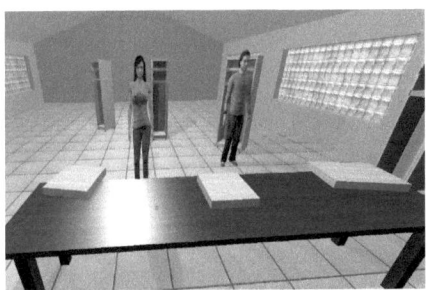 

Fig. 3. Furniture Assembly Scenario (First Person view):
left: before tablet selection   right: before choosing tablet position

- *S1*: Sebastien : *What should we do now?*   [Set-Q(team-next-action)]
- *U1*: Alexandre : *We should place tablets on shelves.*   [Inform(team-next-goal)]
- *S2*: Sebastien : *Ok.*   [Auto-feedback(positive-ack)]
- *S3*: Sebastien : *Should we use the place-tablet plan?*   [Check-Q(action-plan)]
- *U2*: Alexandre : *Yes.*   [Auto-feedback(positive-ack)]
- *S4*: Sebastien : *I will choose the large tablet.*   [Inform(resource-choice)]
  (Sebastien chooses the tablet near to him and go towards shelf;)
  (if user does not make his choice)
- *V1*: Virginie : *Alexandre which narrow tablet will you choose?* [Set-Q(what-resource-choice)]
- *U3*: Alexandre : *I will choose the left tablet.*   [Inform(resource-choice)]
  (user picks the chosen tablet;)

- *V2*: Virginie : *Ok, I will choose the other one.* [Inform(resource-choice)]
  (Virginie picks the other tablet and go towards the shelf;)
  (Sebastien places his tablet on the upper position of the shelf;)
- *S5*: Sebastien : *Inform me when you will finish the activity.* [Directive-request(inform-goal-achieved)]
- *U4*: Alexandre : *Virginie which position will you use to place tablet?* [Set-Q(what-resource-choice)]
- *V3*: Virginie : *I will choose the lower position.* [Inform(resource-choice)]
  (Virginie places its tablet on the shelf)
- *U5*: Alexandre : *Ok, I will place my tablet on upper position.* [Inform(resource-choice)]
  (User places his tablet on the upper position of the shelf)
- *V4*: Virginie : *We have placed all the tablets on shelves.* [Inform(goal-achieved)]

The challenging scenario includes some important characteristics such as collaborative situations to establish common grounding ($S1,U1,S2,S3,U2$), handling resource conflicts ($V1,U3,V2,$), dynamic environment (agents manipulate objects e.g., move tablet), interleaving between communication and actions (agents utter and perform action $S4,U3,V3,U4$), mixed initiative dialogues ($V1,U3,V2$ or $U4,V3,U5$), and both reactive (V3) and proactive (S1,V1) communications.

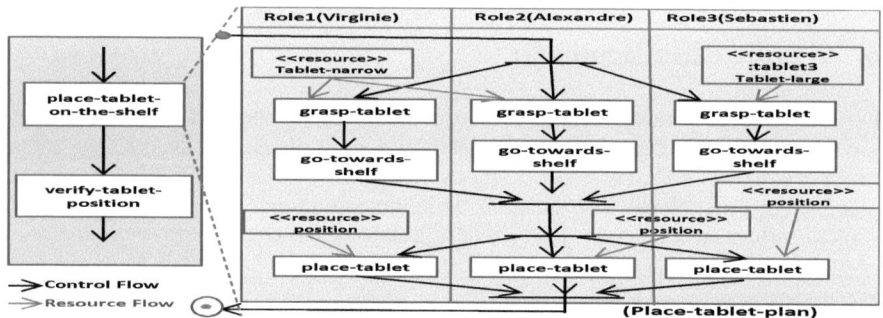

Fig. 4. Partial view of Furniture Assembly plan shared between team members

Table 1. Snapshot of IS for Virginie and Sebastien before initialisation of CCP-1

	R_1 (Virginie)	R_3 (Sebastien)
Information State	*Task-Context*(group-goal("place-tablet-on-the-shelf"))	*Task-Context*(group-goal("place-tablet-on-the-shelf"))

At the beginning, both user and virtual agents have a goal "place-tablet-on-the-shelf". As this goal is shared among team members, it becomes the *group-goal* (Fig. 4). A subset of knowledge of agents is shown in Table. 1. Since, Sebastien has a group-goal in its IS, but has no mutual belief about that goal, the decision making process identifies this collaborative situation that fulfils conditions of CCP-1. The CCP-1 generates *Set-Q(team-next-goal)* dialogue act and generates natural language utterance *S1*. Sebastien interprets utterance *U1* as *Inform(team-next-goal "place-tablet-on-the-shelf")* dialogue act. As Sebastien has the same group-goal, it generates positive acknowledgement *S2* for the user

Table 2. Snapshot of IS for agent Sebastien after establishing joint-goal

	R_3 (Sebastien)
Information State	Cognitive-Context(mutual-belief (group-intention("place-tablet-on-the-shelf") group-goal("place-tablet-on-the-shelf")); Task-Context(group-goal("place-tablet-on-the-shelf") joint-goal("place-tablet-on-the-shelf"))

and creates mutual-belief about group-goal (Table 2). Virginie passively listens to the conversation and updates its IS following CCP-1. Now, to ensure that the each team member will follow the same action plan, Sebastien construct *Check-Q(action-plan)* dialogue act considering that team members have only one plan "place-tablet-plan" to achieve the current group-goal, and generates *S3*. When

Table 3. Snapshot of IS of Virginie after establishing joint-commitment

	Role R_1 (Virginie)
Information State	Cognitive-context(mutual-belief(group-intention("place-tablet-on-the-shelf"); group-goal("place-tablet-on-the-shelf")); Task-Context(group-goal("place-tablet-on-the-shelf") joint-goal("place-tablet-on-the-shelf") joint-intention("place-tablet-on-the-shelf") joint-commitment("place-tablet-on-the-shelf") taskFocus(Intention("grasp-tablet") Intention("place-tablet-on-the-shelf")))

both Sebastien and Virginie receive response *U2* from user, they construct the joint-intention as well as joint-commitment towards the group-goal and update their IS. The decision making process, now, deliberate the plan and computes the new intention as *grasp-tablet* (Table 3). Sebastien chooses the large-tablet as the resource is explicitly defined with the action (Algo. 1, line 2). Virginie needs to perform explicit resource acquisition, as only the resource type is defined for its action which is dependent on user's choice (Fig. 4). As two instances of "Tablet-narrow" are available (Fig. 1:left), and if Virginie has no belief about user choice, it constructs *Set-Q*(what-resource-choice) to ask user to choose one of the tablets (*V1*) (Algo. 1, line 22). When user specifies his choice (*U3*), Virginie chooses the other one (*V2*). After executing last action "place-tablet" by Sebastien from his plan, and as the shared activity is not yet finished, it utters *S5* following CCP-2. When user asks Virginie about its choice of position (*U4*), Virginie interprets it as *Set-Q(what-resource-choice)* and informs its choice (*V3*). Once user places the tablet (*U5*) which is the last action of the shared plan, Virginie informs all the team members that the goal is achieved (*V4*) following CCP-3.

6 Conclusion

The proposed behavioural architecture C^{2}BDI endows agents in the collaborative VE with the ability to coordinate their activities using natural language communication. This capability allows users and agents to share their knowledge. The architecture ensures knowledge sharing between team members by considering deliberative and conversation behaviours, not in isolation, but as tightly coupled components, which is a necessary condition for common grounding and mutual awareness to occur. The collaborative conversational protocols and the resource allocation mechanism enable agents to exhibit human-like proactive conversational behavior, that help users to participate in the collaborative activity. While the implemented scenario already shows the benefits of the solution, the behavior of agents could be enriched both in terms of collaborative team management and in terms of natural language dialogue modelling. Particularly, it would be interesting to endow agents with problem solving capabilities to select their communicative intentions, or to engage themselves into information seeking behaviors and negotiation rounds, as observed in human teamwork [8].

Acknowledgment. This work was partly supported by the ANR (Corvette project ANR-10-CORD-012).

References

1. Barange, M., De Loor, P., Louis, V., Querrec, R., Soler, J., Trinh, T.-H., Maisel, É., Chevaillier, P.: Get involved in an interactive virtual tour of brest harbour: Follow the guide and participate. In: Vilhjálmsson, H.H., Kopp, S., Marsella, S., Thórisson, K.R. (eds.) IVA 2011. LNCS, vol. 6895, pp. 93–99. Springer, Heidelberg (2011)
2. Barange, M., Kabil, A., Chevaillier, P.: The C^2BDI agent architecture for teamwork coordination using spoken dialogues between virtual agents and users. In: Demazeau, Y., Corchado, J.M., Zambonelli, F., Bajo, J. (eds.) PAAMS 2014. LNCS (LNAI), vol. 8473, pp. 315–318. Springer, Heidelberg (2014)
3. Barot, C., Lourdeaux, D., Burkhardt, J.M., Amokrane, K., Lenne, D.: V3S: A virtual environment for risk-management training based on human-activity models. Presence 22(1), 1–19 (2013)
4. Blaylock, N., Allen, J.: A collaborative problem-solving model of dialogue. In: Proc. of the SIGdial Workshop on Discourse and Dialog, pp. 200–211 (2005)
5. Bradshaw, J., Feltovich, P., Johnson, M., Bunch, L., Breedy, M., Eskridge, T., Jung, H., Lott, J., Uszok, A.: Coordination in human-agent-robot teamwork. In: Int. Symposium on Collaborative Technologies and Systems, pp. 467–476 (2008)
6. Bunt, H.: The semantics of dialogue acts. In: Proc. of the 9th Int. Conf. on Computational Semantic, IWCS 2011, Stroudsburg, PA, USA, pp. 1–13 (2011)
7. Chevaillier, P., Trinh, T.H., Barange, M., Devillers, F., Soler, J., Loor, P.D., Querrec, R.: Semantic modelling of virtual environments using MASCARET. In: Proc. of the 4th Workshop on Software Engineering and Architectures for Realtime Interactive Systems, Singapore (March 2011)
8. Clancey, W.J.: Simulating activities: relating motives, deliberation, and attentive coordination. Cognitive Systems Research 3, 471–499 (2002)
9. Clark, H.H., Schaefer, E.F.: Contributing to discourse. Cognitive Science 13, 259–294 (1989)
10. Cohen, P.R., Levesque, H.J.: Confirmations and joint action. In: Proc. of IJCAI 1991, pp. 951–957 (1991)
11. Dignum, F.P.M., Dunin-Keplicz, B., Verbrugge, R.: Agent theory for team formation by dialogue. In: Castelfranchi, C., Lespérance, Y. (eds.) ATAL 2000. LNCS (LNAI), vol. 1986, pp. 150–166. Springer, Heidelberg (2001)
12. Fan, X., Yen, J., Volz, R.A.: A theoretical framework on proactive information exchange in agent teamwork. AI 169(1), 23–97 (2005)

13. Grosz, B.J., Kraus, S.: Collaborative plans for complex group action. AI 86(2), 269–357 (1996)
14. Kopp, S., Pfeiffer-Lessmann, N.: Functions of speaking and acting: An interaction model for collaborative construction tasks. In: Heylen, D., Kopp, S., Marsella, S., Pelachaud, C., Vilhjálmsson, H. (eds.) The First FML Workshop, AAMAS (2008)
15. Kraus, S., Wilkenfeld, J., Zlotkin, G.: Multiagent negotiation under time constraints. AI 75(2), 297 (1995)
16. Rich, C., Sidner, C.L., Lesh, N.: Collagen: applying collaborative discourse theory to human-computer interaction. AI Mag. 22(4), 15–25 (2001)
17. Schmidt, K.: The problem with 'awareness': Introductory remarks on awareness in CSCW. CSCW 11(3), 285–298 (2002)
18. Traum, D., Larsson, S.: The information state approach to dialogue management. In: Kuppevelt, J., Smith, R. (eds.) Current and New Directions in Discourse and Dialogue, Text, Speech and Language Technology, vol. 22, pp. 325–353. Springer Netherlands (2003)
19. Wooldridge, M., Jennings, N.R.: The cooperative problem-solving process. J. of Logic and Computation 9(4), 563–592 (1999)

Agent-Based Simulation of Complex Aviation Incidents by Integrating Different Cognitive Agent Models

Tibor Bosse, Nataliya M. Mogles, and Jan Treur

VU University Amsterdam, Agent Systems Research Group
De Boelelaan 1081, 1081 HV Amsterdam, The Netherlands
{tbosse,nms210,treur}@few.vu.nl

Abstract. Aviation incidents often have a complex character in the sense that a number of different aspects of human and technical functioning come together in creating the incident. Usually only model constructs or computational agent models are available for each of these aspects separately. To obtain an overall model, these agent models have to be integrated. In this paper, existing agent models are used to develop a formal, executable agent model of a real-world scenario concerning an aircraft that descends below the minimal descent altitude because of impaired conditions of the flight crew members. Based on the model, a few proof-of-concept simulations are generated that describe how such hazardous scenarios can evolve.

Keywords: aviation, agent-based simulation, agent model, situation awareness, operator functional state, decision making.

1 Introduction

In analysing hazards and incident scenarios in Air Traffic Management (ATM), agent-based modelling has proved to be a fruitful approach [1,3]. As argued in [11], agent-based modelling has considerable advantages over existing approaches such as STAMP [10] and FRAM [8], which have a qualitative nature. Nevertheless, when studying realistic scenarios, it has been found that many of them show a complex interaction of a number of aspects. Often computational models are available for these aspects, but not for their interaction. To obtain such overall models, multiple model constructs need to be integrated. This can be done on an abstract, conceptual level of descriptions of models by their inputs and outputs (model constructs), but to perform simulations, integration at a more detailed level is required. This paper describes how such an integration at a detailed level can be done and illustrates this for a real-world example.

In order to demonstrate how such an integration of models can take place, an existing ATM scenario was used, which is explained in Section 2. Next, in Section 3 it is shown (on a conceptual level) how this asks for integration of a number of models, including the Operator Functional State model (OFS; cf. [2]), the Situation Awareness model (SA; cf. [9]), and a decision model (DM; inspired by [3]). These are the three models on which this section focuses. In Section 4 a formalisation of the integrated models is presented. In Section 5, simulation experiments with the integrated model are described. The simulations illustrate that the integrated model exhibits realistic behaviour as described in the given scenario, and has the ability to produce alternative behaviours. Finally, the results are discussed in Section 6.

2 Scenario

In a scenario involving a number of adverse factors in addition to a combination of 'get-home-itis' and complacency, this Embraer Phenom 100 Flight Crew was fortunate that Air Traffic Control was able to make a great 'save'. The description of the incident, which was taken from Callback[1], is as follows:

> While on an RNAV approach at night, the Captain and I became disoriented and started to descend to the MDA prior to the Final Approach Fix (FAF). We thought we had already passed the FAF, but in reality we had only passed the intersection before the FAF. Four miles from the FAF, Tower notified us of a low altitude alert and told us to immediately climb to the published altitude. We acknowledged the instruction and corrected our altitude. The published altitude for that segment of the approach was 2,000 feet and we had descended to 1,400 feet.

> There were several causal factors for this event: 1.) It was a long duty day. We had already flown roughly eight hours during the course of the day and this was our fourth leg and last leg home. It was dark and we were tired for sure. 2.) During the final leg to our destination, ATC gave us multiple route changes, speed assignments, vectors and a last minute change to the arrival. There was insufficient time to properly configure and brief the approach and corresponding altitudes. 3.) There was some anxiety about getting below the clouds because there are some unique runway conditions currently at this airport. The first 2,000 feet of the runway were unusable due to routine maintenance and we wanted to make sure we identified the runway early so we could visually verify the new touchdown point. 4.) The morning and afternoon thunderstorms in the vicinity challenged us during the course of the day and they left behind pockets of moderate precipitation and turbulence for the arrival. We had to keep clear of the weather cells and keep up with rapidly changing ATC instructions. 5.) Nourishment. We had each eaten a scant breakfast, taken a late lunch, and completely skipped dinner due to flight requirements. I made several comments that I was ready to get down so I could find a place to get something to eat.

> Looking back on this event, I am most grateful to the safeguards placed within the ATC system. Had we not received the low altitude alert, the history of this particular flight could have been much worse. As the day progressed during long flight legs in rough weather I began to slowly lose my focus and attention to fine detail. Admittedly I was spent. I was safe within legal duty and rest limits, but the anxiety of the trip the night before coupled with the long duty day, dulled my senses and allowed me to slip into a near-lethal combination of "get-home-itis" and complacency.

> I can see now a few variables I could change to prevent this from happening again in the future. First, advise ATC that we need delay vectors to prepare properly for the approach. I know that is a wildly unpopular choice in a very crowded and busy airspace, however it could have afforded us the opportunity to brief and prepare for the approach. Secondly, make sure that I take a moment to get some nourishment before I embark on a full day of flying. Third, make sure I confirm that the other pilot is fully briefed and ready to commence the approach. Finally, make sure that I get proper rest the night before I embark on a long day of flying.

3 High-Level Overview of the Integrated (SA-OFS-DM) Model

This section describes at a high level how the scenario asks for formal integration of the model constructs for Situation Awareness, Operator Functional State, and Decision Making. Parts of the description are taken from [4].

3.1 Separate Model Constructs

The *situation awareness* model [9] is a computational refinement of the conceptual model of Endsley [5], which includes the perception of cues, the comprehension and integration of information, and the projection of information for future events. It consists of 4 main components (see the bottom part of Fig. 1): (1) performance of observations; (2) and (3) belief formation on the current situation (simple and complex beliefs); (4) belief formation on the future situation and (5) mental model. For a detailed description of the model see [9].

---

[1] Callback newsletter. http://asrs.arc.nasa.gov/publications/callback.html. July 10th 2012.

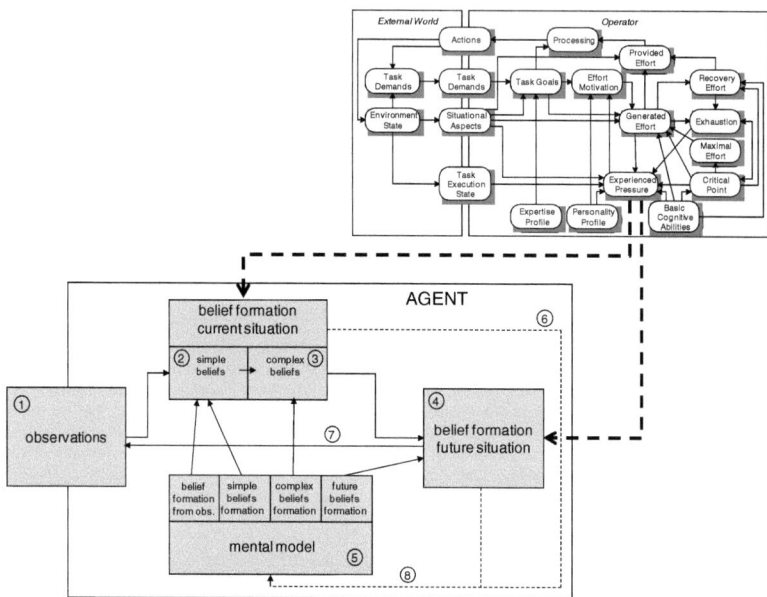

Fig. 1. Integration of Models for OFS and SA

The operator functional state model construct (see top part of Fig. 1) determines a person's *functional state* as a dynamical state, which is a function of task properties and personal characteristics over time. The model is based on two different theories: (1) the *cognitive energetic framework* [7], which states that effort regulation is based on human resources and determines human performance in dynamic conditions, and (2) the idea that when performing physical exercise, a person's generated power can be maintained at some maximal *(critical power)* level without leading to more exhaustiveness [6]. In the upper part of Fig. 1, the concepts on the left hand side denote external factors (such as task demands and environmental conditions), whereas the concepts on the right hand side denote internal states of the operator (such as experienced pressure, exhaustion, and motivation), The concepts in between denote interaction states (i.e., related to the operator's observations and actions). For a detailed description see [2].

The (experienced-based) *decision making* model construct is taken from [3,4]. An extensive description of this model construct is beyond the scope of this paper, but the main idea is that in decision making processes a number of action options are distinguished, and that a model for decision making results from a valuation (e.g., expressed in terms of a real number) for each of the options, in such a way that the action option with the highest associated value is selected to be performed.

3.2 Modelling Interaction between Functional State and Situational Awareness

In many situations in which an operator has a less effective functional state, characterized by high levels of experienced pressure and exhaustion, this affects in a dynamical manner his or her situation awareness, and in turn this impaired situation awareness leads to inadequate decisions. This section focuses on this dynamical interaction pattern. To illustrate this, consider the following: stress or exhaustion may cause a person to make errors in observation (like missing an item on a radar screen), but even when the items have been observed correctly, stress or exhaustion may also induce errors in the way the person processes and interprets the observed items (e.g., even when a pilot observes a low altitude alert, (s)he may interpret this as coherent with approaching an airport and fail to conclude from this that it is necessary to climb to a higher altitude). In terms of the classical sense-reason-act cycle, an operator functional state may influence both the sensing process and the reasoning process, and it may even influence the acting process, which will be explained later.

The scenario described in Section 2 above is a clear example of a situation where functional state affects situation awareness: a pilot misinterprets an important ATC instruction, among others because of fatigue. This is illustrated by the following statement: *'We thought we had already passed the FAF, but in reality we had only passed the intersection before the FAF'*. Hence, although the pilots observed that they had just passed the intersection before the FAF, they interpreted this as having passed the FAF itself. This example illustrates that stress and exhaustion may lead to errors in *interpretation*: they cause human beings to make certain errors in inferences, which they would not have made when they were in their usual functional state. Below, this process of erroneous inference is represented as an incorrect type of belief formation, which is one of the steps modelled in the situation awareness model.

The integration of the models for OFS and SA is visualised in Fig. 1. Note that this picture addresses the case that from the functional state the state of experienced pressure (or stress) influences situation awareness; there are also ways in which exhaustion may affect situation awareness. As shown in Fig. 1, the concept of experienced pressure may interact with concepts in the situation awareness model in two ways: it may impact both the formation of current beliefs and of future beliefs.

In the OFS model the concept of experienced pressure is represented in terms of a variable with a real value in the domain $[0,1]$. For the integration a mechanism was added that models how this variable affects the process of belief formation in the SA model. This mechanism also accounts for having an agent make *incorrect* inferences. To obtain this, an extension of the situation awareness model is needed. This is done by including in the mental model of it a number of incorrect connections between beliefs (e.g., some 'default rules'), which trigger with low strength normally, and to ensure that these connections have a higher probability to be triggered in case the value for experienced pressure is high. This mechanism allows the model to produce errors or perform biased reasoning when somebody is under high pressure.

3.3 Integration with Decision Making

The next step is to integrate the OFS and SA models addressed above with the model DM for decision making, taken from [3]. An overview of the different connections for this integration is shown in Fig. 2. The obtained patterns are as follows:

OFS model → experienced pressure → SA model → adequacy of beliefs

adequacy of beliefs → DM model → adequacy of initiated actions

So, the OFS model affects via experienced pressure the adequacy of beliefs generated by the SA model, and the adequacy of beliefs resulting from the SA model is a basis for adequacy of initiated actions. In short, by high levels of experienced pressure, decisions become less adequate. Furthermore, there is an effect of exhaustion on the readiness or willingness for a human operator to spend effort to get additional observation information at specific issues where needed, for example, to acquire lacking information or get confusing information clarified:

OFS model → exhaustion → SA model → readiness for observation

So, high levels of exhaustion reduce such readiness within Situation Awareness. Moreover, exhaustion also has a similar direct effect on readiness for decision making about and iniatiation of actions in general:

OFS model → exhaustion → DM model → timely initiation of actions

This indicates an effect of exhaustion on readiness for actions to be actually performed when circumstances ask for it. High levels of exhaustion may reduce readiness to undertake any action, as action requires effort, and therefore affects the timeliness of acting; this may imply that in circumstances that require action, such action is not undertaken (or too late). For observation actions in particular the effect on readiness comes from two sides. They have an effect of exhaustion like any other action. But via the SA side they already have another effect from exhaustion. Due to this double effect, high exhaustion levels may even lead to more reduced timeliness of observation actions than of other actions. An overall result may be that in situations of high exhaustion levels, persons tend not to act or act too late, and especially tend not to actively acquire or try to clarify lacking or confusing information. Not initiating observation actions has a negative effect on adequacy of beliefs:

DM model → initiating observation actions → SA model → adequacy of beliefs

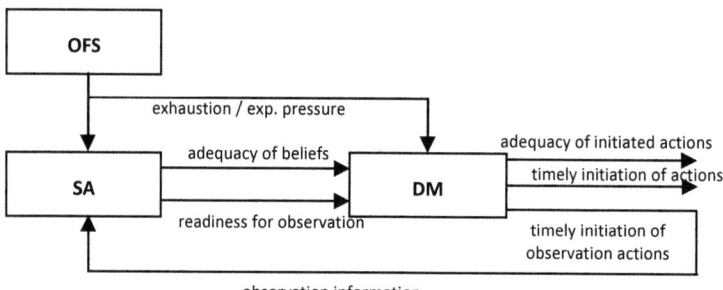

Fig. 2. Integration of Models for Functional State, Situation Awareness, and Decision Making

4 Formalisation of the Integrated Model

This section describes the formalisation of the integrated model. It has an emphasis on the impact of experienced pressure on situation awareness (via interpretation errors, as described above) and decision making. The mechanisms that describe the dynamics of experienced pressure itself (as a result of, among others, high task level) are not shown; for details about this, see [2].

The proposed model consists of five main components: *observations, simple beliefs, derived simple beliefs, complex beliefs* and *actions* (see also Fig. 1). In this model observations from the world are performed by the agent, and these observations are transformed into simple beliefs about the current situation. Simple beliefs concern simple statements that have one-to-one mapping to observations (e.g., an observation of a particular element in a display, an FAF point or an intersection point). Furthermore, simple beliefs provide an input for generation of derived simple beliefs. Derived simple beliefs represent more abstract simple statements about the world that may refer to past situation (e.g., in this scenario the belief that an FAF point has been passed by an aircraft). Derivable simple beliefs are used to generate complex beliefs and based on them also decision-making takes place. The most important formal relations between the variables in the components are as follows.

R1 - Observations

$$V_{observation\_result\_x} = \omega_{observation\_x} V_x \quad (1)$$

This formula determines the activation level of observation of world fact x. These levels have a value within the range of [0, 1], depending on the degree of certainty of an observation. Here, $\omega_{observation\_x}$ is a parameter within the range of [0, 1] that defines the quality of the observation process. In the simulations $\omega_{observation\_x} = 1$ has been taken (assumption of faithful representation of the world by the observation).

R2 - Simple beliefs

$$V_{belief\_simnew} = (1-\beta) * \gamma * V_{belief\_simold} + \beta * th(\tau, \sigma, V_{observation\_new} * \omega_{obs\_simbelief} * (1 + \alpha * EP)) \quad (2)$$

This formula defines how activation of simple beliefs is determined on the basis of observations. Here, β is a recency parameter that defines the contribution of a new observation to the value of a belief, γ is a decay factor for the belief, ω_{obs_belief} is a parameter that defines a connection between observations and simple beliefs.

Furthermore, α is a randomness parameter within a range of [-1, 1] that expresses the random variability of observation interpretation and may contribute to a wrong interpretation of a belief. This models how the extent of error in interpretation depends on experienced pressure with level EP; this experienced pressure (or stress), is what a human agent experiences during demanding task execution. A threshold function is used in this formula in order to translate the level of an observation to a value contributing to the activation value of a simple belief. The threshold function has two parameters: τ and σ that define the threshold value of the function and its steepness respectively.

R3 - Simple derived beliefs

$$V_{belief\_der} = \max(V_{belief\_der1}, V_{belief\_der2} \cdots V_{belief\_dern}) * \omega_{simbelief\_derbelief} \quad (3)$$

This formula defines that only one simple belief with the highest value is propagated further and activates the relevant simple derived belief.

R4 - Complex beliefs

$$V_{belief\_com} = V_{belief\_der} * \omega_{derbelief\_combelief} \quad (4)$$

This formula defines how activation of complex beliefs is determined on the basis of derived beliefs.

R5 - Actions

If $V_{belief\_com} > activation\_threshold$ $V_{action} = 1$
else $V_{action} = 0$ (5)

This formula expresses that if an activation value of a complex belief is higher than a threshold, then a relevant action is performed.

To apply this model to the scenario, it was instantiated as described by Fig. 3.

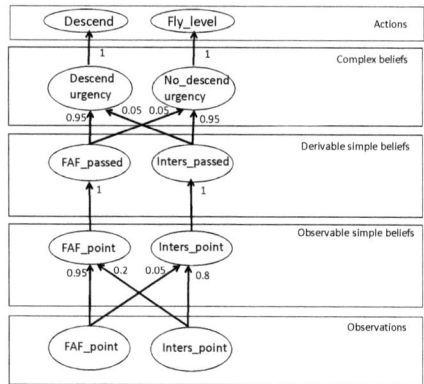

Fig. 3. Instantiation of the Integrated Model to the Scenario

Table 1. Parameter Settings

Parameter	Description	Value
activation_threshold	Beliefs with values above this threshold are activated	0.5
τ_{obs}	Threshold parameter of a threshold function that expresses the value at which an observation to belief contribution of 0.5 is established	0.2
σ_{obs}	Parameter of a threshold function defining the steepness of the curve	0.4
α	Randomness factor that defines the degree of influence of experienced pressure on the formation of simple beliefs from observations	Random value from [-1, 1]
β	Decay factor of simple beliefs	0.8
γ	Recency factor that defines how much a new observation contributes to the formation of a simple belief	0.7
FAF2FAF	Connection value from the observation of an FAF point to a correct simple belief about FAF point	0.95
FAF2intersection	Connection value from the observation of an FAF point to a wrong simple belief about an intersection point	0.05
intersection2intersection	Connection value from an observation of an intersection point to a correct simple belief about an intersection point	0.8
intersection2FAF	Connection value from an observation of an intersection point to a wrong simple belief about a FAF point	0.2[2]
FAF2FAF_passed	Connection value from simple belief about a FAF point to a simple derived belief about passing FAF	1
intersection2inters_passed	Connection value from simple belief about an intersection point to a simple derived belief about passing FAF	1
FAF_passed2desc_urgency	Connection value from simple derived belief about passing FAF to a complex belief about descend urgency	0.95
FAF_passed2nodesc_urgency	Connection value from simple derived belief about passing FAF to a complex belief about no descend urgency	0.05
inters_passed2nodesc_urgency	Connection value from simple derived belief about passing an intersection to a complex belief about no descend urgency	0.95
inters_passed2desc_urgency	Connection value from simple derived belief about passing an intersection to a complex belief about descend urgency	0.05
descend_urgency2action_descend	Connection value from complex belief about descend urgency to a descend action	1
no_descend_urgency2fly_level	Connection value from complex belief about no descend urgency to a fly level action	1

---

[2] Note that this value has been chosen relatively high to represent a 'wishful thinking' process: pilots expect to observe the FAF due to a (possibly unconscious) desire to reach the point of arrival.

An overview of the parameter settings used is given in Table 1. The setting of these values determines how the dynamic Experienced Pressure (EP) variable from the OFS model affects the values of simple beliefs that are formed from observations of an intersection point and a FAF point. In particular, due to the influence of EP and randomness parameter α in formula R2, the value of an erroneous simple belief about passing the FAF point may become higher and thus propagated further to derived simple belief module as only the highest simple belief is taken for further processing.

5   Simulation Results

In order to illustrate how differences in task load influence the dynamics of functional state and situation awareness, in total 10000 simulations were performed (using the Matlab environment): 5000 with a scenario where values of the Task Level (TL) were taken according to the Callback case study and 5000 with a hypothetical scenario where the value of TL is lower. In addition, the relation between Task Level and the probability of incorrect actions was analysed in more detail.

5.1   Simulation of a Scenario with High Task Level

For this scenario, 5000 simulations were performed. In this scenario the Task Level (TL) value in the OFS part of the integrated model varies over time, according to the case study. According to the OFS model [2], TL is a variable that represents the (objective) amount of tasks that are to be done by an operator at a given time point. In principle, the variable ranges over the domain [0, ∞), but in practice values are taken in the domain [100, 500], where 100 represents a situation of relative underload (e.g., for a pilot, flying in mid air without any special demands), and 500 represents a situation of extreme overload (e.g., performing final approach in extreme weather circumstances). To simulate the Callback scenario, TL was set to 200 for the first part of the simulation (representing the beginning of the shift), then to 400 for a while (representing the multiple route changes), and finally to 500 (representing the phase while approaching the destination point).

Of 5000 simulations, there were 32 occurrences of an erroneous belief and hence a wrong descend action. The differences between these simulations are the result of the randomness parameter α in rule R2. Fig. 4 is an example of a simulation in which an erroneous belief occurs. Here, the two graphs at the top indicate states from the Operator Functional State model construct, and the two graphs at the bottom indicate states from the Situation Awareness model construct and the Decision Making model (in particular the state 'Descending action'). As can be seen in Fig. 4, at time point 50 the descend action is performed while there is no observation of the FAF point; instead the intersection point is observed, but erroneously interpreted as FAF (the activation value for the incorrect simple belief about FAF is higher than for the correct belief about intersection point). In the top left part of Fig. 4 it can be seen that the experienced pressure of the agent is increasing with the increase of Task Level and the performance quality is decreasing (top part of the figure).

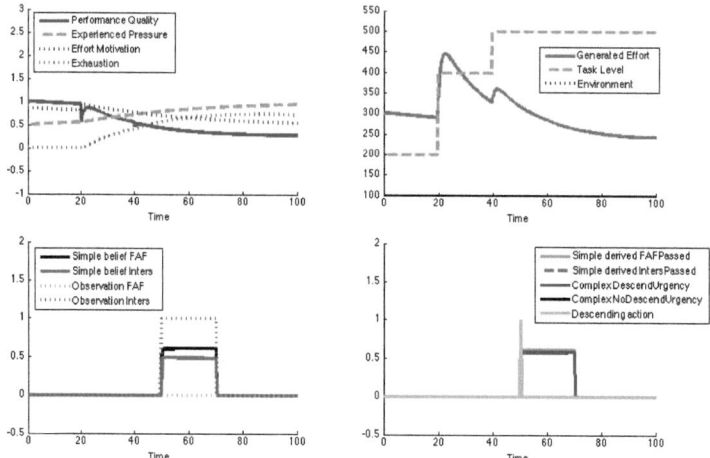

Fig. 4. Wrong descend action is performed as a result of incorrect Situation Awareness

Fig. 5 is an example of a simulation with the same initial settings where no erroneous belief is formed and wrong action is performed, in spite of high experienced pressure. The activation value of the correct simple belief about intersection is higher and propagates further to form a derived simple belief about passing an intersection point.

5.2 Simulation of a Scenario with Medium Task Level

Also 5000 simulations of a hypothetical scenario were performed. Here the Task Level (TL) value in the OFS part of the integrated model stays low (TL=150) during the whole simulation. Of 5000 simulations, there were no occurrences of a wrong

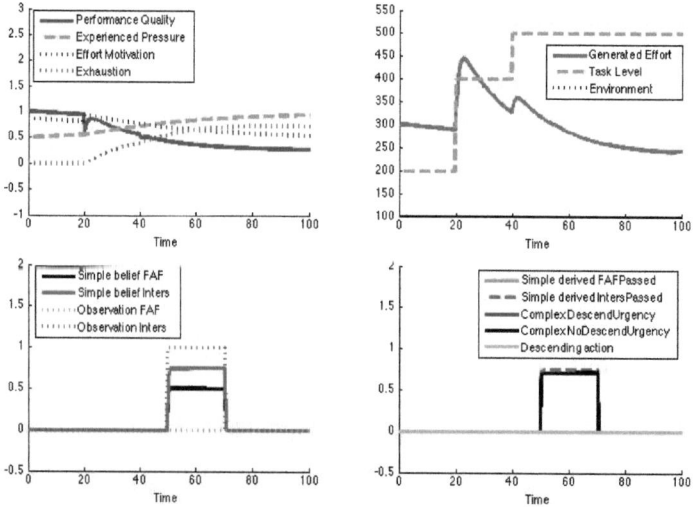

Fig. 5. No descend action is performed thanks to correct Situation Awareness

descend action. Fig. 6 is an example simulation. As can be seen in Fig. 6, no descend action is performed and beliefs about the intersection point are correct. At the top bottom part of Fig. 6 it is shown that the dynamics of Experienced Pressure (EP) of the agent differ from the Callback scenario: it is decreasing instead of increasing. Effort motivation decreases as well, as a result of probably too low task level.

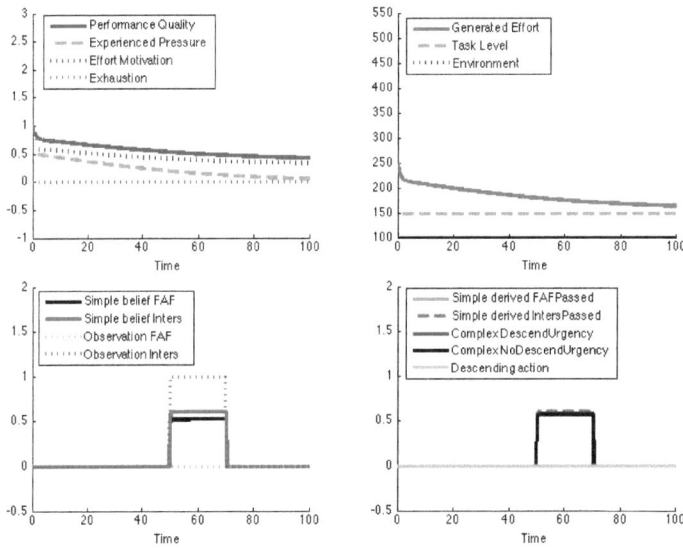

Fig. 6. Hypothetical scenario with low Task Level

5.3 Relation between Task Level and Wrong Actions

To analyse the relation between Task Level (TL) and the probability of incorrect actions in more detail, a number of additional simulations have been run. In these simulations, the value of TL has been varied in a systematic manner with an incrementing interval of 25. It has been done as follows: first, 5000 simulations have been run with the setting TL=100 (during the entire simulation, i.e., TL was not dynamic in these simulations). Next, 5000 simulation have been run with TL=125, then with TL=150, and so on, until TL=500. Totally there were 17 variations of TL. For each of the settings for TL, we counted for how many of the simulations the descend action was performed. The results are shown in Fig. 7, where the x-axis represents TL, and the y-axis the number of incorrect actions recorded.

As can be seen in Fig. 7, the relation between Task Level and the number of wrong descend actions is not linear. In the beginning when TL increases from 100 to 275, there are no wrong actions performed. Further the number of wrong actions systematically increases up to TL=425. With the TL value higher than 425 the number of times when wrong descend actions occur starts fluctuating randomly.

This pattern can be better understood after examining the relations between Task Level and Experienced Pressure (see Fig. 8). This simulation was performed in order to observe the dynamics of EP as a function of TL. Here again 5000 simulations were performed for each level of TL which was kept constant during one simulation. The value of EP was recorded from the last simulation of each TL level and only at one time point that corresponds to the observation of an intersection point by the pilots. As you can see in Fig. 8, the EP curve represents a logistic function that grows rapidly within the range of TL= [150, 300] and stabilizes afterwards when TL=450. It means that after TL higher than 450 EP increases very slowly and making the task more difficult does not influence EP much. This pattern of EP explains the fluctuations of the number of wrong actions in Fig. 7 when TL > 450.

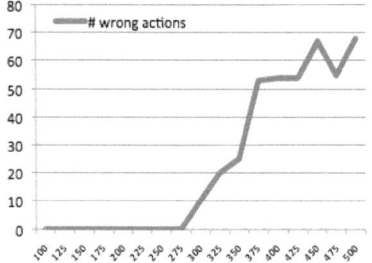 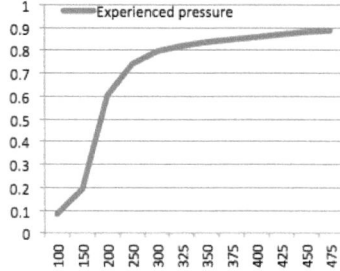

Fig. 7. Relation between *Task Level* (x-axis) and the number of *wrong actions* (y-axis)

Fig. 8. Relation between *Task Level* (x-axis) and *Experinced Pressure* (y-axis)

6 Discussion

The main goal of this paper was to discuss how complex aviation incidents can be modelled by integrating existing computational agent models for different aspects of human functioning. This has been illustrated by a real-world scenario, thereby integrating models for Operator Functional State, Situation Awareness and Decision Making. As also confirmed by a series of interviews with domain experts in ATM (air traffic controllers and pilots), the integrated agent model exhibits realistic behaviour. It shows how accumulation of high workload leads to higher exhaustion and experienced pressure, which in turn affect the situation awareness in such a way that the probability to form erroneous beliefs results increases. As decisions are based on such beliefs, the model shows that therefore wrong descend decisions can be made. Hence, it can provide useful insights in the dynamics of cognitive and physiological processes that affect performance in a non-linear fashion. It can be used by safety experts to make incident and accident predictions given particular circumstances.

For future work, more simulations could be performed, by varying other parameters of the OFS model, such as personality and experience. Also prospective scenarios to make predictions can be investigated. In addition, sensitivity analysis can be performed regarding the adopted parameter values. Finally, on the long term, the model can be embedded into an intelligent support system that is capable of making a detailed estimation of human performance in demanding circumstances.

Acknowledgements. This work is part of the SESAR WP-E programme on long-term and innovative research in ATM. It is co-financed by Eurocontrol on behalf of the SESAR Joint Undertaking (SJU). The paper does not purport to represent views or policies of VU, Eurocontrol or SJU. The views expressed are those of the authors.

References

1. Blom, H.A.P., Bakker, G.J., Blanker, P.J.G., Daams, J., Everdij, M.H.C., Klompstra, M.B.: Accident Risk Assessment for Advanced Air Traffic Management. In: Donohue, G.L., Zellweger, A.G. (eds.) Air Transport Systems Engineering: AIAA, pp. 463–480 (2001)
2. Bosse, T., Both, F., van Lambalgen, R.M., Treur, J.: An Agent Model for a Human's Functional State and Performance. In: Proceedings of WI-IAT 2008, vol. 2, pp. 302–307. IEEE Computer Society Press (2008)
3. Bosse, T., Sharpanskykh, A., Treur, J., Blom, H.A.P., Stroeve, S.H.: Modelling of Human Performance-Related Hazards in ATM. In: Proceedings of ATOS 2012, Delft, The Netherlands (2012)
4. Bosse, T., Sharpanskykh, A., Treur, J., Blom, H.A.P., Stroeve, S.H.: Agent-Based Modelling of Hazards in ATM. In: Proceedings of the Second SESAR Innovation Days, Braunschweig, Germany (2012)
5. Endsley, M.R.: Toward a Theory of Situation Awareness in Dynamic Systems. Human Factors: The Journal of the Human Factors and Ergonomics Society 37(1), 32–64 (1995)
6. Hill, D.W.: The Critical Power Concept. Sports Medicine 16, 237–254 (1993)
7. Hockey, G.R.J.: Compensatory Control in the Regulation of Human Perfomance under Stress and High Workload: A Cognitive-Energetical Framework. Biological Psychology 45, 73–93 (1997)
8. Hollnagel, E.: Barriers and Accident Prevention. Ashgate, Aldershot (2004)
9. Hoogendoorn, M., van Lambalgen, R.M., Treur, J.: Modeling Situation Awareness in Human-like Agents using Mental Models. In: Proceedings of IJCAI 2011, vol. 2, pp. 1697–1704. AAAI Press (2011)
10. Leveson, N.: A New Accident Model for Engineering Safer Systems. Safety Science 42, 237–270 (2004)
11. Stroeve, S.H., Bosse, T., Blom, H.A.P., Sharpanskykh, A., Everdij, M.H.C.: Agent-Based Modelling for Analysis of Resilience in ATM. In: Proceedings of the Third SESAR Innovation Days, Stockholm, Sweden (2013)

A Multi-agent Based Optimised Server Selection Scheme for SOC in Pervasive Environment

Bikash Choudhury, Piyali Dey, Animesh Dutta, and Subhrabrata Choudhury

Multi Agent and Distributed Computing Lab
Department of Information Technology
National Institute of Technology Durgapur, India

Abstract. Recently immense research efforts has been observed towards development of multi-agent based middleware for enabling service oriented computing (SOC) in mobile ad hoc and pervasive environment. The fundamental issues addressed are service discovery, service composition, service replication, service revocation and proper assignment of service request to servers. But, very few proposal considered the total social welfare (sum total of individual utilities) maximisation and self-organised emergence of such systems. In this paper we propose a multi-agent based server selection scheme that ensures maximum social welfare and self organised system emergence by meeting the Quality of Service (QoS) requirement of all service consumers. To achieve this, we formalise it as a multi-agent based distributed constraint optimization problem (DCOP) and solve it using max-sum algorithm. The proposed max-sum algorithm offers significant saving in system wide resource usage and at the same time achieves lower service drop rate and slightly better service completion time. However, the message passing overhead for the max-sum algorithm is higher that limits its practical applicability. To overcome this, we propose a heuristic solution which gives similar gain as offered by max-sum algorithm with substantially lower message passing overhead.

1 Introduction

Service oriented computing (SOC) has penetrated into the core of the Internet. With the evolution of Internet of Services (IOS) [12], the cloud computing [5] solutions are being made available world-wide. Though the virtualisation issues were studied extensively at the beginning of cloud computing solutions, but currently the issue of efficient resource utilisation within the cloud infrastructure has taken up the center-stage of research [11]. Hence, efficient SOC solutions with optimal use of resources within the cloud is very crucial in cloud computing paradigm. So the future challenges of SOC are not only to scale up with the number of user but also to cope with mobility, complex service requirements and heterogeneity(device as well as operating system).

For improved service availability and maintaining desired QoS of services, service oriented middleware (SOM) has been proposed [3] and studied by several researchers. SOM is responsible for provisioning of proper functionalities for deploying, publishing/discovering and accessing services at runtime. SOM also provides support to realize more complex composite services by integrating simpler ones. With the emergence of mobile clouds, an agile and robust SOM implementation for pervasive and ad hoc environment is highly desirable.

The role of SOM in a pervasive environment [1] is more vital and challenging because of the lack of fixed infrastructure, low device capabilities in terms of processing power, memory and bandwidth availability. To address these issues, a SOM, resembling P2P network was proposed in [10]. The characteristics of file based P2P system and service based P2P system are a bit different because in a file based P2P system, the consumer of the file automatically becomes a service provider as the resource is already available with it. However, in a service (compute intensive) based P2P system, the service is to be explicitly replicated in a node.

The fundamental issues in SOM that attracted substantial attention from research community are - dynamic service/server selection, service composition, service replication and service availability. All the above issues have been addressed in the literature [2,4,5,8] but each of the issues were considered as individual problem without making much effort to integrate them. Moreover, very few of them try to optimize system-wide resource usage during the service/server selection including processing power, residual energy, memory and network bandwidth. Recently an integrated service selection and allocation scheme have been proposed in [13], but the authors did not emphasis the network bandwidth although it is an important resource parameter.

In this paper, we propose a multi-agent based server selection scheme that meets the QoS requirements of all service requests in such a way that the overall resource usage in the network is minimised. Here the resources considered are - total remaining processing power, total remaining memory, total remaining energy and total remaining bandwidth over the whole network. We modeled our server allocation problem as a multi-agent based distributed constraint optimization problem (DCOP) and solve it using max-sum algorithm. The proposed max-sum algorithm offers significant saving in system wide resource usage and at the same time achieve lower service drop rate and slightly better service completion time. However the message passing overhead for the max-sum algorithm is higher that limits its practical applicability. To overcome this, we further propose a heuristic that offers the same set of benefits as max-sum at significantly lower message passing overhead.

The rest of the paper is organized as follows. Section 2 presents the proposed system model of multi-agent based pervasive environment. In section 3 we represents our multi-agent based server selection problem as DCOP. Performance metrics of the system are presented in section 4. Section 5 provides a server selection scheme using max-sum algorithm which solves the DCOP problem. In the next section we present a heuristic that almost accurately replaces the max-sum based solution with reduced message passing overhead. Few results are shown in section 7 and finally we conclude in section 8.

2 System Model

The network model can be represented as a graph $G(V, E)$ as shown in the Fig.1 where V is $\{v_1, v_2, ..., v_k\}$ the set of k nodes within the network and E is the set of edges connecting the nodes. The weight of an edge E_{ij} between node v_i and v_j is represented by its corresponding delay D_{ij}. A node v_i contains $\{a_i, s_{ij}\}$ where a_i is the agent associated with node v_i and s_{ij} denotes the set of services provided by v_i and $j = 1, 2, ..., m_i$ (m_i being the maximum number of services at node v_i). In our framework an agent a_i has three interfaces—CI, SI and EAI as shown in Fig. 2. CI stands for client interface that intercepts any service request generated by the node v_i as a client. SI stands for service-interface that handles all issues related to the node when it acts as a server. The third interface is the external agent interface (EAI) through which the agent handles all issues of message passing with any other agent in the system.

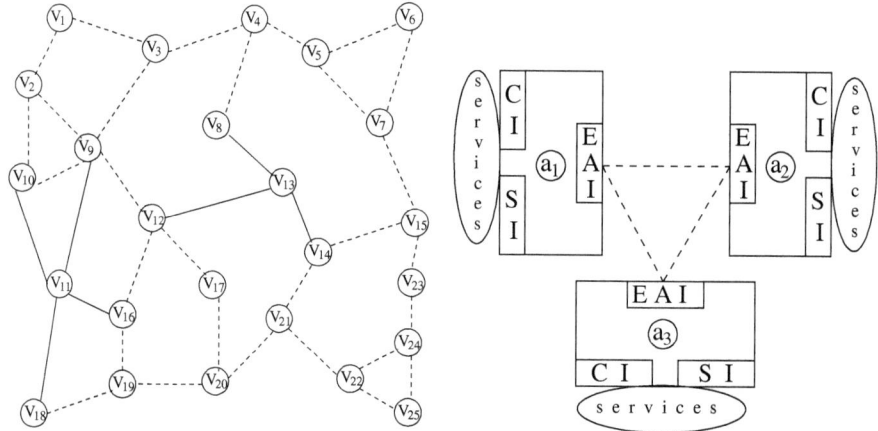

Fig. 1. SOA Based Pervasive Environment   **Fig. 2.** Agents and their Interfaces

Here we consider a scenario in which the set of client nodes and set of server nodes are represented as V_c and V_s respectively. The sets are not necessarily mutually exclusive or in other words a single node may act simultaneously as a server for some services and client for some other services.

Let the set of services being provided at present is $S = \{s_1, s_2, \ldots, s_m\}$. The cardinality of S can be higher than the cardinality of V i.e. $n(S) \geq n(V)$ is possible. This means that a single node $v_i \in V$, may provide more than one service. Under this setting, corresponding to each $s_i \in S$, there is a set of client nodes C_{s_i} that contains all the clients receiving the service s_i. The set C_{s_i} can be expressed as

$$C_{s_i} = {}^{v_1}C_{s_i} \cup {}^{v_2}C_{s_i}, \ldots, {}^{v_k}C_{s_i} = \bigcup_{\forall v_j \in V} {}^{v_j}C_{s_i} \quad (1)$$

where $^{v_j}C_{s_i}$ is the set of client instances at node v_j which are receiving the service s_i. Here the cardinality $n(^{v_j}C_{s_i})$ represents the set of client instances that are receiving the service s_i from the node v_j.

The service s_i may again be provided by multiple nodes and corresponding to each service $s_i \in S$ we get a set of nodes N_{s_i} that provides the service s_i. It should be noted that for each service s_i we obtain a set of nodes V_{s_i} that receives the service s_i. Thus each node $v_j \in V_{s_i}$ will correspond to a set of client nodes $^{v_j}C_{s_i}$ as discussed above.

A service request is denoted as $Req(s_i, QoS)$ where s_i is the service being requested. QoS of a service in general can be defined through service response time (t_r) and service completion time (t_{sc}). We consider the following four kind of services

a) Services where t_r is more important than t_{sc}, classified as *Type1* service (usually end user is a person).
b) Services where t_{sc} is more important than t_r classified as *Type2* service (usually end user is a program).
c) However in some cases the time constraints on both t_r and t_{sc} must be satisfied, classified as *Type3* service.
d) Some services without QoS requirement, classified as *Type4* service.

When a node $v_i \in V$ generates a new service request $Req_i(s_i, QoS)$ the following two cases may arise

1. The QoS requirement of the service can be satisfied by only one of the existing servers. In that case the request is assigned to that particular server.
2. The QoS requirement can be satisfied by more than one server. Then a server assignment algorithm is required to allocate the request to the most suitable server.

In this paper our objective is to design the above server selection algorithm in such a manner that the social welfare (sum of utility of all nodes) of the network is maximized. As the algorithm is invoked right from the birth of the network, the server assignment for service request evolves in such a way that emergence of the system, maintaining maximized social welfare, is guaranteed without compromising the QoS constraints.

3 Problem Formulation Using DCOP

Formally, a DCOP can be defined by the tuple $\{X, D, U, A\}$ where $X = \{x_1, x_2, ..., x_k\}$ set of variable, $U = \{u_1, u_2...u_k\}$ is the set of utility, $D = \{d_1, d_2, ..., d_k\}$ is the set of domain and $A = \{a_1, a_2...a_k\}$ is the set of agent. In our framework we consider a node $v_i \in V$ that contains an agent $a_i \in A$ and the utility of an agent a_i is denoted as u_i. Since a node can simultaneously acts as a service consumer, service provider and service forwarder. Hence the total utility (u_i) of a node v_i can be define as

$$u_i = u_{i_c} + u_{i_s} + u_{i_i} \qquad (2)$$

where u_{i_c} is its utility as a client, u_{i_s} is the utility as server and u_{i_i} is the utility as an intermediate node.

For a particular service request made by a client, we estimate the resource requirement from the whole network to satisfy the QoS of the request. For serving the request, various nodes may play one of the following role – it may act as a server if it is provider of the service, it may play the role of an intermediate node through which the service is provided or it may be a neutral node that neither provides nor forwards the service. We note that the neutral nodes are redundant for finding the appropriate server for a specific service request. Hence to reduce the computational burden, the nodes may be eliminated from the graph where DCOP is being applied. On the other hand, the routes to the set of service providers from the client should be calculated in such a way that the desired routing goal is satisfied. To address both the issues simultaneously, we use an existing multicast routing protocol that returns the most appropriate multicast tree taking the client node as the root of the tree. Though we are working on such optimised multicast tree using multi-agent system, still for the purpose of simplicity and limitation of space, in this work, we use the multicast routing protocol proposed in [14]. This algorithm returns a minimum spanning tree (MST) using the current delay between nodes as the weight. The utility u_i of an agent a_i depends on several parameters such as remaining CPU cycle (R_c), remaining battery power(R_b), remaining memory (R_m) and remaining available bandwidth (R_{bw}) of node node v_i. It can be represented as,

$$u_i = W_C(R_{c_i}) + W_B(R_{b_i}) + W_M(R_{m_i}) + W_{BW}(R_{bw_i}) \qquad (3)$$

where W_C, W_B, W_M, W_{BW} respectively represents the weight assigned to the respective utility parameters. The weights should be chosen in such a way that

$$W_C + W_B + W_M + W_{BW} = 1$$

However, when a new service request is generated there will be several server nodes that can provide the service and the content must be forwarded by all the intermediate nodes that connect a particular server to the requesting client. Hence the MST contains nodes as server or intermediate and client. When examining the total change in utility for selection of a specific server then the utilities of the nodes which are not in the chosen path will not undergo any change and those, participate including server node, change their utility depending on their roles. Hence the utility of a server node and intermediate node respectively changes as follows

$$u_i \leftarrow u_i - \delta^s u_{i_s} \qquad (4)$$

$$u_i \leftarrow u_i - \delta^f u_{i_i} \qquad (5)$$

where $\delta^s u_{i_s}$, $\delta^f u_{i_i}$ represents the additional resource that will be required from the node to satisfy the service request. This will depend on the role of the node i.e., whether it is acting as a service provider or service forwarder. Particularly, when the nodes acts as a service provider, the values of required CPU slots, memory and battery power will be higher than that of the corresponding values when the node works simply as a forwarding node. Hence,

$$\delta^s u_{i_s} > \delta^f u_{i_i} \qquad (6)$$

However when a service is completed the corresponding resources are released and the utility changes as

$$u_i \leftarrow u_i + \delta^s u_{i_s} (\text{or } \delta^f u_{i_i}) \qquad (7)$$

The domain of x_i when the corresponding agent (a_i) is a server or an intermediate node, can be represented as

$$D = \begin{cases} 1 & \text{when node } v_i \text{ is willing to provide/forward the service} \\ 0 & \text{when node } v_i \text{ is not willing to provide/forward the service} \end{cases}$$

For the client node the domain value of x_i is 1 if all requested QoS are satisfied and 0 when any of the requested QoS is not satisfied.

It can be seen that the optimisation function for the pervasive environment can be expressed as the sum of utilities of agents and the agent's goal is to find an assignment X^* for the variables in X that maximises the sum of the utility i.e.,

$$arg \max_{X^*} \sum_{i=0}^{k} U_i \qquad (8)$$

4 Performance Metrics of the System

The performance of a SOM has been traditionally expressed in terms of service response time or request drop rate but for a more comprehensive performance measure, in addition to the aforesaid metric we also introduce the parameter *remaining resources*. The parameters considered here are

1. **Remaining Resources:** This is an important performance indicator as the capacity and life-time of the network is depend on it. The performance of the system can be measured by the available resources $\{R_c, R_b, R_m, R_{bw}\}$. It will be better if the requested service can be served using minimum amount of system resources. The performance of two solutions can be compared by measuring remaining total resources when identical service request pattern is applied to both the system.
2. **Rate of Dropped Request:** The performance of the system is better if the rate of dropped request is lower under identical request scenario. If the total number of request generated in unit time N, and number of dropped request (due to QoS violation) is q, then the drop-rate is $\frac{q}{N}$. This may also be viewed as service availability in the network.

3. **Service Response and Completion Time:** The average service response-time ($\bar{t_r}$) and service completion time ($\bar{t_{sc}}$) are also important performance indicators. But in this case for QoS constraint requests, we assume that QoS (t_r, t_{sc}) has already been taken care of during the formation of MST. However, in some cases where QoS requirement are not stringent both the parameter should be minimised as much as possible.

5 Optimal Server Selection Using MAX-SUM

To solve the DCOP problem as stated above, we observe that

a) The MST can be converted to a factor graph representation that makes it a feasible problem to be solved using max-sum algorithm [7].
b) The network represents a pervasive environment that includes infrastructure-less ad hoc components with diverse heterogeneity which tends to increase message loss probability. It is shown in [6] that max-sum algorithm can provide much superior solution under such environment.

Hence, we solve our server selection problem using max-sum algorithm where each agent belonging to a node, needs to propagate two kinds of messages as shown below

From function to variable

$$P_{n \to m}(x_m) = \max_{X_n \backslash m} [U_n(X_n) + \sum_{m' \epsilon B(n) \backslash m} Q_{m' \to n}(x_{m'})] \qquad (9)$$

From variable to function

$$Q_{m \to n}(x_m) = \sum_{n' \epsilon A(m) \backslash n} P_{n' \to m}(x_m) \qquad (10)$$

where $B(n)$ is the set of variables connected to the function n, A(m) is the set of functions connected to the variable x_m, and finally $X_n \backslash m \equiv \{x_{m'} : m' \epsilon B(n) \backslash m\}$. After some iteration, agent a_i is able to determine the final value of the variable so that the sum total utility of all agents including itself is maximised. It is done by locally calculated function called marginal function, expressed as

$$Z_m(x_m) = \sum_{n \epsilon A(m)} P_{n \to m}(x_m) \qquad (11)$$

Let us consider the network shown in figure 1. Where, node v_{13} requests for a service s_{13} and currently the service is provided by $v_{15}, v_{16}, v_{17}, v_{21}$. Fig.4 represent the corresponding MST. So the member of MST will be $v_{12}, v_{13}, v_{14}, v_{15}, v_{16}, v_{17}, v_{21}$, where v_{12}, v_{14} are the intermediate nodes between client and servers. As mentioned in section 2, a node can acts as a client, server and intermediate, so all agents of respective nodes in the factor graph will calculate their utility using equation (4) and (5), depending on the present role of the agent. After calculating the utility value they will exchange the messages using equation (9), (10). Factor graph for the above example is shown in Fig.3 and the message $P_{14 \to 15}(x_{15})$ is sent from function U_{14} to variable x_{15} and $Q_{14 \to 13}(x_{14})$ is sent from variable x_{14} to function U_{13} on the corresponding factor graph as

$$P_{14 \to 15}(x_{15}) = \max_{x_{13}, x_{14}, x_{21}} [U_{14}(x_{13}, x_{14}, x_{15}, x_{21}) + Q_{13 \to 14}(x_{13}) + Q_{14 \to 14}(x_{14}) + Q_{21 \to 14}(x_{21})]$$

$$Q_{14 \to 13}(x_{14}) = (P_{14 \to 14}(x_{14} + (P_{15 \to 14}(x_{14} + P_{21 \to 14}(x_{14}))$$

Here we do not consider any incentive mechanism. Hence initially all the agents will calculate their utility for all possible options of their domain values. So, the max-sum solutions will converge to a setting where no server provides the service and no intermediate node forwards the service.

But as the solution is not fulfilling the basic objective of providing the service, we assign a large negative utility to the client if it does not receive the service, i.e., when its state is '0'. Now the overall utility will be maximised iff the client node get the service by any one of the server and all intermediate nodes along the path forward it. Finally at any time during the propagation of these messages, agent a_i is able to determine which value it should adopt so that the overall (sum of individual) utility will be maximised.

It was shown in [7] that the max-sum algorithm guarantees convergence within a reasonable number of iteration even when the graph contains a number of loops. But for a acyclic graph with low average degree (as in this case) the exact optimal solution can be achieved within very small number of iteration.

However when it is applied into a large network the message passing overhead is high that limits the applicability of the solution. Hence we propose a heuristic that elaborate in the next section.

6 A Heuristic Based on Distributed Message Passing

In this section we propose a heuristic solution to the problem that can achieve same efficiency with significant reduction of number of overhead messages. We assume that the MST of the network is known to all agents before starting the algorithm and the algorithm starts from leaf of the MST. It should be noted that root of the MST is client and all leaf nodes are server as shown in Fig.4. However, server may also exist in-between root and leaf nodes. The utility values are sent from leaf nodes to the root node. A node waits until it has received utility values from all of its children before comparing (if it is a server) or adding (if it is a forwarder) its own utility value which it sends to its parent. When the root node receives utility values from all of its children then it can chose the best candidate node for the server. The whole procedure is represented in algorithmic form in Algorithm 1.

Algorithm 1. Optimal Message Passing

```
1:  // u_{in}, u_{ic} denotes the utility of a node and list of all childrens utility of
    of a node.
2:  u_{max} ← 0
3:  while till the server is not selected do
4:    for k ∈ v do
5:      if (k == server) then
6:        u_{in} ← calculate utility using equation 4.
7:        compare(u_{in}, u_{ic})
8:        return u_{max}
9:        SentToParent(u_{max})
10:     end if
11:     if (k == intermediate) then
12:       u_{in} ← calculate utility using equation 5.
13:       compare(u_{ic})
14:       return u_{max}
15:       SentToParent(u_{max}+u_{in})
16:     end if
17:   end for
18: end while
19: return u_{max}
```

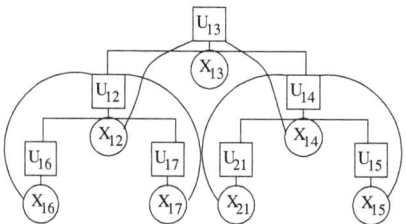 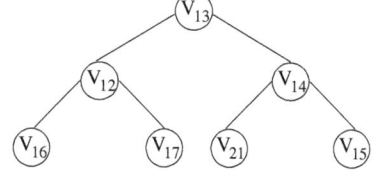

Fig. 3. Factor Graph Representation   **Fig. 4.** MST Representation

Let, node v_{13} requests for the service s_{13} where $v_{12}, v_{15}, v_{16}, v_{17}, v_{21}$ are the service providers and the intermediate nodes between client and servers are v_{12} and v_{14}. So the members of MST are $v_{12}, v_{13}, v_{14}, v_{15}, v_{16}, v_{17}, v_{21}$ where client node v_{13} is the root node. Now all agents (as a server or forwarder) will calculate their utility for the service s_{13} using equation (4) and / or (5) and send it to their respective parent nodes.

Here, node v_{12} itself is a server as well as a forwarder for server node v_{16}. After getting the utility value from server v_{16} agent a_{12} of node v_{12} will compare the utility and send best to its parent node v_{13}. Finally client node v_{13} will be able to select the best server for the service.

It is observed that proposed heuristic solution is more prone to message delivery failure compared to max-sum. The issue is addressed by introducing message retransmission in case of failure.

7 Results and Discussion

In this section we compare the performance of the proposed max-sum and heuristic based server selection algorithm with the existing one [13]. We consider the network model as shown in Fig.1 and simulate it using java agent development framework (JADE) [9]. Here we consider four different types of services as shown in Table 1 where the service request with various QoS pattern are generated following poisson distribution. We assign CPU slots, memory, battery and bandwidth to each of the node by randomly choosing the value from a given set of range. The range of CPU slots, memory, battery and bandwidth are 100 to 1000 megacycles per second (Mc/s), 1MB to 1GB, 0.5 to 5 hrs and 1Mbps to 10Mbps respectively.

Table 1. Service Generation Rate and QoS Pattern

Services	Service Generation Rate	QoS Pattern
$Type1$	20 request/ms	$10ms$, $15ms$, $20ms$
$Type2$	30 request/ms	100 ms, 200 ms, 500 ms
$Type3$	20 request/ms	(10 ms, 100 ms), (15 ms, 200 ms), (20 ms, 400 ms)
$Type4$	30 request/ms	No QoS

Most of the previous works in this area were driven by the objective of minimising the service response time. But as our objective here is to maximise the remaining system resources, we just adhere to a value of response-time and/or completion time, *just enough* to satisfy the QoS of the service request. For the given set of service request the average service completion time for three different schemes heuristic, max-sum and the existing one [13] is shown in Fig.5. It shows that the service completion time is slightly better in our proposed scheme compared to that available using [13]. We normalise the total network resources as unity for three different schemes and show the remaining total network resources in Fig.7. As our proposed algorithms both max-sum and heuristic are invoked right from the birth of the network, they offer higher amount of remaining system resources compared to that obtained using [13]. The gain in resource usage is emphasised at higher values of applied load. Fig.6 shows that the service drop rate in our proposed scheme is less than that of the existing one [13]. Fig.8 shows that the total number of messages sent using max-sum is higher than that in the proposed heuristic. Even though the message passing complexity in [13] is lower but computational complexity is higher as re-optimization scheme is complex. The message passing overhead in our max-sum scheme is higher but computational complexity is significantly lower. However for the heuristic both the computational and message overhead are lower.

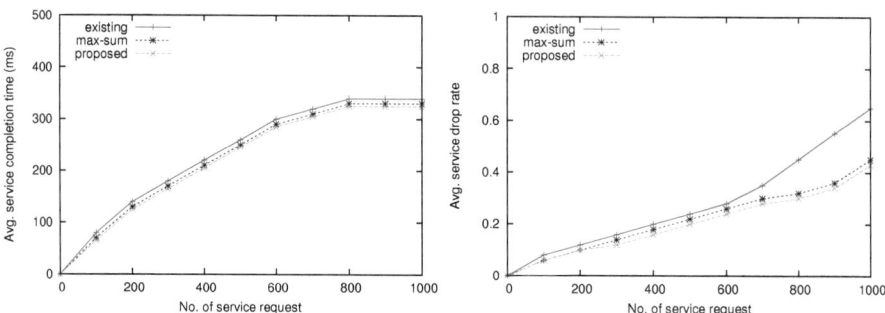

Fig. 5. Average Service Completion Time   **Fig. 6.** Average Service Drop Rate

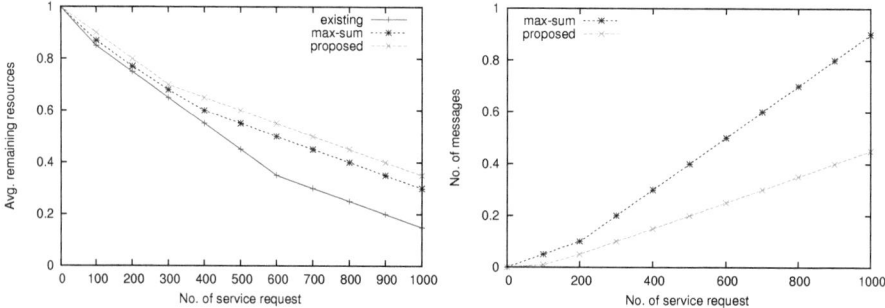

Fig. 7. Remaining Network Resources   **Fig. 8.** Number of Messages Passed

8 Conclusions

In this paper we propose a multi-agent based server selection scheme that ensures maximum social welfare and self organised system emergence by meeting the Quality of Service (QoS) requirement of all service consumers. To achieve this, we formalise it as a multi-agent based distributed constraint optimization problem (DCOP) and solve it using max-sum algorithm. The proposed max-sum algorithm offers significant saving in system wide resource usage and at the same time achieves lower service drop rate and slightly better service completion time. However, the message passing overhead for the max-sum algorithm is higher that limits its practical applicability. To overcome this, we design a heuristic solution which gives similar gain as offered by max-sum algorithm with substantially lower message passing overhead. We propose to extend the algorithm in future to solve the problem of service replication and service migration proactively.

References

1. Adelstein, F., Gupta, S.K., Richard III, G., Schwiebert, L.: Fundamentals of Mobile and Pervasive Computing. McGraw-Hill (2004)
2. Ahmed, A., Yasumoto, K., Shibata, N., Kitani, T., Ito, M.: Dar: Distributed adaptive service replication for manets. In: IEEE International Conference on Wireless and Mobile Computing, Networking and Communications, WIMOB 2009, pp. 91–97 (2009)
3. Caporuscio, M., Raverdy, P.-G., Issarny, V.: Ubisoap: A service-oriented middleware for ubiquitous networking. IEEE Transactions on Services Computing 5(1), 86–98 (2012)
4. Chakraborty, D., Joshi, A., Yesha, Y., Finin, T.: Toward distributed service discovery in pervasive computing environments. IEEE Transactions on Mobile Computing 5(2), 97–112 (2006)
5. Chen, T., Bahsoon, R.: Scalable service oriented replication in the cloud. In: 2011 IEEE International Conference on Cloud Computing (CLOUD), pp. 766–767 (2011)
6. Farinelli, A., Rogers, A., Jennings, N.R.: Agent-based decentralised coordination for sensor networks using the max-sum algorithm. Journal of Autonomous Agents and Multi-Agent Systems (2014)
7. Farinelli, A., Rogers, A., Petcu, A., Jennings, N.R.: Decentralised coordination of low-power embedded devices using the max-sum algorithm. In: Proc. of the 7th Intl. Conf. on Autonomous Agents and Multi-Agent Systems, Estoril, Portugal, pp. 639–646 (2008)
8. He, Q., Yan, J., Yang, Y., Kowalczyk, R., Jin, H.: A decentralized service discovery approach on peer-to-peer networks. IEEE Transactions on Services Computing 6(1), 64–75 (2013)
9. http://jade.tilab.com/
10. Maheshwari, P., Kanhere, S.S., Parameswaran, N.: Service-oriented middleware for peer-to-peer computing. In: 3rd IEEE International Conference on Industrial Informatics, INDIN 2005, pp. 98–103 (2005)
11. Moreno-Vozmediano, R., Montero, R.S., Llorente, I.M.: Key challenges in cloud computing: Enabling the future internet of services. IEEE Internet Computing 17(4), 18–25 (2013)
12. Pan, J., Paul, S., Jain, R.: A survey of the research on future internet architectures. IEEE Communications Magazine 49(7), 26–36 (2011)
13. Sandionigi, C., Ardagna, D., Cugola, G., Ghezzi, C.: Optimizing service selection and allocation in situational computing applications. IEEE Transactions on Services Computing 6(3), 414–428 (2013)
14. Yan, Z., Lee, J.-H., Shen, S., Qiao, C.: Novel branching-router-based multicast routing protocol with mobility support. IEEE Transactions on Parallel and Distributed Systems 24(10), 2060–2068 (2013)

Influence of Participation Rates and Service Level Differentiation on Community Driven Predictions

Rutger Claes, Katrien Van den Berghe, and Tom Holvoet

DistriNet-iMinds, KULeuven, Celestijnenlaan 200A, Leuven, Belgium

Abstract. Anticipatory Vehicle Routing based on Intention Propagation (AVRIP) can help reduce drivers travel times and avoid forming congestion. The route guidance system uses information shared by participating drivers to predict future link traversal times, the time it will take a vehicle to traverse a road at a certain time in the future. Both participating and non-participating drivers benefit from these link travel time predictions. Participating drivers will receive the predictions and will adapt their route to avoid any congestion. Non-participating drivers experience less congestion because of these diversions.

The percentage of drivers participating in the AVRIP guidance is an important factor. This participation rate influences the efficiency of the system in two ways: it affects the accuracy of the predictions and it changes the number of drivers influenced by the predictions.

This paper provides a first study on the influence of the participation rate on the efficiency of AVRIP by varying the participation rate while keeping all other parameters constant in a simulated traffic network.

1 Introduction

Anticipatory Vehicle Routing using Intention Propagation (AVRIP) is a multi-agent system based Advanced Traveller Information System (ATIS). ATIS systems aim to present users with information to assist them in their route choosing process.

The AVRIP system relies on a community of participating drivers willing to share their intention with the AVRIP system. A driver's intention is the route he or she intends to follow. By combining the intentions of all participating drivers, the AVRIP system can estimate the number of vehicles on a road at a future point in time. This information is combined with historical observations to make predictions about the link travel time of the roads. These link travel time predictions, the times it takes a vehicle to traverse a road at a future point in time, are presented back to the driver. The predictions can be used to calculate the fastest route, taking into account future congestion levels.

The benefits of AVRIP as an ATIS have been described earlier [1]. This paper studies on the community driven part of AVRIP and more specifically the relative size of the community of participating drivers. A decentralized ATIS relying on driver participation cannot realistically be deployed at once. The system will undergo an adoption process resulting in varying participation rates. Analyzing the effects of the varying participation rate is necessary as the percentage of drivers participating in the system can influence the accuracy of the system. The study will provide useful information on the effectiveness and challenges throughout this adoption process.

A first consequence of the participation rate is its influence on the prediction process. An insufficient number of participating drivers makes it impossible to accurately predict link travel times. Participating drivers would receive incorrect information leading to inappropriate routing decisions. One research questions looked at in this paper is the minimal populations size required for AVRIP to function.

A second consequence of the participation rate is the influence of participating drivers on the traffic. This effect has been observed by Wunderlich et al. [2]. When facing a congested traffic network, participating vehicles using an advanced traffic information system will start diverting to alternative routes. A small community of participating vehicles would find little traffic on the alternative routes. A large community of participating vehicles could cause congestion on the alternative routes. The situation is reversed for the non-participating drivers. When facing a partly congested network, the congestion will dissolve if enough participating vehicles reroute. The benefit for the non-participating drivers increases when the size of the participating community increases. The benefit for the participating drivers decreases when their community size increases. Whether the findings of Wunderlich et al. hold for AVRIP is the second research question addressed in this paper.

This paper is organized as follows. First a brief overview of the Anticipatory Vehicle Routing using Intention Propagation is given (Section 2). The description is limited to the essentials, further details about AVRIP can be found starting from [1]. Section 3 discusses research related to this paper and in particular the work and experiments by Wunderlich and Kaufman. In Section 4 the experiment setup is described. The results of the simulations are analyzed in Section 5, before drawing conclusions in Section 6.

2 Anticipatory Vehicle Routing Using Intention Propagation

In [1] we propose a decentralized advanced traffic information system based on a multi-agent architecture and Ant Colony Optimization [3]. In this system, vehicle agents represent the interests of the drivers and communicate with infrastructure agents representing the road infrastructure elements such as roads and crossroads. By propagating their intentions, the route the driver intends to follow, the vehicle agents inform the infrastructure agents of their pending arrival. The infrastructure agents in return, use this information to forecast future link traversal times and share these forecasts with the vehicle agents. The forecast information allows the vehicle agents to make better, more informed, decisions.

The system is decentralized, it does not rely on a central component. Vehicle agents are assumed to be deployed in the vehicle they represent. Infrastructure agents are assumed to be deployed near the real-world infrastructure element they represent. This last assumption is not a requirement, the only requirement is that the infrastructure agent has sufficient real-time information about the real-world element it represents and can communicate with vehicle agents.

The intention propagation is initiated by the vehicle agents. At regular intervals, the vehicle agents dispatch mobile agents to inform infrastructure agents of the vehicles' intentions. By traversing the same path as the vehicle plans to take, the mobile agents can interact with all relevant infrastructure agents. Every interaction has two consequences. First, the infrastructure element receives information about a pending visit. Second, the information provided by the infrastructure agent allows the mobile agent to estimate its arrival time at the next infrastructure element. This exchange of information allows the mobile agent to inform subsequent infrastructure agents of its estimated arrival time.

Upon arrival at the vehicles destination, the mobile intention agent will have informed all agents on its path and will have an estimated arrival time for the vehicles destination. This estimated arrival time is communicated back to the vehicle agent and allows it to monitor its estimated arrival time.

The information stored in the infrastructure agent has an expiration time, somewhat similar to how pheromones operate in nature. If the information is not refreshed, it will evaporate. As long as the vehicle remains in traffic and intends to follow its current path, it will send out mobile agents and refresh the information. When the vehicle diverts from its path and chooses a new intention, it does not need to inform all the infrastructure agents on the abandoned path to cancel the visit.

When looking for a route the vehicle agent uses an exploration strategy inspired by Ant Colony Optimization [4]. The vehicle agent dispatches mobile agents similar to the ones used in the intention propagation. These mobile exploration agents are dispatched across possible route alternatives. The alternatives are calculated using the ACO based algorithm described in [4]. Contrary to the mobile intention agents, these exploration agents do not store information on the infrastructure agents. They merely keep track of the estimated arrival times. Upon reaching the destination, the mobile exploration agent informs the vehicle agent of the estimated arrival time for this route alternative.

Infrastructure agents receive information about pending visits in the form of intentions. For every future moment in time, they have a number of vehicles that has committed to pass by. This information, combined with observations of the historic travel times on the road, is used by a neural network to forecast the traversal time at that future moment [5]. It is this information that is shared with the mobile agents.

3 Related Work

In this section we describe related work on several ATIS systems. We focus first on anticipatory ATIS systems: ATIS systems predicting future traffic states in order to guide traffic (Section 3.1). Next we focus on studies looking at multiple user classes in the evaluation of the ATIS (Section 3.2).

3.1 Anticipatory ATIS Systems

ATIS systems taking into account traffic predictions have the potential to not only allow participating drivers to reach their destinations faster, they also have the potential to reduce traffic congestion. By diverting traffic before congestion occurs, the congestion buildup can be avoided.

Wahle and Schreckenberg present a multi-agent based framework combining simulation and real-world traffic data to make short term traffic predictions [6]. They also discuss the need for anticipatory route guidance and the need to model drivers responses to the information they receive but leave the latter as future work.

Kai and Mo also present a real-time traffic information simulation and prediction system [7]. Instead of using neural networks to learn the traffic networks response to traffic, Kai and Mo employ an approach based on support vector machines, namely *Accurate on-line support vector regression* or AOSVR.

Both Wahle and Schreckenberg and Kai and Mo use a combination of historical information, real-time information and simulation to provide the additional information their ATIS's present to the driver. In AVRIP these components are also present, but more implicitly. The neural network training process combines historical information with real-time traffic information to train the networks. When the mobile agents described in Section 2 explore the traffic network they keep track of a time horizon. The route found by the mobile agent combined with time horizon indicating the estimated time of arrival is the equivalent of simulating the route using the information stored in the artificial neural network. The benefit of AVRIP and its use of mobile agents is that information is stored and reasoned on in a decentralized, scalable way.

3.2 Multiple User Classes

Many ATIS systems are presented and evaluated in literature. Authors rarely analyze the impact of partial participation rates on the systems evaluation. Some research on how the information presented by an ATIS system is received by the community of drivers, often dividing the community in multiple classes can be found in literature.

Adler, for example, looks at more fine grained classes for drivers and provides test subjects with different types of information on a hypothetical network to see how they behavior of the test subjects changes due to the information [8]. The classes Adler looks at are (1) basic map information, (2) route guidance, (3) traffic advisory information and finally (4) a combination of route guidance and traffic advisory information. The study presented in this paper is limited to classes (2) and (4), as even the drivers not participating in the ATIS are assumed to have access to basic route guidance.

Peeta and Mahmassani also take into account multiple user classes when evaluating their rolling horizon solution framework [9]. In their paper they argue that (1) online route guidance systems are a necessity because of the dynamic nature of traffic and (2) one should not assume all users have the same access or response to the information provided by an ATIS. These two claims are in line with the position of this paper.

In their paper, Wunderlich et al. present a study similar to the one described in this paper [2]. While the ATIS system described by Wunderlich et al. differs greatly from the one presented in Section 2, the focus of the study was similar: How do multiple user classes influence the impact of the additional information.

The study of Wunderlich et al. is of particular interest because it does not only focus on the overall impact of different user classes (participating and non-participating), but also on the impact of the relative size of the classes on other classes.

The main difference between the ATIS system described in [2] is the systems architecture. Where the architecture described in this paper is fully decentralized, the architecture used by Kauffman is centralized. Many of the research questions are similar though. Much attention is given to the impact of the participation rate on the performance of the guidance system. The evaluation of the centralized guidance system is also based on simulations.

The experiments conducted by Wunderlich et al. show that as the participation rate increases, the benefit for the participating drivers drops. As more and more drivers will be taking the detour, the travel time on the detour will rise and the original congestion will resolve more quickly. A second observation is that for non-participating drivers the effect is the opposite: As the participation rate increases, the non participating vehicles will benefit. These are the observations we set out to verify in our decentralized guidance system.

4 Experiment Setup

In this section we will describe the experiment setup. All experiments are simulation based. The simulation used is described in [10] and uses a spatial model to position vehicles on the road. The vehicles behavior is based on the intelligent driver model [11] combined with the MOBIL [12] lane changing model.

In the simulated scenario two classes of drivers are considered. Drivers participating in the AVRIP guidance system and drivers not participating in the system. Drivers not participating in the system will use an A* based path finding algorithm to calculate their route. Drivers participating in the AVRIP guidance system will use the information obtained from the mobile exploration agents to choose a route and will propagate this using the mobile intention agents. The proportion of drivers participating is what we refer to as the participation rate.

Every simulation uses the same origin destination (OD) matrix. This OD matrix is fully disaggregated, it contains the start time, start location and destination for every vehicle participating in the system. Depending on the participation rate, the vehicles described in the OD matrix are divided between the two classes based on a random number generator.

The AVRIP route guidance system depends on many parameters. During these experiments these parameters were fixed to the ones found in Table 1. These parameters are not guaranteed to be the optimal ones, but previous experiments have shown that they are a good choice [4,5].

The overall experiments setup is as follows: We have constructed one OD matrix. For every participation rate we simulate this OD matrix 20 times, each time with a different random seed. Changing the random seed also affects how the OD matrix is divided between participating and non-participating vehicles.

Coordination mechanisms such as AVRIP are no silver bullets. They can help traffic networks cope with more traffic, increasing their capacity under congestion, but they can only do so for a limited traffic increase. The impact of the coordination system is only noticeable when traffic levels are in this interval. Building an OD matrix for a realistic traffic network in a realistic simulation where traffic levels on all roads are in this interval is nearly impossible. Because of this limitation, we only use a small artificial traffic network. The limited size of the network allows us to thoroughly analyze the simulation outcome.

Figure 1 shows the road network used in the scenarios. The network is constructed as follows: A main traffic axis $A \to F \to E \to B$ is the shortest and - in freeflow traffic - the fastest route between A and B. The route $A \to F \to G \to B$ at the bottom offers an alternative route between A and B, but is slightly slower than the first route. The traffic between A and B is generated so that node E receives a traffic flow just below its capacity. At the top of the network, there is route $C \to E \to D$. When traffic flows across that route, it causes congestion in E for both the $C \to E$ and the $F \to E$ edges. The only way of avoiding the congestion for the $A \to B$ traffic is to use the detour through G.

5 Experiment Analysis

In this section we will analyze the outcome of the experiments. We start by discussing how the vehicles performance is measured. The next step is to analyze the results graphically. Finally we analyze the experienced travel times for all vehicles and look for a statistically significant reduction in travel time using the t-test.

5.1 Travel Time Evaluation

Not all vehicles in the simulation have the same origin destination pair which makes comparison of individual vehicle performance difficult. In order to allow such comparison we introduce a scoring mechanism. In [2], the authors use the average travel times of both participating and non-participating vehicles and compare these averages. We believe using the average travel time has two serious drawbacks: (1) Longer routes will have a greater impact on the end result and (2) by aggregating the performances we loose the information of individual vehicle performances. The second drawback prevents us from looking at the distribution of the results and denies us the possibility to compare the performance of the same vehicle across different simulations.

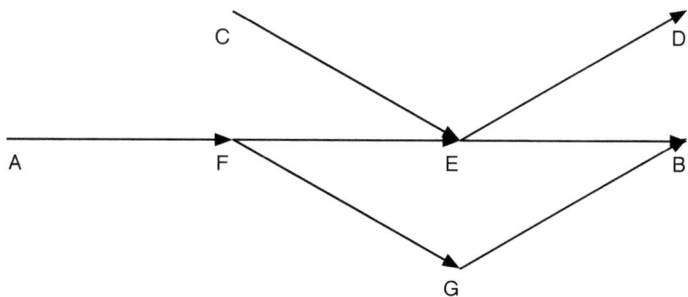

Fig. 1. The road network used in the scenarios. $A \to F \to E \to B$ is the main traffic axis. $A \to F \to G \to B$ is the detour route and $C \to E \to D$ is the congestion causing axis.

Taking these problems into account we score the performance of a vehicle v_i by dividing the vehicles travel time $(t(v_i))$ by the travel time of that same vehicle in a totally unguided traffic situation $t_{p_0}(v_i)$. This last value, $t_{p_0(v_i)}$, is the vehicles travel time in the simulation with a participation rate of zero (p_0), meaning all vehicles use the A* based guidance. We will refer to the quotient of these values as the *Q-score*.

$$Q - score\,(v_i) = \frac{t(v_i)}{t_{p_0}(v_i)} \quad (1)$$

If a vehicle has the same travel time as it does in the p_0 unguided experiment, that vehicles Q-score will be 1. When the vehicle performs better than in the base experiment the Q-score will be lower than 1, when it performs worse the score will be higher than 1.

5.2 Graphical Analysis of Simulation Results

Figure 2 shows the Q-score for participating and non-participating vehicles in all of the experiments. The error bars denote the 95% confidence interval surrounding the average. A first observation that can be made is that the Q-scores of the participating vehicles are lower than those of the non-participating vehicles. As the participation rate increases, both populations start to benefit equally. A trend that is confirmed in Section 5.3. This observation is a validation of the observations made by Wunderlich et al. in [2].

Figure 3a and 3b show the distribution of Q-scores for participating and non-participating vehicles for one simulation in the 10% and 90% participation rate experiments. The histogram combined with the full density line shows the distribution of Q-scores in the experiment while the dashed distribution line allows comparison with the p_0 unguided base case.

As the distributions show the guidance system results in a shift towards the lower Q-scores for most of the vehicles. Here, again, the results indicate that the

Table 1. The parameter values for this set of experiments

Parameter	Value
average injection interval	0,1 ticks (1 s = 1000 ticks)
participation rate	0,1
duration	30 min
reconsideration threshold	0,1
reconsideration rate	10
alpha (ACO)	20
beta (ACO)	30
gamma (ACO)	0,3
rho (ACO)	0,8
phi (ACO)	20
tau_0 (ACO)	50
tau_max (ACO)	1000
max nbr of hops	250
nbr of explorers	10

benefit is greater for the participating vehicles, but that significant number of non-participating vehicles also benefits from the coordination.

To estimate the impact of AVRIP under certain participation rates on the experienced travel times and the resulting congestion in the network we plot the ratio between the actual duration and the static duration vehicles experience on link $F \to E$ against the vehicles arrival time on that road. Figure 4 shows that experienced travel time rises steeply for a participation rate of 10% (Figure 4a on the left). The increase in travel time is less in the case of a participation rate of 50% (Figure 4b in the middle) and is greatly reduced in the case of 90% (Figure 4c on the right).

Based on Figure 4 it appears the information provided by the AVRIP system is able to persuade drivers to choose the alternative road thus avoiding congestion buildup.

5.3 Statistical Analysis of Simulation Results

To verify the impact of using AVRIP we apply a paired t-test to each simulation outcome individually. The hypothesis in this test is that the travel times, not the Q-score, of the vehicles in the experiment are equal to or higher than in the p_0 unguided case. A one-sided paired t-test is then used to reject this null hypothesis

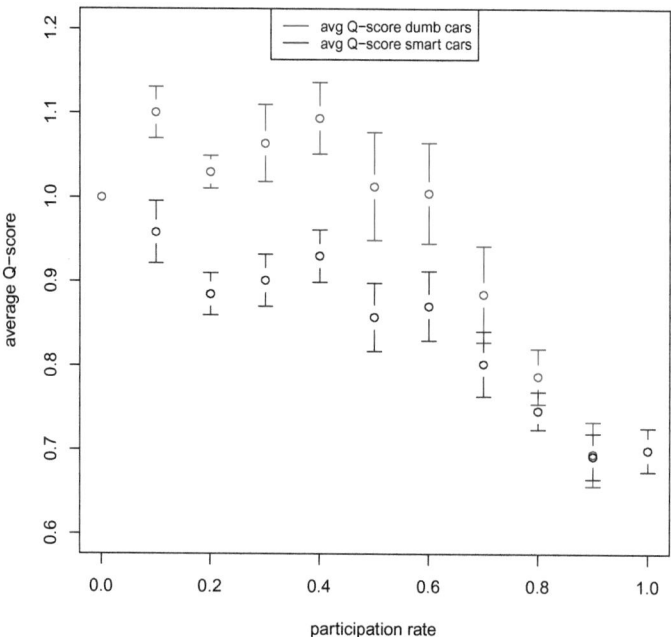

Fig. 2. Q-scores for all simulations with varying participation rates

and conclude that the travel times in the experiment are lower than in the p_0 unguided case. We repeat this process for only the non-participating population, only the participating population and finally the total population. The summary of these tests are in Table 2. The maximum, minimum and average p-values for all experiments are listed along with the number of simulations where the p-value was below 0.05.

As Table 2 shows, the participating vehicles are experiencing lower travel times in nearly all simulations. For the experiment with participation rate $p = 0.1$, only 14 of the simulations result in a statistically significant decrease of travel times. But for simulations with a participation rate of 20% or higher almost all experiments result in successful t-tests. In experiments with high participations rate the non-participating vehicles also benefit and experience reduced travel times. Looking at the last column, we see that for experiments with a participation rate between 20% and 70% the majority of simulations result in statistically relevant reduction in experienced travel times for the entire population. For participation rates above 70%, all simulations result in reduced experienced travel times for the entire population.

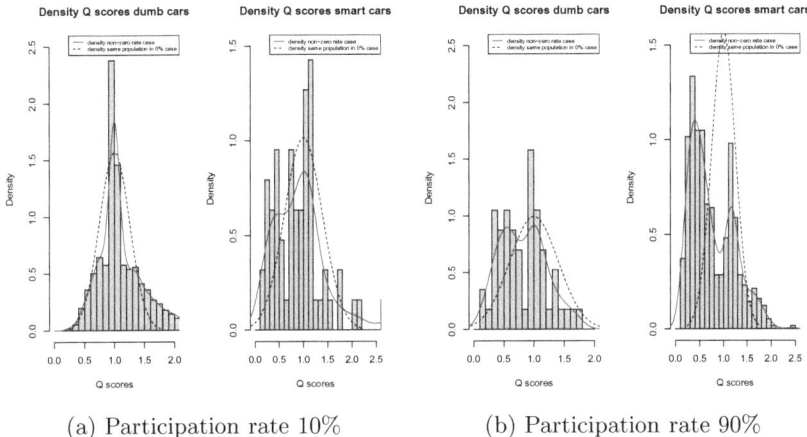

(a) Participation rate 10% (b) Participation rate 90%

Fig. 3. With a participation rate of 90% (right) the dumb vehicles experience less congestion, resulting in lower Q-scores compared to the 10% rate (left)

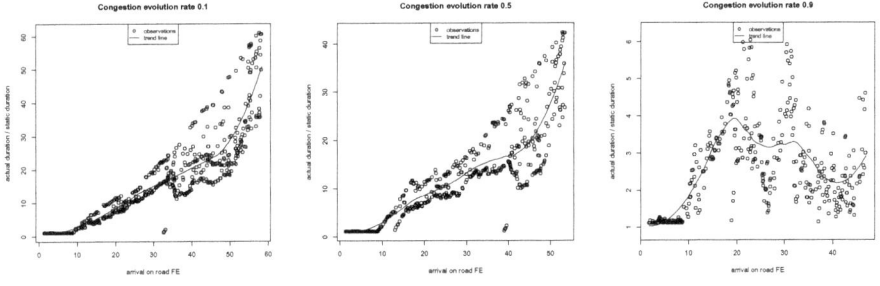

(a) Participation rate 10% (b) Participation rate 50% (c) Participation rate 90%

Fig. 4. Evolution of the congestion rate for participation rates 10%, 50% and 90%

The failure of many of the experiments with participation rates below 20% indicates that this is the critical participation rate needed for the coordination system to successfully assist the drivers with accurate predictions. In participation rates below this boundary, the guidance system fails to forecast the congestion and divert traffic.

Table 2. Summary of the t-test results for all simulations

	non-participating				participating				total population			
p-rate	average	min	max	< 0.05	average	min	max	< 0.05	average	min	max	< 0.05
0.1	6.5E-01	1.8E-03	1.0E+00	4	6.7E-02	4.8E-05	3.4E-01	14	5.1E-01	2.1E-05	1.0E+00	6
0.2	2.2E-01	1.4E-05	9.5E-01	11	4.3E-03	2.5E-11	7.7E-03	20	3.0E-02	1.4E-12	2.9E-01	18
0.3	3.5E-01	2.7E-08	1.0E+00	8	5.9E-03	8.3E-14	1.1E-01	19	1.3E-01	3.0E-19	1.0E+00	15
0.4	6.5E-01	4.0E-15	1.0E+00	4	3.1E-04	2.7E-19	2.8E-03	20	1.2E-01	3.4E-32	7.5E-01	15
0.5	3.6E-01	2.4E-30	1.0E+00	10	1.7E-05	1.5E-32	2.4E-04	20	4.3E-02	2.4E-60	5.9E-01	18
0.6	2.4E-01	1.2E-26	1.0E+00	11	1.2E-02	1.0E-37	2.4E-01	19	5.1E-02	3.6E-61	1.0E+00	19
0.7	7.6E-02	1.6E-25	8.5E-01	18	2.1E-11	6.9E-56	2.5E-10	20	1.2E-08	5.5E-78	2.2E-07	20
0.8	9.1E-05	3.6E-16	1.8E-03	20	2.1E-25	1.0E-59	4.3E-24	20	4.9E-27	1.0E-72	9.8E-26	20
0.9	1.8E-05	5.3E-10	1.7E-04	20	2.3E-39	8.2E-81	3.8E-38	20	3.5E-42	4.2E-89	6.0E-41	20
1.0	NA	NA	NA	NA	2.3E-43	2.2E-86	3.4E-42	20	2.3E-43	2.2E-86	3.4E-42	20

6 Concluding Remarks

In this paper we analyzed the impact of varying participation rates on the efficiency of Anticipatory Vehicle Routing using Intention Propagation. By simulating a small road network under various circumstances, we were able to thoroughly evaluate the travel times for both participating and non-participating vehicles.

As shown in Section 5, the coordination strategy only works if at least 20% of vehicles participate in the guidance mechanism. If less than 20% of the vehicles participate, the participating population not always benefits from the forecast information.

However, if more than 20% of the population participates, the coordination mechanism yields significant decreases in travel times for both participating and non-participating vehicles. The results show that as the participation rate increases, the benefit for the non-participating vehicles is significant. For the participating vehicles the benefits are significant, but stagnate with higher participation rates, something also observed by Wunderlich et al. in [2].

Future work will focus on more large scale and realistic scenarios. The thorough analysis of the artificial network in this paper shows the potential of AVRIP and the influence of the participation rate. Further research confirming these findings in realistic large scale networks is the next step.

References

1. Claes, R., Holvoet, T., Weyns, D.: A decentralized approach for anticipatory vehicle routing using delegate multi-agent systems. IEEE Transactions on Intelligent Transportation Systems 12(2), 364–373 (2011)

2. Wunderlich, K.E., Kaufman, D.E., Smith, R.L.: Link travel time prediction for decentralized route guidancearchitectures. IEEE Transactions on Intelligent Transportation Systems 1(1), 4–14 (2000)
3. Dorigo, M., Maniezzo, V., Colorni, A.: Ant system: optimization by a colony of cooperating agents. IEEE Transactions on Systems, Man, and Cybernetics, Part B: Cybernetics 26(1), 29–41 (1996)
4. Claes, R., Holvoet, T.: Ant colony optimization applied to route planning using link travel time predictions. In: 2011 IEEE International Symposium on Parallel & Distributed Processing Workshops, pp. 358–365 (2011)
5. Claes, R., Holvoet, T.: Ad hoc link traversal time predictions. In: Proceedings of the 14th International IEEE Conference on Intelligent Transportation Systems, pp. 1803–1808 (2011)
6. Wahle, J., Schreckenberg, M.: A multi-agent system for on-line simulations based on real-world traffic data. In: Proceedings of the 34th Annual Hawaii International Conference on System Sciences, p. 9 (2001)
7. Kai, C., Mo, Z.: Design of real-time traffic information prediction and simulation system based on aosvr and on-line learning. In: IEEE International Conference on Vehicular Electronics and Safety, ICVES 2006, pp. 189–193 (2006)
8. Adler, J.: Investigating the learning effects of route guidance and traffic advisories on route choice behavior. Transportation Research Part C: Emerging Technologies 9, 1–14 (2001)
9. Peeta, S., Mahmassani, H.S.: Multiple user classes real-time traffic assignment for online operations: A rolling horizon solution framework. Transportation Research Part C: Emerging Technologies 3, 83–98 (1995)
10. Claes, R., Holvoet, T.: Gridlock: A microscopic traffic simulation platform. In: International Conference on Models and Technologies for Intelligent Transportation Systems (2011)
11. Treiber, M., Hennecke, A., Helbing, D.: Congested traffic states in empirical observations and microscopic simulations. Phys. Rev. E 62, 1805–1824 (2000)
12. Kesting, A., Treiber, M., Helbing, D.: General lane-changing model mobil for car-following models. Transportation Research Record: Journal of the Transportation Research Board 1999, 86–94 (2007)

Anticipatory Coordination of Electric Vehicle Allocation to Fast Charging Infrastructure

Kristof Coninx[1], Rutger Claes[1], Stijn Vandael[1], Niels Leemput[2], Tom Holvoet[1], and Geert Deconinck[2]

[1] iMinds-DistriNet
KU Leuven, 3001 Leuven, Belgium
{firstname.lastname}@cs.kuleuven.be
[2] EnergyVille, Department of Electrical Engineering (ESAT)
KU Leuven, 3001 Leuven, Belgium
{firstname.lastname}@esat.kuleuven.be

Abstract. The limited range of electric vehicles (EVs) in combination with the limited capacity of current fast charging infrastructure are both causes for a limited adoption of EVs. In order to reduce the general inconvenience that EV users experience when having to wait for available fast charging stations and to lessen the danger of damaging the infrastructure by overloading it, an efficient coordination strategy is needed. This paper proposes an anticipatory, decentralised coordination strategy for on-route charging of EVs during lengthy trips in a fast-charging infrastructure. This strategy is compared to a reference strategy that uses global real-time knowledge of charging station occupation. Simulation results using a realistic scenario with real-world traffic data demonstrate that the anticipatory strategy is able to reduce the waiting times for EV users by up to 50% while at the same time decreasing the peak loads of the electricity grid caused by charging EVs by 21%.

1 Introduction

Electric vehicles (EVs) are gaining in popularity with the general public in an effort to reduce the carbon footprint of vehicular transportation by creating environmentally friendly alternatives in the form of Plug-in Hybrid EVs and fully battery-powered EVs. Range anxiety is the term used to describe the fear of becoming stranded by not having enough energy to complete a trip. Although research shows that EV users primarily use their vehicles for relatively short trips [1], the limited range of electrical vehicles is still considered as one of the main causes for the limited adoption of EVs [2], together with the long time needed to recharge the battery. To mitigate the issue of range anxiety, several nations are taking the initiative in deploying electric charging infrastructure to eventually increase the range of EVs. This helps EVs in their efforts to become a completely viable alternative for fossil fuel powered vehicles.

Electric charging infrastructure networks, like road networks are subject to capacity constraints. If there is too much traffic on the network, congestion becomes unavoidable. The same principle applies when considering the collective fast charging capacity of charging stations in an electric infrastructure network. Increasing the load on the charging infrastructure by increasing the number of vehicles that need to charge, causes the waiting times and queueing to increase rapidly, due to the arrival rates becoming greater than the service rates. Prolonged peak loads on these infrastructure elements can also aversely affect the lifespan of the transformers in the electricity grid, driving up the financial cost for the grid operators. Section 2 describes the concrete application problem of this work.

An obvious solution to capacity problems can be found in increasing the capacity but more efficiently using the available infrastructure capacity by use of ICT-based coordination strategies offers another solution to mitigate the symptoms of these capacity problems. Section 3 describes the approach taken to tackle these problems while section 4 elaborates on the proposed coordination strategies.

These coordination strategies will not always be equally beneficial. Therefore it is important to determine in which situations coordination strategies can add value. If there is no traffic, coordination is simply not needed. On the other hand, if there is way too much congestion in the network, even a good coordination mechanism cannot compensate for a significant lack of capacity. Somewhere in between those two extremes, there is an amount of traffic that can cause some congestion while this congestion could still be alleviated by organised coordination. Section 5 describes the realistic scenario used in the experiments including road topology, traffic model and the charging infrastructure model. Section 6 presents the results of the performed experiments while section 8 closes with a general conclusion and some remaining challenges after a discussion of some related work in section 7.

2 Problem Statement

Because this work is focussed on relatively long trips and because for long trips, most often highways are used, this work will only consider Battery EVs travelling on highways. A highway network is modelled as a graph network in which the edges represent the actual highway segments and the nodes represent Points-of-Interest (POI) connecting them. These POIs can be but are not limited to highway access or exit points, highway junctions, rest-areas, gas-stations or electric charging stations. A fleet of battery electric vehicles is modelled to perform trips between pairs of highway access/exit points. These points are randomly chosen and remain fixed for a specific vehicle while the route between these points and any intermediary stops at other POIs are variable. The stops for an EV are described by an itinerary. To simulate EVs having to drive a while before reaching their highway access point and thereby partly depleting their battery before starting the highway trip, the EVs start with a battery state of charge (SoC) drawn from an arbitrarily chosen normal distribution $X \sim \mathcal{N}(\frac{E_{max}}{2}, \frac{E_{max}}{12})$ with E_{max} representing the maximum battery capacity of the vehicles.

These EVs are equipped with agents capable of guiding the decisions on where and when to recharge their batteries during their trips. Keeping into account real-world traffic data presents a very dynamic and large scale environment in which capacity problems quickly become apparent, especially during peak hours. This work is primarily concerned with the problem of finding coordination strategies capable of guiding the charging behaviour of individual agents to globally minimize waiting and queuing times and to avoid excessive peak loading of charging stations in the network. Secondly, this work will determine the scale of traffic for which these coordination strategies pose the biggest benefit. Particularly, these strategies should be scalable and able to cope with the dynamic nature of the problem.

3 Approach

In order to solve the capacity problems in a scalable and dynamic environment, a decentralised and anticipatory strategy is proposed that uses EV intention signalling to anticipate on future station occupation. This strategy is compared to a central, non-anticipatory strategy which has only global real-time knowledge of charging station occupation. These strategies are compared in a realistic scenario using models of a real-world highway network and real-world traffic density data over the course of 24 hours. The traffic density is the percentage of vehicles of a particular vehicle fleet participating in traffic.

The global fleet size for experiments is determined through an analysis of the relation between fleet size and benefits from coordination for a certain amount of available infrastructure capacity. The coordination strategies are evaluated using metrics concerning both parties (EV users and grid operators) to allow an evaluation in terms of real world applicability. The metrics used are the waiting times for EVs at charging stations and the global electrical load of the charging infrastructure. For the experiments, the proposed strategies and scenarios are implemented in the microscopic traffic simulator `Gridlock` [3]. This simulation framework is extended to support EVs, fast charging stations and charging behaviour.

4 Coordination Strategies

4.1 Anticipatory and Decentralised

The anticipatory strategy is based on the DelegateMAS coordination technique [4]. This technique is inspired by ant colonies' foraging behaviour and uses ant agents to perform various tasks such as exploring the environment for information and for propagating the intentions of the owning agent. DelegateMAS has been used as a basis for coordination strategies in several other cases concerning traffic coordination and EV charging behaviour [5,6]. In this work this anticipatory strategy will also be referred to as the DMAS strategy.

For this strategy all EVs are represented by vehicle agents while charging stations are represented by station agents. Vehicle agents start their trip at a highway access node in the the road graph and travel to the highway exit node of their destination by way of a shortest path calculated by an A* Algorithm. Vehicle agents then determine the optimal travel itinerary towards their destination using exploration ants. An itinerary consists of a number of stops at charging stations to recharge when necessary and expected arrival times at those stops. When an itinerary has been decided upon, time window reservations are made at the station agents by use of intention ants.

For this strategy there is no centrally organising entity present in the coordination scheme. All station agents are therefore responsible for retaining and offering information about their occupation state to the outside world. This strategy also anticipates on future occupation of the charging stations in order to determine optimal travel itineraries with the least amount of delay for the total driving times. The prediction of future charging station occupation levels allow for future waiting time estimations in a manner similar to the method described in [7]. Station agents will respond to queries from exploration ants about the expected waiting time at a time in the future. Station agents will calculate the expected waiting time by simulating the real-world processing of the time window reservations by using information about the expected arrival time and the expected battery levels at arrival which are both present in the time window reservations. The optimal travel itinerary is then determined by *exploring* the environment while estimating vehicle travel times and while using time window reservations based on these travel times to declare the agents' *intentions*. The vehicle agents repeat this process when reaching a new node to make sure their decisions are based on the most up to date information about the environment.

Exploration. The exploration component of the vehicle agent is capable of finding the most agreeable itinerary along a certain route by sending out virtual ant agents to explore the environment. The exploration ants simulate travelling along the specified route node by node. These ants simulate the travelling time and battery depletion between the last node and the current node upon arriving at a new node in the path to the destination node. When an exploration ant reaches a charging station node, the ant clones itself and simulates charging at the specified station. This includes calculating the charging time and querying the station agent for the queuing time at the station at the expected moment of arrival. The cloned ant will move along the same path without simulating charging at this node. In this manner, all charging options and combinations along a certain path can be evaluated and when the ants report their itineraries to the vehicle agent, the vehicle agent simply chooses the itinerary with the least total driving time.

Intention Propagation. The intention propagation component of the vehicle agent is capable of signalling its intention of charging at a certain station to the station agent in the form of a reservation. The exploration ants from the previously discussed component provide the estimated arrival times and estimated state of charge upon arrival. Time window reservations are made with these arrival times and the estimated state of charge on arrival at a station.

The *reservations* are perishable and will evaporate if not refreshed. The intention propagation component has to refresh the pheromones periodically to keep the reservation active for a certain station. If at a later point the vehicle agent chooses another station to charge at, the reservation at the previous station will eventually evaporate.

4.2 Non-anticipatory and Centralised

The strategy that acts as a reference strategy uses a station manager component. This component represents a single, central service keeping track of the station occupation of every charging station in real-time. Vehicle agents query this service for the least occupied station within range and choose it as an on-route charging destination. The range is based on the action radius with the current level of charge.

When several stations are in range with the same level of occupation, the closest station is preferred over other stations. The choice of charging destination is not just made once at the start of the trip but vehicle agents recalculate their range and query the station manager for the most suitable charging station in every node and can adapt their previous decisions accordingly.

This strategy is non-anticipatory and uses only information known at the time of querying. This reference strategy is chosen because it focusses on using real-time information to perform navigation and route planning optimizations. The use of real-time traffic information has been a research interest in the context of traffic and navigation in the past. This allows for a realistic base of comparison for the anticipatory strategy.

5 Realistic Scenario

In order to have an evaluation that has real-world relevance, a realistic scenario is used. A highway network in Flanders is chosen and then virtually rebuilt into a format suitable for input into the simulation framework. Vehicle trips are generated in such a manner that all highway segments and intersections are subject to a certain traffic load in all directions while the amount of hourly traffic is based on results of a real-world traffic survey.

5.1 Road Topology

Figure 1 shows a map of the highway network used in this scenario. This highway network has been carefully modelled into an road network graph to make sure the distances between nodes represent the real-world distances. Each highway exit-access pair is represented as a node in the graph, but also roadside truck stops and other highway points of interest are represented as nodes in the graph to allow for easy extension of the graph network.

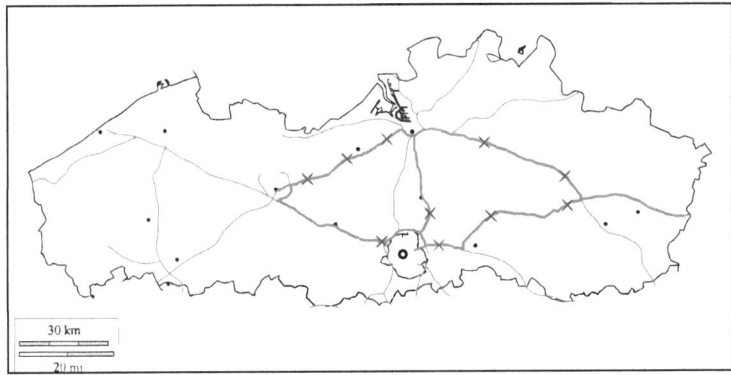

Fig. 1. The road net in Flanders, Belgium, used to perform simulations on. The used network segments are stroked in green while a red × marks a charging station.

5.2 Traffic Model

An other important aspect of using a realistic scenario is the use of a realistic traffic model. The amount of vehicles on the road at any given time constitutes a combination of the traffic density parameter and the traffic fleet size. The fleet size captures the upper bound of the possible amount of traffic described in section 1, while the traffic density varies over the course of 24 hours to accurately follow real-world traffic patterns.

Vehicle Fleet Size. The vehicle fleet size describes the upper bound on the amount of traffic that can be present on an road network and therefore on the amount of vehicles that possibly need to be serviced by the charging infrastructure. A value for this parameter such that coordination can offer benefits is dependent on the capacity of the infrastructure network in question.

This infrastructure capacity can be estimated by aggregating the capacity estimates for infrastructure elements present in the network. These individual capacity estimates are based on a traffic flow with equal inter-departure times to more accurately represent an upper bound on the aggregated capacity that is not influenced by periods of low traffic density.

The hourly capacity of a charging station is estimated by using the following formula:

$$TotC_{hourly}(St_i) = \frac{P_{out}(St_i)}{(C_{battery} - AvgSoc_{arr}(St_i))} * N_{outlet}(St_i)$$

In this formula for estimating $TotC_{hourly}$ for a certain station St_i, the output power of a single charging outlet at St_i is represented as $P_{out}(St_i)$. This output power is the same for all N_{outlet} outlets at St_i. The battery capacity for vehicles accessing the charging stations is represented by $C_{battery}$. This work assumes a fixed battery capacity for all vehicles. Finally the average state of charge for all vehicles accessing St_i is represented as $AvgSoc_{arr}(St_i)$.

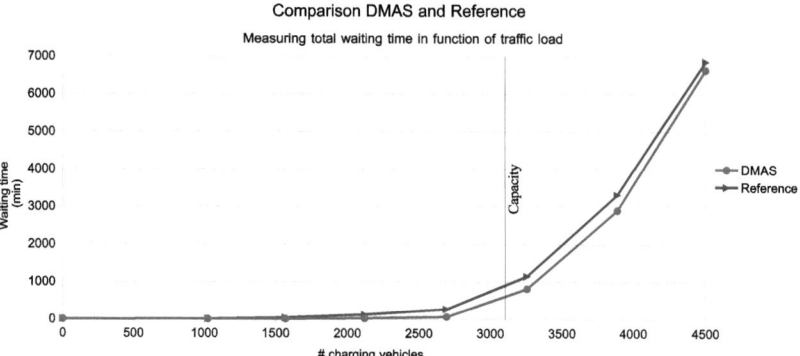

Fig. 2. The anticipatory strategy and the reference strategy both show a super-linear increase in total waiting time beyond the estimated capacity value

Simulation results in Figure 2 show that the total time spent waiting increases super-linearly when the amount of charging vehicles increases. These results also show that the waiting times start to increase when the amount of charging vehicles increases to the value of the estimated capacity of the network.

Traffic Density. The traffic density parameter in this model only represents a relative percentage of vehicles on the road in a fleet of vehicles. The density parameter in this model is based on an availability analysis for mapping EV driving behaviour in Flanders, Belgium [8].

The resulting data from the models of this study is used to construct a traffic model suitable to use as an input source for this scenario. By approximating the hourly traffic densities of [8] as input data and evaluating the throughput of vehicles per hour on the road network, a traffic model is created that approximates the results from the original study closely enough to maintain relevance in a realistic scenario. Figure 3 shows the resulting data from the original study with this approximation and the results from a throughput analysis in context of this scenario.

5.3 Station Location Determination

Research concerning location optimization is often focussed on optimizing locations for charging stations in urban areas. Some strategies for determining locations are discussed in [9–11]. This work focusses more on larger-scale highway networks. Because current-day highways in Belgium are not yet equipped with the charging infrastructure discussed for this scenario, possible locations for deploying charging stations must also allow deployment in the real world. Possible locations alongside the highway sections incorporated in this scenario must therefore meet the following requirements:

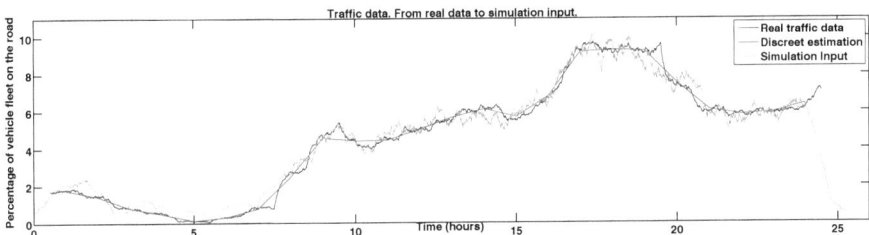

Fig. 3. Real traffic data from a Flemish study using a vehicle travel database is compared to the results from the model used in this scenario. This traffic model is shown to be a good enough approximation to provide a realistic vehicle density for the 24-hour scenario.

- Sufficient surface area in hardened materials (e.g. concrete) is available to physically support vehicles and charging infrastructure.
- The location should be directly accessible from the highway network.
- Connection to the electrical distribution grid should be possible.

A study on the pricing of EV charging, containing models for the required surface area of standard charging stations is used to evaluate possible locations [12]. Valid locations are often found at existing truck stops and fuel stations. First, a set of stations are arbitrarily chosen out of the possible valid locations.

After this initial choice of stations, the model is tested with some uncoordinated traffic and bottlenecks are identified by estimating the station capacity as described in the section about `Vehicle Fleet Size` and comparing it to the traffic throughput. More stations are added when a severe bottleneck is found. The final choice of charging stations offers a balanced scenario with both dense and sparse regions with charging stations.

5.4 Infrastructure Parameters

A charging station in this model is chosen to offer fast-charging at 48 kW per charging outlet. Following [12], a number of 8 charging outlets per station is chosen. 8 EVs can be recharged at the same time for every charging station. For the simulation, there is no maximum queue size for queueing vehicles.

5.5 EV Parameters

For this simulation, only fully battery operated vehicles are used. No Plug-in Hybrid Electric Vehicles are considered because they would not necessarily suffer from limited range or range anxiety. No other non-electric vehicles are participating in the simulation.

The electric vehicle model is based on the specifications of the Nissan Leaf. This encompasses a battery capacity of 24 kWh. The consumption for the vehicle model used for these experiments, is rated at 0.1371 kW per km. This

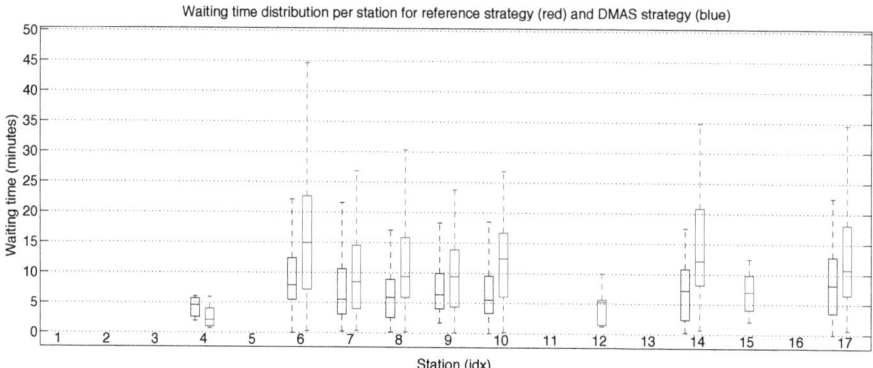

Fig. 4. Box plots for comparing the waiting time distributions per station for both strategies

consumption rate is based on the action radius of the Nissan Leaf (175 km), determined by the New European Driving Cycle (NEDC) and the Leaf's rated battery capacity. The NEDC is a driving cycle similar to driving cycles described in [13], but for vehicle usage in Europe. Further research on electrical vehicle consumption models also warrant an update on the consumption rate used in these vehicle models. A 15% increase to incorporate external factors such as slopes, wind drag and mechanical wear is advised by the EPA [14]. This advise has not been incorporated into the vehicle model used for these experiments.

6 Results

6.1 Waiting Times

The first evaluation of the coordination strategies uses the distribution of vehicle waiting times as a metric. The waiting times at each station are shown for both coordination strategies in Figure 4. This comparison also shows that the distribution of the load between the station remains relatively unaltered but some stations that suffered minimal waiting times under use of the reference strategy, will avoid waiting times using the anticipative strategy. This distribution is a characteristic trait specific to the scenario used in the experiments. The most significant difference between the two results is the scale with which the waiting times are reduced using the anticipative strategy. For some stations (eg. station with index 6) this is a reduction by 50%.

6.2 Infrastructure Load

In this case the instantaneous load on the electrical infrastructure network is defined by the aggregate of the momentary power consumed by the charging stations. A sample of the evolution of this load throughout the day is plotted

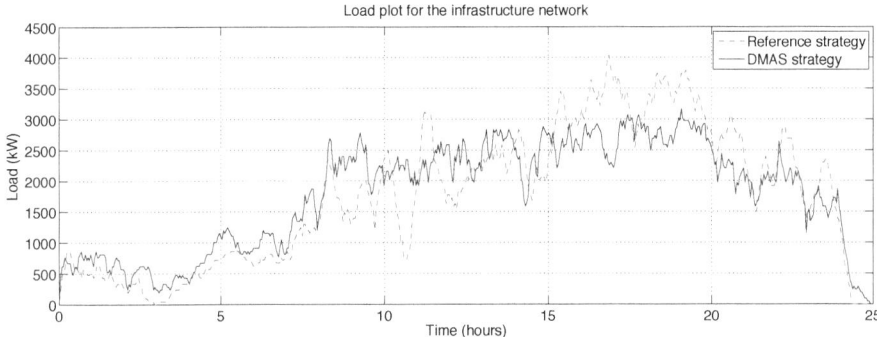

Fig. 5. Plot for the load evolution shows that the anticipatory strategy can reduce load peaks during peak hours

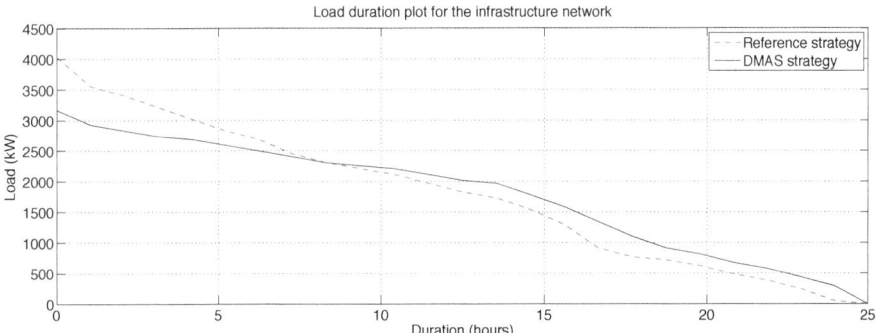

Fig. 6. Plot for the load duration shows that the anticipatory strategy can reduce load peaks during peak hours

in Figure 5 and this figure shows the influence peak hours of traffic have on the charging infrastructure. Figure 6 shows the load-duration curve for the same sample by sorting the instantaneous loads by magnitude. This load-duration curve clearly indicates that the anticipatory solution is capable of reducing the peak loads on the charging infrastructure by 21%.

The benefits the anticipatory strategy presents over the reference strategy is caused by the capability of better reacting to changes in the environment. Using the reference strategy, vehicles decide on charging stations to stop at in the future based on information about how busy the stations are now. In a dynamic environment the situation can change significantly between making the choice and arriving at the station. This is mitigated by re-evaluating the choice of stations repeatedly along the route, but the flexibility EVs have in altering their choices decreases along with the battery levels when driving. Using the anticipatory strategy, the choice of charging stations is always based on how busy the particular stations will be upon arrival or atleast an estimation hereof. This difference in approach is the main cause for the better results that come from using the anticipatory strategy.

7 Related Work

Coordination of EV charging has been an active research topic lately [15]. Several coordination strategies have been proposed to facilitate EV charging with the objective to minimize vehicle waiting times at charging stations [7,16]. The authors of [16] propose strategies requiring global knowledge of charging station occupation over time, in order to optimally plan vehicle to station allocation to minimize certain metrics concerning only EV users, e.g. waiting time. These strategies are evaluated by using a real-world highway segment scenario. The authors of [7] differ from the use of central knowledge of charging station occupation by using reservations and by letting each station simulate their own expected waiting times. They also evaluate their proposed strategies in a artificially designed road network topology.

The work in this paper proposes an anticipatory coordination strategy and evaluates it against a centralised non-anticipatory strategy. As such this work combines the decentralised approach of simulating waiting times from [7] with evaluation in a realistic scenario as proposed in [16] but improves on the use of a single highway segment by using a highway network. The evaluation is also performed from the viewpoint of multiple stakeholders such as EV users and electrical infrastructure maintainers in the context of real-world applicability. In context of the literature overview given in [15], this work proposes a distributed method for coordination on a distribution scale with coupled techno-economic objectives.

8 Conclusion and Remaining Challenges

Offering an infrastructure wherein EV users can recharge their vehicles during their trips significantly increases the action radius of EVs. This work shows that an anticipatory coordination strategy is capable of significantly reducing waiting times for EVs at charging stations by up to 50% when compared to non-anticipatory coordination strategies while at the same time being able to reduce peak loads on the electricity grid by 21%. This work also shows that the saturation of the infrastructure network is an important factor in determining the added value from coordination of EV charging and that organised coordination is most effective when the infrastructure does not suffer from completely insufficient capacity. A realistic scenario is used for the evaluation of the proposed anticipatory coordination strategy for the sake of real-world applicability.

Some challenges remain unaddressed by this work and can be used to improve the realistic setting of the simulated scenario even further. Incorporating realistic location based driving patterns, the use of updated electrical vehicle models in terms of energy consumption, more accurate battery charging models and an even larger highway network are examples of such possible improvements. Furthermore, the evaluation of the anticipatory strategy can be improved upon by comparing it to stronger centralised planning strategies.

References

1. National Household Transportation Survey. Technical report, U.S. Dept. of Transportation (2009)
2. Carley, S., Krause, R.M., Lane, B.W., Graham, J.D.: Intent to purchase a plug-in electric vehicle: A survey of early impressions in large US cites. In: Transportation Research Part D: Transport and Environment, vol. 18, pp. 39–45. Elsevier (2013)
3. Claes, R., Holvoet, T.: GridLock: A microscopic traffic simulation platform. In: International Conference on Models and Technologies for Intelligent Transportation Systems (2011)
4. Holvoet, T., Weyns, D., Valckenaers, P.: Patterns of delegate mas. In: Third IEEE International Conference on Self-Adaptive and Self-Organizing Systems, SASO 2009, pp. 1–9. IEEE (2009)
5. Vandael, S., Holvoet, T., Deconinck, G.: A decentralized approach for public fast charging of electric vehicles using delegate multi-agent systems. In: Proceedings of the Third International Workshop on Agent Technologies for Energy Systems (ATES 2012), Number section 5, p. 6 (2012)
6. Claes, R., Holvoet, T., Weyns, D.: A Decentralized Approach for Anticipatory Vehicle Routing Using Delegate Multiagent Systems. IEEE Transactions on Intelligent Transportation Systems 12(2), 364–373 (2011)
7. Qin, H., Zhang, W.: Charging scheduling with minimal waiting in a network of electric vehicles and charging stations. In: Proceedings of the Eighth ACM International Workshop on Vehicular Inter-Networking, VANET 2011, pp. 51–60. ACM, New York (2011)
8. Van Roy, J., Leemput, N., De Breucker, S., Geth, F., Tant, P., Driesen, J.: An Availability Analysis and Energy Consumption Model for a Flemish Fleet of Electric Vehicles. In: EEVC, Brussels, pp. 1–12 (2011)
9. Hess, A., Malandrino, F., Reinhardt, M.B., Casetti, C., Hummel, K.A., Barceló-Ordinas, J.M.: Optimal deployment of charging stations for electric vehicular networks. In: Proceedings of the First Workshop on Urban Networking, UrbaNe 2012, vol. 1 (2012)
10. Ip, A., Fong, S., Liu, E.: Optimization for allocating BEV recharging stations in urban areas by using hierarchical clustering. In: 6th International Conference on Advanced Information Management and Service, IMS 2010, pp. 460–465. IEEE (2010)
11. Meng, W., Kai, L.: Optimization of electric vehicle charging station location based on game theory. In: Proceedings 2011 International Conference on Transportation, Mechanical, and Electrical Engineering (TMEE), pp. 809–812 (December 2011)
12. Li, Z., Ouyang, M.: The pricing of charging for electric vehicles in China - Dilemma and solution. Energy 36(9), 5765–5778 (2011)
13. United States Environmental Protection Agency: Driving Cycles
14. EPA: Fuel Economy Labeling of Motor Vehicles: Revisions to Improve Calculation of Fuel Economy Estimates (EPA420-R-06-017). Technical report, U.S. Environmental Protection Agency, Washington D.C. (2009)
15. Leemput, N., Van Roy, J., Geth, F., Tant, P., Claessens, B., Driesen, J.: Comparative analysis of coordination strategies for electric vehicles. In: 2011 2nd IEEE PES International Conference and Exhibition on Innovative Smart Grid Technologies (ISGT Europe), pp. 1–8 (2011)
16. Yang, S.N., Cheng, W.S., Hsu, Y.C., Gan, C.H., Lin, Y.B.: Charge scheduling of electric vehicles in highways. Mathematical and Computer Modelling, 1–10 (December 2011)

Bilateral Negotiation of a Meeting Point in a Maze

Fabien Delecroix, Maxime Morge, and Jean-Christophe Routier

Laboratoire d'Informatique Fondamentale de Lille
Université Lille 1
Cité Scientifique- F-59655 Villeneuve d'Ascq
{fabien.delecroix,maxime.morge,jean-christophe.routier}@lifl.fr

Abstract. Negotiation between agents aims at reaching an agreement in which the conflicting interests of agents are accommodated. In this paper, we present a concrete negotiation scenario where two agents are situated in a maze and the negotiation outcome is a cell where they will meet. Based on their individual preferences (a minimal distance from their location computed from their partial knowledge of the environment), we propose a negotiation protocol which allows agents to submit more than two proposals at the same time and a conciliatory strategy. Formally, we prove that the agreement reached by such a negotiation process is Pareto-optimal and a compromise, i.e. a solution which minimizes the maximum effort for one agent. Moreover, the path between the two agents emerges from the repeated negotiations in our experiments.

1 Introduction

Negotiation is a form of interaction in which a group of agents with conflicting interests try to reach a mutually acceptable agreement over some outcomes [1]. The outcome is typically a tasks/resources allocation, a matching between agents or a joint decision. Agents' interests are conflicting in the sense that they cannot be simultaneously fully satisfied. In this perspective, negotiation can be seen as a distributed search through a space of potential agreements [2].

In this paper, we present a concrete negotiation scenario where two agents are situated in a maze and the negotiation outcome is a cell where they will meet. Based on their individual preferences (a minimal distance from their location computed from their partial knowledge of the environment), we propose a negotiation protocol which allows agents to submit more than two proposals at the same time and a strategy which consists in starting from the deal that is best for the agent and then concedes. A concession of an agent means that she proposes a new deal such there is no other preferred alternatives. Formally, we prove that the agreement reached by such a negotiation process is Pareto-optimal and a compromise, i.e. an alternative which minimizes the maximum effort for one agent to reach it. Moreover, the path between the two agents emerges from the repeated negotiations in our experiments.

Paper Overview. Section 2 describes the addressed concrete problem and why the negotiation frameworks in the literature are not sufficient for it. In section 3, we introduce the basic notions in the background of our work. Section 4 proposes a rule for multi-agents decision. Then, we present our negotiation game (Sec. 5). We describe our experiments in section 6. Finally, section 7 concludes.

2 Problem

We consider here two agents which are paratroopers landed at the two opposite corners of a maze. They aim at meeting as soon as possible, i.e minimizing the maximum number of steps for one agent to reach the meeting point. Both of them have a local perception of the environment. Each agent can perceive the walls of her current cell. Moreover, she knows her own location. Contrary to the classical rendezvous problem [3], the agents are allowed to communicate in order to negotiate the meeting point. Moreover, the meeting point can be re-negotiated during the exploration of the maze. The optimal solution for finding a meeting point requires the knowledge of the whole maze. Under this assumption, the agents can compute the shortest path between them and set the meeting point in the middle of it. By contrast, a solution which does not need any prior knowledge consists of pseudo-randomly selecting a meeting point in the first diagonal.

In order to illustrate this problem, we consider a 3×3 maze (cf Fig.1). At the second step of the resolution, Alice is in the cell d while Bob is in the cell f. Each agent computes the distance to reach all the other cells based on its knowledge. For this purpose, an agent takes into consideration the perceived walls and she assumes that there is no wall between the cells it did not visit yet. In other words, the computation is performed by an A-star algorithm where the future path-cost function is the Manhattan distance. For instance, Bob supposes that 3 steps are required to reach the cell c since she is aware there is a wall between c and f, and so it plans to go through e and b. However, this path cannot be followed since there is a wall between e and b the agent is not aware of.

Since we want to minimize the maximum number of steps for an agent to reach the meeting point, the cell e is a good candidate even if d, e and f are Pareto-optimal (see Def. 1). In order to solve this distributed solving problem, we need a negotiation protocol and a strategy which allow to reach a fair solution. It is worth noticing that the communication of their position is not enough to reach a rendezvous with a pure strategy [3]. Moreover, the communication of the wall is useless since the agents explore different parts of the maze.

Related Works. Many negotiation frameworks have been proposed in the literature (see [1] for a survey) depending on the object of negotiation, the agents' preferences (2 or n), the protocol and the strategy. First of all, we consider here 2 agents (the paratroopers) negotiating a single-issue with discrete values (the meeting point).

Model for the Agents' Preferences. Most of the literature assume that the preferences are represented by utility functions in order to negotiate a payoff,

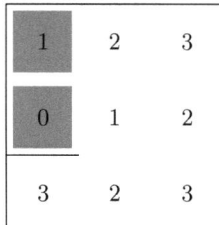 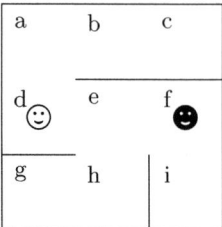 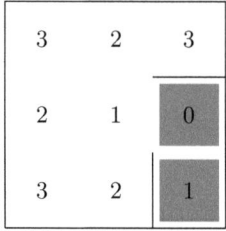

Fig. 1. The maze (at middle) and its internal representation for Alice (at left) and Bob (at right) at time $t = 2$. In the latters, the visited cells are in grey, some walls may be still unknown and each cell is labelled with an estimation of the shortest path length.

i.e a point on the curve of these functions. In our particular example, we can remark that two points are at the same distance of Alice : a and e. Then, we must propose a negotiation strategy based on large preferences for agents. More generally, we will only assume a preference relation which is incomplete in order to consider not only the indifference but also the incomparability between alternatives. [4] allows agents to have a qualitative preference model (i.e. a CP-net) for negotiating. Similarly, we will compute the rank of an alternative using its depth in the preference graph.

Protocol. The negotiation protocol is the set of rules which regulates the exchanges of proposals. It can be symmetric (e.g. [5]) or asymmetric (e.g. [6]). Contrary to [4], our protocol does not give the priority to one agent and each agent can submit more than one alternative at each round: it is required for reaching a fair agreement with large preferences.

Strategy. The negotiation strategy must be set up according to the model for the agents' preferences and the protocol. Its features are the availability of information about opponents and its efficiency. While some negotiation strategies make the assumption of perfect information (e.g. [5]) we think we cannot make such assumption in our context. Most of the existing strategies leads to a Pareto-optimal solution (e.g. [5]). Additionally, we aims at proposing a negotiation process for distributed problem solving which minimizes the maximum effort for one agent. [7] considers social choice theory to allow agents to choose among alternatives based on their social value since it knows the preferences of others. We do not assume here any knowledge about the preferences of the opponents.

In summary, we aim at proposing:

1. a negotiation strategy based on large (and eventually incomplete) preferences which does not assume that agents know the preferences of each other;
2. a protocol which allows more than two offers per round;
3. a fair negotiation process which does not give priority to one agent and which minimize the maximum effort for one agent.

3 Background

In order to represent the taste of the decision maker and to compare the alternatives to each other, we assume here a preference relation on a non-empty finite set of alternatives $\mathcal{X}$, i.e. a preorder relation (reflexive and transitive) denoted $\succsim$. By contrast, the corresponding strict preference relation (denoted $\succ$) is a strict order, i.e. transitive and asymmetric. The indifference relation captures the indifference of the decision maker between alternatives. It means that the decision maker believes that, according to its preferences, there is no real difference between x and y. Moreover, We remark that the preference relation can be incomplete. Two alternatives can be incomparable if it is impossible for the decision maker to compare them. It can be interpreted as a way for the decision maker to refuse to commit due to an uncertain judgment. Contrary to the indifference relation, the incomparability relation is not transitive.

The notion of non-dominance allows to distinguish the alternatives for which there is no preferred alternatives. The set of **non-dominated alternatives** over $\mathcal{X}$ wrt $\succsim$ is the set: $ND(\mathcal{X}, \succsim) = \{x \in \mathcal{X} \mid \forall y \in \mathcal{X}, \neg(y \succ x)\}$. It is worth noticing that there is always at least one non-dominated alternative.

Example 1. *We consider here the set of alternatives $\mathcal{X} = \{a, b, c, d, e, f, g, h, i\}$ and the two preference relations $\succsim_1$ and $\succsim_2$ over $\mathcal{X}$ corresponding to our previous example. In our case, a cell is preferred to another if the estimated distance towards the first cell is at least as good as the second cell. The preference graph of $\succsim_1$ (resp. $\succsim_2$) is represented at left (resp. at right) of Fig. 2 as a directed graph where a node represents an alternative and there is a edge from x to y when x is at least as good as y. We can remark that $ND(\mathcal{X}, \succsim_1) = \{d\}$ and $ND(\mathcal{X}, \succsim_2) = \{f\}$.*

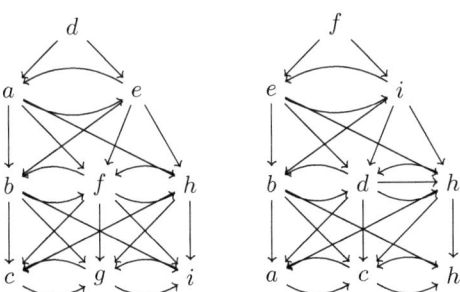

Fig. 2. Preference relation $\succsim_1$ (at left) and $\succsim_2$ (at right)

We focus now on a group of agents (two or more) taking a joint decision. We consider here a non-empty finite set of alternatives $\mathcal{X}$, a set of agents Ω and for each agent $i \in \Omega$, $\succsim_i$ is the preference relation for i over $\mathcal{X}$.

The Pareto rule is used by a group of agents to compare two alternatives. An alternative x Pareto-dominates an alternative y for a group of agents if x is at least as good as y for all the agents and at least one agent strictly prefers x to y. An alternative is Pareto-optimal if it is not Pareto-dominated.

Definition 1 (Pareto). *The **Pareto-dominance** relation $\succ_\Omega \subseteq \mathcal{X} \times \mathcal{X}$ is defined such that $\forall (x, y) \in \mathcal{X}^2$, $x \succ_\Omega y \Leftrightarrow (\forall i \in \Omega, x \succsim_i y) \wedge (\exists j \in \Omega, x \succ_i y)$. The set of **Pareto-optimal** alternatives for Ω over $\mathcal{X}$ is the set $ND(\mathcal{X}, \succ_\Omega) = \{x \in \mathcal{X} \mid \forall y \in \mathcal{X} \; \neg(y \succ_\Omega x)\}$*

It is worth noticing that the Pareto-dominance is a strict order. The Pareto-optimality captures the notion of rationality for multi-agents. Indeed, the alternatives are Pareto-dominated since, from the viewpoint of the group of agents, better alternatives are available. Moreover, there is always a Pareto-optimal alternative. The Pareto-optimality is not a sufficiently discriminatory rule. For instance, in our previous example (cf. Fig. 2), the set of Pareto-optimal alternatives is $\{e, d, f\}$. However, e seems to be more "fair" than d and f.

4 Multi-agents Decision

We aim at setting a rule for multi-agents decision which is Pareto-inclusive and we want to warrant the existence of a solution. We call them compromises.

Like the utility functions allow to evaluate the individual satisfaction of agents, we introduce a rank function for evaluating the effort performed by an agent to accept an alternative.

Definition 2 (Individual rank function). *Let $\succsim_i$ the preference relation of the agent i over $\mathcal{X}$. Our rank function is defined such that :*

$$r(x, \mathcal{X}, \succsim_i) = \begin{cases} 1 & \text{if } x \in ND(\mathcal{X}, \succsim_i) \\ 1 + r(x, \mathcal{X} \setminus ND(\mathcal{X}, \succsim_i), \succsim_i) & \text{otherwise} \end{cases}$$

The rank of an alternative is its level on the preference graph. By taking into account the rank of an alternative, we make the assumption that any concession - the fact to withdraw an alternative for a worst one - of any agent represents the same effort.

In order to obtain Pareto-optimal and fair alternatives, we define the leximin rule on the alternative ranks.

Definition 3 (Leximin Preference). *Let $x, y \in \mathcal{X}$ be two alternatives. We denote $\boldsymbol{x}_r(\Omega) = (x_1, \ldots, x_n)$, the vector of alternative ranks in decreasing order. We say that x is strictly **leximin-preferred** than y (denoted $x \succ_{lex} y$) iff $\exists k \leq n, \forall i < k, x_i = y_i$ and $x_k < y_k$. The **leximin-optimal** set over $\mathcal{X}$ is $ND(\mathcal{X}, \succ_{lex})$.*

The leximin relation is a partial strict order.

All the compromises are Pareto-optimal and there is always one.

Property 1 (Compromises)

1. $Compromises(\mathcal{X}, \Omega) \subseteq ND(\mathcal{X}, \succ_\Omega)$.
2. There always exists $x \in \mathcal{X}$ such that $x \in Compromises(\mathcal{X}, \Omega)$.

Proof 1 (Compromises)

1. Proof by contradiction. Let x be a compromise over $\mathcal{X}$ for Ω. We assume that there is $y \in \mathcal{X}$ which Pareto-dominates x. From Def. 1, we deduce (1) $\forall i \in \Omega, y \succsim_i x$ and (2) there exists an agent $j \in \Omega$ such that $y \succ_j x$. From (1) and Def. 2, we deduce that $\forall i \in \Omega, r(x, \mathcal{X}, \succ_i) \geq r(y, \mathcal{X}, \succ_i)$. From (2) and Def. 2, we deduce there exists an agent $j \in \Omega$ such that $r(x, \mathcal{X}, \succ_j) > r(y, \mathcal{X}, \succ_j)$. From Def. 3, we deduce that $y \succ_{lex} x$ and so x is not a compromise, which is a contradiction.
2. Since the leximin is an order over a non-empty finite set, this set contains at least one minimal element.

We can remark that some Pareto-optimal may not be compromises. In our example (cf. Fig 2), e is the only compromise.

In summary, a compromise captures the fairness of a solution. This rule is Pareto-inclusive and a compromise always exists.

5 Bilateral Negotiation

We propose a bilateral negotiation game in order to reach an agreement. Firstly, we introduce the protocol. Secondly, we present a negotiation strategy. Finally, we evaluate the agreements.

Protocol. Since we do not want to give priority to the agent which speaks first, we consider here a simultaneous game made of several rounds. For this purpose, we introduce an arbitration mechanism[1].

At each round, the arbitrator collects the proposals - each of them is a set of alternatives. The protocol forbids the empty proposals and the repetition of an alternative in two proposals of the same participant. When an alternative is proposed by both participants, the arbitrator closes the game, detects the agreements and informs the participants. Otherwise, it forwards these proposals to the other participant and a new round starts (see Fig. 3).

In the rest of this paper, we denote $p_1(k)$ the proposal of the agent 1 at round $k \geq 1$, i.e. a set of alternatives. At each round t, we denote $H_1(t)$ the history of the proposals of the agent 1 such that $H_1(t) = \bigcup_{k<t} p_1(k)$ and $H(t)$ is the game history $H(t) = H_1(t) \cup H_2(t)$. Moreover, the set of alternatives sent by the agent 1 during the history $H_1(t)$ is denoted $\mathcal{P}_1(t) = \{x \in \mathcal{X} \mid \exists p \in H_1(t), x \in p\}$.

At each round t, if the arbitrator identifies at least one alternative proposed by both participants, the game ends. The arbitrator gives priority to the alternatives which appear earlier in the history (cf. Algo. 1) and it returns this set

---

[1] For clarity, we choose to implement the synchronization with a mediator. However, decentralized solutions are easy to establish.

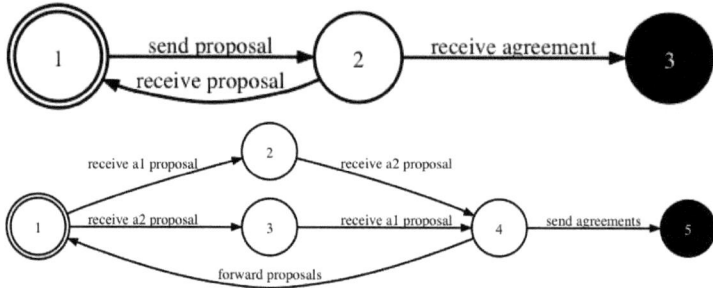

Fig. 3. Protocol for the participants (at top) and for the arbitrator (at bottom). The initial states are represented by double circles and the final ones are in black.

of alternatives, called **agreements**, to the participants. An agreement is not necessarily unique. In order to reach a collective decision, the arbitrator may select one agreement by using a (pseudo-)randomized function.

Algorithm 1. Arbitration

  Data: $H(t)$: history, $p_1(t)$ and $p_2(t)$: proposals
1 **for** $k = 0$ *to* t **do**
2 $\quad$ $A = (p_1(k) \cap p_2(t)) \cup (p_2(k) \cap p_1(t))$;
3 $\quad$ **if** $A \neq \emptyset$ **then**
4 $\quad\quad$ $send(\{a_1, a_2\}, agreement(A))$;
5 $\quad\quad$ **return**;

6 $send(a_2, proposal(p_1(t)))$;
7 $send(a_1, proposal(p_2(t)))$;

Strategy. The strategy of a participant interfaces with the protocol through the condition mechanism of utterance and interpretation of the proposals. Obviously, when an agent receives a proposal, she updates her representation of the history. The content of the proposals is determined by the strategy of the agent.

In this section, we adopt the viewpoint of the agent 1 (since the roles are symmetric). Her strategy (see Algo. 2) is legal: a proposal is not empty and the alternatives are not repeated in its proposals. Moreover, the strategy is rational: the agent chooses among the legal alternatives ($\mathcal{X}'$) those that may be compromises from her viewpoint. The negotiation heuristic consists in choosing among the rational alternatives.

A **conciliatory** agent selects all the rational alternatives in order to reach an agreement as soon as possible ($select(Rat, H(t)) = Rat$). By contrast, other strategies may aim at minimizing the individual rank of an agreement. Since we consider distributed problem solving, we will make the assumption that agents are collaborative and so conciliatory. An agent concedes since she proposes a new deal such there is no other preferred alternatives which are legal.

Algorithm 2. Negotiation strategy

Data: $H(t)$: the history, $\mathcal{X}$: the set of alternatives
1 $\mathcal{X}' = \mathcal{X} \setminus \mathcal{P}_1(t)$;
2 $Rat = ND(\mathcal{X}', \succsim_1)$;
3 $E = select(Rat, H(t))$;
4 $send(arbitrator, proposal(E))$;

Example 2. Let us consider the preferences represented in Fig. 2. We consider the negotiation games where the agent 1 (resp. 2) adopts a conciliatory strategy. In this game, the agent 1 (resp. 2) starts with the alternative d (resp. the alternative f). At the second round, the agent 1 offers both a and e while the agent 2 offers both e and i. Therefore, e is an agreement.

Theoretical Evaluation. We identify here the properties of the agreements.

First, we can remark that the negotiation game always leads to an agreement.

Property 2 (Guaranteed success). *Our negotiation game ends successfully.*

Proof 2 (Guaranteed success). *Since the set of alternatives is finite and the protocol forbids the repetition of alternatives in the proposals of the same agent, the game ends. The set of alternatives with the precedence relation in the history is an non-empty and finite set with a total order. Therefore, this set has always at least one minimal element, i.e. an agreement.*

An agreement reached by a negotiation game between two conciliatory agents is a Pareto-optimal alternative and a compromise.

Theorem 1 (Agreements). *If both participants adopt a conciliatory strategy, then the set of agreements reached $A_{CC} \subseteq \mathcal{X}$ is such that:*

1. $A_{CC} \subseteq ND(\mathcal{X}, \succsim_\Omega)$
2. $x_{CC} \in A_{CC} \Rightarrow compromise(x_{CC}, \Omega, \mathcal{X})$

First, we remark that the timing of proposals depends on their rank.

Lemma 1. *Let $x \in \mathcal{X}$ be an alternative and a negotiation game which stops at time $\theta > 0$. $r(x, \mathcal{X}, \succ_i) < \theta \Rightarrow x \in p_i(r(x, \mathcal{X}, \succ_i))$.*

Proof 3 (Agreements)

1. Let $x \in A_{CC}$ be an agreement. We prove by contradiction that $A_{CC} \subseteq ND(\mathcal{X}, \succsim_\Omega)$. We assume $x \notin ND(\mathcal{X}, \succsim_\Omega)$. Therefore, $\exists y, (y \succ_1 x \land y \succsim_2 x) \lor (y \succ_2 x \land y \succsim_1 x)$. So, $\exists t, y \in \mathcal{P}_1(t) \land y \in \mathcal{P}_2(t) \land (x \notin \mathcal{P}_1(t) \lor x \notin \mathcal{P}_2(t))$. Therefore $x \notin A_{CC}$ which is a contradiction.
2. Let $x \in A_{CC}$ be an agreement and θ the time when the game stops. Proof by contradiction. We assume $x \notin Compromises(\mathcal{X}, \Omega)$. (A)
From (A) and Def. 3 and Prop. 1, $\exists y \in \mathcal{X}, y \succ_{lex} x$. (B)
From Def. 3 and (B), we distinguish 2 cases:

(a) $\max_{a \in \Omega} r(y, \mathcal{X}, \succsim_a) < \max_{a \in \Omega} r(x, \mathcal{X}, \succsim_a)$ (C)
From (C) and Lemma 1, we deduce there exists $t \geq 1$ when both participants play y but only one have played x. Therefore, from Algo. 1, $x \notin A_{CC}$, which is a contradiction.
(b) $\max_{a \in \Omega} r(y, \mathcal{X}, \succsim_a) = \max_{a \in \Omega} r(x, \mathcal{X}, \succsim_a)$ (D) and $\min_{a \in \Omega} r(y, \mathcal{X}, \succsim_a) < \min_{a \in \Omega} r(x, \mathcal{X}, \succsim_a)$ (E).
From (D), (E) and Lemma 1, we deduce that x is played first before y while x and y are played a second time during the same round. From Algo. 1, we deduce that $x \notin A_{CC}$, which is a contradiction.

Actually, the game aims at splitting the effort between the participants.

6 Experiments

Our experiments aim at comparing the improvement of the distributed solving with the negotiation and its communication costs.

The pseudo-random generation of a maze of size $n \times n$ is performed by:

- a pseudo-randomized version of Prim's algorithm. This algorithm results in mazes with many short dead ends and the solution is usually pretty direct as well;
- a depth-first search algorithm. This algorithm results in mazes with fewer but longer dead ends, and the solution is usually very long and twisty.

We pseudo-randomly generate a new $n \times n$ maze, then we try to solve the corresponding problem by:

1. the pseudo-randomly selection of a meeting point in the fist diagonal;
2. the negotiation of the meeting point at each step;
3. the negotiation of the meeting point every 2 steps;
4. the negotiation of the meeting point every 4 steps;
5. the negotiation of the meeting point each time the path length towards the meeting point increases for one agent due to the discovery of a wall.

We consider $n \in [2; 14]$ and for each n, we generate 100 experiments.

In Fig. 4, we consider the maximum number of steps for one agent and the total number for the two agents. Negotiating rather than pseudo-randomly choosing a meeting point improves the time to reach it. More surprisingly, the global satisfaction of the agents is improved by the negotiation in simple mazes. In other words, negotiations may help to find shortest paths.

In Fig. 5, we compare the communication cost of our different strategies in terms of number of negotiations, total number of rounds and total number of proposed alternatives. The results are presented for mazes generated with the randomize version of Prim's algorithm but they are very similar when the depth-first search algorithm is used. Negotiating at each step increases the communication cost with similar results for the number of steps. It seems that the communication cost of the strategies # 3 and # 5 are similar.

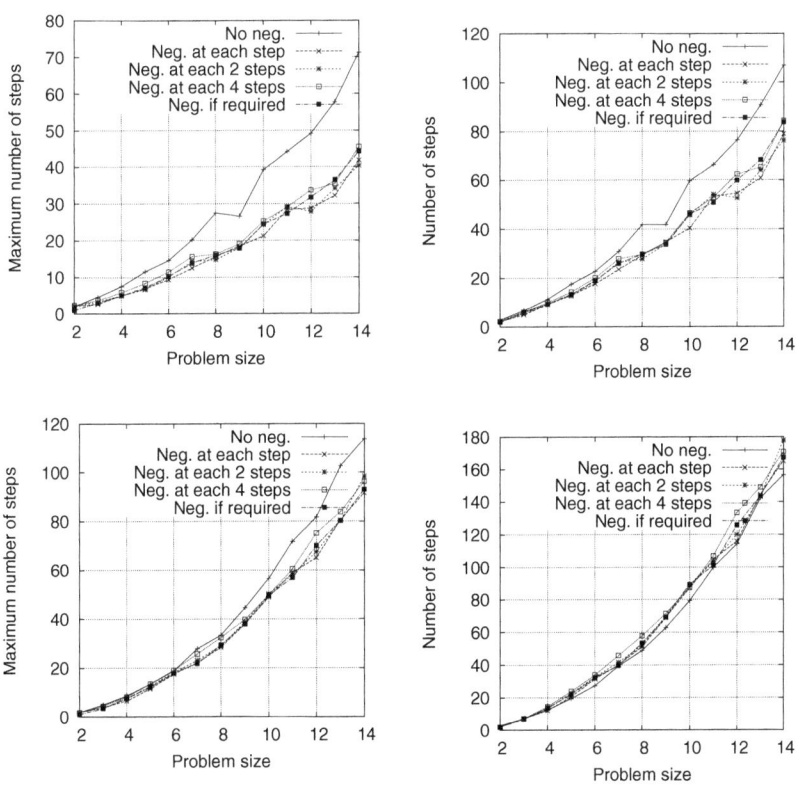

Fig. 4. Maximum number of steps by one agent and the total number of steps performed by two agents with mazes generated with a pseudo-randomized version of Prim's algorithm (top) and with a depth-first search algorithm (bottom).

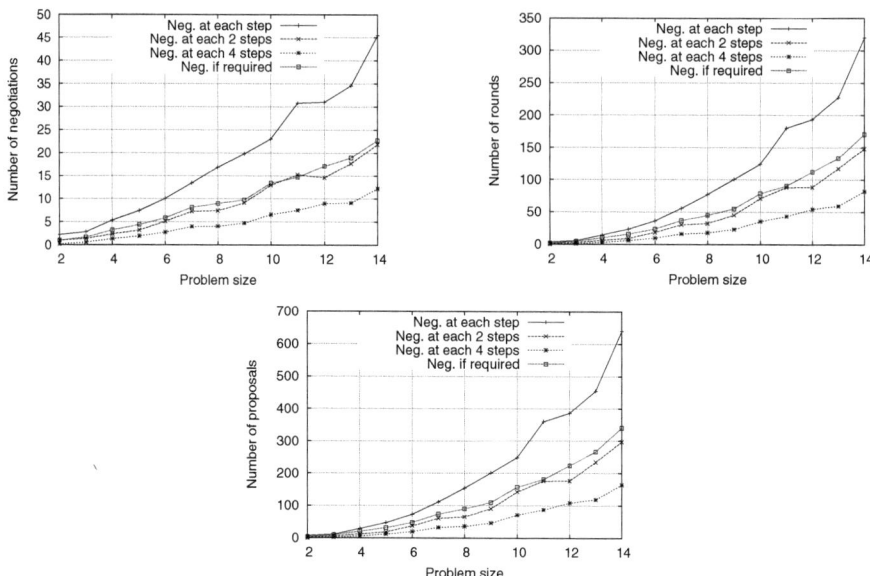

Fig. 5. Number of negotiations (at top), rounds (at center) and proposals (at bottom)

We generate now a 8×8 maze with the pseudo-randomized version of Prim's algorithm and the location of the agents. We partially destroy the walls until the density (nb of walls/nb of initial walls) is d %. Then, we try to solve the corresponding problem with the help of our 5 strategies. We consider $d \in [0; 100]$. For each d, we generate 100 experiments. In Fig. 6, we observe that negotiating rather than pseudo-randomly choosing a meeting point improves the time to reach it. Moreover, we cannot distinguish the efficiency of the different strategies. However, these strategies have different communication cost. For instance, the strategy # 5 is closed to the strategy # 3 when the density is is high.

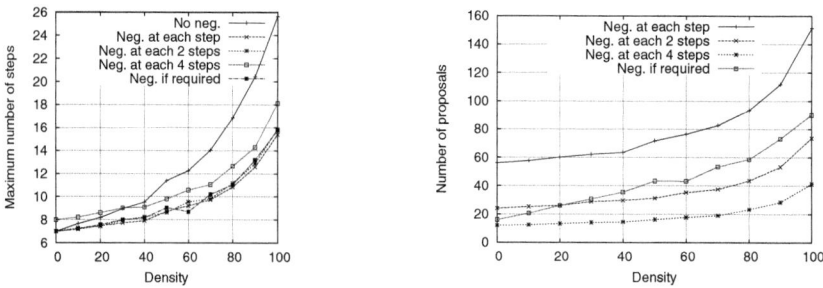

Fig. 6. Number of maximum steps (at left) and proposals (at right) depending on the density of the maze

In order to resume, the strategy #4 seems to be the best one due to the maximum number of steps by one agent and its communication cost whatever the maze is.

7 Conclusion

In this paper, we have proposed a negotiation protocol which allows agents to make more than two offers per round and a negotiation strategy based on large (and eventually incomplete) preferences which does not assume that agents know the preferences of each other. In this way, we have proposed a fair negotiation process which does not give priority to one agent and which minimizes the maximum effort for one agent. We have applied our framework for distributed problem solving. In particular, we have considered the case of two agents in a maze which aims at negotiating a meeting in order to reach it as soon as possible. In our experiments, the negotiation improves the resolution of this problem and the path between the agents emerge from the repeated negotiations.

We are currently extending our bilateral negotiation game to a multi-party negotiation game with more than two agents. Even if our definitions for concessions and compromises are suitable, we adapt the negotiation strategies and the arbitration mechanism. In this way, we will allow more than two agents to negotiate a meeting point.

References

1. Fatima, S., Rahwan, I.: Negotiation and Bargaining. In: Multiagent Systems, pp. 143–176. MIT Press (2013)
2. Jennings, N.R., Faratin, P., Lomuscio, A.R., Parsons, S., Sierra, C., Wooldridge, M.: Automated negotiation: Prospects methods and challenges. GDN 10(2), 199–215 (2001)
3. Alpern, S., Gal, S.: The Theory of Search Games and Rendezvous. Kluwer (2003)
4. Aydoğan, R., Baarslag, T., Hindriks, K.V., Jonker, C.M., Yolum, P.: Heuristic-based approaches for CP-nets in negotiation. In: Ito, T., Zhang, M., Robu, V., Matsuo, T. (eds.) Complex Automated Negotiations. SCI, vol. 435, pp. 115–126. Springer, Heidelberg (2012)
5. Rosenschein, J.S., Zlotkin, G.: Rules of Encounter - Designing Conventions for Automated Negotiation among Computers. MIT Press (1994)
6. Rubinstein, A.: Perfect equilibrium in a bargaining model. Econometrica 50(1), 97–102 (1982)
7. Endriss, U.: Monotonic concession protocols for multilateral negotiation. In: Proc. of AAMAS, pp. 392–399. ACM (2006)

Agent Negotiation for Different Needs in Smart Parking Allocation*

Claudia Di Napoli[1], Dario Di Nocera[2,**], and Silvia Rossi[3]

[1] Istituto di Calcolo e Reti ad Alte Prestazioni
Consiglio Nazionale delle Ricerche, Napoli, Italy
claudia.dinapoli@cnr.it
[2] Dipartimento di Matematica
Università degli Studi di Napoli "Federico II", Napoli, Italy
dario.dinocera@unina.it
[3] Dipartimento di Ingegneria Elettrica e Tecnologie dell'Informazione
Università degli Studi di Napoli "Federico II", Napoli, Italy
silvia.rossi@unina.it

Abstract. Smart Cities are experiencing a growing interest from different research areas. One of the challenges of Smart Cities is the design of an effective City Parking System that may contribute to improve the city life in terms of gas emission and air pollution in city centers, but also the everyday life of city dwellers by facilitating to park with the support of automatic parking services. In this work, an investigation on the use of software agents negotiation to accommodate both user and vendor requirements on a parking space is carried out. It is shown that agent negotiation allows to assign parking spaces in an automatic and intelligent manner by taking into account that users have their own needs regarding parking location and price, while parking vendors have their own needs regarding efficient allocation of parking spaces, and city regulations.

Keywords: Agent negotiation, multi-agent systems, smart parking, smart cities.

1 Introduction

Smart Cities initiatives are focused on different themes relevant to increase the state of innovation of European and worldwide cities in order to: increase the quality of life of city-dwellers, enhance the efficiency and competitiveness of the economy, move towards the sustainability of cities by improving resource efficiency and meeting emission reduction targets.

---

* The research leading to these results has received funding from the EU FP7-ICT-2012-8 under the MIDAS Project (Model and Inference Driven - Automated testing of Services architectures), Grant Agreement no. 318786, and the Italian Ministry of University and Research and EU under the PON OR.C.HES.T.R.A. project (ORganization of Cultural HEritage for Smart Tourism and Real-time Accessibility).
** Ph.D. scholarship funded by Media Motive S.r.l Napoli (Italy), POR Campania FSE 2007-2013.

One of the challenging problems to be addressed is parking in urban areas. It is widely recognized that drivers searching for a parking space in wide urban areas waste time and fuel, so increasing traffic congestion and air pollution [7]. It is not always possible to address the problem by creating more parking spaces, but rather "intelligent" parking facilities are necessary.

The use of advanced technologies, including vehicle sensors, wireless communications, and data analytics, is the base for the efficient allocation, monitoring, and management of smart parking solutions for future Smart Cities in order to improve urban mobility strategies. Most of the research projects concerning smart parking systems focus on ways to collect and publish live parking information to drivers so they can be informed of available parking spaces near to the destination they require. At the same time, many companies are developing electronic parking systems allowing for a wide variety of available payment methods in conjunction with the dissemination of parking availability information. Nevertheless, they lack of intelligent features allowing not only to advise motorists of available car parks in multiple zones, but more importantly to help them in making decisions on where to park.

Mechanisms to manage the relationship between supply and demand are necessary to provide user-oriented automatic parking services that take into account both drivers preferences, and parking vendors requirements together with social benefits for the city, such as a reduction of traffic in city centers by limiting parking in that area [8].

In this context, we investigate the possibility to use software agent negotiation to address some of the challenges concerning smart parking and mobility pricing strategies. Software agents are software programs situated in some environment, continuously active, capable of autonomous actions (either proactive or reactive), and of working on tasks on behalf of users. These programs differ from regular software because they are personalized, continuously running, and to a certain extent autonomous, so making them suitable to assist buyers in the search and selection of products [5]. Software agents are able to communicate with other agents, and to negotiate over a set of issues [3]. Automated software agent negotiation is crucial to address the demands for systems composed of agents that represent different individuals or organizations and that are capable of reaching agreements through negotiation [4].

The present work proposes an automated negotiation mechanism among a software agent that models a Parking Manager responsible for providing parking spaces, and a software agent acting on behalf of a motorist user searching for a parking space in the city center of a urban area. Negotiation is used in order to accommodate both users and providers needs that are different and, more importantly, conflicting. In fact, the Parking Manager has the objective to sell parking spaces to make a profit, but to prevent, as much as possible, motorists to park in the city center, while users would prefer to save as much money as possible, but to park close to the city center location they require. The allocation of the parking space is the result of a negotiation process between the Parking

Manager and the user having their own private utility functions respectively to make a parking space offer, and to evaluate whether to accept a received offer.

2 Automated Negotiation for Parking Allocation

Usually, parking applications provide users with available parking spaces among which to select the preferred one according to their own preferences, if possible. In the Smart Cities of the future, users should be equipped with applications able to carry out this selection automatically, and more importantly, to take into account different requirements for a parking space based on user profiles (e.g. business, tourist, generic) that may have different preferences on parking attributes. Furthermore, in order to help refining the selection process, additional information may be used (that could come from other sources of information), such as unavailability of public transportation at the required time, the necessity to reach different locations once the car has been parked, the possibility to find other attractions in the area, and so on.

Another problem of parking in big cities is the fragmentation of public and private parking providers, each one adopting their own technology to collect occupancy data that, as such, cannot be easily shared among different owners or made accessible by user-friendly applications. In order to provide motorists with smart parking applications, the first step would be to encourage public and private parking providers to share their data and to build smart parking software applications that coordinate individual parking solutions for end users without involving them in the fragmentation of parking owners. At the same time, individual parking owners should be made aware of the benefits of providing such a global parking provision showing them that the coordinated provision of parking solutions still guarantees their individual income and fair competition by better exploiting the parking spaces offered in a city. Furthermore, a coordinated parking system allows to gather information to dynamically change the price of the offered parking spaces according to market-based evaluations based on the flow of user requests and the occupancy of the car parks in a given time interval (e.g., the price could decrease according to the occupancy of the parking, or to the time requested by the user), their geographical location, and so on.

In this context, automated negotiation may address some of these issues by allowing car park owners and users to negotiate over parking space attributes whose values may depend on dynamic information and on users' and car park owners' preferences. Different user profiles may be modeled by using different utility functions to evaluate parking offers. It is assumed that car park owners (that can be both public and private) agree to subscribe to a Coordinated Parking System by making it available a given number of parking spaces managed by a Parking Manager Agent (PM). It is responsible for their coordinated reselling to provide a better distribution of vehicles in the managed car parks. Its objective is to sell parking spaces to make a profit, but also to prevent, as much as possible, motorists to park in the city center, so improving the city life by decreasing the circulation of cars in the city center. Motorists are modeled as User Agents (UAs) interacting with the PM to submit requests for parking spaces specifying their own preferences on where to park, but also trying to pay as little as possible. Automated negotiation between the PM and the UA is used to find a parking space allocation that accommodates their needs up to a certain extent, i.e. by finding an acceptable compromise for the involved negotiators.

The length of the negotiation process could prevent its use in real-world scenarios, so we adopt a flexible negotiation mechanism, proposed in [1], that allows to dynamically set the negotiation duration according to the number of available parking spaces that is known only at the time of a request, and so it cannot statically included in the negotiation mechanism.

2.1 The Negotiation Model

The adopted negotiation mechanism, reported in [1], is used in the present work as a bi-lateral negotiation whose protocol is based on a Contract Net Iterated Protocol, and it may be iterated for a variable number of times until a deadline is reached or the negotiation is successful. Each iteration is referred to as a negotiation *round*, and the deadline is the number of allowed rounds.

According to the protocol, at the first negotiation round the UA submits its request for a parking space specifying the preferred location area in the city center, and the requested time interval. The PM replies sending an offer for a parking space, waiting for an acceptance or rejection from the UA. If the offer is accepted the negotiation ends successfully, otherwise a new round is started, if allowed by the protocol. The PM will send as many offers as the number of allowed rounds, that of course cannot be greater than the number of available parking spaces.

In the proposed negotiation, utility functions are used to model the different needs of the PM and the UA: the PM uses the value of the utility functions to decide which offer to send, while the UA uses the utility function to evaluate whether accept or reject the received offer. The utility U for an agent x is a function that depends on the specific agent x, and on an offer o_i made by the agent y (with $x = y$ or $x \neq y$) such as $U_x(o_y) : D_1 \times \cdots \times D_r \to [0,1]$, where $D_1, \ldots, D_r$ are the value domains of the r negotiation issues. The issues for the PM are the car park availability and its distance from the city center, while the issues for the UA are the parking space price, the distance of the car park from the requested location, and the same distance evaluated in terms of travel time from the requested location. So, the utility functions for the PM and the UA have the following domains:

$$U_{PM}(offer_{PM}(k)) : availability \times distance\_from\_city\_center \to [0,1]$$
$$U_{UA}(offer_{PM}(k)) : price \times GPS\_distance \times time\_distance \to [0,1]$$

where, the co-domain $[0,1]$ indicates that the functions are normalized.

Utility functions are modeled as linear functions (as will be explained in the following Sections) resulting from the weighted sum of the considered issues. Different *weights* can be associated to the considered parking attributes, so modeling the different importance of the attributes for different classes of users, and even

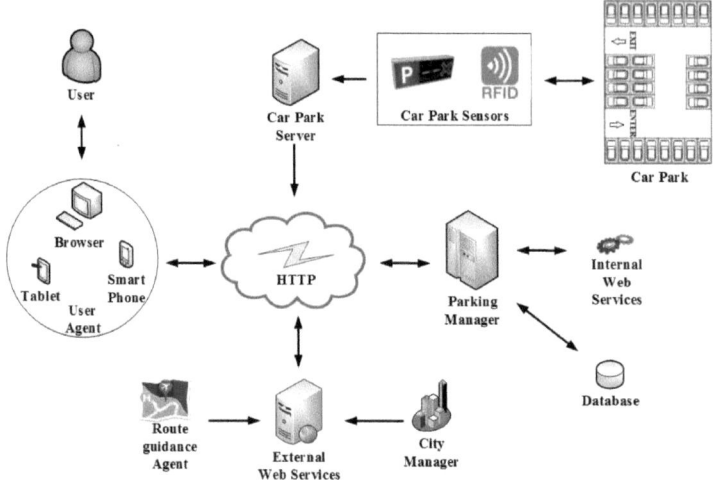

Fig. 1. Coordinated Car Parking Service architecture

for different Parking Managers. It should be noted that an offer proposed by the PM in a negotiation round cannot be considered available in the successive rounds once rejected by the UA, since it may be allocated to a different user, or its price may change according to the number of requests.

3 The Coordinated Parking System

In order to provide motorists with an automatic parking system, first of all it is necessary to provide them with logistic information about available car parks in a specific area, upon a user request. It is assumed that motorists interact with a Coordinated Parking System, as shown in Figure 1, by submitting a request for a parking space to the Car Park Server through several devices (e.g. Tablet, Smart-Phone, PDA or PC) using a city map to select the area where he/she would like to park, and an interface to indicate his/her parking preferences. The PM is responsible for processing the request: it queries an internal database (Database) to retrieve information on the available car parks, and it relies on specific applications to extract car park availability when the request is processed, and to collect relevant information on city regulations, or on events that may affect public transportation.

Each car park is characterized by the following parameters:

car_park= <park_id, park_GPS_location, ref_price_unit,
park_capacity, sector>

where park_id is the unique identifier of the car park, park_GPS_location is its GPS location, ref_price_unit is the default time unit price for a parking space, park_capacity is the total number of parking spaces in the car park, and

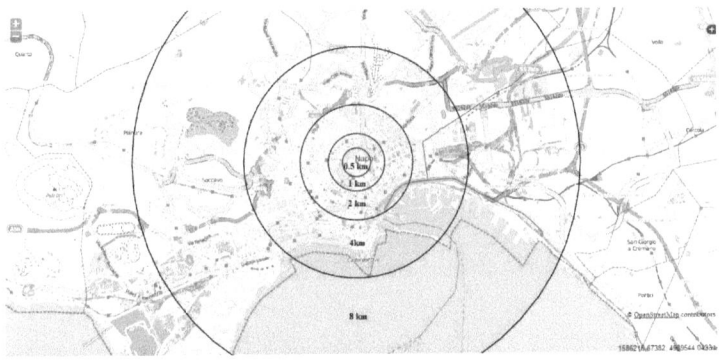

Fig. 2. A representation of city sectors

sector represents the geographical location of the car park with respect to the city center. A sector identifies a ring and its value is an integer computed as follows:

$$sector = \begin{cases} 0 & distance\_from\_city\_center < min\_range \\ 1 + \lfloor log_2(distance\_from\_city\_center/min\_range) \rfloor & otherwise \end{cases}$$

where min_range is the radius of the area of (sector=0), and $distance\_from\_city$ represents the distance between the car park location and the city center (located in the area of sector=0).

The distribution of sectors starting from the city center is shown in Fig. 2 and it is used to model the reliance of the price offered for a parking space on the distance between the car park and the city center (as it will be shown in Section 3.1).

A UA request park_req is composed of values referred to the parking space attributes that are relevant for the user to decide where to park:

park_req= <id_req, dest_GPS_location, start_time,

end_time, reserv_time>

where id_req is the unique identifier of the user request, dest_location represents the GPS location of the destination the user wants to reach, the interval (end_time - start_time) represents the time the user wants to park for, and reserv_time is a flag used to distinguish between on-demand or advance requests. For the time being, only advance requests are considered since for on-demand requests different assumption on the evaluation of car park occupancy should be considered.

With a static selection, the PM will select car parks considering only to meet the user requirements in terms of location, and available parking spaces for the required time interval. If there is no parking space meeting the requirements, a static mechanism will end up with no solutions for the driver request.

A dynamic selection of parking spaces implies the evaluation of criteria that may not be explicitly expressed by the user, and that can influence both the selection of parking spaces offered by the PM, and the evaluation of the received offer. By using an automated negotiation mechanism for a dynamic selection of parking spaces, it is possible to propose offers that do not strictly meet the user requirements, but that are a result of an evaluation of the available parking spaces against parking space attributes that are relevant to the PM, and whose values may depend on dynamic information, such as the car park occupancy. On the other hand, a received offer is evaluated by the UA against parking space attributes that are relevant to the UA and whose importance (i.e. the weight associated to each attribute) may vary for different users.

3.1 The Parking Manager Model

As described earlier, the proposed negotiation mechanism is not based on the exchange of offers and counteroffers, since UA may only accept or reject offers. So, the PM may compute the set of offers it will propose during negotiation, at the first round. The set of possible offers is computed by selecting first a set of car parks that meet the following requirements:

- the distance (referred to as park_GPS_distance) of the car park location (park_GPS_location) from the destination (dest_GPS_location) set by the user, is within a given distance (referred to as the location_tolerance),
- the car park have spaces available for the time interval specified by the user at the time t the request is issued.

The location_tolerance is set by the PM in such a way to include also car parks that are not in the city center, and consequently they may be far from the dest_GPS_location specified by the user, since the PM tries to prevent users from parking in the city center and to maximize the occupancy of car parks not located in the city center. In order to incentivize users to park outside the city center and in car parks with more parking spaces available, the PM calculates the unit price to offer for a parking space by considering that car parks located in the city center are more expensive (according to the distribution reported in Figure 1), and by applying a discount factor that depends on the car park occupancy at the time the request is processed, related to the its total capacity. Hence, the park_price_unit for a selected car park is dynamically computed as follows:

$$\text{park\_price\_unit} = \text{max\_price} - 2^{\text{sector}} \cdot (u_p/2) + \left(1 - \frac{\text{park\_availability}}{\text{park\_capacity}}\right) \cdot u_p$$

where, max_price is the maximum time unit price among the selected car parks, park_availability is the number of parking spaces available for the time interval (end_time - start_time) requested by the UA, park_capacity is the total number of parking spaces, and u_p is a unit of price (e.g., 1 euro). It is assumed that park_availability is retrieved through a specific service invoked by the PM at the time the request is processed. The PM includes in the offer also the time necessary to travel from park_GPS_location to the dest_GPS_location by using public transportation (dest_time_distance). It is assumed that this information is retrieved with the support of external services. So, an offer of the PM is:

$$\text{offer(k)} = <\text{park\_id}, \text{park\_GPS\_distance}, \text{dest\_time\_distance},$$
$$\text{park\_price\_unit}>$$

Once the PM computes the set of possible offers, it needs to establish which one to offer at each negotiation round, i.e. it needs to establish its concession strategy during negotiation. In order to do so, the PM uses a private utility function to rank the selected car parks. The evaluation function used by the PM to compute the utility of each car parking ($offer_{PM}(k)$) is the following:

$$U_{PM}(offer_{PM}(k)) = \sum_{i=1}^{n}(\alpha_i * \frac{q_{i,k} - \min_j(q_{i,j})}{\max_j(q_{i,j}) - \min_j(q_{i,j})}) \quad (1)$$

where n is the number of issues the agent is evaluating, $q_{i,k}$ is the value of the i-th issue of the k-th car park, $\min_j(q_{i,j})$ and $\max_j(q_{i,j})$ are respectively the minimum and the maximum values of the i-th issue among all the car parks selected by the PM, and the constants α_i are weights associates to the different issues with $\sum_{i=1}^{n} \alpha_i = 1$. As previously described, the issues for the PM are:

$q_1 = dist(\text{park\_GPS\_location}, \text{center\_GPS\_location})$
$q_2 = \text{park\_availability}$

Once the set of offers is ordered according to the utility values of Eq. 1, the PM sends as first offer the one with the highest utility value, and it concedes in utility offering, at each negotiation round, parking spaces with a monotonically decreasing value of its own utility. The PM will end the negotiation with a failure if all the car parks selected have been offered and not accepted. If an offer is accepted by the UA, then the negotiation ends successfully.

3.2 The User Agent Model

The evaluation function used by the UA to compute the utility of each offer proposed by PM is the following:

$$U_{UA}(offer_{PM}(k)) = \left[1 - \sum_{i=1}^{m} \beta_i * \frac{q_{i,k} - c_i}{h_i - c_i}\right] \quad (2)$$

where, m is the number of issues the agent is evaluating, $q_{i,k}$ the value i-th issue of the k-th offer, c_i is the preferred value over the i-th issue, h_i are constant values introduced for normalizing each term of the formula into the set [0,1], and β_i are weights associates to the different issues with $\sum_{i=1}^{m} \beta_i = 1$. Moreover, we assume that the preferred c_i values are reasonable with respect to each considered issue, i. e. the preferred user values are not unreasonable in relation to the issue (this means that the user cannot ask for a parking space for free!). If $q_{i,k} - c_i < 0$ than the term is set to zero.

As previously described, the issues for the UA are:

q_1 = park_price_unit
q_2 = park_GPS_distance
q_3 = park_time_distance

At each round, the UA calculates its utility for the received offer according to Eq. 2, and it accepts it only if the utility value is greater then a predefined threshold. Otherwise, it rejects the offer and waits for another offer, or for a message of negotiation end.

4 Experimental Analysis

A preliminary set of experiments was carried out in order to determine whether the negotiation is a viable approach in order to meet both users and parking managers requirements.

The experiments simulate 150 different queries made by users by selecting a destination on the interactive map of the city provided by the Coordinated Parking System, and associating to the destination the time interval which the user wants to park for. The destinations selected by the users are located in sectors two and three on the city map. For each query a negotiation run takes place. At the first negotiation round, the PM selects the car parks according to the query as reported in Section 3.1. Parking identifiers and locations are extracted from the OpenStreetMap database [2] of the city of Naples (Italy), while routing information (dest_GPS_distance and dest_time_distance) are retrieved through the use of Google MAPs API [6]. The occupancy of car parks is randomly generated for each negotiation run.

The weights in the utility formulas are equally distributed among issues (α_i = 0.5 and β_i = 0.33 for all i), while, for each issue i, h_i and c_i are dynamically set respectively to $max_j(q_{i,j})$ and $med_j(q_{i,j})$ (i.e., the maximum and the medium value for the current issue). The UA accepts an offer if its utility for that offer is greater than a threshold value set to 0.6 for the experiments.

4.1 Experimental Results

The first experimental results are summarized in Table 1 in case of successful negotiations. In particular, the table reports the maximum, the minimum and the mean value (with the standard deviation), obtained at the end of each negotiation run, of the number of selected car parks (# available parks), the number of negotiation rounds (# Rounds), the parking spaces available in the car park (Availability), the distance between the selected car park and the city center (Distance), the distance between the selected car park and the user's destination (Route), the parking space unit price (Price), the travel time to reach the destination from the car park (Time), the PM utility (PM Utility), and the UA utility (UA Utility).

The mean value of rounds (that is the number of offers sent by the PM) is very low with respect to the mean number of car parks selected by PM for the

Table 1. Experimental Data collected in 150 runs

	max_value	min_value	mean_value
# Available parks	14	10	11 ± 2
# Rounds	9	1	3.3 ± 2.5
Availability	237	1	110 ± 58
Distance (m)	7339	1948	3495 ± 360
Route (m)	4355	649	1105 ± 160
Price (u_p)	8.9	5.1	7.6 ± 0.3
Time (s)	3046	457	927 ± 211
PM Utility	0.97	0.03	0.62 ± 0.22
UA Utility	0.75	0.10	0.68 ± 0.06
PM Utility without Neg			0.35 ± 0.27
UA Utility without Neg			0.71 ± 0.04

Fig. 3. User Agent and Parking Manager Utilities

experiments. This means that the negotiation ends before the PM offers all the selected car parks, and the obtained mean utilities values for the UA and PM show that the requirements of both parties can be met in a satisfactory way.

With the same settings we evaluated the PM and the UA mean value utilities obtained in the case the complete set of offers selected by the PM is known to the UA as well (the last two rows in Table 1), as shown in Figure 3 that reports a graphical representation of the different utility values respectively for the PM and the UA on the interactive city map. In this case the UA would select the offer that maximizes its own utility (in the average 0.71), that corresponds to a low utility for the PM (in the average 0.35). As expected, in this way, the UA requirement are privileged with respect to the PM ones.

In Table 2 experimental results are reported for two negotiation runs with the same query, but varying the occupancy of the selected car parks. The Table reports the values of the issues of each offer for both the PM and UA and their utilities. According to the negotiation mechanism, at each negotiation round the PM selects the offer with the best utility value, among the remaining offers.

Table 2. Negotiation on a single query

# Rounds	ID	Availability	Distance	Price	Route	Time	PM Utility	UA Utility
1°	417856728	78	3530	7, 78	1849	1676	0.77	0.19
2°	2204657189	27	4389	5, 14	2151	1951	0.65	0.18
3°	1495201878	40	3719	7, 30	1442	1110	0.59	0.45
4°	2245281153	87	2357	7, 59	1030	720	0.58	0.62

# Rounds	ID	Availability	Distance	Price	Route	Time	PM Utility	UA Utility
1°	2204658556	171	3712	7, 46	1126	848	0.72	0.53
2°	2239471042	237	2273	7, 99	1263	1013	0.56	0.43
3°	2204657189	2	4389	5, 82	2151	1951	0.50	0.11
4°	2204657190	7	3946	7, 86	1525	1790	0.41	0.19
5°	1495201878	18	3719	7, 52	1442	1110	0.40	0.39
6°	417856728	36	3530	7, 92	1849	1676	0.40	0.18
7°	2245281149	138	2434	7, 17	883	725	0.39	0.63

The negotiation ends as soon as the UA utility for an offer is greater than its threshold value. As shown in Table 2, varying the occupancy of the selected car parks impacts the length of the negotiation (i.e., the number of rounds necessary to reach an agreement).

5 Conclusions

Parking in populated urban areas is becoming a challenging problem requiring smart technologies in order to assist users in finding parking solutions, so improving the time necessary to find parking spaces. In this way, it is possible to decrease traffic congestion, and to improve the everyday life of city dwellers. In the present work, we investigated the possibility to use software agent negotiation to address the parking problem by taking into account not only motorists preferences regarding parking location, but also parking vendors preferences regarding car park occupancy, and social city benefits by incentivizing to park outside the city center. We use a flexible negotiation mechanism to find parking solutions that represent a compromise among different needs: a user who prefers to park close to the city center, the car park vendors who prefer to sell parking spaces in less occupied car parks, and a city manager who tries to limit the circulation of cars in city centers. At this purpose, a Coordinated Car Park System is proposed in order to provide a coordinated selling of parking spaces belonging to different car parks, managed by a single software entity, the Parking Manager.

We show that an automated negotiation mechanism between the Parking Manager and motorists represented by User Agents, allows to find this compromise, through the use of utility functions for the involved negotiators that manage different needs to be dynamically evaluated, and help users in their decision making process. The first experiments carried out shows that negotiation is a viable and promising approach since a solution is found before all the selected car parks are proposed to users. The second experimental result shows that car parks occupancy have an impact on the length of negotiation and further experiments will be carried out to find the relation between the occupancy percentage and the length of negotiation.

We plan to extend the experimentation by including different User Agents with different utility functions and weights for the issues that negotiate with the Parking Manager, so to show the suitability of multi-agent negotiation to model real-world scenarios.

References

1. Di Napoli, C., Pisa, P., Rossi, S.: Towards a dynamic negotiation mechanism for qos-aware service markets. In: Pérez, J.B., et al. (eds.) Trends in Practical Applications of Agents and Multiagent Systems. AISC, vol. 221, pp. 9–16. Springer International Publishing, Switzerland (2013)
2. Haklay, M., Weber, P.: Openstreetmap: User-generated street maps. IEEE Pervasive Computing 7(4), 12–18 (2008)
3. Jennings, N.R., Faratin, P., Lomuscio, A.R., Parsons, S., Sierra, C., Wooldridge, M.: Automated negotiation: prospects, methods and challenges. Int. Journal of Group Decision and Negotiation 10(2), 199–215 (2001)
4. Lopes, F., Wooldridge, M., Novais, A.: Negotiation among autonomous computational agents: principles, analysis and challenges. Artificial Intelligence Review 29(1), 1–44 (2008)
5. Nwana, J.S.: Software agents: An overview. Int. Journal of Group Decision and Negotiation 11(3), 205–244 (1996)
6. Pan, B., Crotts, J., Muller, B.: Developing web-based tourist information tools using google map. In: Sigala, M., Mich, L., Murphy, J. (eds.) Information and Communication Technologies in Tourism 2007, pp. 503–512. Springer Vienna (2007)
7. Polycarpou, E., Lambrinos, L., Protopapadakis, E.: Smart parking solutions for urban areas. In: 2013 IEEE 14th International Symposium and Workshops on a World of Wireless, Mobile and Multimedia Networks (WoWMoM), pp. 1–6 (2013)
8. Teodorović, D., Lučić, P.: Intelligent parking systems. European Journal of Operational Research 175(3), 1666–1681 (2006)

Design of Forces Driving Adaptation of Agent Organizations

Sergio Esparcia[1], Olivier Boissier[2], and Estefanía Argente[1]

[1] Departamento de Sistemas Informáticos y Computación
Universitat Politècnica de València
Camino de Vera s/n, 46022 - Valencia, Spain
{sesparcia,eargente}@dsic.upv.es
[2] Fayol Institute
École Nationale Supérieure des Mines de Saint-Étienne
158 Cours Fauriel, 42023 - Saint-Étienne, France
olivier.boissier@emse.fr

Abstract. Adaptation is an important feature of human organizations. Being able to change allows them not only to survive, but to evolve to get new advantages from new situations happening in their environment or from inside the organization. The same way human organizations do, agent organizations should be able to adapt. Even if adaptation is addressed in the literature, it lacks the ability to clearly manage the reasons for change. These reasons are known in the social science bibliography as forces that drive the organizational change. These forces were introduced in a previous work in the computational domain, but only for the analysis phase of the engineering of agents organizations. In this work, a set of templates is presented to define these forces at design time. These templates have been applied in the design of components for detecting the 'obtaining resources' force, which have been implemented using Jason agents and CArtAgO artifacts within an agent organization.

Keywords: multi-agent systems, agent organizations, adaptation, driving forces.

1 Introduction

As stated in the studies of human organizations by Organizational Theory[1] (OT) [15], these structures are dynamic and able to adapt at runtime. The OT is one of the inspirations for Organization-Centered Multi-Agent Systems[2] (OCMAS) [10] developers. Multiple proposals have been presented to design and implement such systems, like [7,8,11], most of them focusing on the way the change is done, or the cost of this change in the organization. However, they do not take into account the reasons that make human organizations to change, leaving aside the forces that drive organizational change, which are an important concept when dealing with adaptation. These forces have been

---

[1] Organizational theory is the sociological study of formal social organizations, such as businesses and bureaucracies, and their interrelationship with the environment where they operate.
[2] Organization-Centered Multi-Agent Systems are Multi-Agent Systems where organizational elements (such as structure, goals, roles, norms, etc.) are explicitly defined.

widely studied by Social Sciences researchers such as Aldrich [2] and Lewin[3] [13]. Aldrich classifies forces into *external* and *internal* forces, depending on where the pressure for change comes from. A force is external if the reason for change comes from the organizational environment, and internal if this reason comes from inside the organization. Moreover, forces have been introduced in [9] for the analysis of OCMAS where two sets of guidelines for expressing a force are proposed: (i) *condition factors* detecting the action of the force and (ii) *solutions* for reacting to the force in the organization.

The objectives of this paper are: (i) to take the existing guidelines described in [9], which are used for the analysis of the forces, to a more formal description that works as a design step, (ii) to show how this description facilitates the implementation of forces, and finally (iii) to implement the condition factors and solutions of the forces as adaptation mechanisms distributed among agents (implemented as Jason agents [6]) and artifacts (implemented using the CArtAgO platform [16]), which can be accessed by Jason agents. Both Jason and CArtAgO are part of the JaCaMo framework [5]. Due to the lack of space, we focus on the force named **'Obtaining resources'** [2] at the design and implementation phases of an agent organization. It is an external force that states that a failure when obtaining resources can drive to an organizational change to guarantee organizational survival. Therefore, it could be necessary for organizational survival to improve the way in which resources are obtained. For example, by extending the organization to a place where resources are easily obtained, or by reaching an agreement with another organization that has a better access to the required resources.

The rest of this paper is structured as follows: Section 2 positions our contribution in the context of previous works on adaptation in agent organizations. Section 3 presents the templates to describe a force at the design time. Section 4 presents the room allocation case study. Section 5 presents the definition of a force at the design time, using the **Obtaining resources** force as an example. Section 6 describes the implementation of this force. Finally, Section 7 presents the conclusion of this paper as well as the future work on this topic.

2 Adaptation in Agent Organizations

Several works deal with adaptation in OCMAS. This section focuses on some of them to highlight the main directions that have been explored so far. Some works approach adaptation from the knowledge and skills required by the agents. For instance, DeLoach *et al.* [7] define adaptive organizations as distributed systems that can autonomously adapt to their environment thanks to organizational knowledge, based on the current goals and capabilities. In [12], the adaptation is considered from the coordination point of view by defining a *reorganization group* composed of different roles,[4] responsible of executing the *reorganization scheme*, a plan to realize the adaptation process.

---

[3] Lewin states that change is only carried out if the forces supporting the change are stronger than the forces against the change.

[4] *OrgManager* role is in charge of managing the adaptation process, *Monitor* role monitors the organizational activity, *Historian* role maintains history of the organization, *Designer* role analyzes the organization so as to identify problems and propose alternatives, and *Selector* role is in charge of selecting one of these alternatives.

Other works focus on the adaptation process itself seeing it as a state transition problem. For instance, in [8], authors propose a formal semantics framework where adaptation is treated as a design issue where changes of the organization are represented as transitions between states. Two activities are considered to realize this adaptation: (i) evaluation of the current organizational state, computing its 'distance' to the desired state; and (ii) change of organizational elements (structure, agent population, objectives) in order to achieve the desired state. The proposed strategy to decide about adaptation is based on the cost of this adaptation. A similar cost-based adaptation framework is also proposed in [1]. The costs are based on concepts like *Organization Transition Impact* and *Organization Utility*. They propose a Multi-dimensional Transition Deliberation Mechanism (MTDM) where three types of transition are considered, depending on the organizational dimension that changes: role reallocation transition, acquaintance transition, and agent population transition.

Even though these works are proposing complementary and interesting approaches for dealing with adaptation, they mainly focus on the management of the process to carry the changes out. They do not specify the reasons for change which is an important topic when dealing with adaptation. For instance, in [11] authors present a model for organizational change which states that a change in an organization is provoked by two opposing forces: *resistant* forces and *driving* forces towards a new organization. Based on these forces, authors propose a change along a three-phase process: (i) *unfreezing phase*, where the driving forces are stronger than resistant forces; (ii) *movement phase*, where all the changes are carried out; and (iii) *equilibrium*, after all changes have been deployed, where resistant forces are stronger than driving forces.

However, the authors of [11] do not specify the reasons of these forces to appear in an organization. Knowing the specific reasons of the forces facilitates the task of offering better solutions to the problems caused by such forces. Since the OT studies these forces, we are working on their definition into the OCMAS domain. After having defined a set of guidelines for the analysis phase in [9], we propose in this paper to go a step further in this direction by proposing templates to identify, describe, and implement these forces.

3 Templates to Define Forces

Force detection has to be carried out along the organizational life-cycle. For that purpose, guidelines may help to develop tools to identify the factors and the solutions of forces. The factors express the conditions making possible to state if the force is currently active or not. The solutions express the actions to execute in the organization in order, either to take advantage of the benefits that the force may imply, or to minimize the possible damages produced by the force in the organization. The guidelines presented in [9] focus on the analysis step, identifying and describing the factors and solutions using plain text and include one table for factors and force description, and another table depicting the solutions. In this paper, since it is addressing the design phase, we propose templates[5] for identifying and describing the factors and solutions of forces.

---

[5] We use the word template to differentiate the products of the design step from the guidelines produced at the analysis step, and also from the design patterns from software engineering.

Their contents are more formal, closer to an actual implementation. In this case, a force is defined by means of a template, where the factors and solutions are pointed out. Both are fully described in separate tables making possible to reuse a factor or a solution in the definition of another force.

A force (Table 1) is defined by its name, a textual description, a type stating if the force is internal or external, a set of factors participating on the detection of the action of the force, a force detection condition, a set of solutions and a selection criteria among the solutions. The force detection condition is a boolean expression bearing on the factors.

Table 1. Force description template

Field	Description
Name	Name of the force.
Description	Textual description of the force acting over the organization.
Monitor	The role of the organization responsible of monitoring the force.
Type	*Internal* or *external*.
Factors	Names of factors involved in the detection of the force.
Force detection condition	Logical combination of factors stating that the force is in action.
Solutions	Solutions that can be applied in case the force is active.
Solution choice criteria	Depicts how a solution is chosen.

Since we are defining templates to be filled along the organization definition, rather than guidelines, references to the organizational model such as roles, goals, etc. may appear in the definition of the factors and solutions.

3.1 Factors Stating That a Force Is Acting

Table 2 defines the components of the factors for expressing the conditions testing that a force is acting over the organization. A factor is a set of monitoring mechanisms in the organization to detect if the force is acting, and it is characterized by its name, a description, the parameters referring to organizational values, and the condition which states when the factor is active.

Table 2. Force factor description template

Factor	
Name	The name of the factor that helps identifying the force.
Description	Textual description of the factor.
Parameters	Organizational elements concerned by the action of the force, which help in the detection of its action.
Condition	The condition stating the relations among the parameters that help in the detection of the action of the force.

3.2 Solutions to Face the Force

Table 3 defines the actions that should be carried out in the organization in order to take advantage or to prevent damage from the force that has been detected. Each solution is described by a name, a textual description, a condition that points out the particular factors that need to be satisfied to execute this solution, the parameters involved in the actions of the solution, the actions to execute, and the roles of the organization that will be in charge of executing the solution.

Table 3. Force solution description template

Field	Description
Name	Name of the solution.
Description	Text describing this solution.
Condition	The condition (related to factors) that must hold in order to apply this solution.
Parameters	Describes the elements that have to be known prior to apply the solution.
Actions	The set of actions that must be carried out to apply this solution.
Cost	The cost of applying this solution to the organization.
Roles	The responsible roles for applying this solution.

4 Case Study

A case study is employed to illustrate the use of the templates from the previous section. This case study focuses on how to manage the distribution of activities assigned to the different rooms of a smart building in a university.[6] The three types of activities that a room can carry out are: teaching, meeting, and brainstorming. Fig. 1 represents the organizational model issued from the analysis phase. This model is based on the graphical notation used by the GORMAS[7] methodology [4].

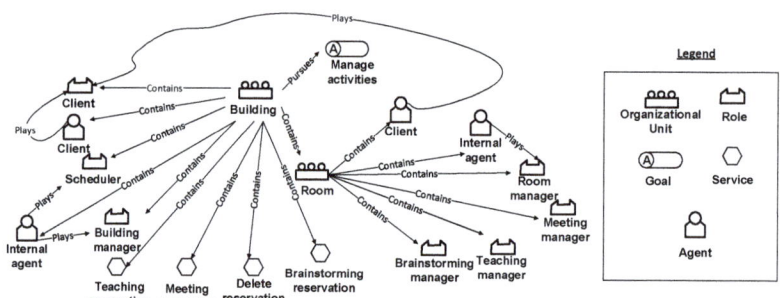

Fig. 1. Structural dimension of the building represented with the GORMAS notation

As it can be seen in Fig. 1, the organization is composed of a **Building** organizational unit, which contains **Room** units, as many as needed. Each Room unit represents the way agents and services governing the room will be organized. It contains an Internal agent that plays the **Room Manager** role and one of the following roles: **Teaching Manager**, **Meeting Manager**, **Brainstorming Manager**. At the system initialization it only plays the Room Manager role, which is in charge of managing utilities, equipment, and other tasks related to the room management. With the objective of specifying the activity to be carried out in a specific Room at a specific time, the Internal Agent also plays one of any of the other three roles, which are exclusive between them, since a Room can only develop one type of activity at the same time. In each Room, there can

---

[6] This case study is inspired in [17].
[7] GORMAS is an agent-oriented software engineering methodology for the analysis, design, and implementation of OCMAS. It has been chosen because the authors have a high knowledge of it, thus facilitating the definition of the case study.

be **Client** agents that request activities. The type of activities of each Room is changed dynamically depending on the requests issued by the Client agents. All Rooms are equipped to be able to develop any of the three types of activities at any time.

Additionally, the Building unit also contains the roles **Client** (played by the Client agents), and **Scheduler** and **Building Manager**, played by Internal Agents. The Building Manager specifies the type of the activities to be carried out in each Room by assigning a specific role (Brainstorming, Meeting, or Teaching Manager) to each Internal Agent playing the Room Manager role. The agents populating the Building unit are in charge of achieving the Manage Activities goal to assure a correct organizational performance. Finally the Building Unit is composed of one service for deleting existing reservations and three types of reservation services: **Teaching Reservation**, **Meeting Reservation**, and **Brainstorming Reservation**.

The scheduling of activities that are carried out in the Rooms of the Building are controlled by the Scheduler. The Clients of the Building (external agents) send their petitions (that include the type of room, the day, the start time and the duration of the activity expressed in number of hours) to the Scheduler, who is responsible of assigning a specific activity to a room at the required time. In this application, the organization may be subject to many sources of change. For example, the number of requests received by the organization or the number of clients populating the organization are two of these sources.

In this paper, we focus on the aforementioned **Obtaining Resources** external force. In this case study, the resources are considered to be the rooms. Access to the rooms is managed by the reservation services. Therefore, it is considered that the access to a resource fails if the access to the service that manages the Room fails. The solution for this force implies changing the role of some Room Managers, or adding new virtual Rooms to the organization.

5 Description of Forces at the Design Step

In this paper we want to go one step further from [9] where the forces were described by means of the guidelines using plain text descriptions. Following the templates defined in Section 3, forces will be described using a formal language, which will connect the description of the forces with the organizational definition in GORMAS notation. Each element of the organizational model has associated properties or functions. They are accessed using the notation *element.property* (for accessing properties) or *element.function(parameters)* (for accessing functions). This section presents the design phase, where the templates to describe a force are filled, making references to the organizational model presented in Fig. 1. The following subsections define the *Obtaining resources* force, including the factors and solutions. Section 6 describes how an implementation of the case study has been carried out, including elements for dealing with the Obtaining resources force.

Additionally, aside from the functionalities of the organizational elements, generic functions refer to the actions for adding or removing organizational elements (e.g. *AddRole, DeleteOrgUnit, GetRole, LeaveRole, etc.*). To structure these actions in an adaptation process one may use sequence operator (;), choice operator (|), parallel execution (||), optional execution ([ ]), iteration (a^n) to order the different actions when adapting.

5.1 *Obtaining Resources* Force at the Design Time

In the room allocation scenario, the services that are considered to check if the Obtaining resources force is triggered or not are the services to make a reservation (one for each type of room). A service is considered to fail if the request for a service is not fulfilled because there are not enough available rooms. In this case, it is necessary to modify the type of activity the rooms have been assigned to allow the organization to satisfy the requirements of their Clients. This operation is done by modifying the role assigned to one of the Room Managers whose controlled Room has an empty schedule. The Obtaining Resources external force is described in Table 4. Its triggering factor is *FailedServiceCallsRate* and two solutions are defined: *ChangeRoomActivity* and *ExtendBuilding*. Their description is depicted in the next subsections.

Table 4. Definition of the Obtaining resources force, design step

Field	Description
Name	ObtainingResources
Description	A resource cannot be allocated by a service of an organization.
Monitor	Monitor element
Type	External
Factors	FailedServiceCallsRate
Force Detection Condition	FailedServiceCallsRate.Condition = TRUE
Solutions	$sol_1 = ChangeRoomActivity$, $sol_2 = ExtendBuilding$
Solution choice criteria	$max(utility_{sol1}, utility_{sol2}, utility_{noSol})$

FailedServiceCallsRate Factor. This factor (Table 5) takes into account the failures of the reservation services in a time duration *dur* and is activated if failure rate is higher than 1 - QoS. The Quality of Service (QoS) [14] defines the expected success rate when calling a service. For example, in the case of having a QoS of 90%, the maximum allowed failure rate is 10%. Each service has a different QoS, so the factor will be differently triggered depending on each service.

To detect whether the factor is active in the organization, the number of requests for activities and the number of failures of such requests by the Reservation service are considered. In our application, a request is defined as a tuple $r = \{type, time, status\}$. Let us define the set $R_{dur,res} = \{r | r.type = res \land res = \{teaching, meeting, brainstorming\}\}$ as the set of requests received by the (teaching, meeting, or brainstorming) reservation service in the period of time *dur*, and the set $R'_{dur,res} = \{r \in R_{dur,res} | r.status = fail\}$ that records the number of failures on requests to the (teaching, meeting, or brainstorming) reservation service during the same period of time. The failure rate for the service *Reservation* for a time period *dur* is calculated as:

$$Monitor.Failures(Reservation, dur) = \begin{cases} \frac{|R'_{dur,Reservation}|}{|R_{dur,Reservation}|} & : |R_{dur,Reservation}| \neq 0 \\ 0 & : |R_{dur,Reservation}| = 0 \end{cases} \quad (1)$$

where *Reservation* is a parameter representing the type of reservation service to be checked (i.e., *TeachingReservation*, *MeetingReservation*, or *BrainstormingReservation*) according to our organizational model. Then, if the failure rate is higher than the expected one, it is necessary to apply one of the two possible solutions, described in the next subsection.

Table 5. Description of the FailedServiceCallsRate factor, design step

Factor	
Name	FailedServiceCallsRate
Description	If the failed service calls rate (i.e., requesting a spot for developing an activity) is higher than the allowed failure rate threshold, then the force is considered as acting.
Parameters	$Reservation \in \{TeachingReservation, MeetingReservation, BrainstorminReservation\}, dur$
Condition	$Monitor.Failures(Reservation, dur) > ((1 - Reservation.QoS) * Monitor.Requests(Reservation, dur))$

Applying the Solution of the Force. After the detection of the force, it is necessary to take a decision about the adaptation action to develop into the building. In our use case, the Obtaining Resources Force defines two possible solutions: ChangeRoomActivity and ExtendBuilding (cf. Table 6 and 7). As can be seen in the solution choice criterion of the force in table 4, the solution which provides the highest utility will be deployed.

The first solution (cf. Table 6) consists, as expressed in the field 'Action', in the modification of the type of activity being developed inside one or more rooms, to get free spots in the schedule for developing activities. Once the FailedServiceCallsRate is active, the Scheduler builds the *RoomManagerList* set, containing pairs of the form $\langle rm_i, nr_i \rangle$ containing the Room Manager agent (rm_i) of $Room_i$ whose role is required to change, and the new role that the agent will take (nr_i). This gives the $Room_i$ the opportunity to host a new type of activities. This solution is, in most situations, the less costly. This cost is calculated as:

$$cost(ChangeRoomActivity) = \sum_{\forall \langle rm_i, nr_i \rangle \in RoomManagerList} (CostPlay(nr_i) + CostChange(rm_i.Role, nr_i) - CostPlay(rm_i.Role)) \quad (2)$$

This is, for each room that might change its type of activity, it is calculated the cost of having the new role in the organization compared to the cost of the current role the room manager is playing, and also the cost of changing from one role to another. Playing a role has a cost because depending on the role, a different subset of the room equipment is used, thus having different costs in terms of energy consumption, etc.

The second solution proposed by this force (cf. Table 7) is to extend the building with more virtual rooms to make possible more activities in it at the same time. This change will suppose adding one or more Room organizational units inside the building. The types of the rooms to be added are described inside the *NewRoles* set. Each role in this set corresponds to a type of room to be added. Therefore, for each role nr_i in the set, the BuildingManager adds a new room $Room_i$ to the building by using the function *AddOU*, then adds a new internal agent $RoomManager_i$ in this room (*AddAgent*), and finally assigns the role $nr_i \in NewRoles$ to this newly created agent. The cost of this solution is calculated as the cost of creating all the new rooms. Creating a room implies to add a new organizational unit (*CostAddOU*), a new internal agent that manages the room (*CostAddAgent*), and also includes the cost of this agent playing a specific role (*CostPlay*). Then, this cost is calculated as:

Table 6. ChangeRoomActivity solution, design step

Field	Description
Name	ChangeRoomActivity
Description	The type of activity being carried out in a room is modified by changing the role of the room manager agent.
Condition	FailedServiceCallsRate
Parameters	$RoomManagerList = \{\langle rm_i, nr_i \rangle,$ where $rm_i \in RoomManager \wedge$ $nr_i \in \{MeetingManager, TeachingManager, BrainstormManager\}$
Actions	$\forall \langle rm_i, nr_i \rangle \in RoomManagerList : rm_i.LeaveRole(Role); rm_i.GetRole(nr_i)$
Cost	$\sum_{\forall \langle rm_i, nr_i \rangle \in RoomManagerList}(CostPlay(nr_i) + CostChange(rm_i.Role, nr_i) - CostPlay(rm_i.Role))$
Roles	Scheduler

$$cost(ExtendBuilding) = |NewRoles| * (CostAddOU(Room) +$$

$$CostAddAgent(InternalAgent)) + \sum_{nr_i \in NewRoles} CostPlay(nr_i) \quad (3)$$

Table 7. ExtendBuilding solution, design step

Field	Description
Name	ExtendBuilding
Description	The building is extended with new rooms that allow it to fulfil all the received petitions.
Condition	FailedServiceCallsRate
Parameters	$NewRoles = 2^{\{MeetingManager, TeachingManager, BrainstormManager\}}$
Actions	$\forall nr_i \in NewRoles : Building.AddOU(Room_i); Building.AddAgent(RoomManager_i);$ $RoomManager_i.GetRole(nr_i)$
Cost	$|NewRoles| * (CostAddOU(Room) + CostAddAgent(InternalAgent)) + \sum_{nr_i \in NewRoles} CostPlay(nr_i)$
Roles	Building manager

5.2 Selection between Solutions

As stated in [1], to select between different options for change it is necessary to have a utility function that has to express the costs and benefits (both direct and indirect) of both the current and future states of the system, as well as the adaptation costs.

In some situations two forces may apply their solutions to the same organizational elements, thus being necessary to take a decision about which option to take. For this reason, applying the solution for one of these forces may make the organization to solve the effects of both forces. Therefore, in order to exactly choose one of those solutions, the one which maximizes the utility is selected.

For calculating the utility, not only the cost of applying the solution is taken into account, but also the cost of having failures, and the benefits obtained by the organization. In the case of the *Obtaining resources* force, its benefits are represented as the requests that have been correctly placed in a room. Therefore, the utility of a solution to this force is calculated as:

$$utility_{sol} = benefit_{sol} - (cost(sol) + cost_{sol}(Failures)) \quad (4)$$

where $benefit_{sol}$ is the benefit obtained for placing the activities into the schedule of the rooms, calculated as $benefit_{sol} = AccReq * UnitBen$ where $AccReq$ is the number of requests accepted and placed in the schedule of a room and $UnitBen$ is the unitary benefit of having a request correctly scheduled. $cost(sol)$ is the cost associated to the solution *sol*. Finally, $cost_{sol}(Failures)$ is the cost of the remaining failures among the requests, calculated as $cost_{sol}(Failures) = RemFails * UnitFail$, where $RemFails$ is the number of remaining failures after applying the solution, and $UnitFail$ is the unitary cost of having a failure in the organization.

Then, the action to apply in the organization is decided following this equation:

$$max(utility_{sol1}, utility_{sol2}, utility_{noSol}) \qquad (5)$$

where $utility_{sol1}$ is the utility of the first solution, $utility_{sol2}$ is the utility of the second solution, and $utility_{noSol}$ is the utility without applying any solution. As it can be noticed, in some situations where the cost of applying the solution is too high it is recommended to not take any action because it is the option with the maximum utility.

Applying the solution of a force could provoke the triggering of a factor of another force. Then, an action to solve the newly appeared force would have to be taken.

6 Implementation

In order to exemplify the implementation of the forces described in the previous section in the context of the use case described in Section 4, let us set a scenario with a building of three rooms (*room*1, *room*2, and *room*3) each being able to host one of the three following activities: teaching, meeting, and brainstorming. Each room is managed by a room manager (*RoomManager*1, *RoomManager*2, and *RoomManager*3, respectively) which has to check that the room is properly running. The building manager sets the following QoS: 90% for teaching, 60% for meeting, and 50% for brainstorming reservations.[8] At the start of a week, the rooms can be randomly distributed, or they can follow the distribution of the week before. In this example, they are randomly distributed.

This scenario, as described in Section 4, is based on the GORMAS organizational model. Agents and forces are implemented using Jason [6], for programming autonomous agents, and CArtAgO [16] for programming environment artifacts. Both components are available in the Multi-Agent Programming framework JaCaMo [5] that provides the infrastructure and abstractions for running distributed multi-agent systems combining agents, artifacts and organizations.

- **Agents** are: *Building manager* (responsible of selecting the solution and to apply the ExtendBuilding solution), *client* (generates a request for activity), *room manager* (manages the room and the role it plays is the activity carried out inside the room), and *scheduler* (distributes the petitions around the different rooms, calculates the failures of the petitions, and is responsible of the ChangeRoomActivity solution). Each type of agent has a different set of skills and capabilities, related to the roles defined at the design time.
- **Artifacts**, implemented as CArtAgO classes, provide functionalities to the agents. The *monitor* and *room* artifacts store the number of requests and occupancies. The *room* artifact is controlled by the *room manager* agent. The *monitor* artifact (mentioned in Table 4) controls that the behavior and performance of the system is

---

[8] Such QoS mean that the building management will only accept a maximum of 10%, 40%, and 50% of failures for teaching, meeting, and brainstorming requests for activities, respectively.

correct by checking the factor of the *Obtaining resources* force (by taking into account the QoS of each service). To carry out the experimentations, a *date generator* artifact generates random requests of activities in the system.

At the first execution cycle, the building manager creates both the Monitor artifact and the date generator artifact. Additionally, in this phase each of the defined room manager agents randomly receives a type of role (teaching, meeting, and brainstorming), creates the room artifact it manages, and sends this information to the scheduler.

Then, on each execution cycle, each client executes an operation of the date generator artifact to generate a random petition for an activity. Each petition for a room includes a specific day of the week (from Monday to Friday), with a specific start time (from 9am to 6pm, in 1-hour intervals, thus having the opportunity to start the activity in 10 different hours each day), and a length (of 1, 2, or 3 hours). In this example, the duration *dur* taken into account when monitoring the organization refers to a week. All clients send this information to the Scheduler, which tries to allocate all the petitions around the different rooms at the required times. After all the requests have been processed, and after deciding whether they can be allocated into a room or not (failures are calculated using Equation 5.1), the Monitor artifact reacts and computes if an adaptation is required or not, following the condition of Table 5. Then, the Monitor sends a specific signal if an adaptation is required. As previously stated, an adaptation is required if any of the values of the QoS is lower than the acceptable value. In order to do this, the monitor counts the different types of the petitions separately, and then checks the QoS for all the reservation services (*TeachingReservation*, *MeetingReservation*, *BrainstormingReservation*).

In this case, the building manager requests the Monitor artifact to compute the utility of the two possible solutions (described in Tables 6 and 7) so as to decide which solution to apply, or to not take any further action.

Some experimentation has been carried out. However, due to the lack of space, this section only focuses on how a design template is implemented.

7 Conclusions and Future Work

In this work, templates for the design of the forces that drive organizational change, including the factors that help to detect if they are active or not, and the solutions that will take advantage of the forces or to prevent damage to the organization, have been defined. They have been used to implement the concept of forces into an OCMAS with adaptation features. These templates extend the guidelines presented in [9] that are used during the analysis phase of the development process.

As future work, more forces based on this example will be designed and implemented, and also different case studies will be studied. Finally, the implementation of the force detection and solution will be applied in other MAS-supporting frameworks such as THOMAS [3].

Acknowledgment. This work is supported by the MINECO/FEDER grant TIN2012-36586-C03-01, the TIN2009-13839-C03-01 project of the Spanish government, and CONSOLIDER-INGENIO 2010 under grant CSD2007-00022.

References

1. Alberola, J.M., Julian, V., Garcia-Fornes, A.: A cost-based transition approach for multi-agent systems reorganization. In: 10th International Conference on Autonomous Agents and Multiagent Systems, vol. 3, pp. 1221–1222. IFAAMAS (2011)
2. Aldrich, H.: Organizations evolving. Sage Publications Ltd. (1999)
3. Argente, E., Botti, V., Carrascosa, C., Giret, A., Julian, V., Rebollo, M.: An abstract architecture for virtual organizations: The thomas approach. Knowledge and Information Systems 29(2), 379–403 (2011)
4. Argente, E., Botti, V., Julian, V.: GORMAS: An organizational-oriented methodological guideline for open MAS. In: Gleizes, M.-P., Gomez-Sanz, J.J. (eds.) AOSE 2009. LNCS, vol. 6038, pp. 32–47. Springer, Heidelberg (2011)
5. Boissier, O., Bordini, R.H., Hübner, J.F., Ricci, A., Santi, A.: Multi-agent oriented programming with jacamo. In: Science of Computer Programming (2011)
6. Bordini, R.H., Hübner, J.F., Wooldridge, M.: Programming multi-agent systems in AgentSpeak using Jason, vol. 8 (2007), Wiley.com
7. Deloach, S.A., Oyenan, W.H., Matson, E.T.: A capabilities-based model for adaptive organizations. Autonomous Agents and Multi-Agent Systems 16(1), 13–56 (2008)
8. Dignum, V., Dignum, F.: Towards formal semantics for reorganization. Technical report UU-CS (2006)
9. Esparcia, S., Argente, E.: Forces that drive organizational change in an adaptive virtual organization. In: 2012 Sixth International Conference on Complex, Intelligent and Software Intensive Systems (CISIS), pp. 46–53. IEEE (2012)
10. Ferber, J., Gutknecht, O., Michel, F.: From agents to organizations: An organizational view of multi-agent systems. In: Giorgini, P., Müller, J.P., Odell, J.J. (eds.) AOSE 2003. LNCS, vol. 2935, pp. 214–230. Springer, Heidelberg (2004)
11. Hoogendoorn, M., Jonker, C., Schut, M., Treur, J.: Modeling centralized organization of organizational change. Comput. Math. Organ Theory 13(2), 147–184 (2007)
12. Hubner, J., Sichman, J., Boissier, O.: Moise+: towards a structural, functional, and deontic model for mas organization. In: Proc. of Int. Conf. on Autonomous Agents and Multiagent Systems, pp. 501–502. ACM (2002)
13. Lewin, K., Cartwright, D.: Field theory in social science. Harper & Brothers (1951)
14. Papazoglou, M.P.: Service-oriented computing: Concepts, characteristics and directions. In: Proc. Web Information Systems Engineering, WISE 2003, pp. 3–12. IEEE (2003)
15. Pugh, D.S., Weber, M.: Organization theory: selected readings. Penguin (1971)
16. Ricci, A., Piunti, M., Viroli, M., Omicini, A.: Environment programming in cartago. In: Multi-Agent Programming, pp. 259–288. Springer (2009)
17. Sorici, A., Boissier, O., Picard, G., Santi, A.: Exploiting the jacamo framework for realising an adaptive room governance application. In: Proc. DSM 2011, TMC 2011, AGERE 2011, AOOPES 2011, NEAT 2011, & VMIL 2011, pp. 239–242. ACM (2011)

Practical Multi-Agent System Application for Simulation of Tourists in Madrid Routes with INGENIAS

Iván García-Magariño

Departamento de Ingeniería Informática y Organización Industrial,
Facultad de Enseñanzas Técnicas,
Universidad a Distancia de Madrid,
Collado Villalba, Madrid, Spain
ivan.garcia-magarino@udima.es

Abstract. The tourism can promote a way out of the crisis in Spain and other European countries. In fact, some research projects are funding the development of applications that can increase the tourist activities in different cities. In particular, this work has been supported in a research project in this context for Madrid routes. This work presents a Multi-agent System (MAS) that simulates the tourist behaviors when signing up for a set of Madrid routes. The goal of this application is to guide the tourism experts for selecting a set of routes that are useful for promoting tourism in Madrid, in a balanced way, so that the different tourism locations are full but not overcrowded. This MAS has been developed following the INGENIAS methodology, with an adaptation for MAS simulations. The resulting application has been run with 92 agents and 50 iterations over 10 Madrid routes, showing results that allow tourism experts to improve the set of the offered Madrid routes.

Keywords: Agent-oriented software engineering, INGENIAS, multi-agent system, simulation, tourism.

1 Introduction

The recommender systems for tourism routes have increased in the late years. In particular, the review article of Gavalas et al. [5] analyzes and classifies the tourist recommender systems in the mobile devices, showing the recent increment of the number of these systems. In addition, the tourism has effects on the economics of cities, as stated in the review of Song et al. [14]. Hence, the tourist recommender systems can influence in the tourism of certain cities, and consequently in their economics.

The current work is based on the assumption that the core of the tourist recommender systems is the underlying set of routes and their recommended suitability for the different kinds of tourists. For this reason, this work proposes a MAS that simulates tourists that choose routes from a set of these with some suitability ranks attached, showing how many tourist people sign up for each route. This simulation can assist tourism experts in improving the set of tourist routes for a given city before the recommender system is actually publicly deployed, avoiding overcrowded and non-profitable routes as much as possible.

There are several works that use MASs for simulation in different aspects of cities such as [12], but they are not strictly related to tourism. The existing works related to tourism simulations like [1] does not take the improvement of a set of urban routes into account. The existing 3D tourism simulation environments, e.g. [9], neither addresses the objective of the current work. Thus, to the best of author's knowledge, the presented MAS is novel in its objectives. The improvements of the current work over the literature are further discussed later in this paper when presenting the related works.

The presented MAS considers five types of tourists, which are singles, couples, families with babies, families without babies, and groups of friends. Each of these tourist types is represented with a different agent type. In addition, there is a simulator agent that guides all the simulation and present the analysis of the results to the user. Furthermore, a route manager agent is in charge of managing the access to the different tourist routes.

The development of the presented MAS has followed the INGENIAS methodology [13]. In particular, the development of this MAS has been inspired by the adaptation of INGENIAS for simulation presented in [6]. As a proof of concept, this article presents the execution of the presented MAS application alongside an example of experimentation. The interested practitioners can download the presented executable MAS application from the web [3].

This work belongs to the context of a research project about tourist information systems for promoting cultural urban routes, with Madrid historic center region as a pilot project, supported by the Hergar foundation (see acknowledgments section for further details). In this project, tourism experts are committed to propose a set of routes that are useful for presenting routes for all kinds of tourists. One of the goals of this project is to provide a set of routes that distribute the tourists in a balanced way among the routes, according to certain numbers of tourists of each type, in order to avoid overcrowded routes and non-profitable routes. For achieving this goal, the tourism experts require a simulation as the one presented in this paper, so that they can properly assess the different sets of routes. In particular, this work addresses this need by means of a MAS.

The remaining of this paper is organized as follows: the next section presents the related works indicating the improvement of the current work over the literature; section 3 describes the modeling and development of the MAS following the INGENIAS methodology by presenting the most relevant diagrams in the INGENIAS notation; section 4 determines an adaptation framework for making the generated programming code more efficient in simulations; section 5 shows the MAS running for simulating the tourists in Madrid routes, presenting the Graphical User Interface (GUI) of the simulator and analyzing the obtained results; finally section 6 mentions the conclusions of this work and the future lines of research.

2 Related Works

To begin with, there are several works that use MASs for simulating different aspects of cities. For instance, Nguyen et al. [12] present a MAS that simulates the different kinds of transportation in a city. This work takes travel, parking and transportation strategies into account. In addition, Mustapha et al. [10] simulate natural disaster complex systems with a MAS. Its main goal is to guide rescue teams in an effective organization for saving as much lives as possible in natural disasters. In this line of research, Wijerathne et al. [16] present a MAS for simulating the evacuation of urban areas. In this simulation, they show the effectiveness of a navigation algorithm that allows a massive number of people to rapidly evacuate from a large urban area. Similarly, Wagner et al. [15] have developed a MAS for simulation the evacuation of crowded places such as auditoriums and stadiums where there is uncontrolled fire, in order to establish the necessary measures beforehand, so that the consequences in real fire situations are mitigated. All the aforementioned works have in common with the current work that use MASs for simulating scenarios beforehand in order to improve the organization or measures when the real situations occur. However, none of these works uses the MAS simulation for guiding tourism experts for providing suitable sets of tourist routes, as this work does for promoting urban tourism in a particular city.

There are works that concretely apply simulations related to tourism. Specifically, Balbi et al. [1] have constructed a MAS for assessing the impact of weather conditions on the alpine tourism. Their system mainly considers three factors, which are the weather conditions (snow cover and temperature), numbers of the different kinds of tourists and the type of market competition. In addition, they use eight different kinds of tourist agents. This work is similar to the current one in two factors: (1) both works use MAS simulations in the tourism context (2) both works use similar number of tourist profiles. However, there are two main differences. Firstly, the tourism environments are different (alpine areas opposed to urban areas). Secondly, the improvement objective is quite different; the former work is aimed at improving the infrastructures from the winter industries point of view, while the latter work pursues the improvement of the set of offered tourist routes. Moreover, Hamilton el al. [8] present a simulation that analyzes the influence of international tourism in the climate, population and income of different countries. This work is based on data on departures and arrivals for 207 countries, and concludes that the influence of international tourism is higher in population and income than in climate. Nonetheless, the goal of the current work is different, since it is aimed at promoting the tourism in a particular city instead of forecasting its international influence in different countries.

Some works relate to the simulation of tourism situations with 3D environments. In the education context, Hsu [9] uses the Second Life 3D virtual environment for making eight students train tourism situations in these environments with considerably less cost than training in real scenarios. In the e-Marketplace context, the work of Gärtner et al. [4] provides a mechanism for mapping the gap between software agents and 3D environments, for allowing agent-mediated

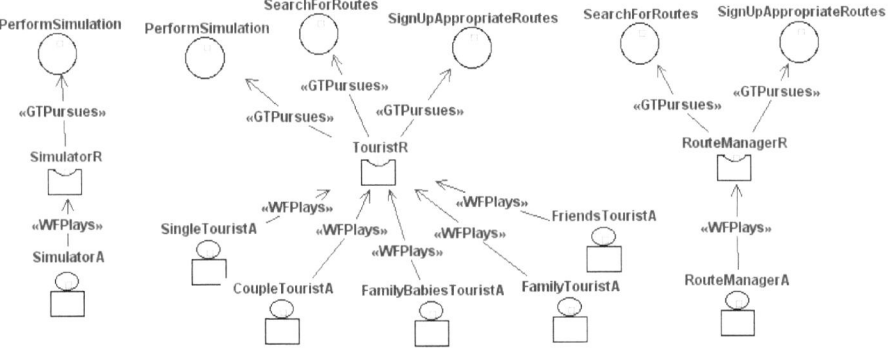

Fig. 1. The definition of agents with the INGENIAS notation

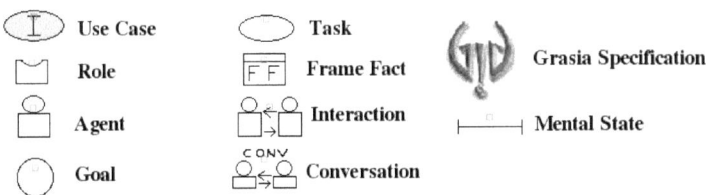

Fig. 2. Main concepts of the INGENIAS notation

e-Marketplace in immersive 3D virtual environments. On the contrary, none of these works is specifically aimed at obtaining an appropriate set of tourist routes for a given city, as it is addressed by the current work.

3 Definition of a MAS for Tourist Simulation with INGENIAS

The presented MAS contains three different roles and six agent types for allowing users to simulate the tourists choosing routes of a particular city. These three roles and six agent types are graphically presented in Figure 1 with the INGENIAS notation, alongside the goals of the MAS. It is worth mentioning that this diagram uses the -R suffix for roles and the -A suffix for agents, in order to avoid conflict of names in an abbreviated way. In order to make this diagram and the following ones understandable, the main concepts of the INGENIAS notations are determined in Figure 2.

The MAS has the following roles with the corresponding agents:

– *Simulator Role*: The agent playing this role is in charge of conducting the whole simulation. In particular, the simulator agent plays this role. This agent provides a GUI, so that the human expert can configure the parameters of the simulation and execute it. When the human expert asks this agent to

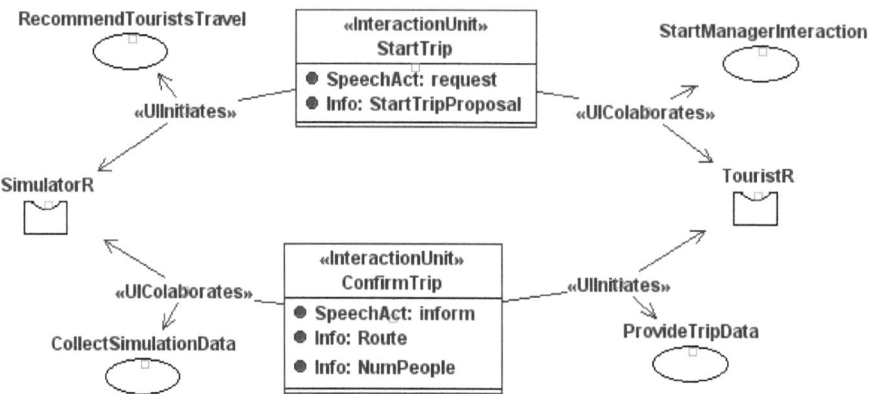

Fig. 3. Interaction between the Simulator agent and the agents playing the Tourist role

conduct the experiment, this agent initializes the remaining agents according to the established parameters, and starts the necessary interactions to make the other agents run for the simulation.
- *Tourist Role*: This role gathers all the agent types that represent the different kinds of tourists. This role defines the common interactions to all the kinds of tourists. These interactions mainly concern (1) the execution of search for a trip when the simulator agent asks so, and (2) the selection of routes by communicating with the Route Manager agent. The agents of this role represent both individual people and groups of people. Thus, each agent can represent a different number of people. This role is played by the following agent types:
  - *Single Tourist Agent*: This agent represents a single person that is interested in visiting the city of the simulation.
  - *Couple Tourist Agent*: This agent impersonates a couple that plans to travel to the city of the simulation.
  - *Family Babies Tourist Agent*: This agent represents a family with at least one baby under two years old. The family can also have other children of whatever age.
  - *Family Tourist Agent*: This agent conforms a family with at least one child, and all the children must be above two years old.
  - *Friends Tourist Agent*: This agent represents a group of several friends.
- *Route Manager role*: This role manages the routes of a city. This role is the responsible for accessing the routes when an agent playing the Tourist role requires so. In addition, the agent playing the route manager role provides rank recommendations for each presented route from zero to ten according to the specific kind of a particular tourist agent. This role is played by the Route Manager agent.

When a user asks the Simulator agent to run a simulation through the GUI, the simulator agent initializes the tourist agents, and starts interactions with

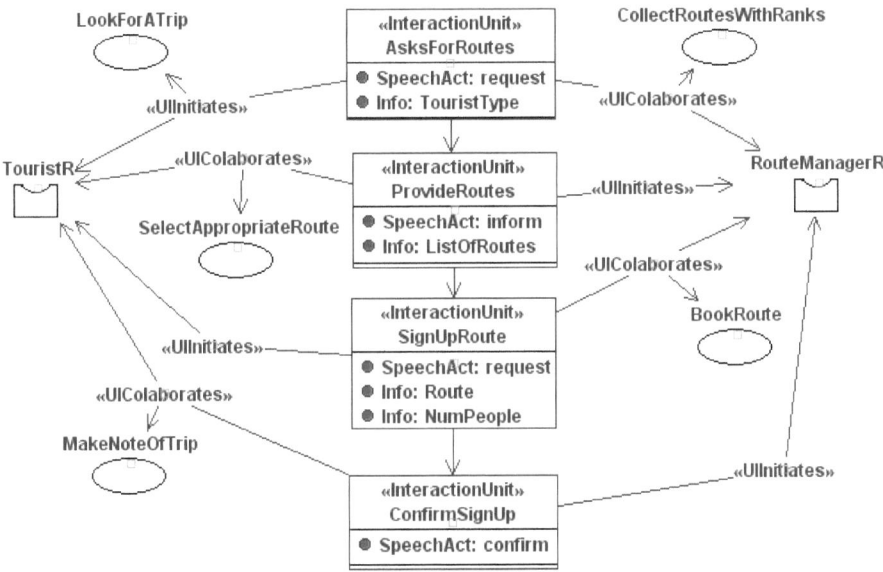

Fig. 4. Interaction between the agents playing the Tourist role and the Route Manager agent

these. In particular, the interaction between the simulator role and the tourist role is determined in the diagram of Figure 3. In this interaction, the simulator agent sends a broadcast message to all the agents playing the tourist role for proposing them to start a trip, by means of the task named *Recommend Tourist Travel*. Each tourist agent will start a negotiation interaction with the route manager role for obtaining a trip that suits its type, in the task titled *Start Manager Interaction*. After selecting the appropriate route, the tourist agent provides the data of (1) the route and (2) the number of people that the tourist agent represents. Both pieces of information are transferred by means of Route and NumPeople frame facts, and are established in the *Provide Trip Data* task. The simulator agent collects the data of each tourist agent in the *Collect Simulation Data* task. After several rounds of trips, the simulator agent extracts the relevant information and presents it to the user. The number of rounds of trips is one of the parameters established for the simulation in the GUI by the user.

The interaction between the tourist role and the route manager role is defined in Figure 4. In this interaction, a tourist agent starts looking for a trip in the corresponding task. The tourist agent sends an interaction unit (also known as message in other methodologies) with the type of tourist, and the route manager agent collects all the available routes in the system for the given city alongside the recommendation ranks of each route for the corresponding tourist type. The list of routes is sent back to the tourist agent, by means of the *List of Routes* frame fact. After this, the tourist agent selects a route from the provided list of routes. In order to simulate the selection of routes, the tourist agent randomly

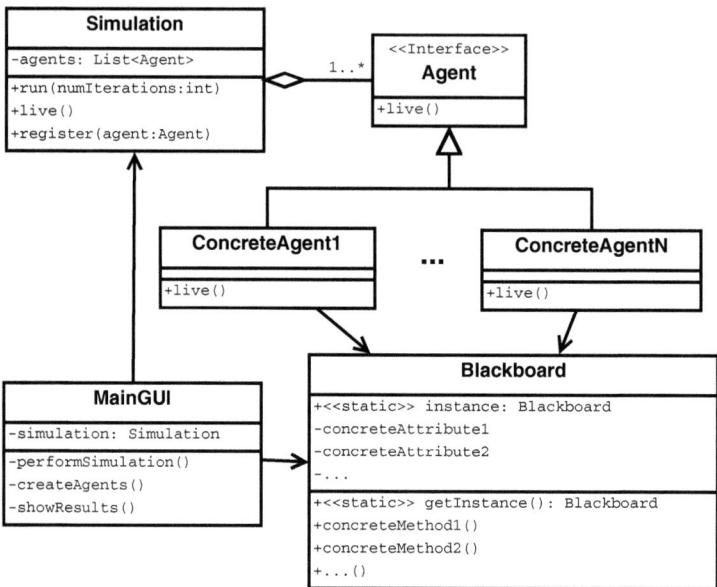

Fig. 5. Integration of blackboard simulation within INGENIAS

chooses a route, but with a probability weighted by the rank recommendations for each route and the corresponding tourist type. Then, the tourist agent asks the route manager to book the route for the given number of people that the tourist agent represents, by means of the *Sign Up Route* interaction unit. The manager agent books the route and confirms the operation to the tourist agent. The tourist agent makes note of the booked route, and sends back this route along with the number of people finishing the other interaction between the simulator agent and the tourist agent, which was previously described.

The complete definition of all the INGENIAS diagrams of the MAS is omitted in this paper for the sake of brevity. From all the corresponding INGENIAS diagrams, the programming code was generated by means of the INGENIAS Development Kit (IDK) [7].

4 Adaptation of the Generated Code for the Extensive Tourist Simulation

The INGENIAS Agent Framework (IAF) is the IDK plugin that generated the programming code for the MAS specified in the previous section. However, due to the high number of agents that are necessary in these kinds of simulations, this paper presents an adaptation framework to fasten the communications between agents. This framework has been applied in the presented MAS. This adaptation is in a similar vein of the work of Gómez-Sanz et al. [6].

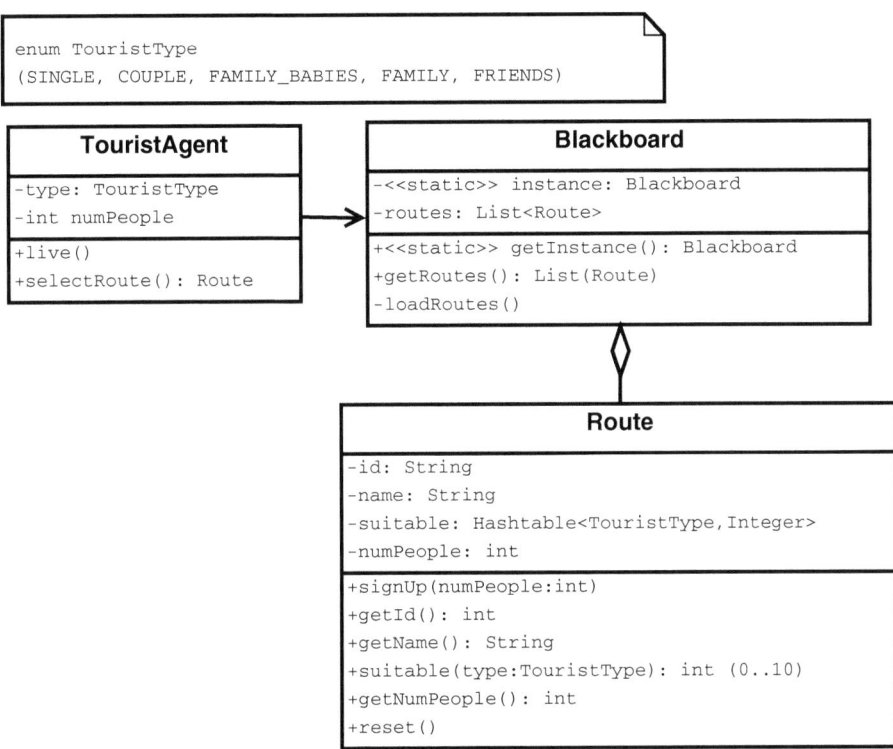

Fig. 6. Particularization of blackboard simulation for tourist routes

In particular, an excerpt of the proposed simulation framework is presented in Figure 5. In this framework, the communications of agents are performed trough Java method calls, instead of using high-consuming messages through the JADE platform [2]. The Simulation class contains all the agents within a list. All the agents have the live method, in which they perform their activities periodically. The communications are performed through a blackboard represented with a class. In this manner, all the agent can implicitly communicate through the Blackboard, saving the time and costs of resubmitting the information. All the agents can access to the Blackboard through the Singleton pattern [11].

An excerpt of the particularization of the aforementioned simulation framework for the presented MAS is shown in Figure 6. Since all the tourist agent types have very similar operations except for the tourist type that is provided to the route manager agent, a unique class is implemented for all the tourist agents, and this class has an attribute that specifies the tourist type from an enumeration type. This class is called TouristAgent, and also has an attribute for indicating the number of people each agent represents.

It is worth mentioning that the route manager agent storages the routes in the blackboard, and these routes are also stored alongside the number of people signed to each route, by means of the numPeople attribute of the Route class.

In this manner, at the end of the simulation, the simulator agent can directly retrieve the number people signed for each route, which is the relevant information presented to the users. The Route class provides methods for safely signing up tourist people in each route and retrieving the relevant information.

5 Simulation Experimentation of Tourists in Madrid Routes

For the experimentation of this MAS, an application is provided to the tourism experts. Figure 7 shows this application running. This application is available from the author's website [3] for practitioners. This application is distributed as an executable jar file, and one needs to download this file and to have installed the Java SE Runtime Environment (JRE) version 7u45 (or above) for running the application.

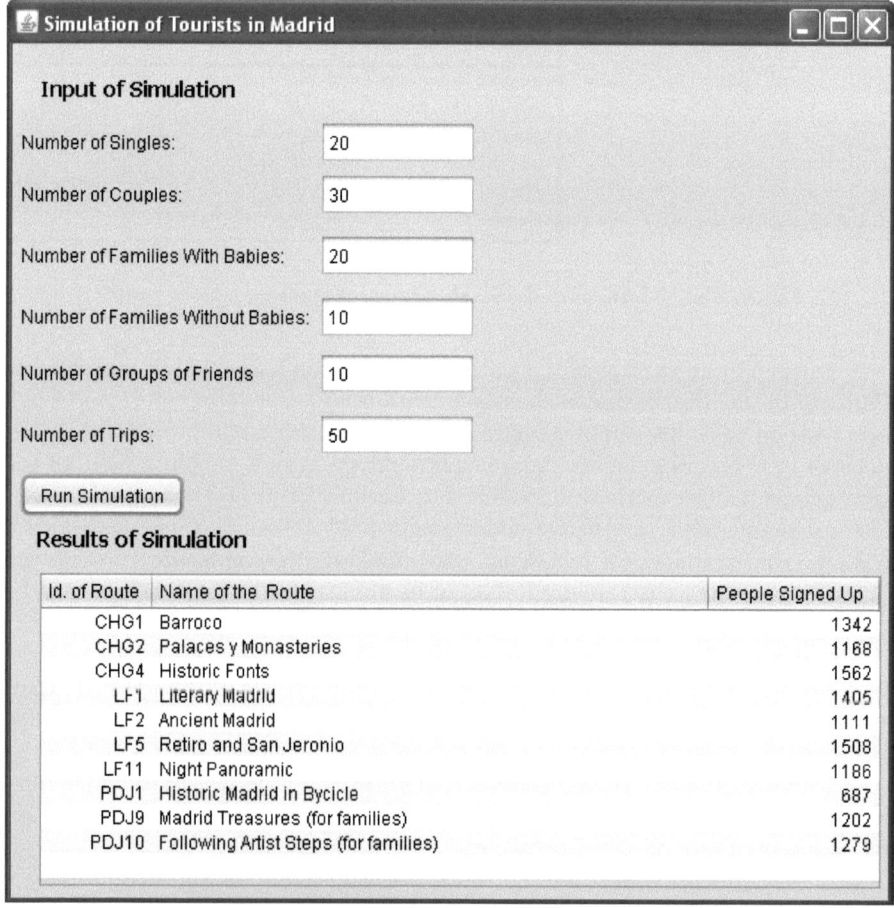

Fig. 7. Practical application of simulation of tourists in Madrid routes

In this experimentation, the tourism experts provided a set of routes in the historic center of Madrid, and a subset of ten routes was included in the application for the simulation. The application lets users determine the number of each kind of tourist individuals or groups (i.e. singles, couples, families with babies, families without babies, groups of friends). In addition, the user can also determine the number of trips, which represent the number of iterations in which the tourists select routes.

In this simulation application, each family (with or without babies) has a random number of members from three to six, while each group of friends has a random number of members from two to ten.

Once a user sets all the available parameters of the simulation in the GUI, they can press the Run Simulation button, and the results are displayed in the bottom part of the application. In particular, the identifier and name of each route is presented alongside the number of people signed up to it after all the simulation.

Specifically, Figure 7 shows the results of the simulation for 20 singles, 30 couples, 20 families with babies, 10 families without babies, and 10 groups of friends, with 50 iterations (trips). As one can observe, the Historic Fonts route is overcrowded with 1562 people signed up, while the Historic Madrid in Bicycle route can be non-profitable with only 687 people signed up. The tourism exerts can reflect on these results, in order to select another subset of Madrid routes that produces a more balanced distribution of tourist people.

6 Conclusions and Future Work

On the whole, this paper presents a practical MAS application for simulating the tourist selection of routes in a particular city. This MAS has been developed with the INGENIAS methodology, and the generated programming code has been adapted for the simulation. In particular, this MAS has been applied to guide tourism experts in obtaining an appropriate set of routes of the historic center of Madrid.

As future work, a short-term goal is to apply this MAS to larger sets of Madrid routes to further assess the usefulness of this MAS. Tourist experts are planned to be surveyed about this MAS to obtain their feedback. In addition, the presented MAS is planned to be experienced with routes of several European cities with different cultural features, so that the experience is wider to assess this approach. The MAS is planned to be extended to let users simulate sets of routes of several cities and towns of a particular region, to predict the behavior of tourists in a region. In this manner, experts can achieve proper distributions of tourist loads among different cities and towns of a given region. In this extension, the results will include a new column for indicating the city or town of each route, and the application will analyze and present the results gathering the tourist people signed up to the routes of each city and each town. The types tourists will also be extended distinguishing for instance between young and old couples or using another set of tourist types extracted from tourism literature. Furthermore, the proposed adaptation framework for simulations is planned to be provided in a more automated way, maybe as a new IDK plugin. Finally, the suitability ranks of each route can be determined with data-mining techniques from the features of the route such as length, duration time and cultural type.

Acknowledgments. This work is supported by the project *Los Sistemas de Información Turística como herramientas tecnológicas para incrementar la operatividad turística de los itinerarios culturales urbanos: El centro histórico de Madrid como proyecto piloto* (SIT-MAD) funded by the Hergar Foundation with grant FH-2012-03. This work has also been done in the context of the project *Social Ambient Assisting Living - Methods* (SociAAL), supported by Spanish Ministry for Economy and Competitiveness, with grant TIN2011-28335-C02-01.

References

1. Balbi, S., Giupponi, C., Perez, P., Alberti, M.: A spatial agent-based model for assessing strategies of adaptation to climate and tourism demand changes in an alpine tourism destination. Environmental Modelling & Software 45, 29–51 (2012)
2. Bellifemine, F.L., Poggi, A., Rimassa, G.: Developing multi-agent systems with JADE. In: Castelfranchi, C., Lespérance, Y. (eds.) ATAL 2000. LNCS (LNAI), vol. 1986, pp. 89–103. Springer, Heidelberg (2001)
3. García-Magariño, I.: Webpage of Iván García-Magariño: Additional Material for Papers (February 2014), http://ivangarciamagarino.net23.net (last accessed February 26, 2014)
4. Gärtner, M., Seidel, I., Froschauer, J., Berger, H.: The formation of virtual organizations by means of electronic institutions in a 3D e-Tourism environment. Information Sciences 180(17), 3157–3169 (2010)
5. Gavalas, D., Konstantopoulos, C., Mastakas, K., Pantziou, G.: Mobile recommender systems in tourism. Journal of Network and Computer Applications (2013) (in press)
6. Gómez-Sanz, J.J., Fernández, C.R., Arroyo, J.: Model driven development and simulations with the INGENIAS agent framework. Simulation Modelling Practice and Theory 18(10), 1468–1482 (2010)
7. Gomez-Sanz, J.J., Fuentes, R., Pavón, J., García-Magariño, I.: Ingenias development kit: a visual multi-agent system development environment. In: Proceedings of the 7th International Joint Conference on Autonomous Agents and Multiagent Systems: Demo Papers, pp. 1675–1676. International Foundation for Autonomous Agents and Multiagent Systems (2008)
8. Hamilton, J.M., Maddison, D.J., Tol, R.S.: Climate change and international tourism: a simulation study. Global Environmental Change 15(3), 253–266 (2005)
9. Hsu, L.: Web 3D simulation-based application in tourism education: A case study with Second Life. Journal of Hospitality, Leisure, Sport & Tourism Education 11(2), 113–124 (2012)
10. Mustapha, K., Mcheick, H., Mellouli, S.: Modeling and simulation agent-based of natural disaster complex systems. Procedia Computer Science 21, 148–155 (2013)
11. Nguyen, D.: Design patterns for data structures. In: Proceedings of the Twenty-Ninth SIGCSE Technical Symposium on Computer Science Education, SIGCSE 1998. ACM SIGCSE Bulletin, vol. 30, pp. 336–340. ACM (1998)

12. Nguyen, Q.T., Bouju, A., Estraillier, P.: Multi-agent architecture with space-time components for the simulation of urban transportation systems. Procedia-Social and Behavioral Sciences 54, 365–374 (2012)
13. Pavón, J., Gómez-Sanz, J.J.: Agent oriented software engineering with INGENIAS. In: Mařík, V., Müller, J.P., Pěchouček, M. (eds.) CEEMAS 2003. LNCS (LNAI), vol. 2691, pp. 394–403. Springer, Heidelberg (2003)
14. Song, H., Dwyer, L., Li, G., Cao, Z.: Tourism economics research: A review and assessment. Annals of Tourism Research 39(3), 1653–1682 (2012)
15. Wagner, N., Agrawal, V.: An agent-based simulation system for concert venue crowd evacuation modeling in the presence of a fire disaster. Expert Systems with Applications 80(3), 255–275 (2014)
16. Wijerathne, M.L.L., Melgar, L.A., Hori, M., Ichimura, T., Tanaka, S.: Hpc enhanced large urban area evacuation simulations with vision based autonomously navigating multi agents. Procedia Computer Science 18, 1515–1524 (2013)

Domain and Subtask-Adaptive Conversational Agents to Provide an Enhanced Human-Agent Interaction

David Griol, José Manuel Molina, and Araceli Sanchis de Miguel

Computer Science Department
Carlos III University of Madrid
Avda. de la Universidad, 30, 28911 - Leganés, Spain
{david.griol,josemanuel.molina,araceli.sanchis}@uc3m.es

Abstract. One of the most demanding tasks when developing conversational agents consists of designing the dialog manager, which decides the next system response considering the user's actions and the dialog history. A previously developed statistical dialog management technique is adapted in this work to reduce the effort and time required to design the dialog manager. This technique allows not only an easy adaptation to new domains, but also to deal with the different subtasks by means of specific dialog models adapted to each dialog objective in the domain of a multiagent system. The practical application of the proposed technique to develop a conversational agent providing railway information shows that the use of these specific dialog models increases the quality and number of successful interactions with the agent in comparison with developing a single dialog model for the complete domain.

Keywords: Human-agent interaction, User interfaces, Conversational agents, Speech interaction, Information systems, Statistical methodologies.

1 Introduction

Spoken conversational agents or dialog systems are computer programs that receive speech as input and generate as output synthesized speech, engaging the user in a dialog that aims to be similar to that between humans [1, 2]. Thus, these interfaces make technologies more usable, as they ease interaction [3], allow integration in different environments [4], facilitate the interaction with multiagent systems [5, 6] and make technologies more accessible, especially for disabled people [7].

Usually, conversational agents carry out five main tasks: Automatic Speech Recognition (ASR), Spoken Language Understanding (SLU), Dialog Management (DM), Natural Language Generation (NLG), and Text-To-Speech Synthesis (TTS). These tasks are typically implemented in different modules of the system's architecture.

The goal of speech recognition is to obtain the sequence of words uttered by a speaker. It is a very complex task, as there can be a great deal of variation in the input the recognizer must analyze, for example, in terms of the linguistics of the utterance, inter and intra speaker variation, the interaction context and the transmission channel. Once the speech recognizer has provided an output, the system must understand what the user said. The goal of spoken language understanding is to obtain the semantics from the recognized sentence. This process generally requires morphological, lexical, syntactical, semantic, discourse and pragmatical knowledge.

The dialog manager decides the next action of the system, interpreting the incoming semantic representation of the user input in the context of the dialog. In addition, it resolves ellipsis and anaphora, evaluates the relevance and completeness of user requests, identifies and recovers from recognition and understanding errors, retrieves information from data repositories, and decides about the next system's response. Natural language generation is the process of obtaining sentences in natural language from the non-linguistic, internal representation of information handled by the dialog system. Finally, the TTS module transforms the generated sentences into synthesized speech.

In order to enable rapid deployment of these agents, markup languages such as VoiceXML[1] have been widely adopted as they reduce the time and effort required for system implementation. However, typically hand-crafted dialog management strategies using rules and heuristics still involve a very costly engineering cycle in the system development with this approach [8]. As an attempt to reduce this cost and carry out rapid system prototyping, statistical approaches are gaining increasing interest [9–11].

Statistical approaches enable automatic learning of dialog strategies, thus avoiding the time-consuming process that hand-crafted dialog design involves. Statistical models can be trained from real dialogs, modeling the variability in user behaviors. Although the construction and parameterization of these models depend on expert knowledge about the interaction domain, the objective is to develop systems that are more robust for real-world conditions, and easier to adapt to different users and tasks [9].

The most widespread methodology for machine-learning of dialog strategies consists of modeling human-computer interaction as an optimization problem using Partially Observable Markov Decision Processes (MDP) and reinforcement methods [12]. The main drawback of this approach is that the large state space of practical domains makes its direct representation intractable [13].

In this paper we adapt a statistical approach for the development of dialog managers [10], which is mainly based on the use of a classification process for the estimation of a statistical model from the sequences of the system and user dialog acts obtained from a set of training data. This technique has been previously applied to develop dialog managers for domains of different complexity [10]. This paper is specially focused on the adaptation and evaluation of this technique when specific dialog models are learned for each dialog subtask instead of learning

---

[1] http://www.w3.org/TR/voicexml20/

a single dialog model for the complete conversational agent. To do this, the training data is divided into different subsets, each covering a specific dialog objective or subtask. We propose to use our approach to learn specific dialog models for each dialog subset instead of using the complete training data to learn a single dialog model for the task. These specific dialog models are selected by the dialog manager once the objective of the dialog has been detected, using the generic dialog model until this condition has been fulfilled.

We have applied the proposed methodology to develop two versions of a conversational agent providing railway information in Spanish. The first one uses a generic dialog model and the second one uses specific dialog models for each dialog objective. An in-depth comparative assessment of the conversational agents has been completed using both real users and a user-agent simulation technique recently developed [14]. The results of the evaluation show that the specific dialog models allow a better selection of the next system responses, thus increasing the number and quality of successful interactions with the agent.

The rest of the paper is organized as follows. Section 2 describes our proposal for developing statistical dialog managers with specific dialog models. Section 3 shows a practical implementation of our proposal to generate a specific system. In Section 4 we discuss the evaluation results obtained by comparing two baseline versions of the system with a context-aware version that adapts its behavior integrating our proposal. Finally, in Section 5 we present the conclusions and outline guidelines for future work.

2 Our Proposed Methodology for Dialog Management

This section summarizes the proposed dialog management technique and the practical implementation proposed in this paper by means of specific dialog models for each subtask.

2.1 Proposed Statistical Methodology

In order to control the interactions with the user, our dialog manager represents dialogs as a sequence of pairs (A_i, U_i), where A_i is the output of the dialog manager (the system answer) at time i, and U_i is the semantic representation of the user turn (the result of the understanding process of the user input) at time i; both expressed in terms of dialog acts [10]. Each dialog is represented by:

$$(A_1, U_1), \cdots, (A_i, U_i), \cdots, (A_n, U_n)$$

where A_1 is the greeting turn of the system, and U_n is the last user turn. We refer to a pair (A_i, U_i) as S_i, the state of the dialog sequence at time i.

In this framework, we consider that, at time i, the objective of the dialog manager is to find the best system answer A_i. This selection is a local process for each time i and takes into account the previous history of the dialog, that is to say, the sequence of states of the dialog preceding time i:

$$\hat{A}_i = \underset{A_i \in \mathcal{A}}{\operatorname{argmax}} P(A_i|S_1, \cdots, S_{i-1}) \qquad (1)$$

where set $\mathcal{A}$ contains all the possible system answers.

Following Equation 1, the dialog manager selects the following system prompt by taking into account the sequence of previous pairs (A_i, U_i). The main problem to resolve this equation is regarding the number of possible sequences of states, which is usually very large. To solve the problem, we define a data structure in order to establish a partition in this space, i.e., in the history of the dialog preceding time i. This data structure, which we call *Dialog Register* (DR), contains the information provided by the user throughout the previous history of the dialog. After establishing the equivalence relation in the histories of dialogs, the selection of the best A_i is given by:

$$\hat{A}_i = \underset{A_i \in \mathcal{A}}{\operatorname{argmax}} P(A_i|DR_{i-1}, S_{i-1}) \qquad (2)$$

Each user turn supplies the system with information about the task; i.e., the user asks for a specific concept and/or provides specific values for certain attributes. However, a user turn can also provide other kinds of information, such as task-independent information (for instance, *Acceptance*, *Rejection*, and *Not-Understood* dialog acts). This kind of information implies some decisions which are different from simply updating the DR_{i-1}. Hence, for the selection of the best system response A_i, we take into account the DR that results from turn 1 to turn $i-1$, and we explicitly consider the last state S_{i-1}.

As stated before, the DR contains information about concepts and values for the attributes provided by the user throughout the previous history of the dialog. For the dialog manager to determine the next answer, we have assumed that the exact values of the attributes are not significant. They are important for accessing databases and for constructing the output sentences of the system. However, the only information necessary to predict the next action by the system is the presence or absence of concepts and attributes. Therefore, the codification we use for each field in the DR is in terms of three values, $\{0, 1, 2\}$, according to the following criteria: (0) The concept is unknown or the value of the attribute is not given; (1) the concept or attribute is known with a confidence score that is higher than a given threshold; (2) the concept or attribute has a confidence score that is lower than the given threshold. To decide whether the state of a certain value in the DR is 1 or 2, the system employs confidence measures provided by the ASR and SLU modules.

2.2 Proposed Implementation by Means of Specific Dialog Models

As a practical implementation of this methodology, in this paper we propose the use of two modules. The first module deals with the detection of the specific dialog objective described by the user. This detection is based on the specific semantic information regarded to the task that is provided by the SLU module. This module also updates the *Dialog Register* that contains the complete list of features provided by the SLU module through the dialog history until the current moment. Until a specific problem is detected, a generic model learned with all the training dialogs is used for the selection of the next system response.

Once the objective of the dialog has been detected, a second module uses a specific dialog model learned for each subtask to select the next system response. To do this, we propose to solve Equation 2 by means of a classification process. This way, every dialog situation (i.e., each possible sequence of dialog acts) is classified taking into account a set of classes $\mathcal{C}$, in which a class contains all the sequences that provide the same set of system actions (responses). The objective of the dialog manager at each moment is to select a class of this set $c \in \mathcal{C}$, so that the system response is the one associated with the selected class.

The classification function can be defined in several ways. We have previously evaluated six different definitions of such a function: a multinomial naive Bayes classifier, an n-gram based classifier, a decision tree classifier, a support vector machine classifier, a classifier based on grammatical inference techniques, and a classifier based on artificial neural networks [10]. The best results were obtained using a multilayer perceptron (MLP) [15] where the input layer holds the input pair (DR_{i-1}, S_{i-1}) corresponding to the dialog register and the state. The values of the output layer can be seen as an approximation of the a posteriori probability of the input belonging to the associated class $c \in \mathcal{C}$. Figure 1 shows the described scheme for the practical implementation of the proposed dialog management technique and its interaction with the rest of the modules in the conversational agent.

3 Practical Application

Within the framework of the DIHANA project, a mixed-initiative conversational agent was developed to provide a railway information system using spontaneous speech in Spanish [16]. The system integrates the CMU Sphinx-II system speech recognition module[2]. As in many other conversational agents, the semantic representation chosen for dialog acts of the SLU module is based on the concept of frame [17]. This way, one or more concepts represent the intention of the utterance, and a sequence of attribute-value pairs contains the information about the values given by the user. For the task, we defined eight concepts and ten attributes. The eight concepts are divided into two groups:

1. *Task-Dependent Concepts*: they represent the concepts the user can ask for (*Timetables, Fares, Train-Type, Trip-Time,* and *Services*).
2. *Task-Independent Concepts*: they represent typical interactions in a dialog (*Acceptance, Rejection,* and *Not-Understood*).

The attributes are: *Origin, Destination, Departure-Date, Arrival-Date, Class, Departure-Hour, Arrival-Hour, Train-Type, Order-Number,* and *Services*. A total of 51 responses were defined for the system, corresponding to the request of

---
[2] cmusphinx.sourceforge.net

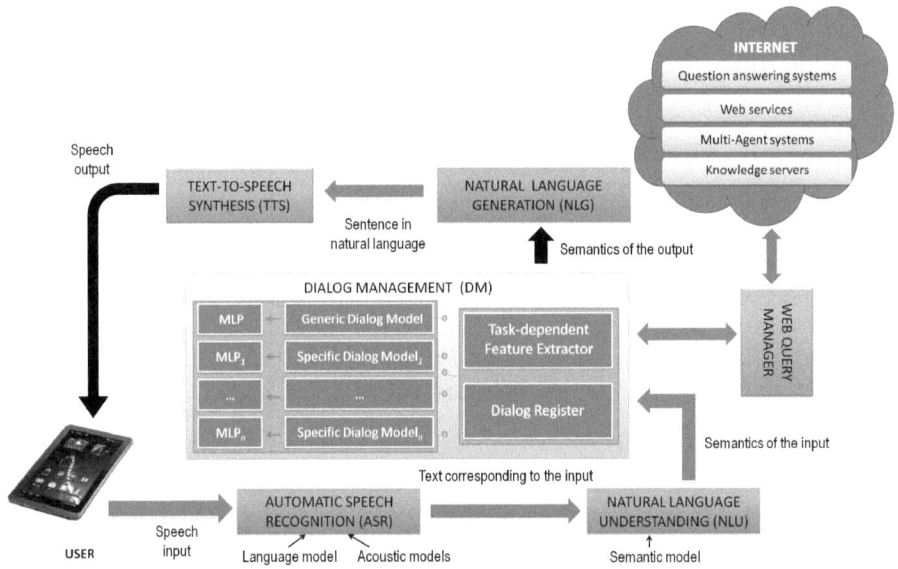

Fig. 1. Scheme of the complete architecture for the development of enhanced conversational agents

the different concepts or attributes, the confirmation of these attributes, the provision of information, and the opening and closing of the dialog. The DR defined for the task consists of the five possible task-dependent concepts and ten attributes previously enumerated.

Regarding the application of the proposed dialog management technique, Figure 2 shows an excerpt of a dialog for the conversational agent. Using the previously described codification for the DR, when a dialog starts (in the greeting turn) all the values in the dialog register are initialized to "0". The information provided by the users in each dialog turn is employed to update the previous DR and obtain the current one, as Figure 2 shows.

This figure shows the semantic interpretation and confidence scores (in brackets) for a user's utterance provided by the SLU module. In this case, the confidence score assigned to the attribute *Date* is very low. Thus, a "2" value is added in the corresponding position of the DR_1. The concept (*Hour*) and the attribute *Destination* are recognized with a high confidence score, adding a "1" value in the corresponding positions of the DR_1. As the input to the MLP is generated using DR_1, the codification of the labeling of the last system turn (A_1), and the task-independent information provided in the last user turn (none in this case), the dialog manager selects to confirm the departure date. This process is repeated to predict the next system response after each user turn.

The NLG module translates the semantic representations of the system dialog acts to sentences in Spanish. Our technique consists of having a set of

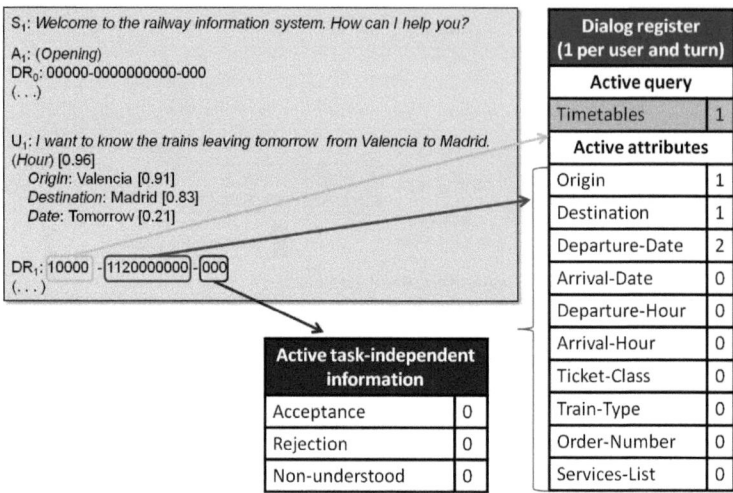

Fig. 2. Excerpt of a dialog with its correspondent *Dialog Register* and active task-independent information for one of the turns

templates associated to each one of the different dialog acts, in which the names of the attributes are shown. These names are replaced by the values recognized in order to generate the final answer for the user. For the speech output, we have integrated the Festival speech synthesis system[3]. The specific information relative to our task is stored in a PostGres database using information that is dynamically extracted from the web.

An initial corpus of 900 dialogs (10.8 hours) was acquired for the task by means of the Wizard of Oz technique with 225 real users [16]. A set of 20 scenarios was used to carry out the acquisition. Each scenario defined one or two objectives to be completed by the user and the set of attributes that they must provide, as Figure 3 shows. The corpus consists of 6,280 user turns, with an average number of 7.7 words per turn. Using this corpus, two versions of the conversational agent have been developed. The first one (*Conversational Agent 1*) uses a generic dialog model for the task, which has been learned using the 900 dialogs. The second one (*Conversational Agent 2*) also employs 20 specific dialog models learned using only the corresponding dialogs acquired for each one of the scenarios.

4 Results of the Evaluation

The conversational agent described in the previous section allows two operation modes. First, the system uses the ASR and the SLU modules for the normal interaction between the agent and the real users. Second, the agent allows the automatic acquisition of dialogs by means of a recently developed user-agent simulator [14]. The following subsections describes the evaluation of the two versions of the conversational agent by means of both techniques.

[3] www.cstr.ed.ac.uk/projects/festival

Code	Objective	Information provided by the user
A0	To obtain Timetables	Destination, Date
A1	To obtain Timetables	Destination, Date, Hour
A2	To obtain Timetables and Types of Trains	Destination, Date
A3	To obtain Timetables	Destination, Date, Train-Type
A4	To obtain Timetables	Destination, Date, Hour, Train-Type
A5	To obtain Timetables	Origin, Destination, Date, Hour
A6	To obtain Timetables and Types of Trains	Origin, Destination, Date
A7	To obtain Timetables	Origin, Destination, Date, Train-Type
A8	To obtain Timetables and Types of Trains	Origin, Destination, Date, Hour
A9	To obtain Timetables	Origin, Destination, Date, Hour, Train-Type
B0	To obtain Timetables and Fares	Destination, Date
B1	To obtain Timetables and Fares	Destination, Date, Hour
B2	To obtain Timetables and Fares	Destination, Date, Train-Type
B3	To obtain Timetables and Fares	Destination, Date, Hour, Train-Type
B4	To obtain Timetables and Fares	Origin, Destination, Date, Hour
B5	To obtain Timetables and Fares	Origin, Destination, Date, Train-Type
B6	To obtain Timetables and Fares	Origin, Destination, Date, Hour, Train-Type
B7	To obtain Fares	Destination, Date, Train-Type
B8	To obtain Fares	Origin, Destination, Date, Train-Type
B9	To obtain Fares	Origin, Destination, Date, Hour, Train-Type

Fig. 3. Set of different scenarios defined for the railway task

4.1 Evaluation with a User Simulator

A total of 1,000 dialogs have been acquired for each of the 20 designed scenarios by means of the interaction of the conversational agents with a brute-force automatic user simulator. The following measures were defined to compare the two corpus acquired with the conversational agents: number of successful dialogs, average number of user turns, number of different dialogs (taking into account their labeling in terms of frames and not the exact values of the attributes), the number of repetitions and user turns of the most seen dialog (in term of frames), the number of user turns of the shortest and longest dialogs, and the number of repeated dialogs (also in term of frames). Table 1 shows the result of the evaluation.

As it can be observed, the number of successfully simulated dialogs increases in most of the scenarios using the proposed technique with specific dialog models for each one of them (from a total of 6,100 successful dialogs acquired with the *Conversational Agent 1* to 8,720 successful dialogs acquired with the *Conversational Agent 2*). The user-agent simulator was developed to generate unsupervised dialogs, that is why a high amount of unsuccessful interactions were generated. In addition, there is a reduction in the average number of turns required to fulfill the objectives using the *Conversational Agent 2* (from an average of 5.7 turns using the *Conversational Agent 1* to 4.9 turns using the *Conversational Agent 2*). This general reduction in the number of turns is generalized also to the case of the longest, shortest and most seen dialogs for the *Conversational Agent 2*. Both results are specially remarkable for the most complicated subtasks, in which two objectives must be fulfilled and users must provide a large number of attributes.

On the other hand, the number of repetitions of the most seen dialog and the number of repeated dialogs is increased using the *Conversational Agent 2*. This can be explained due to the more reduced number of dialogs used to learn

Table 1. Results of the evaluation using a generic dialog model (top) or specific dialog models (bottom) and the user simulator

Conversational Agent 1										
	A0	A1	A2	A3	A4	A5	A6	A7	A8	A9
Number of successful dialogs	771	547	25	475	493	562	25	459	28	487
Average number of user turns	4.3	5.2	5.4	5.4	5.5	5.3	5.8	5.4	6.2	5.6
Number of different dialogs	489	500	24	438	476	493	25	437	28	466
Number of repetitions most seen dialog	70	10	2	8	5	14	1	7	1	6
Number of user turns most seen dialog	2	4	3	2	2	7	8	7	8	2
Number of user turns shortest dialog	2	2	3	2	2	2	3	2	3	2
Number of user turns longest dialog	8	8	8	8	8	8	8	8	8	8
Number of repeated dialogs	19	16	0	11	11	6	0	14	0	12
	B0	B1	B2	B3	B4	B5	B6	B7	B8	B9
Number of successful dialogs	290	215	185	167	210	184	194	247	273	263
Average number of user turns	5.6	6.2	6.2	6.2	6.3	6.0	6.3	5.6	5.6	5.8
Number of different dialogs	259	213	182	167	208	184	193	244	267	259
Number of repetitions most seen dialog	9	1	2	1	2	1	2	2	5	2
Number of user turns most seen dialog	3	3	4	4	4	8	3	3	2	5
Number of user turns shortest dialog	3	3	3	3	3	3	3	2	2	2
Number of user turns longest dialog	8	8	8	8	8	8	8	8	8	8
Number of repeated dialogs	5	1	3	3	2	3	3	3	5	5
Conversational Agent 2										
	A0	A1	A2	A3	A4	A5	A6	A7	A8	A9
Number of successful dialogs	831	484	96	279	353	749	403	760	391	636
Average number of user turns	3.7	4.6	5.4	3.8	4.3	3.8	5.2	4.7	4.9	4.3
Number of different dialogs	277	353	69	180	266	460	291	456	326	402
Number of repetitions most seen dialog	124	18	7	23	10	31	21	35	11	54
Number of user turns most seen dialog	2	2	4	7	3	4	8	2	3	4
Number of user turns shortest dialog	2	2	4	2	2	3	3	2	3	2
Number of user turns longest dialog	8	8	8	8	8	8	8	8	8	8
Number of repeated dialogs	14	9	1	9	5	13	2	11	2	10
	B0	B1	B2	B3	B4	B5	B6	B7	B8	B9
Number of successful dialogs	403	195	120	207	429	357	291	445	627	664
Average number of user turns	4.9	5.6	5.5	5.9	5.3	5.7	5.8	4.9	4.4	4.5
Number of different dialogs	252	178	111	187	389	336	278	318	438	547
Number of repetitions most seen dialog	51	4	4	4	6	3	4	23	19	18
Number of user turns most seen dialog	3	3	4	3	3	3	3	8	2	2
Number of user turns shortest dialog	3	3	3	3	3	3	3	2	2	2
Number of user turns longest dialog	8	8	8	8	8	8	8	8	8	8
Number of repeated dialogs	6	4	3	0	5	5	3	3	8	7

the specific dialog models, which reduces the space of dialog states in order to select the next system prompt. However, the *Conversational Agent 2* allows generating more different dialogs (from 5,552 different dialogs obtained with the *Conversational Agent 1* to 6,114 different dialogs with the *Conversational Agent 2*), then increasing the variability of the simulated corpus.

Additionally, we grouped all user and system actions into three categories: "goal directed" (actions to provide or request information), "grounding" (confirmations and negations), and "other". Table 2 shows a comparison between these categories. As can be observed, the dialogs provided by the *Conversational Agent 2* have a better quality, as the proportion of goal-directed actions is higher than the values obtained for the *Conversational Agent 1*.

4.2 Evaluation with Real Users

Secondly, we have evaluated the conversational agents with recruited users and the same set of scenarios previously described. A total of 100 dialogs for each

Table 2. Proportions of dialog spent on-goal directed actions, ground actions and other possible actions

	Conversational Agent 1	Conversational Agent 2
Goal-directed actions	67.21%	73.43%
Grounding actions	31.64%	25.54%
Rest of actions	1.15%	1.03%

agent was recorded from the interactions of 5 users (one dialog for each scenario acquired by each user). The same set of previously described measures was used to complete an objective evaluation. As shown in Table 3, the results of the evaluation confirm the conclusions extracted from the evaluation with the user-agent simulator, obtaining a large number of successful dialogs with also a reduced number of turns when the *Conversational Agent 2* was used.

Table 3. Results of the objective evaluation with recruited users

	Conversational Agent 1	Conversational Agent 2
Number of successful dialogs	84%	92%
Average number of user turns	6.4	5.6
Number of different dialogs	76%	85%
Number of repetitions most seen dialog	5	8
Number of user turns most seen dialog	6	5
Number of user turns shortest dialog	5	3
Number of user turns longest dialog	12	10
Number of repeated dialogs	6	9

In addition, we asked the recruited users to complete a questionnaire to assess their subjective opinion about the agents performance. The questionnaire had six questions: i) Q1: *How well did the system understand you?*; ii) Q2: *How well did you understand the system messages?*; iii) Q3: *Was it easy for you to get the requested information?*; iv) Q4: *Was the interaction with the system quick enough?*; v) Q5: *If there were system errors, was it easy for you to correct them?*; vi) Q6: *In general, are you satisfied with the performance of the system?* The possible answers for each one of the questions were the same: *Never/Not at all, Seldom/In some measure, Sometimes/Acceptably, Usually/Well,* and *Always/Very Well*. All the answers were assigned a numeric value between one and five (in the same order as they appear in the questionnaire).

Table 4 shows the average results of the subjective evaluation using the described questionnaire. It can be observed that using either *Conversational Agent 1* or *Conversational Agent 2* the users perceived that the system understood them correctly. Moreover, they expressed a similar opinion regarding the easiness for correcting system errors. However, users said that it was easier to obtain the information specified for the different objectives using *Conversational Agent 2*, and that the interaction with the system was more adequate with the proposed dialog manager. Finally, the users were more satisfied with the system employing *Conversational Agent 2*.

Table 4. Results of the subjective evaluation with real users (For the mean value M: 1=worst, 5=best evaluation)

	Conversational Agent 1	Conversational Agent 2
Q1	M = 4.53, SD = 0.41	M = 4.71, SD = 0.33
Q2	M = 3.67, SD = 0.32	M = 3.92, SD = 0.28
Q3	M = 3.81, SD = 0.54	M = 4.29, SD = 0.32
Q4	M = 3.64, SD = 0.29	M = 4.33, SD = 0.29
Q5	M = 3.47, SD = 0.55	M = 3.54, SD = 0.53
Q6	M = 3.75, SD = 0.43	M = 4.32, SD = 0.37

5 Conclusions and Future Work

In this paper, we have adapted a statistical methodology for the development of conversational agents and the optimization of dialog strategies. The methodology is based on the estimation of a statistical model from the sequences of system and user dialog acts obtained from a set of training data. The selection of the next system response is carried out by the dialog manager using two modules. The first module is used to detect the specific objective described by the user based on the specific task-dependent semantic information provided by the SLU module. The second module is based on a classification process that takes into account the history of the dialog by means of a data structure and selects the specific dialog model generated by means of a MLP. We have defined a codification of this information to facilitate the correct operation of this classification function.

The results of the evaluation of our proposal for a conversational agent providing railway information show that the number of successful dialogs is increased in comparison with using a generic dialog model for the task. Also, these dialogs are statistically shorter and present a better quality in the selection of the system responses. For future work, we want to consider the incorporation in the DR of additional information regarding the user, such as specific user profiles adapted to the interaction domain. Finally, we also want to evaluate our proposal with additional domains and wider populations.

Acknowledgements. This work was supported in part by Projects MINECO TEC2012-37832-C02-01, CICYT TEC2011-28626-C02-02, CAM CONTEXTS (S2009/TIC-1485).

References

1. Pieraccini, R.: The Voice in the Machine: Building Computers that Understand Speech. The MIT Press (2012)
2. López-Cózar, R., Araki, M.: Spoken, Multilingual and Multimodal Dialogue Systems. John Wiley & Sons Publishers (2005)
3. Hempel, T.: Usability of Speech Dialog Systems: Listening to the Target Audience. Springer (2008)
4. Heinroth, T., Minker, W.: Introducing Spoken Dialogue Systems into Intelligent Environments. Kluwer Academic Publishers (2012)

5. Rodríguez, S., de Paz, Y., Bajo, J., Corchado, J.M.: Social-based Planning Model for Multi-agent Systems. Expert Systems with Applications 38(10), 13005–13023 (2011)
6. Corchado, J., Tapia, D., Bajo, J.: A multi-agent architecture for distributed services and applications. Computational Intelligence 24(2), 77–107 (2008)
7. Vipperla, R., Wolters, M., Renals, S.: Spoken dialogue interfaces for older people, pp. 118–137. IOS Press (2012)
8. Rojas-Barahona, L., Giorgino, T.: Adaptable dialog architecture and runtime engine (adarte): A framework for rapid prototyping of health dialog systems. International Journal of Medical Informatics 78, 56–68 (2009)
9. Schatzmann, J., Weilhammer, K., Stuttle, M., Young, S.: A Survey of Statistical User Simulation Techniques for Reinforcement-Learning of Dialogue Management Strategies. Knowledge Engineering Review 21(2), 97–126 (2006)
10. Griol, D., Molina, J.M., Callejas, Z.: Bringing together commercial and academic perspectives for the development of intelligent AmI interfaces. Journal of Ambient Intelligence and Smart Environments 4, 183–207 (2012)
11. Paek, T., Pieraccini, R.: Automating spoken dialogue management design using machine learning: An industry perspective. Speech Communication 50(8-9), 716–729 (2008)
12. Levin, E., Pieraccini, R., Eckert, W.: A stochastic model of human-machine interaction for learning dialog strategies. IEEE Transactions on Speech and Audio Processing 8(1), 11–23 (2000)
13. Young, S., Schatzmann, J., Weilhammer, K., Ye, H.: The Hidden Information State Approach to Dialogue Management. In: Proc. ICASSP 2007, pp. 149–152 (2007)
14. Griol, D., Carbó, J., Molina, J.: An Automatic Dialog Simulation Technique to Develop and Evaluate Interactive Conversational Agents. Applied Artificial Intelligence 27(9), 759–780 (2013)
15. Borrajo, M., Baruque, B., Corchado, E., Bajo, J., Corchado, J.: Hybrid neural intelligent system to predict business failure in small-to-medium-size enterprises. International Journal of Neural Systems 21(4), 277–296 (2011)
16. Griol, D., Hurtado, L., Segarra, E., Sanchis, E.: A Statistical Approach to Spoken Dialog Systems Design and Evaluation. Speech Communication 50(8-9), 666–682 (2008)
17. Minsky, M.: A Framework for Representing Knowledge. McGraw-Hill (1975)

Dynamic Scheduling of Ready Mixed Concrete Delivery Problem Using Delegate MAS

Shaza Hanif and Tom Holvoet

Department of Computer Science
KU Leuven

Abstract. Delegate MAS is a bio-inspired coordination mechanism that is geared at large-scale and dynamic applications. It is used for coordination and control applications, such as decentralized management of traffic and logistics. While using Delegate MAS, agents behave selfishly and try to maximize their own utility. It is unclear that with such selfish behaviour, complex and constrained scheduling problem can also be solved. In these problems, coping with dynamism in stressful scenarios is very challenging. In this paper, we present our experience of using Delegate MAS for a constrained problem. As a case study, we use dynamic ready mixed concrete delivery problem. We characterized input scenarios of our case study into unique attributes. By empirical evaluation, we have found that using Delegate MAS as coordination mechanism results in consistent performance when scale and stress of the problem is increased.

1 Introduction

Decentralized Coordination and Control (C & C) applications are among the few significant research domains for Multi-Agent Systems (MAS). Designing a coordination mechanism for C & C applications in dynamic environments is challenging. Because of decentralization, agents in these systems lack access to global system changes. Thus, making effective local decisions that emerge to serve the global objective is arduous. The biological systems that constitute individuals living in colonies, led some researchers to investigate the coordination mechanisms inspired by nature. Delegate MAS [8] is such a coordination mechanism used in MAS. It is inspired by social insects that live in colonies, like ants and termites. It has proved to be an effective coordination mechanism for C & C applications in several domains [16,5]. However, agents using Delegate MAS behave selfishly; every agent aims at maximizing its individual gain. With such selfish behaviour it may not be possible to solve a complex and constrained scheduling problem.

We use the case study of Ready Mixed Concrete delivery (RMC) problem and investigate if despite selfishness of Delegate MAS, agents are able to dynamically cope with the constraints of the problem. RMC is a transport scheduling problem, related to the category of pick-up and delivery problems. Scheduling for RMC problem in a dynamic environment is a challenge because the information changes in real-time. There are hard constraints while devising the truck schedules due to the perishable nature of concrete. For instance; 1) the time between the successive deliveries of an order must not exceed 30 minutes (see LT in Table 1). 2) Consider that while the construction is in progress, a truck is broken down during its delivery to an order, introducing a dynamic event. A new truck needs to be scheduled which also has to abide by the constraint of not exceeding the time beyond 30 minutes from the last delivery. When real time changes are accommodated, we refer such problem as *dynamic RMC problem*.

We address dynamic RMC problem by developing a decentralized C & C software for scheduling trucks. It is a MAS simulation, in which agents generate schedules by coordinating with each other using Delegate MAS. The application domain is very challenging due to the constrained nature of the problem and the fact that interdependency between individual scheduling units (that is deliveries) is high. In this paper, we present our experience of using Delegate MAS as a coordination mechanism to address dynamic RMC. A thorough evaluation of the coordination mechanism is conducted by multiple problem scale and varying degree of stressfulness in a typical day.

The main contributions of this paper are the following. 1) We identify, describe and use an interesting application for MAS based approaches 2) We investigate potential of Delegate MAS as a coordination mechanism on a very complex problem of dynamic RMC. 3) We present characterization of dynamic RMC problem scenarios into Stress, Dynamism and Scale (see Section 4.1) for conducting evaluation.

In Section 2 details about the dynamic RMC problem are given. We report on our decentralized coordination mechanism of Delegate MAS in Section 3. Experiment setup and evaluation of coordination mechanism is described in Sections 4 and 5. In Section 6, the background and related work is described. Finally, Section 7 concludes the paper.

2 Case Study - Dynamic RMC Problem

In this section we describe dynamic RMC problem, motivation of using it and related notation. Dynamic RMC problem considers a set of orders that need to be fulfilled by delivering concrete from several Production Sites (PSs), using a fleet of concrete delivery trucks. One Delivery refers to a round trip of a truck; that means it gets loaded from a PS, travels to an Order Site (OS), unloads at the OS and then returns to a PS to be prepared and loaded for the next delivery.

Typically, the ordered amount of concrete is more than the capacity of a single truck, necessitating a sequence of deliveries by multiple trucks. A Truck is always required to be loaded to its full capacity, otherwise due to less quantity CPT (see Table 1) is disturbed. The problem is dynamic because of the delivery failures caused by the truck breakdowns in a day. These breakdowns could be a result of a technical fault in the truck or due to traffic jams. Orders also dynamically arrive in the system during the day.

2.1 Why Dynamic RMC?

Dynamic RMC problem is well suited as a case study because: 1) It is inherently decentralized, making it feasible to map the real life entities to the agents in a decentralized MAS [3]. 2) Since Delegate MAS is geared towards dynamic environment, our case study is suitable as it involves dynamism. 3) Dynamic RMC problem has hard constraints, enabling us to analyse if Delegate MAS is performing well for the constrained problems. 4) The research conducted for dynamic RMC problem, can help us address similar transportation problems like split delivery problem and perishable goods, such as yogurt and milk transportation.

2.2 Problem Description and Notation

After giving motivation for using this problem, in this section we define the problem notation. Table 1 shows abbreviations necessary to be elaborated before proceeding forward to the next sections.

Table 1. Notation related to dynamic RMC problem, chosen values represent the values used by an RMC company

Term name	Explanation	Notation	Typical Value	Chosen Value
Lag Time	Time between two consecutive deliveries. (*minutes*)	LT	0 to 30	30
Concrete Perish Time	Maximum time, concrete can remain in truck(*minutes*)	CPT	90 to 110	100
Unloading Rate	The rate of unloading by truck at an OS ($m^3/hours$)	ULR	10 to 20	10
Concrete Loading Time	Time required by a PS to load a truck (*minutes*)	CLT	2 to 10	5
Start Time delay	The delay in delivery time for first delivery, from the requested start time of an OS (*minutes*)	$STdelay$	depends on schedule	-

We begin with a set of locations L, used to represent the physical locations in real world. Both PSs and OSs are situated at fixed locations. Distance between two locations is considered constant and is represented by d.

$L = \{l_0, l_1, ..., l_n\}$, set of locations
$d(l_i, l_j) \in \mathbb{R}^+$ (distance between l_i and l_j)

Production Site use fully automated processes to load a truck according to an order's requirement. PS services one truck at a time, by first cleaning and then loading. Because of fully automated processes of today's PS, it takes as less as 2 minutes (see CLT in Table 1) to service a truck [18]. We therefore assume that, a PS is available all the time for loading. In our notation, set P represents set of PSs:

$P = \{p_0, p_1, ..., p_n\}$, set of PSs
p_i^l = location of production site p_i from L (constant)

Order represents information about required quantity of concrete, unloading time for the first delivery (called start time of the order), and location of the OS. Set O is defined as:

$O = \{o_0, o_1, ..., o_n\}$, set of orders
o_i^q = quantity of order o_i
o_i^{st} = start time for order o_i
o_i^l = location of order o_i from L

Order delivery represent single delivery. As mentioned earlier, multiple trucks are required to deliver concrete for an $o_i \in O$. The notation for deliveries is given below:

$o_i D = \{o_i d_0, o_i d_1, ..., o_i d_n\}$, set of deliveries of an order o_i
$o_i d_k^{ut}$ = unload time of kth delivery of order o_i
$o_i d_k^q$ = quantity of kth delivery of order o_i

These sequence of deliveries need to be scheduled subject to following constraints:

- Sum of concrete delivered by all n deliveries for an order o_k should be equal to total quantity o_k^q ordered by order o_k.
$$\sum_{i=0}^{n} o_k d_i^q = o_k^q, \quad \forall o_k \in O, \forall o_k d_i \in o_k D$$
- Every delivery of an order o_k should be started after start time of an order o_k^{st}:
$o_k d_i^{st} \geq o_k^{st}, \quad \forall o_k \in O, \forall o_k d_i \in o_k D$
- At Order site, one truck can be unloaded at a time, resulting no overlap between two consecutive deliveries of an order o_k:
$o_k d_i^{ut} > o_k d_j^{ut} + (o_k d_i^q / ULR), \quad \forall j > i, \forall o_k \in O, \forall o_k d_i \in o_k D$
- The time between two consecutive deliveries of an order o_k should not exceed LT (Table 1).
$o_k d_{i+1}^{ut} \leq o_k d_i^{ut} + (o_k d_i^q / ULR) + LT, \quad \forall o_k \in O, \forall o_k d_i \in o_k D$

Delivery Truck set is represented by V. They represent the only mobile entity in the dynamic RMC problem. They start from a PS and at the end of day, return back to the nearest PS. After loading once, a truck cannot serve multiple OSs. Every time after serving a delivery, it must return back to a PS.

Notation for delivery trucks is given as below:

$V = \{v_0, v_1, ..., v_n\}$, set of trucks
v_i^c = capacity for truck v_i
v_i^{tt} = total distance travelled by truck v_i

Truck schedule is a list of delivery jobs, to be carried out by a truck. A job is formally represented as follows:

$v_i J = \{v_i j_0, v_i j_1, ..., v_i j_n\}$, set of jobs of a truck v_i
$v_i j_k^{st}$ = start time of kth job of truck v_i
$v_i j_k^{et}$ = end time of kth job of truck v_i

$v_i j_0 = o_x d_2$ denotes that truck v_i's first delivery job is to serve order o_x's second delivery. Figure 1 shows a typical schedule of a truck v_i. It has two jobs $v_i j_0$ and $v_i j_1$, with the first job further elaborated using our notation. Notably, once concrete is loaded in the truck, it must not take more than CPT (see Table 1), until it is fully unloaded at the OS.

Dynamism is due to the truck breakdowns, resulting delivery failures. Trucks can break at any time in a day (see Section 4.1).

2.3 Functional Requirements

Our goal for dynamic RMC problem is to serve maximum orders despite truck breakdowns during the day. However, every scheduling problem requires to be

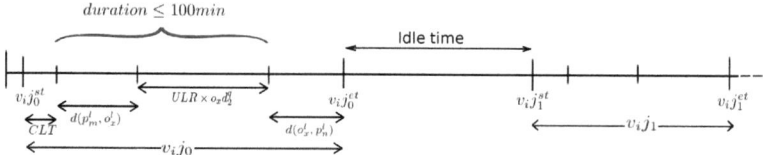

Fig. 1. Partial schedule of a truck v_i; two delivery jobs are defined

optimized for some objective function. The optimization objectives for our dynamic RMC problem are to minimize the objectives listed below. Weights are assigned in consultation with a concrete delivery company.

1. The per Order Start Time Delay; $w_l = 10$.
2. The per Order Wasted Concrete; $w_w = 10$.
3. The per Truck Traveling Time; $w_t = 20$.

Converting a multi-objective optimization into a scalarize optimization problem [2] results:

Objective function value = $\min \left(w_l \times (perOrderStartTimeDelay) + w_w \times (perOrder- WastedConcrete) + w_t \times (perTruckTravellingTime) \right)$
Implies that:

$$\text{Objective function value} = \min \left(\sum_{i=0}^{n} o_i^{st} w_l + \sum_{i=0}^{n} o_i^{wq} w_w + \sum_{k=0}^{m} v_k^{tt} w_t \right)$$

where n and m represents total number of orders and trucks respectively.

The main functional requirement for dynamic RMC is to produce a continually updating schedule of delivery trucks and not a static schedule. The schedule of each truck is a list of delivery jobs. An example of such schedule is shown in Figure 1.

3 Approach to Address the Dynamic RMC Problem

In this section, we explain details about simulation, agents and coordination between agents using Delegate MAS. In our simulation, the real life problem entities defined in the previous section are directly mapped to the agents. Time it takes for a truck to travel from one location to an other location is assumed constant. Internally, our agents are modelled as BDI agents [7]. We abstract the underlying communication infrastructure used by the agents.

In our simulation, the physical world is simulated with an environment, where different entities like OS, PS and truck are situated [15]. There are two types of agents; Order agent and Truck agent, residing on the problem entities $o_i \in O$ and $v_i \in V$. Trucks are mobile, they are driven by the Truck agents. For instance, a Truck agent can make its truck move to a PS and get loaded by concrete. There is no agent on a PS, but a PS can communicate and store information. Once appeared in simulation, OS and PS remain immobile.

Order Agent: An Order agent responsible for $o_i \in O$, ensures that all its desired quantity of concrete is served, without violating any hard constraints like exceeding CPT or LT (see Table 1). According to o_i^{st}, at t_0 Order agent announces the time at which it requires its first delivery. This announced time is called *interested time* as shown in Figure 2(a). If at t_1 after scheduling this delivery, still there is remaining concrete, it will announce next interested time. After each announcement of *interested time*, it waits for Truck agent proposals for making delivery. For the best proposal based on objective function (see Section 2.3), it replies with $SEEMS\_OK$ message, and $REJECT$ all other proposals. Since ants are sent periodically, the conversation matures. Further dialogue between Truck agent and Order agent is shown in Figure 2(b). Thus Order agent continues to schedule its deliveries until all the concrete is booked by Truck agents.

Truck Agent: In contrast, a Truck agent is responsible for constructing the schedule for its truck while taking into account the scalarized objective function (see Section 2.3). It explores the environment to search orders according to the truck's schedule. Once a suitable order is found, it sends a proposal to make delivery for the order. Such a proposal gets replied by the Order agent with a response of either $REJECT$ or $SEEMS\_OK$ (see Figure 2(b)).

Interaction via Delegate MAS: Agents coordinate using Delegate MAS via environment: Agents disseminate their information, and later collect the relevant information from the environment [8]. They delegate part of their responsibilities to the Delegate MAS component, which communicates with the environment using light weight agents called ants. Adhering to the patterns of Delegate MAS [9], we used two types of Delegate MASs: Exploration ants for collecting the relevant information from the environment and Intention ants for communicating decisions taken by the agents. Both Delegate MASs send ants periodically. We illustrate our coordination mechanism in three steps as below:

Step 1: Order agent sends messages to those PSs from which it can receive delivery without violating CPT limit (see Table 1). These messages contain information of *interested time* and travel distance to the PS. Consequently, each PS will have a list of Order agents with there interested times and travel distances maintained in a table called Order table.

Step 2: Truck agent uses Delegate MAS for exploring the environment for delivery jobs. It sends an exploration ant (ExpAnt) to a PS with an updated schedule of truck where it reads the Order table. For each entry in the Order table, ExpAnt verifies if the truck might be able to serve the delivery job towards that Order agent. For each verified Order agent, ExpAnt clones itself and moves towards it for further exploration. The ExpAnt enquires on reaching the Order agent, that if truck makes the delivery, is there any wasted concrete or lag time involved. Lag time is measured by the difference between proposed time and interested time, while for wasted concrete procedure at Figure 3(a) is used. ExpAnt then puts delivery job in truck's schedule and moves back to a randomly selected PS. The ExpAnt continues until specific number of delivery jobs are explored (see Table 2). At the end, the ExpAnt returns back to the Truck agent.

Step 3: When the exploration ants returns back to the Truck agent, a best ant is selected based on its explored job schedule using heuristic given in Figure 3(b). Truck agent then sends intention ants with the best ExpAnt's schedule to make the bookings at the PSs for loading and at Order agents for corresponding unloading of deliveries.

All these ants are periodically sent by agents. Specifically, intention ants, keeps on refreshing their Truck agent's bookings from $SEEMS\_OK$ to $WEAK\_ACCEPT$ and then to $STRONG\_ACCEPT$ as shown in Figure 2(b). MAS is allowed to converge with Truck agents making their schedules according to Order agent requirements.

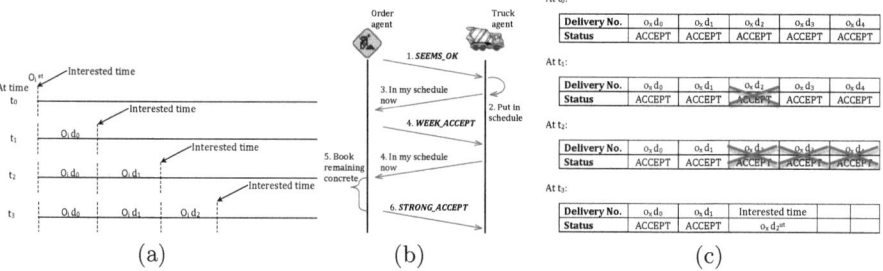

Fig. 2. (a)Change in *interestedtime* after booking of each delivery (b) An abstract view of coordination between Order agent and Truck agent. Delivery status evolves from $SEEMS\_OK$ to $STRONG\_ACCEPT$ in multiple steps (c) Change in order plan, when one of o_x's delivery o_xd_2 Failed at t_1. Order starts to re-plan all future deliveries after o_xd_2

Handling Dynamism: In case of a truck breakdown, the deliveries in its schedule are failed. Truck agent stops sending refresh intention ants. An Order agent detects this failure since its booking is not refreshed. It adjusts its current plan by announcing new *interested time* and sending delivery job $REJECT$ messages to other Truck agents if required. The Order agents may have all the deliveries booked or may be in the process of booking deliveries. As shown in Figure 2(c), due to failure of o_xd_2 at t_0, Order agent starts rebooking all the deliveries that appear after the failed delivery. It announces new interested time as $o_xd_2^{ut}$.

If an Order agent does not get all its concrete booked until ST_DELAY_LIMIT (Table 2), it changes its plan for o^{st}. Instead of starting at o^{st}, it starts order at $o^{st} + ST\_DELAYED\_BY\_PERIOD$. Whenever intention ants visit Order agent for refreshing the bookings related to previous plan, they are replied $REJECT$. On receiving $REJECT$, Truck agents remove the jobs from their schedules.

4 Simulation and Experiment Setup

Before stating evaluation of our communication mechanism, this section describes input, output and experiment setup. We simulated dynamic RMC problem using Rinsim [11] framework.

```
procedure GETWASTEDCONCRETE(truckCapacity, truckDeliveryTime)
    a = truckCapacity − truckDeliveryTime
    if a < 0 then
        wasted = 0
    else
        wasted = a
    end if
    return wasted
end procedure
```
(a)

```
del0Score(schedule)  = //score based on number of
                       first deliveries of orders
optiScore(schedule)  = //score based on optimization
                       objectives.
procedure COMPARE(schedule1, schedule2)
    a = truckCapacity − truckDeliveryTime
    if del0Score(schedule1) ≠ del0Score(schedule2) then
        return argmin(del0Score(schedule1), del0Score(schedule2))
    else
        return argmin(optiScore(schedule1), optiScore(schedule2))
    end if
end procedure
```
(b)

Fig. 3. (a) Order calculation of wasted concrete. (b) Heuristic for selecting Exploration ant with best schedule.

4.1 Input Instances

Our simulator is given input in the form of input instances. An input instance contains problem details mentioned in Section 2 except details about Order delivery and Truck schedule. These input instances are based on real life data taken from an RMC production company.

An input instance is defined as combination of three sets O, V and P, all situated in region of $50 \times 50 km^2$. For all input instances, there are always three PSs at fixed locations making P always fixed. Sets O and V vary for each input instance. The input is categorized in three dimensions to better understand its characteristics and get finer analysis of simulation output. These categories are:

Dynamism: For all input instances, we assume that 20% of total trucks may fail at random (using uniform distribution). Though orders also arrive dynamically, their effect is negligible since each order o_i is announced three hours before its o_i^{st}.

Scale: As the name indicates, Scale is used to give notion of problem size. We use a number of trucks to express Scale. If Scale is 20 then 20% dynamism means four of the trucks may fail during the day. Due to the failure, their delivery jobs are re-booked by corresponding Order agents. The variance in the number of orders for an input instance is captured by Stress.

Stress: It is the most complex and novel characteristic of an input instance. It is a theoretical measure based on average concrete a single truck can deliver in a day. Each truck may take approximately two hours to complete a delivery. Thus in a typical day of 16 hours, a maximum of 8 deliveries are possible to be served by a truck. For instance, a Scale of 6 means, 6 trucks have a potential to serve approximately 48 delivery jobs. But practically, due to time the constraints, it is seldom the case that trucks use their full potential. Stress of an input instance is calculated as follows:

$$Stress = \frac{Load}{Total number truck \times deliverable concrete per truck per second}$$
where $Load = \frac{Total Amount Of Concrete By All Orders}{Total Number Of Loaded Seconds Considering Unloading Rate}$

For example if an input instance I_1 has two orders with $o_1^{st} = 11:00, o_1^q = 20m^3$

and $o_2^{st} = 13:00, o_2^q = 10m^3$. Therefore,
$$I_1^{load} = 2.8 \ mm^3/sec$$
$$I_1^{Stress} \text{ considering 1 truck} = 2.0$$
$$I_1^{Stress} \text{ considering 2 trucks} = 1.0$$
Defining Stress help us to compare two input instances with different total concrete required but same number of available trucks. We are able to make statements like output is better for Stress = 0.9 but not for Stress = 1.2. For instance, if the Stress = 0.1, irrespective of the Scale, scheduling can be done manually. Typically the Stress of 1.0 puts a reasonable load on trucks.

Input Instance Generation: The input instance are generated using an input generator. The input generator selects a Scale, randomly picks number of orders and for each order randomly picks its quantity. Each order requires multiple deliveries ranging from 3 to 8. Then Stress is calculated based on formula mentioned above. In this way, hundreds of input instances are generated. If required, there is also an option in input generator to generate file of a specific Stress, Scale value.

4.2 Experiment Setup

In this section, we describe parameter settings and types of experiments that we conducted for evaluation.

There are several parameters related to our communication model that are used as input to the simulation (Table 2). The parameter values are tuned by exhaustive runs of simulation and by experience. Instead of generating a concrete schedule of trucks in a single shot, simulation runs continuously and manages schedules through out the day.

Table 2. Simulation parameters

Parameter name	Description	Selected Value
Exploration_limit	Number of deliveries, that an exploration ant is allowed to explore for its Truck agent	2 orders
Order_inform_interval	Periodic interval for informing *interested time* to orders	$100sec$
Exploration_Interval	Periodic interval for sending Exploration ants	$60sec$
Intention_Interval	Periodic interval for sending Intention ants	$100sec$
Intention_evaporation	Interval to evaporate intention when not refreshed by Truck agent	Intention Interval $+30sec$
ST_delay_limit	Time passed after which due to not booking all concrete, Order agent decides to delay start time	$30min$
ST_delay_by_ period	Time by which start time is delayed	$30min$

Table 3. Experiment Setup

Instance detail	No of instances	No of runs
Stress Experiment	For both Scale = 10 and 14, each Stress 10 instances	For each instance 20 runs
Scale Experiment	For both Stress = 0.8 and 1.0, each Scale 10 instances.	For each instance 20 runs

Two types of experiments are conducted for for evaluating our coordination mechanism. For both experiments, dynamism is fixed to 20%. In **Stress experiment**, we investigate performance of our coordination mechanism while varying the amount of Stress. For **Scale experiment**, we investigate if the coordination mechanism scales well with varying problem sizes. Figure 4 shows results for our experiments. Table 3 shows our experiment set up where for each of the 20 runs, different random seeds are used.

5 Evaluation

In this section we present evaluation for our coordination mechanism. Two metrics are used for evaluation:
1) **Percentage Delivered concrete:** It expresses percentage of concrete that is delivered by trucks from total concrete ordered by all orders.

$$\%ageOfDeliveredConcrete = \frac{concretedDeliveredByTrucks - wastedConcrete}{totalConcreteOrderedByOrders}$$

2) **Optimization function value:** Although its not our objective to optimize, rather we wanted to deal with maximum orders served, yet this metric helps us investigate if the same sized input instances optimize differently when Stress is varied. The value is calculated using formula given in Section 2.3

Results and Discussion

Figure 4 shows results of evaluation. Each dot in a figure means an average of 10 input instances, with each input instance run 20 times taking variable random seeds.

In Figure 4(a) the evaluation metric are plotted for two different problem sizes to analyse impact of increasing Stress. We notice that as Stress increases, performances starts decreasing. In more stressful scenario's, due to dynamism and time constraints, it is expected that lesser amount of concrete would be successfully delivered. Figure 4(b) shows that before Stress reaches near 0.9, objective function value is increasing, indicating additional orders are served. After Stress 0.9, it stabilizes, since what ever orders are added, trucks are no more able to serve them.

For the two problem sizes, we observed that Delegate MAS shows consistent performance. Overall similar percentage of concrete is delivered for both problem scales. The consistence with increase in Scale is more obvious in Figure 4(c). Here Scale is ranging from 6 to 18, yet agents are able to deliver nearly 90% of concrete at Stress 0.8 and approximately 80% of concrete for Stress 1.0. Figure 4(d) is actually not an evaluation, rather it shows demand and supply of concrete during a typical day. The red line shows demand at each hour of the day, while blue shows supply. By the end of the day it appears that supply is more than demand, this is due to unavoidable wasted concrete delivered by trucks. Figure 4(e) shows screen shot of a very trivial scenario. We note that, despite with Delegate MAS the individual agent decisions seemed selfish, when observed globally didn't emerged selfish any more.

6 Related Work

We position our work from two perspectives: 1) Ant based coordination in MAS, due to their relevance with Delegate MAS. 2) Other approaches that address RMC problem are discussed.

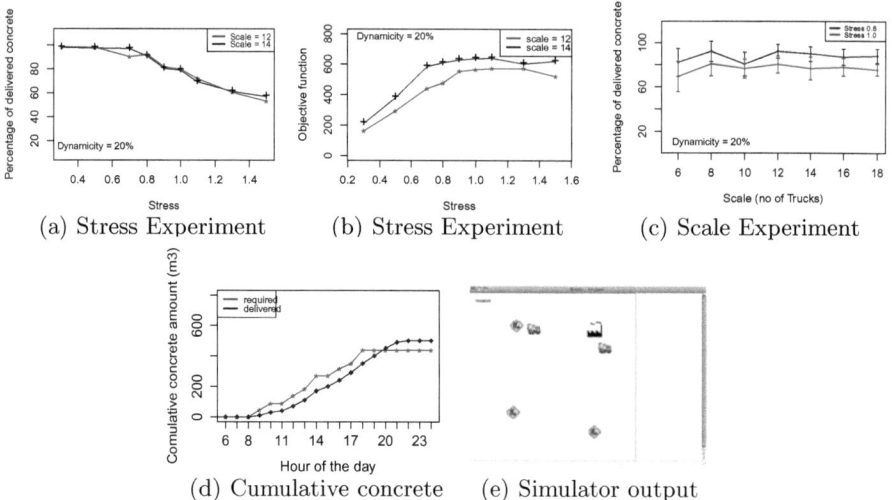

Fig. 4. (a), (b) As Stress increases, lesser orders are served. (c) As Scale increases, performance is consistent. (d) Supply and demand of concrete during the day, (e) Screen shot of simulator showing a production site, two trucks serving 3 of the orders.

6.1 Ant Based Coordination Mechanisms

In recent decade, there has been considerable research interests in using decentralized mechanisms inspired by stigmergy and swarm intelligence. In several application domains, emergent properties are achieved by such mechanisms. These include intrusion detection in computer networks [4], manufacturing control [10] and unmanned vehicle coordination [14]. In our Delegate MAS approach, the intention ants resemble these stigmergic mechanisms, since ants drop intentions, which if not refreshed, evaporate with the passage of time. Exploration ants are however different and are more related to smart messages, with explicit behaviour and state [9]. Since our implementation of Delegate MAS is according to [9], where task of coordination with environment is delegated to a component within an agent, we consider it rather unique as compared to other stigmergic approaches. Our ants are also similar to poly-agents used by Parunak [13].

6.2 RMC Problem

Research presented for RMC problem mostly uses combinatorial optimization techniques [1]. There are some efforts that use stochastic models [17] or genetic algorithms [12] as well. These mechanisms attempt to solve RMC problem by generating static output, where as we solve the dynamic RMC problem. To the best of our knowledge, the only work that addresses partially dynamic RMC is by Hoffman and Durbin [6]. They have a planner component that plans for already known information and a runtime component that can handle dynamic events. We address dynamic RMC without any static components, and can cope with truck break downs during the day.

7 Conclusion

In this paper we presented our experience of using Delegate MAS with very constrained and complex scheduling problem. We used dynamic RMC problem as a case study. Using Delegate MAS as a coordination mechanism, when any of the Stress or Scale is increased, we notice a consistent performance in terms of total concrete delivered and optimization objective. We found that apparently self centred local decisions emerge to the globally significant behaviour.

In future, we plan to add coalitions on top of the Delegate MAS. We also have plans to use an opportunity of substituting a simple heuristic with some advance decision mechanism.

References

1. Asbach, L., Dorndorf, U., Pesch, E.: Analysis, modeling and solution of the concrete delivery problem. European Journal of Operational Research 193(3), 820–835 (2009)
2. Collette, Y., Siarry, P.: Multiobjective optimization: principles and case studies. Springer (2003)
3. Fischer, K., Müller, J.P., Pischel, M.: Cooperative transportation scheduling: an application domain for dai. Applied Artificial Intelligence 10(1), 1–34 (1996)
4. Foukia, N.: IDReAM: Intrusion detection and response executed with agent mobility. In: Brueckner, S.A., Di Marzo Serugendo, G., Karageorgos, A., Nagpal, R. (eds.) ESOA 2005. LNCS (LNAI), vol. 3464, pp. 227–239. Springer, Heidelberg (2005)
5. Hanif, S., van Lon, R.R.S., Gui, N., Holvoet, T.: Delegate MAS for large scale and dynamic PDP: A case study. In: Brazier, F.M.T., Nieuwenhuis, K., Pavlin, G., Warnier, M., Badica, C. (eds.) Intelligent Distributed Computing V. SCI, vol. 382, pp. 23–33. Springer, Heidelberg (2011)
6. Hoffman, K., Durbin, M.: The dance of the thirty ton trucks. Operations Research 56(1), 3–19 (2008)
7. Holvoet, T., Valckenaers, P.: Beliefs, desires and intentions through the environment. In: Proceedings of the Fifth International Joint Conference on Autonomous Agents and Multiagent Systems, pp. 1052–1054. ACM (2006)
8. Holvoet, T., Valckenaers, P.: Exploiting the environment for coordinating agent intentions. In: Weyns, D., Van Dyke Parunak, H., Michel, F. (eds.) E4MAS 2006. LNCS (LNAI), vol. 4389, pp. 51–66. Springer, Heidelberg (2007)
9. Holvoet, T., Weyns, D., Valckenaers, P.: Patterns of Delegate MAS. In: Third IEEE International Conference on Self-Adaptive and Self-Organizing Systems, SASO 2009, pp. 1–9. IEEE (2009)
10. Karuna, H., Valckenaers, P., Saint-Germain, B., Verstraete, P., Zamfirescu, C.B., Van Brussel, H.H.: Emergent forecasting using a stigmergy approach in manufacturing coordination and control. In: Brueckner, S.A., Di Marzo Serugendo, G., Karageorgos, A., Nagpal, R. (eds.) ESOA 2005. LNCS (LNAI), vol. 3464, pp. 210–226. Springer, Heidelberg (2005)
11. van Lon, R.R.S., Holvoet, T.: Rinsim: a simulator for collective adaptive systems in transportation and logistics. In: 2012 IEEE Sixth International Conference on Self-Adaptive and Self-Organizing Systems (SASO), pp. 231–232. IEEE (2012)

12. Naso, D., Surico, M., Turchiano, B., Kaymak, U.: Genetic algorithms for supply-chain scheduling: A case study in the distribution of ready-mixed concrete. European Journal of Operational Research 177(3), 2069–2099 (2007)
13. Van Dyke Parunak, H., Brueckner, S.A., Weyns, D., Holvoet, T., Verstraete, P., Valckenaers, P.: E pluribus unum: Polyagent and delegate MAS architectures. In: Antunes, L., Paolucci, M., Norling, E. (eds.) MABS 2007. LNCS (LNAI), vol. 5003, pp. 36–51. Springer, Heidelberg (2008)
14. Van Dyke Parunak, H., Brueckner, S., Sauter, J.: Digital pheromone mechanisms for coordination of unmanned vehicles. In: Proceedings of the First International Joint Conference on Autonomous Agents and Multiagent Systems: Part 1, pp. 449–450. ACM (2002)
15. Weyns, D., Holvoet, T.: A reference architecture for situated multiagent systems. In: Weyns, D., Van Dyke Parunak, H., Michel, F. (eds.) E4MAS 2006. LNCS (LNAI), vol. 4389, pp. 1–40. Springer, Heidelberg (2007)
16. Weyns, D., Holvoet, T., Helleboogh, A.: Anticipatory vehicle routing using delegate multi-agent systems. In: IEEE Intelligent Transportation Systems Conference, ITSC 2007, pp. 87–93. IEEE (2007)
17. Yan, S., Lin, H.C., Jiang, X.Y.: A planning model with a solution algorithm for ready mixed concrete production and truck dispatching under stochastic travel times. Engineering Optimization 44(4), 427–447 (2012)
18. Yan, S., Lai, W., Chen, M.: Production scheduling and truck dispatching of ready mixed concrete. Transportation Research Part E: Logistics and Transportation Review 44(1), 164–179 (2008)

Handling Safety-Related Non-Functional Requirements in Embedded Multi-Agent System Design

Jean-Paul Jamont, Clément Raievsky, and Michel Occello

Université de Grenoble Alpes, Laboratoire LCIS, Valence, France
firstname.lastname@lcis.grenoble-inp.fr

Abstract. Appropriate handling of safety-related non-functional requirements is crucial in the deployment of embedded multi-agent systems. In order to capture these requirements, a dedicated activity has been added to the DIAMOND multi-agent design methodology. The purpose of this paper is to present how safety-related requirements are identified during this activity and how they can be integrated in the resulting multi-agent system. We illustrate our approach with an industrial collective robotics application.

Keywords: non-functional requirements, agent oriented software engineering, embedded systems.

1 Introduction

Rising availabilities of low cost wireless communication devices and battery performances improvement makes it possible to build embedded computing systems as composed sets of autonomous operating units. Besides measuring and actuation tasks, most aspects of control and decision-making are becoming decentralized. Integration of hardware concerns remains a key problem in the deployment of multi-agent systems (MAS) in industrial contexts [1]. Another crucial issue of such systems is their dependability, which refers to both their availability and their safety. Indeed, regarding availability, downtime following a failure have to be avoided. Regarding safety, it is necessary to guarantee the absence of danger for people and assets. Dependability must be analyzed according to risk analysis criteria (probability of occurrence, severity) and regulations criteria (standards).

These considerations apply to the numerous areas of application of embedded MAS (eMAS) like collective robotics. When these robots share their environment with human operators, safety is a crucial concern, enforced by law. MAS contributions also appear in daily environment managing applications such as indoor building comfort control or air quality system management. In all these domains, safety is expressed as a set of non-functional constraints which must be taken into consideration at all the levels of MAS design.

The DIAMOND method [2] is dedicated to the design and implementation of embedded MAS. This paper discusses its activity which involves MAS safety related non-functional requirements (NFR) identification and their integration into agents. This activity highlights the specific operating modes of eMAS such as calibration of sensors and actuators of agents' or other (not autonomous) devices.

In Section 2, we present the context of our contribution. We pay attention to work focusing on taking NFR in MAS into account. In Section 3, we present the DIAMOND activity which enables non-functional constraints handling from the point of view of the group of agents. A use case of collective robotics in a manufacturing context is presented in Section 4 to illustrate the details of this activity. Before concluding, we discuss the integration of these requirements into agents at an individual level (Section 5).

2 Context

The main specificity of embedded systems in the MAS context is the importance of physical deployment. Therefore designing embedded MASs requires to deal with NFR related to deployment. These requirements include safety concerns and must be included in all the design and implementation phases of a eMAS development process.

Addressing NFR and how design processes can be driven by these abstract requirements is very recent. These considerations are starting to be included in the latest extensions of some of the leading multi-agent methodologies (e.g. [3] with O-Mase or [4] with RE-Gaia). Tropos [5] enable to build a system model that is incrementally refined where NFR are seen as softgoals (an objective without clear-cut criteria). An analysis [6] shows that ADELFE [7] takes into account some NFR in its third activity regarding storage of large data volumes, capacities of human-machine interaction, and system availability under the form of prerequisites. They even consider some running constraints such as distribution or multi-task capabilities.

As embedded systems are closely related to physical systems, their action may be harmful to their environment or people. Leveson [8] states that accidents involving complex systems are caused by misinterpreted or incorrectly carried out interactions between humans and machines. Risks and hazards must thus be considered both in the design and running phase of eMAS. However, the safety problem is rarely addressed. Some work focus on security, such as the inviolability of systems [5], but these approaches do not address physical applications nor user safety. Ensuring safety in MAS is therefore an interesting question which leads us to distinguish a global level regarding requirement specifications for the whole system on one hand, and a local level concerning how these requirements will be implemented in the decentralized systems at the design level on the other hand. Indeed, some studies about hazard in complex systems [9] claim that the approach must use a risk-based, whole-system model but that the analysis can be achieved only by evaluating exposure to risk, either suffered by or caused by, each entity in the system.

Classical industrial techniques have been applied to the MAS domain: for example the failure modes and effects analysis (FMEA) is a qualitative hazard identification that uses past experience to identify potential failure modes, study the effects of these failures, and how they can affect users. [10] proposed an agent structure to ensure safety management in a MAS by means of faulty diagnosis diagram thus trying to address limitations of FMEA in complex distributed systems. Influenced by FMEA, [11] proposes an interesting language to express self-management aspects that leads to self-protection and self-configuration aspects. [12] presents safety as a quality attribute for a MAS and proposes to improve a multi-agent methodology using Hazard and Operability (HAZOP) studies. The HAZOP approach is a systematic procedure aimed at determining the causes and consequences of deviations from normal behavior. Several industrial applications using MAS have involved some HAZOP rules [13,14].

3 Non-Functional Requirements Capture

This section describes our approach which consists in proposing an easy to use graphical tool to enable the identification of the non-functional requirements allowing to mainly guarantee the absence of danger for people and assets.

Positioning the Activity in the DIAMOND Methodology. The DIAMOND multi-agent design approach uses five main stages arranged in a spiral-shaped life cycle. In the *requirement analysis* stage, the analyst defines what the user needs and characterizes global functionalities. It begins with the analysis of the system's physical context (e.g. identifying work flows and main tasks). Then, the different actors and their participative use cases (using UML use case diagrams) are identified and the service needs of these actors are specified (using UML sequence diagram).

As already stressed out, working with physical systems forces the designer to not only specify the way the system will run autonomously in normal conditions but also to identify the desired behaviour in many special circumstances, directly related to the embedded aspect of the system: Which state must the system be in when going under maintenance? How to calibrate the system components? In which state must all components be when an emergency stop occurs (e.g. a robot enter a forbidden area)? The *particular mode analysis* activity[1] is dedicated to answer these questions by taking the embedded context into account and structuring the global operation of the system. This activity requires to ask design-oriented questions at the beginning of the project. It thus decreases the number of iterations in the analysis phase by including potential human interventions in general requirements as soon as possible.

This activity allows the designer to take the physical safety of users into account according to sixteen different dynamical defined states, called procedures, grouped into three categories (see Figure 1).

---

[1] This activity is strongly inspired by the GEMMA Guide [15]. It is a methodology used by automation engineers to coordinate GRAFCETs (a particular type of FSM) in the context of programmable logic controller centralized systems.

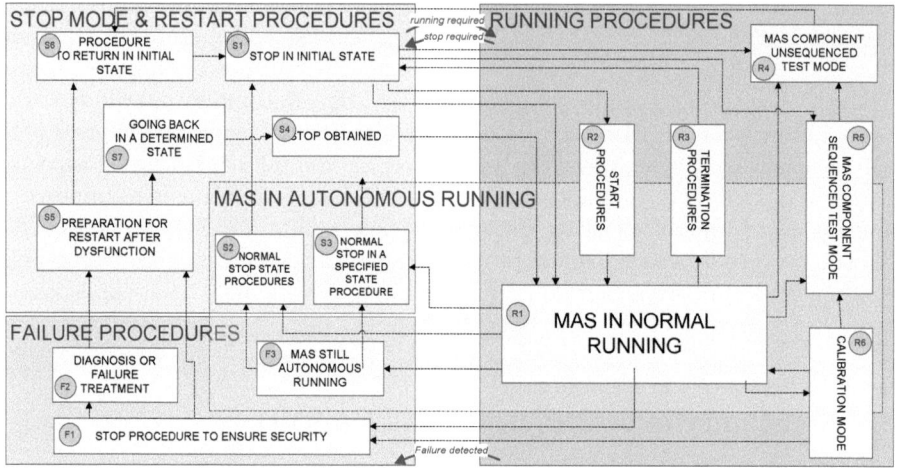

Fig. 1. Particular mode study in DIAMOND

The *running procedures* (see Table 1) focus on defining the states during which the system is autonomously operating toward satisfying or to being able to satisfy its functional requirements. The *stop procedures* are related to the different procedures to stop the MAS because of external reasons (such as missing raw material in the case of manufacturing control). The *failure procedures* regroup safety procedures (e.g. allowing a maintenance team to work on the system) or specific rules enforcing restricted running modes.

Using this tool may seem to guide the designer toward a centralized resolution of the problem. However this tool is used at a preliminary stage. The detection of transition conditions between states may be distributed and each procedure can be a decentralized decision process. The autonomy of the MAS is not strictly linked to the categories. In each of the three categories, some procedures are carried out autonomously while the others are executed by external operators.

Activity Running. Figure 1 shows the guide provided to assist the designer in identifying the different operating modes at the MAS global scale and to capture non-functional requirements. This guide is a kind of checklist to ensure that the designer has not forgotten to bring its attention to a MAS particular modes. Similarly to GEMMA, each procedure is characterized by (1) the symbolic name that specifies the mode family (Si, Ri, Fi), respectively (Stop, Run, Failure) and (2) the name of the procedure, e.g. "MAS sequenced test mode" is associated with the procedure $R5$.

The *running modes* (Table 1) are the procedures during which the MAS operates autonomously to meet functional requirements. These procedures include calibration and adjustment of the system. They specify in particular MAS cold starts (all hardware and software components of the MAS were switched off and must therefore be initialized) and MAS hot starts (some MAS components had lost their status due to a failure or an error (e.g. power supply problem) and must be re-initialized).

Table 1. Description of running procedures (R), stop and restart procedures (S) and failure procedures (F)

State	Description
R1	*Nnormal running:* MAS is running in normal conditions, agents are autonomous.
R2	*Start up procedures:* Initialization proc. which are prerequisites of normal running modes.
R3	*Termination procedures:* Groups operations required before shutting down the MAS.
R4	*MAS unsequenced test mode:* Running modes that put some agents in a state that allows an operator to check them.
R5	*MAS sequenced test mode:* Procedures that put some agents in a semi-autonomous mode, allowing an operator to carry out more complex, potentially automatic, tests on them. Agents can still make use of their coordination capabilities.
R6	*MAS components calibration mode:* Calibration procedures for sensors and actuators.
S1	*Initial stop state:* Agents are powered on but their autonomous behavior is not activated.
S2	*Normal stop requested:* MAS has been asked to stop. It is responsible for putting itself in an appropriate state.
S3	*Specific stop state requested:* The MAS has been asked to stop in a specific and identifiable state. As long as this state is not reached, the MAS continues its autonomous execution.
S4	*Obtained stop:* The MAS is stopped, in a specific, identified state. It is possible to cleanly restart the MAS from this state.
S5	*Recovery:* All manual operations required by a restart are carried out.
S6	*MAS reset to initial state:* During this state we can manually control components of the MAS to set it into the initial stop state.
S7	*Specific state requested:* In this state, the MAS is manually or automatically set back into a state from which it can resume autonomous operation.
F1	*Safety-related procedures:* refers to specific actions which have to be taken in emergency situations. It includes stops, but also commands to limit the consequences of the failure.
F2	*Trouble shooting and repair procedures:* allows an operator to check the MAS after a failure and to take the required actions before being able to restart the MAS.
F3	*MAS still in autonomous running:* Under certain circumstances, it is necessary to keep a partially autonomous behavior while restricting its behavior. Some components of the MAS can be stopped or replaced.

The stopping and suspending procedures (Table 1) capture operation required to put the MAS in a suspended state or to switch it off. These are required procedures since a MAS cannot run indefinitely. As in traditional embedded systems, we distinguish fencing and safety-related interruptions. Fencing refers to normal stopping conditions. (e.g. the MAS working session is completed, MAS operation is temporarily interrupted by an operator with authority). Safety-related interruptions are, for example, triggered by human operators using a punch button (emergency stop), by sensors (e.g. an ultrasonic barrier detecting someone entering a dangerous area), or virtual sensors (e.g. a monitoring process evaluates the reaction time of an operator as incorrect or reject a given instruction as suspicious). Of course, safety-related suspension of operation have always the highest priority and are the subject of many European standards (e.g. EN292, EN418) and international standards (e.g. ISO 10218, ISO 11161, ISO 13855).

Failure modes (Table 1) allow the designer to specify the safety procedures associated with a failure or incident. For example, when a failure occurs, it must be signaled (e.g. visual and/or aural alarm). Since all failures are not predictable, the MAS will need to adapt and try to recover from them and, in critical cases, operators will have to trigger failure procedure.

Using Paths to Design a MAS. The graph of Figure 1 can be used as a checklist to ensure that no important class of procedure has been left out. The life cycle of the MAS running can be characterized by identifying some predefined loops in this study guide. This kind of paths may also be used at runtime, by the MAS itself, to evaluate the current situation as usual or not. As an instance, the loop S1 → R1 → S2 → S1 is the normal running cycle of the MAS. In the beginning, the MAS is stopped. Then an operator with authority requests the MAS to operate autonomously to meet functional requirements. When the work session is completed, it informs the MAS that it must stop. Finally the MAS returns to its initial normal state.

4 Illustration

In this section, we first briefly present a case study that involves robotized manufacturing control. We then illustrate the operation of collecting non-functional requirements in this context.

Problem Description. We are interested in the coordination and control of the internal logistics of a manufacturing department (Figure 2). This description comes from [16]. Finished parts have to be delivered at a given due date for assembly in another department. Parts are transported in containers by two robots. Typically, a container holds about 10 parts, but this may vary. The system comprises a grid of container storage spaces, distributed across the manufacturing department. The system also comprises 8 workstations with varying properties and capabilities. Workstations have two or three locations at which a container can be placed. An operator picks parts out of one container, processes them in a pipelined fashion on the machines in his/her workstation, and places processed parts in another container at her/his workstation. Robots, moving over rails, normally transport the containers. They can carry two containers almost in the same time at any given time. In addition, carts handled by human operators can also transport parts (without the container), which also is how the parts travel to the assembly department when they are finished.

We consider the following multi-agent solution that (1) gives manufacturing orders to workstations, (2) assigns operators to workstations depending on their qualification, (3) controls both robots that carry containers between workstations in the same workshop and from a workshop to another and (4) does not control machines/tools at workstations. The *production line* includes the MAS and the workstations.

Capture of Non-Functional Requirements. We are interested here to identify different type of NFR like the safety, the availability and the recoverability. Here are some running modes that can be defined:
- RUNNING: The MAS is operating autonomously (R1).
- START: The workshop supervisor starts the production line by selecting the "n" position (b_{on}) putting the system in the R2 state. In this state the first robot ($r1$) is going in front of the workstation 1 ($w1$), a condition noted $r1@w1$.

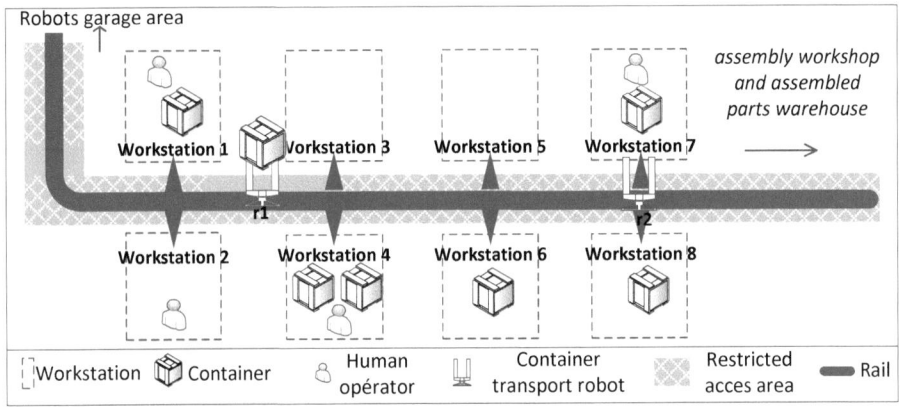

Fig. 2. Illustration of the study case

The second robot is going to workstation 7 (trying to make $r2@w7$ true). Once robots are in place, maintenance operators make a visual check of them. The production then starts when the workshop supervisor presses a dedicated push button (b_{scy}).

• CLOSE: When the workday is over, the workshop supervisor press on the push button (b_{scy}). Normal operation of the production line will stop: the robots must return to their docking stations (MAS is in the transient state S2 as long as the condition $r1@d1.r2@d2$ is not verified). Meanwhile, maintenance operators clean machines/tools on each workstation. When a workstation is clean, the operator presses the pulse button $b_{net}(i)$ with i the workstation identifier. System "production line" is switched off (MAS in $S1$) when the workshop supervisor set the global control switch to "off" ($/b_{on}$).

• MAINTENANCE: Using the *RobotCtrl* software, created by the team that implemented the MAS, the maintenance team monitors agents state while they are running autonomously (software use case denoted *AutoRobots*). They observe in particular the state of the effectors and sensors. When they detect a failure, they put the system in the "MAS component sequenced test" mode (R5) and replay collaborative tasks such as transferring a container from one robot to another to locate the problem. This running mode include the calibration operation that the maintenance team will have to carry out, ideally outside of production hours but sometimes while production is active. Examples of devices that can be calibrated are (1) encoders that compute distance traveled by robots from the number of rotations of the wheel motors and (2) the pressure of the pneumatic cylinders that catch containers to avoid damaging them. This mode allows the maintenance team to diagnose, debug, and test the MAS and is therefore an important tool to support the collaboration between the maintenance operators and the MAS development team.

- SAFETY: The system must stop, regardless of the state of the MAS, as soon as a human operator enters in the working area of the robots. This situation is detected when (1) one of the workstation emergency stop buttons is on ($b_{ES}(i)$ with i the workstation identifier), (2) the workshop supervisor emergency stop button is on ($b_{ES}(0)$) or (3) the ultrasonic barrier is crossed d_{ult}. After having detected such a situation, the MAS is in state E1. The safety/quality manager comes in the workshop and makes a statement of the problem that caused the emergency stop decision. Procedures may be subsequently revised to take those situations into account. The maintenance team is responsible for restoring the system to its initial correct state. After these operations, the workshop supervisor presses the button b_{scy}. Causing the robot agents to check their own integrity (MAS in state S5). When a system restart is requested (by pressing again b_{scy}), agents go back to the last correct state stored before the emergency stop (MAS in state S7). When operations associated with this state are completed, the MAS switches to state S4. Pressing b_{scy} will allow the MAS to resume its autonomous running.

The synthesis of this capture is shown in Figure 3. Devices that give safety-related information to the MAS and which allow it to detect transitions can external to the MAS. s_{on} is the main production line switch. It allows an operator to switch the MAS on (s_{on}) or off ($/s_{on}$). b_{scy} is a pulse button used to indicate the beginning of a cycle. $b_{ES}(i)$ are mushroom buttons with key release ($i = 0$: emergency stop general button, $i \in [1,8]$: workstations emergency stop buttons). $b_{net}(i)$ are pulse button which enable an operator to report that workstation i has been cleaned. d_{ult} is the ultrasonic barrier. Event d_{ult} is triggered when an object crosses the ultrasonic barrier.

5 Integrating Non-Functional Requirements into Agents

The integration of non-functional requirements in agents' individual behaviours has two aspects. On one hand agents' behaviour must ensure that the identified NFR are satisfied using the perceptions of the agents. On the other hand, the detection of an abnormal situation by an agent must be shared with the other agents to make a collective response possible.

Integrating Non-Functionnal Requirements into the Individual Behaviours. The different states in Figure 3 capture the different contexts in which the agents will be running. These states do not need to be explicitly represented within the agents' decision-making process. However the designer have to give the agents means to detect transitions in their running context and to change their behavior accordingly. One of the purposes of the presented activity is to ensure that no state that can be anticipated will be left out when designing agents' behaviours. One way to ensure that, is to associate a behaviour to each identified state. Some agents may not be concerned/sensitive to a particular context but all agents must take into account the safety procedures.

Handling Safety-Related NFR in Embedded Multi-Agent System Design 167

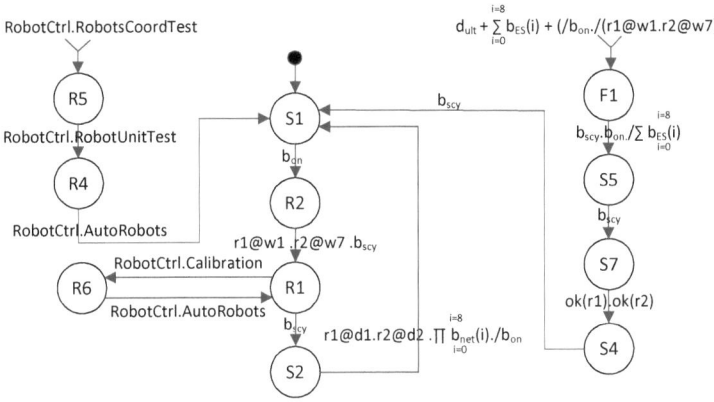

Fig. 3. Synthesis of requirements capture

Table 2 shows the behavior to adopt according to the context (the mode) for the previously presented case study. In our simplified use cases, we focus on robot agents.

Table 2. Behavioral changes related to context grouped by type of mode

Mode	Associated behavior
R1	Behavior meets the functional requirements
R2	Robot r1 goes to docking station d1 and robot r2 goes to docking station d2.
R4	Robots wait for commands from an operator. They perform tasks requested via their communication interfaces.
R5	Robots complete their tasks and save their operational contexts. The operator imposes goals to the agents. They execute a plan to accomplish this goal. Before leaving this state they restore their contexts.
R6	The robot agent which must be calibrated completes its task, saves its operational context and thenadopts the same behavior that in R4 (but parameters values have changed).
F1	The operational context is not stored. Robot agents stay still and maintain their actuators in position. The robot has a battery dedicated to this. Indeed, it is important to keep the manipulated containers in place (in case of a fall, content can be deteriorated, operators may be injured).
S1	Robots are in "energy saving" mode.
S2	Robot agent r1 goes to docking station d1 and robot r2 goes to docking station d2.
S4	Robots wait for the order to start their functional autonomous running behavior.
S5	The concerned robot agent completes its task and saves its operational context. It then performs local tests. As long as a problem persists, it remains in this state. When its tests pass, it is ready to switch to another state.
S7	Agents are restoring the last stable saved state.

Once influence of contexts on agents' behaviours has been defined, the designer should specify how the context is perceived by agents, e.g. local perceptions from their own sensors, information exchanged via a communication interface, individually established reasoning. The main constraint on this specification is that each transition impacting the behavior of an agent must be completely expressed from its own representation of the world.

A way to integrate the requirements in the agents decision process consists in defining different behaviors for the different modes. These behaviors are then switched according to the local perceptions. In our method, behavior of agents is built by integrating (1) the individual behavior of agents, (2) the social behavior that allows the agents to find in the group the missing information/skills to achieve a goal and (3) the constraints coming from non-functional requirements (which have potentially not been included yet in the definition of the first two points).

For each identified integration problem (e.g. incompatibility of individual behavior and social behavior, behavior which violates a strong non-functional requirement), we should change the behavior to meet the requirements.

Generating and Sharing an Alertness State. It is often not possible, and even not desirable, that all agents involved in the control of a distributed system have access to all available information. However it is of tremendous importance that the group of agent is able to react collectively to a situation that threaten the NFR. To give this ability to a system, we propose a mechanism inspired by the ones at work in collective emotions. Emotion plays a significant role in collective behaviours [17] and ensure short-term and long-term group cohesion [18] [19].

To address the problem of NFR integration in the collective behaviour, we propose to add an implicit and shared state of *alertness* to the system.

The three main problems to tackle when trying to give collective emotions to a MAS are: 1) How to generate an emotional state in each agent, individually? 2) How to propagate this emotional state through the group? 3) How emotion-related information from other agents will modify agents' behaviour?

In a nutshell, human emotion starts by an increase in the arousal of the person. This arousal then triggers simultaneously an hedonistic evaluation (appraisal) of the situation and an increase in the person's readiness [20]. The situation appraisal confirms or refutes that the situation is abnormal and refines the emotional response. The emotional state resulting from this process modifies the way the world is perceived, how the next actions are carried out, and sometimes initiates dedicated behaviours.

As the alertness state we propose is only related to NFR, its generation is based on the satisfaction or not of these requirements. Therefore, when the current situation fails to meet the identified NFR, an alertness episode is elicited.

Sharing this state between agents is carried out by broadcasting signals. These signals do not carry any information, their presence or absence is the only information monitored by agents. This characteristic decreases the sensibility of the state sharing to communication failures and make it possible to use low bandwidth communication channels, resistant to industrial environments. Propagation of the alertness signal allows agents that have not directly perceived an occurring abnormal situation to prepare by modifying their behaviour.

The influence of alertness messages on an agent's alertness depends upon the frequency and duration of the alertness signals reception. As long as the reception frequency of alertness signals f_s is higher than a threshold S_f, that is to say as long as the agent receives information indicating that an abnormal situation is occurring, its alertness n increases linearly. As soon as the reception frequency is lower than the threshold S_f, its alertness decreases according to the function introduced by [21] about emotional variables evolution. Alertness of an agent is thus expressed by equation 1:

$$n(t) = \begin{cases} n(t_0) + \alpha \cdot (t - t_0) & \text{if } f_s(t) > S_f \\ n(t_1) \cdot e^{-\beta \cdot (t-t_1)} & \text{else} \end{cases} \quad (1)$$

where α and β are linear increasing and decreasing factors, respectively. t_0 is the time at which $f_s(t)$ has become greater than S_f and t_1 is the time at which $f_s(t)$ has become lower than S_f.

To address the third question, the alertness of an agent can influence the way it perceives and/or acts on its environment. An agent can modify the way it perceives its environment by modifying raw data pre-processing, increasing the priority of these processing, or an increasing of the sampling frequency of raw data. The adaptation of the agent's behaviour can be achieved by modulating parameters or initiating new ones according to its alertness.

It is possible to modify the alertness state of an agent by monitoring the recurrence of identified paths (end of Section 3) in the global state of the MAS at an inadequate frequency.

6 Conclusion

This article described a design activity that was added to the DIAMOND methodology to take into account the non-functional requirements related to the safety of embedded MASs. This activity gives designers a framework dedicated to the analysis of eMASs behaviour and especially to the safety-related aspects of their physical deployment. We also presented a graphical synthesis of the various running modes of an eMAS that can be used to check that no required operating mode has been left out during the analysis. Furthermore, this graphical tool allows designers to identify standard and abnormal paths going through different operating modes. Integrating such an activity in a methodology permit to take safety-related concerns into account all through the design process and, therefore, to deploy MASs in the real world more serenely.

We are working on the formalization of our activity using SPEM (Software and System Process Engineering Metamodel).

References

1. Pechoucek, M., Mark, V.: Industrial deployment of multi-agent technologies: review and case studies. Autonomous Agents and Multi-Agent Systems 17, 397–431 (2008)
2. Jamont, J.-P., Occello, M.: Designing embedded collective systems: The diamond multiagent method. In: 19th IEEE Int. Conf. on Tools with AI, vol. 2. IEEE (2007)
3. Harmon, S.J., DeLoach, S.A., Robby: Abstract requirement analysis in multiagent system design. In: Proc. of the IEEE/WIC/ACM Int. Conf. on Intelligent Agent Technology, pp. 86–91. IEEE (2009)

4. Blanes, D., Insfran, E., Abrahão, S.: Re4gaia: A requirements modeling approach for the development of multi-agent systems. In: Ślęzak, D., Kim, T.-H., Kiumi, A., Jiang, T., Verner, J., Abrahão, S. (eds.) ASEA 2009. CCIS, vol. 59, pp. 245–252. Springer, Heidelberg (2009)
5. Bresciani, P., Perini, A., Giorgini, P., Giunchiglia, F., Mylopoulos, J.: Tropos: An agent-oriented software development methodology. JAAMAS 8(3), 203–236 (2004)
6. Werneck, V., Kano, A.Y., Cysneiros, L.M.: Evaluating adelfe methodology in the requirements identification. In: 10th Work. in Requirements Engineering (2007)
7. Picard, G., Gleizes, M.P.: The adelfe methodology - designing adaptive cooperative multi-agent systems. In: Methodologies and Software Engineering for Agent Systems: The AOSE Handbook, ch. 8, pp. 157–176. Kluwer Publishing (2004)
8. Leveson, N.G.: A new accident model for engineering safer systems. Safety Science 42(4), 237–270 (2004)
9. Alexander, R., Alexander-Bown, R., Kelly, T.: Engineering safety-critical complex systems. In: Proceedings of the 1st CoSMoS Workshop (September 2008)
10. Ebrahimipour, V., Rezaie, K., Shokravi, S.: Enhanced fmea by multi-agent engineering fipa based system to analyze failures. In: Proc. of Reliability and Maintainability Symposium (RAMS) 2010, pp. 1–6 (January 2010)
11. Rodriguez-Fernández, C., Gómez-Sanz, J.J.: Self-management capability requirements with selfmml & ingenias to attain self-organising behaviours. In: Proc. of the 2nd Int. Workshop on Self-organizing Architectures, pp. 11–20. ACM (2010)
12. Sterling, L., Taveter, K.: The Art of Agent-Oriented Modelling. MIT Press (2009)
13. Lakner, R., Nemeth, E., Hangos, K.M., Cameron, I.: Agent-based diagnosis for granulation processes. In: 16th Euro. Symp. on Comp. Aided Process Eng. (2006)
14. Johnson, C.: The glasgow-hospital evacuation simulator: Using computer sim to support a risk-based approach to hospital evacuation. Technical report, Univ. of Glasgow (2005)
15. Adams, G., Paques, J.J.: Gemma, the complementary tool of the grafcet. In: Proc. of the 4th Annual Canadian Conf. on Programmable Control and Automation Technology Conference and Exhibition, Toronto, Canada. IEEE (1988)
16. Valckenaers, P.: Benchmark description manufacturing control. Technical report, TFG SO d'AgentLink III (2004)
17. Barsade, S., Gibson, D.E.: Group emotion: A view from top and bottom. In: Research on Managing in Groups and Teams, vol. 1, pp. 81–102. JAI Press (1998)
18. Aubé, M.: From Toda's urge theory to the commitment theory of emotions. Grounding Emotions in Adaptive Systems, special issue of Cybernetics and Systems: An International Journal 32(6), 585–610 (2001)
19. Hatfield, E., Cacioppo, J.T., Rapson, R.L.: Emotional contagion. Current Directions in Psychological Science 2(3), 96–99 (1993)
20. Frijda, N.H.: The emotions. Studies in Emotion and Social Interaction. Cambridge University Press, Cambridge (1986)
21. Picard, R.: Affective Computing. MIT Press, Cambridge (1995)

The Multi-agent Patrolling Problem
Theoretical Results about Cyclic Strategies

Fabrice Lauri, Jean-Charles Créput, and Abderrafiaa Koukam

IRTES-SeT
Rue Thiery-Mieg, Belfort, France

Abstract. Patrolling an environment consists in visiting as frequently as possible its most relevant areas in order to supervise, control or protect it. This task is commonly performed by a team of agents that seek to optimize a performance criterion generally based on the notion of node idleness, that is the period during which a node remains unvisited. For some patrolling strategies, the performance criterion may be unbounded or the classical iterative evaluation algorithm may be ineffective to rapidly provide this performance criterion. The contribution of this paper is fourfold. Firstly we extend the formulation of the classical multi-agent patrolling problem. Secondly we define a large class of multi-agent patrolling strategies, the consistent cyclic patrolling strategies, where every agent may visit some nodes once before ultimately visiting the same set of nodes infinitely often. Idleness-based performance criteria considered in this paper to evaluate such strategies are always bounded. Thirdly we provide theoretical results about the computation time required for evaluating efficiently and accurately any consistent cyclic strategy. Fourthly we propose an efficient and accurate evaluation algorithm of polynomial complexity based on these theoretical results.

Keywords: Multi-agent patrolling, cyclic strategies, theoretical results.

1 Introduction

A patrol is a mission involving a team of several individuals whose goal consists in *continuously* visiting the relevant areas of an environment, in order to efficiently supervise, control or protect it. A group of drones searching for wildfires in order to contribute in the forest conservation, a team of vaccum cleaning robots searching for dirt, postmen on their daily rounds, or a squad of marines securing an area are all examples of patrols. Performing such a task implies that all of the involved members coordinate their actions efficiently.

In this paper, we focus on the multi-agent patrolling problem of a known environment represented by a graph. Techniques solving this problem can be used in numerous applications, including the rescue by robots of people in danger after a disaster [13,6] or the protection of a territory to face enemy threats [5,13,2,9]. The multi-agent patrolling problem in known environments has been formulated recently [10]. This problem consists in determining a patrolling strategy that minimizes a given performance criterion. A patrolling strategy is made up of several individual patrolling strategies, one for each involved agent. An individual strategy indicates which graph nodes an agent has to visit. It can be defined prior to the patrol or while the agents are patrolling. The performance criterion which evaluates a patrolling strategy is generally based on the notion of node idleness [10], which represents the duration a node remains unvisited. The idleness of a node is zero when an agent is on the node and it increases as soon as the agent leaves the node. In [9,1,14,3,4,7,8,11,13], many patrolling strategies have been devised and experimentally validated using an evaluation criteria based on idleness. For example, one of this performance criterion, the worst idleness, consists in determining the largest period a node remains unvisited when agents follow a given patrolling strategy. This criterion is particularly adapted when some geographically distributed information has to be collected very frequently. In this paper, we focus on the framework using the worst idleness performance criterion. As all the state-of-the-art algorithms generating patrolling strategies only yield approximate solutions to this complex problem, they all require an efficient algorithm to accurately evaluate a given strategy. We provide thereafter the theoretical proofs for designing such an evaluation algorithm.

The contribution of this paper is fourfold. Firstly we extend the formulation of the classical multi-agent patrolling problem (see Section 2). Secondly we define a large class of multi-agent patrolling strategies, the cyclic patrolling strategies (see Section 4), where every agent may visit some nodes once before ultimately visiting the same set of nodes infinitely often. One of the main advantages of these cyclic strategies stems from the fact that they can be evaluated in a finite number of iterations. Another advantage is to be represented by a data structure whose size is finite. Thirdly we provide theoretical results about the computation time required for the evaluation of a cyclic strategy to converge (see Section 5). These results can be extended to the evaluation of the strategies studied by Chevaleyre [3], as cyclic strategies are generalizations of single-cycle strategies, partition-based strategies and mixed strategies. Fourthly we propose an efficient and accurate evaluation algorithm, of polynomial complexity, based on these theoretical results (see Section 6). In the remainder of this paper, Section 3 adresses the related works about the multi-agent patrolling problem, and concluding remarks and future research directions are given in Section 7.

2 Problem Formulation

The environment that has to be patrolled consists of a directed connected graph $G = (\mathcal{V}, \mathcal{E}, c)$. $\mathcal{V}$ represents the strategically relevant areas and $\mathcal{E} \subset \mathcal{V}^2$ the means of transport between them. A cost $c(x, y) \in \mathbb{R}$ is associated with any edge $(x, y) \in \mathcal{E}$. It may measure the distance (in meters for example) required to reach node y from node x. The cost function $c : \mathcal{E} \to \mathbb{R}$ satisfies the following properties: $c(x, y) \geq 0$ for any $(x, y) \in \mathcal{E}$ and $c(x, y) = 0$ iff $x = y$.

Let $r < |\mathcal{V}|$ denote the number of agents patrolling graph G. Each agent i is assumed to be located at node $sn_i \in \mathcal{V}$ prior to the patrolling and to possess a movement speed $s_i > 0$ (in m/s for instance). Node sn_i represents the deployment site of agent i. Agent i reaches node y from node x after $\frac{c(x,y)}{s_i}$ units of time (seconds for instance).

With any node x is associated an *instantaneous node idleness*, which represents the time period this node remains unvisited, and a *discount factor* $\gamma_x \in \mathbb{R}_{+*}$ [1], which influences the increase in the node idleness. When any node receives the visit of an agent, its idleness drops to zero. If node x has been left unvisited for a period Δt, its idleness equals $\gamma_x \Delta t$.

Let $\mathcal{I} = (G, r, \overrightarrow{sn}, \overrightarrow{s}, \overrightarrow{\gamma})$ be an instance of the multi-agent patrolling problem, where G is the patrolling graph, r the number of patrolling agents, $\overrightarrow{sn} \in \mathcal{V}^r$ the agent deployment sites, $\overrightarrow{s} \in \mathbb{R}^r_{+*}$ the agent speeds and $\overrightarrow{\gamma} \in \mathbb{R}^r_{+*}$ the discount factors of the nodes. Solving the multi-agent patrolling problem on $\mathcal{I}$ consists in elaborating a coverage strategy $\pi^\mathcal{I}$ of graph G by r agents such that any node of G is visited infinitely often. Such a patrolling strategy must optimize a given quality criterion. For the sake of clarity, a multi-agent patrolling strategy will be from now on noted π whenever there is no ambiguity on the instance $\mathcal{I}$.

Let Π be the set of all the multi-agent patrolling strategies $\pi = (\pi_1, \pi_2, \cdots, \pi_r)$ where any individual strategy $\pi_i : \mathbb{N}_* \to \mathcal{V}$ maps a discrete time space into the node set, with $\pi_i(1) = sn_i$. $\pi_i(j)$ denotes the j-th node that agent i has to visit, with $\pi_i(j+1) = x$ only if $(\pi_i(j), x) \in \mathcal{E}$.

We are concerned with determining patrolling strategies that minimize the idleness of any node $x \in \mathcal{V}$. Several criteria have been devised in [10] in order to evaluate the quality of a multi-agent patrolling strategy on a graph. For the sake of theoretical analysis, only the criterion based on the *worst idleness* will be used in this paper. The interested reader can consult Machado *et al.* [10] for other evaluation criteria. Knowing that the chosen criterion, that is the worst idleness of the graph, upper bounds the others ([3]), minimizing it implies minimizing the others.

All of the evaluation criteria can be formulated from the notion of instantaneous node idleness (INI). Assuming the agents follow strategy π on graph G, the INI $I^\pi_t(x) \in \mathbb{R}_{+*}$ of node x at time t is the elapsed *discounted* duration since this node has received the visit of an agent. If node x has been visited at time t by an agent and if Δt is the elapsed time since the last visit at node x, then the instantaneous idleness of node x at time $t + \Delta t$ is given by: $I^\pi_{t+\Delta t}(x) = \gamma_x \Delta t$

Discount factors can be used to set *visit priorities* on nodes. The higher the discount factor, the faster the idleness of the corresponding node grows. By convention, at initial time, $I^\pi_0(i) = 0$, for any strategy π and for any node $i = 1, 2, \cdots, |\mathcal{V}|$.

Evaluating the multi-agent patrolling strategy π using the worst idleness criterion consists in using the following equation:

$$WI^\pi = \limsup_{t \to +\infty} WI^\pi_t \qquad (1)$$

---

[1] $\mathbb{R}_{+*} = \{x \in \mathbb{R} | x > 0\}$

where WI_t^π denotes the *instantaneous worst graph idleness* which is the highest instantaneous node idleness over the set $\mathcal{V}$ of nodes of G at time t, that is: $WI_t^\pi = \max_{x \in \mathcal{V}} I_t^\pi(x)$.

Solving the multi-agent patrolling problem thus consists in determining a strategy $\pi^* \in \mathrm{argmin}_{\pi \in \Pi} WI^\pi$ such that for any strategy π, $WI^{\pi^*} \leq WI^\pi$.

3 Related Works

In [10,9], several multi-agent architectures and multi-agent patrolling strategy evaluation criteria were addressed. [1] improved the best architectures proposed by [9]. They have devised agents able to exchange messages freely and conduct negotiations about the nodes they have to visit. Chevaleyre [3] has formulated the patrolling problem in terms of a combinatorial optimization problem. He first proved that a patrolling strategy involving one agent could be obtained using an algorithm that solves the *Graphical Traveling Salesman Problem*. In this variant of the *Traveling Salesman Problem*, graphs are not necessarily complete. He then studied several possible classes of multi-agent patrolling strategies and showed that they all were able to reach close to optimal performance. In [14], the agents are able to learn to patrol using the Reinforcement Learning (RL) framework. All of the previously described approaches were evaluated in [1] and were compared in several configurations. Lauri et al. [7,8] proposed several Ant Colony Optimization techniques, assuming all of the agents are deployed from the same initial node. Marier et al. [11] define the multi-agent patrolling problem as a Generalized Semi-Markov Decision Process (GSMDP). This mathematical model can handle continuous time and uncertainties in the execution of a patrol. Finally, Poulet et al. [13] formulate another version of the multi-agent patrolling problem, by introducing priorities on the nodes, metric performance criteria and an agent population whose size is dynamic.

In [12], the authors show that the existing multi-agent patrolling strategy search techniques have several limitations. The lack of study about the flexibility of the proposed approaches or about the efficacity of the computation resources, along with the deterministic aspect of many existing centralized approaches are part of the emphasized limitations. From a theoretical point of view, we believe that other strong limitations of some of the techniques presented above consist in using classes of patrolling strategies whose performance criteria are not well defined or using an inaccurate evaluation algorithm. Indeed, on the one hand, there exist some multi-agent patrolling strategies that have a unbounded worst idleness, for example. Trivially, these can be obtained when a node is not visited infinitely often by at least one agent, or when visits to some nodes become more and more rare. On the other hand, evaluation of patrolling strategies currently relies on an iterative algorithm, called *SEPS* (*Standard Evaluation of Patrolling Strategies*) in the rest of the paper. This algorithm updates the value of the performance criterion (the worst idleness for example) by simulating the agents' movements. It ends after T iterations, but this parameter may have been specified inadequately by the user. Briefly, we will show in Section 5 that, for consistent cyclic strategies especially, there exists T^* such that equation 1 can be rewritten as $WI^\pi = \limsup_{t \to T^*} WI_t^\pi$. An inaccurate value of the worst idleness WI may be found by $SEPS$ when $T < T^*$.

4 Cyclic Multi-agent Patrolling Strategies

Cyclic multi-agent patrolling strategies are generalizations of single-cycle strategies, partition-based strategies and mixed strategies defined by Chevaleyre [3]. They are particularly adapted to represent tasks that consist in collecting geographically distributed information very frequently and as fast as possible.

A multi-agent patrolling strategy π is cyclic iff each of its individual strategy π_i is parameterized by a tuple (μ_i, l_i) where: $\mu_i = (\mu_i(1), \mu_i(2), \ldots, \mu_i(N_i))$ is a finite sequence of N_i nodes, $l_i \in \{1, 2, \ldots, N_i\}$, $\mu_i(1) = sn_i$, $\mu_i(l_i) = \mu_i(N_i)$, and such that:

$$\pi_i(j) = \begin{cases} \mu_i(j) & \text{for } j < N_i \\ \mu_i(l_i + (j - l_i) \mod (N_i - l_i)) & \text{for } j \geq N_i \end{cases} \quad (2)$$

The individual patrolling strategies in a cyclic multi-agent patrolling strategy are characterized by the existence of a cycle and possibly of a precycle. The patrolling cycle $\text{cyc}(\pi, i)$ of agent i in a cyclic multi-agent patrolling strategy π is the finite sequence of nodes of π_i visited infinitely often by agent i, that is $\text{cyc}(\pi, i) = (\pi_i(l_i), \pi_i(l_i + 1), \cdots, \pi_i(N_i))$. The precycle of agent i in a cyclic multi-agent patrolling strategy π is the sequence of nodes of π_i visited only once by agent i from its deployment site sn_i to the node $\pi_i(l_i)$ beginning its patrolling cycle. Whenever $l_i = 1$, there is no precycle in π_i. A cyclic multi-agent patrolling strategy is consistent if any node of G is visited infinitely often by at least one agent in its patrolling cycle. In the sequel, Π^{cyclic} denotes the set of all the consistent cyclic multi-agent patrolling strategies for a given instance.

Let us consider the graph represented in figure 1 that has to be patrolled by 2 agents both deployed on node 1. Let $\pi = (\pi_1, \pi_2)$ be a patrolling strategy, such that: $\pi_1 = ((1, \mathbf{4,7,8,6,5,4}), 2)$, and $\pi_2 = ((\mathbf{1,2,3,2,1}), 1)$. where the patrolling cycles are written in bold. In this patrolling strategy, agent 1 visits infinitely often the nodes $4, 7, 8, 6$ and 5 : these nodes form its patrolling cycle. The precycle of agent 1 is represented by the path $(1, 4)$. Agent 2 directly performs its cycle, composed by nodes $1, 2$ and 3, without being entered previously within a pre-cycle.

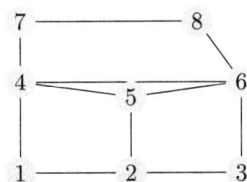

Fig. 1. Example of a patrol graph (8 nodes, 11 edges)

5 Evaluation of Cyclic Strategies

Determining an optimal strategy π^* that minimizes equation 1 involves evaluating several strategies $\pi \in \Pi^{cyclic}$ before finding it. The efficiency of an algorithm capable of approximately solving an instance of the multi-agent patrolling problem then strongly depends on the computation time required to evaluate a multi-agent patrolling strategy. The more strategies evaluated in a given time period, the more likely it is that good strategies are determined by an approximate algorithm. This section provides theoretical results about the efficient and accurate evaluation of the worst idleness of cyclic patrolling strategies.

In the sequel, the following notations are used:

- $\mathbb{I}_{\{p\}}$ is the function that returns 1 if the predicate p is satisfied and 0 otherwise.
- $c(\pi_i, x) = \sum_{k=1}^{j-1} c(\pi_i(k), \pi_i(k+1))$ is the cost of the path from the deployment site $\pi_i(1)$ to node $x = \pi_i(j)$.
- $\mu = (\mu(1), \mu(2), \cdots, \mu(N_\mu))$ is a path of N_μ nodes from $\mu(1)$ to $\mu(N_\mu)$, where $\mu(j+1) = x$ only if $(\mu(j), x) \in \mathcal{E}$.
- $c(\mu) = \sum_{k=1}^{N_\mu - 1} c(\mu(k), \mu(k+1))$ is the cost of μ.
- $E(\mu) = \{\mu(k) | 1 \leq k \leq N_\mu\}$ is the set of nodes appearing in a sequence of nodes μ.
- $n^\pi(x) = \sum_{k=1}^{r} \mathbb{I}_{\{x \in E(cyc(\pi, k))\}}$ is the number of agents visiting node x in their patrolling cycle.
- $n^{\pi_i}(x) = \sum_{j=l_i}^{N_i} \mathbb{I}_{\{x = \pi_i(j)\}}$ is the number of times node x appears in the patrolling cycle of π_i.
- $WI_T^\pi(x) = \limsup_{t \to T} I_t^\pi(x)$ is the worst idleness of node x after a time period T when agents follow the patrolling strategy π.
- $WI^\pi(x)$ is the worst idleness of node x when agents follow π during a time period ensuring its convergence. In other words, $WI^\pi(x) = WI_\infty^\pi(x)$.
- $WI_T^\pi = \limsup_{t \to T} WI_t^\pi$ is the worst idleness of graph G after a time period T when agents follow the patrolling strategy π.

The problem we are faced with here can be formulated as follows:

Identify the necessary and sufficient conditions that determine, for any $\pi \in \Pi^{cyclic}$, the time period T^π ensuring that $WI^\pi = \limsup_{t \to T^\pi} WI_t^\pi$, that is such that, $\forall T > T^\pi$, $\limsup_{t \to T} WI_t^\pi = \limsup_{t \to T^\pi} WI_t^\pi$.

Let $P_x(n)$ be the following property defined for any node x:

$P_x(n)$: "The worst idleness $WI^\pi(x)$ of any node $x \in \mathcal{V}$ visited by n agents converges after a time period $T_x(n) = \min\{T_{x,i}\}_{1 \leq i \leq n}$, where $T_{x,i}$ corresponds to the time period agent i needs to visit node x exactly $n^{\pi_i}(x) + \mathbb{I}_{\{x \neq \pi_i(l_i)\}}$ times[2].

---

[2] For the sake of clarity, the n agents of indices $i = 1, 2, \ldots, n$ are assumed to visit node x.

We are about to prove by induction in theorem 1 that $P_x(n)$ is true for all n. The demonstration of this theorem relies on two lemmas. Lemma 1 gives an upper bound on the worst idleness of any node x visited infinitely often by only one agent. This upper bound is used in lemma 2 to state that the above property $P_x(n)$ is true for $n = 1$.

Lemma 1. *The worst idleness of a node x visited infinitely often by only one agent i, that is such that $x \in E(\mathrm{cyc}(\pi, i))$ and $n^\pi(x) = 1$, satisfies:*

$$WI^\pi(x) \leq \frac{\gamma_x}{s_i} \max\{c(\mathrm{cyc}(\pi, i)), c(\pi_i, x)\} \tag{3}$$

Proof. Let t_x be the elapsed time until the first visit at node $x \in E(\mathrm{cyc}(\pi, i))$. Then, prior to the actual patrolling, the worst idleness of node x after a time period t_x is equal to:

$$WI^\pi_{t_x}(x) = \limsup_{t \to t_x} I^\pi_t(x) = \frac{\gamma_x}{s_i} c(\pi_i, x)$$

The worst idleness of x has converged after a time period $T > t_x$ that corresponds to the time span agent i needs to complete its patrolling cycle once and come back to node x. If node x appears only once in $\mathrm{cyc}(\pi, i)$ or if it is the beginning node of the patrolling cycle and it appears exactly two times in π_i, that is $n^{\pi_i}(x) = 1 + \mathbb{I}_{\{x = \pi_i(l_i)\}}$, then its worst idleness satisfies:

$$WI^\pi(x) = \begin{cases} WI^\pi_{t_x}(x) & \text{if } \frac{\gamma_x}{s_i} c(\mathrm{cyc}(\pi, i)) \leq WI^\pi_{t_x}(x). \\ \frac{\gamma_x}{s_i} c(\mathrm{cyc}(\pi, i)) & \text{otherwise} \end{cases}$$

If $n^{\pi_i}(x) > 1 + \mathbb{I}_{\{x = \pi_i(l_i)\}}$, then the above equality becomes a lower inequality. Hence in the general case, $WI^\pi(x) \leq \frac{\gamma_x}{s_i} \max\{c(\mathrm{cyc}(\pi, i)), c(\pi_i, x)\}$.

Lemma 2. *The worst idleness of a node x visited infinitely often by only one agent i is ensured to converge after a time span $T_{x,i}$ that corresponds to the time span agent i needs to visit node x $n^{\pi_i}(x) + \mathbb{I}_{\{x \neq \pi_i(l_i)\}}$ times exactly. In other words, $P_x(1)$ is true.*

Proof. Proof of lemma 1 reports that the worst idleness of a node x visited infinitely often by only one agent i is ensured to converge once agent i has completed its patrolling cycle once and has come back to x. If $x = \pi_i(l_i)$, then x appears at least two times in $\mathrm{cyc}(\pi, i)$. In this case, the worst idleness of x has converged once x has been visited exactly $n^{\pi_i}(x)$ times. If $x \neq \pi_i(l_i)$, then x appears at least one time in $\mathrm{cyc}(\pi, i)$. In this case, the worst idleness of x has converged once x has been visited exactly $n^{\pi_i}(x) + 1$ times.

Theorem 1. *The worst idleness $WI^\pi(x)$ of any node $x \in V$ visited by n agents converges after a time span $T_x(n) = \min\{T_{x,i}\}_{1 \leq i \leq n}$, where $T_{x,i}$ corresponds to the time period that agent i needs to visit node x exactly $n^{\pi_i}(x) + \mathbb{I}_{\{x \neq \pi_i(l_i)\}}$ times.*

Proof. Let us suppose that $P_x(n)$ is true and prove by induction that $P_x(n+1)$ is also true. $P_x(n+1)$ means that: "The worst idleness $WI^\pi(x)$ of any node $x \in \mathcal{V}$ visited by $n+1$ agents converges after a time span $T_x(n+1) = \min\{T_x(n), T_{x,n+1}\}$". If $T_x(n) \leq T_{x,n+1}$, since $P_x(n)$ is true, then $WI^\pi(x) = WI^\pi_{T_x(n)}(x)$. If $T_{x,n+1} < T_x(n)$, that is if agent $n+1$ visits node x more rapidly than the others, then $WI^\pi(x) = WI^\pi_{T_{x,n+1}}(x)$. Hence $WI^\pi(x) = WI^\pi_{T_x(n+1)}(x)$ which states that $P_x(n+1)$ is true assuming $P_x(n)$ is true. As $P_x(1)$ is true (lemma 2) and $\forall n, (P_x(n) \Rightarrow P_x(n+1))$, then $P_x(n)$ is true for all n.

The following corollary can be deducted from this theorem:

Corollary 1. *The worst idleness of each node x converges after a time period $T_x(n^\pi(x))$, that is:*

$$WI^\pi(x) = WI^\pi_{T_x(n^\pi(x))}(x) = \limsup_{t \to T_x(n^\pi(x))} I^\pi_t(x) \qquad (4)$$

Proof. Each node x is visited infinitely often by $n^\pi(x)$ agents. Hence, by using theorem 1, $WI^\pi(x) = WI^\pi_{T_x(n^\pi(x))}(x)$.

We now demonstrate in the following theorem that the worst idleness converges once the worst idlenesses of every node have converged.

Theorem 2. *The worst idleness of graph G when agents follow π converges after a time period T^π, that is $WI^\pi = \limsup_{t \to T^\pi} WI^\pi_t$, where:*

$$T^\pi = \max_{x \in \mathcal{V}} T_x(n^\pi(x)) \qquad (5)$$

T^π represents the time period required so that the worst idleness of every node of G has converged. T^π also corresponds to the time span elapsed so that each agent i visits every node x of its patrolling cycle $n^{\pi_i}(x) + \mathbb{I}_{\{x \neq \pi_i(l_i)\}}$ times.

Proof. Equation 1 can be reformulated as:

$$\begin{aligned}
WI^\pi &= \max_{x \in \mathcal{V}} \limsup_{t \to +\infty} I^\pi_t(x) \\
&= \max_{x \in \mathcal{V}} WI^\pi(x) \\
&= \max_{x \in \mathcal{V}} \limsup_{t \to T_x(n^\pi(x))} I^\pi_t(x) \qquad (6) \\
&= \limsup_{t \to T^\pi} \max_{x \in \mathcal{V}} I^\pi_t(x) \qquad (7) \\
&= \limsup_{t \to T^\pi} WI^\pi_t
\end{aligned}$$

Equation 6 leads to equation 7 by using equation 5.

Finally, theorem 3 below introduces the stopping criteria of the evaluation algorithm *AECPS* presented in the next section.

Theorem 3. *The following propositions are equivalent:*

- T^π corresponds to the time span elapsed so that each agent i visits every node x of its patrolling cycle $n^{\pi_i}(x) + \mathbb{I}_{\{x \neq \pi_i(l_i)\}}$ times.
- T^π corresponds to the time span elapsed so that each agent i visits M_i nodes in its cycle, where $M_i = \sum_{x \in E(cyc(\pi,i))} (n^{\pi_i}(x) + 1)$.

Proof. When agent i has completed its patrolling cycle the first time, each node x has been visited $n^{\pi_i}(x)$ times. The second patrolling cycle allows agent i to visit each node one more time, for a total of visited nodes equal to M_i.

6 Evaluation Algorithm

In this section, we present the algorithm *AECPS* (*Accurate Evaluation of Cyclic Patrolling Strategies*). This algorithm evaluate in a efficient and accurate ways, grounded on the theoretical results presented previously, any cyclic multi-agent patrolling strategy. An empirical comparison between *AECPS* and *SEPS* is given in Section 6.2.

6.1 Algorithm *AECPS*

Require: Patrol graph G, number of agents r, agents' speeds $\vec{s}$, discount factors $\vec{\gamma}$, cyclic patrolling strategy π.
Ensure: Worst idleness WI.

1: $I(x) \leftarrow 0$ for every node $x \in V$
2: $WI \leftarrow 0$
3: **for** every agent $i \in [1; r]$ **do**
4:     $cn(i) \leftarrow 1$
5:     $pn(i) \leftarrow 2$
6:     $d(i) \leftarrow c(\pi_i(cn(i)), \pi_i(pn(i)))$
7:     $n(i) \leftarrow \sum_{x \in E(cyc(\pi,i))} (n^{\pi_i}(x) + 1)$
8: **end for**
9: **repeat**
10:     $\Delta_t \leftarrow \min_{i \in [1;r]} \frac{d(i)}{s_i}$
11:     **for** every node $x \in V$ **do**
12:        $I(x) \leftarrow I(x) + \gamma_x \times \Delta_t$
13:     **end for**
14:     $WI \leftarrow \max(WI, \max_{x \in V}\{I(x)\})$
15:     **for** every agent $i \in [1; r]$ **do**
16:        $d(i) \leftarrow d(i) - \Delta_t \times s_i$
17:        **if** $d(i) = 0$ **then**
18:            **if** $cn(i) \geq l_i$ **and** $n(i) > 0$ **then**
19:                $n(i) \leftarrow n(i) - 1$

```
20:         end if
21:         Update indices cn(i) and pn(i).
22:         d(i) ← c(π_i(cn(i)), π_i(pn(i)))
23:         I(π_i(cn(i))) ← 0
24:     end if
25: end for
26: until n(i) = 0 for every agent i ∈ [1; r]
```

The data structures used to compute the worst idleness WI of graph G are initialized from line 1 to line 8. These data structures represent: the instantaneous idleness $I(x)$ of each node x, the worst idleness WI of graph G, the index $cn(i)$ of the current node of each agent i, knowing that the current node of agent i is given by $\pi_i(cn(i))$, the index $pn(i)$ of the next node that each agent i must reach, the total number $n(i)$ of nodes that each agent i must visit once it has entered its cycle, and the distance $d(i)$ between the current node of each agent i and its next node. Line 10 computes the minimal period required by one of the agents to reach the next node. Lines 11 to 13 update the instantaneous idlenesses of the nodes. The update of the worst idleness WI is carried out in line 14. From line 16 to line 24, each agent i moves during a period Δ_t on the edge linking its current node to its next node according to its individual patrolling strategy π_i. If some agent i reach its next node (lines 16 and 17), the current and the next nodes (line 21) along with the distance between them (line 22) are updated for ensuring the next agent movement. Lines 18 to 20 decrease the number of nodes that remains to be visited once agent has entered its patrolling cycle. At line 23, the idleness of the current node is set to zero. The agents' movements stop when the convergence of the worst idleness criterion has been reached. This happens when every agent i has visited a total number $n(i)$ (value initialized at line 5) of nodes in its cycle (test at line 26).

6.2 Empirical Comparison between *AECPS* and *SEPS*

To emphasize on the importance of having an efficient and accurate evaluation algorithm, we have conducted several experiments by using some of the graphs commonly used by the community [10,3,1,7,8] for this problem. The same patrolling strategies were evaluated successively by the algorithms *AECPS* and *SEPS*. The results of these experiments are reported in Table 1.

In this table, k is the number of iterations performed by algorithm *AECPS*, T is the number of iterations specified in algorithm *SEPS*, and WI denotes the value of the worst idleness ultimately determined. The durations shown in the table are expressed in seconds and represent the computation times of 1000 successive evaluations of a patrolling strategy. The empirical worst idlenesses that have converged to the theoretical ones are shown in bold.

One may notice that the algorithm *AECPS* determines the theoretical worst idleness in minimum computing time for most of the patrolling strategies. Because of the bound specified in lemma 1, upon which are based all the subsequent

Table 1. Empirical comparison between the proposed algorithm $AECPS$ and the standard evaluation algorithm $SEPS$. Computing time is expressed in seconds.

	# agents	k	AECPS WI	Time	SEPS $T=50$ WI	Time	SEPS $T=100$ WI	Time	SEPS $T=500$ WI	Time
Hub 20 nodes 19 edges	5	235	**2344**	0.12	2011	0.028	2252	0.055	**2344**	0.26
	10	219	**2367**	0.158	2228	0.036	2348	0.071	**2367**	0.34
	15	46	**2141**	0.047	**2141**	0.054	**2141**	0.104	**2141**	0.53
MapA 50 nodes 104 edges	5	190	**4026**	0.077	2768	0.021	**4026**	0.042	**4026**	0.20
	10	322	**2520**	0.16	1854	0.026	2469	0.051	**2520**	0.24
	15	434	**2477**	0.25	1725	0.035	2432	0.064	**2477**	0.29
	20	543	**2348**	0.36	1569	0.041	2090	0.075	**2348**	0.35
MapB 50 nodes 69 edges	5	246	**1044**	0.196	600	0.04	981	0.087	**1044**	0.36
	10	429	**836**	0.367	419	0.05	629	0.097	**836**	0.434
	15	500	**728**	0.48	402	0.059	557	0.113	**728**	0.48
	20	634	**583**	0.64	370	0.068	481	0.128	**583**	0.56
Town 330 nodes 522 edges	5	3068	**104634**	9.13	11052	0.13	16328	0.27	56909	1.85
	10	4080	**66819**	11.72	9203	0.15	13679	0.30	34174	1.80
	15	5097	**51548**	14.80	10620	0.16	13046	0.32	26874	1.86
	20	6786	**46692**	19.56	9142	0.17	12397	0.34	22877	1.84

theorems, $AECPS$ may use a number of iterations greater than necessary. Yet, these results perfectly illustrate the difficulty to master the trade-off between the evaluation accuracy and the computation time in the algorithm $SEPS$, especially when the number of nodes of the graph and the number of agents are high. This trade-off no longer exists when using the algorithm $AECPS$.

7 Conclusion and Future Works

The techniques solving the multi-agent patrolling problem can be used in numerous applications, ranging from the management of information networks, control of mobile and multiple patrolling robots (like in mobile wireless sensor networks) to the enhancement of non-player character behaviors in computer games, to name a few. As the multi-agent patrolling problem may be considered as NP-hard, only approximate solutions can be obtained for large instances. The pioneer work that has been conducted in this article is to deliver rigourous proofs about the computation time required for accurately and efficiently evaluating any multi-agent patrolling strategy belonging to the new introduced class of cyclic patrolling strategies. Cyclic patrolling strategies are generalizations of previously studied patrolling strategies like single-cycle strategies, partition-based strategies and mixed strategies. One research direction that might be followed consists in designing and experimentally validating algorithms that efficiently generate cyclic multi-agent patrolling strategies. Another research direction consists in providing a better bound in the proof to reduce computation time.

References

1. Almeida, A., Ramalho, G.L., Santana, H., Azevedo Tedesco, P., Menezes, T., Corruble, V., Chevaleyre, Y.: Recent Advances on Multi-Agent Patrolling. In: Bazzan, A.L.C., Labidi, S. (eds.) SBIA 2004. LNCS (LNAI), vol. 3171, pp. 474–483. Springer, Heidelberg (2004)
2. Bošanský, B., Lisý, V., Jakob, M., Pechoucek, M.: Computing Time-Dependent Policies for Patrolling Games with Mobile Targets. In: International Joint Conference on Autonomous Agents and Multi-Agent Systems (2011)
3. Chevaleyre, Y.: Theoretical Analysis of the Multi-Agent Patrolling Problem. In: International Joint Conference on Intelligent Agent Technology, pp. 302–308 (2004)
4. Chevaleyre, Y.: The Patrolling Problem: theoretical and experimental results. In: Combinatorial Optimization and Theoretical Computer Science. Wiley (2007)
5. Jiang, A., Yin, Z., Zhang, C., Tambe, M., Kraus, S.: Game-theoretic Randomization for Security Patrolling with Dynamic Execution Uncertainty. In: International Joint Conference on Autonomous Agents and Multi-Agent Systems (2013)
6. Kitano, H.: RoboCup Rescue: A Grand Challenge for Multi-Agent Systems. In: Proceedings of the 4th International Conference on Multi Agent Systems, pp. 5–12 (2000)
7. Lauri, F., Charpillet, F.: Ant Colony Optimization applied to the Multi-Agent Patrolling Problem. In: IEEE Swarm Intelligence Symposium, Indianapolis, Indiana, USA (2006)
8. Lauri, F., Koukam, A.: A Two-Step Evolutionary and ACO Approach for Solving the Multi-Agent Patrolling Problem. In: IEEE World Congress on Computational Intelligence, Honk-Kong, Chine (2008)
9. Machado, A., Almeida, A., et al.: Multi-Agent Movement Coordination in Patrolling. In: Proceedings of the 3rd International Conference on Computer and Game (2002)
10. Machado, A., Ramalho, G., et al.: Multi-Agent Patrolling: An Empirical Analysis of Alternatives Architectures. In: Proceedings of the 3rd International Workshop on Multi-Agent Based Simulation, pp. 155–170 (2002)
11. Marier, J.-S., Besse, C., Chaib-draa, B.: A Markov Model for Multiagent Patrolling in Continuous Time. In: Leung, C.S., Lee, M., Chan, J.H. (eds.) ICONIP 2009, Part II. LNCS, vol. 5864, pp. 648–656. Springer, Heidelberg (2009)
12. Portugal, D., Rocha, R.: A Survey on Multi-robot Patrolling Algorithms. In: Camarinha-Matos, L.M. (ed.) DoCEIS 2011. IFIP AICT, vol. 349, pp. 139–146. Springer, Heidelberg (2011)
13. Poulet, C., Corruble, V., Seghrouchni, A., Ramalho, G.: The Open System Setting in Timed MultiAgent Patrolling. In: IEEE/WIC/ACM International Conferences on Web Intelligence and Intelligent Agent Technology (2011)
14. Santana, H., Ramalho, G., et al.: Multi-Agent Patrolling with Reinforcement Learning. In: Proceedings of the 3rd International Joint Conference on Autonomous Agents and Multi-Agent Systems, pp. 1122–1129 (2004)

Representation of Interactions in a Multi-Level Multi-Agent Model for Cartography Constraint Solving

Adrien Maudet[1], Guillaume Touya[1], Cécile Duchêne[1], and Sébastien Picault[2]

[1] Université Paris Est, IGN, Laboratoire COGIT, Saint-Mandé, France
{adrien.maudet,guillaume.touya,cecile.duchene}@ign.fr
[2] LIFL, Université Lille 1, Villeneuve d'Ascq, France
sebastien.picault@lifl.fr

Abstract. The objective of cartographic generalisation is to simplify geographic data in order to create legible maps when scale decreases. It often requires to reason at different levels of abstraction (e.g. a building, a city). To automate this process, Multi-Agent approaches have been used for several years. Map objects (e.g. buildings) are modelled as autonomous entities that try to solve constraints through appropriate transformations. Yet, those approaches are not able to deal with all situations that appear between cartographic objects in a map. Indeed, though a map intrinsically involves objects that belong to several description, scale or organisation levels, there is no explicit multi-level representation in agent-based cartographic models. Thus we assume that the use of a multi-level multi-agent model would improve the automated generalisation process. Especially, the PADAWAN model is a multi-agent model offering multi-level capabilities which meet quite well the requirements for the multi-level organisation of cartographic objects. In this paper, we expose how we use this model on the one hand, to reify multi-level relations between cartographic agents, and on the other hand, to represent the constraints and the actions proposed to solve them, as interactions between the agents.

Keywords: Cartography, Cartographic Generalisation, Multi-Level Modelling, Spatialised Problems, Interactions Modelling, Constraints Solving.

1 Introduction

Map creation is a process with several stages aiming at drawing a legible map from geographic information. Today, geographic information is stored in databases where different objects (e.g. building, roads) are implemented with geometric shapes (e.g. point, polyline, polygon) and other non-geometric attributes (e.g. road name, building type). One characteristic of a map is its scale. Depending on the scale, information will not be shown, because room to display the same portion of the real world is smaller at a smaller scale. Among differences we may state various modifications, for instance: symbols may be changed (e.g. a building may be symbolised with its original shape, or a specific symbol depicting its function); the shape may be simplified (the detail of the line of a road may be more or less precise); some objects are not always displayed (i.e. small paths are not displayed on a road map, but they are displayed on a town map); some objects may be shown as a whole (i.e. close buildings in district centres are shown as a whole instead of being individually drawn).

All these modifications are motivated by the need to fit for the visual perception levels of the final user of the map. Yet, the information needs to remain semantically true (e.g. if the position of a building is allowed to change, it is not allowed to go to the other side of the road).

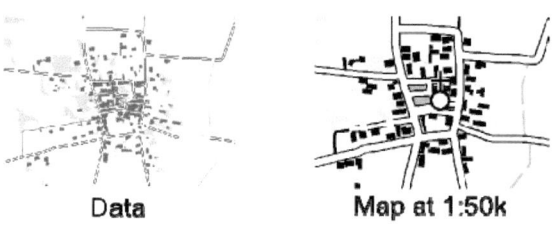

Fig. 1. Initial data generalised at the 1:50 000 scale

This simplification process is called cartographic generalisation. Figure 1 shows an instance of generalisation. Its automation is a complex question. First, specific transformation algorithms have been designed in order to simplify the shape of objects, modify them and satisfy readability constraints (e.g. buildings must be above a minimum size, symbols have to be sufficiently spaced). But some algorithms involve several objects, and some objects are involved in more than one algorithm. The application of the appropriate algorithms to satisfy the constraints of objects of a map is a research question in geographic information science. Some solutions have been proposed. Among the different approaches, some are based on multi-agent models [1], [2], [5], [8], [11]. In multi-agent approaches for generalisation, geographical objects are modelled as agents trying to satisfy their own constraints. Some of these models handle the organisation in levels of geographical objects, because it has been shown that generalisation sometimes requires to reason on groups of objects considered as a whole [20] (e.g. a building is a part of an urban block, i.e. a portion of space bounded by roads). However, this organisation is rigid and the unsolved issues involve more complex relations between geographic objects, especially when they belong to several organisation or description levels [13]. Thus, we assume that using a more flexible multi-levels formalism may help us to tackle the unsolved issues. The purpose of this paper is to explain the whole approach, and develop the first steps of our ongoing work, consisting in defining a generic model to express multi-level interactions in an agent oriented approach for generalisation, and adapting behaviours of agents from existing models to the new one.

The paper is organised as follows. Related works on multi-agent systems for generalisation and on geographical multi-level organisation are presented in section 2. Two opposite solutions (multi-model vs. improved multi-level approaches) are discussed in section 3; then section 4 addresses the issue of adapting one of the multi-level solutions to the existing multi-agent constraint-solving systems. Implementation and results are presented in section 5, before we give some perspectives on this work.

2 Multi-Agent Approaches for Automated Generalisation

In multi-agent generalisation models, the agents are either geographical entities (e.g. buildings, roads, towns) [5, 8, 11, 18], or the points that compose their geometry ([1, 11]. The purpose of these agents is to solve constraints that express some legibility conditions about geographical objects, as well as characteristics preservation conditions. Constraints affect either a single object (e.g. a minimum size constraint: a building must remain large enough to fit a perception threshold), or two objects (e.g. a proximity constraint: a road and a building must stay close to each other), or a group of objects (e.g. a density preservation constraint on an urban block involving all the buildings inside it).

In order to solve these constraints, geographic objects modelled as agents apply algorithms modifying their own geometry: the building grows bigger to satisfy its minimal size constraint; the building steps back from the road in order to satisfy the proximity constraints; the urban block eliminates some of its buildings in order to maintain its density while its buildings grow. The way the application of algorithms works depends on the different models. Among them, we are especially interested in AGENT, CartACom and GAEL, which are complementary to each other, and which all extend the model by [1]. This section briefly describes these three models, and then explains why the way relations are described may require a new perspective to go further in automatic generalisation quality.

2.1 AGENT, CartACom and GAEL Multi-Agent Models for Generalisation

AGENT ([2], [18], also formalised by [7]) is a model describing a hierarchical structure between agents: micro agents describe basic geographical entities (e.g. buildings, roads) and meso agents describe more complex entities composed by other agents, micro or meso (e.g. an urban block is composed of buildings). Meso agents share a hierarchical relation with their components. As explain in [19], this hierarchical relation implies different roles for a meso: coordinator, when the meso acts as a scheduler and activate its components; as a legislator, when the meso modifies its component and as a controller when the meso controls the result of the generalisation of its components. The behaviour of the agents follows a trial-and-error life cycle chaining constraints assessment, transformation, improvement evaluation, and commit or backtrack. It has an in-depth backtrack capability, resulting in an informed exploration of a states tree (described e.g. in [22]). AGENT proves effectiveness in urban zones, where the geographical entities are organised in hierarchies, and for the generalisation of roads, where a road may be subdivided into parts, which may generalise themselves, but need an agent to supervise the operations and maintain continuity between sections.

CartACom [3], [5] is a model managing transversal relations between agents. All agents interact in a same level. Here, constraints are shared by two agents and are called relational constraints. To satisfy them, an agent may either modify its own geometry, or try to modify the agent sharing the relation, which, due to the autonomy of the agents, requires to dialogue with it: ask, wait for an answer, and adapt its behaviour to the response. The behaviour of the agents follows a life cycle similar to the one of AGENT but where only the last action can be backtracked. The scheduling of the agents is managed by a common scheduler, which uses some specific rules, like giving priority to an agent who just received a message. CartACom proves effectiveness in rural zones, where the density of objects is low.

The GAEL model [8] subdivides micro objects into primitives (points, segments, triangles) called submicro objects. Points of micro objects are modelled as agents trying to satisfy constraints to maintain the shape of related submicro objects. Micro objects are modelled as agents too, and share some constraints with other geographic agents like in CartACom. When a micro object is activated as a GAEL agent, it activates its point agents, and after acting, each point agent activates neighbouring points. GAEL proves effectiveness for the generalisation of background field objects (e.g. relief) consistently with foreground elements (e.g. rivers, roads, buildings).

When focusing on the multi-level aspect of these three models, different organisations may be noticed. In CartACom, all objects belong to the same level. AGENT suggests a tree-like structure, where components are part of meso objects, and modifications on these parts modify the meso agent itself. GAEL introduces interactions between two levels: micro and submicro, but in very specific ways. The ways levels and relations are modelled in these three models are very specific, and these models fail to handle more complex situations.

2.2 Unsolved Issues and New Kinds of Relations

Those approaches of automated generalisation cover a lot of situations, but some cases are not well handled yet. We assume that agent oriented models may be used to handle these cases. But, as explained in the previous section, existing agent oriented models only enable to model specific kinds of interactions between geographical objects. The issues we want to solve involve different kind of multi-level relations. For instance, in figure 2, there are three recognisable levels: the micro objects level (buildings and roads), the urban blocks level, and between both, the aggregate level involving two adjacent buildings. The aggregate is, like the buildings, part of the urban blocks, and inside this urban block may need to interact as a whole with other buildings. But the adjacent buildings, although they are part of an aggregate, need to individually maintain their transversal relations with other buildings. Then, a solution to automatically generalise this situation requires:

— transversal relations between micro objects,
— hierarchical relations
  • between micro objects and the urban block,
  • between buildings and the aggregate,
  • between the aggregate and the urban block,
— diagonal relations between the aggregate and the buildings outside this aggregate.

In [13], other situations are exhibited. In particular, different kinds of hierarchical relations need to be modelled. An inclusion relation (i.e. a bus station on a road) [10] is different from a composition relation (i.e. a building is a part of an urban block). All these situations require a more flexible and more generic way to express relations and interactions between objects in different levels. This is why we propose to explore the use of a multi-level model.

Fig. 2. Two adjacent buildings compose an aggregate. Aggregated buildings need to have normal interactions for buildings, but the aggregate also needs to interact as a whole.

3 A Multi-Level Models to Better Handle Relations

In this section, we expose our approach, consisting in using an appropriate existing multi-level model. Our objective is to get a model making explicit both hierarchical and transversal relations. First, we will explain why a multi-model approach is not suitable, then we will introduce the model we chose to base on while explaining why it was chosen.

3.1 Multi-model Solutions

The goal of our work is not the mere fusion of existing models into a single one, but the design of a new one with more flexibility, in order to manage new kinds of interactions. These considerations are quite decisive in the choice of adaptations that have to be made to the existing models. Using a multi-model solution for generalisation was previously explored in [4] where three scenarios are introduced so as to improve multi-agent solution for generalisation. First, a multi-model method for generalisation was proposed, and developed in [24]. The purpose of this model is to identify areas, and apply the more appropriate process (a process may be an agent-oriented method or another kind of process, like a least square optimisation solution proposed by [9]). This solution provides good results, but is dependent on the processes capacity to handle all situations.

Second, a multi-agent multi-model system where agents may behave alternately as AGENT agents and CartACom agents was proposed. This kind of approaches raises several issues such as detecting the appropriate model in each situation, or ensuring the consistency of internal data used by a model when another one is used. Some methods are suggested in the simulation literature, like in [26]. But, the way to detect the need to change model is specific to each situation. Adding mechanisms for detecting model commutations seems very redundant with the existing constraints, which are already used as controller. We believe that generalisation requires an alternative solution. It may be to have all information in a same level, in order to choose in a single process which agent will be activated, and which algorithm will be apply. This implies to have a single model mimicking the behaviour of all three existing models.

3.2 A Multi-Level Multi-Agent Model: PADAWAN

As exposed in [15], there has been a recent raise of the issue of multi-level modelling in multi-agent systems. Having analysed and compared existing multi-level multi-agent models with regards to the needs in cartographic generalisation, including [6], [14], [21], [23], [25], our choice was to use the PADAWAN model [16], where the non-tree-like organisation of levels and the flexible definition of environment seem wide enough to model the complex relations between our geographical objects.

PADAWAN is a multi-level multi-agent model for simulation, allowing agents to get relations in several environments. It relies upon an interaction-oriented approach (IODA) [12]. The expression of agents' behaviour in the IODA formalism is based on interactions, that describe through a condition/action rule a behaviour that occurs between two entities. The entities involved in an interaction are a source, i.e. an agent, and a target, which may be one or several agents, or the source itself – for reflexive interactions. The behaviour of agents of a given environment is expressed using an interactions matrix. When an interaction between a family of sources and a family of targets is feasible, it is assigned to the intersection of the line of the source and the column of the target. This assignment links an interaction to a priority of execution and a maximum distance between the source and the target.

The description of an interaction consists in three distinct aspects: a trigger, preconditions and actions to do. The trigger expresses the motivation for the agent to do the interaction (e.g. in an ecosystem simulation "eat" may have "be hungry" as trigger). Preconditions express external conditions to satisfy ("get some food"). Both criteria need to be satisfied in order for an interaction to become feasible. Trigger, preconditions and actions are described using abstract primitives, which are to be concretely implemented by agents.

Compared with IODA, PADAWAN includes a multi-environment aspect. Agents may be situated inside one or more environments, and each environment may be encapsulated inside an agent, so that environments might be interlinked in a non-treelike way. Each environment gets its own interaction matrix, allowing the definition of behaviour rules specific to each environment. Added to the expression of relations between hosted agents, this matrix allows the expression of relations between a host and the hosted agent.

4 Adapting AGENT and CartACom

In order to build the new model, we have to express the behaviour of original generalisation models within the PADAWAN paradigm, while gaining genericity. The adaptation of interactions from AGENT and CartACom models is the first step of our process seeking to solve remaining generalisation issues.

4.1 Differences between Simulation and Problem Solving

While PADAWAN is designed for multi-agent simulation, map generalisation is a constraint-driven problem. In the first case, the objective is to simulate a phenomenon in order to make observations on a system. In a constraints solving problem, the objective is to obtain satisfying results with a minimum cost. Thus, the definition of the perception of the environment by an agent will not be motivated by the intention of realism (i.e. the range of the field of vision of an animal), but instead by care of efficiency: an agent will perceive all necessary things in order to be generalised at best. In both situations, the perception will be limited, but by differently defined criteria. Similar differences occur when considering life cycle and time aspects.

These differences are not, a priori, an issue to the adaptation of PADAWAN to the solving of cartographic generalisation problems. The perception of the environment in PADAWAN is implemented at the interaction matrix level. Regarding life cycle, the PADAWAN interactions selection process is used in a specific life cycle. This aspect is developed in the next sections.

4.2 Inversion of the Perspective

In figure 3, the processing schemas of both AGENT and CartACom on one hand, and PADAWAN on the other hand, are displayed. The behaviour of agents in AGENT and CartACom is motivated by constraints. During its life cycle, an agent questions its constraint having priority to be solved, and this constraint returns a set of actions that the agent may try to execute. For instance, a building agent needs to satisfy its minimum size constraint. The agent then questions this constraint, and the constraint returns the following set of actions to try: {"Grow up", "Change geometry to a bigger rectangle", "Eliminate yourself"}).

An action in a PADAWAN interaction can easily be taken from an AGENT/CartACom action. Rules defined in the constraints of AGENT/CartACom models are merged with PADAWAN preconditions. The notion of constraint satisfaction naturally brings around the use of unsatisfaction as an interaction trigger.

Regarding the choice, by the agent, of the next action (resp. interaction) to execute, the perspective between AGENT/CartACom and PADAWAN is reverted: in AGENT, the agent chooses the next constraint to satisfy, and then deduces the next action to try (the first one in the list of actions to try it returns); in PADAWAN, the agent chooses its interaction from the whole set of the feasible ones. In other words, the entry point is constraints in AGENT, but interactions in PADAWAN. The switch is non-trivial, because in AGENT an action may be proposed by several constraints, and an action proposed by a constraint may be discouraged by another one. The first step of the adaptation of the action from AGENT and CartACom is to establish a way to express the opinion that a constraint may have on the realisation of an action.

4.3 Behaviour of the Agents

In existing generalisation models, a constraint may take a stand for (or against) an action in four different ways. In order to formalise this report, we introduce the notion of advices of a constraint. The four possible advices that a constraint may express are:

— *indifferent*, the default one, when there is no prior generalisation knowledge about the influence of the execution of an action on the satisfaction of this constraint,
— *favourable*, only when the constraint is unsatisfied, and generalisation knowledge assumes a positive influence of the action execution on the constraint satisfaction,

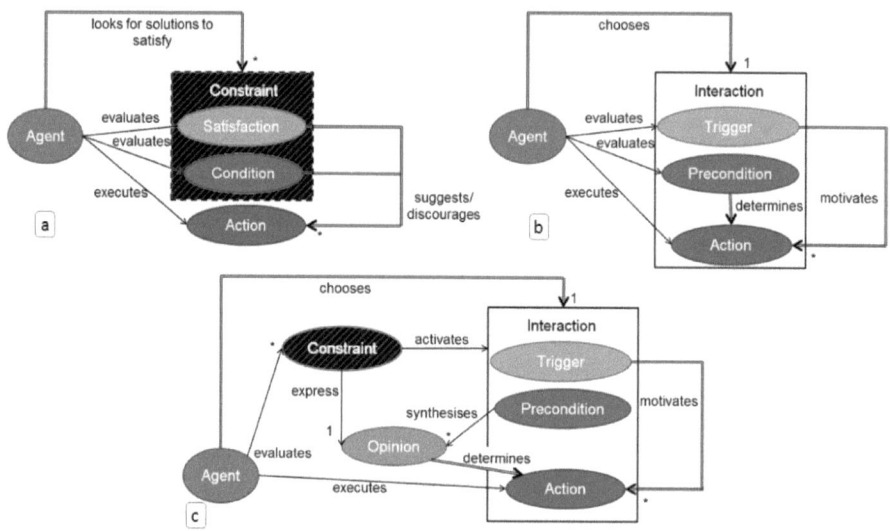

Fig. 3. (a) exposes the mechanism of AGENT and CartACom, (b) exposes the mechanism of PADAWAN, (c) is our proposal to use specific aspects of generalisation models in the PADAWAN models

- *unfavourable*, opposite of the previous one, when the execution of the action is *a priori* negative for the constraint,
- *opposite*, when the impact of the execution of the action will certainly be damaging, and may cause irreparable mistakes.

For instance, for a building, the unsatisfied "Squareness" constraint (expressing the willingness to replace almost right angles by strictly right angles) will be favourable to the "Simplify in Rectangle" action, but the "Preservation of the concavity" constraint (for objects with a concave shape) will be unfavourable to this action. Synthesising advices of constraints, an interaction may be a priori:

- *feasible*, if at least one constraint is favourable, and the others are in the worst case indifferent;
- *feasible, but risky*, if at least one constraint is favourable, at least one is unfavourable, and none is opposite;
- *unfeasible*, when at least one is opposite, or when there is no favourable constraints.

The precondition notion of PADAWAN is substituted by this advice model. This allows a first selection of feasible interactions, but it is not sufficient to choose the best interaction. In the AGENT and CartACom models, the constraint having priority is selected according to following factors, in order of decreasing importance: the importance of the constraint (a constraint will not be relaxed before another one with a lower importance), the current unsatisfaction, and a weight factor given by the constraint for the action. At the moment, we use here a basic heuristic that needs to be enhanced. For the adaptation of PADAWAN, we use the notion of trigger to organise interactions.

The constraint aspect of AGENT, CartACom and GAEL was translated into the PADAWAN paradigm using this expressed advice model. Interactions were defined and included in interaction matrices sets, specific to some concrete experiments describes in section 5. We defined new life cycles for the agent based on these matrices. These life cycles are based on the PADAWAN life cycle, but add adaptations specific to our generalisation problem. One of the adaptations is the fact that the life cycle of an agent in generalisation allows to revert a modification, if a modification is assessed as having a negative effect on constraints satisfaction. So, when the original PADAWAN life cycle for simulation chooses one action sequence, in our model for generalisation, the agent identifies a ranked list of possible actions, and tries and tests the first one. If one of them gives a perfect solution (all constraints are satisfied), the life cycle is over. If the impact is positive, but not perfect, the model proposes another list of realisable interactions, computed from the new result, and tries another one. If the impact is negative, the interaction is cancelled, and the next one in the list is tried. Two life cycles have been implemented with simple and extended backtracking respectively, corresponding to the original CartACom and AGENT life-cycles.

5   Implementation and Results

Our first experiment was to try to reproduce the existing models results with the PADAWAN paradigm. To do that, we used the matrices shown on figure 4a for AGENT and on figure 4b for CartACom. As we can see, no interaction between host agent and hosted agents may be seen in the CartACom matrix, and no action between two hosted elements may be seen in the AGENT matrix which translates the fact that interactions between agents are hierarchical in AGENT and transversal in CartACom. We used the life-cycles with simple and extended backtracking for CartACom and AGENT respectively. As a result, we managed to reproduce the results of the original models, in term of effectiveness (the quality of the results is the same), and in term of efficiency (the number of time-consuming operations is the same).

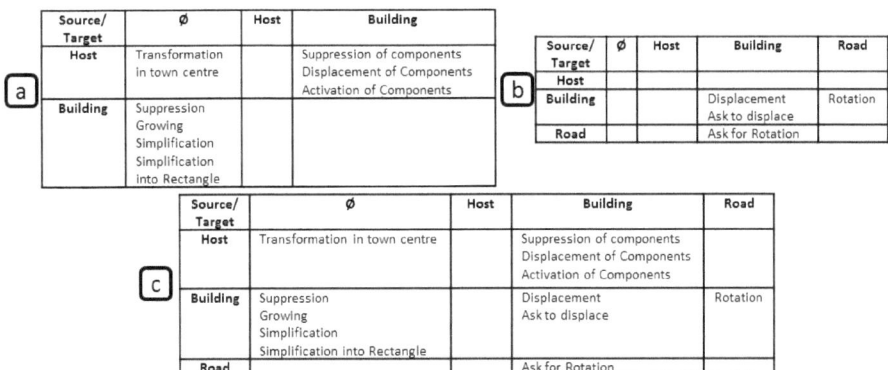

Fig. 4. Different matrices for our experiments. (a) matrix for urban an urban block in AGENT, (b) matrix for the map environment in CartACom, (c) matrix for urban block in our combined experiment.

For our second experiment, we tried to mix agent behaviours stemming from both AGENT and CartACom models, on a simple application case (to begin) that however is a remaining problem of generalisation. When generalising urban areas with buildings to a scale of 1:25k or smaller, we want to ensure that buildings almost parallel to a road change to strictly parallel. Indeed, the exact relative orientation of a building is, for this kind of scale, information surplus. Applying the rotation operation, based on a relational constraint of parallelism, is already done in rural areas using CartACom. We want here to introduce this transformation also when generalising an urban area with the AGENT paradigm. We use the matrix given in figure 4c, and the life cycle with simple backtracking. The main difficulty was to calibrate the parameters controlling the order in which the actions are tried. This calibration was done empirically, with progressive refinement. Despite this methodology not being satisfactory, we managed to get some satisfying results, as shown in figure 5. This proves that we may add new interactions in a simple way, and opens perspectives for solving more complex problems using interactions that are not purely hierarchical or transversal.

  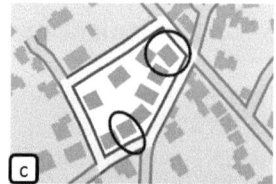

Fig. 5. (a) non-generalised data, (b) generalised data in 1:25k, using AGENT (only the central block was generalised), (c) generalised data using our PADAWAN modelling with buildings aligned to the road

6 Conclusion and Perspectives

In order to solve remaining generalisation issues, we showed that modelling interactions of agents using a multi-level formalism is quite helpful. Therefore, we used a multi-level simulation model and proposed an adaptation for the specificities of a constraints driven problem. As a first step, we manage to reproduce the results of existing models, and to solve some relatively simple issues handling multi-level relations, like the orientation of building in urban area (Figure 5), or the generalisation of dead-ends and of their neighbourhood [13].

In this paper, we presented the first steps of a work in progress with imperfect results demanding manual corrections. Our next step will be to propose a generic way to orchestrate possible interactions and to calibrate parameters used to order possible interactions. Another point is to propose a better heuristic for selecting interactions. Then, we will propose a solution to integrate the GAEL agents behaviour in our system, focusing on topographic maps with trekking and tourism data upon.

References

1. Baeijs, C., Demazeau, Y., Alvares, L.: SIGMA: Application of Multi-Agent Systems to Cartographic Generalization. In: Perram, J., Van de Velde, W. (eds.) MAAMAW 1996. LNCS, vol. 1038, pp. 163–176. Springer, Heidelberg (1996)
2. Barrault, M., Regnauld, N., Duchêne, C., Haire, K., Baeijs, C., Demazeau, Y., Hardy, P., Mackaness, W., Ruas, A., Weibel, R.: Integrating Multi-agent, Object-oriented, and Algorithmic Techniques For Improved Automated Map Generalization. In: 20th International Cartographic Conference, vol. 3, pp. 2110–2116 (2001)
3. Duchêne, C.: Généralisation cartographique par agents communicants: le modèle CartA-Com. PhD Thesis, Université Paris 6 – Pierre et Marie Curie, Paris, France (2004)
4. Duchêne, C., Gaffuri, J.: Combining three multi-agent based generalisation models: AGENT, CartACom and GAEL. In: 13th International Symposium on Spatial Data Handling, pp. 277–296 (2008)
5. Duchêne, C., Ruas, A., Cambier, C.: The CartACom model: transforming cartographic features into communicating agents for cartographic generalisation. International Journal of Geographic Information Science 26(9), 1533–1562 (2012)
6. Ferber, J., Michel, F., Baez, J.: AGRE: Integrating environments with organizations. In: Weyns, D., Van Dyke Parunak, H., Michel, F. (eds.) E4MAS 2004. LNCS (LNAI), vol. 3374, pp. 48–56. Springer, Heidelberg (2005)
7. Fernandes, K.: Systèmes Multi-Agents Hybrides: Une approche pour la Conception des Systèmes Complexes. PhD Thesis, Université Joseph Fourier, Grenoble, France (2001)
8. Gaffuri, J., Duchêne, C., Ruas, A.: Object-field relationships modelling in an agent-based generalisation model. In: Proceedings of 11th ICA Workshop on Generalisation and Multiple Representation, Montpellier, France (2008)
9. Harrie, L., Sarjakoski, T.: Simultaneous graphic generalization of vector data sets. Geoinformatica 6(3), 221–233 (2002)
10. Jaara, K., Duchêne, C., Ruas, A.: A model for preserving the consistency between topographic and thematic layers throughout data migration. In: 15th International Symposium on Spatial Data Handling (SDH 2012), Bonn, Germany (2012)
11. Jabeur, N., Boulekrouche, B., Moulin, B.: Using multiagent systems to improve real-time map generation. In: Lamontagne, L., Marchand, M. (eds.) Canadian AI 2006. LNCS (LNAI), vol. 4013, pp. 37–48. Springer, Heidelberg (2006)
12. Kubera, Y., Mathieu, P., Picault, S.: IODA: an interaction-oriented approach for multi-agent based simulations. Journal of Autonomous Agents and Multi-Agent Systems (JAAMAS) 23(3), 303–343 (2011)
13. Maudet, A., Touya, G., Duchêne, C., Picault, S.: Improving multi-level interactions modelling in a multi-agent generalisation model: first thoughts. In: Proceedings of 16th ICA Workshop on Generalisation and Multiple Representation, Dresden, Germany (2013)
14. Minar, N., Burkhart, R., Langton, C., Askenazi, M.: The Swarm simulation system: A toolkit for building Multi-Agent simulations. Technical Report 96-06-042, Santa Fe Institute (1996)
15. Morvan, G.: Multi-level agent-based modelling – A literature survey, http://arxiv.org/abs/1205.0561
16. Picault, S., Mathieu, P.: An Interaction-Oriented Model for Multi-Scale Simulation. In: 22nd International Joint Conference on Artificial Intelligence (IJCAI/AAAI), Barcelona, Spain, pp. 332–337 (2011)

17. Renard, J., Gaffuri, J., Duchêne, C.: Capitalisation problem in research –example of a new platform for generalisation: CartAGen. In: 12th ICA Workshop on Generalisation and Multiple Representation, Zürich, Switzerland (2010)
18. Ruas, A.: Modèle de généralisation de données géographiques à base de contraintes et d'autonomie. PhD Thesis, Université Marne La Vallée (1999)
19. Ruas, A.: The Roles of Meso Objects for Generalisation. In: 9th International Symposium on Spatial Data Handling, Beijing, China, vol. 3b, pp. 50–63 (2000)
20. Ruas, A., Plazanet, C.: Strategies for automated map generalisation. In: 7th International Symposium on Spatial Data Handling (SDH 1996), Delft, Netherlands, pp. 319–336 (1996)
21. Soyez, J.-B., Morvan, G., Dupont, D., Merzouki, R.: A Methodology to Engineer and Validate Dynamic Multi-level Multi-agent Based Simulations. In: Giardini, F., Amblard, F. (eds.) MABS 2012. LNCS, vol. 7838, pp. 130–142. Springer, Heidelberg (2013)
22. Taillandier, P., Gaffuri, J.: Improving map generalisation with new pruning heuristics. International Journal of Geographical Information Science 26, 1309–1323 (2012)
23. Taillandier, P., Vo, D.A., Amouroux, E., Drogoul, A.: GAMA: A simulation platform that integrates geographical information data, agent-based modeling and multi-scale control. In: Cousineau, G., Curien, P.-L., Robinet, B. (eds.) LITP 1985. LNCS, vol. 242, pp. 242–258. Springer, Heidelberg (1986)
24. Touya, G., Duchêne, C.: CollaGen: Collaboration between automatic cartographic generalisation processes. In: Advances in Cartography and GIScience, pp. 541–558 (2011)
25. Vo, D.A., Drogoul, A., Zucker, J.D.: An operational Meta-Model for handling multiple scales in Agent-Based simulations. In: International Conference on Computing & Communication Technologies, Research, Innovation, and Vision for the Future (2012)
26. Yilmaz, L., Lim, A., Bowen, S., Ören, T.: Requirements and Designs Principles for Multisimulation with Multiresolutions, Multistage and Multimodels. In: Proceedings of the 2007 Winter Simulation Conference (2007)

Practical Application of Matchmaking Problem: Trainee Allocation for Teachers

Maxime Morge and Eric Piette

Laboratoire d'Informatique Fondamentale de Lille
Université Lille 1
Cité Scientifique- F-59655 Villeneuve d'Ascq
`maxime.morge@univ-lille1.fr, eric.piette@gmail.com`

Abstract. In this paper, we tackle a complex real-world problem: trainee allocation for primary school teachers in a French teaching Academy. This complex real-world problem can be reduced into the well-known Hospitals / Residents (HR) problem. However, the most difficult part consists of generating the preference lists according to the real constraints, priorities and wishes. Additionally, we adapt the $\mathbb{S}wing$ method to the HR problem and we apply it to this real-world problem in order to balance the different objectives. In this way, the $\mathbb{S}wing$ method decreases the management cost of the operation.

1 Introduction

Many real-world problems can be understood as matchmaking problems in which two sets need to be paired up: the assignment of junior physicians to hospitals [1], staff to faculties [2], students to colleges [3], children to schools [1,4], online matrimony [5], etc. Whatever the application domains are, the problem consists in finding the best matching between individuals. This problem was first studied in [6] which provides a constructive proof showing that every instance admits at least one admissible solution.

In this paper, we tackle a complex real-world problem: trainee allocation for primary school teachers in a French teaching Academy (in French, IUFM). For this purpose, the University Institute for Teachers Training has a program to allocate training practices according to the desiderata of trainees and the constraints of the supervisors. In order to be assigned, each teacher selects and orders two areas where she wants to be assigned. Additionally, priority is given to trainees having more children, then those working part-time and finally those with no car. Conversely, the diplomas of supervisors and the distances between the trainees and the supervisors allows to prioritize them. In order to manage the increasing number of recruitments, the allocation, which is performed manually, must be automated. It is worth noticing no optimization method can be applied due to scalability issues. This complex real-world problem can be reduced into the well-known Hospitals / Residents (HR) problem [6]. However, the most difficult part consists of generating the preference lists according to the real constraints, priorities and wishes. Additionally, when we apply the existing algorithm for solving this problem we promote one community (e.g. the average distance) or another (e.g. the priority over trainees). Actually, even if the solution given by the Gale-Shapley algorithm is stable, it is the best one for one community but the worst for the other community [7]. By contrast, a recent method aims at reaching "fair" outcome: $\mathbb{S}wing$ [8]. In this paper, we adapt the $\mathbb{S}wing$ method to the HR problem and we apply it to a complex real-world problem in order to balance the different objectives. Since some constraints are relaxed, the $\mathbb{S}wing$ method decreases the management cost of the operation.

The paper is organized as follows. Section 2 introduces the background of our work. We adapt the $\mathbb{S}wing$ method in order to tackle this problem. Then, we present the real-world problem we address and we compare the solutions computed by the modified $\mathbb{S}wing$ method with some classical algorithms. Finally, section 5 discusses some related works and section 6 concludes.

2 Background

The Hospitals / Residents (HR) problem was first defined in [6]. This problem is a many-one generalization of the well-known Stable Marriage Problem.

In the HR problem, each man corresponds to a resident and each woman corresponds to a hospital which can potentially be assigned to multiple residents up to some fixed capacity.

Definition 1 (HR). *An instance of **Hospitals / Residents problem** of size (n, m), with $n \geq 1$ and $m \geq 1$, is a couple $HR = \langle H, R \rangle$ with $|H| = n$ and $|R| = m$ defined such that:*

- $H = \{h_1, \ldots, h_n\}$ *is a set of n hospitals. Each hospital $h \in H$ has a positive integral capacity, denoted c_h, indicating the number of posts that h has. Each hospital $h \in H$ has a preference list, denoted π_h, in which its ranks an acceptable set of residents in strict order;*
- $R = \{r_1, \ldots, r_m\}$ *is a set of m residents, each resident $r \in R$ has a preference list, denoted π_r, in which she ranks an acceptable set of hospitals in strict order.*

Given any individual $z \in H \cup R$, and given any potential partners $p_1, p_2 \in H \cup R$, z is said to prefer p_1 to p_2 if both p_1 and p_2 are in π_z and p_1 precedes p_2 on z's preference list π_z.

A solution for an instance of HR is an assignment of residents in posts for each of the hospitals. The assignment of a resident is an hospital, possibly none (denoted θ). The posts of an hospital are residents, possibly the empty set. Obviously, the assignment is mutual. Considering the assignment M, if $a_M(r_k) = \theta$, r_k is said to be unassigned, otherwise r_k is assigned. Similarly, a hospital $h_k \in H$ is undersubscribed, full or oversubscribed if the corresponding number of residents in posts (denoted $|p_M(h_k)|$) is less than, equal to, or greater than c_k, respectively. In a **matching**, no resident is assigned to an unacceptable hospital, no hospital offers a post to an unacceptable resident, each resident is assigned to at most one hospital and no hospital is oversubscribed.

A matching for an instance of HR is **stable** there is no potential couple, called blocking pair, which threats the current matching. A blocking pair prefers to be assigned together rather than according to the current matching. Considering a matching M for a HR problem, a couple (h, r) is blocking if r prefers h to her current assignment and: either h is undersubscribed; or h prefers r to at least one of its posts. A stable matching is called an admissible solution.

[6] provides a constructive proof showing that every instance of HR admits at least one admissible solution: an algorithm called the resident-oriented Gale-Shapley algorithm (RGS for short). In RGS, each unassigned resident, which is not desperate (alone and with a non-empty preference list), sends a proposal to her preferred hospital which accepts. If this latter is oversubscribed, then the hospital fires the worst resident having a post in this hospital. If the hospital is full, it deletes from its preference list all the residents who are worst than the residents having a post and reciprocally.

A counterpart of the RGS algorithm, known as the hospital-oriented Gale-Shapley algorithm (HGS for short), involves hospitals offering posts to residents. In HGS, each hospital which is not desperate (undersubscribed and with at least one resident in its preference list which is not assigned to it) proposes a post to the best one who accepts. If the resident was already assigned to a different hospital, then the resident is first unassigned. Then, the resident deletes from her preference list all the hospitals which are worst than the current hospital and reciprocally.

The RGS algorithm terminates with the resident-optimal stable matching (denoted M_r) in which each assigned resident has the best hospital that she could achieve in any stable matching and each unassigned resident is unassigned in every stable matching. M_r is worst-possible for the hospitals : if M is any other stable matching, then every hospital $h \in H$ prefers each resident in $p_M(h)$ to each resident in $p_{M_r}(h) \setminus p_M(h)$. The HGS terminates with the hospital-optimal stable matching (denoted M_h) in which every full hospital h is assigned with its c_h best partners and every undersubscribed hospital is assigned to the same set of residents in every stable matching. In M_h, each assigned resident has the worst hospital that she could achieve in any stable matching and each unassigned resident is unassigned in every stable matching. In general, there may be other stable matchings which cannot be reached by these two algorithms.

3 Swing

We adapt here the method $\mathbb{S}wing$ which was initially proposed in [8] to solve Stable Marriage Problem in order to tackle HR. $\mathbb{S}wing$ may reach some stable matchings which are not the output of RGS and HGS.

In the RGS and HGS algorithms, each community is given a role (proposer or responder). In the $\mathbb{S}wing$ method, the agents (residents or hospitals) alternatively play both of them in many bilateral negotiations from which the solution emerges. $\mathbb{S}wing$ realizes the minimal concession strategy [9] to reach a stable matching in order to be more equitable than the outputs of RGS and HGS. Based on this strategy, an agent goes first to its preferred partner. If that fails, the agent concedes, which consists in the withdrawal of its expectation, and so it sends a proposal to the following partners in its preference list. Meanwhile, the potential partners play the role of responder: these agents receive some proposals they can accept or reject depending on their concession levels. When all the agents are fully assigned or desperate, the $\mathbb{S}wing$ method stops.

The $\mathbb{S}wing$ method adopts an agent-based methodology for solving an economics problem of matchmaking since it focus on the interaction between the agents and the link between their satisfaction and the market. In the $\mathbb{S}wing$ method, each hospital and each resident is represented by an **agent** $a \in H \cup R$. At each step, the agent a is represented by a concession level ($\kappa_a \in [0, |\pi_a|]$) and its assignment status ($\sigma_a \in \{\top, \bot\}$). We note $\pi_z[1]$ the most preferred partner of z, $\pi_z[2]$ the second most preferred partner of z, and so on. If $\pi_z[k] = \lambda$, then $regret_z(\lambda) = k$. We define the concession level as the maximum rank in the preference list that the agent considers as acceptable at a certain time. $\kappa_z = 1$ means that the agent focus on its most preferred partner and so the other potential partners are not acceptable. A resident r is fully assigned ($\sigma_r = \top$) if she is assigned ($a_M(r) \neq \theta$). A hospital h is fully assigned ($\sigma_r = \top$) if it is full ($|p_M(h)| = c_h$). Initially, $\sigma_a = \bot$ and $\kappa_a = 1$ for all the agents. The preference lists π_a are different from one agent to another.

In $\mathbb{S}wing$, hospitals propose and residents respond alternatively (cf Algo. 1). In the odd steps, the hospitals play the role of proposers and the residents play the role of responders. In the even steps, the roles are swapped. Each proposer sends a proposal to the acceptable partners from the preferred ones to the least preferred ones. As soon as a responder accepts this proposal:

1. the proposer and the responder may divorce;
2. the proposer and responder are assigned;
3. the concession level of the proposer/responder are moved such that, if they are fully assigned, then they will only accept better partners.

It is worth noticing that, at each step, a proposer stops to send proposals as soon as it is fully assigned. If all the responders reject its proposals, the proposer will concede. When all the agents are fully assigned or desperate, the $\mathbb{S}wing$ method stops. An agent is desperate if this is an hospital (resp. a resident) which is undersubscribed (resp. unassigned) and it has reached the maximal concession level (the preference list has been fully explored).

At each step, the proposer and the responder may divorce (cf Algo. 2). If a member of the new couple is fully assigned, its previous (or one of its previous) partner is unassigned and so this latter may need to concede.

4 Practical Application

In this section, we present the real-world problem we tackle: the trainee allocation for primary school teachers in a French teaching Academy. For this purpose, the

Algorithm 1. $\mathbb{S}wing$ method

Data: $HR = \langle H, R \rangle$
Result: a assignment M

1 $M \leftarrow \emptyset$;
2 $step \leftarrow 0$;
3 **while** $\exists a \in \mathcal{A}, \sigma_a = \bot \wedge \kappa_a < |\pi_a|$ **do**
4   **if** $step$ is $even$ **then**
5        $proposers \leftarrow R$;
6        $responders \leftarrow H$;
7   **else**
8        $proposers \leftarrow H$;
9        $responders \leftarrow R$;
10   **forall the** $p \in proposers$ **do**
11   **for** $(i = 1 ; i \leq \kappa_p ; i++)$ **do**
12          $r \leftarrow \pi_p[i]$;
13   //p sends a proposal to r
14   **if** $regret_r(p) \leq \kappa_r$ **then**
15   //r accepts this proposal
16             $divorce(p,r)$;
17   **if** p is a $Resident$ **then**
18                $res \leftarrow p$;
19                $hos \leftarrow r$;
20   **else**
21                $res \leftarrow r$;
22                $hos \leftarrow p$;
23             $a_M(res) \leftarrow hos$;
24             $p_M(hos) \leftarrow p_M(hos) \cup \{res\}$;
25             $\sigma_{res} \leftarrow \top$;
26             $\kappa_{res} \leftarrow regret_{res}(hos) - 1$;
27   **if** $\sigma_{hos} = \top$ **then**
28                $\kappa_{hos} \leftarrow regret_{hos}(res) - 1$;
29   **else**
30                $\kappa_{hos} \leftarrow regret_{hos}(res) + 1$;
31   **break**;
32   **else**
33   //r rejects this proposal
34   **if** $\sigma_p = \bot$ **then**
35             $\kappa_p \leftarrow min(\kappa_p + 1, |\pi_p|)$;
36    $step++$;
37 **return** M

Algorithm 2. a and b may divorce

Data: a and b

1 **if** a *is a Resident* **then**
2 $\quad\mid\quad r \leftarrow a$;
3 $\quad\mid\quad h \leftarrow b$;
4 **else**
5 $\quad\mid\quad h \leftarrow a$;
6 $\quad\mid\quad r \leftarrow b$;
7 **if** $\sigma_r = \top$ **then**
8 $\quad\mid\quad h_2 \leftarrow a_M(r)$;
9 $\quad\mid\quad$ **if** $\sigma_{h_2} = \top$ **then**
10 $\quad\mid\quad\quad\mid\quad \kappa_{h_2} = min(regret_{h_2}(r) + 1, |\pi_{h_2}|)$;
11 $\quad\mid\quad a_M(r) \leftarrow \theta$;
12 $\quad\mid\quad p_M(h_2) \leftarrow p_M(h_2) \setminus \{r\}$;
13 **if** $\sigma_h = \top$ **then**
14 $\quad\mid\quad r_2 \leftarrow min_p(h)$;
15 $\quad\mid\quad a_M(r_2) \leftarrow \theta$;
16 $\quad\mid\quad p_M(h) \leftarrow p_M(h) \setminus \{r_2\}$;
17 $\quad\mid\quad \sigma_{r_2} = \bot$;
18 $\quad\mid\quad \kappa_{r_2} = min(regret_{r_2}(h) + 1, |\pi_{r_2}|)$;

University Institute for Teachers Training (in French IUFM) has a program to allocate training practices according to the desiderata of trainees and the constraints of the supervisors. We show here how this real-world problem is modeled and can be computed with the HR solving methods.

4.1 Overview

Each teacher must complete 3 internships, one per each quarter. Conversely, each supervisor can manage at most 2 trainees for each quarter. The region is divided into some areas and subareas. Each subarea is composed of cities where schools are located. In order to be assigned, each teacher expresses two wishes, i.e she selects and orders two areas where she wants to be assigned.

The problem is represented in Fig. 1 with an ER-model. The supervisors teach in different classrooms. Each classroom is included in one or more levels. The French primary education is divided into three levels:

- level L1 includes 3 classrooms called TPS, PS and MS;
- level L2 includes 3 classrooms called GS, CP and CE1;
- level L3 includes 3 classrooms called CE2, CM1 and CM2.

When a supervisors teaches in a classroom which is included in a level, we consider she teaches at this level. However, if she simultaneously teaches in GS and MS (or PS), then we consider she also teaches at level L1.

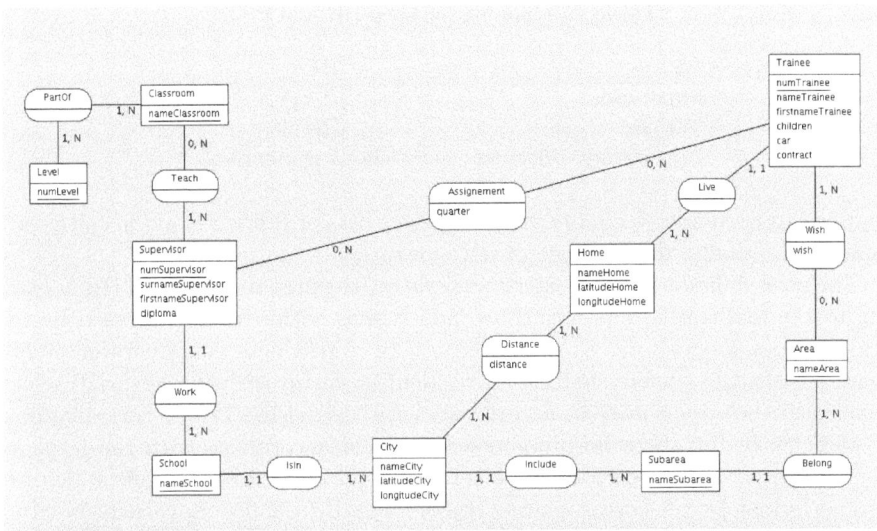

Fig. 1. ER model representing the inputs and the output of the problem

The IUFM aims at assigning an internship per quarter for each trainee respecting her wishes. Moreover, the IUFM wants to minimize the refunding due to the travels. That is the reason why we add the relation "Distance" between the homes of trainees and the cities where schools are. The distinction between these two entities allows to decrease the number of distances which are computed.

Priority is given to trainees having more children, then those working part-time and finally those with no car. Conversely, the diplomas of supervisors (EMF, CAFIPEMF or MAT) allows to prioritize them. Finally, the IUFM aims at minimizing the number of employed supervisors.

4.2 Mapping

An instance of **Primary School Teachers problem** (PST) is a couple PST = $\langle S, T \rangle$ where S is a set of supervisors and T is a set of trainees. An instance of PST can be reduced into 3 instances of HR, each of them corresponding to a quarter. In order to solve an instance of PST, we generate the corresponding instances of HR, solve them and translate the solutions.

Let us consider an instance of PST. In order to reach the assignment W_i for the quarter i, we transform PST into an instance HR_i in order to compute a matching with RGS, HGS or $\mathbb{S}wing$. This matching M_i allows to deduce W_i. Informally, the transformation is performed using Tab. 1.

The mapping between the agents for an instance PST and the agents for an instance of HR is performed by a bijection. For each quarter, the corresponding instance of HR is generated and resolved. Therefore, M_i is translated into W_i.

The transformation of an instance of PST into an instance of HR is performed in 3 steps. Firstly, supervisors are mapped to hospitals and trainees are

Table 1. Mapping between HR and PST

PST	HR
Supervisor	Hospital
Trainee	Resident
Constraints, priorities, and wishes	Preference list

mapped to residents. Secondly, the preference lists of residents and hospitals are generated. Finally, the instance of HR is returned.

The most difficult part consists in generating the preference lists of HR according to the real constraints, priorities, and wishes within PST expressed by the trainees and supervisors. The preference lists of residents are generated as follows. Firstly, the preference list of a resident is set up with the hospitals which map with the supervisors in accordance with the wishes of the corresponding trainee. Secondly, these hospitals are divided in accordance with the levels of the corresponding supervisors in order to give priority to the levels which are not performed by the corresponding trainee. Finally, the hospitals corresponding to supervisors who teach in classrooms already practiced by the corresponding trainee are deleted. The generation of the preference lists for the hospitals is performed as follows. For each hospital, the preference list is set up with the residents who consider it. Residents are sorted according to the number of children of the corresponding trainee, then according to the working time, and finally according to the car.

4.3 Experiments

We consider here data for the 2012 trainee allocation. 356 junior teachers must find 3 training practices supervised by one of the 783 senior teachers. As described previously, we transform this instance of PST into 3 instances of HR. Then, we resolve them using RGS, HGS or $\mathbb{S}wing$ (see Algo. 1). It is worth noticing no optimization method have been applied such as SMP2 [10] or DisFC [11] due to scalability issues. The experiments have been performed by a MacBookPro (2.6 GHz Intel Core i7 with 8 Go RAM). Each method reaches a solution in around twenty minutes. 80 % of the computational time is consumed by the generation of the preference lists which are different for each quarter since: i) the supervisors must be sorted according to the wishes, the diplomas, the distance and the levels which are not performed; ii) the trainees must be sorted according to the number of children of the corresponding trainee, then according to the working time, and finally according to the car. The assignments are denoted W_{RGS}, W_{HGS} and $W_{\mathbb{S}wing}$.

Table 1 compares the outcomes of the three methods. We can note that all the trainees are allocated according to these methods. Indeed, the number of available supervisors is greater than the number of trainees. Contrary to HGS, the RGS algorithm - which promotes the trainees - and the $\mathbb{S}wing$ method, allow (almost all trainees) to perform a training practice at each level. Whatever the method used, all the matchings are compliant with the wishes expressed by the trainees. Even if the HGS algorithm does not give priority to trainees, HGS as the RGS algorithm give the priority to the first wishes of trainees. Its seems that this soft constraint is relaxed by the $\mathbb{S}wing$ method. The average distance between the home of a candidate and the place of the training practice is lower for W_{RGS} (promoting trainees) than W_{HGS}. The average distance for $W_{\mathbb{S}wing}$ is in between. Since some constraints are relaxed, the $\mathbb{S}wing$ method allows to decrease the cost of management (by reducing the number of employed supervisors) much more than HGS and RGS.

Table 2. Overview (at top) and distribution of trainees/diplomas (at bottom)

Criteria	W_{RGS}	W_{HGS}	$W_{\mathbb{S}wing}$
Trainees with 3 practices	356	356	356
Trainees with 3 levels	348	266	356
Trainees with wish # 1	185	190	65
Average distance (km)	22.26	29.29	23.58
Nb of supervisors	496	348	64

Diploma	W_{RGS}	W_{HGS}	$W_{\mathbb{S}wing}$
EMF	41.23 %	32.02 %	15.78 %
CAFIPEMF	39.13 %	27.05 %	6.89 %
MAT	18.76 %	21.16 %	10.14 %

Table 1 shows the distribution of supervisors over diplomas. For instances, 41.23 % of supervisors having the best diploma (EMF) are required by the RGS algorithm. The RGS and HGS algorithms employ the supervisors with the best diplomas as much as possible. The RGS algorithm involves more specifically the supervisors with the best diplomas since the preference list of the trainees are generated depending on these diplomas. Since the $\mathbb{S}wing$ method involves only 64 supervisors (12 with EMF, 44 with CAFIPEMF and 7 with MAT), it is hard to say if the matching takes into account the diplomas of the supervisors.

As said previously, priority is given to trainees having more children, those working part-time and finally those who have no car. Table 3 summarizes for each of these categories, the number of trainees and the average distance. In 2012, few trainees having children are involved. That is the reason why we cannot check that the average distance decreases when the number of children increases. If we consider only trainees with no child, it seems that the trainees working part-time are promoted. Since the trainees with no car represent two-thirds of the cohort, the corresponding rule cannot be applied whatever the algorithm is.

Table. 4 summarizes and compares the outcomes of our three methods. ++, +, and -, means that a criteria is completely, moderately and badly fullfilled respectively. According to our experiments, no method seems to satisfy all the criteria. While RGS seems to give priority to trainees (level coverage, average distance, diploma), HGS is adapted to give priority to the supervisors (i.e. children, part-time, car). The $\mathbb{S}wing$ method balances both aspects. Actually, this

Table 3. Average distances for trainees

Nb of child.	Work. time	Car	Nb of trainee	W_{RGS}	W_{HGS}	W_{swing}
4	Part	No	0	-	-	-
		Yes	0	-	-	-
	Full	No	1	2.01	20.20	2.01
		Yes	0	-	-	-
3	Part	No	0	-	-	-
		Yes	0	-	-	-
	Full	No	2	5.84	67.90	6.78
		Yes	0	-	-	-
2	TPS	No	0	-	-	-
		Yes	0	-	-	-
	Full	No	1	45.79	45.80	45.79
		Yes	5	10.79	16.30	11.45
1	TPS	No	0	-	-	-
		Yes	1	6.92	73.90	7.38
	Full	No	12	17.03	20.20	17.35
		Yes	2	6.34	81.90	8.18
0	TPS	No	13	7.58	15.00	7.94
		Yes	9	19.39	16.30	19.92
	Full	No	202	27.43	35.70	29.01
		Yes	108	20.42	22.60	17.68

method seems to relax the constraints related to the wishes. Since these constraints have been relaxed, the $\mathbb{S}wing$ method allows to increase the coverage of levels and to decrease the number of supervisors who are employed and so, the management cost of the matching.

5 Related Works

The most famous real-world application for matchmaking problems is the National Resident Matching Program (NRMP) which manage the entry-level labor market for new physicians in the United States [1]. Each year, approximately 20,000 jobs are filled. In 2012, 38,777 aspiring medical residents applied for 26,772 available resident positions. For this purpose, each applicant submits a rank order list of positions for which she has interviewed and each residency program submit a rank order list of applicants they have interviewed and the number of positions to fill. Even if the number of participants for this application is greater than in our experiments, it is a straightforward application of the HR problem while solving a PST problem requires the generation of complex preference lists.

College admissions in China are centralized processes via standardized tests [3]. Therefore, the same preferences list is generated according to the test scores for all the schools. The Gale-Shapley algorithm is used for public school admissions in Boston and New-York [1]. Since, the inputs include the preferences of pupils over school and the priority levels of pupils (a pupil has priority to attend the

Table 4. Comparison of the methods for solving HR applied to an instance of PST

Criteria	RGS	HGS	$\mathbb{S}wing$
3 training practices	++	++	++
3 levels	+	−	++
Wishes	+	+	−
Distance	++	−	+
Nb. of supervisors	−	+	++
Priority to diplomas	++	+	?
Priority to children	?	?	?
Priority to part-time	+	+	+
Priority to "no car"	−	−	−

same school as an older sibling, pupils who are living in the school's walk zone have priority), the generation of the preference lists for schools is quite simple. In the daycare system in Denmark [4], priorities are imposed by local municipality (e.g. all schools give priority to their currently enrolled children and to the children with special needs). Therefore, the generation of priority is also straightforward.

In [5], the application domain is online matrimony in India. They propose to generate the preference list of participants according to the characteristics of the potential partners using fuzzy analytical hierarchy process considering multiple criteria. This method performs pairwise comparison of candidates attribute-wise since both women and men value physical attributes, such as age and weight, and those choices are assortative along age, height and education. Even if this application requires the generation of complex preference lists, the resulting matching is not evaluated.

6 Conclusion

In this paper, we have addressed a complex real-world problem: trainee allocation for primary school teachers in a French teaching Academy. Since we have presented the inputs and the outputs of such problem called Primary Schools Teachers (for short, PST), we have shown that an instance of PST can be reduced into 3 instances of the well-known Hospitals / Residents (HR) problem. However, this transformation requires the generation of complex preference lists. The preference list of each resident takes into account the wishes of the corresponding trainees, the diplomas of the supervisors, the distance between them, etc. The preference list of each hospital takes into account the priority over trainees which depends on the number of children, if they are part-time and if they have cars. In order to solve the corresponding instances of HR, we have tried the classical algorithms (the resident-oriented Gale-Shapley algorithm and the hospital-oriented Gale-Shapley) and we have also adapted a "fair" method called $\mathbb{S}wing$. Our first experiments seem to be in conformance with the fact that this latter balances the criteria which promote the trainees (e.g. average distance) and the criteria which promote the supervisor (i.e the priority over the trainees). Since some constraints are relaxed, the $\mathbb{S}wing$ method decreases the number of supervisors who are employed and so the management cost of the operation. However, it would be interesting to confront our first conclusion with the data of future campaigns.

References

1. Roth, A., Peranson, E.: The redesign of the matching market for american physicians: Some engineering aspects of economic design. AER 89(4), 748–780 (1999)
2. Baiou, M., Balinski, M.: Admissions and recruitment. AMM 110(5), 386–399 (2003)
3. Zhang, H.: Analysis of the Chinese college admission system. PhD thesis, University of Edinburgh (2009)
4. Kennes, J., Monte, D., Tumennasan, N.: The daycare assignment problem. Technical report, Department if Economics and Business, Aarhus University (2011)
5. Joshi, K., Kumar, S.: Matchmaking using fuzzy analytical hierarchy process, compatibility measure and stable matching for online matrimony in india. Journal of MCDA 19, 57–66 (2012)
6. Gale, D., Shapley, L.S.: College admissions and the stability of marriage. AMM 69, 9–14 (1962)
7. Knuth, D.: Mariage stables. Les Presses de l'Université de Montréal (1971)
8. Everaere, P., Picard, G., Morge, M.: Minimal concession strategy for reaching fair, optimal and stable marriages (extended abstract). In: Proc. of AAMAS, pp. 1319–1320 (2013)
9. Rosenschein, J., Zlotkin, G.: Rules of encounter: designing conventions for automated negotiation among Computers. MIT press (1994)
10. Gelain, M., Pini, M., Rossi, F., Venable, K., Walsh, T.: Local search algorithms on the stable marriage problem: Experimental studies. In: Proc. of ECAI, pp. 1085–1086 (2010)
11. Brito, I., Meseguer, P.: Distributed stable matching problems. In: van Beek, P. (ed.) CP 2005. LNCS, vol. 3709, pp. 152–166. Springer, Heidelberg (2005)

A Control Architecture of Complex Systems Based on Multi-agent Models

Tomás Navarrete Gutiérrez[1], Laurent Ciarletta[2], and Vincent Chevrier[2]

[1] Public Research Centre Henri Tudor (CRPHT),
Resource Centre for Environmental Technologies (CRTE)
6A avenue des Hauts-Fourneaux
L-4362 Esch-sur-Alzette, Luxembourg
tomas.navarrete@tudor.lu
[2] Université de Lorraine, LORIA, INRIA-Lorraine
Vandoeuvre-lès-Nancy
F-54506, France
{vincent.chevrier,laurent.ciarletta}@loria.fr

Abstract. The challenge we address in this work is the control of complex systems. We consider techno-social systems which share with complex systems some characteristics like big number of entities, autonomous entities, pre-existing systems, and multiple levels of organization.

Our proposal is based on the multi-agent paradigm to model the complex system, to forecast its evolution and to assess the impact of control actions on it. Our solution is an exogenous architecture of the system to control using an equation-free approach based on multi-agent model. An example implementation of the architecture is presented on a free-riding problem of peer-to-peer file sharing networks. Implementation results demonstrate that our architecture can control such a network.

Our contributions are i) to demonstrate the feasibility of our approach and its ability to control a system and, ii) to show that the modularity of the architecture enables to tackle issues related to the use of multi-agent paradigm in the context of control of complex systems.

1 Introduction

The objective of our work is to make a concrete link between multi-agent model simulation and external control of complex systems. The control of complex systems obliges to overcome a series of difficulties related to complex systems characteristics: local interactions produce the global outcomes of the system, complex systems are decentralized systems made of autonomous entities, they are not easily (or at least usefully) modeled by analytical models, preexisting complex systems may not be legally, or technically stopped or tampered with in order to control them. One major difficulty that any control mechanisms of a complex system faces is modeling the evolution of the system behavior. Overcoming this difficulty means to characterize the evolution of the behavior of the target system by taking into consideration the different levels of a complex system (local and global for example) and the emergence of global outcome from local interactions.

Multi-agent paradigm is well suited for modeling complex systems, because it can take into consideration the following characteristics of complex systems: many autonomous entities, different levels of organization, sensitivity to initial conditions and non-linear dynamics. It has been identified as suitable to model or engineer specific domains like sociology[1], biology[2], urban studies[3], wireless communications[4], or traffic[5].

Within the multi-agent paradigm, the global dynamics of a system, at the macroscopic level, is not given in advance (opposite to the analytical models) but is the outcome of the interaction of each agent's behavior, at the microscopic level. The advantages of this approach are that: it can represent and simulate open systems; it can take into consideration, from the moment of creating the model, the dynamic and heterogeneous characteristics of the individual behaviors; and finally, it can analyze the importance of a local behavior on the global functioning of the system[6].

In this article, we consider the special case of complex techno-social systems [7,8]. These systems are made of humans and artificial entities (cars, routers, servers, telephones, electricity lines). Specifically, we focus on techno-social systems out of control, that cannot be "stopped" to modify their behavior and guide them to a particular state. Controlling a system means applying (control) actions to modify the course of its behavior. The choice of the action to apply is made by using a predictive model of the system. In the case of complex systems, these actions are at local level but their effects are global. Controlling a complex system implies to have a predictive model that includes both aspects in order to assess the impact of a local action at global level. Additionally, we consider the case where endogenous control mechanisms (if any) of a given system are insufficient.

In this article, we investigate the use of a multi-agent system as model of complex systems. Such system can elicit (by testing) the link between local actions and collective outcome.

Our work is guided by the question: **How can we use multi-agent model simulation to control a techno-social system from the outside?**

The contribution of this paper is the description of a generic architecture to achieve an exogenous control and its assessment through a peer-to-peer example.

The paper is organized as follow. In the next section we present related work, we then present the case study on which we will implement our proposal. The presentation of our proposition is divided in two parts: first we describe the principles of the architecture and then we outline the specific implementation of our architecture within the example case. Afterwards, we present experiments and results obtained with our architecture and finally our conclusions.

2 Related Work

We present here work that also applies the multi-agent paradigm to the control of complex systems.

Organic Computing (OC) is a German research initiative whose object of study are technical complex systems [9]. The main idea behind OC is that technical systems share characteristics such as emergence and self-organization with living (organic) systems. Living systems are considered to deal with the control problem through self-* properties. Therefore, other systems could also benefit (particularly when dealing with control) from having self-* properties as well as from learning.

Self-organization is a process where a system changes its internal organization to adapt to changes in its goals and the environment without *explicit external control* [10]. [11] argue that control feed-back loops are useful to engineer self-organizing (a form of complex systems or at least systems sharing properties with complex systems) software systems. The point of view of engineering self-organizing systems is that, the autonomy of the elements should lead to a coherent global behavior. However, solely defining a system with autonomous elements cannot give guarantees about the global behavior of the system. Empirical approaches have demonstrated the feasibility of self-organizing systems [12].

Emergent engineering is a methodological framework for deploying large-scale networked systems. It is illustrated with self-organized security scenarios [13]. It involves an abstract model of programmable network self-construction in which nodes execute the same code, yet differentiate according to position. It relies on defining the basic entities and the mechanisms by which these entities are able to create reliable architectural components. Control is broken down and locally distributed to every entity of the system.

All the previous related works propose example applications that tackle the problem of control from a "design" or "engineering" point of view and as such, they are hardly applicable without major modifications to preexisting systems. Our proposal is to envisage a control mechanism from an exogenous perspective.

3 Case Study

In this part, we present the system to control, namely the *target system*. It is a peer-to-peer (p2p) network where peers are connected in a network of a certain topology. Peers have a "free-market" behavior: they share if they have an interest in doing so.

Peer-to-peer file sharing networks like BitTorrent, Kademlia or eDonkey are techno-social systems sharing some characteristics with complex systems [14], namely those we are interested in: they are composed of autonomous participants, they may have millions of participants, because of their self-organizing and open nature they exhibit nonlinear behaviors and it is not simple to gather information from them [15,16].

We are particularly interested in a collective phenomenon present in p2p networks: free-riding. In p2p file sharing networks each member of the network or "peer" is supposed to contribute to the system by sharing its files in return for being able to download files from other peers [17]. Free-riding in a p2p file-sharing network means to be able to download files from other peers without sharing any. Extensive presence of free-riders in a network can degrade its performance up to the point of rendering it useless, that is why it is important to control their presence [18,19].

As target system we use a peer-to-peer network simulator since it is not easy to directly work with an already deployed file-sharing network because of technical and legal reasons. A simulator allows us to measure every parameter of the system and hence, better assess the performance of the architecture. Another advantage is the possibility to reproduce the experiments, impossible otherwise within a real peer-to-peer network. A precise description of the simulator implementation is provided in [20], we used the simulator "PeerSim" [21], developed within the European projects "Bison" and "DELIS".

The agent's definition is inspired from [22]. An agent decide to share (or not) according to its generosity and to the proportion of other peers that share in its neighborhood. We will use different definitions of the neighborhood parametrized by a "depth". The network is defined by a constant number of agents, its topology built from a Watts and Strogatz algorithm [23] can produce different families of graphs by only changing the value of a parameter (namely p).

In brief, agent's parameters are its sharing state ($Sharing_i$), its generosity (θ_i) and the depth of the neighborhood (d). The network is characterized by its size (N) and its structure (parametrized by p).

The initial proportion of peers that share is given by X_{init} parameter.

4 The Architecture

4.1 Definition and Principles

We add a control architecture (called C) to an existing system (the target system T). The objective of C is to keep T in a given state. This architecture works in a feedback loop. It observes this system, forecasts its evolution through multi-agent simulations and determines the most appropriate action to apply through (again) multi-agent simulations. This architecture is based on the following principles.

Feedback Loop. System C will influence system T in order to make the output y of T be as close as possible to a reference value. The output of system T is used as input for system C which in turn will produce an output that will become the input of system T.

Exogenous Implementation. The exogenous principle of the architecture is twofold. First, it is exogenous because system C is meant to be an independent system. That is, if it stops working, it shall not prevent system T from working. Second, it is built under the hypothesis that the preexisting system T cannot be stopped to add the architecture as a control mechanism.

Equation-Free Modeling. Equation-free refers to a paradigm for multiscale computation and computer-aided analysis[24,25]. The central idea is to avoid the explicit definition of coarse equations by using short bursts of appropriately initialized fine-scale simulation.

The main idea behind the equation-free approach is the use of microscopic models to do macroscopic analysis of a model. In our case, we use microscopic models to determine the state of the target system as well as the effects of control actions. These models are simulated models given at a local description level namely multi-agent models.

4.2 Overview of the Architecture

We shall only give here a broad description of the architecture (see [26] for the full generic definition).

The architecture is composed of different blocks in charge of the different functions of the architecture. *Observe Target System* provides the architecture with information observed from the target system. *Estimate Future State* executes the multi-agent model simulation to estimate the target system. *Simulate Control Actions* executes the multi-agent model simulation of possible control actions effects. *Apply Control Actions* effectively applies control actions.

The execution flow of our architecture can be summarized as follows.

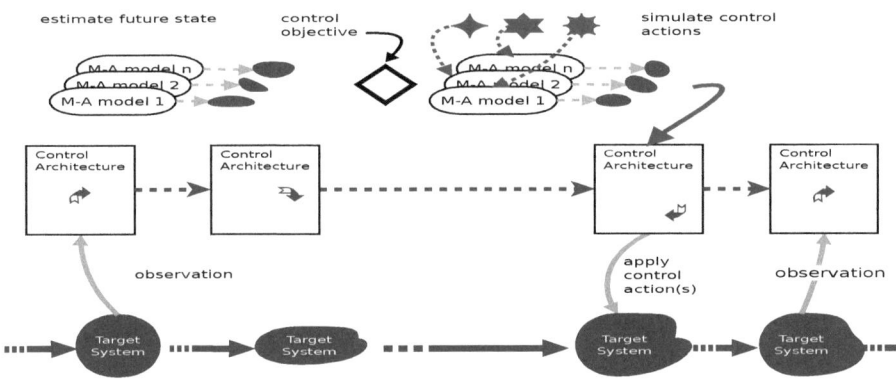

Fig. 1. Item flow of the blocks in the architecture

The first activity executed is to provide one (or more) multi-agent model(s) with data based on the observation of the target system and to simulate it (them) up to a time horizon corresponding to the control objective in order to obtain an (several) estimation(s) of the future state of the target system. Then, this estimated future state is compared to the control objective to see if any actions are required. If control actions are required, they are determined by simulation models and then applied. If no control actions are necessary, the main control loop restarts. This execution flow is illustrated in figure 1.

5 Implementation in the Case Study

For the p2p free-riding phenomenon, each of the blocks were instantiated as follows.

Observe p2p Network. A peer is randomly selected from the target system, its internal characteristics ($Sharing_i$ and θ_i) and the list of its neighbors are recorded. The neighbors of the peer are put in a queue of peers to sample. The next peer from the queue is sampled and so on, until q peers have been sampled.

Estimate Future Contribution Level. We define a multi-agent model called $M_{topological}$ where the agents represent the peers of the target system and are organized in a network. The network in $M_{topological}$ is identical to the sampled graph. Each agent is identical to its corresponding peer (same characteristics) and we suppose it follows the same decision function.

The future contribution level is estimated by running a $M_{topological}$ instance initialized by the above mentioned information.

Simulate Control Actions. Acting on the target system consists in tricking peers to make them share. We have settled a maximum number of peers to control (cf. table 1). The different control actions tested consist of different amounts of peers to be controlled.

In the experiments, we will test two different ways to select the peers to trick: random selection and based on an importance metric relative to the portion of the network sampled.

Criteria to Select the Control Action. The criteria used to decide which control action is the best one is the gain in contribution level.

6 Experiments

We have conducted a series of experiments with two aims. In the first set of experiments, we wish to demonstrate the possibility of controlling a system with our architecture. In the second one, we focus on issues related to multi-agent simulation and illustrate how the modularity of the architecture ease their study.

6.1 Controlling the Target System

Experimental Setup. We define different target system specifications that differ according to the node number ($N = 1000$ or $N = 10000$), the network family (structured $p = 0$, small world $p = 0.25$, semi-structured $p = 0.50, 0.75$ or random $p = 1$). For all scenarios, the target system is configured with the parameters indicated in table 1. We generated 1000 instances of the target system for each family of networks and peers number, each instance was initialized to have an initial contribution level of 0.18.

In the control architecture, we use different metrics to choose the node on which apply the control action (random, betweenness and HITS). Each importance metric to select the peers to trick was tested on each of the generated instances of the target system.

Table 1. Parameters values of the target system and the architecture used in the first set of experiments

Parameter	Changes in the experiments	
	Yes	No
N	1000, 10000	
$\theta \sim U(0, \theta_{max})$		$\theta_{max} = 10$
p	0, 0.25, 0.50, 0.75, 1	
d		1
x_{init}		0.018
q		6
maximum number of peers to trick		10
strategy to choose peers to trick	random, betweenness, hits	

For each experiment, we measured the number of times that the final contribution level x_f reached a value higher or equal than 0.50.

Nominal Behavior of the Target Systems. It refers to the behavior of the target system without our control architecture. Table 2 summarizes the nominal behavior of the different families for each scenario. In the majority of scenarios, free-riding is present.

Table 2. Nominal behavior of the target system. Number of experiments (out of 1000) where the final contribution level was higher or equal to 0.50 for each network family ($p = 0, 0.25, 0.50, 0.75, 1$).

	$x_f \geq 0.50$				
	$p=0$	$p=0.25$	$p=0.50$	$p=0.75$	$p=1$
$N = 1000$	1	468	41	0	0
$N = 10000$	0	195	0	0	0

Results. We present the results for each of the scenarios and for each of the metrics in table 3: the control architecture reduced the free-riding phenomenon. This demonstrates that the architecture is able to control the target system.

The best performance in the experiments was achieved with the small world network family. In semi-structured networks, the architecture succeeded only in the $N = 1000$ scenarios. For the other scenarios, the architecture could not control the system at all.

We can notice that a random selection as metric can slightly increase the performance of the architecture.

6.2 Multi-agent Related Issues

The objective in these experiments is to study the influence of the specific issues of multi-agent model simulation in the performance of the architecture: having

Table 3. Results summary. Number of experiments (out of 1000) where the final contribution was higher or equal to 0.50 for each network family ($p = 0, 0.25, 0.50, 0.75, 1$).

	$x_f \geq 0.50$				
	$p=0$	$p=0.25$	$p=0.50$	$p=0.75$	$p=1$
$N = 1000$					
random	8	955	688	13	0
betweenness	8	962	653	4	0
hits	9	917	641	4	0
$N = 10000$					
random	0	578	0	0	0
betweenness	0	570	0	0	0
hits	0	429	0	0	0

multiple models producing multiple future state predictions, changing the time horizons of the simulations, the amount of information gathered from the target system.

During experiments, we will vary the amount of information gathered from the target system, the numbers of models used for simulation and the time horizons for system state prediction.

Experimental Setup. We chose only one kind of target system and made variations on the architecture implementation.

The specification of the target systems is the same as that of the previous set of experiments. Here we present the different values given to the parameters that changed with respect to previous experiments.

- $N = 1000$
- The graph linking the agents was generated with the Watts and Strogatz algorithm with $p = 0.25$.
- $X_{init} = 1\%$

Architecture Implementation. We focus here on the changes towards the previous implementation of our architecture.

We varied here the size of the sample used to observe the target system: $q = \{1, 5, 20, 50, 100\}$ in the *Observe p2p network* block.

In multi-agent model simulation, we used two different time horizons $t_a = \{1, 15\}$ to estimate the future state of the target system.

In the architecture, multi-agent simulations are used in the *Estimate future contribution level* and *Simulate control actions* blocks. For simplicity, we shall focus on using ten instances of $M_{topological}$ at the same time for the *Estimate future state* block. This implies that we shall directly initialize 10 instances of the topological model at the same time at the first time step of simulation and let them simulate for a specified time horizon.

The model used is the same as the one of the previous set of experiments. To initialize the values for the parameters of the model, we first gather information from the target system as previously described in 5. We sample the target system starting at a randomly chosen peer. We repeat this 10 times, each time with a different random initial peer.

Each model provides a prediction of the system state. To select among these multiple predictions, we compare at each time step the previous prediction of the contribution level with the observed contribution level at the current time step. The importance of the criteria is that the model with the least error is the one to be used in the *Simulate control actions* block.

We also change the maximum number of peers to trick (namely $maxspins = \{10, 30\}$).

Nominal Behavior for Target System. It exhibits two different behaviors given the same initial conditions. In 71% of cases, we have a network with a majority of free-riders, and in 29% of cases, we have a majority of sharing peers.

Experiments and Results. The experiments were conducted varying parameters as mentioned above. Each configuration was repeated 100 times.

The results are summarized in table 4. From the results, we can see that implementing multiple models in the *Estimate future state* yields better results, compared to those of the previous set of experiments. In the implementation with only one model of the previous set of experiments, for network family $p = 0.25$ we managed to augment, in average, 47% the cases where $x_f \geq 0.50$ (see table 3). In this implementation with ten models, we see an average augmentation of almost 70% (target system stabilizes at $x_f < 0.50$ in 29% of cases).

Table 4. Control results with direct initialization. Percentage of experiments where the final contribution level was higher or equal to 0.50 for each sample size ($q = 1, 5, 20, 50, 100$). *N.A.:* Not tested because with a sample size of $q = 1$, we assumed that we could not trick more peers than sampled.

t_a	max. peers to trick	$x_f \geq 0.50$ q				
		1	5	20	50	100
1	10	99%	95%	94%	89%	64%
15	10	85%	86%	84%	75%	100%
15	30	N.A.	100%	100%	100%	97%

6.3 Discussion

The preceding results demonstrate the feasibility of our approach through its implementation in a concrete case. It is important to notice that the architecture succeeded in controlling the system with few resources: less than 10% (resp. 1%) of sample nodes to observe the target system in the $N = 1000$ (resp. $N = 10000$) scenario and 1% (resp. 0.1%) of peers to trick to achieve the control.

As we used different multi-agent simulations to determines the system evolution and the effects of possible actions, a decision should be made to select the "best" model. In the experiments of 6.2, the criteria was the quality of the predictions. In this particular implementation the variable to control is global, and thus, we selected a criteria that compares the global outcome of the simulations. Nonetheless, we can imagine criteria related to local characteristics of the system (e.g. the amount of correct sharing state (of each peer) predictions). This would imply that a correspondence between the agents and the peers in the network exists (whether direct or indirect).

This previous criteria selected one model *and* its results. Instead of limiting to one result, we could be interested in using all the results by aggregating them. In the case of a global variable, we can imagine aggregating in a mean value the results of all the instances we simulated, or taking a median value from the observed results. But, once again, we could imagine that the variable to control is local. In this case, we would also have to define a way to compare the local characteristics in the results of each model to the other models.

7 Conclusions

In this article, we proposed a coherent architecture integrating multi-agent simulation in a control loop using the equation-free approach to control complex system. The architecture has the form of a generic pattern where several multi-agent simulations can be used to estimate the future state of the target system and the effects of local control actions.

This architecture was implemented in an experimental platform and applied to the free-riding problem in p2p file sharing networks. This implementation illustrated how each component of the architecture can be instantiated. We have demonstrated that the architecture can attain control of a system under conditions where the expected behavior cannot be reached with a nominal behavior. We also showed how its modular design enables to study issues related to the control of complex systems and to the improvement of performances.

Using multi-agent simulation requires to establish a relationship between the model and the target system: the validity and calibration of models, and the translation of entities from the target system to the elements of the model. We showed that the modular design of the architecture is convenient to investigate such issues and to assess the decision made. This modular design also enables to incrementally improve a specific implementation.

As perspectives, the generic and modular design of the architecture would allow to explore the following aspects:

- The application example we used can be further investigated along different dimensions to better assess the architecture: open target system, heterogeneous behaviors of peers, noise on the observations, etc.
- The different operating regimes of the target system lead to an implementation where one model would be used for the slow regime and one for the fast regime. The kind of regimes are already a hint on how to select the model to use: for fast regimes of the target system (implying fast state changes) one could be compelled to use models that keep the pace with the target system

(give fast but inaccurate results) and for slow regimes, one could use models that are not as fast as the target system (giving very accurate results but requiring significant time).
– Also we consider worthy to study different ways to make evolve the models used in the architecture, like learning techniques, or genetic algorithms.

References

1. Phan, D., Amblard, F. (eds.): Agent-based modelling and simulation in the social and human sciences. GEMAS Studies in Social Analysis. Bardwell (2007)
2. Grimm, V., Railsback, S.: Individual-based modeling and ecology. Princeton Univ. Pr. (2005)
3. Galland, S., Gaud, N., Demange, J., Koukam, A.: Environment Model for Multiagent-Based Simulation of 3D Urban Systems. In: The 7th European Workshop on Multi-Agent Systems, EUMAS 2009 (2009)
4. Jamont, J.P., Occello, M., Lagrèze, A.: A multiagent approach to manage communication in wireless instrumentation systems. Measurement 43(4), 489–503 (2010)
5. Mandiau, R., Champion, A., Auberlet, J., Espié, S., Kolski, C.: Behaviour based on decision matrices for a coordination between agents in a urban traffic simulation. Applied Intelligence 28(2), 121–138 (2008)
6. Van Dyke Parunak, H., Savit, R., Riolo, R.L.: Agent-Based Modeling vs. Equation-Based Modeling: A Case Study and Users' Guide. In: Sichman, J.S., Conte, R., Gilbert, N. (eds.) MABS 1998. LNCS (LNAI), vol. 1534, pp. 10–25. Springer, Heidelberg (1998)
7. Vespignani, A.: Predicting the behavior of techno-social systems. Science 325(5939), 425 (2009)
8. Parke, T., et al.: The social constructions of technological systems: New directions in the sociology and history of technology. The MIT Press (1987)
9. Würtz, R.P.: Organic Computing. Understanding Complex Systems, vol. 21. Springer, Heidelberg (2008)
10. Di Marzo Serugendo, G., Gleizes, M.P., Karageorgos, A.: Self-organization in multi-agent systems. Knowledge Engineering Review 20, 165–189 (2005)
11. Brun, Y., Di Marzo Serugendo, G., Gacek, C., Giese, H., Kienle, H., Litoiu, M., Müller, H., Pezzè, M., Shaw, M.: Engineering self-adaptive systems through feedback loops. In: Cheng, B.H.C., de Lemos, R., Giese, H., Inverardi, P., Magee, J. (eds.) Self-Adaptive Systems. LNCS, vol. 5525, pp. 48–70. Springer, Heidelberg (2009)
12. Wolf, T.D., Holvoet, T., Samaey, G.: Engineering Self-Organising Emergent Systems with Simulation-based Scientific Analysis. In: Proceedings of the Fourth International Workshop on Engineering Self-Organising Applications, Universiteit Utrecht, pp. 146–160 (2005)
13. Ulieru, M., Doursat, R.: Emergent engineering: a radical paradigm shift. International Journal of Autonomous and Adaptive Communications Systems 4(1), 39–60 (2011)
14. Shahabi, C., Banaei-Kashani, F.: Modelling P2P data networks under complex system theory. Int. J. Comput. Sci. Eng. 3(2), 103–111 (2007)
15. Aidouni, F., Latapy, M., Magnien, C.: Ten weeks in the life of an eDonkey server. In: IEEE International Symposium on Parallel & Distributed Processing, IPDPS, pp. 1–5. IEEE (2009)

16. Stutzbach, D., Rejaie, R.: Capturing accurate snapshots of the Gnutella network. In: INFOCOM 2005. 24th Annual Joint Conference of the IEEE Computer and Communications Societies. Proceedings IEEE, vol. 4 (March 2005)
17. Androutsellis-Theotokis, S., Spinellis, D.: A survey of peer-to-peer content distribution technologies. ACM Computing Surveys (CSUR) 36(4), 335–371 (2004)
18. Krishnan, R., Smith, M.D., Tang, Z., Telang, R.: The impact of free-riding on peer-to-peer networks. In: Proceedings of the 37th Annual Hawaii International Conference on System Sciences, p. 10 (January 2004)
19. Zghaibeh, M., Harmantzis, F.: Revisiting free riding and the Tit-for-Tat in BitTorrent: A measurement study. Peer-to-Peer Networking and Applications 1(2), 162–173 (2008)
20. Ciarletta, L., Chevrier, V., Navarrete Gutierrez, T.: Multi-agent simulation based governance of complex systems: architecture and example implementation on free-riding. In: ENC 2013, Mexican International Conference on Computer Science, MORELIA, Mexique (October 2013)
21. Jelasity, M., Montresor, A., Babaoglu, O.: A modular paradigm for building self-organizing peer-to-peer applications. In: Proceedings of the International Workshop on Engineering Self-Organising Applications (July 2003)
22. Feldman, M., Papadimitriou, C.H., Chuang, J., Stoica, I.: Free-riding and whitewashing in peer-to-peer systems. IEEE Journal on Selected Areas in Communications 24(5), 1010–1019 (2006)
23. Watts, D., Strogatz, S.: Collective Dynamics of 'small-world' networks. Nature 393, 440–442 (1998)
24. Samaey, Y.K.G.: Equation-free modeling. Scholarpedia 5(9), 4847 (2010)
25. Siettos, C.: Equation-Free multiscale computational analysis of individual-based epidemic dynamics on networks. Applied Mathematics and Computation 218(2), 324–336 (2011)
26. Navarrete Gutierrez, T.: Une architecture de contrôle de systèmes complexes basée sur la simulation multi-agent. Thesis (in english), Université de Lorraine (October 2012)

Monitoring Oil Pipeline Infrastructures with Multiple Unmanned Aerial Vehicles

Jakub Ondráček, Ondřej Vaněk, and Michal Pěchouček

Agent Technology Center, Department of Computer Science, FEE,
Czech Technical University, Technická 2, Praha 6, Czech Republic
http://agents.fel.cvut.cz

Abstract. Effective monitoring of oil pipeline systems is an important task due to a very high environmental cost of an undetected oil spill. For this task, we focus on the utilization of unmanned aerial vehicles (UAV) and we formalize the problem of optimal pipeline monitoring with multiple mobile agents as a mathematical program which captures properties of the problem, including environmental sensitivity and motion constraints of the UAVs. We design two algorithmic extensions which push inherent scalability limits of this problem. Finally, we show that even with limited scalability, we are able to find optimal solutions for real-world sized problems and show a promising way to approximately solve larger scenarios.

Keywords: Optimization, Unmanned Aerial Vehicles, Mathematical Programming, Infrastructure Security.

1 Introduction

Oil pipeline systems belong to a set of critical infrastructures which are vital for contemporary society, however, by their inherent spread throughout a wide area and poisonous fluid transported, they pose a serious threat to the environment. Additionally, many oil pipeline infrastructures have obsolete equipment and underdeveloped monitoring systems. Only in Nigeria, between 1976 and 1996, authorities report 4647 incidents of oil pipeline damage; these incidents resulted into spills of over 2 millions of barrels of oil with a great negative impact on local mangrove forests with precious fauna.

With the spread of new technologies, new possibilities for pipeline systems monitoring are emerging. We focus on the utilization of a set of unmanned aerial vehicles (UAV) equipped with a leak detection sensors; the UAVs periodically patrol the oil pipeline system for a potential damage. Mobile UAVs with high resolution sensors greatly enhance the security of oil transfer compared to static sensors, as static sensors are typically able to only detect leakage at a certain place, however, they are unable to track the damage, take high-resolution pictures from required angles and they cannot be easily reassigned to perform another monitoring task.

We address the problem of designing a set of algorithms able to compute optimal trajectories for a set of UAVs with their mobility restrictions. The problem of trajectory design for one or more mobile units over a monitored area is not a new one [1–3]. However, the existing approaches have a specific set of restrictions and the area being monitored differs from a pipeline tree-like structure so any of the existing approaches cannot be–to our best knowledge–directly reused.

Extending the work of Nigam and Kroo [1], we formalize the problem as planning of multiple trajectories on a graph. We introduce two different environment representations, we provide a mixed-integer mathematical program for computing trajectories for each UAV, minimizing the total potential damage possibly caused (using environmental sensitivity index maps), and we provide two algorithmic improvements to speed up the solutions process.

The results show that the model contains scalability bottlenecks, such as the number of agents and the planning horizon. However, even with limited scalability, we are able to compute optimal solution for graphs with 50–100 nodes with 10 agents in tens of minutes which are promising results for possible deployment of UAVs for oil pipeline system monitoring.

2 Related Work

Decision making for improved risk management of oil pipeline infrastructures is a well studied subject. Recently, Dawotola et al. [4] introduce a set of decision methods for risk management of oil and gas pipelines. Prasanta et al. [5] propose a risk-based decision support system that reduces the amount time spent on inspection using Multi-Criteria Decision Analysis framework. When narrowing down to individual pipeline monitoring approaches, Tapanes [6] solves a problem of real-time pipeline integrity monitoring where he uses a Fiber Optic Technology. Jawhar [7] solves the problem of pipeline infrastructure monitoring with Wireless Sensor Networks. His work is based on static sensors deployment; however, we are interested in using mobile sensors, such as UAVs and in the design algorithms for their movement.

If we look at the problem of trajectory planning for one or more UAVs, Nigam and Kroo [1] solve the problem of persistent surveillance with a focus on creating a trajectory for UAVs with respect to aircraft dynamics. They formalize the problem as a semi-heuristic patrolling algorithm for a single UAV and its extension for multiple UAVs. Presented algorithms are suitable for trajectory design, however, we plan over a different environment and we thus have a different set of constraints. Jakob et al. [2] solve the problem of coordination and planning for aerial surveillance. They decompose the problem into two sub-problems: the problem of single-area surveillance and the problem of allocation of UAVs to multiple areas. They use area decomposition approach as we do, however our environment model and utility function differ. Pasqualetti et al. [3] solve the problem of cooperative patrolling using graph theory. Their work is similar to ours in patrolling a set of points with priorities, however; their approach is not directly applicable because they look only for solutions with non-intersecting trajectories. Finally, Chevaleyre [8] solves another patrolling problem on a graph.

The problem is formalized as a computation of trajectory minimizing time lag between two visits in each node. We extend this work by considering multiple agents with real-world restrictions.

3 Domain Description

The main purpose of this work is to design an optimal oil pipeline patrolling mechanism to detect pipeline damage with proactive methods, i.e., detect the oil pipeline damage as soon as possible and minimize the resulting loss using mobile units equipped with damage sensors. The solution is applicable to any overground pipeline systems. There are several types of events potentially causing oil pipeline damage. These events can be categorized into the following classes [9]: corrosion, operational failure, mechanical failure, natural hazards and third party activity. We focus on all events except the third party activities as we assume no strategic element behind the events and we assume the events to have a purely random nature.

Typically, the pipeline systems are monitored using a number of static sensors, such as optical fibers, pressure sensors or volumetric difference measurements. These systems suffer from a limited number of types of events they can detect and they provide reactive observations—they report an event after the a harmful event was caused. Additionally, some of these systems have a high rate of false alarms. Mobile sensors such as UAVs equipped with a camera are more difficult to deploy, however, they can detect problems before an actual damage, the range of detectable events is large and false positives can be typically minimized by repeated measurements with differing parameters. We thus focus on mobile sensors for pipeline damage detection[1].

Typically, the pipelines span over a larger area with unequal sensitivity to damage. To model the sensitivity of the environment, a mapping between complex properties of the environment and a numerical scale is required. We utilize Environmental Sensitivity Index (ESI) [10] which quantifies the difficulty of removing the effects of oil spills on biological resources (such as oil-sensitive animals and rare plants), biological habitats (which are used by oil-sensitive species or are themselves sensitive to oil spills) and human-use resources which have an added value to human activities. To each segment of the oil pipeline, we assign a single number from the ESI map. ESI takes values from 1 to 10 where 1 is the lowest sensitivity of the area to oil spills and 10 is the highest with highest recovery costs. We use the scale in a linear manner, however in general, there is no problem of using a non-linear scale (or rescale the ESI scale non-linearly).

Problem Statement

The problem can be stated as a problem of design of monitoring trajectories for a group of UAVs equipped with sensors for damage detection over a graph

---

[1] However, our solutions is applicable jointly with static sensors, such as optical fibers providing additional information to the UAVs.

like structure with heterogeneous costs assigned to each node in the graph. The UAVs fly autonomously from and to a base and their movement is not restricted by the pipeline.

4 Formal Model of the Problem

Formally, the problem of oil pipeline monitoring using multiple UAVs can be seen as an optimization problem with multiple mobile agents optimizing a joint criterion function. In following sections, we abstract the environment into a graph, we explicitly define the movement of agents on the graph and we formulate the utility function to be optimized as a cost of potential damage to the environment. We use mathematical programming which allows us to capture constraints posed on the mobility of agents easily.

4.1 Environment Representation

We work with two possible types of environment representation; both of them are discretization of continuous areas. In the first case we leverage the graph-like structure of the oil pipeline systems and represent the environment by a tree graph $G = (N, E)$. The set of nodes N represents monitored parts of area. The nodes are placed on the junctions of the pipeline system and on the pipeline, such that the distance between the two nodes (i.e. the length of the edge connecting these nodes l) equals to the diameter of the agent's sensor. Every two nodes which represent adjacent pipeline parts in the original pipeline system are connected by a directed edge $e \in E$, where E is a set of all edges (i.e., for each pair of nodes n and m, we have a pair of edges $e(n, m)$ and $e(m, n)$).

In the second case the environment is tilled into a grid covering the pipeline system with hexagon tiles having diameter equal to the agent's sensor. The hexagon grid is represented by a directed graph $G_h=(N_h, E_h)$. Nodes $n \in N_h$ represent the centers of hexagon tiles. Directed edges $e \in E_h$ of length l connect nodes of neighboring tiles.

The two representations are displayed in Figure 1. Figure 1a displays the oil pipeline system. Figure 1b shows a tree graph representation and Figure 1c shows the hexagon grid created over the oil pipeline system.

In each graph, there is one or more nodes denoted as a base $B \in \mathbf{B}$. Each agent k has a single base ^kB assigned from which it starts and after a defined period of time returns to. One base can be used by multiple agents.

Finally, we add a loop edge $\lambda(n)$ into every node in the graph to represent a possibility of an agent staying in a node for some time.

4.2 UAV Movement

The UAVs are represented as K mobile agents moving over the graph. In general, the agents can have differing speeds $\{s_1, s_2, \ldots, s_k\}$. To capture the movement

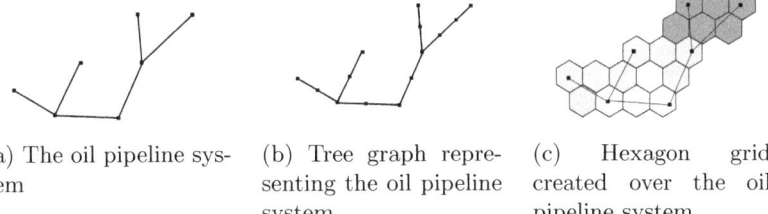

(a) The oil pipeline system   (b) Tree graph representing the oil pipeline system   (c) Hexagon grid created over the oil pipeline system

Fig. 1. Two representations of the environment considered in our model. The directions of edges are omitted for a better readability.

of UAVs, we discretize the time dimension and we plan the movement of the agents for T time steps.

If an agent k with a speed s_k transits an edge e with a length l, it requires $\sigma_k = l/s_k$ time steps, where σ_k has to be an integer. Thus, all speeds have to be scaled properly in the model to meet this constraint.

We introduce *edge-presence* variable ${}^k a_e^t$ which is set to 1 if the agent k is on the edge e in the time step t. Additionally, using ${}^k a_e^t$, we define *edge-entry* variable ${}^k r_e^t$ for each agent and each time step:

$$ {}^k r_e^t = \max\{{}^k a_e^t - {}^k a_e^{t-1}; 0\} \qquad (1) $$

This variable is expressed using two edge-presence variables: if the agent k wasn't in step t on the edge e and it was on the edge e in step $t+1$, then it entered the edge and the corresponding edge-entry variable is set to 1 (and zero in all other cases).

As an agent moves through a graph, we assume it covers by its sensor always only a single node. We introduce an indicator variable ${}^k x_n^t$ set to 1 if the k-th agent ${}^k a$ covers a node n at time step t and to zero otherwise. We consider a node n covered (i.e., a part of the environment along a pipeline being inspected) if the agent is on the loop edge $\lambda(n)$ (the first summand), on the second half of the incoming edge to n (the second summand) or on the first half of the outgoing edge from n (the third summand):

$$ {}^k x_n^t \leq {}^k a_{\lambda(n)}^t + \sum_{\substack{e \in in(n) \\ e \neq \lambda(n)}} \sum_{i=\max\{t-\sigma_k+1;0\}}^{\max\{t-\lfloor \sigma_k/2 \rfloor;0\}} {}^k r_e^i + \sum_{\substack{e \in out(n) \\ e \neq \lambda(n)}} \sum_{i=\max\{t-\lfloor \sigma_k/2 \rfloor+1;0\}}^{t} {}^k r_e^i \qquad (2) $$

where functions $in(n)$ and $out(n)$ return incoming and outgoing edges of the node n respectively.

4.3 Utility Function

Given the problem objectives, we aim to minimize the time of all parts of the oil pipeline system being unobserved by some UAV, weighted by the sensitivity of the area given by the ESI map. Formally, we minimize weighted age of information (AoI, measured in time steps) for all nodes in the graph.

For a node $n \in N$ and for a time step $t \in T$, we can compute a cost of a potential damage caused from the last visit (when no damage was found; in case of a damage detection, the trajectory planning process switches to another phase which is not considered here). If an agent covers a node in a given time step, AoI of that node is set to zero. If no agent covers the node, the AoI is incremented in each time step for a predefined value. The age of information at a node n at a time step t is defined recursively as:

$$AoI_n^t = \begin{cases} 0 & \text{if } \exists k, k \in K, {}^k x_n^t = 1 \\ AoI_n^{t-1} + 1 & \text{otherwise} \end{cases} \quad (3)$$

The first case reflects the coverage of the node n by an agent (captured in ${}^k x_n^t$). AoI is incremented by one if no agent is covering the node n.

Using AoI and properties of the environment, we can define cost of expected damage c_n^t for each node at each time step:

$$c_n^t = AoI_n^t \cdot ESI_n \cdot l_n \cdot f_n \quad (4)$$

The cost is given by the age of information (capturing number of steps when the node was not covered) multiplied by the value from the ESI map for the node n ESI_n, by the length l_n of the oil pipeline system within the sensor radius around a node n and by the failure rate f_n. Where the failure rate represent *damageability* of a given pipeline segment. It also represents another degree of freedom of our model and it can be replaced by a parameter supplied by subject matter experts. In our case the failure rate consists of two elements. The first element is inner pressure and the second one is a set of pipeline parameters (age, corrosion) and area properties (humidity, stability of the subsoil, temperature variations), which influence pipeline damageability [11].

For given system, ESI_n, l_n and f_n are fixed. We can thus replace the multiplication term by a constant $C_n = ESI \cdot l_n \cdot f_n$, reformulating the cost to:

$$c_n^t = AoI \cdot C_n \quad (5)$$

By combining the equation (3) and (5) we get:

$$c_n^t = \begin{cases} 0 & \text{if } \exists k \in K, {}^k x_n^t = 1 \\ c_n^{t-1} + C_n & \text{otherwise} \end{cases} \quad (6)$$

And we can express the utility for the system and time horizon T as:

$$U = \sum_{t \in T} \sum_{n \in N} c_n^t \quad (7)$$

The problem can be then specified as a problem of design of a constrained movement of agents such that the utility defined in equation (7) is minimized.

4.4 Multi-agent Model

With all definitions in place, we can introduce a mathematical model minimizing utility defined by (7) with a set of constraints imposed by the movement of UAVs. The model is valid for any oriented graph $G(N, E)$ with edges of equal length:

$$min \sum_{t \in T} \sum_{n \in N} c_n^t \quad (8)$$

$$c_n^t \geq c_n^{t-1} + C_n - M \cdot \sum_{k \in K} {}^k x_n^t \quad \forall n \in N, \forall t \in [1, T] \quad (9)$$

$$c_n^t \geq 0 \quad \forall n \in N, \forall t \in T \quad (10)$$

$$c_n^0 = 0 \quad \forall n \in N \quad (11)$$

$$\sum_{f \in out(n)} {}^k a_f^t \leq {}^k a_{\lambda(n)}^{t-1} + \sum_{\substack{e \in in(n) \\ e \neq \lambda(n)}} {}^k a_e^{\max\{t-\sigma_k; 0\}} \quad \forall n \in N, \forall k \in K, \forall t \in [1, T] \quad (12)$$

$$\sum_{e \in E} {}^k a_e^t \leq 1 \quad \forall k \in K, \forall t \in T \quad (13)$$

$$\sum_{e \in E} {}^k a_e^0 = 0 \qquad \sum_{e \in out({}^k B)} {}^k a_e^1 = 1 \quad \forall k \in K \quad (14)$$

$$\sum_{e \in in({}^k B)} {}^k a_e^{T-\sigma_k} = 1 \quad \forall k \in K \quad (15)$$

$${}^k r_e^t \geq {}^k a_e^t - {}^k a_e^{t-1} \quad \forall e \in E, \forall k \in K, \forall t \in [1, T] \quad (16)$$

$${}^k r_e^t \geq 0 \quad \forall e \in E, \forall k \in K, \forall t \in [1, T] \quad (17)$$

$${}^k x_n^t \leq {}^k a_{\lambda(n)}^t +$$

$$+ \sum_{\substack{e \in in(n) \\ e \neq \lambda(n)}} \sum_{i=\max\{t-\sigma_k+1; 0\}}^{\max\{t-\lfloor \sigma_k/2 \rfloor; 0\}} {}^k r_e^i +$$

$$+ \sum_{\substack{e \in out(n) \\ e \neq \lambda(n)}} \sum_{i=\max\{t-\lfloor \sigma_k/2 \rfloor+1; 0\}}^{t} {}^k r_e^i \quad \forall n \in N, \forall k \in K, \forall t \in [1, T] \quad (18)$$

$${}^k a_e^t, {}^k r_n^t \in \{0; 1\} \quad {}^k x_n^t \in R \quad \forall k \in K, \forall e \in E, \forall t \in T \quad (19)$$

$$c_n^t \in R \quad \forall n \in N, \forall t \in T \quad (20)$$

Equation (8) is the criterion minimizing the utility function. Equations (9)–(11) describe the advancement of cost on nodes in time (see section 4.3). Equation (12) guarantees continuity of agents' movement: it defines movement of the k-th agent from a loop of n or any incoming edge of n to any outgoing edge of n. Equation (13) defines that the k-th agent is in time t located on at most one edge. Equation (14) initializes the position of the agents. In time step $t = 0$ agents are not located on any edge. In time step $t = 1$, agents have to be located on any edge leading from the base (including a loop edge, allowing waiting in a base). Equation (15) defines that the agent has to be on an edge $e \in in(^kB)$ at σ_k time steps before the end of the planning horizon such that it lands in the base ^kB in time step T. Equations (16) and (17) integrate the edge entry conditions. Equation (18) express the coverage of nodes in terms of agent's movement on the edges (see section 4.2 for a detailed explanation). When the program is solved, the trajectories of the agents can be reconstructed from decision variables $^ka_e^t$.

Endurance of Agents. One of the real-world UAV restrictions is that each agent has a maximum flying endurance representing how many time steps an agent can fly without recharging. To incorporate this restriction, we define maximum endurance ^kD for each agent k and we add a variable ^kd_t for all agents and time steps $t \in T$ which represents how many time steps the agent have been away from its base, i.e., the flight time of the agent. These properties are reflected in equations (21). The agent's endurance is computed in the following way. If the agent is not located in its base at a current time step, then the flight time is increased by 1 according to equation (22). Otherwise, the result of the equation (22) is negative and the flight time of the agent is set to 0 according to the stronger restriction (21) (we assume that the agent needs just one step for the recharging in its base).

$$^kd^t \geq 0 \quad ^kd^t \leq {}^kD \qquad \forall k \in K, \forall t \in T \qquad (21)$$
$$^kd^t \geq {}^kd^{t-1} + 1 - M \cdot {}^kx^t_{kB} \qquad \forall k \in K, \forall t \geq 1, t \in T \qquad (22)$$
$$^kd^t \in \{0; {}^kD\} \qquad \forall k \in K, \forall t \in T \qquad (23)$$

These constraints can be appended to the model described above to integrate the endurance restrictions on the UAV flight time.

5 Solution Approach

Due to the fact that the model with extensions is computationally hard, we developed two modifications of a standard algorithm with a better scalability. The first one is an algorithm based on the decomposition of a given area into subareas and execution of the computation for each sub-area separately in a way that the optimal solution is still maintained. The second modification is a sub-optimal iterative algorithm which iteratively constructs a joint plan by computing a sub-plan for a single agent at a time and fixing plans of the others. We use IBM CPLEX 12.5 for solving our models.

5.1 Area Decomposition

The decomposition algorithm is based on the idea that with multiple bases, the agents starting in different bases with a limited endurance are able to reach only a subset of nodes in the graph. If the reachable areas do not intersect for two or more groups of agents, we can decompose the problem and solve the problem for the two reachable areas separately.

Our algorithm works in the following way: first, for each base $B^i \in \mathbf{B}$, we find all reachable nodes N^i from that base. The reachable nodes are nodes with a distance from base shorter than one half of the range of the agent with the best ratio of speed and endurance which is located in a base.

Second, we remove all nodes from the graph $G(N, E)$, which are not reachable from any base and create a *reachable graph* $G'(N', E')$ containing only reachable nodes without edges connected to unreachable nodes.

Third, we decompose the reachable graph into a number of sub-graphs:

$$G_1(N_1, E_1) \cup G_2(N_2, E_2) \cup \cdots \cup G_n(N_n, E_n) = G'(N', E')$$

where each sub-graph contains one or more base. For any two sub-graphs $G_i(N_i, E_i)$ with bases $B_i^1, \ldots B_i^n$ and $G_j(N_j, E_j)$ with bases $B_j^1, \ldots, B_j^m$, the following holds:

$$N_i = N_i^1 \cup \cdots \cup N_i^n, \quad N_j = N_j^1 \cup \cdots \cup N_j^m, \quad N_i \cap N_j = \emptyset$$

The edge sets E_i and E_j are subsets of E' connecting only nodes N_i and N_j respectively. Having the sub-graphs, we can compute solution for each sub-graph separately without negatively affecting the quality of the solution.

5.2 Iterative Algorithm

The main scalability drawback of the original approach is computation of all trajectories for all agents at once. By decomposing the problem and computing one trajectory at a time, we can significantly speed up the solution process with the trade-off of loosing optimality guarantees. The iterative process is performed as follows: in each iteration, we pick one agent and we compute its trajectory using the original model, but fixing all trajectories of other agents computed in previous iterations and not considering the rest of the agents whose trajectory was not computed yet. The iterative process stops when the utility cannot be improved by re-computing a new trajectory for any of the agents. This algorithm might terminate with a sub-optimal solution. We quantify the trade-off between speed and optimality in the following section.

6 Evaluation

In the evaluation we focus on two main properties: scalability and quality of our approach. The scalability of the model with respect to parameters is measured first, pinpointing the main bottlenecks of the model. Additionally, we compare the speed of computation of the three main programs: full model, decomposition algorithm and iterative algorithm, together with quantification of quality vs. optimality trade-off. Finally, we focus on the quality difference between different area representations, i.e., the tree graph and hexagon grid.

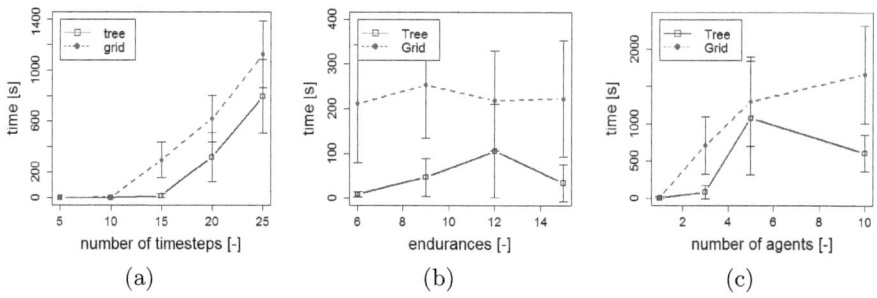

Fig. 2. Scalability of the model with respect to main parameters: number of time steps (a), endurance of the agents (b) and number of agents (c). Full computation without decomposition or iterative process was used.

For the evaluation, unless stated otherwise, we have used the following default configuration: the ESI values are set in rage 1–10 and sampled randomly from a normal distribution; agents have speeds sampled uniformly from a set of values $\{\frac{1}{3}, \frac{1}{2}, 1\}$. The default scenarios have randomly generated tree graphs with 50 nodes. When comparing the tree graph and grid representation, the grid is created from the tree graph by creating a convex hull. We considered two bases randomly positioned in a graph, 15 time steps and endurance of 10 time steps for all agents. Every instance of scenario was repeated 50 times with random parameters re-sampled; all tests were performed on 8-core Intel Xeon with 8 GB of memory.

Scalability. The scalability of the algorithm does not directly depend on the number of nodes (i.e., size of the graph) neither on the number of bases, however, rather on the planning horizon, i.e., the number of time steps (Figure 2a) where the dependency is exponential. Interestingly, there is no direct scalability bottleneck in the endurance of agents (Figure 2b). Higher endurance allows higher number of possible trajectories; however, if the endurance is equal to the number of time steps, the performance can be actually better in comparison with a shorter endurance.

The algorithm scales reasonably with the number of agents. Figure 2c shows the dependency of computation time on the number of agents on a graph with 100 nodes, 18 time steps, endurance of 18 and 5 bases randomly positioned in a graph. The dependency is not monotonic due to the distribution of agents into different bases. For a high number of agents, some of the newly added agents do not contribute to the quality of solution anymore (visible in case of the tree graph) and the solution may be found even faster.

If we look at different representations of the area, Figures 3a and 3b compare the scalability of all three algorithms on grid and tree representation. Due to the smaller size of the tree graph and lower number of possible paths, all algorithms scale better on tree graphs.

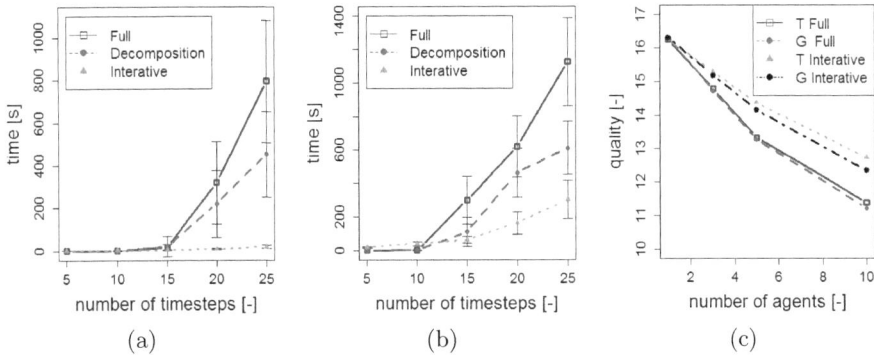

Fig. 3. Scalability of three different computation techniques on tree graphs (a) and grid graphs (b). Comparison of solution quality (lower is better) on tree and grid representation for full and iterative algorithms (c).

Solution Quality. Focusing on the quality of solutions, Figure 3c compares the cost of solution for the two representations. It can be seen that the quality is practically equal, it is thus not beneficial to represent the area as a grid (typically used in related work [1]). Finally, we compare the quality of the solution for optimal approach (i.e., full algorithm) and sub-optimal approach (i.e., iterative algorithm). From figures 3a and 3b we can see that iterative algorithm scales one to two orders of magnitude better, however, the quality of solution computed by the iterative algorithm is approx. 15% worse than the optimal solution (see Figure 3c). This shows a promising way of scaling the algorithm while keeping the quality in reasonable bounds.

7 Conclusions

Monitoring of oil pipeline infrastructures is vital for early detection of an environmental damage from an oil spill. Utilization of UAVs is one of possible ways how to effectively monitor the oil pipeline system; however, new algorithms have to be designed to efficiently navigate the UAVs. We have proposed a model of the problem with two possible area representations, extending the existing state of the art. We have incorporated a number of real-world constraints such as UAV speed and endurance, allowing design of more realistic trajectories. We have introduced two scalability improvements to be able to solve the model on real-world scenarios, preferring either quality of the solution or scalability of the computation. We have quantified main bottleneck parameters of the model and have shown that we are able to compute an optimal solution on real-world sized instances of the problem. The model does not consider an intelligent adversary which is causing a non-negligible amount of damage. This aspect would require utilization of the game-theoretic framework and it is subject to future research. Additionally, robustness extensions considering environmental conditions affecting the UAVs [12] are currently being integrated into the system.

Acknowledgements. This research was funded by the Office of Naval Research Global (grant no. N62909-11-1-7034). We also thank to the reviewers for insightful comments.

References

1. Nigam, N., Kroo, I.: Persistent surveillance using multiple unmanned air vehicles. In: 2008 IEEE Aerospace Conference, pp. 1–14. IEEE (2008)
2. Jakob, M., Semsch, E., Pavlíček, D., Pěchouček, M.: Occlusion-aware multi-uav surveillance of multiple urban areas. In: 6th Workshop on Agents in Traffic and Transportation (ATT 2010), pp. 59–66 (2010)
3. Pasqualetti, F., Durham, J.W., Bullo, F.: Cooperative patrolling via weighted tours: Performance analysis and distributed algorithms (2012)
4. Dawotola, A.W., van Gelder, P., Vrijling, J.: Multi criteria decision analysis framework for risk management of oil and gas pipelines. In: RELIABILITY, Risk and Safety, pp. 307–314. Taylor & Francis Group, London (2010)
5. Dey, P.K., Ogunlana, S.O., Naksuksakul, S.: Risk-based maintenance model for offshore oil and gas pipelines: a case study. Journal of Quality in Maintenance Engineering 10(3), 169–183 (2004)
6. Tapanes, E.: Fibre optic sensing solutions for real-time pipeline integrity monitoring. In: Australian Pipeline Industry Association National Convention, pp. 27–30 (2001)
7. Jawhar, I., Mohamed, N., Shuaib, K.: A framework for pipeline infrastructure monitoring using wireless sensor networks. In: Wireless Telecommunications Symposium, WTS 2007, pp. 1–7. IEEE (2007)
8. Chevaleyre, Y.: Theoretical analysis of the multi-agent patrolling problem. In: Proceedings of IEEE/WIC/ACM International Conference on Intelligent Agent Technology (IAT 2004), pp. 302–308 (2004)
9. Achebe, C.H., Nneke, U.C., Anisiji, O.E.: Analysis of oil pipeline failures in the oil and gas industries in the niger delta area of nigeria, 1274–1279 (2012)
10. Michel, J., Hayes, M.O., Brown, P.J.: Application of an oil spill vulnerability index to the shoreline of lower cook inlet, alaska. Environmental Geology 2(2), 107–117 (1978)
11. Hopkins, P.: The structural integrity of oil and gas transmission pipelines (2002)
12. Selecký, M., Váňa, P., Rollo, M., Meiser, T.: Wind corrections in flight path planning. International Journal of Advanced Robotic Systems 10 (2013)

Planning When Goals Change: A Moving Target Search Approach

Damien Pellier[1], Humbert Fiorino[1], and Marc Métivier[2]

[1] Laboratoire d'Informatique de Grenoble
110 avenue de la Chimie BP 38053 Grenoble
[2] Université Paris Descartes
45, rue des St Pères, 75006 Paris

Abstract. Devising intelligent robots or agents that interact with humans is a major challenge for artificial intelligence. In such contexts, agents must constantly adapt their decisions according to human activities and modify their goals. In this paper, we tackle this problem by introducing a novel planning approach, called Moving Goal Planning (MGP), to adapt plans to goal evolutions. This planning algorithm draws inspiration from Moving Target Search (MTS) algorithms. In order to limit the number of search iterations and to improve its efficiency, MGP delays as much as possible triggering new searches when the goal changes over time. To this purpose, MGP uses two strategies: Open Check (OC) that checks if the new goal is still in the current search tree and Plan Follow (PF) that estimates whether executing actions of the current plan brings MGP closer to the new goal. Moreover, MGP uses a parsimonious strategy to update incrementally the search tree at each new search that reduces the number of calls to the heuristic function and speeds up the search. Finally, we show evaluation results that demonstrate the effectiveness of our approach.

1 Introduction

Service robots performing simple domestic tasks begin to enter our daily lives. Still, many breakthroughs must be made in navigation, perception and sensors, energy management, mechatronics etc. But whatever the progresses made in these areas, one prominent issue is robot usability and their ability to adapt their decisions according to human activities. In such contexts, robots must constantly cope with events that modify their goals and disrupt their plans.

In order to tackle this problem, we propose in this paper a new planning algorithm that interleaves on-line planning and execution, called MGP (Moving Goal Planning) and built on the MTS (Moving Target Search) search strategy. MTS algorithms are search algorithms designed for path-finding and for real-time moving targets (an agent, "the hunter", follows a moving target, "the prey") interleaving path-finding toward the prey and hunter displacements. MTS algorithms are based on heuristic search (distance calculation) and, to our knowledge, have not been used for task planning. Thus, we propose to capitalize on recent advances in these two areas to devise a new and efficient planning algorithm able to adapt its plan when its goal changes over time as a new approach for continual planning [1].

The rest of the paper is organized as follows: Section 2 gives the state of the art; Section 3 formally introduces the moving goal planning problem and describes our algorithm; Section 4 presents the algorithms evaluation; Section 5 concludes and proposes possible avenues for future extensions.

2 Related Work

In task planning, the design of agents evolving in dynamic environments and able to adapt the execution of their current plan to goal changes is mainly studied in two different ways: rebuilding a plan from scratch or repairing it so that it can be executed in the new context. Although in theory both approaches are equally expensive in the worst case [2], experimental results show that plan repair is more efficient than replanning from scratch [3]. Preserving plan stability is another argument in favor of the plan repair strategy [4].

In path-finding, the agent's adaptation to dynamic environments is also a challenging issue especially in computer games to solve the Moving Target Search (MTS) with respect to real-time responses, large-scale search spaces and limited computation resources. In essence, a MTS algorithm interleaves path-finding and action execution for a "hunter" agent chasing a moving target – the "prey" – over a large map or grid. Since the pioneering works of Ishida [5], MTS approaches fall into two categories according to the strategy used to reuse the information collected in past searches.

The first strategy consists in using a heuristic to guide the search and learn shortest path distances between pairs of locations on a map. At each search, the heuristic is more informative and the search is sped up. The original MTS algorithm was an adaptation of the Learning Real-Time A* algorithm (LRTA*) [6] for a moving target. This approach was shown to be complete in turns based settings when the target periodically skips moves but it is subject to heuristic depressions and lost of information when the target moves [7]. Currently, the state-of-the-art algorithms with this first strategy are variants of the AA* algorithm [8]: MTAA* [9] and GAA* [10]. All these algorithms must use admissible heuristics to ensure their soundness and completeness.

The second strategy consists in reusing incrementally the search tree between two successive searches. The first algorithms based on this strategy are D* [11] and its successors. These algorithms were devised for replanning in unknown or changing environments and are both based on backward chaining. They perform correctly when the environment does not change much during the search. Otherwise, their performances are bypassed by simple successive calls to A* every time the target moves [10]. As for FRA* [12], changes in the environment are not taken into account but it performs properly when the target moves over time. FRA* is based on the A* forward search. Every time the target moves, FRA* adapts quickly the search tree and recalls A* on the new search tree. FRA* is currently the most efficient MTS algorithm. However, the adaption of the search tree is widely dependent on the grid representation of the environment. In order to apply FRA* on more generic environments, a variant called GFRA* [13] (Generalized Fringe-Retrieving A*) has been recently proposed. Contrary to FRA*, GFRA* uses arbitrary graphs, including the state lattices used for Unmanned Ground Vehicles navigation. Finally, Sun at al. [14] proposes an algorithm called I-ARA*, which is the first incremental anytime search algorithm for moving target search. I-ARA* operates like repeated ARA* [15], except that it also uses incremental search as used in GFRA* to speed up the search by adapting the tree search and by reusing the information from the previous search.

To summarize, algorithms based on heuristic guidance (the first strategy) are more appropriate for environment changes rather than goal changes. On the other hand, algorithms based on incremental search (the second strategy) are efficient with goal changes but operate with less generic environments. Among them, GFRA* seems the more interesting to use for task planning mainly for two reasons: (1) it is based on a heuristic forward search as the most powerful state-of-the-art planners and (2) it can work with non-admissible heuristic function as it is often the case in task planning.

3 Moving Goal Planning

3.1 Problem Formulation

We address sequential planning in the propositional STRIPS framework [16]. All sets are finite. A *state* s is a set of logical propositions. An *action* a is a tuple $a = (pre(a), add(a), del(a))$ where $pre(a)$ are the action's *preconditions*, $add(a)$ and $del(a)$ are its positive and negative *effects*. The state s' is reached from s by applying an action a according to the transition function γ: $s' = \gamma(s, a) = (s - del(a)) \cup add(a)$ if $pre(a) \subseteq s$, undefined otherwise.

The application of a sequence of actions $\pi = \langle a_1, \ldots, a_n \rangle$ to a state s is recursively defined as $\gamma(s, \langle a_1, \ldots, a_n \rangle) = \gamma(\gamma(s, a_1), \langle a_2, \ldots, a_n \rangle)$. A Moving-Goal Pursuit problem is a tuple (A, s_t, g_t): at a given timestamp t, an agent is in a state s_t; g_t is its current goal (s_t and g_t are sets of propositions) and A is the set of actions that it can perform. It executes actions in order to reach its goal and the goal can change at any time. The agent has no information on how the goal changes over time. A *plan* is a sequence of actions $\pi_t = \langle a_1, \ldots, a_n \rangle$ ($a_i \in A$) such that the goal $g_t \subseteq \gamma(s_t, \pi_t)$ and g_t is *reachable* if such a plan exists. A goal state is a state s such that $g_t \subseteq s$. At a given time t, a Moving-Goal Pursuit problem is solved if $g_t \subseteq s_t$: the agent has reached its goal.

3.2 Algorithm

The MGP pseudocode is given in Algo. 1. MGP takes as input a Moving Goal Pursuit problem (A, s_0, g_0). The variables g and s denote respectively the current goal and the current state set initially to g_0 and s_0 (i is the search iteration counter).

MGP iterates a search procedure (line 2) as long as the current goal has not been reached. The Search procedure is detailed in section 3.3. This procedure builds a search tree whose nodes are states and edges are actions. The search procedure fails if the current goal has not been reached and MGP fails (line 3). This is the case when the planning problem is unsolvable. Otherwise MGP postpones as much as possible triggering a new search and expansion of the search tree (while-loop line 4) and it extracts a plan from the search tree (lines 5). The while-loop ends when the goal evolves out of the search tree, i.e., none of the nodes is a goal state (procedure OpenCheck), or when the goal *significantly* changes (procedure PlanFollow). These two procedures are detailed in section 3.3.

As long as the goal is reachable with the extracted plan or does not significantly change, MGP executes the actions of this plan and update its current state (line 7). The goal changes are provided by the procedure UpdateGoal (line 8). Then, if MGP reaches its current goal, it returns success (line 9). Otherwise, MGP reduces its search tree to the subtree whose root is the current state s (DeleteStatesOutOfTree, line 10). If the new goal is in this subtree and a new search can be postponed, MGP extracts a new plan and executes its actions to reach the new goal. Otherwise, MGP updates the heuristic values of the search tree nodes according to the new goal (line 11) (UpdateSearchTree procedure detailed in the next section) and finally increments its search iteration counter (line 12) and expands its search tree (line 3).

Algorithm 1. MGP(A, s_0, g_0)

1   $s \leftarrow s_0, g \leftarrow g_0, i \leftarrow 1$
2   **while** $g \not\subseteq s$ **do**
3   **if** Search(A, s, g, i) *fails* **then return** Failure
4   **while** OpenCheck(g) *and* PlanFollow(s, g) **do**
5   Extract a solution plan π from the search tree
6   **while** $(g \not\subseteq s$ *and* $g \subseteq \gamma(s, \pi))$ *or* (PlanFollow(s, g) *and* $\pi \neq \emptyset)$ **do**
7            $a \leftarrow$ get and remove the first action of π, execute a, $s \leftarrow \gamma(s, a)$
8            $g \leftarrow$ UpdateGoal(g) ;; *simulate goals change*
9   **if** $g \subseteq s$ **then return** Success
10   DeleteStatesOutOfTree(s)
11   UpdateSearchTree(s, g, i)
12    $i \leftarrow i + 1$

3.3 Implementation

In this section, we describe the MGP implementation. The search tree is represented by two lists denoted OPEN and CLOSED: the OPEN list contains the pending states of the search and the CLOSED list contains the explored states.

Weighted A* as Search Strategy. Contrary to GFRA* that uses A* as basic search algorithm, MGP uses the Weighted-A* search strategy. This variant of A* overestimates the cost of the heuristic value according to a ratio w. The evaluation function $f(s)$ for a state s is $f(s) = g(s) + w \times h(s)$ where $g(s)$ is the cost to reach s from the initial state s_0 and $h(s)$ the estimated cost from s to the goal g. The greater w, the greater is the weight of the heuristic in the guidance of the search. Usually, using Weighted A* with an informative and admissible heuristic speeds up the search but breaks up the optimality of the solution plans. This approach is relevant because it is more important to find quickly a good solution than to find an optimal solution that will become outdated after a goal change. We show that using Weighted-A* instead of A* significantly improves the MGP performances (see section 4). Moreover, Weighted-A* does not impair the soundness and the completeness of MGP. The Weighted-A* algorithm used in our approach is a modified version of the classical algorithm. It takes as input a search problem (A, s, g), a ratio w and the search iteration counter i. For each state, it maintains three values: the g-value and the h-value of the state, and the parent pointer $parent(s)$ that points to the parent state of s in the search tree. At the first procedure call, the OPEN and CLOSED lists hold the initial state of the search problem such as $g(s) = 0$ and $h(s) = H(s, g)$ where H is the heuristic function that estimates the cost from the initial state s to the goal g.

Search Delaying Strategies. In order to limit the number of search iterations and to speed up the algorithm performances, MGP delays as much as possible starting new searches when the goal changes. MGP uses two novel and different strategies.

Open Check (OC). MGP checks if the new goal is still in the search tree. In that case, a new plan can be extracted in the current search tree. Contrary to GFRA* that only checks the states in the CLOSED list, MGP also checks the pending states in the OPEN list. This checkout avoids useless searches and readjustments of the search tree.

Plan Follow (PF). MGP estimates whether executing the actions of the current plan brings it closer to the new goal. Each time the goal changes and before starting a new search, MGP evaluates if the new goal is close to the previous one and determines if the current plan can still be used. This test is based on the heuristic function and the computation of an inequality between the current state s, the previous goal p and the new goal g: $H(s, g) \times c > H(s, p) + H(p, g)$ where c is called the delay ratio. MGP follows the current plan while the inequality is true, i.e., until it estimates that a straightforward plan from the current state s to the new goal g is better than achieving the previous goal and then finding a new plan from the previous goal to the new goal. Values of $c > 1$ allow us to adjust the delay before a new search. As searches are expensive, delaying them speeds up the algorithm but alters plan quality (see section 4).

Incremental Updates of the Search Tree. MGP incrementally updates the search tree at each new search (see Algo. 1 line 14). Contrary to GFRA* that updates the heuristic value of all the states of the search tree with respect to the new goal, MGP uses a parsimonious strategy to reduce the number of calls to the heuristic function. To this purpose, MGP clears the OPEN list, adds the current state and updates its h-value by calling the heuristic function H. To indicate

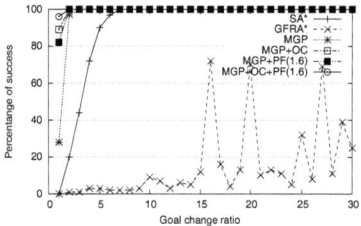
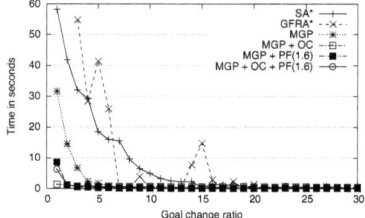

(a) Percentage of success with respect to the goal change ratio.

(b) Search time with respect to the goal change ratio.

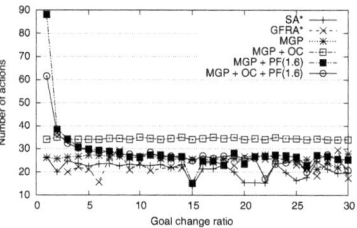

(c) Plan length with respect to the goal change ratio.

Fig. 1. Global analysis of Blockworld problem 20

that the heuristic value of the current state is up-to-date, MGP sets its iteration value to the MGP iteration counter. During the search, each time a state in the CLOSED list is encountered with an iteration value smaller than the iteration counter, it is added into the OPEN list and its h-value is updated. This strategy has two advantages: (1) it reduces the number of states generated by reusing the states in the CLOSED list during a search and (2) it reduces significantly the time needed to update the heuristic values by limiting the updates to the states explored during the new search.

4 Experiments and Evaluation

The objective of these experiments is to evaluate the performances of MGP with respect to the different search delaying strategies: Open Check (OC) and Plan Follow (PF). MGP is compared with the state-of-the-art algorithm GFRA* and the naive approach Successive A* (SA*) that consists in calling A* each time the goal changes. The benchmarks used for the evaluation are taken from the International Planning Competition (IPC). We use the non-admissible heuristic function of FF [17] to drive the search. We evaluate six algorithms: Successive A* (SA*), GFRA*, MGP without search delaying strategy (MGP), MGP with Open Check (MGP+OC), MGP with Plan Follow (MGP+PF) and MGP with both strategies (MGP+OC+PF).

4.1 Simulation of the Goal Changes

Classically, MTS algorithms assume that the moving target, the "prey", always follows the shortest path from its current position to a randomly selected and unblocked position. Each time the prey reaches this position, a new position is randomly selected and so on. Every n moves, the prey remains idle, allowing the "hunter" to catch it. As this approach is not transposable to task planning, we change the goal by randomly applying an action to the current goal state. This process is repeated many times to make the goal more difficult to reach. The new goal is always reachable from the current goal, but it is not guaranteed that MGP will reach it since it may evolve so quickly that MGP cannot reach it. This simulation of goal changes is more challenging than the one classically used to compare MTS algorithms: in our experiments, the goal does not change as a function of the executed actions but in a real time manner as a function of the time needed to find a solution plan. Thus, the more an algorithm takes time to find a solution, the more the goal evolves and becomes difficult to reach. To parametrize the goal evolution, a counter t is incremented every time a state is explored during the Weighted-A* search and every time the heuristic function is called to update a state h-value. These two procedures are the most time consuming. The number n of actions applied to the goal state is computed as follows: $n = (t - t_p)/g_r$ where t_p denotes the previous value of the counter t and g_r the goal change ratio. Hence, g_r allows us to adjust the swiftness of goal changes: small goal ratios mean fast goal changes and high goal ratios slow goal changes.

4.2 Experiment Framework

Each algorithm was tested 100 times on a planning problem with a given goal change ratio. Each test was conducted on an Intel Xeon 4 Core (2.0Ghz) with a maximum of 4 Gbytes of memory and was allocated a CPU time of 60 seconds.

In a first stage, the algorithms are tested with the IPC-2 Blockworld benchmark in order to measure their respective performances with respect to the goal change ratio. In a second stage, we have tested the impact of the delay ratio and of the heuristic weight in the performances of the best algorithm observed at the first stage. In a third stage, we have tested the algorithms on a large set of planning domains and problems.

The performances presented are: (1) the success percentage, i.e., the number of times the algorithm succeed to reach the goal, (2) the search time and (3) the plan length.

4.3 Algorithms Comparisons on Blockworld

In this section, we present a comparison of the six algorithms SA*, GFRA*, MGP, MGP+OC, MGP+PF and MGP+OC+PF on the IPC-2 Blockworld P20 with respect to the goal change ratio and we give an overview of their respective performances on Blockworld domain. The delay ratio is arbitrary set to 1.6

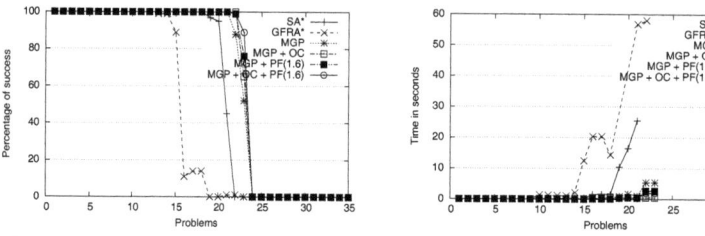

(a) Percentage of success with respect to the problems.

(b) Search time with respect to the problems.

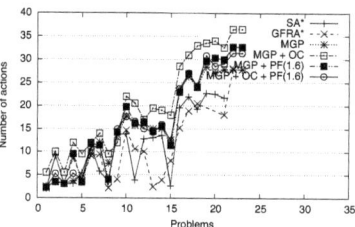

(c) Plan length with respect to the problems.

Fig. 2. Global analysis of Blockworld domain

for MGP+PF and MGP+OC+PF and the heuristic weight is set to 1 for all algorithms. Both parameteres are studied section 4.4.

Study in the Blockworld P20. Figures 1(a), 1(b), 1(c) show the results obtained in terms of percentage of success, search time and plan length. Regarding the percentage of success, the best algorithm is MGP+OC+PF. Even with a goal change ratio $g_r = 1$, MGP+OC+PF has a success rate above 95%. The other search delaying strategies are less efficient but obtain more than 80% of success. The naive approach SA* needs a goal change ratio 5 times bigger to obtain the same percentage of success. GFRA* does not reach this percentage of success even with a goal change ratio 30 times bigger. Finally, GFRA* is outclassed by the other algorithms. In terms of search time, the best algorithm is MGP+OC. Then, we have MGP+OC+PF, MGP+PF and MGP. Finally, we have SA* and far away GFRA*. MGP+OC is very efficient with Blockworld P20. Indeed, the new goal is often contained in the open list of A*. Moreover, OC+PF enhances significatively the naive version of MGP wrt search time but not plan length. This can be explained by the optimistic behaviour of the PF variants of MGP: when they make bad choices, the cost to pay is higher. In terms of plan length, MGP and its variants produce longer plans than SA* and GFRA*. Two reasons explain this difference. First, the OC strategy checks if the new goal was already explored and then extracts directly a new plan from the search tree. This cannot guarantee that the extracted plan is the shortest because the search tree was not built for this goal. Second, the PF strategy, as shown by the figure 2(c), tends to increase plan length. However, plan length narrows with the increase of the goal change ratio and it is largely compensated by better search times and percentages of success.

Overview of the Blockworld Domain. Figures 2(a), 2(b) and 2(c) show respectively the results obtained in terms of percentages of success, search time and plan length for all the problems of the blockworld benchmark. The problems are ordered with respect to their complexity. In these experiments, the goal change ratio is set to 5 to convert a large range of problems. The other parameters are unchanged: each experiment is repeated 100 times and 60 seconds is allocated for each experiment. In terms of percentage of success, the results are identical to Blockworld P20. GFRA* is widely outclassed. Its percentage of success decreases to 20% from P16. Then, we have SA* which reaches 40% of success at P21. Then, we have the variants of MGP. Their percentages of success starts decreasing between the P22 and P23. Even if the results are comparable, MGP+OC+PF performs better (90% of success) on P23 than MGP+PF (80% of success), MGP+OC (70% of success) and MGP (50% of success). These results are similar on search time. Different variants of MGP outperform SA* and GFRA* with search time less than 5 seconds. Here again, as for the problem P20, MGP+OC performs slightly better. Finally, in terms of plan length, the results on the other problems of Blockworld confirm the results on P20. SA* and GFRA* plans are shorter than for the MGP variants.

4.4 Impact of the Delay Ratio and the Heuristic

In this section, we evaluate the impact of the delay ratio and the heuristic weight on MGP+OC+PF which is the most efficient variant of MGP. On all tests, we use the same problem (blockworld P20). Since MGP+OC+PF have a success rate that is always close to 100%, we only present search time and plan length results in this section.

Impact of the Delay Ratio. Figure 3(a) and 3(b) show respectively the search time and the plan length wrt. the goal change ratio. We can make three observations. First, we see that the delay ratio significantly increases the performances. For instance, MGP+OC+PF with a delay ratio of 2 is 6 times quicker than with a delay ratio of 0 when the goal change ratio $g_r = 1$. Second, search time and plan length converge quickly on the same values with respect to the increase of the goal change ratio. With $g_r \geq 4$, the delay ratio has no impact on the search time and the plan length. Third, increasing the delay ratio augments the plan length and reduces the search time. Consequently, the delay ratio must be a tradeoff between the plan length and the search time.

Impact of the Heuristic Weight. Figures 4 shows respectively search time and plan length wrt. the heuristic weight of MGP+OC+PF. The heuristic weight w significantly increases the performances (MGP+OC+PF is 4 times quicker with $w = 2.0$ than with $w = 1.0$ for a goal change ratio $g_r = 1$). In addition, the impact of w on the plan length is not significant: whatever the heuristic weight, plan lengths are close for a given goal change ratio.

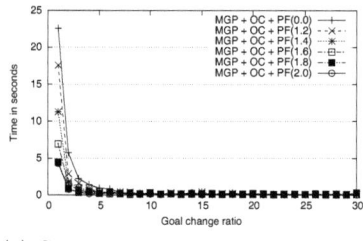 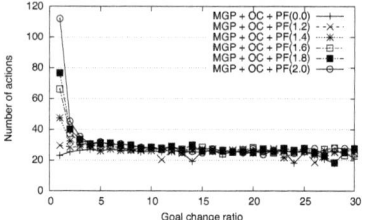

(a) Search time with respect to the delay & goal change ratios.

(b) Plan length with respect to the delay & goal change ratios.

Fig. 3. Delay ratio impact in Blockworld P20

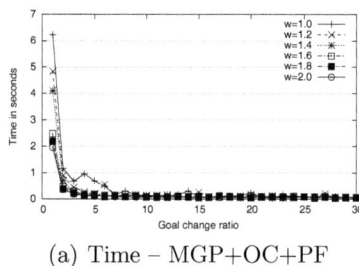 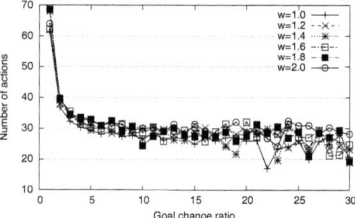

(a) Time – MGP+OC+PF

(b) Plan length – MGP+OC+PF

Fig. 4. Heuristic weight impact in Blockworld P20

Table 1. Comparison of search time

Problem	SA*	GFRA*	MGP	OC	PF	OC+PF
airport p16	3,38	0,91	0,20	0,18	0,17	0,12
airport p19	-	13,48	0,40	0,36	0,37	0,21
depot p03	8,12	-	2,40	1,28	1,67	0,78
depot p07	-	-	7,41	6,42	1,73	1,13
driverlog p03	0,03	0,02	0,33	0,22	0,18	0,17
driverlog p06	13,57	-	4,32	5,50	5,53	4,35
elevator p30	24,85	23,69	29,32	3,23	2,22	1,46
elevator p35	23,04	-	-	44,60	35,31	20,80
freecell p20	10,94	-	-	4,72	6,20	3,65
freecell p26	48,76	-	56,61	26,70	32,12	24,20
openstack p06	55,58	55,80	55,20	54,03	48,69	36,30
openstack p07	54,55	57,51	57,35	50,33	46,13	43,32
pipeworld p04	0,50	17,73	1,68	0,49	0,55	0,48
pipeworld p08	-	-	18,02	13,89	13,70	12,51
pathway p02	15,60	9,52	6,92	3,53	2,83	1,74
pathway p04	-	-	-	-	8,05	4,39
rover p03	23,35	14,17	3,72	2,85	2,15	1,87
rover p07	-	-	-	23,51	-	22,54
satellite p03	-	17,26	9,36	3,67	4,56	3,18
satellite p06	-	-	-	-	-	8,97

4.5 Performance Overview

In this section, we give an overview of the algorithms' performances on different IPC domains: table 1 shows the search time, table 2 shows the percentage of success and table 3 presents the plan length. Each algorithm has been run 100 times to obtain statistically relevant results. Each experiment was allocated a CPU time of 60 seconds. The delay ratio was set to 1.6 and the goal change ratio to 100. The experimentation was carried out on *all problems of each domain* and tables 1, 2 and 3 are parts of our results. The problems were chosen to show the

Table 2. Comparison of percentage of success

Problem	SA*	GFRA*	MGP	OC	PF	OC+PF
airport p16	97	100	100	100	100	100
airport p19	-	72	81	100	100	100
depot p03	10	-	99	30	60	100
depot p07	-	-	33	12	14	88
driverlog p03	100	100	100	100	100	100
driverlog p06	1	-	1	56	88	98
elevator p30	69	99	91	100	100	100
elevator p35	1	-	-	19	5	55
freecell p20	39	-	-	99	100	100
freecell p26	56	-	1	100	100	100
openstack p06	77	48	62	70	96	99
openstack p07	44	15	21	100	99	99
pipeworld p04	99	7	99	99	98	100
pipeworld p08	-	-	48	70	60	76
pathway p02	100	100	100	100	100	100
pathway p04	-	-	-	-	22	48
rover p03	48	8	99	99	94	99
rover p07	-	-	-	32	-	52
satellite p03	-	1	4	16	15	52
satellite p06	-	-	-	-	-	28

Table 3. Comparison of plan length

Problem	SA*	GFRA*	MGP	OC	PF	OC+PF
airport p16	80,98	80,98	79,15	81,25	80,81	81,12
airport p19	-	91,98	90,12	91,52	90,62	91,14
depot p03	20,80	-	21,73	21,67	25,18	22,83
depot p07	-	-	25,24	23,08	26,00	24,74
driverlog p03	7,30	4,14	8,42	11,57	12,57	9,57
driverlog p06	12,00	-	14,00	15,00	11,23	16,91
elevator p30	29,20	27,88	27,33	28,42	27,74	28,80
elevator p35	34,00	-	-	33,05	32,20	32,18
freecell p20	29,97	-	-	29,99	29,99	29,99
freecell p26	37,02	-	38,00	37,01	37,01	37,01
openstack p06	50,41	51,13	51,28	50,68	50,06	50,54
openstack p07	51,12	52,14	50,76	51,25	50,72	51,02
pipeworld p04	3,21	11,86	7,61	9,19	10,20	8,12
pipeworld p08	-	-	18,21	21,09	19,76	21,02
pathway p02	27,18	26,39	26,27	26,93	37,02	40,76
pathway p04	-	-	-	-	34,92	35,12
rover p03	44,53	44,73	44,40	44,54	44,66	44,24
rover p07	-	-	-	43,20	-	43,50
satellite p03	-	42,00	26,00	24,69	32,12	25,80
satellite p06	-	-	-	-	-	26,00

performances' decrease of the algorithms as observed in Blockworld between the problems 15 and 24.

In terms of search time, MGP+OC+PF is broadly quicker than the other algorithms. Moreover, MGP+OC+PF outclasses MGP with one search delaying strategy (either OC or PF) as well as SA* and GFRA*. Likewise, MGP+OC+PF outclasses the other algorithms in terms of percentage of success. However, MGP sometimes fails on problems solved by SA* (Elevator P35 and Freecell P26) even if MGP is broadly better than SA* and GFRA*. Finally, in terms of plan length, all algorithms find plans with close lengths.

To summarize the evaluation, OC and PF increase the performances of MGP, which performs better than SA* or GFRA*. The combination of OC+PF strategies give better results than MGP with one search delaying strategy. The results obtained on different domains and problems confirm that MGP+OC+PF is the best algorithm and GFRA* is outdistanced because it updates the heuristic value of all states of the search tree at each incremental search.

5 Conclusion

In this paper, we have proposed a novel approach to planning, called MGP, which considers plan adaptation to constantly changing goals as a process pursuing "moving" goals. MGP is based on an incremental Weighted-A* search and interleaves planning and execution when the goal changes over time. In order to limit the number of search iterations and to improve its efficiency, MGP delays as much as possible starting new searches when the goal changes. To this purpose, MGP uses two search delaying strategies: Open Check (OC) that checks if the new goal is still in the search tree and Plan Follow (PF) that estimates whether executing the actions of the current plan brings MGP closer to the new goal. Moreover, MGP uses a parsimonious strategy based on an incremental update of the search tree at each new search in order to reduce the expensive calls to the heuristic function.

We have experimentally shown that MGP outperforms the naive approach SA* and the state-of-the-art approach GFRA*. We have shown that the combination of the search delaying strategies OC+PF gives better performances than one search delaying strategy. Moreover, the delay ratio of the Plan Follow (PF) strategy must be a tradeoff between plan length and search time while the heuristic weight in the WA* search enhances the search time.

We are currently pursuing two concurrent lines of work: (1) generating goal changes based on domain-dependent strategies and real-world applications and (2) extending our approach to real-time planning where search and execution are time bound.

References

1. Pellier, D., Fiorino, H., Métivier, M.: A new approach for continual planning. In: AAMAS, pp. 1115–1116 (2013)
2. Nebel, B., Koehler, J.: Plan reuse versus plan generation: A theoretical and empirical analysis. Artificial Intelligence 76, 427–454 (1995)
3. van der Krogt, R., de Weerdt, M.: Plan repair as an extension of planning. In: ICAPS, pp. 161–170 (2005)
4. Fox, M., Gerevini, A., Long, D., Serina, I.: Plan stability: Replanning versus plan repair. In: ICAPS, pp. 212–221 (2006)
5. Ishida, T., Korf, R.: Moving target search. In: IJCAI, pp. 204–210 (1991)
6. Korf, R.: Real-Time Heuristic Search. Artificial Intelligence 42(2-3), 189–211 (1990)
7. Melax, S.: New approaches to moving target search. In: AAAI Falls Symp. Game Planning Learn., pp. 30–38 (1993)
8. Koenig, S., Likhachev, M.: Adaptive A*. In: AAMAS, pp. 1311–1312 (2005)
9. Koenig, S., Likhachev, M., Sun, X.: Speeding up moving target search. In: AAMAS (2007)
10. Sun, X., Koenig, S., Yeoh, W.: Generalized adaptive A*. In: AAMAS, pp. 469–476 (2008)
11. Stenz, A.: The focused D* algorithm for real-time replanning. In: IJCAI, pp. 1642–1659 (1995)
12. Sun, X., Yeoh, W., Koenig, S.: Efficient incremental search for moving target search. In: IJCAI, pp. 615–620 (2009)

13. Sun, X., Yeoh, W., Koenig, S.: Generalized Fringe-Retrieving A*: Faster Moving Target Search on State Lattices. In: AAMAS, pp. 1081–1088 (2010)
14. Sun, X., Yeoh, W., Uras, T., Koenig, S.: Incremental ARA*: An Incremental Anytime Search Algorithm for Moving Target Search. In: ICAPS (2012)
15. Likhachev, M., Gordon, M., Thrun, S.: ARA*: Anytime a* with provable bounds on sub-optimality. In: NIPS (2003)
16. Finke, R., Nilsson, N.: STRIPS: A new approach to the application of theorem proving to problem solving. Artificial Intelligence 3-4(2), 189–208 (1971)
17. Hoffmann, J., Nebel, B.: The FF Planning System: Fast Plan Generation Through Heuristic Search. JAIR 14(1), 253–302 (2001)

Agent Clusters: The Usual vs. The Unusual

Kavin Preethi Narasimhan and Graham White

Cognitive Science Research Group
School of Electronic Engineering and Computer Science
Queen Mary University of London, London E1 4NS

Abstract. Conversational clusters refer to groups of two or more people engaged in face-to-face interaction, wherein the arrangement of people's bodies in space determines the spatial layout of clusters. Existing computational models have mostly focused on simulating 'circular' agent clusters. This paper questions the realistic appeal of a circular manifestation for conversational clusters. As a comparative case study, two contrasting models have been implemented: Model 1, like existing approaches, simulates circular agent clusters; whereas Model 2 yields agent clusters of various shapes. Outcomes of the two models are then compared with video data of naturally occurring conversational clusters. Comparison shows that neither Model 1 nor Model 2 are fully self-contained to simulate realistic shapes for agent clusters. Results also demonstrate that circle isn't the only plausible spatial manifestation for conversational clusters.

Keywords: agent-based simulation, conversational clusters, F-formation, spatial relations, social norm.

1 Introduction

Casual face-to-face conversations often begin with participants exchanging salutations, followed by standing reasonably close and facing one another so that seeing or hearing won't be a problem. Two or more people engaged in face-to-face interaction in this way may be identified as a conversational cluster. These clusters are integral social units that have distinct spatial boundaries made manifest by interlocutors' collective body positions and orientations – like dots connected to form a whole. In turn, the spatial manifestation of a cluster helps in preserving the integrity of an ongoing conversation by insulating it against disturbances. E.g., If we were to walk in a corridor and find a group of people talking ahead of us, more often than not we'd avoid walking through the group. Even if forced to walk through (e.g., due to a narrow corridor), we'd either dip our heads or utter "sorry!" as we walk through. Likewise, an outsider's presence within a group wouldn't go unnoticed. Evidently so, the spatial manifestation of a conversational cluster makes us sensitive to its existence.

There have been attempts to synthesize conversational clusters for the purposes of social behaviour modelling for agents featuring in games, training systems etc. Some of these models have succeeded in simulating evidently circular conversational clusters. There are propositions endorsing a circular spatial layout for conversational clusters involving three or more people, e.g., Goffman's (1963) proposal of an "eye-to-eye ecological huddle", Kendon's (1990) theory of F-formations etc. But circles isn't the only possible spatial manifestation for conversational groups. Neither do theories of human behaviour favour this unanimous assumption. Surprisingly however, existing models simulate near perfect circular spatial configurations, almost all the time.

Moreover, even theories that embrace circularity do not favour it being imposed forcefully – it is rather suggested that, over time, circles emerge as a consequence of interlocutors' spatial-orientational readjustments with respect to one another. However, in existing models, circularity has been the principal factor driving agents' actions with respect to one another. That is to say, agents are explicitly obliged to form *only* circles in the event of face-to-face encounters. Lastly, most of the existing models haven't gone beyond using post-experiment questionnaires to verify the efficiency of their approach. As known from [7, p. 2], questioning people directly about a social phenomenon isn't hugely beneficial either because people aren't aware of any such phenomenon, or even if there are genuine reasons, people are not obliged to disclose it.

To this end, this paper performs a case study of two different models: Model 1, which explicitly enforces circularity akin to the existing approaches, and Model 2, which simulates conversational clusters as an emergent phenomenon. Outcomes of the two models are then compared with videos of people conversing in groups during parties. Comparison accounts for if and how the respective models simulate realistic shapes for conversational clusters. The rest of this paper is organized as follows. Section 2 reviews existing models to simulate conversational clusters. This section also highlights how, despite all superficial differences, the core concept remains unchanged across models. Section 3 reviews theoretical underpinnings for Models 1 & 2 described in section 4. Comparing outcomes from the respective models with videos of naturally occurring conversational clusters is presented in section 5, followed by conclusions of the study in section 6.

2   State of the Art

Currently, there are only two overarching approaches to simulate conversational clusters: one seeks to use external authority to organize agents into clusters (e.g., [9]); another approach coerces conversing agents to form circular arrangements (e.g., [8], [10], [14], [16]). In [9], a manager module makes decisions regarding organizing individual puppet agents into interactional groups. However, in naturally occurring conversations, there is no external authority controlling the emergence of clusters – participants within a cluster are alone responsible for its existence and integrity [4]. E.g., if we are at a party, we don't expect to be told how and where to stand with respect to our friends or family.

In contrast to the manager-puppet approach, the social force model proposed in [8] allows agents to make autonomous spatial decisions when forming conversational clusters. Based on this rather intuitive approach, [9] was then hugely modified in [10], to simulate clusters alongside rendering fluctuations that occur within. Here, fluctuations refer to the positional and orientational re-adjustments made by agents to accommodate changes affecting the cluster – like entry of a new member into the cluster, exit of a current member etc. Changes like this often involve active members of the cluster re-adjusting their position and orientation to compensate for any imbalances caused by the fluctuation [4].

In essence, the core concept used in [8] and [10] works as follows. Once two or more agents are engaged in conversation, a *social force field* is established between them. Apart from that, there is a set of individual forces constantly acting upon each individual agent. The net effect of these forces motivate an agent's spatial course of action, i.e., re-adjustments in position and orientation. In addition, the individual forces are modelled such that an agent is obliged to contribute to the stability of the cluster in which it participates. Stability here is realized in terms of sustaining the net social force field between interactant agents. An extension of this concept was later proposed in [14] to include an additional set of territorial constraints when influencing agents' movement decisions. Furthermore, in [16], another enhancement concerning the realistic and fluid rendering of fluctuations was proposed.

Despite the variations, establishing and sustaining a mean social force field between interacting agents has been the controlling idea of all the models reviewed so far. Outcomes from these models show agent clusters that are almost perfectly circular in shape. Does this mean a circular layout is the only plausible spatial manifestation for conversational clusters? Do humans actually form perfectly (or almost perfect) circular conversational clusters all the time? Answering these questions requires systematic probing.

Some further notes before proceeding. Research in robotics has focused on conversational clusters, too – e.g., [13] and [15]. Nonetheless, the embodiment of agents along with the kind of sensory inputs it makes available, the terrain in which agents work etc., are significantly different between agents residing in virtual environments and robots residing in the real world. So a one-on-one comparison isn't reasonable. Simulating conversational clusters also tends to be compared with crowd and pedestrian simulations (e.g., [6,11]), or flocking behaviour (e.g., [5]). But flocks, crowd and pedestrian simulations deal with much bigger agent units that do not synthesize the spatial-orientational dynamics that are characteristic of conversational clusters.

3 Theoretical Underpinnings

Our models are based on the following concepts concerning human face-to-face conversations:

Spatial Zones around an Individual. According to Hall (1969), there are four distinct zones of space surrounding every individual – intimate (extending outwards upto 1.5 feet from an individual), personal (between 1.5 feet and 4 feet), social (between 4 feet and 12 feet), and public (beyond 12 feet). Among these, the area just outside the personal zone is identified as being ideal for face-to-face conversations. This is because at an interpersonal distance of about 4 feet, interlocutors have full visual and auditory access to one another.

Individual Transactional Segment. According to Kendon (1990), assuming that a hypothetical line is drawn extending outwards from the center of an individual's midriff, there is an area of space called the *transactional segment*, which extends upto 45 degrees [3] on either side. At all times, an individual endeavours to protect his transactional segment from external interventions, so as to perform his intended activities in an unobstructed manner. The extent of an individual's transactional segment varies depending upon the kind of activity being performed [12]. For conversations though, it extends up to 4 feet from an individual's body [3]. Figure 1 depicts the different spatial zones around an individual and his transactional segment.

Overlapping Transactional Segments (O-Space). Unlike being alone, engaging in collaborative activities like face-to-face conversations, makes interlocutors want to overlap their individual transactional segments. This is so they can have complete visual and auditory access to one another. The hypothetical space that arises out of overlapping individual transactional segments is referred to as an o-space [4]. A conversational cluster becomes a distinct social unit with the emergence of an o-space. Sustaining the integrity of an o-space is key to maintaining the flow of conversation within, as well as safeguarding the cluster from external disturbances. Figure 2 depicts the o-space formed by two agents that are spatially organized in a vis-à-vis arrangement.

F-Formation. Whenever the spatial arrangement of interlocutors leads to the emergence of an o-space, a conversational cluster becomes an F-formation. The spatial-orientational manoeuvres undertaken by interlocutors to sustain an o-space is referred to as the F-formation system. Both these concepts serve to provide an analytical framework to study conversational clusters as spatial units of interaction [4].

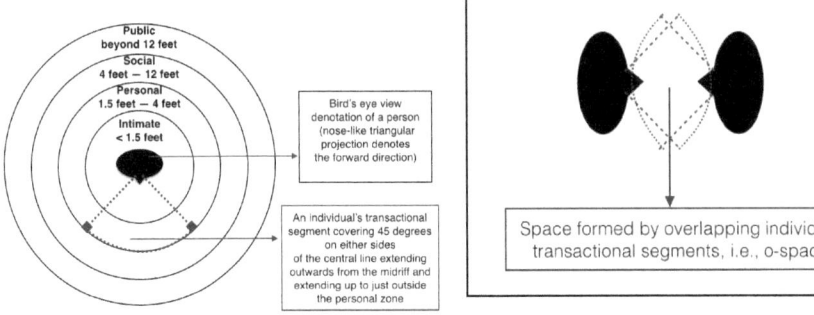

Fig. 1. Spatial zones around an individual and his transactional segment

Fig. 2. The o-space

Contemplating on the models reviewed in section 2 in light of the theories just discussed, it appears that the social force model targets establishing and sustaining an equivalent of o-space to simulate conversational clusters. However, F-formation and the o-space within it, are joint spatial structures that emerge from overlapping individual transactional segments. This logically means, if there is a way to simulate conversational clusters by enforcing the existence of o-space (or its synthetic equivalent), there should also be a way of letting o-space emerge eventually from overlapping individual transactional segments. The following section explores both possibilities.

4 Formalizing Theories: Our Algorithm

4.1 The Simulation Platform

Kendon's (1990) and Deutsch's (1977) representation of humans as blobs with pointed noses motivated us to use a similar representation for agents. The pointed noses indicate the direction in which agents move within a 1200*700 (in pixels) bounded X-Y frame. There are 25 agents in total – each identified by a unique number on their blob-shaped head. This strength was chosen only so there are neither too many nor too little agents within the simulation window. Figure 3 shows the blob-shaped agent, figure 4 denotes an arc-shaped transactional segment covering 45 degrees on either side of the central line extending outwards from an agent's nose and extending up to just outside the (virtual equivalent) of personal zone. Figure 5 shows an instantaneous capture of the simulation window with 25 agents spread across. Of these, agents with transactional segments are the ones that are stopped, while others were in motion at the time of generating the screen capture. Agents and the simulations have been implemented using Processing[1].

Fig. 3. Blob shaped agent **Fig. 4.** Agent & its transactional segment **Fig. 5.** The simulation window

4.2 Basic Working

When the simulation is running, each agent assumes one of the following states: stopped, walking or readjusting. When the simulation begins, each agent starts moving from a random (x,y) position in a random direction pointed to by its

---
[1] http://www.processing.org

nose. This state is referred to as *walking*. At every time step t of the simulation, an agent stores and updates the following information in its state parameter: (i) its (x,y) position; (ii) the direction θ in which it is facing; (iii) a list of neighbours (i.e., other agents within its personal zone – as defined in section 3); and (iv) its current state (i.e., whether stopped, walking or readjusting). Movement of an agent is realized by updating its (x,y) position over time. An agent stops walking whenever it recognizes other agents within, or on the boundary of, its personal zone. This state is referred to as being *stopped*.

In the stopped state, an agent might re-adjust its spatial stance (position and/or orientation) with respect to its neighbours depending upon Model 1 or Model 2. This state is referred to as *readjusting*. Then, after a prefixed stopping time, which is the same for both Models 1 & 2, an agent disengages from its neighbours and moves away. The same disengagement mechanism is used for both Models 1 & 2 – a vector pointing away from the locations of its neighbours is used for steering away (similar to the steering away mechanism proposed in [5]).

Models 1 and 2 both operate on a given agent together with its neighbours. The difference is that, for Model 1, an agent's neighbours will consist of its neighbours, *their* neighbours, and so on, whereas for Model 2, it will just be an agent's immediate neighbours.

4.3 Model 1: A Globally Driven Model

This model explicitly motivates nearby agents that are stopped to form a circular o-space. Once established, sustaining the circular o-space governs all future changes to interactant agents' position and orientation. The primary input variables used are loc_{self} (location of self) and $\text{loc}_{\text{neighbour}}$ (location of neighbour)[2]. Based on these input parameters, the following calculations are made to compute a net force that motivates an agent (i.e., self) to resort to a stable position and orientation:

Compute centroid C of $\{\text{self} \cup \text{neighbours}\}$:

$$C = \frac{\text{loc}_{\text{self}} + \Sigma \text{loc}_{\text{neighbours}}}{|\text{neighbours}| + 1} \quad (1)$$

Compute the average distance from self to C:

$$E_p = \frac{d_{\text{self},C} + \Sigma_{\text{neighbours}} d_{\text{neighbour},C}}{|\text{neighbours}| + 1} \quad (2)$$

Make distance from self to C, $d_{\text{self},C} = E_p$ by moving an appropriate distance towards or away from C. As will have been evident from the formulas, Model 1 coerces nearby agents to maintain an equal distance from their collective centroid. This eventually leads agents to being organized in a circular arrangement. Examples of cluster formations resulting from this model are shown in figures 6, 7 & 8.

---

[2] 'self' denotes the agent which currently acts based on Model 1 and 'neighbour' denotes every other agent within self's list of neighbours.

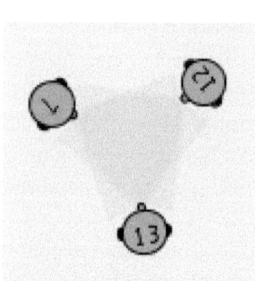 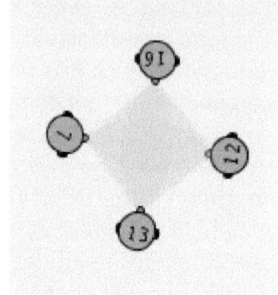 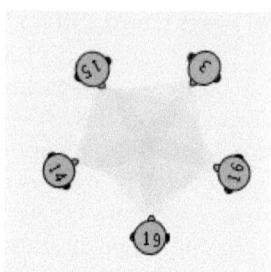

Fig. 6. Model 1: Cluster with 3 agents   **Fig. 7.** Model 1: Cluster with 4 agents   **Fig. 8.** Model 1: Cluster with 5 agents

4.4 Model 2: A Locally Driven Model

Unlike the global strategy used in Model 1, Model 2 motivates self to alter its position and orientation with a view to maximize the overlap of its individual transactional segment with those of its immediate neighbours alone. Agents start off from the same state as in Model 1: stopped and ready to form conversational clusters by readjusting their spatial stance. They operate on the following input parameters: loc_{self}, θ_{self} (orientation of self), $\text{loc}_{\text{neighbour}}$ and $\theta_{\text{neighbour}}$ (orientation of neighbour) to compute a net force that motivates self to re-adjust its position and/or orientation:

Firstly, for each agent in neighbours, compute the heading of a vector pointing from loc_{self} to $\text{loc}_{\text{neighbour}}$. If this heading is greater than 45 degrees (meaning outside the transactional segment), accumulate the excess angle in a variable θ_{excess}. Based on the net value of θ_{excess}, compute the redefined target location as:

$$t_{\text{redefined}} = \{\text{loc}_{\text{self}}.x + \cos(\theta_{\text{self}} + \theta_{\text{excess}}), \\ \text{loc}_{\text{self}}.y + \sin(\theta_{\text{self}} + \theta_{\text{excess}})\} \quad (3)$$

Divide $t_{\text{redefined}}$ by n, where n represents the total number of neighbours that lie beyond self's hypothetical transactional segment. Compute local centroid (i.e., for immediate neighbours alone) C of $\{\text{self} \cup \text{neighbours}\}$:

$$C = \frac{\text{loc}_{\text{self}} + \Sigma \text{loc}_{\text{neighbours}}}{|\text{neighbours}| + 1} \quad (4)$$

Compute distance from self to $t_{\text{redefined}}$ as $\overline{d}_{\text{self-to-redefined}}$. Then, compute the average distance from self to C:

$$\overline{d}_{\text{self-to-C}} = \frac{d_{\text{self},C} + \Sigma_{\text{neighbours}} d_{\text{neighbour},C}}{|\text{neighbours}| + 1} \quad (5)$$

Finally, motivate an agent to move towards or away from C until $\overline{d}_{\text{self-to-redefined}} = 0$. Figures 9, 10 & 11 are all examples of clusters resulting from Model 2. From the figures, it will be evident how, unlike Model 1, Model 2 encourages more open arrangements, where every agent resorts to a position and orientation that maximizes the overlap of its individual transactional segment with those of its immediate neighbours.

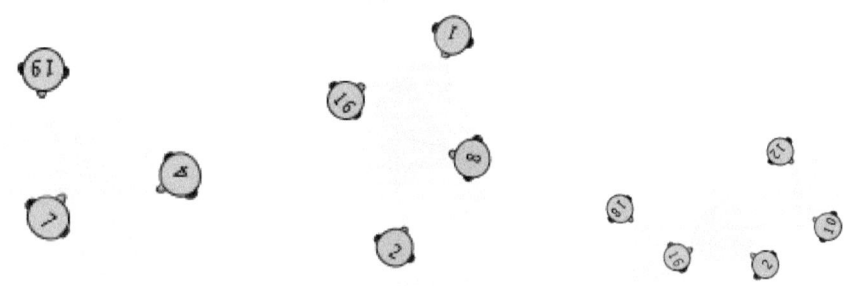

Fig. 9. Model 2: Cluster with 3 agents

Fig. 10. Model 2: Cluster with 4 agents

Fig. 11. Model 3: Cluster with 5 agents

5 Discussion

At the outset, comparing figures 6, 7 and 8 with figures 9, 10 and 11, it would appear that unlike Model 2, Model 1 simulates spatially well-delineated conversational clusters that are almost circular in shape. The question at issue here is whether this corresponds with the reality of human behaviour. We collected videos of naturally occurring conversational clusters that were filmed on three different occasions at drinks reception parties following events at University. Recordings were made by fixing cameras to the false ceiling so that an almost overhead view of the space could be achieved. Multiple cameras were used to capture the entire area where people conversed during the respective parties. For ethical reasons, participants were informed about the filming, however, it appeared that people in practice were not very aware of it. Total duration of the party, total number of people involved and the number of conversational clusters differed on each occasion. Among these, the longest-lasting cluster (we call it F1) that was observed lasted about 55 minutes. F1 also involved a lot of dynamics – entry of new members, exit of current members, re-entry of members, the group breaking out to form co-located sub-groups etc. Owing to the dynamics involved, F1 was chosen for further investigation. Figures 12, 13, 14, 15 & 16 show a candidate set of images representing the spatial organization of interactants in F1 at various timestamps (in hh:mm:ss).

Even a mere visual inspection of the images of F1 suggests that conversational clusters are not perfectly circular all the time. The actual spatial manifestation of F1 debunks some of the common assumptions made when simulating conversational clusters. Firstly, circle isn't the only possible spatial manifestation for conversational clusters. In fact, non-circular arrangements (e.g., people standing slightly behind one another, one person standing at the pivoted end of an elongated parallelogram etc.) were more common than circular arrangements. Secondly, closed arrangements and circular arrangements are not consequential of one another. That is, not all closed arrangements were circular (e.g., there were elliptical configurations). Conversely, not all seemingly circular arrangements were fully closed. E.g., if an existing member left a circular arrangement, it was not always the case where others re-organized their positional orientations, almost instantaneously (like in [16]), to compensate for the loss and close the arrangements. There were extended time intervals, where clusters remained open. Lastly, it was never the case where circular arrangements once established were never disturbed. Circularity eventually emerges at some point, and subsequently dissolves as time progresses only to be re-established again.

Fig. 12. F1 at 00:24:04   **Fig. 13.** F1 at 00:24:14   **Fig. 14.** F1 at 00:26:49

For further analysis, F1 was sampled at one frame for every 30 seconds of its entire duration (i.e., 55 minutes) to form the dataset representing a naturally occurring human conversational cluster.Corresponding to F1, the biggest and the longest lasting agent clusters were also identified from the screen recordings made of Models 1 & 2 – each run with 25 agents for a total duration of 30 minutes – referred to as M1 and M2 respectively. Again, M1 and M2 were each sampled at one frame for every 30 seconds of their entire duration (i.e., 25 minutes for both M1 & M2) to form the samples for agent clusters simulated using Model 1 and Model 2 respectively. It is true that for both Models 1 & 2 the biggest agent clusters in each case lasted for the same duration. This could be attributed to Models 1 & 2 both adopting the same stopping time and disengaging mechanism for agents. Nonetheless, as will become evident from subsequent analysis, dynamics of the models in terms of change in participation, shape etc., was quite different between M1 & M2.

F1, M1 and M2 were categorically coded to identify if the clusters are open or closed and circular or non- circular at the chosen frame. Here, open means there is sufficient space in between interlocutors (or agents) for outsiders to

Fig. 15. F1 at 00:47:08   **Fig. 16.** F1 (F1a, F1b & F1c) at 00:52:22

step in without too much hassle, closed means the space between interlocutors is tight for outsiders to step in without hesitation or appropriate intimation. Judgements on circular versus non-circular shapes for clusters are based on how the shape looks roughly, e.g., if the shape has no pivoted corners and is more on the circular end of an ellipse then it is roughly a circle. Two trained coders coded 10% of the entire dataset (110 images for F1, 50 images each for M1 & M2) to calculate Cohens Kappa for inter-rater agreement using the chosen coding scheme. This showed good agreement (Kappa= 0.765, 95% CI (0.464,1.000)) for the open versus closed rating, and very good agreement (Kappa = 0.900, 95% CI (0.710 to 1.000)) for the circular versus non circular rating. Table 1 summarizes the frequency for F1, M1 & M2 being identified as open, closed, circular and non-circular spatial arrangements.

Table 1. Classification of open vs. closed and circular vs. non-circular clusters

Cluster	Open	Closed	Circular	Non-circular
F1	48.18%	51.8%	49.09%	50.9%
M1	2%	98%	98%	2%
M2	84%	16%	14%	86%

From table 1, it is evident that neither Model 1 nor Model 2 fully replicate F1's figures for being open vs. closed or circular vs. non-circular. At the most basic level, similarities only extend to F1 and M1 being more closed than they are open, and F1 and M2 being more non-circular than they are circular. Outcomes also suggest that Model 1 simulates predominantly closed and circular clusters whereas Model 2 simulates predominantly open and non-circular clusters. Neither resembles F1 which has an almost equal distribution of all cases. On the other hand, figures reported in table 1 are based on the spatial layouts of F1, M1 and M2 at discrete time steps. Measurements are static in the sense that they present an overall summary but do not capture the spatial dynamics of conversational clusters over time. But F1 actually goes through lots of changes. E.g., in a roughly five minute interval, F1 goes from being one big group to many small co-located sub-groups (see figures 15 and 16). In this regard, it appears that Model 2 performs better than Model 1. Once an o-space is established, an obligation to maintain its circularity at all times prevents Model 1 from allowing agents to form sub-groups; whereas the local optimization strategy adopted in Model 2 allows agents to occasionally form sub-groups.

6 Conclusion

There are four main contributions in this paper. Firstly, there is full specification for a simplified version of the social force model (i.e., Model 1) that simulates predominantly circular agent clusters. Secondly, there is full specification for Model 2, which simulates variably shaped agent clusters. Thirdly, a comparative study to show that neither models are fully self-contained to simulate agent clusters that comprehensively resemble human conversational groups. Last and more importantly, the disintegration and re-integration of F1 over time has brought to the fore an important aspect that requires further probing. Kendon (1990) proposed that an F-formation usually lasts until the last participant leaves and may undergo several changes during its lifetime. But there has been no systematic inquiry into how this happens. Model 2, with its ability to recreate some of the spatial dynamics of F1, has a potential for further research in this direction.

The proposed work also has some shortcomings. Firstly, time plays an important role in the spatial manifestation of conversational clusters. Future analysis should therefore account for time as a causal factor. Secondly, instead of just one cluster like F1, a more comprehensive dataset including clusters of different sizes, shapes and duration have to be used for the case study. Lastly, a reliable comparison of models versus films requires that objects like furniture should also be modelled in the simulations.

Acknowledgements. We would like to thank QMUL CDTA and The Rabin Ezra Scholarship Trust for funding this research. We also thank our colleagues in the Cognitive Science research group at QMUL and the wider scientific community for all their suggestions and feedback regarding this work.

References

1. Goffman, E.: Behavior in public places: Notes on the social organization of gatherings (1963)
2. Hall, E.T., Hall, E.T.: The hidden dimension, p. 119. Anchor Books, New York (1969)
3. Deutsch, R.D.: Spatial structurings in everyday face-to-face behavior: a neurocybernetic model. Association for the Study of Man-Environment Relations (1977)
4. Kendon, A.: Conducting interaction: Patterns of behavior in focused encounters (1990)
5. Reynolds, C.W.: Steering behaviors for autonomous characters. In: Game Developers Conference, vol. 1999, pp. 763–782 (1999)

6. O Sullivan, C., Cassell, J., Vilhjlmsson, H., Dobbyn, S., Peters, C., Leeson, W., Dingliana, J.: Crowd and group simulation with levels of detail for geometry, motion and behavior. In: Third Irish Workshop on Computer Graphics, vol. 1, p. 4 (2002)
7. Gilbert, N., Troitzsch, K.G.: Simulation for the social scientist. McGraw-Hill International (2005)
8. Jan, D., Traum, D.R.: Dynamic movement and positioning of embodied agents in multiparty conversations. In: Proceedings of the Workshop on Embodied Language Processing, pp. 59–66. Association for Computational Linguistics (June 2007)
9. Vilhjalmsson, H., Merchant, C., Samtani, P.: Social puppets: Towards modular social animation for agents and avatars. In: Schuler, D. (ed.) Online Communities and Social Comput., HCII 2007. LNCS, vol. 4564, pp. 192–201. Springer, Heidelberg (2007)
10. Pedica, C., Vilhjálmsson, H.H.: Social perception and steering for online avatars. In: Prendinger, H., Lester, J.C., Ishizuka, M. (eds.) IVA 2008. LNCS (LNAI), vol. 5208, pp. 104–116. Springer, Heidelberg (2008)
11. Silveira, R., Prestes, E., Nedel, L.P.: Managing coherent groups. Computer Animation and Virtual Worlds 19(3-4), 295–305 (2008)
12. Kendon, A.: Spacing and orientation in co-present interaction. In: Esposito, A., Campbell, N., Vogel, C., Hussain, A., Nijholt, A. (eds.) Second COST 2102. LNCS, vol. 5967, pp. 1–15. Springer, Heidelberg (2010)
13. Yamaoka, F., Kanda, T., Ishiguro, H., Hagita, N.: A model of proximity control for information-presenting robots. IEEE Transactions on Robotics 26(1), 187–195 (2010)
14. Pedica, C., Hgni Vilhjlmsson, H.: Spontaneous avatar behavior for human territoriality. Applied Artificial Intelligence 24(6), 575–593 (2010)
15. Shi, C., Shimada, M., Kanda, T., Ishiguro, H., Hagita, N.: Spatial Formation Model for Initiating Conversation. In: Robotics: Science and Systems (2011)
16. Pedica, C., Vilhjlmsson, H.H.: Lifelike interactive characters with behavior trees for social territorial intelligence. In: ACM SIGGRAPH 2012 Posters, p. 32. ACM (August 2012)

An Agent-Based Architecture to Model and Manipulate Context Knowledge

Ludo Stellingwerff and Giovanni E. Pazienza

Almende BV,
Westerstraat 50, Rotterdam 3016 DJ,
The Netherlands
{ludo,giovanni}@almende.org

Abstract. The proliferation of devices endowed with an extensive variety of sensors, continuous connection to social networks, and a significant computing power has opened up countless new visionary applications: the context, meant as all data influencing the behaviour of the user and the application, plays a key role in modern life. However, defining an adequate framework to model and manipulate this context is still an open issue. In this paper, we propose a Context Aware Programming Environment (CAPE) to tackle this problem and present an agent-based architecture implementing it. Also, we discuss a practical application of our approach in the domain of emergency management.

Keywords: Context aware programming, agent-based systems, human-centric design.

1 Introduction

Nowadays, ubiquitous interconnected electronic devices are not anymore passive machines operated *by* humans but rather active computational components cooperating *with* humans. This paradigm shift has given birth to several scientific disciplines which have considered how humans can profit – without being overwhelmed – from such a huge amount of data.

In our work, we create innovative software tools facilitating the use of context data (which generically include all data sources having an influence on the user's behaviour) in practical applications. Specifically, in this paper we outline a novel ontology-based extensible model of the context (which is partially based on the classical approach proposed in [11] and [14]) and a framework, called Context Aware Programming Environment (CAPE), to manipulate context data. Furthermore, we suggest that an agent-based architecture is ideal to realise these kind of scalable and flexible software implementations and present in detail one specific use case related to emergency response. In general, we do not aim at going beyond the state of the art on context-aware systems (see [3] for a extensive, though slightly outdated, survey) but we want to propose an original and sound point of view on these issues which can be then used to build working software applications.

This paper is structured as follows: in Sec. 2, we introduce the definition and the model of the human-centric context; in Sec. 3, we describe an agent-based architecture of CAPE, discussing the motivations for it as well as a practical use case; in Sec. 4, we draw the conclusions of our work.

2 Defining and Modelling the Human-Centric Context

2.1 What Is a Human-Centric Context?

There are countless definitions of the term *context* (see [3] and [9] for a comprehensive survey, and [4] for a more recent one but applied to a specific area); here, we adhere to perhaps the classical one given in [1] for which context is:

"[...] any information that can be used to characterize the situation of entities (i.e., whether a person, place or object) and is considered relevant to the interaction between a user and an application [...]".

In our work, we emphasise the role of humans (especially end users, but also app developers) and hence we talk about the 'human-centric context' as everything affecting directly the behaviour of the human players of the system. For instance, the temperature is not per se part of the human-centric context unless it affects the behaviour of a user, for instance by influencing him to enter a room or buying an ice cream (similarly as what suggested in [12], for instance). Also, in our view the context does not imply only an unidirectional data flow ('sensing' the context and 'acting' on it) but a bidirectional one: the context may give feedback to the user about the context interpretation (e.g., suggesting the user to move, thus changing his position) or modify its sources (e.g., adding contacts to a contact list).

Our suggestion is to divide context data sources into three categories:

- *physical sensors*, which refer to real-time data describing the 'physical world' (such as temperature, pressure, and position);
- *virtual sensors*, which refer to the real-time data describing the 'virtual world' (such as contacts, agenda, and weather forecast);
- *historical data*, which refer to the past history of both virtual and physical sensors (usually stored in a database).

Note that a similar approach (though limited only to the location of the user and with a different clustering into three classes) was proposed in [10].

2.2 The Four Cornerstones of the Human-Centric Context Model

In order to act on the human-centric context, it is first necessary to devise an adequate model of it. Of course, the most natural approach (also called 'ontology-based') is to provide an *a priori* description of the context instances, which could be done by an expert of the users' activities. Several practical implementations of it have been proposed (a popular one was described in [14]), however in practice it leads to semantic rich models that are hard to use and fit only to a very specific application. If these ontologies are more generic and extensible (as suggested in numerous scientific works, [11] being among the most prominent ones) makes the context knowledge modelling and presentation difficult to achieve, as the context is by nature nearly unlimited in scope. Other approaches to tackle this issue include the inference of the human-centric information (as proposed in the 5W1H method [8]) and the model of the context via the interactions between user and environment (so-called 'interaction traces' [5]) are equally valid, but they always imply some drawbacks to use the model in practical applications. More approaches, often suffering from similar limitations, can be found in [3].

In our work, we advocate for abstracting the user-context information from sensor data, which is a relatively common approach [3]. As pointed out in [5], these transformation rules may not be reliable and precise, but we accept such limitations for the sake of having an effective and easy-to-understand method to succeed in this scenario. In general, we model the context around the human actors, using focused terminology and semantic interpretation: as such, the model is human-centric.

Our model consists of four cornerstones which are concisely described as follows:

i) *State*: it describes the user's situation from the physical (e.g., location, activity), emotional (e.g., mood, expectations), and social (e.g., appointments, social engagement) viewpoint as the result of aggregating physical/virtual sensor data;

ii) *Timeline*: it adds the dimension of time to the user' state introducing information about his past and future, and hence including historical data too;

iii) *Network*: it adds the dimension of space (not necessarily in a physical meaning, but especially in the sense of relationship) to the user' state describing his interactions with other users (for instance, via social nets, contact details, or shared events);

iv) *Dialog*: it describes the communication with the user and offers access to all channels available to the user.

Of course, this is only one of the many possible representations of the human-centric context; nevertheless, we consider that it includes all necessary and sufficient features to give a adequate description of the context, and for this reason we have based our work on it.

An example may help to understand how these four features can be used, for instance with a user having with himself a personal device while riding a bicycle. In that case, the *state* part of the context would include the information that the user is on a bicycle (since he is moving slowly, but not walking); the *timeline* part would add the information that the user always bikes around that time, and the possibly he commutes by bicycle and the ride will be finished by a given time; the *network* part may communicate with other people/objects along his way, possibly a friend who is biking in the neighbourhood; the *dialog* part would offer the access to all communication channels that are available to the user at that point, which for instance may include phone calls but not instant messages. Thanks to this representation of the context and by using the CAPE framework described below, a developer may easily create an app that connects two users biking and possibly go towards the same direction (because of historical data or information stored in the personal agendas) by prompting a phone call between the two of them.

2.3 Working with the Human-Centric Context

The main challenge in manipulating the human-centric context is to provide the application (developer) with an environment to access the model of the context and to interact directly with the user via different means thus modifying his context. In our vision, this issue can be tackled via a Context-Aware Programming Environment (CAPE) that interacts with the context data via public APIs, as any program would do, but has some specific mechanisms to communicate with the human beings as well. In particular, on the developer's side, it simplifies the access to context information by providing native proxy-like APIs (where the plural emphasises the fact that it applies to a number of different programming environments), whereas on the user's side it provides a seamless interaction with human beings via UIs, instant-messaging applications, or directly by changing his context (for instance, modifying the agenda or forwarding phone calls). A representation of the role of CAPE is shown in Fig. 1.

Therefore, the role of CAPE is twofold: from the infrastructural point of view, it interfaces the context (from which it collects raw data), the application (developer), and the user; from the applicative point of view, it transforms context data into meaningful information modelled via the four cornerstones.

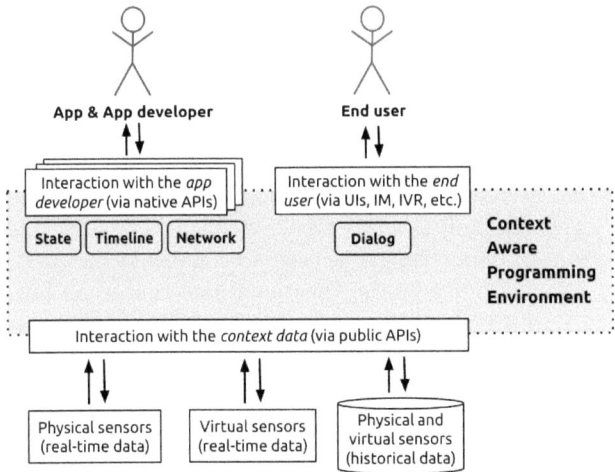

Fig. 1. The Context-Aware Programming Environment interfaces the three key players of the user-centric context system: end user, application (developer), and context data

3 The Role of Agents in Working with the Human-Centric Context

3.1 Motivations for Using an Agent-Based Approach for CAPE

The first step to implement the Context-Aware Programming Environment devised above is to propose a feasible architecture for it, which must meet key requirements such as scalability (in principle, there should be no limit to the number of data sources forming the context and to the number of users involved in the scenario), extensibility (new devices and context sources may become part of CAPE on the fly), and reusability (the impact of the overhead required by the introduction of new devices and context sources should be minimal). In general, classical data distribution architectures are not suitable to be used in this application, due to the heterogeneous nature of the context sources. For example, a publish-subscribe architecture may fit the *state* viewpoint of the context, but it is relatively ill-suited for the *network* one due to the highly structured nature of its data. Not to mention that the control of data authorization poses very different challenges from those regarding data quality and robustness.

In our approach, we propose to implement CAPE via an agent-based software architecture, where the whole work of context data collection, filtering, aggregation, and manipulation is done by software CAPE agents interacting in a multi-agent systems fashion. A crucial benefit of software agents is their ability to facilitate bidirectional asynchronous communication; in the framework of CAPE, this feature provides devices with the possibility to be data providers (e.g., sensors), application runtime environments, and communication channel with the end user. Therefore, context-aware applications no longer need to choose between accessing sensors directly or using a context server, because CAPE offers both these options: hence, each device becomes – through its agents – a context server as well as a context data client application.

3.2 A Multilayered Architecture of CAPE

Following a similar rationale as other well-known approaches [7,2], we propose a layered conceptual architecture of CAPE (shown in Table 1) corresponding to a practical implementation of it, further described in the rest of this paper.

Though these layers may appear generic and not specific to CAPE, the peculiar features can be found in the functionalities that each layer has and in how it has been implemented. Of course, this architecture refers to the specific approach taken in the current implementation (i.e., agent-based) and to the implementation with the Eve agent platform, which will be detailed in Sec. 3.4; a concise description of the layers is given in the following:

1. Application layer: this layer offers an API to connect to CAPE, either by subscribing to context data sources or by retrieving information produced in the 'multiagent system' layer; also, it offers the possibility to do dynamic queries over the processed information coming from the lower layer.

An Agent-Based Architecture to Model and Manipulate Context Knowledge   261

Table 1. Layered conceptual architecture of CAPE for the agent-based implementation

1. *Application* layer
(CAPE client API)
2. *Multiagent system* layer
(CAPE agents)
3. *Agent platform* layer
(Eve agents)
4. *ICT infrastructure* layer
(OpenLDAP, OpenID, and Prosody XMPP servers)

2. Multiagent system layer: this layer comprises the multiagent system model of the context, which consists of CAPE agents producing information about the context modelled via the aforementioned four cornerstones (state, timeline, network, dialog); such information is obtained by aggregating, filtering, and manipulating the context data.

3. Agent platform layer: this layer concerns the practical implementation of the 'multiagent system' layer, for instance thanks to the agent platform 'Eve' (see Sec. 3.4) which ensures the possibility to include agents running on heterogeneous environments, such as mobile devices, servers, browsers, or in the cloud.

4. ICT infrastructure layer: the function of this layer is obvious; in the current version of CAPE, this layer is composed of: i) an OpenLDAP server for managing accounts; ii) an OpenID server connected to the OpenLDAP server for handling the unified user authentication; iii) a Prosody XMPP server that uses the OpenLDAP server for the authorization of the agents via SASL. The support for external OpenID services (from Google, Facebook, etc) will be added in the near future.

In fact, one may argue that layer 2 could avoid the agent-based approach altogether, which is indeed a valid option. However, there are several benefits in using a multi-agent approach and some of them will be highlighted in Sec. 3.5, which refers to a practical use case we have tackled. In general, the fact of relying on a multi-agent approach moves the complexity towards the individual agents rather than to a monolithic solution allows the application to be more flexible and to work seamlessly on different environments.

3.3 Notes on the CAPE Multiagent System (Layer 2)

In the CAPE multiagent system there are two classes of agents: the 'personal' and the 'context' ones (see Fig. 2). The former run on the personal devices of the end users (or they can result from the aggregation of a group of close agents running on cloud servers) and their main task is to handle the bidirectional communication with the user, thus incarnating the 'dialog' viewpoint of the context;

the latter run in the cloud and they collect, filter, and aggregate all context data. As it traditionally occurs in multiagentsystems [15], tasks are carried out via the collaboration of multiple agents. In CAPE, the actual computational work is done by context agents, to which the work is delegated by the personal agents. The relation of delegation between the personal and the context agents is an important part of the authorization model; part of the delegation can include the exchange of trust tokens (e.g., OAuth tokens).

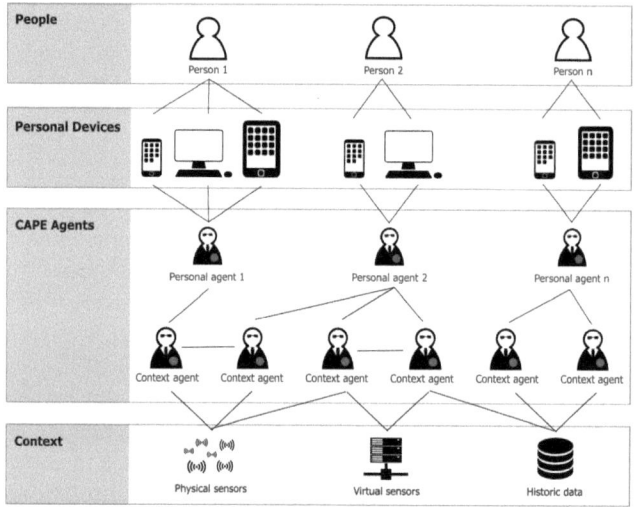

Fig. 2. The multiagent system implementation of CAPE: each person, who can use different devices, is represented by a single personal agent whereas several context agents collaborate to distill information from the context data sources

In this framework, there is no need of a complex directory of agents because each personal agent knows the delegates and can remember the addressing information to contact the agents when needed (of course, provided that each personal agent has knowledge of the existence and location of agents it can instantiate, which can for instance hardcoded in the personal agents). Also, CAPE agents do not need to be developed from scratch: some useful hints can be found in [16].

3.4 Notes on the Eve Agent Platform (Layer 3)

Choosing an appropriate agent platform to implement CAPE agents is not straightforward: unfortunately, many of the traditional agent platforms are usually tied to a single programming language (Java, in general) and they are built to be deployed in a closed and controlled environment (operating system or simulation environment) where agents can live and interact with each other. In general, these platforms suffer from issues connected to scalability and robustness, mainly because of the presence of central directory services (which require

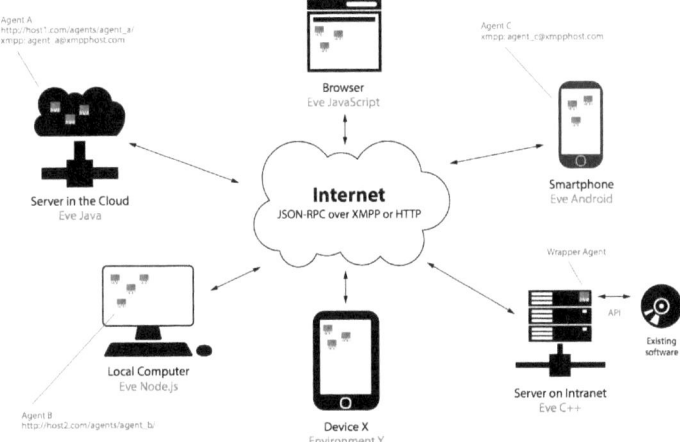

Fig. 3. Conceptual architecture of the agent platform 'Eve', which has been used in layer 3 of the CAPE reference implementation presented in this paper. Heterogeneous devices hosting Eve agents can communicate via the internet by using the XMPP protocol (from [6]).

memory to be stored) and to the amount of manual setup to add new agents, especially when the platform runs in a heterogeneous environment.

For this reason, the ideas behind CAPE have encouraged us to develop a brand new agent platform called 'Eve', which has been described in detail in [6]. Eve, whose conceptual architecture is shown in Fig. 3, is very scalable and suitable to be applied in heterogeneous environments, such as those considered in CAPE. Eve is fully web-based and each Eve agent has its own URLs, which implies that from a practical point of view there is no upper bound to the number of new agents that can be added to the system without degrading its performances. Eve is also fully decentralised, thus there is neither central coordination nor centrally-stored list of all available agents. Moreover, the state persistency in Eve is offloaded from the agents to the environment (i.e., the states of the agents are distributed), which makes Eve insensitive to server/device failures. Although the network transport layer can contain single points of failure, Eve itself is a distributed agent platform, with no single point of failure by design. Among the other advantages, we can emphasise that Eve is platform-independent since agents can live on any device (smartphones, robots, servers or, more generically, in the cloud) – which is another requirement for CAPE – as well as language-independent because it dictates only the communication protocol (JSON-RPC) which works over existing transport layers (HTTP, XMPP); all interactions among Eve agents are asynchronous and request-driven. The XMPP layer also provides basic authentication and authorization services between agents. Of course, this description is sufficient to have only a shallow knowledge about Eve; more details about Eve can be also found in [6] and in [13].

All these characteristics make Eve an ideal candidate to be used in layer 3 of CAPE; as already mentioned above, other agent platforms could be used as well, even though their characteristics may hamper the interoperability, scalability, and robustness of the particular implementation, especially when it is deployed on a heterogeneous network of devices.

3.5 Example of a Use Case: Emergency Management

As a practical application of the work described above, we give a brief overview of the CAPE-based coordination platform for the volunteers of the Royal Netherlands Sea Rescue Institution (KNRM is the Dutch acronym), which is the Dutch organization aimed at saving lives at sea: it has 39 lifeboat stations along the Dutch coasts and it relies on the effort of thousands of volunteers distributed across the Netherlands. When an alert is issued, crews of volunteers (usually 7) have to be quickly formed and the skipper is coordinating all efforts.

Before CAPE was used, each time that an alert was issued a number of rescuers much larger than the crew size was summoned; the redundancy was compensating the fact that potential rescuers could not be available or had been slowed down by external events – such as weather conditions or traffic jams – on their way to the meeting point. Also the reverse situation used to happen: some rescuers may have arrived to the vessel only to find out that it had already left. The main problem of that approach is that all notifications were done through pagers and coordinated by the skipper: therefore, the necessary continuous communication between the skipper and the crew members was time-consuming and ineffective, which is particularly critical in a life threatening situation.

The current implementation strongly relies on CAPE to manage and combine the information coming from multiple data sources, such as the alert system, the personal agendas of the skippers and the rescuers, the weather forecast, and the traffic conditions. Each volunteer has still his own pager that is now equipped with a *personal agent* which, when prompted, can communicate its state (not available or available within a given time frame); also, there is a *coordination agent* (which is the personal agent of the skipper) that takes care of handling all information from the different personal agents and controls the amount of rescuers available. Such coordination agent may autonomously take low-level decisions (especially related to the communication with the personal agents) and assist a human coordinator in taking high-level decisions (such as those concerning the final assessment of the specific volunteers that will form a rescue team). In this framework, even when the personal pager of a rescuer is switched off or out of battery, his 'virtual' counterpart will continue to exist and interact with the rest of the multi-agent system. All privacy and trust issues are managed directly by the Eve system; in this specific case, the system knows what personal devices (and hence personal agents) belong to the network and since the context data are wrapped into the information by the *context agents* it is not necessary to disclose sensitive information such as the exact location of a user or the details of his personal agenda. The application has been validated in real-life experiments and it is currently in use at KNRM.

From a technical point of view, this CAPE implementation makes use of the possibility of Eve to let software agents communicate over XMPP (via the Jabber chat protocol), allowing direct access to agents running on mobile devices as well as to agents running on cloud servers. As such, the CAPE framework bridges the gap between cloud and mobile devices. An excerpt of the CAPE client API for this use case is shown in Table 2; of course, it contains some generic methods which can find application in wider scenarios. As evident in this example, the fact that CAPE provides an API to the developer encapsulates the specific details of the agent platform thus reducing the learning curve to that of using standard libraries.

Table 2. Excerpt from the CAPE client API for the use case described in Sec. 3.5

Method	Description	Example
getState	Retrieve the value of the state variables	location = getState("location", "Hans")
setState	Set the value of the state variables	setState("team id", "4")
sendNotification	Notify the user (no answer requested)	sendNotification("A team is forming up")
sendMessage	Notify the user and expect answer	available = sendMessage("Are you available now?",["yes", "no"])
addContact	Add an entry to the contact list	addContact("name": "Hans", ...)
getContacts	Add all entries from the contact list	contacts = getContacts()

4 Conclusions

The current technological framework calls for effective solutions to model context knowledge and to work with it. In this paper, we have offered an innovative insight into this subject and presented an implementation of a novel agent-based architecture that can be used in practical applications.

The first part of this paper has concerned a general discussion about the so-called human-centric context, which puts a special emphasis on the human players of the system (end users and app developers). We have proposed to model this context via four 'cornerstones' which summarise how both the user and the application (developer) see the information obtained interpreting the data of the context sources. Also, we have introduced the concept of Context-Aware Programming Environment (CAPE) which acts as an interface between the context and the humans and the application, both at an infrastructural level (managing the bidirectional communication between humans and context) and at an applicative level (offering a way to interact with the context and the humans).

The second part of this paper has concerned the agent-based implementation of CAPE, achieved thanks to the agent platform Eve. We have discussed how CAPE agents forming a multiagent system can be used to filter and aggregate sensor data, and hence to obtain and manipulate context information. Current applications of CAPE range from emergency management (which has brought up as an emblematic example in this paper) to health management, where for instance the context is defined by physiological/environmental variables monitored by the sensors of a mobile device. Of course, the future practical application domains are countless from a practical point of view, and the flexible agent-based architecture of CAPE is suitable to be easily tailored to specific use cases.

References

1. Abowd, G.D., Dey, A.K.: Towards a better understanding of context and context-awareness. In: Gellersen, H.-W. (ed.) HUC 1999. LNCS, vol. 1707, pp. 304–307. Springer, Heidelberg (1999)
2. Ailisto, H., Alahuhta, P., Haataja, V., Kyllönen, V., Lindholm, M.: Structuring context aware applications: Five-layer model and example case. In: Proceedings of the Workshop on Concepts and Models for Ubiquitous Computing, pp. 1–5 (2002)
3. Baldauf, M., Dustdar, S., Rosenberg, F.: A survey on context-aware systems. International Journal of Ad Hoc and Ubiquitous Computing 2(4), 263–277 (2007)
4. Bellavista, P., Corradi, A., Fanelli, M., Foschini, L.: A survey of context data distribution for mobile ubiquitous systems. ACM Computing Surveys (CSUR) 44(4), 24 (2012)
5. Cram, D., Fuchs, B., Prié, Y., Mille, A.: An approach to user-centric context-aware assistance based on interaction traces. In: Modeling and Reasoning in Context, MRC 2008 (2008)
6. de Jong, J., Stellingwerff, L., Pazienza, G.E.: Eve: A novel open-source web-based agent platform. In: 2013 IEEE International Conference on Systems, Man, and Cybernetics (SMC), IEEE (2013)
7. Dey, A.K., Abowd, G.D., Salber, D.: A conceptual framework and a toolkit for supporting the rapid prototyping of context-aware applications. Human-computer Interaction 16(2), 97–166 (2001)
8. Hong, D., Schmidtke, H.R., Woo, W.: Linking context modelling and contextual reasoning. In: 4th International Workshop on Modeling and Reasoning in Context (MRC), pp. 37–48. Citeseer (2007)
9. Hong, J.-Y., Suh, E.-H., Kim, S.-J.: Context-aware systems: A literature review and classification. Expert Systems with Applications 36(4), 8509–8522 (2009)
10. Indulska, J., Sutton, P.: Location management in pervasive systems. In: Proceedings of the Australasian Information Security Workshop Conference on ACSW Frontiers 2003, vol. 21, pp. 143–151. Australian Computer Society, Inc. (2003)
11. Korpipaa, P., Mantyjarvi, J., Kela, J., Keranen, H., Malm, E.-J.: Managing context information in mobile devices. IEEE Pervasive Computing 2(3), 42–51 (2003)
12. Nguyen-Vuong, Q.-T., Agoulmine, N., Ghamri-Doudane, Y.: A user-centric and context-aware solution to interface management and access network selection in heterogeneous wireless environments. Computer Networks 52(18), 3358–3372 (2008)

13. Stellingwerff, L., Pazienza, G.E.: Practical applications of the web-based agent platform Eve. In: Demazeau, Y., Corchado, J.M., Zambonelli, F., Bajo, J. (eds.) PAAMS 2014. LNCS (LNAI), vol. 8473, Springer, Heidelberg (2014)
14. Strang, T., Linnhoff-Popien, C., Frank, K.: CoOL: A context ontology language to enable contextual interoperability. In: Stefani, J.-B., Demeure, I., Zhang, J. (eds.) DAIS 2003. LNCS, vol. 2893, pp. 236–247. Springer, Heidelberg (2003)
15. Wooldridge, M.: An introduction to multiagent systems (2008), `Wiley`
16. Ahrndt, S., Lützenberger, M., Heßler, A., Albayrak, S.: HAI–A Human agent interface for JIAC. In: Klügl, F., Ossowski, S. (eds.) MATES 2011. LNCS, vol. 6973, pp. 149–156. Springer, Heidelberg (2011)

Practical Applications of the Web-Based Agent Platform 'Eve'

Ludo Stellingwerff, Jos de Jong, and Giovanni E. Pazienza

Almende BV,
Westerstraat 50, Rotterdam 3016 DJ,
The Netherlands
{ludo,jos,giovanni}@almende.org

Abstract. The existing approaches to build multi-agent systems fail at addressing the challenges posed by the current technology, where ubiquitous interconnected electronic devices are no more passive machines operated by humans but rather active computational components cooperating with humans. In order to tackle this problem, we have created a novel open-source web-based agent platform called 'Eve' that features some specific characteristics (e.g., platform and language independence, openness) that make it particularly suitable to be deployed in real-life applications. In this paper, we discuss the main features of Eve and present several use cases in which it has been successfully applied.

Keywords: agent platforms, multiagent systems, interoperability.

1 Introduction

Nowadays, both humans and software applications can be considered as entities with some degree of autonomy that interact with each other and with the environment without need of centralized coordination. In this framework, devices are modelled as agents that mimic some of the characteristics of human beings: they are autonomous (i.e., capable of taking decisions), intelligent (i.e., capable of adapt their behaviour on the basis of available data), and social (i.e., capable of communicating with humans as well as other agents). Therefore, the fundamental tool to handle (and profit from) such a complex yet promising scenario is to build an effective multi-agent system (MAS) [11] tailored for this novel technological context. A MAS is usually developed on an agent platform, which is usually chosen among the several dozens already available on the market (a good yet not recent overview can be found in [13]). Nevertheless, the great majority of them – usually Java based – consist of a closed and controlled environment (operating system or simulation environment) where agents can live and interact with each other. In general, these platforms suffer from connected to the scalability and to the robustness, mainly because of the presence of central directory services (which require memory to be stored) and to the amount of manual setup to add new agents, especially when the platform runs in a heterogeneous environment.

In order to overcome these problems, we propose 'Eve' [8] that is an agent platform specifically thought to be deployed on a diverse distributed environment. Eve is inspired by the principles of human-agent collectives described CHAP [17] and in ORCHID [15], in which agents (both human and software) collaborate in a seamless and effective way. Eve has been the key component of several successful applications, especially in the fields of emergency management, smart grids, energy consumption optimisation, and coordination of complex tasks. In this paper, we also discuss several of these practical use cases, emphasising that they are just a few of those in which such innovative agent platform may find application.

The paper is structured as follows: in Sec. 2, we describe the architecture and the main features of Eve; in Sec. 3, we illustrate a few practical examples in which Eve has already found application; in Sec. 4, we draw the conclusions of our work.

2 Summary of the Main Features of Eve

2.1 Conceptual Architecture

From the architectural overview of Eve shown in Fig. 2, it is possible to catch a glimpse of its main features. It should be evident that Eve can be deployed on a number of different devices (smartphones, servers, local PCs, etc.) hosting different environments (JavaScript, Android, C++, etc.), all connected to the internet via the JSON-RPC protocol.

Thanks to this approach, Eve has some distinctive characteristics. First of all, Eve is platform independent since agents can live on any device: smartphones, robots, servers or, more generically, in the cloud. Second, Eve is language independent[1] because it dictates only the communication protocol (JSON-RPC) which works over existing transport layers (HTTP, XMPP) and a simple API, as described in and Table I. Third, Eve is an open agent platform: each agent has its own public[2] URLs and hence existing Eve-systems can be easily connected to the others. Furthermore, non-Eve systems can be connected to the Eve platform by making its API available via an Eve agent acting as a wrapper.

The architecture of Eve leads to further advantages among which is worth to emphasize the following ones:

Scalability: Eve is fully web-based and hence, from a practical point of view, there is no upper bound to the number of new agents that can be added to the system without degrading its performances.

Robustness: the state persistency in Eve is offloaded from the agents to the environment (i.e., the states of the agents are distributed), which makes Eve

---

[1] Currently, there are two mature implementations of Eve (one in Java and the other in JavaScript) whereas a third one (in Python) is in an embryonic stage.
[2] Authorization mechanisms have already been implemented, in case the application needs them.

insensitive to server/device failures. Although the network transport layer can contain single points of failure, Eve itself is a distributed agent platform, with no single point of failure by design.

Massive parallelization of the workload of an agent: agents can be multiplexed (i.e., multiple instances of the same agent sharing the same state can exist at once). Traditional agent platforms have 1 thread per agent; in contrast, Eve allocates up to n threads (where n has virtually no upper bound) when the agent is heavily loaded and no thread at all when the agent is idle. This approach has the additional advantage of reducing resource consumption for idle agents.

Seamless migration: In Eve, there is no difference in accessing local or remote agents, as agents are fully location agnostic. This feature allows seamless migration of agents between run-time environments.

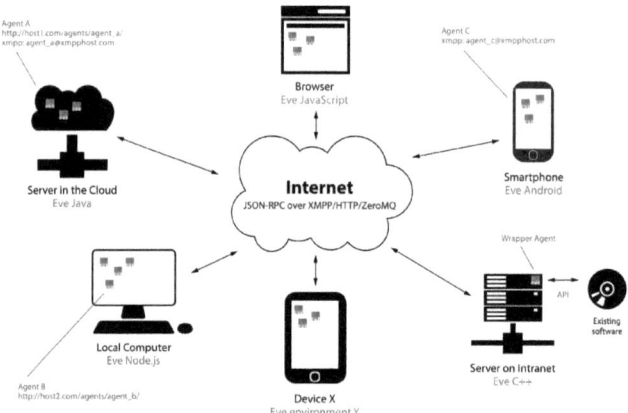

Fig. 1. Conceptual architecture of the Eve, showing that it can be deployed in a heterogeneous environment where different devices are connected to the internet via the JSON-RPC protocol

Eve is a fully decentralized system: there is neither central coordination nor centrally-stored list of all available agents. Interactions among agents are asynchronous and request-driven; agents get to know each other via the so-called shared services (e.g., acting in the same calendar or registering at the same locations service). Eve agents communicate via regular HTTP POST requests or via XMPP messages through the JSON-RPC protocol, which is a simple protocol using JSON (JavaScript Object Notation) to format requests and responses.

2.2 What Is an Eve Agent?

Defining what exactly an agent is has been a long-standing issue. However, there is a general agreement over the basic capabilities that an agent needs, as proposed in [19]:

- *Autonomy*: agents should be able to perform the majority of their problem-solving tasks without the direct intervention of humans or other agents, and they should have a degree of control over their own actions and their own internal state.
- *Social ability*: agents should be able to interact, when they deem appropriate, with other software agents and humans in order to complete their own problem solving and to help others with their activities where appropriate.
- *Responsiveness*: agents should perceive their environment (which may be the physical world, a user, a collection of agents, the Internet, etc.) and respond in a timely fashion to changes which occur in it.
- *Proactiveness*: agents should not simply act in response to their environment, they should be able to exhibit opportunistic, goal-directed behaviour and take the initiative where appropriate.

This description fits very well to the way in which Eve agents have been devised; in particular, an Eve agent consists of: i) *code* containing the agents logic, which allows an agent to perform its tasks, take initiatives, learn, react, cooperate, negotiate, etc.; ii) *communication facilities* allowing the agent to interact with other agents (currently over HTTP and XMPP); iii) *clock*, enabling the agent to schedule tasks for itself; iv) *memory*, a place where the agent can store its state and history.

All Eve agents have a set of standard methods available, described in detail in Table 1. In particular, we have created methods to retrieve the agent id (*getId*), type (*getType*), version (*getVersion*), and description (*getDescription*). Also, there is a method to get all URLs of an agent (*getURLs*), and to subscribe (*onSubscribe*) or unsubscribe (*onUnsubscribe*) from the agent events.

2.3 Short Notes about FIPA Compliancy

Eve has been conceived to allow developers easy access to agent concepts – such as time autonomy and direct interagent communication – and its architecture relies in large part on existing technologies and infrastructures. These choices have led us to a pragmatic approach concerning the a priori compliancy to FIPA specifications. As a result, Eve is not fully FIPA compliant by design.

A through discussion of the motivations behind this choice is beyond the scopes of this paper. However, we would like to emphasise that the last version of FIPA specifications is from 2000 (revised in 2002) [2], and that in some cases they do not align with the modern netcentric approach of agent systems. For instance, FIPA specifications mandates hat an agent system defines a directory facilitator; Eve goes beyond this concept, letting agents know each other via shared services, thus avoiding the need for a global registry of agents. Also, it is the underlying

Table 1. Set of standard methods available to all Eve agents

Method	Description
getId	Retrieve the agent id. In Eve, an agent may have multiple URLs but only one id. The agent id is not globally unique, since agents running on different platforms may have the same id.
getType	Retrieve the agent type, which is typically the class name of the agent.
getVersion	Retrieve the agent version number.
getDescription	Retrieve a description of the agent functionality.
getURLs	Retrieve an array with the agent URLs. An agent can have multiple URLs for different transport services, such as HTTP and XMPP.
getMethods	Retrieve a list with all available methods.
onSubscribe	Subscribe to an event of this agent; the provided callback URL and method will be invoked when the event is triggered.
onUnsubscribe	Unsubscribe from one of this agent events.

assumption of FIPA that agent- systems should form a common global ontology and a common API using a globally accepted language. This strict coupling (at specification level) may even limit the interoperability between agent-systems and complicate the development. In our experience, it is more effective favour loose coupling between agents and bridge systems by injecting ontology-mapping translation agents, using ad hoc (but well documented) languages.

There is some evidence [1] that FIPA has a roadmap for introducing several compliance levels: from minimal-FIPA compliance level, which represents the lowest requirements, up to a full-FIPA compliance level, which comprises all current mandatory parts of normative specifications. This process is still ongoing, but our belief is that Eve will have an intermediate-FIPA compliance level.

2.4 On the Comparison with Related Approach

Nowadays, there are numerous widely-employed agent platforms, such as JADE [7], AgentScape [16], and A-globe [18], only to mention a few. Performing a throughout comparison between Eve and all of them is out of the scopes of this paper, which is rather focused on the practical applications of Eve. However, it is worth to mention that a fair comparison of Eve with existing agent platforms is difficult to make, mainly for two reasons. First, the core concepts of Eve are different from those of traditional agent platforms: Eve is fully web-based and lacks of any 'centralised' feature, and its main strengths are in the fact of beings platform-independent and easily deployable, which are difficult to translate into numbers. Second, there is very little literature about the comparison of multi-agent systems: some recent works (e.g., [9]) makes some original proposal – based on some classical works [12] – which is though not applicable to Eve because Eve has been built to operate in different context; [10] proposes yet another approach, which though focuses on a very particular aspect possibly missing the overall evaluation. Curiously, some concrete effort to define common criteria to evaluate different systems was made in the past (see [14]) but the current technological framework condemns to early obsoleteness any effort of this sort.

Still, in the near future we plan to publish an ad-hoc paper dedicated to this issue which may help to define at least some preliminary metrics to evaluate the performances of Eve.

3 Examples of Practical Applications of Eve

Eve has already been used in several commercial and research projects covering different scientific fields. In the following, we describe a four existing practical applications of Eve, even though more are expected to be implemented in the near future. What we report here is a summary of the work carried out; more details and demos can be found on the Eve website [6].

3.1 Autonomous (Re)scheduling of Appointments

In the last two decades, there has been a major shift towards calendaring software to keep track of events and (re)schedule appointments. Especially when several people are involved, these tasks can be a tedious time-consuming burden as, in general, different calendaring softwares do not interact seamlessly with each other. As a consequence, people waste a considerable amount of time *scheduling* rather than *doing*.

In order to tackle this issue, Eve has been successfully used to build an agent-based scheduling system, whose conceptual architecture is shown in Fig. 2. It is composed of four kinds of agents:

- *personal agents*, which are the virtual counterpart of each user, and hence they represent the users' preference and learn autonomously the user preferences (e.g., working shifts) based on the past meetings;
- *meeting agents*, which negotiate and schedule the appointments based on the information coming from all other agents;
- *context agents*, which have access to the users' calendar by communicating with the servers (Gmail, Exchange, etc.) and to other context data – such as traffic conditions and weather – that may influence the behaviour of the users.
- *location agents*, which are a special kind of context agents whose sole task is connecting to location services and calculate travel times between user locations.

Whenever needed, a meeting agent negotiates with the personal agents of all participants as well as with other existing meeting agents in order to find the most convenient time slot and location for the meeting, and reschedule it when the circumstances change. This process is totally transparent to the user,

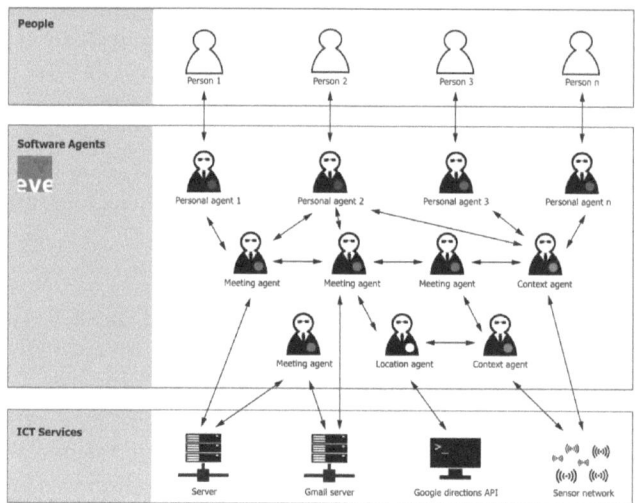

Fig. 2. Conceptual architecture of the Eve-based autonomous scheduling multiagent system

who may – but is not required to – interact with his own personal agent via smartphone apps, web interfaces, instant-messaging (e.g., chat), and standard telephone through Interactive Voice Response. Therefore, as a result of the application of Eve, the slow and cumbersome communication between humans, or between a human and his calendaring software, can be substituted (or at least facilitated) by the fast and seamless communication between software agents.

Eve is specifically suited to this application for a number of reasons: first, it is language- and environment- independent and hence Eve agents can be easily developed for the different OS hosted on the personal devices; second, the fact that Eve is fully decentralised allows this system to rely on a very limited amount of messages, as devices (better to say, *personal agents*) can autonomously take peer-to-peer actions, without communication to a central unit; third, Eve agents are lightweight, and thus particularly fit to devices which may have limited memory and processing power.

3.2 Emergency Management

Natural disasters and accidents do not take into account municipal or national borders; in fact, in case of a large-scale incident, such as a terrorist attack or a major fire, different agencies from different regions or even countries have to work together and it is often very difficult, because of incompatible systems, organizational structures and protocols. This is the main motivation behind the BRIDGE [4] project, whose main goal is to develop a platform to provide technical support for multi-agency collaboration in large-scale emergency relief efforts, taking care of their (IT) systems, people, and protocols. In this framework, agent technology is very useful to solve communication and collaboration problems, especially because a multi-agent system can make sure that the right information is passed to the right agencies and that the relevant experts are involved. Therefore, a passive communication infrastructure can be transformed into an active system that can initiate connections.

In the BRIDGE project, Eve is used to model and support the various emergency response resources involved: different software agents are used to represent interests of different parties, and thus quickly negotiate and collaborate. Also, the software agents are mainly meant to perform rapid, repetitive tasks, such as quick communication or aggregation of data whereas people are involved when difficult tasks must be executed or decisions made. Through negotiation between Eve agents, ad hoc groups of resources are formed to handle tasks. The agents also obtain, aggregate and interpret sensor data, which is then communicated to field commanders and to other agents, thus providing situational awareness. The Eve agents are run on a cloud platform and on mobile smartphones, whereas the communication between the Eve agents and other components of the BRIDGE platform is done through the EDXL-RM protocol.

There are at least two key aspects of Eve emphasised in this application: first, the fact that being language- and platform- independent Eve can act as a middleware among devices of different nature; second, the fact that the combination of local and cloud counterparts of Eve agents makes the system particularly robust to infrastructural failures (which are critical in emergency managing situations) as well as to the fact that portables devices can be switched off or out of battery (which would allow the 'cloud' agents to be still active anyway).

3.3 Energy-Efficient Data Centres

Renewable energy sources – such as wind, water and solar energy – are not predictable and hence power suppliers can therefore not guarantee a completely 'green' energy supply during peak hours. In case of high demand, they are forced to rely on dirty energy produced by diesel-fuelled generators, or they have to transport energy from faraway sources. In the case of data centers, it would be ideal to estimate their power needs in order to allow power suppliers can better anticipate future energy demands. This is the rationale behind the All4Green project [3], which brings together relevant stakeholders to create a 'sustainable ICT ecosystem' for the datacenter sector. By enabling datacenters, power suppliers and end-users to communicate their expected supply and demand, ICT resources can be better allocated to provide requested services, while saving energy and reducing greenhouse gas emissions.

In the All4Green project, Eve is used to negotiate the most efficient energy balance between energy providers and large- scale energy users, specifically data centers. The context of this negotiation process is given in the form of GreenSLA contracts, which offer a template for energy profiles of data centers. By communicating the expected energy profiles, the energy providers provide a goal for the Eve agents to work towards. Also, Eve has a communication middleware role: the toolset has offered an in-place replacement of a Springframework SOAP stack, still adhering and actively enforcing the (Java Interface) contract between the communicating partners; this is achieved through the proxy-agent generation of Eve. The way in which Eve has been used in this project also shows that Eve can work properly in a strict Java EE infrastructure.

Similarly as before, the role of Eve as a communication middleware is emphasised in this application; also, the fact that Eve agents are proactive and are able to carry out autonomously even complex negotiation tasks is particularly critical too.

3.4 Dynamic Management of Smart Grids

The energy market suffers from structural inertia: in theory, energy prices should follow a standard supply-and-demand-mechanism; in practice, the market is not able to adapt to the rapid changes in supply and demand of energy. One of the reasons behind this mechanism is that the current energy grid is still based on a centralized and inflexible management of supply and demand of energy, but the modern energy market is becoming much more dynamic. The current grid is not prepared for a distributed energy market, in which individual households cause energy supply peaks by generating their own solar power on a sunny day. Managing this scenario by applying an Internet-of-Things-approach is the motivation of the INERTIA project [5], which that aims to model and use the energy flexibility of terniary buildings to lower peak electricity demand. At each building, INERTIA will support the building manager with making optimal decisions and taking limited control of Distributed Energy Resources (DERs). Many of such buildings will be connected with a hub, where energy flexibility can be pooled and traded with energy providers (or other consumers).

Within INERTIA, Eve is used as an integration platform for the software that will run at each building. This is achieved by wrapping numerous pieces of existing and new software within Eve agents, elegantly separating the means of communication from the functionality within the agents. As the different software components are written in different languages, the fact that Eve is language independent can ease development. As some of the software components implements cross-cutting concerns, the Eve based architecture also performs a function similar to aspect-oriented programming: it facilitates loose coupling between the agents implementing the cross-cutting concern and the rest of INERTIA. Moreover, agents that consist of small bits of logic such as a learning algorithm can be instantiated as often as required effortlessly.

Besides Eve as an architectural solution, Eve agents are also used to represent and interact with the physical reality: users, DERs, and spaces (which can contain multiple users and DERs). Such an agent representation will allow the end users to acquire a complete breakdown of the aggregated energy use and flexibility to the level of individual consumers and DERs, helping analysis and improvement of energy performance. One of the key benefits of using Eve agents is their ability to migrate: agents representing humans can associate with different space agent to represent moving from one room to another and migrate to a whole new server to represent moving from one office building to the next (e.g., when changing jobs).

Finally, ongoing development of Eve implementations are expected to allow the user interfaces of the agents to be conveniently dynamic and modular.

This application relies on all aspects of Eve emphasised in the previous three applications: its role as a middleware among different platforms; the fact that it is language-independent and lightweight, which then makes it particularly suited to be deployed in an heterogeneous Internet-of-Things approach; its robustness, which is particularly critical when managing electric grids.

4 Conclusion

In this paper, we have introduced the main characteristics of Eve, a novel agent platform that has been explicitly devised to be applied in the current technological framework composed of a multitude of devices based on different platforms and programming languages, and described a few successful practical applications of it.

Eve is intrinsically platform- and language- independent and it can be considered as one of the precursors of a new generation of agent platforms, which will be drastically different from (and hence difficult to compare to) the current ones. Among the other features, we want to emphasize that Eve is a fully decentralized open agent platform: agents have their own public URLs but there is no centrally- stored list of all available agents. These characteristics make Eve very scalable (one could claim that the system is as scalable as the web itself) and robust. As future developments of Eve, we plan to extend the number of working implementations beyond the current ones, which are in Java and JavaScript.

Currently, Eve has been applied to several areas, including emergency management, smart grids, energy-efficient data centers, and context interpretation. In each of them, Eve has proved to be an effective solution to problems that otherwise would have been hard to solve, especially those connected to the interoperability of heterogeneous devices. Among the new applications on which we are currently working, we can mention a new system to capture and interpret non-conformity events in a large manufacturing company where Eve will be used as the infrastructure for an Internet of Things approach.

Acknowledgement. This research has been partially funded by the European Union Seventh Framework Programme under grant agreements no. 261817 (BRIDGE project), no. 288674 (All4Green project), and no. 105543 (INERTIA project). The authors are grateful to Andries Stam, Rick van Krevelen, Remco Tukker, and Janny Remakers for their support writing this paper.

References

1. Minimal FIPA and FIPA compliance levels work plan (2001), http://www.fipa.org/docs/wps/f-wp-00018/f-wp-00018.html
2. FIPA specifications (2002), http://www.fipa.org/specifications/
3. All4Green project (2012), http://www.all4green-project.eu/

4. Bridging resources and agencies in large-scale emergency management, BRIDGE project (2012), http://www.bridgeproject.eu/en
5. INERTIA project (2013), http://www.inertia-project.eu/
6. Eve - a web-based agent platform (2014), http://eve.almende.com/
7. Bellifemine, F., Poggi, A., Rimassa, G.: Jade: a fipa2000 compliant agent development environment. In: Proceedings of the Fifth International Conference on Autonomous Agents, pp. 216–217. ACM (2001)
8. de Jong, J., Stellingwerff, L., Pazienza, G.E.: Eve: a novel open-source web-based agent platform. In: 2013 IEEE International Conference on Systems, Man and Cybernetics. IEEE (2013)
9. Di Bitonto, P., Laterza, M., Roselli, T., Rossano, V.: Evaluation of multi-agent systems: Proposal and validation of a metric plan. In: Nguyen, N.T. (ed.) Transactions on CCI VII. LNCS, vol. 7270, pp. 198–221. Springer, Heidelberg (2012)
10. Ben Hmida, F., Lejouad Chaari, W., Tagina, M.: Performance evaluation of multiagent systems: Communication criterion. In: Nguyen, N.T., Jo, G.-S., Howlett, R.J., Jain, L.C. (eds.) KES-AMSTA 2008. LNCS (LNAI), vol. 4953, pp. 773–782. Springer, Heidelberg (2008)
11. Jennings, N.R., Sycara, K., Wooldridge, M.: A roadmap of agent research and development. Autonomous Agents and Multi-agent Systems 1(1), 7–38 (1998)
12. Kusek, K.J.G.J.M.: A performance analysis of multi-agent systems. International Transactions on Systems Science and Applications 1(4) (2006)
13. Leszczyna, R.: Evaluation of agent platforms. European Commission, Joint Research Centre, Institute for the Protection and Security of the Citizen, Ispra, Italy, Tech. Rep. (2004)
14. Occello, M., Guessoum, Z., Boissier, O., et al.: Un essai de définition de critères pour l étude comparative de plates-formes multi-agents. Technique et Science Informatiques (TSI) 21(4) (2002)
15. U. of Southampton. The ORCHID project. (2014), http://www.orchid.ac.uk/
16. Overeinder, B.J., Brazier, F.M.T.: Scalable middleware environment for agent-based internet applications. In: Dongarra, J., Madsen, K., Waśniewski, J. (eds.) PARA 2004. LNCS, vol. 3732, pp. 675–679. Springer, Heidelberg (2006)
17. Serban, R., Guo, H., Salden, A.: Common hybrid agent platform–sustaining the collective. In: 2012 13th ACIS International Conference on Software Engineering, Artificial Intelligence, Networking and Parallel & Distributed Computing (SNPD), pp. 420–427. IEEE (2012)
18. Šišlák, D., Rollo, M., Pěchouček, M.: A-globe: Agent platform with inaccessibility and mobility support. In: Klusch, M., Ossowski, S., Kashyap, V., Unland, R. (eds.) CIA 2004. LNCS (LNAI), vol. 3191, pp. 199–214. Springer, Heidelberg (2004)
19. Wooldridge, M., Jennings, N.R.: et al. Intelligent agents: Theory and practice. Knowledge Engineering Review 10(2), 115–152 (1995)

Multi-Armed Bandit Policies for Reputation Systems

Thibaut Vallée, Grégory Bonnet, and François Bourdon

Normandie Université, France
UNICAEN, GREYC, F-14032 Caen, France
CNRS, UMR 6072, F-14032 Caen, France
firstname.lastname@unicaen.fr

Abstract. The robustness of reputation systems against manipulations have been widely studied. However, the study of how to use the reputation values computed by those systems are rare. In this paper, we draw the analogy between reputation systems and multi-armed bandit problems. We investigate how to use the multi-armed bandit selection policies in order to increase the robustness of reputation systems against malicious agents. To this end, we propose a model of an abstract service sharing system which uses such a bandit-based reputation system. Finally, in an empirical study, we show that some multi-armed bandits policies are more robust against manipulations but cost-free for the malicious agents whereas some other policies are manipulable but costly.

1 Introduction

In a multi-agent system, when an agent cannot carry out a task alone, it needs to delegate it to another agent. In such systems, agents need to share skills and knowledge, and thus agents are both service consumers and providers. However, as large open multi-agent systems allow heterogeneous agents to interact, some agents can provide bad quality services due to computation or network failures, or even due to malicious behaviours. For instance, such problems as corrupted files (failures) and viruses (malicious behaviours) spreading are common in peer-to-peer file sharing systems (as Gnutella [1]). A common way to help agents to select with whom they will interact[1] is to use a reputation system. Such systems allow agents to ask services to other agents whom have been advised by a third-party. Agents evaluate their past interactions and compute a value which represents how they trust each other agent with whom they have interacted. These trust values are communicated by the agents and agregated through feedbacks. Then these feedbacks are used to compute a reputation value for each agent, that is assumed to reflect their reliability as service providers. Many reputation systems have been proposed but, in those systems, a malicious agent can lie, collude with other agents, introduce many false identities called Sybil agents, leave and join the system with a new identity, or change its behaviour in order

---

[1] We say that two agents interact when one provides a service to the other.

to manipulate its reputation value. Several works propose reputation systems which are robust to a specific manipulation. However those studies focus on how the trust and reputation values are computed but not on how the agents will use it. Indeed, the policy used to select providers impacts the system. If each agent interacts only with the one which has the best reputation value, it will be hard for a single malicious agent to provide many bad services. However, such a policy leads few service providers to be overloaded while other providers never interact. Conversely, if an agent selects randomly with whom it will interact, the system opens but the reputation value is useless: malicious agents can easily provide bad services. Moreover, many reputation systems are robust to one-shot manipulations but sensitive against collusions of agents that execute a long-term manipulation. For instance, on eBay [2], an agent can behave in a good way for many low-priced transactions in order to increase its reputation value and can behave badly for rare high-priced transactions. The problem of selecting with whom interacting based on past observations has been widely studied in the context of multi-armed bandit (MAB). In this paper, we propose to investigate how using the MAB policies in a reputation system can decrease the number of manipulations efficiently. Our work is organized as follows. We present in Section 2 the literature in the field of reputation systems, their manipulations and the field of MAB. In Section 3, we propose a model of service sharing system and draw the analogy between this model and the Multi-Armed Bandit problem. We present in Section 4 some canonical policies and manipulations. Finally, we present in Section 5 an empiric study of the performance of the system when a coalition of agents tries to manipulate it.

2 Related Work

Trust was introduced by Marsh [3] in the context of multi-agent systems. This notion formalizes an estimation of the future behaviour of an agent when there exists a risk of unexpected behaviour. Three fundamental axioms define what a reputation system is [4]: (1) the agents in the system will interact in the future; (2) feedbacks, called trust values, on the interactions between agents must be shared with the other agents; (3) those feedbacks must be used to help consummers to decide which will be their next providers. Thus, in reputation systems, the trust value of an agent about another is the evaluation of the past interactions by the former about the latter. Then, the reputation of an agent is an agregation of all the trust values about this agent. Many reputation systems have been proprosed [4–11]. They can be classified in three families: symmetric (e.g. eBay's reputation system [4]), assymmetric global (e.g. Google's Page Rank) and assymmetric personnalized (e.g. maxflow-based algorithm). Two of the more common reputation systems are BetaReputation [6] and EigenTrust [7]. BetaReputation uses a Beta density function to compute the probability that an agent exhibits a good behaviour. EigenTrust uses the same algorithm than Google's Page rank: given a graph which represents the trust values between the agents, the reputation of an agent is the probability than a random walker passes by the node corresponding to this agent. Let us notice that EigenTrust is known to be manipulable by a simple coalition of agents [12]. The problem of the robustness of reputation systems has been strongly studied [10, 11, 13]. Cheng and Friedman [13] proved that no symmetric reputation system can be robust to false-identity collusions and only assymetric reputation systems can be robust if they satisfy some strong conditions. Altman *et al.* [11] defined, among other axioms for reputation and ranking systems, the incentive compatibility which corresponds to a robustness against manipulation, and they proved that most of the ranking systems do not satisfy it. However, both Cheng and Friedman, and Altman *et al.* considered manipulations at a given instant: a system is robust if the manipulation does not change the reputation value (or rank) at the time the manipulation is perfomed. They do not investigate if it is possible to manipulate the reputation system over time. Indeed, some manipulations as strategic oscillation [14] are built to manipulate the reputation systems on a long term. Moreover, most of those papers consider specific manipulations but do not study how using the reputation values to select the most reliable agents can impact the system robustness. Pinyol and Sabater [15] highlighted the notion of learning/adaption strategy which is how the agents use the reputation to adapt their behavior for future interactions. Although most of the reputation systems do not offer clear strategies, a similar problem of selection has been studied in another context: the multi-armed bandit problem (MAB) [16]. The canonical definition of this problem is the following. Let us consider a gambling machine with multiple arms. Each arm has an unknown reward function. Thus, the problem is which arm an agent needs to pull in order to maximize its reward? Many models of MAB have been studied (for instance with multiple players [17], stochastic or stationary policies [18]). All these models propose selection policies to minimize the agent's regret: the difference between the reward it obtained and how much it could had won if it had always pulled the best arm. All this policies, such as UCB, Poker, ε-greedy [19, 20], are a compromise between pulling the arm which has the best expected reward and pulling another arm in order to increase the agent's knowledge on the reward distributions (known as the exploration - exploitation compromise). In this paper, we propose to draw an analogy between both problems: the selection of agents evaluated by a reputation value and the selection of arms evaluated by an estimated reward function. We investigate how using MAB policies in a reputation system impacts of the manipulations, which had not been studied to the best of our knowledge.

3 A General Model Using Reputation System

The aim of a reputation system is to help each agent to determine with which agent it will interact in order to achieve its goal. In this section, we propose a general application where the agents must interact with the others and use a reputation system. In such system, the agents use a policy in order to select with whom interact. By analogy with the multi-armed bandit problem, we propose to used the MAB policies in such system.

3.1 A Service Sharing System Model

Considering a multi-agent system where each of them can provide some services. In order to be general, we consider abstract services. A such system is called a *service sharing system*: when an agent needs a service that it cannot provide itself, it ask this service to another agent.

Definition 1. *A service sharing system is a tuple $\langle N, S \rangle$ where N is a set of agents and S a set of available services. We denote by $N_x \subseteq N$ the set of agents that can provide the service $s_x \in S$.*

Definition 2. *In a service sharing system, an agent $a_i = \langle \vec{\varepsilon_i}, v_i, T, f_i, \pi_i \rangle$ is an entity which can consume and provide services where: $\vec{\varepsilon_i}$ is its expertise vector; v_i is its evaluation function; T is the matrix of trust values; f_i is its reputation function; π_i is its policy.*

The *expertise* of $a_i \in N$ for the service $s_x \in S$, denoted $\varepsilon_{i,x}$, is the capacity for a_i to performs s_x with a good quality when another agent asks it to. Even if the quality of a service depends on the expertise of the provider, it is subject to the consumer evaluation. This evaluation can be based on many factors. For instance, in peer-to-peer file sharing systems, the quality can be evaluated on the download latency, the file quality and so on, such as it can take many kind of values: booleans, $[-1; 1]$, $\mathbb{N}$, $\mathbb{R}$ or any other representation. In order to stay general, we assume that for all agents $a_i \in N$, a_i evaluates the services with its *evaluation function* $v_i : S \to V$ where V is a common codomain for all agents. We assume that the agents agregate their past experiences in a trust matrix (denoted T) and use feedbacks to share with the others their observations. The agents can provide a feedback each time they receive a service, or only when it is necessary to avoid communication flooding. The trust value of the agents represents only how each agent evaluates the service that it received from the others. The reputation of an agent a_i is the agregation of all the local trust values about a_i. In this article, we do not focus ourselves on how the reputation is computed. We only assume that each agent uses a *reputation fonction* $f_i : N \times S \to \mathbb{R}$. Hence each agent can compute alone with its knowledge of T the reputation of the other agents for each service. We make no assumption on the reputation function and allow two agents to use different reputation functions. The reputation of the agents is assumed to represent if they can provide a given service with a good quality. The *policy* of the agent $a_i \in N$ defines how it uses those reputations in order to select an expected good service provider: $\pi_i : S \to N_x$. We do not make any assumption on how the policy is computed and allow the agents to follow differents policies. The Figure 1 resumes the different interactions between agents in this application. The arrow 1 represents service requests from a_i to other agents (selected by the policy). The arrow 2 represents this service as provided. On the other side, arrows 3 and 4 are respectivly service requests from an agent a_j to a_i and the service that a_i provides to a_j. We represent the feedbacks by arrows 5, 6, 7 and 8 (respectivly a feedback request from a_i to a_j, a feedback answer from a_j to a_i, a feedback request from a_j to a_i and a feedback answer from a_i to a_j).

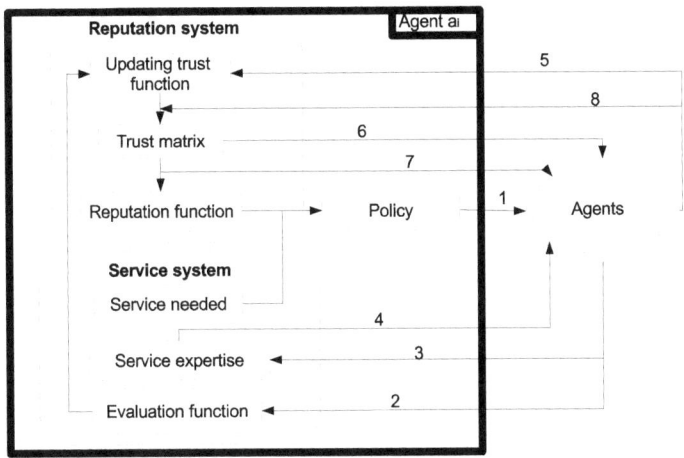

Fig. 1. Interactions between agents in the service sharing system

3.2 Analogy with Multi-Armed Bandit Problems

The aim of the policy in the service sharing system is to determinate to which agent asking a service. Such problem is related to a multi-armed bandit problem. Let us consider a player and a gambling machines with multiple arms. Each of these arms has an unkown reward function. The problem is which arm the player needs to pull in order to obtain the best possible reward? Both problems, service sharing and multi-armed bandit, use past observations to estimate the future service quality/reward of an agent/arm if it is selected/pulled. Thus, we can modelise a service sharing system with a MAB where each agent is in the same time a player and a gambling machines, and each arm corresponds to a service that the agent can provide.

Definition 3. *Let a $\langle N, S \rangle$ be a service sharing system. The corresponding MAB is defined by the set of M multi-armed bandits where $|M| = |N|$ and $\forall a_i \in N, \forall s_x \in S : a_i \in N_x$, there exists one and only one arm $m_{i,x}$ on the slot machine m_i. The expected reward of the arm $m_{i,x}$ is $\varepsilon_{i,x}$.*

In this MAB, agents communicate to share their observations. A such exchange of knowledge allows the agents to use the past experiences of the others in order to approximate the expected the reward of each arm. However, some feedbacks can be deceitful. The reputation system in this MAB helps the agents to agregate theirs observations. In this context, the agents can compute a reputation value for each arm. This value does not correspond exactly to the expected reward. Indeed, if an agent uses EigenTrust as reputation function, the reputation of an arm is the ratio of reward that it had provided on the sum of all reward. However, we assume that for two arms $m_{k,x}$ and $m_{k',x}$, $f_i(m_{k,x}, s_x) > f_i(m_{k',x}, s_x)$ implies that the expected reward of the first is better

Table 1. Analogy between the service sharing system and MAB

	Service sharing system	**MAB**
Aim	Maximize the services quality	Maximize the reward
Actors	Agents (consumers)	Players
	Agents (providers)	Bandits
Interactions	Asking a service	Pulling an arm
Capacity	Expertise	Reward distribution function
Gain	Service quality	Reward
Observations	Trust matrix	Past observations
Communication	Feedback on another agent	Feedback on a arm
Reputation	Expected behaviour	Expected reward
Policy	Gives the next service provider	Gives the next arm to pull
Manipulations	Malicious agents	Adversarial players

than the reward of the second. As both are correlated (the arm with the best reputation is the one with the best expected reward), we consider that reputation of an arm is an approximation of the expected reward. Table 3.2 sums up the analogy between the services sharing system and a MAB. Based on this analogy, we propose to use canonical policies of multi-armed bandit problems in a service sharing system.

4 Agents Strategies

In this section, we define firstly the MAB policies in our model. Secondly, as some malicious agents can try to manipulate this system, we define some threats models. Finally, in order to evaluate the impact of the policies against this manipulations, we define several performance metrics.

4.1 Policies from Multi-Armed Bandit Problem

To resolve the multi-armed bandit problem, many solutions have been studied [21, 22]. We adapt two of them, UCB and ε-greedy policies, and propose a third: the ε-elitist policy. All of them make a compromise between optimizing the reward and exploring the system in order to refine the agent's knowledge.

The main algorithm to solve MAB problems is UCB (Upper Confidence Bound). UCB allows the agent to select another machine than the one which has the best expected reward in order to increase its knowledge about the system. We recall we assume that the reputation of an agent is an approximation of the expected quality of a service that it can provide.

Definition 4. *An agent follows UCB policy if it selects the agent $a_j \in N_x$ which maximizes $f_i(a_j, s_x) + \sqrt{\frac{2\ln(1+n_x)}{1+n_{j,x}}}$ where $n_{j,x}$ is the number of services s_x that has provided a_j to a_i and n_x is the number of services s_x that a_i has received.*

An intuitive policy for an agent is to ask services to the agent which has the best reputation value. Such policy is called *elitism* and the agent which has the best reputation value will be always solicited. Another trivial policy called *uniform policy* consists in selecting a_j uniformly at random in N_x, and to not use the reputation of the agents. Thus, we propose to use the ε-greedy policy [21] that is a mixed policy between elitism and uniform policy.

Definition 5. *An agent $a_i \in N$ follows an ε-greedy policy if it selects the provider $a_j \in N_x$ which have the best reputation value with a probability of $1 - \varepsilon$ and, with a probability ε, it selects a provider uniformly at random in N_x.*

Notice that if $\varepsilon = 0$ this policy is elitism, and if $\varepsilon = 1$ the policy is uniform. We propose also a third policy called the ε-elitism policy. Intuitively, an agent which follows this policy selects the future provider randomly within the $\varepsilon \times |N_x|$ agents which have the best reputation values.

Definition 6. *Let $N'_x \subseteq N_x$ such that $|N'_x| = \lceil \varepsilon \times |N_x| \rceil$ and that $\forall a_j \in N'_x, \nexists a_k \in N_x \setminus N'_x : f_i(a_j, s_x) < f_i(a_k, s_x)$. An agent $a_i \in N$ follows an ε-elitist policy if it selects uniformly at random a_j in N'_x.*

4.2 Threat Model

As we intend to investigate the policies robustness to malicious behaviors, we assume firstly that an agent is honest if the quality of its services are in accordance with its expertise vector and if its feedbacks about another agent are its trust value about this latter. In opposite, we define a malicious agent as an agent which provides willingly a service with a bad quality or gives a false feedback about an agent. We make two assumptions on the malicious agents in our system. Firstly, all malicious agents are in a coalition (denoted $\mathcal{M} \subset N$) as if it exists two coalitions, both coalitions try to manipulate the other as if it is composed of honest agents. Secondly, they aim at maximizing the number of bad services that they provide as if a malicious agent a_i provides only good services, the agents which interact with are satisfied and a_i cannot be considered as malicious. Remark we consider coalitions as reputation systems are robust to single malicious behaviours but still vulnerable to collusion [10]. Moreover, any single malicious agents can use false identities (called Sybil [23]) in order to form a coalition with itself. It exists many manipulations as slandering, promotion, withewashing [10] that aim at modifying the malicious agents' reputation values. Those manipulations can be applied in a single timestep. Moreover, some manipulations as the oscillating manipulation apply over time. In order to consider the worst possible setting, we agregated slandering, promotion, withewashing and oscillating manipulation in a single malicious behaviour. Let a malicious coalition $\mathcal{M}$ which is splitted in two subsets $\mathcal{M}_1$ and $\mathcal{M}_2$. At each timestep, the malicious agents apply the following strategy:

- the agents of $\mathcal{M}_1$ slander the agents of $N \setminus \mathcal{M}$;
- the agents of $\mathcal{M}_2$ promote the agents of $\mathcal{M}_1$;

- the agents of $\mathcal{M}_1$ provide willingly "bad" services;
- the agents of $\mathcal{M}_2$ provide their services with respect of their expertise factor;
- when $a_i \in \mathcal{M}_1$ has a low reputation value, it whitewashes. An agent of $\mathcal{M}_2$ changes its behaviours and joins $\mathcal{M}_1$ and the new identity a_{n+1} joins $\mathcal{M}_2$.

When a coalition of agents manipulate the system, they impact the performance of the system. Thus, we define how to evaluate this impact.

4.3 System Evalutation

In order to evaluate the performance of those policies, we propose some metrics of performance. A common metrics for MAB is the *regret* [21, 22]. Intuitivly, the regret of an agent is the difference between the reward that it could have won if it had interacted with the provider whom had the best reputation and the reward that it has obtained. The aim of our model is to maximize the number of good services provided. Thus, we define the system efficiency as the complementary of the regret.

Definition 7. *Let R_i be the set of services that have received the agent a_i and let R_i^+ be the set of good services that it received. The efficiency of the system is the ratio:* $\sum_{a_i \in N} |R_i^+| \;/\; \sum_{a_i \in N} |R_i|$

In opposite, the malicious agents search to maximize the number of bad services that they provide. However, manipulating the system has a cost for the malicious agents. Indeed, in order to maintain a good reputation, the agents provide sometimes good services that is in opposite to their goal. We define hence a malicious cost measure.

Definition 8. *Let P_i be the set of services that the agent a_i has provided and let P_i^+ be the set of good services that it has provided. The manipulation cost is the ratio:* $\sum_{a_i \in M} |P_i^+| \;/\; \sum_{a_i \in N} |P_i|$

As we consider open multi-agent systems, some policies, such as the elitism, make that a small subset of the agents will provide the services, and thus those agents can be overloaded. Moreover, only this subset of agents will see their reputation value updated. As in [7] we mesure the load balancing in the system.

Definition 9. *Let $N_t \subseteq N$ be the subset of agents that have provided services at the timestep t. The load balancing is the ratio:* $|N_t| \;/\; |N|$

Those three metrics are defined in order to evaluate the robustness of the system against a malicious coalition. The system efficiency defines how much the malicious agent provide bad services. The manipulation cost represents how much the malicious agents must pay in order to manipulate. The load distribution represents how the policy impacts the openness property of the system.

5 Experiences

In this section, we evaluate the policies against a malicious coalition. To the best of our knowledge, there is no other works to compare with as we do not evaluate the reputation systems but the policies that use such systems.

5.1 Protocol

For simplicity, we assume that only one service is provided: sharing a file. At each timestep, each agent asks to another agent a file that it does not have. We also assume that providing a file is completed in a single timestep. We do not limit the number of files that can be provided by an agent in one step. The expertise of the agents is drawing uniformly at random. As in our model, we make no assumption on the reputation system used, we study here our policy on two canonical reputation system: EigenTrust [7] and BetaReputation [6]. We assume that the agents detect immediatly if the file they received is good or not. We investigate the uniform, UCB, ε-greedy and ε-elitist (with $\varepsilon \in [0;1]$) policies. In these experiences, we consider a coalition of malicious agents which applies the thread model given in Section 4.2. We initialize the simulations with 100 agents which interact during 100 timesteps. At each timestep, we consider that it has a probability of 0.01 that an honest agent joins or leaves the system in order to simulate an open system. At $t = 100$, we introduce 10 malicious agents which try to manipulate the system during 1000 timesteps in order to simulate a malicious coalition trying to manipulate a running system. We reiterate those simulations 50 times and compute the average metrics with their 95% confidence intervals. Although, all the results are dependent on a huge number of parameters, we claim these results give us insights about the policies distinctive features. For instance, increasing the number of malicious agents simply decreases the system efficiency and increases the manipulation cost (all other things being equal).

5.2 Results and Analysis

For readability, we present only four policies: uniform, UCB, 0.2-elitist and 0.2-greedy. The uniform policy is used as a baseline. The main result of this empirical study is that the policy used influences the robustness of the reputation system against manipulations. UCB is clearly sensitive to a strategic manipulation but is costly for the malicious agents. In the over side, the robustness of a reputation system which uses a ε-greedy policy depends essentially on the robustness of its reputation function. Morever, even if the malicious agents provides a small set of bad services, manipulating the ε-greedy policy is costless. Finally, using a ε-elitist policy is a compromise between UCB and ε-greedy policy. Figure 2 shows the system efficiency under the policies. As we can see, the UCB policy is clearly sensitive to a malicious coalition, even with a BetaReputation wich is more robust to the manipulation than EigenTrust. In the other side, the 0.2-greedy policy is robust to the manipulations on BetaReputation system but not on EigenTrust. As it is a manipulable reputation function, the malicious agents can easily have

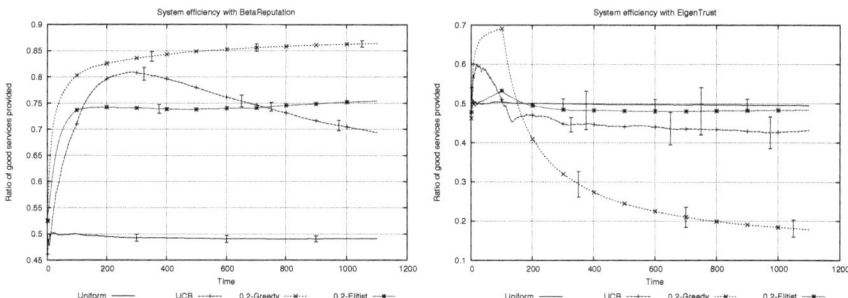

Fig. 2. System efficiency

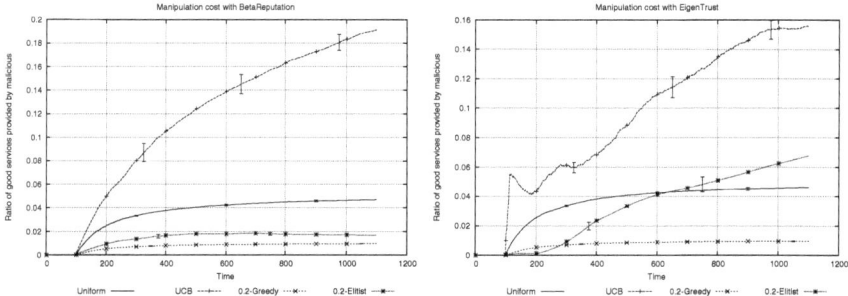

Fig. 3. Manipulation cost

a good reputation value and the greedy policy selects them. Hence, we assume that the robustness of the greedy policy is linked to the reputation function used, which is not the case for UCB. Denote that the 0.2-elitist policy is less effective than the 0.2-greedy with BetaReputation system but less manipulable with EigenTrust. UCB policy is clearly manipulable. However, the Figure 3 shows us that UCB is also costly for the malicious agents. In order to maintain a good reputation values, the malicious agents must provide more good services than bad services. Indeed, the manipulability of UCB comes from the fact that it selects the providers on whom the consumer has the least knowledge. Hence, in order to manipulate the system, the malicious agents need to frequently whitewash which is very costly. On the other side, the 0.2-greedy policy is almost cost-free for the malicious agents. In EigenTrust, the malicious agent can provide a large number of bad services without providing good services in order to increase their reputations values. The 0.2-elitist policy is a compromise between manipulation efficiency and cost: the malicious agents can provide bad services but they must provide good services too. The load balancing presented in Figure 4 shows us the degree of openness of the system. Remark that the greedy policy always selects a small subset of agents. As this policy selects the agents with the best reputation values, the probability for a new agent to be selected is small. Hence, using a greedy policy implies that new agent cannot be selected. Thus, this policy is effective against whitewashing but at the cost of the openness of system.

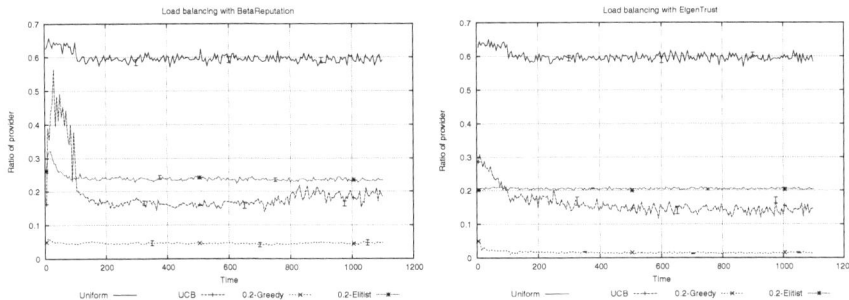

Fig. 4. Load balancing

Moreover, if a malicious agent manages to have a better reputation value than honests agents (for instance promotion and slandering with EigenTrust), this malicious agent is always selected and hence can provide bad services. UCB selects a greater subset of providers. Indeed, this policy allows the agent to explore the agents that they do not know. Hence UCB is more sensitive to whitewashing but also more open than greedy policy. To conclude this empirical study, UCB is manipulable but also very costly for the malicious coalition, and the robustness of a services sharing system which uses a ε-greedy policy depends on the robustness of its reputation function. Moreover, manipulating such policy is almost cost-free. A ε-elitist policy is a compromise between robustness and cost of the manipulation. We show also that the robustness against whitewashing has a cost on the openness property of the system.

6 Conclusion

In this paper, we propose a model for service sharing system which combines reputation systems and selection policies. As the problem of selection policy in services sharing systems and in multi-armed bandits are closely related, we propose to use multi-armed bandits policies in the service sharing system in order to fight against malicious agents. We study empiricaly the impacts of canonicals policies on manipulations. These policies are either sensitive against manipulations but costly for the malicious agents, or dependent on the reputation function robustness but almost cost-free. Finding a selection policy which is in the same time robust against manipulations, costly for the malicious agents and that does not impact the openness of the system is still an open problem. In a future work we intend to modelise a reputation multi-armed bandit where feedbacks could be seen as pulling a specific arm of a bandit. Moreover, we expect to clearly distinguish the trust in the expertise and the trust in the feedbacks. As there is no reputation function robust against all manipulations, we propose to aggregate several reputation functions in order to increase the robustness. A such problem has been considered on the multi-armed bandit problem by Auer [18] where players have a set of policies for choosing the best action.

References

1. Adar, E., Huberman, B.A.: Free riding on Gnutella. First Monday (2000)
2. Dini, F., Spagnolo, G.: Buying reputation on eBay: Do recent changes help? IJEB, 581–598 (2009)
3. Marsh, S.P.: Formalising trust as a computational concept. PhD thesis, University of Stirling (1994)
4. Resnick, P., Kuwabara, K., Zeckhauser, R., Friedman, E.: Reputation systems. ACM Communications, 45–48 (2000)
5. Page, L., Brin, S., Motwani, R., Winograd, T.: The PageRank citation ranking: bringing order to the Web. Technical report, Stanford InfoLab (1999)
6. Jøsang, A., Ismail, R.: The Beta reputation system. In: 15th BledEC, pp. 41–55 (2002)
7. Kamvar, S.D., Schlosser, M.T., Garcia-Molina, H.: The EigenTrust algorithm for reputation management inP2P networks. In: 12th WWW, pp. 640–651 (2003)
8. Jøsang, A., Ismail, R., Boyd, C.: A survey of trust and reputation systems for online service provision. Decision Support Systems, 618–644 (2007)
9. Rahbar, A.G.P., Yang, O.: PowerTrust: A robust and scalable reputation system for trusted peer-to-peer computing. In: IEEE PDS, pp. 460–473 (2007)
10. Hoffman, K., Zage, D., Nita-Rotaru, C.: A survey of attack and defense techniques for reputation systems. CSUR (2009)
11. Altman, A., Tennenholtz, M.: An axiomatic approach to personalized ranking systems. JACM (2010)
12. Cheng, A., Friedman, E.: Manipulability of PageRank under Sybil strategies. In: 1st NETECON (2006)
13. Cheng, A., Friedman, E.: Sybilproof reputation mechanisms. In: 3rd P2PECON, pp. 128–132 (2005)
14. Srivatsa, M., Xiong, L., Liu, L.: TrustGuard: countering vulnerabilities in reputation management for decentralized overlay networks. In: 14th WWW, pp. 422–431 (2005)
15. Pinyol, I., Sabater-Mir, J.: Computational trust and reputation models for open multi-agent systems: a review. Artificial Intelligence Review, 1–25 (2013)
16. Robbins, H.: Some aspects of the sequential design of experiments. Bulletin of the AMS, 527–535 (1952)
17. Liu, K., Zhao, Q.: Distributed learning in multi-armed bandit with multiple players. IEEE SP, 5667–5681 (2010)
18. Auer, P., Cesa-Bianchi, N., Freund, Y., Schapire, R.E.: Gambling in a rigged casino: the adversarial multi-armed bandit problem. In: 36th FOCS (1995)
19. Vermorel, J., Mohri, M.: Multi-armed bandit algorithms and empirical evaluation. In: 16th ECM, pp. 437–448 (2005)
20. Auer, P., Ortner, R.: UCB revisited: Improved regret bounds for the stochastic multi-armed bandit problem. In: Periodica Mathematica Hungarica, pp. 55–65 (2010)
21. Auer, P., Cesa-Bianchi, N., Fischer, P.: Finite-time analysis of the multiarmed bandit problem. In: Machine Learning, pp. 235–256 (2002)
22. Wang, Y., Audibert, J.Y., Munos, R.: Algorithms for infinitely many-armed bandits. In: NIPS, pp. 1729–1736 (2008)
23. Douceur, J.R.: The Sybil attack. In: Druschel, P., Kaashoek, M.F., Rowstron, A. (eds.) IPTPS 2002. LNCS, vol. 2429, pp. 251–260. Springer, Heidelberg (2002)

MASSA: Multi-Agent System to Support Functional Annotation

Daniela Xavier[1,2], Berta Crespo[3], Rubén Fuentes-Fernández[4], and Jorge J. Gómez-Sanz[4]

[1] Dept. of Biochemistry and Molecular Biology I,
Universidad Complutense de Madrid, Avd. Complutense s/n, 28040 Madrid, Spain
[2] GARP (Genomic and RNA Profiling Core),
Department of Molecular and Human Genetics, Baylor College of Medicine,
One Baylor Plaza, 77030 Houston, USA
[3] Dept. of Fish Physiology and Biotechnology,
Instituto de Acuicultura de Torre la Sal,
Consejo Superior de Investigaciones Científicas (CSIC), Torre la Sal,
Ribera de Cabanes s/n, 12595 Castellón, Spain
[4] Dept. of Software Engineering and Artificial Intelligence,
Universidad Complutense de Madrid, C/ Profesor José García Santesmases s/n,
28040 Madrid, Spain

Abstract. Functional annotation aims to predict the biological function of DNA sequences. This complex and time-consuming task has to process huge amounts of data and get high quality results. In order to guarantee the quality of the outcome, the annotation should be carried out by human experts, but the great volume of biological data produced lately demands a high degree of automation. The features of this problem (i.e., knowledge-based, distributed resources, and an evolving environment) make it suitable for an agent approach. This paper presents MASSA, a Multi-Agent System to support functional annotation. MASSA combines the potentialities of the agent approach with a Rule-Based Expert System to reproduce the annotation steps, including the human reasoning, at the inference stage. The expert system integrates knowledge on Biology and tools. A case study on the annotation of sequences of four phylogenetically distinct species illustrates the results and use of MASSA.

Keywords: Functional annotation, Multi-Agent System, Rule-based Expert System, Bioinformatics.

1 Introduction

Predicting the biological function of Deoxyribonucleic Acid (DNA) sequences is one of the many challenges Bioinformatics faces. This task, called *functional annotation*, has to be as accurate and reliable as possible due to its impact in further researches [11]. In order to guarantee the quality of the annotation, experts should manually annotate each sequence. However, the great volume of genomic data generated lately makes this practice only suitable for few sequences or model organisms. The automatic annotation, on the other hand, rapidly processes big data sets at low cost, but produces less accurate results.

The annotation process involves many tasks, such as, comparing sequences, accessing information resources, and inferring the function. Though there is a variety of tools that supports experts in these tasks, they present some limitations. First, some tools (or their outcome) are not quite intuitive for the final users. Second, they are in general standalone programs, so users have to combine their results manually. Third, they encapsulate knowledge in the code of their components, what hinders the expert involvement on creating and validating it. Finally, these tools are not designed in general to evolve, though this should be a core feature given their domain. For instance, the majority of them use biological information stored in multiple and heterogeneous databases, which are distributed and constantly being updated. Their proper maintenance largely depends on being able to integrate easily new or modified information sources.

In order to address these issues, some works have considered the combined use of Expert Systems (ESs) and Multi-Agent Systems (MASs). On one side, ESs [9] are a well-known approach to avoid the expert bottleneck when automating processes. In particular, Rule-Based ESs (RBESs) are suitable to deal with factual and heuristic knowledge, like that used at the inference stage of functional annotation [28]. On the other side, agents have proved to be useful for applications that imply repetitive and time-consuming activities, and also require knowledge management, such as integrating multiple information sources and tools, and modeling complex dynamic systems [12].

Nevertheless, this last group of systems also presents its own open issues. Most of them [6,8] still encapsulate relevant parts of knowledge in code. Besides, the applied knowledge is mainly related to the flow of data between basic tools [6,8], with only some rules dealing with expert heuristics [15]. This puts aside the core of the usual process of experts, which is on biological constraints and relationships. Finally, they seem not to apply well-founded methodological approaches in their development, at least according to information in literature.

This paper presents MASSA (*MAS to Support functional Annotation*), which overcomes some of the previous limitations. This is achieved through a design focused on an expert-oriented management of knowledge and facilitating evolution and maintenance. MASSA combines an agent-oriented approach with RBESs to infer accurate annotations and being also able to take advantage of distributed computational resources, collect data from different sources, and maintain its data sources up to date. The work applies two state-of-the-art methodologies: INGENIAS [18] for the MAS; and CommonKADS [22] for modeling the knowledge employed for the RBES, as described in [28].

MASSA includes two main subsystems. *MASSAPipe* manages a flexible pipeline of traditional Bioinformatics tools and databases in order to collect the basic information for the process. *MASSAInference* integrates the RBES that makes the inference applying knowledge on Biology and Bioinformatics tools.

The rest of the paper discusses these aspects in detail. Section 2 introduces briefly the annotation problem. MASSA is presented in Section 3, and Section 4 describes its functioning and performance for a set of sequences. Section 5 reviews the related work. Finally, Section 6 discusses some conclusions and future work.

2 Biological Background

In most organisms, the hereditary information is stored in macromolecules called Deoxyribonucleic Acid (DNA). *Genes* are segments of DNA that are responsible for the transmission of genetic traits from an organism to its descendants. Genes can code polypeptide molecules called *proteins*.

A protein can be understood as a chain of amino acids (i.e., *primary structure*) that folds into itself, creating two-dimension structures (i.e., *secondary structure*) such as turns, helixes, or sheets. These elements are packed in the space into compact globular units, forming the *tertiary structure*.

The protein's role is directly related to its tertiary structure. Some regions of the protein's primary structure may vary substantially without affecting its biological function. However, some regions are crucial for the protein's function and preserved over evolutionary time, like *domains* and *conserved sites*.

A protein *family* is a set of proteins that share an evolutionary relationship and have a significant similarity in primary structure and/or with similar tertiary structure and function. The members of a protein family are called *homologs* and are usually identical across a 25% or more of their sequences. Two *homologs* are said to be *paralogs* if they are found in the same species, or *orthologs* if they belong to different species.

The *functional annotation* aims to predict the protein's function of a given sequence. This prediction can be done from the tertiary structure, but this involves time-consuming, labor-intensive, and expensive processes, which are only affordable for few sequences. The function can also be obtained from the primary structure, but it is a NP-complete problem [7], and hence frequently unfeasible computationally. An alternative method is taking advantage of evolutionary relationships. Orthologs often preserve their biological role, and thus identifying them allows transferring functional information between genes from different organisms with a high degree of reliability [21]. Since finding orthology is not a trivial task, its prediction can be complemented with other features, such as conserved domains and residues, to enhance the quality of the annotation.

Many tools support the different steps of the annotation process. BLAST [2] (and its many derivatives such as BLASTP, BLASTX, TBLASTX, BLASTN, and RPS-BLAST) is one of the most popular. It is used to look for regions of local similarity between a query sequence and a target dataset. Popular tools are also those to recognize domains (e.g., InterProScan [20]), and to predict orthology (e.g., Orthostrapper [23]).

There is a great amount of genetic information publicly available that can be used in the annotation process. There are databases for genes (e.g., GenBank [4]), protein data (e.g., Entrez Protein [17] and UniProt [13]), domains and families (e.g., Conserved Domains Database (CDD) [14]), and for ontologies (e.g., GO [24]). These databases are updated regularly, and some of them make available for download pre-formatted Search Databases (SDBs) ready to use with BLAST, like Non-Redundant proteins (NR) and CDD, both from the National Center for Biotechnology Information (NCBI) [16].

3 MASSA Architecture

MASSA combines a MAS with a RBES to generate accurate functional annotations and overcome domain constraints. These include: evolving and heterogeneous knowledge to consider; multiple tools to combine without standardized common interfaces; distributed data sources frequently updated and with different structures; heavy computation tasks and queries that frequently make use of shared computational resources. MASSA is organized in subsystems that can handle simultaneously multiple user requests (see Fig. 1).

An annotation request to MASSA comprises a FASTA file and, optionally, a Configuration File (CF). FASTA [16] is a standard text-based format to specify nucleotide or peptide sequences. The CF contains a list of *tasks* and their parameters to be used in the pipeline. Experts usually include this information to adjust the process.

Each request is linked to a *project*, which has assigned its own execution *environment*. The *environment* includes a *container* for the group of agents working in it, and an outcome database for intermediate results, named the Result Database (RDB). The RDB stores the information on annotation candidates, which will be used later in the inference process. The system divides each request in smaller chunks, called *tasks*, in order to parallelize as much as possible its processing. A *task* can involve the execution of one or more tools, scripts, or complementary jobs, depending on its goal. In the case that a *task* executes more than one step, it can be decomposed into *subtasks*.

The structure of MASSA is mainly organized around two subsystems, *MASSAPipe* and *MASSAInference*, and several agents that provide shared services. MASSAPipe aims to execute an annotation pipeline of traditional Bioinformatics tools. MASSAInference infers the best annotation based on the data previously acquired and the set of rules in its Knowledge Base (KB). Although these subsystems work together in MASSA, their modular design makes possible to use them separately. The other agents are related to standard services (e.g., lifecycle management and yellow pages), user interface, and work coordination.

MASSA start-up initializes only three agent instances: an *Interface Agent* (IA) to manage the user interface; a *Launcher Agent* (LA) to launch projects; and an *External Information Updater Agent* (EInfoUA) to update files from external sources. The IA receives user requests and passes them to the LA. Then, the LA creates a *Controller Agent* (CA) for each request. The CA is responsible for managing global aspects of the request *project* and coordinating the other agents in MASSA working for it, including the communications with the IA. The CA decomposes the work in the *project* and delegates it to the relevant agents. First, agents in MASSAPipe gather the required information, and when they finish, the CA uploads the resulting information to the RDB. After that, agents in MASSAInference calculate their annotation, that the IA returns as the answer to the request.

MASSA is mainly implemented in Java, using Jade [3] for the MAS and Drools [25] for the RBES. The system also contains scripts in Perl to manipulate Bioinformatics-specific information, and uses MySQL for database management.

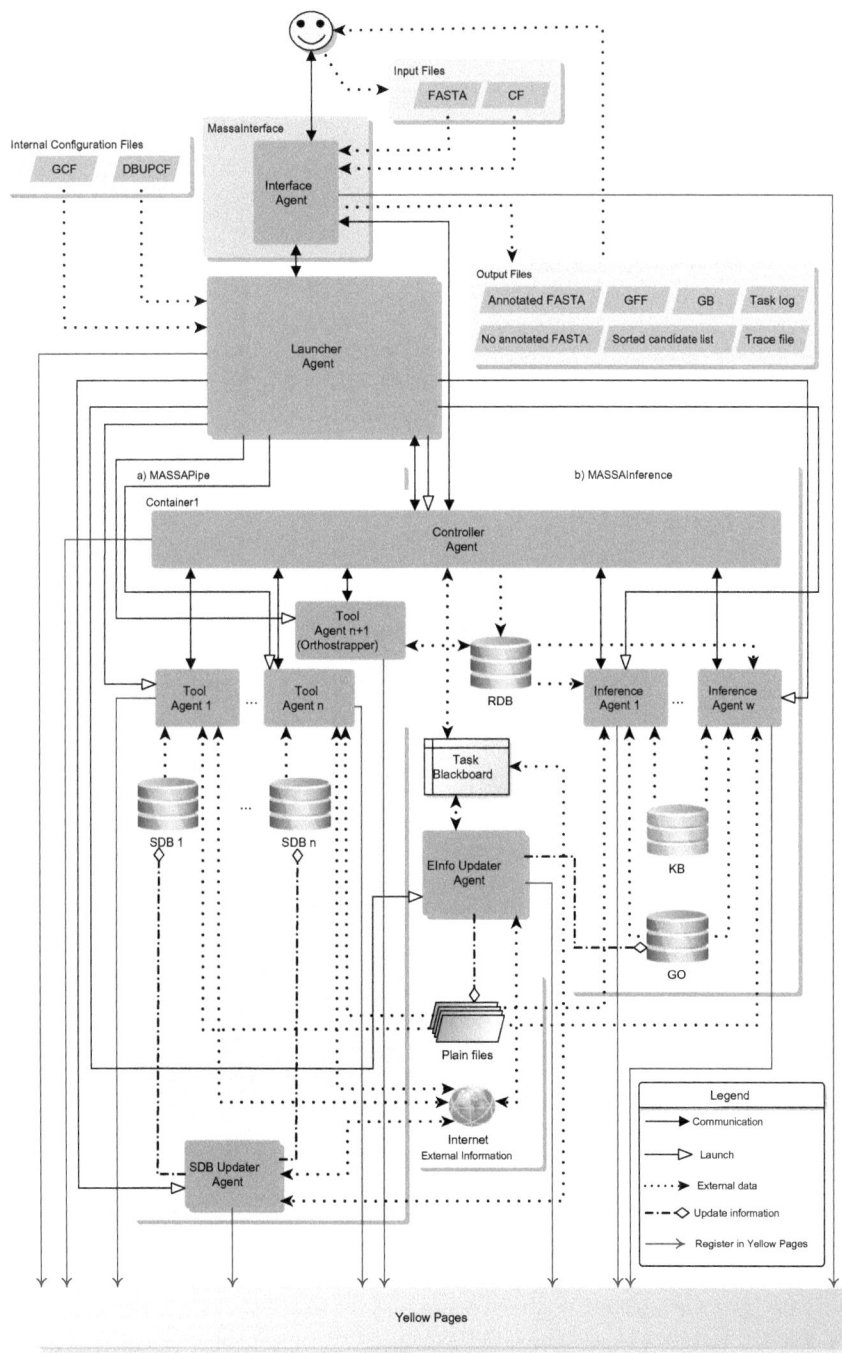

Fig. 1. MASSA architecture

The rest of the section further discusses the two MASSA subsystems: MASSAPipe (see Section 3.1) and MASSAInference (see Section 3.2).

3.1 MASSAPipe

MASSAPipe manages the annotation pipeline. It executes tools and scripts that search in SDBs to get likely candidates for the annotation. It is also responsible for storing the information obtained and updating some of the default SDBs and files from their original sources.

MASSAPipe includes three types of agents:

- The *Tool Agent* (TA) wraps tools and scripts. It also accesses remote databases (e.g., Entrez Protein [17] and CDD [14]) and external files in order to get relevant information that may increase the accuracy of the annotation.
- The *Search Database Updater Agent* (SDBUA) updates the SDBs from its source remote servers. It controls resource usage for these tasks, the availability of the remote sources, and performs error recovery.

The activities of the MASSAPipe subsystem start when the LA creates the CA and its *environment* to meet a request. This includes creating a RDB, where the *task* outcomes will be stored, and launching TAs for the *tasks* in the request, though limited by the system workload and resources.

The CA checks whether all input files specified in the CF are available. Then, it processes the *tasks* to perform. These *tasks* are mainly searches in SDBs through tools like BLAST [2] or InterProScan [20]. As they are independent, the CA processes them in parallel. Each *task* is decomposed into *subtasks* that are stored in a queue and assigned to the available TAs. The TAs gather their information on candidate annotations as files in the GFF format [26], and after completing the assigned *task* they remove themselves from the *container*.

When the TAs complete the search *tasks*, the CA uploads the resulting files into the RDB of the *project*. Then, it sends a message to the TA responsible for executing Orthostrapper [23]. This TA uses some of the RDB information to predict orthology and updates the RDB with the obtained outcome. After that, the IA informs the user that this step is finished. The CA, in turn, changes the status of the job to "Finished", and tells the last TA to finish itself.

3.2 MASSAInference

MASSAInference is the part of the system that assigns automatically functional annotations. Its key agent is the *Inference Agent* (InfA), which manages the RBES. The InfA provides the rule engine with data retrieved from the RDB on candidate annotations for a query sequence. It also accesses local information (files and a database) to get the GO terms used to enrich the inferred annotation.

The KB contains rules that take into account different candidate features. The rules score and assess these features, and sort the candidates. The best situation happens when the query sequence present similarities with data from protein databases (i.e., there are similar homolog candidates), along with additional indicators such as orthology likelihood and domain information. If there is no match to homolog candidates, the system tries to infer the annotation based on domain alignments. When this also fails, the sequence is added to a "Not annotated" list. The resulting sorted list starts with the candidate that has the most likely and informative annotation.

This subsystem starts working when the CA is notified that all the agents in the pipeline have finished. Then, it notifies the LA that it can proceed to the next step, and the LA launches as many InfAs as defined in the CF. The CA divides the work between the InfAs based on the number of query sequences and InfAs available. An InfA queries the RDB one sequence at time, obtaining the features of the candidate, and processing them according to the rules in the KB. Based on these rules, the candidate lists are created. When an InfA completes its *task*, it notifies that to the CA.

As InfAs finish their *tasks*, the CA asks them to self-destroy. When all InfAs have finished, the CA informs the IA that the annotation is done, and removes its *container* (together with itself) from the platform. Then, the IA notifies the user and makes the outputs available, mainly the sorted list of candidate annotations.

MASSA was designed to be able to evolve. Its modular and flexible architecture, together with its well-supported base frameworks, make this goal feasible. Adding a new tool to the pipeline is straightforward. It just requires describing the new task (i.e., a new Java class for it) and adding in the CA the code to ask for its execution. If the task introduces a new feature for the annotation process, the InfA has also to be programmed to deal with it, and new rules have to be defined. The later can be done just by modifying the rules flat file of the KB.

4   Case Study

With the purpose of testing the system, 2128 annotated sequences from four phylogenetically distinct species - *Homo sapiens* (532), *Gallus gallus* (596), *Drosophila melanogaster* (500), and *Xenopus tropicalis* (500) - were submitted to the system. Seven *tasks* were executed: FASTA to GFF, BLASTX against NR, BLASTX against UniProt, InterProScan, RPS-BLAST against CDD, and Orthostrapper. Parameters like the e-value threshold ($<= 1.0E^{-20}$ for BLASTX and $<= 1.0E^{-05}$ for RPS-BLAST) and number of InfA to perform the prediction (6) were also set.

After getting the input, the IA sends a message containing this information to the LA. The LA reads the message, and creates the container (*Container-1*) and its respective RDB (*massa_Container_1*). Based on the message, the LA launches on *Container-1* a CA and seven TAs (one for each task). Then, the LA forwards the message received to the CA and informs this agent that it can start the MASSAPipe workflow.

The CA checks the existence of the input files and splits each *task* into *subtasks*. For instance, the RPS-BLAST *task* is divided into a list of *subtasks*: *FastaTranslate*, *RPS-BLAST*, and *BLAST2GFF*. This *task* is carried out as follows.

At first, the CA informs the TA *Container-1_rpsBlast_1*, in charge of the RPS-BLAST *task*, that it should execute the *FastaTranslate subtask*. After finishing this *subtask*, the TA sends a message to the CA reporting the completed status of the *subtask*, and waits for the next command. The CA, in turn, checks the *subtask* list and assigns the *RPS-BLAST subtask* to the *Container-1_rpsBlast_1* TA. When this job is done, this agent informs the CA, which sends it the last *subtask*, *BLAST2GFF*. While performing it, the agent accesses online information from CDD and the local GO data in order to improve the quality of the information. At the GFF formatting stage, just target sequences with "informative" annotations are included into the GFF, that is, terms like "unnamed protein" or "unknown domain" are ignored. After completing the last *subtask*, the TA sends a message to the CA, which asks it to remove itself from the container. This procedure is done for all defined *tasks* (i.e., FASTA to GFF, BLASTX against NR, BLASTX against UniProt, InterProScan, and RPS-BLAST against CDD) in parallel, except for Orthostrapper.

When all the parallelizable *tasks* are done, the CA uploads the GFF files generated into the *massa_Container_1 database*. Once the data transference is completed, the CA informs the TA responsible for the Orthostrapper *task* (i.e., *Container-1_orthology*) it can start. *Container-1_orthology* accesses the RDB in order to get the information to accomplish its goal, and then uploads the result obtained into the RDB. After that, this agent sends a message to the CA informing its job is done and leaves the container. The CA, in turn, informs the IA and the LA that MASSAPipe has finished, and the IA forwards this message to the user. The LA launches four InfAs, and sends a message to the CA telling it can start MASSAInference.

The CA queries the RBD to get the number of query sequences to be annotated (e.g., 532 for *Homo sapiens*), divides the work based on the InfA number set in the CF (i.e., 6 InfAs) and sends a message to each InfA with the range of sequences they have to annotate. For example, *Container-1_Inference_1* is in charge of the first 90 sequences, *Container-1_Inference_2* annotates the next 90, and so on. An InfA infers one annotation at time, but all InfAs work in parallel.

The annotation inference is performed based on the rules described in the KB. These rules take into consideration the orthology, the domains found in the sequence, the conserved sites, the existence of GO terms, the bit score, the e-value, and the percentage of identity. The best-case scenario uses all these features to infer an annotation.

The results from MASSA were manually compared with the original ones by an expert, and 93.7% of the sequences were predicted correctly using the homology candidate approach. 0.28% of the sequences were annotated only with domain information, and 0.47% of the sequences could not be annotated. The rest of the sequences, 5.55%, was not satisfactorily annotated. This issue can be caused by sequences that are not correctly annotated or have questionable annotations because of the lack of consensus in the biological community. These results are promising according to experts, but additional comparison with human experts and tools is required.

5   Related Work

Nowadays, a range of tools that support the functional annotation process are publicly available. In general, these tools are standalone programs that do not communicate with each other, what encumbers the whole process. In order to overcome this hurdle, systems that integrate some of these tools have been developed using different approaches.

Systems like the Ensembl Analysis Pipeline (EAP) [19] and FIGENIX [10] are RBEs developed to accomplish the functional prediction. Although they are quite successful in this task, they constrain users because of their design and considered requirements. For instance, EAP can only deal with complete genomes, thus it is not suitable for DNA sequences out of this context. FIGENIX is only available through a Web service, presenting all the limitations related to this approach (e.g., applicable tools, parameters, and databases, and small input size), which precludes expert users from taking advantage of all their expertise.

More complex systems that combine MASs and RBEs have also been developed, though this approach is less popular. Examples of them are GeneWeaver [6], BioMas [8], and EDITtoTrEMBL [15]. They are mainly focused on wrapping a variety of tools and databases, but pay less attention to develop ESs that integrate knowledge. Their ESs are more related to managing the tool pipeline than to biological issues. Moreover, some of these systems do not integrate true ESs, but components that apply expert knowledge. For instance, BioMas includes an algorithm for deducing appropriate electronic GO annotations by mapping terms from different ontologies [8]. However, this knowledge is hard-coded in a component and not available in a KB as in true ESs [9].

Another issue is the use of infrastructures with limited support, or even developed *ad-hoc* for a particular system. For instance, EDITtoTrEMBL integrates a RBES based on logic programming with Well-Founded Semantics eXtended for explicit negation (WFSX) [1]. This is a less extended formalism than those present in, for instance, Drools [25] or the Semantic Web Rule Language (SWRL) [5], which have bigger communities supporting them. This support brings important benefits regarding development, maintenance, and extension of tools. Nevertheless, there are not studies evaluating whether experts have more or less difficulties to work with different formalisms, so the choice of a suitable one remains an open issue.

Finally, there are also methodological aspects. It is well-known that systematic approaches from Software and Knowledge Engineering facilitate the development of complex systems, but the literature does not document their application for the aforementioned systems. The lack of engineering methodologies does not only affect the development of systems, but also the repeatability, understanding, and analysis of these processes, as well as their functionalities and outcomes.

6   Conclusions

This work presents MASSA, a MAS with a RBES for functional annotation. It addresses three key problems of current annotation tools. Firstly, it uses the

RBES to mimic expert reasoning at certain points of the process, which allows generating more precise outcomes and reducing expert workload. Secondly, the explicit and declarative representation of knowledge as rules facilitates a greater involvement of experts in their specification and validation. Thirdly, applying the agent paradigm facilitates overtaking the environment hurdles of this problem (i.e., distribution, heterogeneity, and high pace of evolution in tools and data sources), and integrating the knowledge management.

MASSA does not only facilitate the annotation process, but also presents other remarkable features to boost and improve the process. It is able to deal with different databases, maintain the data up to date, take advantage of the available computational resources, and report all the reasoning process applied to come to the annotation. Regarding knowledge, it takes into consideration, among others, orthology, existence of domains, conserved sites, level of relevance of the annotation, and GO terms. All these features aggregate quality to the prediction. MASSA was able to produce accurate annotations for 93.7% of the 2128 sequences tested, what is a very encouraging result.

As far as we can ascertain, this approach has not been widely used to tackle this problem, since most of the MAS annotators developed to date lack of ESs. Also, some of the considered features appear in previous systems, but they do not do it in an integrated way. Moreover, the combination of MASs and RBESs seems to be quite suitable and advantageous for several Bioinformatics problems. Therefore, this work does not only intend to propose a possible solution to the functional annotation problem, but also to encourage the application of similar strategies in this field.

MASSA is ongoing work with several open lines for improvement. The system still has to be tested and assessed more extensively for other sequences and species. Besides, more complex performance tests should be carried out as well. This will be facilitated by making the system, its code, and results publicly available for the community. MASSA also needs to incorporate support for additional resources, such as methods for identifying conserved residues that affect function and for predicting transmembrane regions. In line with this, new rules will be added to the KB. These will allow representing the expert knowledge still missing regarding the annotation process in general, and also integrating properly the new resources. Another improvement could come from specializing the InfAs in different subtypes that work with different KBs representing the perspectives of multiple human experts. This differentiation would also require setting up some negotiation mechanism among agents that allow them arriving to a common (or at least most recommended) annotation. Regarding the system interface, we intend to follow the workflow management system trend, like in [27], to allow the user easily define the pipeline for each project.

Acknowledgments. This work has been done in the context of the projects "Aquagenomics" (CSD2007-00002) funded by the Consolider-Ingenio 2010 program of the Spanish Ministry of Education and Science, and "Social Ambient Assisting Living - Methods (SociAAL)" (TIN2011-28335-C02-01) supported by the Spanish Ministry for Economy and Competitiveness. Also, we acknowledge support from the "Red Científico-Tecnológica en Ciencias de los Servicios" (TIN2011-15497-E) and the "Programa de Creación y Consolidación de Grupos de Investigación" (UCM-BSCH GR35/10-A).

References

1. Alferes, J.J., Pereira, L.M.: Reasoning with Logic Programming. LNCS, vol. 1111. Springer, Heidelberg (1996)
2. Altschul, S.F., Madden, T.L., Schäffer, A.A., Zhang, J., Zhang, Z., Miller, W., Lipman, D.J.: Gapped BLAST and PSI-BLAST: a new generation of protein database search programs. Nucleic Acids Research 25(17), 3389–3402 (1997)
3. Bellifemine, F., Poggi, A., Rimassa, G.: JADE: a FIPA2000 compliant agent development environment. In: Proceedings of the 5th International Conference on Autonomous Agents (AGENTS 2001), pp. 216–217. ACM (2001)
4. Benson, D.A., Cavanaugh, M., Clark, K., Karsch-Mizrachi, I., Lipman, D.J., Ostell, J., Sayers, E.W.: GenBank. Nucleic Acids Research 41(D1), D36–D42 (2013)
5. Bodenreider, O., Stevens, R.: Bio-ontologies: current trends and future directions. Briefings in Bioinformatics 7(3), 256–274 (2006)
6. Bryson, K., Luck, M., Joy, M., Jones, D.T.: Agent interaction for Bioinformatics data management. Applied Artificial Intelligence 15(10), 917–947 (2001)
7. Crescenzi, P., Goldman, D., Papadimitriou, C.H., Piccolboni, A., Yannakakis, M.: On the complexity of protein folding. In: 2nd Annual International Conference on Computational Molecular Biology (RECOMB 1998), pp. 61–62. ACM (1998)
8. Decker, K., Khan, S., Schmidt, C., Situ, G., Makkena, R., Michaud, D.: BioMAS: a multi-agent system for genomic annotation. International Journal of Cooperative Information Systems 11(03n04), 265–292 (2002)
9. Giarratano, J.C., Riley, G.: Expert Systems: Principles and Programming. Computer Science Series. PWS Publishing Company (1998)
10. Gouret, P., Vitiello, V., Balandraud, N., Gilles, A., Pontarotti, P., Danchin, E.G.: FIGENIX: Intelligent automation of genomic annotation: expertise integration in a new software platform. BMC Bioinformatics 6, 198 (2005), http://www.ncbi.nlm.nih.gov/pubmed/16083500
11. Lehninger, A.L., Nelson, D.L., Cox, M.M.: Lehninger Principles of Biochemistry, 5th edn. W. H. Freeman & Company (2008)
12. Luck, M., Merelli, E.: Agents in Bioinformatics. Knowledge Engineering Review 20(2), 117–125 (2005)
13. Magrane, M., UniProt Consortium: UniProt knowledgebase: a hub of integrated protein data. Database 2011, bar009 (2011)
14. Marchler-Bauer, A., Lu, S., Anderson, J.B., Chitsaz, F., Derbyshire, M.K., DeWeese-Scott, C., Fong, J.H., Geer, L.Y., Geer, R.C., Gonzales, N.R., Gwadz, M., Hurwitz, D.I., Jackson, J.D., Ke, Z., Lanczycki, C.J., Lu, F., Marchler, G.H., Mullokandov, M., Omelchenko, M.V., Robertson, C.L., Song, J.S., Thanki, N., Yamashita, R.A., Zhang, D., Zhang, N., Zheng, C., Bryant, S.H.: CDD: conserved domains and protein three-dimensional structure. Nucleic Acids Research 41(D1), D348–D352 (2013)
15. Möller, S., Leser, U., Fleischmann, W., Apweiler, R.: EDITtoTrEMBL: a distributed approach to high-quality automated protein sequence annotation. Bioinformatics 15(3), 219–227 (1999)

16. NCBI: http://www.ncbi.nlm.nih.gov, (accessed December 20, 2013)
17. NCBI Resource Coordinators: Database resources of the National Center for Biotechnology Information. Nucleic Acids Research 41(D1), D8–D20 (2013)
18. Pavón, J., Gómez-Sanz, J.J., Fuentes, R.: The INGENIAS methodology and tools. In: Agent-Oriented Methodologies, pp. 236–276. Idea Group Publishing (2005)
19. Potter, S.C., Clarke, L., Curwen, V., Keenan, S., Mongin, E., Searle, S.M.J., Stabenau, A., Storey, R., Clamp, M.: The Ensembl Analysis Pipeline. Genome Research 14(5), 934–941 (2004)
20. Quevillon, E., Silventoinen, V., Pillai, S., Harte, N., Mulder, N., Apweiler, R., Lopez, R.: InterProScan: protein domains identifier. Nucleic Acids Research 33(2), W116–W120 (2005)
21. Remm, M., Storm, C.E.V., Sonnhammer, E.L.L.: Automatic clustering of orthologs and in-paralogs from pairwise species comparisons. Journal of Molecular Biology 314(5), 1041–1052 (2001)
22. Schreiber, G., Akkermans, H., Anjewierden, A., de Hoog, R., Shadbolt, N., Van de Velde, W., Wielinga, B.: Knowledge Engineering and Management – The CommonKADS Methodology. MIT Press, Cambridge (2000)
23. Storm, C.E.V., Sonnhammer, E.L.L.: Automated ortholog inference from phylogenetic trees and calculation of orthology reliability. Bioinformatics 18(1), 92–99 (2002)
24. The Gene Ontology Consortium: Gene Ontology: tool for the unification of Biology. Nature Genetics 25(1), 25–29 (2000)
25. The JBoss Drools Team: Drools expert user guide (May 2012), http://docs.jboss.org/drools/release/5.4.0.Final/drools-expert-docs/pdf/drools-expert-docs.pdf (accessed December 20, 2013)
26. Welcome Trust Sanger Institute: GFF (General Feature Format) specifications document. (December 2012), http://www.sanger.ac.uk/resources/software/gff/spec.html (accessed December 20, 2013)
27. Wolstencroft, K., Haines, R., Fellows, D., Williams, A., Withers, D., Owen, S., Soiland-Reyes, S., Dunlop, I., Nenadic, A., Fisher, P., Bhagat, J., Belhajjame, K., Bacall, F., Hardisty, A., de la Hidalga, A.N., Balcazar Vargas, M.P., Sufi, S., Goble, C.: The taverna workflow suite: designing and executing workflows of web services on the desktop, web or in the cloud. Nucleic Acids Research 41(W1), W557–W561 (2013)
28. Xavier, D., Morán, F., Fuentes-Fernández, R., Pajares, G.: Modelling knowledge strategy for solving the DNA sequence annotation problem through CommonKADS methodology. Expert Systems with Applications 40(10), 3943–3952 (2013)

A Multi-agent System for Nested Inquiry Dialogues

Chunli Yan, Juan Carlos Nieves, and Helena Lindgren

Department of Computing Science, Umeå University, SE-901 87 Umeå, Sweden

Abstract. Generating and evaluating arguments are two important aspects in argumentation-based dialogue systems. In current research, however, generating and evaluating arguments are normally treated separately. Also, there are rarely implementations of the approaches in real applications. In this paper, we generate inquiry dialogues and evaluate arguments during the dialogue procedure simultaneously. Furthermore, we have implemented this approach in a real medical domain and demonstrated a practical example extracted from this application.

Keywords: Inquiry dialogue, Argumentation framework, Multi-agent system.

1 Introduction

Argumentation has become a core technology in Artificial Intelligence [1,2] and multi-agent systems [3]. The most well-known argumentation framework is the abstract argumentation framework (AAF) presented by Dung in 1995 [4]. There are extensive works on extending AAF, such as value-based argumentation framework [5], bipolar argumentation framework [6] and preference-based argumentation framework [7]. These frameworks mainly focus on the *evaluation* of arguments, calculating the acceptability of arguments.

In softwares that apply the formal augmentation framework to multi-agent systems, it is also important to have specific steps for agents to *generate* dialogues. Black and Hunter [3] do provide a specific strategy for generating dialogues. Their approach has the advantage of providing a specific strategy for agents to follow when choosing which legal move to make where there are more than one, in contrast to most other work [8]. In this paper, we further use queue data structure to reduce the workload compared to [3].

Black and Hunter [3] separate the process of constructing and evaluating arguments. However, Gordon et al. [9] argue that these two should be considered together. Therefore, in this paper we propose a solution, where the evaluation work is conducted within the inquiry dialogues, i.e., we allow the agents to come to partial conclusions within the nested dialogues, which is a method in which the strongest arguments are aggregated to serve the argument evaluation for deciding upon the major topic. We modify the theoretical framework presented by Black and Hunter in [3], and improve the algorithm for implementation.

In medical domain, it is common that different physician has his/her own knowledge and viewpoint. The medical rules coming from different guidelines may conflict with each other as well. It leads to contradictory data, which can affect the judgment of physicians. The approach we present in this paper can catch the contradictory data and do reasoning so as to get optimal result to improve the accuracy of diagnosis. In fact, we have already implemented this approach in a real medical software of diagnosing dementia disease.

The paper is organized as follows. Next section presents how arguments and dialogues are formalized. In Section 3 the developed methods for dialogue generation are described. In Section 4 an example in a real application is described. In Section 5 we compare our approach with papers [3] and [9], and the paper ends with conclusions.

2 Argumentation System

This section presents an argumentation system and a definition of dialogues used in our approach. Our approach is based on both *Defeasible Logic Programming* [10] and *inquiry argumentation systems* [3]. We begin by presenting the syntax of the knowledge base of each of our agents.

2.1 Defeasible Knowledge Base

We adapt the notion of defeasible facts and rules presented in [10]. Therefore, a *literal* denotes either an atom α or its negation $\neg \alpha$. The symbols, such as binary connectives $\wedge$, quantifiers $\exists$, $\forall$, implication $\rightarrow$, negation $\neg$ are the same as in first-order logic.

As it is done in defeasible programming [10], a **rule** is denoted as:

$$\alpha_1 \wedge \cdots \wedge \alpha_n \rightarrow \beta$$

such that α_i ($1 \leq i \leq n$) and β are literals. α_i ($1 \leq i \leq n$) is called **premise** of the rule and β is called **conclusion** of the rule. Given a rule $r = \alpha_1 \wedge \cdots \wedge \alpha_n \rightarrow \beta$, $concl(r) = \beta$.

A **fact** is a rule with a empty set of premises and is denoted by a literal α which is the conclusion of the rule. Rules, in defeasible programming, can be categorized as either *strict rules* or *defeasible rules*. A strict rule specifies that a literal (*i.e.* β) is always a consequence of a finite set of literals (*i.e.* $\alpha_1, \ldots, \alpha_n$), which can never be defeated [10]. A defeasible rule can be defeated by other rules with higher priority.

In order to add a priority level to each rule, the concept of belief is defined as follows:

Definition 1. A **belief**, denoted by B, is a tuple of the form (ϕ, L) where ϕ is a rule and $L \in \mathbb{N}$ which denotes a **preference level** of the belief. Given a belief (ϕ, L), if ϕ is a fact, then (ϕ, L) is called a *state belief*; otherwise, it is called a *domain belief*.

Following the convention in paper [3], we stipulate if there are two beliefs (ϕ_1, L_1) and (ϕ_2, L_2) and $L_1 < L_2$, then (ϕ_1, L_1) is more preferred than (ϕ_2, L_2). If a set of beliefs has the same preference level, we assume neither is preferred over the other.

In order to provide a given agent with a knowledge base, a belief base is defined as follows:

Definition 2. A **belief base** of an agent $x \in \{1, 2\}$, denoted by Σ_x, is a finite set of beliefs.

In the following sections, we use x to present one agent and $\hat{x}$ to present the other one, such that if $x = 1$ then $\hat{x} = 2$, and vice versa.

In order to project a set of rules from a belief base of a given agent x with respect to a particular conclusion, we are going to define the concept of *related belief base* as follows:

Definition 3. The **related Belief Base** about literal α with respect to agent x, denoted by Σ_x^α is defined as follows:

$$\Sigma_x^\alpha = \{(\phi, L) | (\phi, L) \in \Sigma_x \text{ and } (concl(\phi) = \alpha \text{ or } concl(\phi) = \neg\alpha)\}$$

We use the function $relatedBeliefBase_x(\alpha)$ to return Σ_x^α from Σ_x.

Let us illustrate the definition with the following example:

Example 1. Let Σ_1 be the belief base of agent 1 which is of the form $\{(\neg a, 1), (b, 3), (a \to c, 2), (b \to a, 2), (d \to e, 2), (\neg a \land \neg b \to \neg c, 2)\}$. Hence, some of examples of related belief bases are:

$relatedBeliefBase_1(a) = \{(\neg a, 1), (b \to a, 2)\}$;
$relatedBeliefBase_1(b) = \{(b, 3)\}$;
$relatedBeliefBase_1(c) = \{(a \to c, 2), (\neg a \land \neg b \to \neg c, 2)\}$.

We will define three relations between a belief and a fact: *defend*, *attack* and *irrelevant*.

Definition 4. Let B be a belief, such that $B = (\alpha_0, L_0)$, if it is a state belief; or $B = (\alpha_1 \land ... \land \alpha_n \to \alpha_0, L_0)$ if it is a domain belief. Let α be a fact, then:

1. If $\alpha_0 = \alpha$, we say the belief B **defends** the fact α.
2. If $\alpha_0 = \neg\alpha$, we say the belief B **attacks** the fact α.
3. If α_0 equals neither α nor $\neg\alpha$, we say that the belief B is **irrelevant** to the fact α.

Let us illustrate Definition 4 with the following example:

Example 2. Let Σ_1 be the belief base introduced in Example 1. We can observe that: $(\neg a, 1)$ attacks a; $(b, 3)$ defends b; $(a \to c, 2)$ defends c, $(b \to a, 2)$ defends a, $(d \to e, 2)$ defends e, $(\neg a \land \neg b \to \neg c, 2)$ attacks c. Except these relations, the others relations are irrelevant relations. For instance, $(\neg a, 1)$ is irrelevant to e.

2.2 Dialogues Representation

Inquiry dialogues, among other types of dialogues, were defined by Walton and Krabbe [11], as having the purpose to collaboratively build new knowledge. In our approach, two agents take part in the proof process (an inquiry dialogue) of a topic in which these two agents do not know if the topic is true or false. Each agent has its knowledge about the given topic. However, they are not able to prove the truth of the topic by themselves; hence, they need to collaborate in order to come up with a conclusion. Their goal is to find and to verify the evidence with respect to a given topic. The goal of an inquiry dialogue is to prove or disapprove the hypothesis in a proof process of a collaborative reasoning.

In order to formalize our dialogue system, we follow the dialogue style introduces by Black and Hunter [3]. Two participating agents use *moves* to communicate with each other in our argumentation system. Three types of moves are allowed: *open*, *assert* and *close*. An *open* move means that an agent opens a new dialogue. An *assert* move means that an agent believes that a given belief is true. A *close* move means that an agent wants to close the current dialogue; however, if another agent does not agree, this dialogue will not be closed.

We use two kinds of inquiry dialogues in our framework: *warrant inquiry* (wi) dialogue and *argument inquiry* (ai) dialogue. A move m is a tuple of the form:

$$m = \langle agent,\ move\ type,\ dialogue\ type,\ topic \rangle$$

in which *agent* denotes which agent makes this move, *move type* denote the kind of move: open, assert, close, and *dialogue type* can be either wi or ai. If the move is an open/close wi move, *topic* is a fact; if it is an open/close ai move, *topic* is a domain belief; otherwise, *topic* is a state belief. Since we have two types of inquiry dialogues and three types of moves, there are six types of move formats which are presented in Table 1.

Table 1. Move format

Move	dialogue	Format
Open	wi	$\langle x, open, wi, \alpha \rangle$
Open	ai	$\langle x, open, ai, (\alpha_1 \wedge ... \wedge \alpha_n \rightarrow \beta, L) \rangle$
Assert	wi	$\langle x, assert, wi, (\alpha, L) \rangle$
Assert	ai	$\langle x, assert, ai, (\alpha, L) \rangle$
Close	wi	$\langle x, close, wi, \alpha \rangle$
Close	ai	$\langle x, close, ai, (\alpha_1 \wedge ... \wedge \alpha_n \rightarrow \beta, L) \rangle$

- $\langle x, open/close, wi, \alpha \rangle$ means that agent x opens/closes a wi dialogue and the topic of the dialogue is α.
- $\langle x, open/close, ai, (\alpha_1 \wedge ... \wedge \alpha_n \rightarrow \beta, L) \rangle$ means that agent x opens/closes an ai dialogue and the topic of the dialogue is $(\alpha_1 \wedge ... \wedge \alpha_n \rightarrow \beta, L)$.
- $\langle x, assert, wi, (\alpha, L) \rangle$ means that this move is within a wi dialogue and (α, L) defends / attacks the topic of this dialogue and agent x asserts that (α, L) is true.

– $\langle x, assert, ai, (\alpha, L) \rangle$ means this move is within an ai dialogue and agent x asserts that (α, L) is true and α is one of the ai topic's premises. Let us observe that (α, L) is not from the agent's belief base. It is from the result store (which will be described in next section) that has already been proved to be true by the two agents.

In order to formalize our dialogue system, we follow the definitions about *dialogue, sub-dialogue* and *well-formed dialogue*, which were introduced by Black and Hunter [3]. Therefore, we only give a brief descriptions of these. For detailed descriptions of these concepts, we refer the interested reader to [3].

Definition 5. A **dialogue** D_r^t (r,t $\in \mathbb{N}$ and r$\leq$ t) is a sequence of moves $[m_r, \ldots, m_t]$ with two agents participating in that: (1) the first move of the dialogue is an open move; (2) each agent takes its turn to make moves. A **sub-dialogue** is a sub-sequence of another dialogue. A **well-formed dialogue** is a dialogue where (1) the last two moves must be close moves made by two agents successively which means both agents agree to close the dialogue; (2) this dialogue only terminates once; (3) all its sub-dialogues are also well-formed and terminate before their parent dialogue.

3 Modeling Dialogues

In this section, we go through the details of generating dialogues and evaluating arguments. We first define some notations (data structures: PBQ, QS, CS and RS and outcomes of dialogues: $Outcome_{ai}$ and $Outcome_{wi}$) needed to generate the dialogues, then give the specific protocols for generating the two different dialogues: wi and ai. The purpose of wi dialogue is to generate several arguments defend or attack its topic and compare these arguments. The purpose of ai dialogue is to detect if the topic rule is fulfilled, i.e., if all its premises can be proved to be true, and generate an argument if so.

In a wi dialogue, we use a *Possible Beliefs Queue (PBQ)* to store the belief's *relatedBeliefBase* according to a topic, so that it can pick up the first belief from this queue when it needs to make a move.

Definition 6. A **Possible Beliefs Queue (PBQ)** is a queue of beliefs that the agent can legally use for selecting the next move for the current wi dialogue. Let D_r^t be the current dialogue and $\mathcal{I}$ be the set of participants. For all $x \in \mathcal{I}$,

$$PBQ_x^t(\alpha) = \begin{cases} relatedBeliefBase_x(\alpha), & \text{iff } m_t = \{x, open, wi, \alpha\} \text{ or} \\ & m_{t-1} = \{\hat{x}, open, wi, \alpha\} \\ relatedBeliefBase_x(\alpha) - (\phi, L), & \text{iff } m_t = \{x, open, ai, (\phi, L)\} \\ relatedBeliefBase_x(\alpha) - (\alpha, L), & \text{iff } m_t = \{x, assert, wi, \alpha\} \\ PBQ_x^{t-1}(\alpha), & otherwise \end{cases}$$

When agent x opens a wi dialogue with topic α, it updates its PBQ according to $relatedBeliefBase_x(\alpha)$ and next time, agent $\hat{x}$ updates its PBQ. Within the wi dialogue, the agent retrieves and deletes the first belief in its PBQ and use this for its next move. Only when the agent's PBQ is empty, i.e., it has nothing more to say about the current wi topic, it makes a close wi move.

When an agent opens an argument inquiry dialogue with the topic (Φ, L), a query store associated with this topic is created which is shared between two agents. Within an ai dialogue, if an agent needs to make a move, it can consult query store and get the first fact in it and make an open wi move.

Definition 7. A **query store** QS_Φ^t is a finite queue of facts such that

$$QS_\Phi^t = \begin{cases} \{\alpha_1, ..., \alpha_n\}, & \text{iff } m_t = \langle x, open, ai, (\alpha_1 \wedge ... \wedge \alpha_n \rightarrow \beta, L) \rangle \\ QS_\Phi^{t-1} - \alpha, & \text{iff } (m_t = \langle x, open, wi, \alpha \rangle \text{ or } m_t = \langle x, assert, ai, (\alpha, L) \rangle) \\ & \text{and } \alpha \in QS_\Phi^{t-1} \\ \emptyset, & \text{iff } \alpha_i \in QS_\Phi^{t-1} \text{ and } m_t = \langle x, close, wi, \alpha \rangle \text{ and} \\ & m_{t-1} = \langle \hat{x}, close, wi, \alpha \rangle \text{ and } Result(\alpha) \neq T \\ QS_\Phi^{t-1}, & \text{otherwise} \end{cases}$$

When an agent makes an open ai move, the premises of its topic rule are stored in a query store. Within this ai dialogue, if the move $\langle x, open, wi, \alpha \rangle$ or $\langle x, assert, ai, (\alpha, L) \rangle$ is made, query store removes α. Another case is, within the ai dialogue, if a wi dialogue terminates (whose topic is a premise of this ai dialogue topic) and this premise can not be proven true ($Result(\alpha) \neq T$ is given in definition 11), then a conclusion that the ai's topic is not fulfilled can be made without any further steps. The query store is thus emptied.

PBQ and QS are two core data structures we use for storing beliefs and selecting next moves. They are two *queues* so that they follow the fundamental principle of queues, such as *first in first out (FIFO)*. We also can use some common operations to these two queues. Each agent has its own PBQ which both facts and rules are stored in it. PBQ is used for agent to select the next exact move in wi dialogue. If the first belief in PBQ is a rule, the agent makes an *open ai* move; else if the belief is a fact, it makes an *assert wi* move; else the queue is empty and it makes a *close wi* move. Both agents share the same QS which only stores facts. QS is used for agents to select move in ai dialogue. If QS is empty, the agent makes a *close ai* move; else it makes an *open wi* move.

Whenever an agent takes part in a dialogue, its commitment store will be update. In order to identify the state of the commitment store of each agent which participate in a given dialogue D_r^t, CS_x^t denotes the commitment store of the agent x and t denotes a point in the dialogue D_r^t.

The update of commitment store (CS), outcome of ai dialogue ($Outcome_{ai}$) and outcome of wi dialogue ($Outcome_{wi}$) are recursive. For updating CS, we need to get $Outcome_{ai}$. For getting $Outcome_{ai}$, we need to calculate $Outcome_{wi}$. For calculating $Outcome_{wi}$, we need to know CS.

The update of the commitment stores of each agent is done as follows ($Outcome_{ai}$ will be defined in definition 9).

Definition 8. Let D_r^t be the current dialogue and $\mathcal{I}$ be the set of participants. For all $x \in \mathcal{I}$,

$$CS_x^t = \begin{cases} \emptyset, & \text{iff } t = 0, \\ CS_x^{t-1} \cup \{(\alpha, L)\}, & \text{iff } m_t = \langle x, assert, wi, (\alpha, L)\rangle, or \\ & Outcome_{ai}(D_r^t) = (\alpha, L) \\ CS_x^{t-1}, & \text{otherwise.} \end{cases}$$

According to Definition 8, the commitment store of each agent is updated whenever it performs an assert wi move or when the ai dialogue closes. An important consequence of this update is that the information which is added to the commitment store is public to the other agents which are taking part in the given dialogue.

When an ai dialogue terminates, its outcome is calculated. If all the premises of its topic are considered to be true ($Outcome_{wi} = \langle T, l\rangle$, which is given in definition 10), the outcome is a belief constructed with the rule's conclusion and a calculated preference level; otherwise, the outcome is empty.

Definition 9. Let D_r^t be a well-formed argument inquiry dialogue and $(\alpha_1 \wedge ... \wedge \alpha_n \to C, L))$ be its topic. **Outcome of argument inquiry dialogue** is a function that:

$$Outcome_{ai}(D_r^t) = \begin{cases} \{(C, L')\}, & \text{iff } \forall \alpha_i (i \in \{1, ..., n\} \text{ and } Outcome_{wi}(D_{r_i}^{t_i}) = (T, l_i) \text{ and } \\ & Topic(D_{r_i}^{t_i}) = \alpha_i) \text{ and } L' = max(l_1, ..., l_n, L) \\ \emptyset, & Otherwise \end{cases}$$

Within a wi dialogue, several arguments defending or attacking the topic α may be generated. When this wi dialogue terminates, its outcome is calculated according to an algorithm which will be given in Table 2. The outcome is a tuple $\langle r, l\rangle$ where $r \in \{T, F, U\}$. If the defending arguments win, $r = T$ meaning α is $True$; Else if the attacking arguments win, $r = F$ meaning α is $False$. In both cases, l is a natural number which can be calculated from the algorithm. However if the two sides are well matched, $r = U$ which means the result is undetermined and l is empty.

Definition 10. Let D_r^t be a well-formed argument inquiry dialogue and α be its topic. **Outcome of warrant inquiry dialogue** is a function such that: $D_{wi} \mapsto \{T, F, U\} \times (\mathbb{N} \cup \emptyset)$.

Before giving the algorithm, let us show several functions used in the algorithm.

The first function F_d is to get all the beliefs that defend a topic α from a set of domain belief bases Λ.

The second function F_a is to get all the beliefs that attack a topic α from Λ.

The third function LS is to get the smallest preference level from a nonempty set Λ.

The forth one F_l is to get all the beliefs with a particular preference level from Λ.

The last one $Amou$ is to get the number of the beliefs in Λ.

The main idea about the algorithm is as follows. First, classify beliefs from the union of two commitment stores into two sets: Λ_d and Λ_a - according to if the belief defends or attacks a given topic. Second, get the smallest preference levels (the highest priority) from each set and compare these two numbers. Third, the set with smaller number wins. However if they have the same number, remove the beliefs with the smallest preference level from each set and get two new sets. We compare the new sets until one set wins or both become empty.

Now we can give the algorithm to get $Outcome_{wi}$ in Table 2.

Table 2. Algorithm of getting $Outcome_{wi}(D_r^t)$

Input: a warrant inquiry dialogue D_r^t with α as its topic; Output: $\langle r, l \rangle$.
1 $\Lambda_d = F_d(CS_x^t \cup CS_{\hat{x}}^t, \alpha)$ and $\Lambda_a = F_a(CS_x^t \cup CS_{\hat{x}}^t, \alpha)$.
2 If $\Lambda_d = \emptyset$ and $\Lambda_a = \emptyset$, then $r = U$ and $l = \emptyset$.
3 Else if $\Lambda_d \neq \emptyset$ and $\Lambda_a = \emptyset$, then $r = T$ and $l = LS(\Lambda_d)$.
4 Else if $\Lambda_d = \emptyset$ and $\Lambda_a \neq \emptyset$, then $r = F$ and $l = LS(\Lambda_a)$.
5 Else

– If $LS(\Lambda_d) < LS(\Lambda_a)$, then $r = T$ and $l = LS(\Lambda_d)$.
– Else if $LS(\Lambda_d) > LS(\Lambda_a)$, then $r = F$ and $l = LS(\Lambda_a)$.
– Else
  • If $Amou((\Lambda_d)) > Amou((\Lambda_a))$, then $r = T$ and $l = LS(\Lambda_d)$.
  • Else if $Amou((\Lambda_d)) < Amou((\Lambda_a))$, then $r = F$ and $l = LS(\Lambda_a)$.
  • Else $\Lambda_d = \Lambda_d - F_l(LS(\Lambda_d))$ and $\Lambda_a = \Lambda_a - F_l(LS(\Lambda_a))$ and loop from step 2 again.

It could be the case that different rules have the same premise. If the premise has already been proved before (a wi dialogue with this premise as topic has already terminated), the system should not prove it twice. Otherwise, it is a repetitive work. We use *result store* to save the intermediate result.

Definition 11. A result store RS is a set of tuples $\langle \alpha, Outcome_{wi}(D_r^t) \rangle$ where α is a defeasible fact and the topic of D_r^t is α. If $Outcome_{wi}(D_r^t) = \langle r, l \rangle$, r is returned by a function $Result(\alpha)$ such that $Result(\alpha) = r$; while l is natural number and returned by a function $PL(\alpha)$ such that $PL(\alpha) = l$.

Now we give the protocols for generating warrant inquiry dialogue and argument inquiry dialogue in table 3 and 4.

4 Example

We implemented our approach in a medical application diagnosing dementia disease [12]. Here we use a study case as an example to illustrate how we generate nested dialogues and make decision about a topic.

Table 3. Step of Warrant Inquire Dialogue Protocol

---

1. Agent x starts a warrant inquire dialogue D_r^t with the topic α: $m_r = \langle x, open, wi, \alpha \rangle$.
2. Both agents x and $\hat{x}$ update their possible belief queue according to Definition 6.
3. Agent $\hat{x}$ performs the moves m_i ($i \in \{r+1, r+3, \ldots, t_1\}$) and x performs the moves m_j ($j \in \{r+2, r+4, \ldots, t_2\}$), such that $t = max(t_1, t_2)$ and the difference between t_1 and t_2 is 1. Both m_i and m_j are of the following form:

   - $\langle \hat{x}, assert, wi, (\alpha, L) \rangle$ such that $(\alpha, L) \in PBQ_{\hat{x}}^t(\alpha)$. The commitment store of the agent $\hat{x}$ is updated according to Definition 8.
   - $\langle \hat{x}, open, ai, (\alpha_1 \wedge \cdots \wedge \alpha_1 \rightarrow \alpha, L) \rangle$ such that $(\alpha_1 \wedge \cdots \wedge \alpha_1 \rightarrow \alpha, L) \in PBQ_{\hat{x}}^t(\alpha)$.
   - $\langle \hat{x}, close, wi, \alpha \rangle$ if the agent is unable to perform one of the previous steps.

4. When the dialogue closes, the result store is updated according to Definition 11.

Table 4. Step of Argument Inquire Dialogue Protocol

---

1. Agent x starts a warrant inquire dialogue D_r^t with the topic α: $\langle x, open, ai, (\alpha_1 \wedge \cdots \wedge \alpha_1 \rightarrow \alpha, L) \rangle$.
2. The query store is updated according to Definition 7.
3. Agent $\hat{x}$ performs the moves m_i ($i \in \{r+1, r+3, \ldots, t_1\}$) and x performs the moves m_j ($j \in \{r+2, r+4, \ldots, t_2\}$), such that $t = max(t_1, t_2)$ and the difference between t_1 and t_2 is 1. Both m_i and m_j are of the following form:

   - $\langle \hat{x}, assert, ai, (\alpha, L) \rangle$ such that $(\alpha, L) \in RS$.
   - $\langle \hat{x}, open, wi, (\alpha, L) \rangle$ such that $(\alpha, L) \in QS_\Phi^t$. The query store is updated according to Definition Definition 7.
   - $\langle \hat{x}, close, ai, \alpha \rangle$ if the agent $\hat{x}$ is unable to perform the previous step.

4. When the ai dialogue terminates, the outcome of the dialogue is calculated according to Definition 9; and the commitment store is updated according to Definition 8.

In this example, there are two agents: physician agent (PA) and domain agent (DA). PA diagnoses a patient and suspects that she has got a mild cognitive impairment. However PA has not enough experience to make a decision. Therefore, PA collaborates with DA in a diagnostic dialogue with the purpose to validate the hypothesis.

All the moves generated by two agents during the dialogue are shown with natural language in Fig.1. In the figure, each line starts with a number, followed by the agent name and the context of the move which means at which step, which agent (PA/DA) presents this move context. The whole figure is a wi dialogue with the topic *Mild Cognitive Impairment (MCI) is present* made by PA (can be seen from step 1 in Fig.1). Under this dialogue, there are several nested ai dialogues whose information are collapsed and can be shown by clicking the corresponding triangles (e.g. 2, 126...) in the application.

PA initiates a wi dialogue (step 1). PA and DA update their PBQs according to definition 6. DA has at least five rules in its PBQ now since we can see five ai

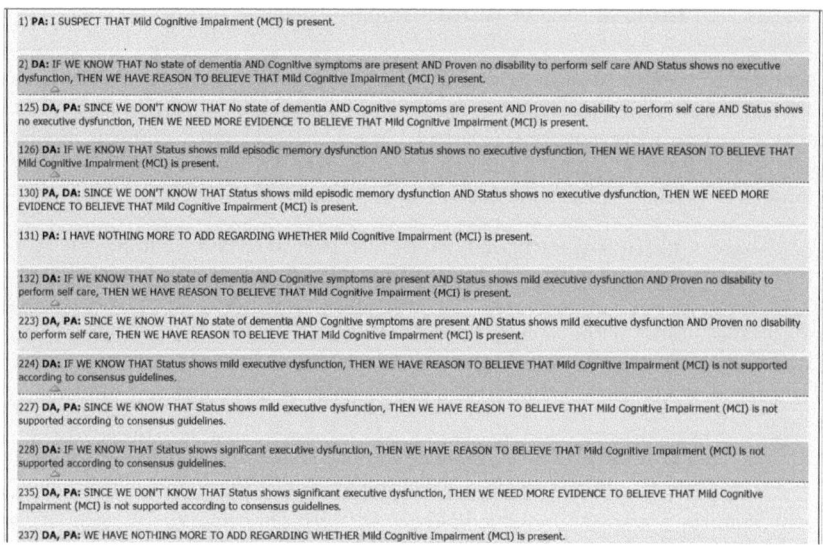

Fig. 1. Moves generated by the two agents

dialogues (from steps 2, 126, 132, 224 and 228) in the picture. DA picks up the first one in its PBQ and opens an ai dialogue (definition 6) in step 2 and stores the premises to QS (definition 7). At next step (step 3, which is not shown in the figure), DA opens a nested wi dialogue with the first premise in QS as its topic (definition 7). When the nested wi dialogue closes, its result is stored in RS (definition 11). When the nested ai dialogue closes, its outcome is stored in CS (definition 8). In this example, the outcome of one ai dialogue (from step 132 to 223) defends the topic *Mild Cognitive Impairment (MCI) is present* and the other (from step 224 to 227) attacks it. Then at the last step, the agents compares these two following the comparison algorithm presented after the definition 11. If the preference level of the rule used in the former ai dialogue is smaller/bigger than the second one, the result should be *Mild Cognitive Impairment (MCI) is present* is *True/False*. In this example, the two preference levels are equal and there are no more arguments, which defend/attack the topic. Therefore, the result about the topic is *Undetermined*.

5 Related Work

There are extensive research done on formal argumentation with focus on the evaluation of arguments, such as Dung's abstract argumentation framework [4] and its successors [5,6,7]. There are surprisingly few contributions, which focus on both constructing and evaluating arguments according to a set of potentially defeasible rules and facts. We have already mentioned the inquiry dialogue systems presented by Black and Hunter's [3], which is similar in some aspects to the approach presented in this paper. Both adapt Defeasible Logic Programming for representing the beliefs; define the same move types; and generate warrant inquiry and argument inquiry dialogues. However, the two approaches have significant differences, mainly in the different protocols used for generating the sequence of moves and the evaluation mechanism.

Black and Hunter divide the dialogue systems into two processes: the construction of arguments and the evaluation of arguments. They first generates a set of arguments during the inquiry dialogue and then constructs a dialectical tree with these arguments to evaluate the acceptability of the root node. When implementing the system, each process needs to use at least one loop, which is unnecessarily time-consuming. By contrast, we construct and evaluate arguments simultaneously. In our approach, the evaluation is accomplished within the dialogue procedure.

In order to restrict the discussion scope, we allow a wi dialogue to be nested in an ai dialogue while it is not allowed in [3]. We do like this because we want to avoid the following situation: within an ai dialogue with the topic ($\alpha_1 \wedge ... \wedge \alpha_n \to \alpha$), agent x discusses one premise and agent $\hat{x}$ another, then the agents will be confused by the dialogue. For each premise α_i, a wi dialogue may be opened and two agents are only limited to talk about α_i until the dialogue ends.

Both approaches can select a single next move within a set of possible legal next moves which makes it stronger than other dialogue approaches presented in research literature. In [3] each move content is assigned arbitrarily a unique number and these numbers are compared according to a function to determine the next move. We use queue, since queue has the inherent feature of FIFO. Specifically, we save possible next Open wi and Assert ai moves in QS and Open ai and Assert wi moves in PBQ. Therefore, we resolved the problem without additional workload.

Our evaluation mechanism is somewhat similar to Carneades [9]. The Carneades model can be mapped to our approach. A statement node in Carneades is the same as a literal (premise and conclusion) in our model and an argument node can be mapped as a rule in ours. Supporting and contradictory arguments can be mapped as two conflict rules so that their conclusions are α and $\neg \alpha$ respectively. The result of a wi dialogue is like the acceptability of a statement and the result of an ai dialogue is like the defensibility of an argument. The decision about the outcome of a wi/ai dialogue is recursive and the process is comparable to what Carneades does in the acceptability of statement and the defensibility of an argument.

However there are two significant differences between Carneades and our work. 1) Carneades does not define dialogue protocol, roles and speech acts; while these are the main building blocks in our paper. 2) The Carneades model focuses on persuasion dialogue while ours is on inquiry dialogue.

6 Conclusions

In this paper we present our framework for generating inquiry dialogues and comparing arguments. We supply details that allow agents to select a precise step at each particular time, not only give them several legal moves. Following our approach, a dialogue can be generated and a result will be reached. In this framework, we generate two kinds of inquiry dialogues: warrant inquiry dialogue and argument inquiry dialogue. The goal of a warrant inquiry dialogue is to determine if its topic is true, false or undetermined. The goal of an argument inquiry dialogue is to generate a valid argument. Two kinds of dialogues are nested within each other in order to reach a valid decision. We have implemented our approach in a real medical application and received positive feedback.

Finally, the human agent needs to be able to participate both in the dialogue, aggregating arguments and evaluating the arguments. Therefore, in future work, the implemented multi-agent system will be extended in the relevant domain. Moreover, we will improve the visualization of the dialogue procedure with a graph similar to [9] so that it can become more intuitive.

Due to the page limit here, we would rather provide the formal properties (soundness and completeness) in a longer version of this paper.

References

1. Bench-Capon, T.J.M., Dunne, P.E.: Argumentation in artificial intelligence. Artificial Intelligence 171(10-15), 619–641 (2007)
2. Nieves, J.C., Osorio, M., Cortés, U.: An overview of argumentation semantics. Computación y Sistemas 12(1), 65–88 (2008)
3. Black, E., Hunter, A.: An inquiry dialogue system. Autonomous Agents and Multi-Agent Systems 19(2), 173–209 (2009)
4. Dung, P.M.: On the acceptability of arguments and its fundamental role in nonmonotonic reasoning, logic programming and n-person games. Artificial Intelligence 77(2), 321–357 (1995)
5. Bench-Capon, T.J.M.: Persuasion in practical argument using value-based argumentation frameworks. Journal of Logic and Computation 13(3), 429–448 (2003)
6. Amgoud, L., Cayrol, C., Lagasquie-Schiex, M.C., Livet, P.: On bipolarity in argumentation frameworks. International Journal of Intelligent Systems 23(10), 1062–1093 (2008)
7. Amgoud, L., Cayrol, C.: A reasoning model based on the production of acceptable arguments. Annals of Mathematics and Artificial Intelligence 34(1), 197–215 (2002)
8. Parsons, S., Wooldridge, M., Amgoud, L.: On the outcomes of formal interagent dialogues. In: Second International Conference on Autonomous Agents and Multi-Agent Systems (AAMAS 2003), Melbourne, Australia, pp. 616–623 (2003)
9. Gordon, T.F., Prakken, H., Walton, D.: The carneades model of argument and burden of proof. Artificial Intelligence 171(10), 875–896 (2007)
10. García, A.J., Simari, G.R.: Defeasible logic programming: An argumentative approach. Theory and Practice of Logic Programming 4(1-2), 95–138 (2004)
11. Walton, D.: The New Dialectic: Conversational Contexts of Argument. University of Toronto Press, Toronto (1998)
12. Yan, C., Lindgren, H.: Hypothesis-driven agent dialogues for dementia assessment. In: International Workshop on Agents Applied in Health Care (AAHC 2013), Murcia, Spain (2013)

The C²BDI Agent Architecture for Teamwork Coordination Using Spoken Dialogues between Virtual Agents and Users

Mukesh Barange, Alexandre Kabil, and Pierre Chevaillier

ENIB–UEB, Lab-STICC, France

Keywords: Human interaction with autonomous agents, Cooperation, Dialogue Management, Decision-Making, Resource Sharing.

1 Introduction

In Collaborative Virtual Environments (VEs) for Training, users have to learn how to perform a collaborative task and also how to coordinate with teammates' activities. Efficient coordination requires teammates to exchange information about their beliefs, goals and plans. The collaborative-conversational BDI agent (C²BDI) endows virtual agents with first, deliberative capabilities about the interdependency of their activities, and second, with task-oriented conversational capabilities that support multiparty spoken dialogues helping them to coordinate their activities with teammates [2]. This proposed solution has been used in two virtual reality applications: a real training scenario [1] and an application dedicated to scientific experiments [2]. The main motivations of this last was to control the characteristics of the collective activity and to be more extensible.

2 Main Purpose

The C²BDI architecture treats both deliberative and conversational behaviours uniformly as guided by the goal-directed shared activity (Fig. 1). It extends the Information State (IS) by adding *task context* to it. IS represents the context model of the agent which not only contains information about the current context of the dialogue, but also that of the collaborative task. The originality of the model lies first on the role of dialogue, that modifies together the believes, the desire and the plan of the agent, and second on the collaborative characteristics of the agent's activity. To achieve coordination among teammates, the C²BDI uses *collaborative conversational protocols* (CCPs), and *resource allocation mechanism* (RAM) which have been defined in [2].

This paper mainly focuses on first, how agents update their beliefs from the perception, plan deliberation, or from dialogues, and second, how the spoken dialogues are processed and generated by them to support team coordination to achieve shared goal. A key issue was that tasks could be done using different plans of actions, and for that agents had to achieve users commitment on the way to do it, where users were not instructed to follow any predefined plans.

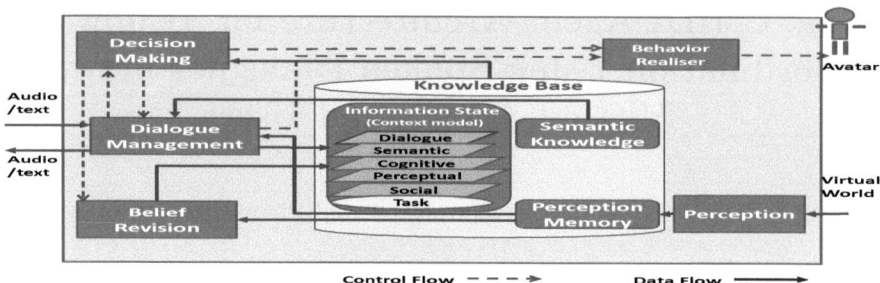

Fig. 1. Components of C²BDI Agent architecture and data flow

3 Demonstration

Technical Architecture: The technical architecture is mainly composed of dialogue manager and Unity3D interface (Fig. 2). Each C²BDI agent is associated with a virtual human and controls its behaviors. User interacts with VE through her avatar. C²BDI agent sends service messages to the associated virtual human to perform actions chosen by the decision-making module or by the dialogue manager (turn-taking behavior). The rendering system realises the requested actions and sends action events (begin, end) towards corresponding C²BDI agent. The conversation manager deals with automatic-speech-recognition (ASR) and text to speech synthesis (TTS). The message manager handles the dispatching of perception information and service messages.

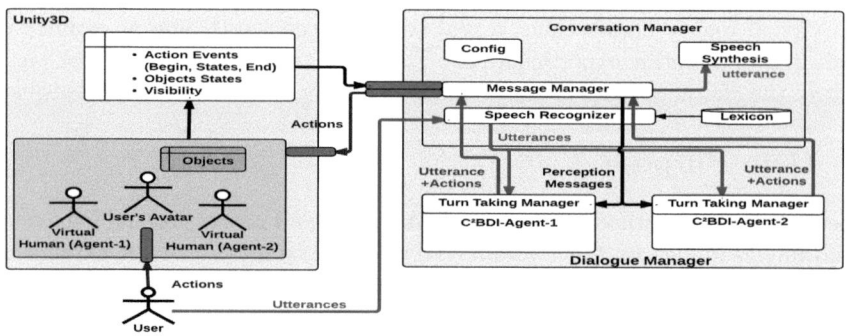

Fig. 2. Technical Architecture: Data flow between different components

Belief-Revision: The belief-revision specialises the classical mechanism of BDI. Since, the state of VE can be changed due to interactions by team members, the belief-revision periodically updates knowledge base of the agent. It ensures the coherence of knowledge elements acquired from the perception of the VE and from the natural language spoken dialogues. The beliefs in C²BDI agent are the instantiation of the semantic knowledge at any time. When agent perceives an action, it updates the belief about the current state of the performer with respect to the shared plan. Moreover, it also updates beliefs about the resource allocation by teammates through their perceived actions. It updates the beliefs about the states of objects (resources) when it perceives the object. Furthermore, it also updates belief about the task in progress, resource allocation etc. through the means of dialogue processing.

Natural Language Processing: The ASR recognises spoken phrases with confidence level. The C²BDI agent uses the rule based approach [3] for natural language understanding (NLU) and generation (NLG). When it receives an utterance, the turn-taking manager determines the sender and the addressee(s) based on the analysis of the utterance phrase, and the orientation and position of virtual humans. The agent then uses NLU templates to construct the utterance semantic form using semantic knowledge and *perception context*, and also performs pronoun resolution. For example, when the agent receives an utterance "which tablet will you choose?", it is matched with one of the templates as shown below, and generates the semantic form "Set-Q(what-resource-choice Self Tablet future)" considering that the dialogue is addressed to the agent.

```
(nlu-rule:  input:  {[which] [concept($res)] alt({[will] [you]} { [you] [will]}) [select]}
      output:  ({Set-Q([what-resource-choice] @myself() @concept-class($res) [future]) }) )
```

The dialogue contents are identified using the semantic knowledge and the contextual information from the IS. Here, @concept-class($res) determines the class of the resource using semantic knowledge. NLU rules are then used to construct the dialogue act (DA) corresponding to utterance semantic form [4]. It then add the DA to the addressee's-dialogue-act in *dialogue context*. The dialogue manager processes these DAs and updates IS based on update rules. The reactive behavior of C²BDI then apply selection rules on updated IS to compute new communicative intentions (e.g., reply to an information seeking question) and adds it to the agenda in the *semantic context* of IS. When the agent has a communicative intention, it constructs corresponding dialogue act, and selection rules are applied which modify IS and generate next dialogue moves. For example, the agent generates Inform(resource-choice) as next move, in response to the information seeking set-Q(what-resource-choice). If the agent has the belief about the resource to be used in next action (e.g., tablet-large), it generate the semantic form inform(resource-choice $addressee tablet-large future). Template based NLG rules (e.g., as shown below) are then used to generate utterance corresponding to semantic form, based on the current context from IS. Thus, the agent generates the utterance "I will choose the large tablet".

```
(nlg-rule:
input:  { inform([resource-choice] [token($addressee)] [concept($res)]) [future]}
effect: talk({ optional($addressee,) "I will" alt([choose][use][select])
      @article(@concept-gender($res) @concept-number($res) definitive) @concept-name($res)} ) )
```

Context Management: The C²BDI agent updates its IS based context model when (i) it processes an utterance, or it has an intention to say something; and (ii) during the belief-revision and decision-making. The *dialogue context* is updated during the processing of utterances by modifying the information about the addressees, identified dialogue acts, next moves etc. similar to [4]. The processing of the task-oriented dialogue results in creating new beliefs about the task and allocated resources, and thus, modifies the *semantic context*. The processing may also result in adding expectations of information in *semantic context*. In a human-agent team, the user's behavior is uncertain, i.e., user may not necessarily follow the coordination protocols. The agent updates its beliefs using perception information, therefore, it can make the expectations to be true from the observation of actions of user perceived by the agent, or from the information provided by other team members.

The decision-making process deliberates the plan, and can add the current intention to the *task-focus* in *task context*, or can identify collaborative situations (e.g., satisfying the conditions of CCPs, need to handle resource allocation). These situations add new communicative intentions to the agenda in the *semantic context* of IS. C^2BDI provides the proactive communication behavior based on the anticipation of the needs of other teammates. Moreover, handling collaborative situations using CCPs results in modifying *cognitive context* by creating or modifying mutual beliefs, and modifying the *task context* by creating or updating beliefs about its individual- and joint- goals, desires and intentions. The RAM updates the *semantic context* by creating new communicative intentions in agenda to inform or request about resource management, and also updates beliefs about the resource allocation among team members. The belief-revision also modifies the *perceptual context* which contains information to which the agent pays attention during conversation and during the realisation of the task. This information is used, in particular, for the resolution of pronouns and the instantiation of contextualised semantic knowledge of the agent. If the task-focus contains primitive action, the agent selects this action and sends it towards associated virtual human to realize it.

4 Conclusion

This demo shows that C^2BDI ensures knowledge sharing between team members by considering deliberative and conversation behaviours as tightly coupled components. The system is being used in the Corvette project to analyse users's interactions with virtual agents. First results indicate a good coordination between users and the virtual agents.

Acknowledgment. This work was partly supported by the ANR (Corvette project ANR-10-CORD-012).

References

1. Barange, M., Kabil, A., De Keukelaere, C., Chevaillier, P.: Communicative capabilities of agents for the collaboration in a human-agent team. In: The 7th Int. Conf. on Advances in Computer-Human Interactions, Barcelona, Spain (March 2014)
2. Barange, M., Kabil, A., De Keukelaere, C., Chevaillier, P.: Task-oriented conversational behavior of agents for collaboration in human-agent teamwork. In: Demazeau, Y., Corchado, J.M., Zambonelli, F., Bajo, J. (eds.) PAAMS 2014. LNCS (LNAI), vol. 8473, pp. 25–37. Springer, Heidelberg (2014)
3. Barange, M., De Loor, P., Louis, V., Querrec, R., Soler, J., Trinh, T.-H., Maisel, É., Chevaillier, P.: Get involved in an interactive virtual tour of brest harbour: Follow the guide and participate. In: Vilhjálmsson, H.H., Kopp, S., Marsella, S., Thórisson, K.R. (eds.) IVA 2011. LNCS, vol. 6895, pp. 93–99. Springer, Heidelberg (2011)
4. Bunt, H.: The semantics of dialogue acts. In: Proc. of the 9th Int. Conf. on Computational Semantics, IWCS 2011, Stroudsburg, PA, USA, pp. 1–13 (2011)

Agent Based Simulation for Creating Ambient Assisted Living Solutions

Pablo Campillo-Sanchez and Jorge J. Gómez-Sanz

Departamento de Ingeniería del Software e Inteligencia Artificial,
Facultad de Informática
Universidad Complutense de Madrid,
Madrid, Spain
{pabcampi,jjgomez}@ucm.es

Abstract. This demo shows how the development of Ambient Assisted Living systems can be enhanced with the assistance of agent technology. Concretely, this demo introduces advances in the PHAT framework to create what we call Virtual Living Labs. This Virtual Living Lab reproduces realistic conditions of an application working inside embedded hardware that can run Android OS. The concrete situations to reproduce are captured using SociAALML, a modeling language that is being tested in the context of Parkinson's patients. This information is later on processed to create scenarios in the Virtual Living Lab.

Keywords: Agent-oriented software engineering, assisted living, modeling, multi-agent system, ontology, Parkinson's disease.

1 Introduction

An Ambient Assisted Living (AAL) applications is a system that increases the quality of living of elderly by assisting them. The development of AAL system for specific collectives, like Parkinson, is reduced. Parkinson's Disease (PD) is an illness with a high impact in the elderly. Parkinson's patients (PPs) have problems controlling movements, and this is hard to compensate. However, some improvement can be made, like providing stimulus to the patient when they remain still and unable to continue moving. Readers can find a more detailed description of PD and some ideas for improvement in our previous analysis [1].

In the project SociAAL[1], we work under the hypothesis that we could produce more affordable AAL applications for PPs if we had an account of the needs of these patients, and if we could test the intended AAL system in a less expensive way. This approach would save costs firstly because it would tell developers what functionalities are actually demanded, reducing the risks of developing the wrong system; and secondly, because the kind AAL development we pursue requires using a real Living Lab, which are expensive. A Living Lab is a room or a house where the AAL system is deployed and subject of evaluation.

---

[1] SociAAL website: http://grasia.fdi.ucm.es/sociaal

In this demo, we elaborate on how SociAAL develops solutions in both directions using concepts and technology borrowed from agent research. Agent research provides useful concepts for capturing behavioral information of PPs. Also, this information is realised later on through Multi-Agent Based Simulations, using MASON platform, that capture the daily living of the patients and permits to validate AAL systems.

Our contribution in this demo is twofold. First, we present SociAALML, a domain specific modeling language for capturing activities of the daily living of PPs. This language is introduced in section2. Second, we introduce the concept of Virtual Living Lab with our current implementation of PHAT [2]. A Virtual Living Lab aims to provide early testing for developers that permits to reduce the amount of time invested in the real, and expensive, Living Lab. This concept is more properly presented in section 3.

2 SociAALML, A Modeling Language Based on Social Principles

SociAALML is a modeling language for capturing requirements related to daily situations that PD patients meet. The language is built using INGENME[2] meta-modeling framework and is being tested against a collection of interviews made in a field study.

In the 2, there is a brief declaration of one patient in one of the interviews. Each patient has a profile that serves to characterize their capabilities and how the disease is affecting them. This is captured with the ParkinsonProfile element. Other elements affecting the behavior of the patient is the social profile, which refers to the influences of the people around the patient, the culture, and the society itself. Other different diseases may appear and condition the behavior of the patient, like the blood return disease. These aspects do condition the daily activities of the patient, which are captured by the ADL Profile. The language permits also to characterize how each daily activity is affected by the specific symptom. The idea is to collect a library of ADL (Activities of Daily Living) and reuse them along the different kinds of actors. Also, we would accumulate symptoms and reuse them directly, or combining them. Once properly defined, these models are processed to generate documentation, but also to parameterize the Virtual Living Lab which will be introduced in the next section.

3 PHAT, A Virtual Living Lab Concept

The Virtual Living Lab, to be credible, needs to immerse AAL applications completely in the virtual environment. PHAT [2] is a framework that produces 3D simulations representing the outcome of the interaction between an AAL system and some virtual characters. Using a physics engine, PHAT can simulate different collision between objects producing new situations a developer may not

---

[2] http://ingenme.sf.net

Fig. 1. An excerpt of patient case study using SociAALML

have expected. As an excerpt of what we can do, the environment permits to reproduce effects like sound attenuation due to the distance or having a camera too close to a wall to show anything. The behavior of the actors is implemented using MASON platform. To facilitate MaSON programming, we provide with abstractions of 3D elements that can be used in the MASON coding.

In a PHAT scenario, the developer identifies actors and their particularities. Since SociAAL is about Parkinson's patients, PHAT includes some disease specific features that aims to capture what we have found in the field studies. As section 2 has introduced, actors can have regular activities which are conditioned by the conditions of the patient. In the case of figure 2, the patient shows shaking moves which may appear in some cases. These moves are a challenge, for instance, if you intend to identify when the patient has fallen. The relative, in the same case study, is in the kitchen preparing diner. In this scenario, the quality of the relative is increased because there is a monitoring system, represented by the three abovementioned devices, that permits the relative to pay less attention to the patient. In the case of the patient, it increases the autonomy because it is not necessary to have the relative watching everytime. With this purpose in mind, a developer would have to produce the necessary software that would run into the different parts of this monitoring system.

PHAT allows to integrate virtual devices in the environment with full sensory integration. These devices are supposed to run Android OS (any version), like many of the current smartphones available today, though Android OS is capable of running into other hardware. There is actual support to embed Android in other typical smart home hardware in the Android developer site. We use official Android emulators for each device. This facilitates the portability of developed apps to the target platform. These apps have access to the sensory elements of the device and would be able to generate instructions for other elements, like triggering alarms or switching on Smart TVs.

In figure 2, there are three devices: one attached to the hand of the patient, another to the hand of his relative, and a third attached to the bathroom. The relative and patient's devices have a camera that is active anytime. The device of the bathroom has a microphone that is listening to nearby sounds. The integration of devices and environment is rather complete. The environment feeds the devices with accelerometer information, image streams, sounds (including attenuation due to the distance of the source of sound), even user input. The later is a feature under development that our virtual characters use to interact with the devices.

Fig. 2. A running instance of PHAT showing a Parkinson's patient and a relative

4 Conclusions and Future Work

Using agent research results, we are creating a modeling language and an agent based platform to aid us building our Virtual Living Lab concept. Both elements are being applied to rethink how Ambient Assisted Living systems are developed. The final goal is to reduce the costs of producing applications for Parkinson patients, though these principles can be applied to people in different situations.

Acknowledgements. This work has been done in the context of the project *Social Ambient Assisting Living - Methods* (SociAAL), supported by Spanish Ministry for Economy and Competitiveness, with grant TIN2011-28335-C02-01.

References

1. Arroyo, M., Finkel, L., Gomez-Sanz, J.J.: Requirements for an intelligent ambient assisted living application for parkinson patients. In: Corchado, J.M., et al. (eds.) PAAMS 2013. CCIS, vol. 365, pp. 441–452. Springer, Heidelberg (2013)
2. Campillo-Sanchez, P., Gómez-Sanz, J.J., Botía, J.A.: Phat: Physical human activity tester. In: Pan, J.-S., Polycarpou, M.M., Woźniak, M., de Carvalho, A.C.P.L.F., Quintián, H., Corchado, E. (eds.) HAIS 2013. LNCS, vol. 8073, pp. 41–50. Springer, Heidelberg (2013)

A Microscopic Traffic Simulation Platform for Coordinated Charging of Electric Vehicles

Kristof Coninx and Tom Holvoet

iMinds-DistriNet
KU Leuven, 3001 Leuven, Belgium
{firstname.lastname}@cs.kuleuven.be

Abstract. Gridlock is a microscopic traffic simulation platform and is now extended with electric vehicle support. Simulations for coordination mechanisms concerning on-line charging of electric vehicles on highway networks are performed using this simulation platform. The platform offers a means for gathering and processing simulation data and the real-time visualisation of simulation state aspects such as traffic density and charging station occupation.

1 Introduction

Electric vehicles (EVs) are gaining in popularity in an effort to reduce the carbon footprint of vehicular transportation by creating environmentally friendly alternatives in the form of Plug-in Hybrid EVs and fully battery-powered EVs but the limited driving range is still considered as one of the main causes for the limited adoption of EVs, together with the long time needed to recharge the battery. Electric charging infrastructure will need to be built. These networks will, however, be subject to capacity constraints.

If there is too much traffic on the network, congestion becomes unavoidable. Increasing the load on the charging infrastructure by increasing the number of vehicles that need to charge, causes the waiting times and queueing to increase rapidly. Prolonged peak loads on these infrastructure elements can also aversely affect the lifespan of the transformers in the electricity grid, driving up the financial cost for the grid operators.

More efficiently using the available infrastructure by use of ICT-based coordination strategies offers a solution to mitigate the symptoms of these capacity problems. The primary goal of the work in [1] is finding coordination strategies capable of guiding the charging behaviour of individual agents to globally minimize waiting and queuing times and to avoid excessive peak loading of charging stations in the network.

2 Main Purpose

This paper demonstrates the simulation platform used for evaluating coordination mechanisms for on-line allocation of electric vehicles to fast charging

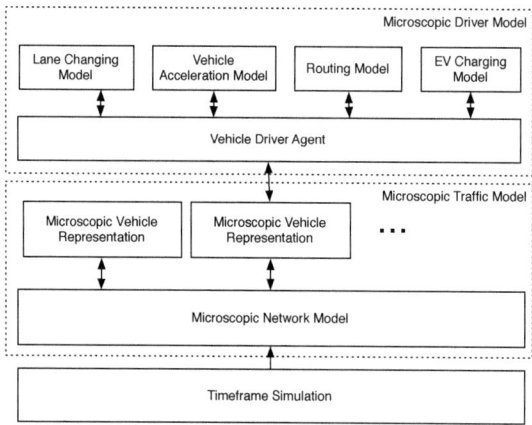

Fig. 1. Structure of simulation platform

infrastructure in [1]. The simulation platform is based on `Gridlock` [2] and has been extended to support EVs, fast charging stations, charging behaviour and coordination mechanisms. Afterwards, a realistic scenario is implemented in the simulator and multiple simulation experiments are performed with rudimentary visualisations.

3 Demonstration

3.1 Gridlock

`Gridlock` is a microscopic traffic simulator and simulates vehicles in traffic on a microscopic scale. Consecutively, the platform allows for macroscopic evaluation of simulation experiments. In a microscopic simulation, all vehicles are represented as separate entities with their own behaviours. Every second in simulation time the effects of these behaviours are calculated and updated throughout the model. This platform also allows for the implementation of custom event listeners using a Publish-Subscribe model to gather and aggregate simulation data. The platform architecture is represented in Figure 1.

3.2 Topology

The simulation scenario implemented for the experiments in [1] is chosen for its real-world relevance and this section will demonstrate how it is constructed. A highway network in Flanders, Belgium is virtually rebuilt into a format suitable for input into the simulation platform. Different points-of-interest (POI) are identified along the highway such as gas stations, truck stops and highway access points. The distances between these POI are measured by using the average of measurements by different on-line map tools. These point coordinates and their inter-point distances are then converted into an annotated weighed graph

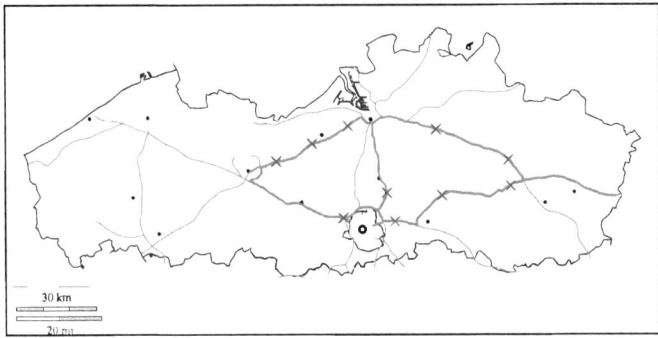

Fig. 2. The road net in Flanders, Belgium, used to perform simulations on. The used network segments are stroked in green while a red × marks a charging station.

structure wherein the weights represent the real world distances between nodes. The coordinates themselves are artificially created for easy visualisation purposes. This explains why the visualised graph does not look completely similar to the real-world highway topology but for simulation purposes the represented distances are accurate. Figure 2 shows the real-world highway network and chosen charging stations while Figure 3 displays the road network as visualised by the simulation platform.

3.3 Visualisation

Traffic Density. Besides drawing the network graph, the visualisation also represents how many vehicles are present on the different edges in the graph. A vehicle driving on an edge has the coordinates of the nodes that edge connects distorted by a small amount of Gaussian noise. These distorted coordinates are connected and stroked in red. Figure 4 shows this effect where no two vehicle paths on the same edge are drawn between the same two points on screen. More vehicles present on a certain edge will show as a more pronounced *glow* compared to edges with less traffic present.

The specific amount of vehicles on the road is determined by a traffic generator which takes an input file with the relative amount of vehicles on an hourly basis. This relative amount is in relation to a global fleet size set in the simulation configuration file.

Charging Station Load. The nodes in the graph that function as a representations of charging stations are colour coded. The possible colours can range from blue meaning no vehicles have charged here to green, yellow and red representing <33,3%, <66,6% and <100% occupation relative to the maximum amount of station load observed in the system so far. This is therefore a relative representation of the current load in relation to the maximum observed load for the whole simulation run. The nodes that remain blue for the duration of a simulation are

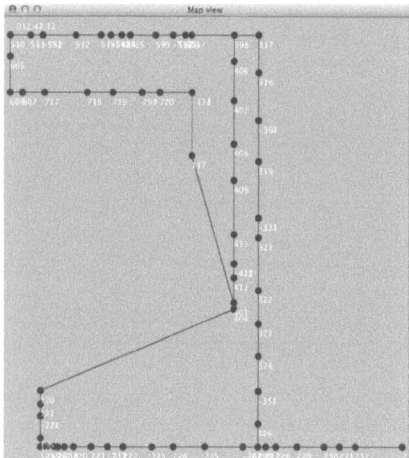 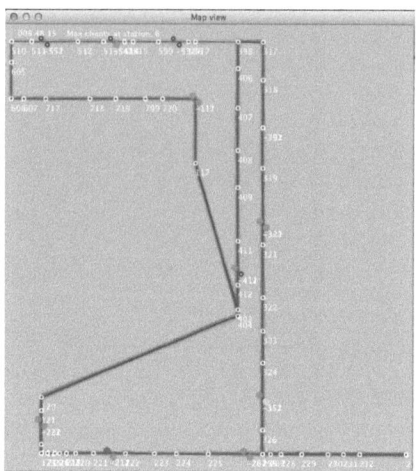

Fig. 3. The visualisation of the bare highway network

Fig. 4. The visualisation of the highway traffic densities and station loads

indicative that these stations might actually be obsolete because they are not used by vehicles to charge at.

4 Conclusion

This paper shows some aspects about the real time visualisation capabilities of the Gridlock simulation platform and its extension for electric vehicles. Gridlock is used as a simulation tool for research concerning coordination mechanisms for on-line charging of Electric Vehicles in traffic and for evaluating possible charging station topologies. The simulation tool is demonstrated by using a scenario based on a real-world highway network with real world traffic data.

References

1. Coninx, K., Claes, R., Vandael, S., Holvoet, T., Deconinck, G.: Anticipatory Coordination of Electric Vehicle Allocation to Fast Charging Infrastructure. In: Demazeau, Y., Corchado, J.M., Zambonelli, F., Bajo, J. (eds.) PAAMS 2014. LNCS (LNAI), vol. 8473, Springer, Heidelberg (2014)
2. Claes, R., Holvoet, T.: GridLock: A microscopic traffic simulation platform. In: International Conference on Models and Technologies for Intelligent Transportation Systems (2011)

Bilateral Negotiation of a Meeting Point in a Maze: Demonstration

Fabien Delecroix, Maxime Morge, and Jean-Christophe Routier

Laboratoire d'Informatique Fondamentale de Lille
Université Lille 1
Cité Scientifique- F-59655 Villeneuve d'Ascq
{fabien.delecroix,maxime.morge,jean-christophe.routier}@lifl.fr

Abstract. Negotiation between agents aims at reaching an agreement in which the conflicting interests of agents are accommodated. In this demonstration, we present a concrete negotiation scenario where two agents are situated in a maze and the negotiation outcome is a cell where they will meet. Their individual preferences match with a minimal distance computed from their partial knowledge of the environment. We illustrate a bargaining protocol which allows agents to submit several proposals at the same round and a negotiation strategy which consists in starting from the best deal for the agent and then concedes. The path between the agents emerges from the repeated negotiations.

1 Introduction

Multiagents systems (MAS) is a paradigm to analyze, to design and to implement systems made of autonomous entities interacting each other. These systems are characterized by oppositions. These conflicts exist since agents have a local perception of the environment and/or their own goals. In a MAS, the agents, even if they are self-interested, must collaborate to reach their goals. Negotiation is a form of interaction to reach a mutual agreement. This agreement can be a resource allocation [1–6], a 2-side matching [7] or a collective decision [8]. The goals of the agents are conflicting since they cannot be fully satisfied at the same time. In this perspective, negotiation is a distributed search in a potential agreements space [9].

Many complex negotiation environments can be considered: multi-party negotiation (with more than two agents), multi-issue negotiation (the potential agreements space is multi-dimensional), argumentation-based negotiation (offer are attacked/defended), assumptions over the agents' preferences (reservation value, discount factor, deadline, etc.). Based on the principle of parsimony, we study proposal-based bilateral single-issue negotiation in a companion paper [10]. We illustrate here our negotiation game in a concrete scenario where two agents are situated in a maze and the negotiation outcome is a cell where they will meet.

2 Main Purpose

Tab. 2 situates our negotiation environment [10] wrt related works.
Many different negotiation environments have been studied in the literature:

- the object of negotiation can be single-issue or multi-issue, with discrete or continuous issues;
- the agents' preferences (2 or more) can be captured by preference relations (denoted $\succsim$) or utility functions (denoted u);
- the negotiation protocol can be symmetric or asymmetric, simultaneous or successive, continuous or discrete, with or without deadline;
- the knowledge of agents about the opponents can be perfect or imperfect.

We distinguish two approaches to design multiagents negotiation. In the game-theoretical approach, the negotiation environment is restricted to formally validate the properties of the outcome (optimality) and of the process (stability, computational complexity, distribution, etc.). In the heuristic-based approach the negotiation environment is realistic but the properties are empirically evaluated. The imperfect information is the major difficulty for the first approach. However, since we adopt the heuristic-based approach, we think this assumption is crucial for practical application.

Table 1. Analysis grid of the literature according to the negotiation environment.

	Nb agents	Object	Pref.	Protocol	Deadline	Information
[1]	2	single continuous	u	symmetric simultaneous	no	perfect
[2]	2	single continuous	u	asymmetric successive	no	perfect
[3]	2	multi continuous	u	asymmetric successive	yes	perfect / imperfect
[4]	2	single continuous	u	asymmetric successive	yes	imperfect
[5]	2	single continuous	u	asymmetric continuous	yes	imperfect
[6]	n	multi continuous / discrete	u	asymmetric continuous	yes	imperfect
[7]	n	single discrete	$\succsim$	asymmetric successive	no	imperfect
[8]	2	single discrete	$\succsim$	asymmetric continuous	yes	imperfect
[10]	*2*	*single discrete*	$\succsim$	*symmetric simultaneous*	*no*	*imperfect*

3 Demonstration

We consider here two agents, Alice and Bob, which are paratroopers landed in an unknown maze. They aim at meeting as soon as possible, i.e minimizing the maximum number of steps for an agent to reach the meeting point. Both of them have a local perception of the environment. Each agent can perceive the walls of her current cell. Moreover, she knows her own location. Additionally, the agents are allowed to communicate in order to negotiate the meeting point. The meeting point can be re-negotiate during the exploration of the maze. The optimal solution for finding a meeting point requires the knowledge of the whole maze. Under this assumption, the agents can compute the shortest path between them and set the meeting point in the middle of it. By contrast, a solution which does not need any prior knowledge consists of pseudo-randomly selecting a meeting point in the maze.

In order to illustrate this problem, we consider a 3×3 maze (cf Fig.1) at the second step of the resolution. Each agent computes the distance to reach all the other cells based on her knowledge. For this purpose, an agent takes into consideration the perceived walls and she assumes that there is no wall between the cells she did not visit yet. In other words, the computation is performed by an A-star algorithm where the future path-cost function is the Manhattan distance. Since we want to minimize the maximum number of steps for an agent to reach the meeting point, the cell with the red flag is a good candidate. In order to solve this distributed solving problem, we use the negotiation protocol and strategy of [10] which allow to reach a fair solution.

Fig. 1. The maze (at middle) and its internal representation for Alice (at left) and Bob (at right) at time $t = 2$. In the latters, the visited cells are in grey, some walls may be still unknown and each cell is labelled with an estimation of the shortest path length.

Our demonstration exhibits the behaviours of agents exploring several mazes. These behaviours are the result of iterated negotiation games that take into account the information gathered by the agents during the exploration.

4 Conclusion

In this demonstration, we have illustrated a negotiation protocol which allows agents to make more than two offers per round and a negotiation strategy based on large (and eventually partial) preferences which does not assume that agents know the preferences of each other. In this way, we have demonstrated a fair negotiation process which does not give priority to one agent and which minimizes the maximum effort of one agent. We have applied our framework for distributed problem solving. In particular, we have considered the case of two agents in a maze which aims at negotiating a meeting in order to reach it as soon as possible. The path between the agents emerges from the repeated negotiations.

We are currently extending our bilateral negotiation game to a multi-party negotiation game where more than two agents play and observe moves.

References

1. Rosenschein, J., Zlotkin, G.: Rules of Encounter - Designing Conventions for Automated Negotiation among Computers. MIT Press (1994)
2. Rubinstein, A.: Perfect equilibrium in a bargaining model. Econometrica 50(1), 97–102 (1982)
3. Fatima, S.S., Wooldridge, M., Jennings, N.R.: Multi-issue negotiation with deadlines. Journal of Artificial Intelligence Research 27, 381–417 (2006)
4. Gatti, N., Giunta, F.D., Marino, S.: Alternating-offers bargaining with one-sided uncertain deadlines: an efficient algorithm. Artificial Intelligence 172(8-9), 1119–1157 (2008)
5. Sandholm, T., Vulkan, N.: Bargaining with deadlines. In: Proc. of AAAI, pp. 44–51 (1999)
6. Faratin, P., Sierra, C., Jennings, N.R.: Negotiation decision functions for autonomous agents. Robotics and Autonomous Systems 24(3-4), 159–182 (1998)
7. Morge, M., Picard, G.: Privacy-preserving strategy for negotiating stable, equitable and optimal matchings. In: Demazeau, Y., Pěchouček, M., Corchado, J.M., Pérez, J.B. (eds.) Adv. on Prac. Appl. of Agents and Multi. Sys. AISC, pp. 97–102. Springer, Heidelberg (2011)
8. Aydoğan, R., Baarslag, T., Hindriks, K.V., Jonker, C.M., Yolum, P.: Heuristic-based approaches for CP-nets in negotiation. In: Ito, T., Zhang, M., Robu, V., Matsuo, T. (eds.) Complex Automated Negotiations. SCI, vol. 435, pp. 115–126. Springer, Heidelberg (2012)
9. Jennings, N., Faratin, P., Lomuscio, A., Parsons, S., Wooldridge, M., Sierra, C.: Automated negotiation: Prospects methods and challenges. Group Decision and Negotiation 10(2), 199–215 (2001)
10. Delecroix, F., Morge, M., Routier, J.C.: Bilateral negotiation of a meeting point in a maze. In: Demazeau, Y., Corchado, J.M., Zambonelli, F., Bajo, J. (eds.) PAAMS 2014. LNCS (LNAI), vol. 8473, pp. 86–97. Springer, Heidelberg (2014)

Using Negotiation for Parking Selection in Smart Cities[*]

Claudia Di Napoli[1], Dario Di Nocera[2,**], and Silvia Rossi[3]

[1] Istituto di Calcolo e Reti ad Alte Prestazioni - C.N.R., Napoli, Italy
claudia.dinapoli@cnr.it
[2] Dipartimento di Matematica - University of Naples "Federico II", Napoli, Italy
dario.dinocera@unina.it
[3] Dipartimento di Ingegneria Elettrica e Tecnologie dell'Informazione
University of Naples "Federico II", Napoli, Italy
silvia.rossi@unina.it

Keywords: Agent negotiation, multi-agent systems, smart parking, smart cities.

1 Introduction

Parking in urban areas is becoming a big concern for its environmental and economic implications. Smart parking systems are considered essential to improve both city life in terms of gas emission and air pollution, and motorists life by making it easier to park. Supporting technologies are emerging at the industrial level to easily locate available parking spaces, to automate parking payments, and to collect useful data on consumer demand. Most of the research projects concerning smart parking systems focus on ways to collect and publish live parking information and many companies are developing electronic parking systems allowing for a wide variety of available payment methods.

Nevertheless, the full potentiality of smart parking systems is still far to come, and it represents a big challenge for the future of Smart Cities. New approaches are necessary to better mange and regulate parking supply and demand relying on decision mechanisms to help locating and assigning parking spaces in an intelligent manner. Such mechanisms are necessary to provide user-oriented automatic parking services that take into account both drivers preferences, and parking vendors requirements together with social benefits for the city, such as a reduction of traffic by limiting parking in city center [1].

In this paper we show the use of a software agent negotiation mechanism in order to establish an agreement between parking providers and parking requestors that accommodates their respective requirements on a parking space, in terms of its location and cost for the requestors, and in terms of income and city regulations for the the vendor, to obtain an efficient parking allocation and traffic redirection.

---

[*] The research leading to these results has received funding from the EU FP7-ICT-2012-8 under the MIDAS Project no. 318786, and the Italian Ministry of University and Research and EU under the PON OR.C.HE.S.T.R.A. project.
[**] Ph.D. scholarship funded by Media Motive S.r.l, POR Campania FSE 2007-2013.

2 Main Purpose

In the present work, a Car Park System is intended as a complex application composed of different devices and services. The system provides the user with a city map to select the area he/she would like to park, and also an interface to indicate his/her parking preferences. The Parking Manager (PM) is responsible for processing the request. It queries external/internal databases to retrieve information on the available car parks. Also it may invoke additional external services to collect information on city regulation and/or events, or other relevant information, such as an estimation of the time necessary to arrive to the user destination from a specific car park.

An automatic negotiation mechanism is used between two agents: the PM and a User Agent. In the present work we adopt the negotiation mechanism reported in [2], whose protocol is based on the Iterated Contract Net Protocol. Both PM and UA preferences over the attributes to be negotiated upon, are modeled through utility functions based on the Multi-Attribute Utility Theory defined on independent issues [3]. The utility function of the PM depends on the car park availability at the moment the request is received, and on the distance of the car park from the city center. In this way, the issues considered in the PM utility function take into account the preference of the PM to propose first car parks that are both less occupied and not located in the city center (to reduce the influx of cars in city centers). The issues considered in the UA utility function take into account the preference of the UA concerning the parking space price, and its location with respect to the preferred final destination.

3 Demonstration

A running example of a negotiation, where we evaluate the utility obtained by the PM and the UA when an agreement is achieved, is reported. In this example the weights in the utility functions are equally distributed among the considered issues.

The example starts with a request issued by a hypothetical user specifying the destination he/she wants to reach, selected on interactive city map provided by a specific service, and the time interval he/she wants to park for. The UA sends a "call for parking" to the PM. A graphical representation of the use case described above is reported in the Figure 1, where the destination selected by the user is identified with the down arrow.

At the first round, the PM selects a list of car parks around the user's destination, and it calculates the ranking of the selected car parks based on its utility. The PM found ten car parks with parking spaces available around the requested area within a predefined tolerance distance. Parking identifiers and locations are extracted from the OpenStreetMap database [4] of the city of Naples (Italy), while routing information are evaluated through the use of Google MAPs API [5]. The occupancy of car parks is randomly generated. In the Figure 1(a), the selected car parks are reported with labels specifying the corresponding park ids and their utility values, as evaluated by the PM.

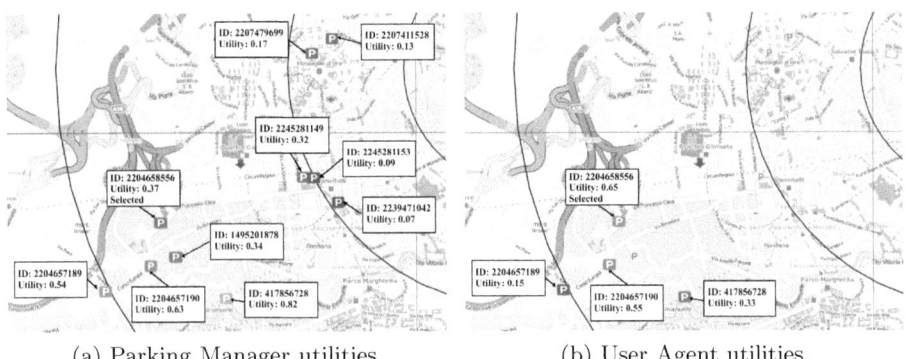

Fig. 1. Parking Manager and User Agent Utilities

Table 1. Negotiation on a single query

Rounds	ID	Spaces	Dist (m)	Price (€)	Route (m)	Time (s)	U_{PM}	U_{UA}
1°	417856728	109	3187	7.99	1516	1384	0.82	0.34
2°	2204657189	41	4036	5.61	1818	2183	0.63	0.16
3°	2204657190	41	3594	7.98	1192	871	0.54	0.55
4°	2204658556	18	3359	7.46	891	646	0.37	0.66

At each negotiation round, the PM offers to the UA the parking space with the highest utility value (in this example it offer a car park with utility equals to 0.82). The UA accepts (rejects) the offer if its utility for that offer, is higher (lower) than the threshold value. The first PM offer corresponds to an utility for the UA equals to 0.33. Hence, the offer is rejected because it is lower than the threshold value (equals to 0.6), and the UA starts another round of negotiation. The negotiation ends at the fourth round, when the UA accepts an offer with utility equals to 0.66 (corresponding to an utility for the PM equals to 0.37). It should be noted that an offer proposed by PM in a negotiation round is not considered available in future rounds once it is rejected. This assumption models the possibility that a rejected parking space may be offered to another user in the meantime, or its price may change according to the parking market trends. In the Figure 1(b), car parks offered by the PM during negotiation are reported with labels specifying the corresponding park ids and their utility values, as evaluated by the UA.

In Table 1 we summarized all the relevant information at each negotiation round, reporting the number of parking spaces available in a car park (Spaces), its distance from the city center (Dist), the unit price (Price) to be paid for the parking space, and the distance of the car park from the destination set by the UA, calculated both in length and in time (Route and Time), as obtained by querying a service of Google Maps. This information is necessary to allow the PM and the UA to calculate their utility values (U_{PM} and U_{UA}) for the car parks. In this specific run, the negotiation ends after four rounds with an utility of the PM equals to 0.37 and for the UA equals to 0.66. Note that while the utility of the PM is not particularly high (because of the few parking spaces available in the car parks), the PM still manages to allocate a parking space in only four rounds of negotiation, being able to reach a compromise by offering a car park that is not the closest to the user's destination, but still acceptable by the user in terms of time necessary to reach the destination from the car park location, and that is not too close to the city center.

4 Conclusions

Parking in populated urban areas is becoming a challenging problem requiring smart technologies in order to assist users in finding parking solutions, to shorten the time necessary to find parking spaces. In this way, it is possible to decrease traffic congestion, and to improve the everyday life of city dwellers.

In the present work, we show the use software agent negotiation to address the parking problem by taking into account not only motorists' preferences regarding parking locations, but also parking vendors preferences regarding car park occupancy, and social city benefits (e.g. less traffic congestion in city centers, so encouraging the diffusion of pedestrian areas). We use a flexible negotiation mechanism to find parking solutions that represent a compromise among different needs: a user who prefers to park close to the city center, the car park vendors who prefer to sell parking spaces in less occupied car parks, and a city manager who tries to limit the circulation of cars in city centers. The automated negotiation mechanism allows to formulate offers that do not strictly meet the user requirements, and to find parking solutions that are a result of a negotiation process between the PM and the UA upon parking attributes that are evaluated differently by the negotiators. The proposed framework allows also to model different user's profiles since the evaluation of the parking space attribute values may vary for different classes of users.

References

1. Teodorović, D., Lučić, P.: Intelligent parking systems. European Journal of Operational Research 175(3), 1666–1681 (2006)
2. Di Napoli, C., Pisa, P., Rossi, S.: Towards a dynamic negotiation mechanism for qoS-aware service markets. In: Pérez, J.B., et al. (eds.) Trends in Pract. Appl. of Agents & Multiagent Syst. AISC, vol. 221, pp. 9–16. Springer, Heidelberg (2013)
3. Barbuceanu, M., Lo, W.-K.: Multi-attribute utility theoretic negotiation for electronic commerce. In: Dignum, F.P.M., Cortés, U. (eds.) AMEC 2000. LNCS (LNAI), vol. 2003, pp. 15–30. Springer, Heidelberg (2001)
4. Haklay, M., Weber, P.: Openstreetmap: User-generated street maps. IEEE Pervasive Computing 7(4), 12–18 (2008)
5. Svennerberg, G.: Beginning Google Maps API 3. Apress (2010)

Developing Multimodal Conversational Agents: From the Use of VoiceXML to Android-Based Applications

David Griol, José Manuel Molina, and Araceli Sanchis de Miguel

Computer Science Department
Carlos III University of Madrid
Avda. de la Universidad, 30, 28911 - Leganés, Spain
{david.griol,josemanuel.molina,araceli.sanchis}@uc3m.es

Abstract. The current industrial development of commercial conversational agents and dialog systems deploys robust interfaces in strictly defined application domains. However, commercial systems have not yet adopted new perspectives proposed in the academic settings, which would allow straightforward adaptation of these interfaces. In this paper, we propose two approaches to bridge the gap between the academic and industrial perspectives in order to develop conversational agents using an academic paradigm for dialog management while employing the industrial standards, like the VoiceXML language or the Android OS. Our proposal has been evaluated with the successful development of different spoken and multimodal systems.

Keywords: Human-agent interaction, User interfaces, Conversational agents, Spoken and Multimodal interaction, Statistical methodologies.

1 Introduction

Speech Technologies and Language Processing have made possible the development of a number of new applications which are based on conversational agents [1]. Speech access is then a solution to the shrinking size of mobile devices (both keyboards to provide information and displays to see the results). Besides, speech interfaces facilitate the access to multiagent systems [2], especially in environments where this access is not possible using traditional input interfaces (e.g., keyboard and mouse). It also facilitates information access for people with visual or motor disabilities.

In this paper we describe two approaches than can be used to bridge the gap between the academic and industrial perspectives in order to develop dialog systems using an academic paradigm based on a statistical dialog management technique [3] combined with the industrial standards, like the VoiceXML standard[1] or the Android OS [4]. This makes it possible to obtain new generation

---

[1] http://www.w3.org/TR/voicexml20/

interfaces without the need for changing the already existing commercial infrastructures. The first approach is oriented to the development of spoken conversational agents, while the second approach also allows to develop systems dealing with multimodal inputs and outputs.

2 Main Purpose

Our first approach to integrate statistical methodologies in industry applications combines the flexibility of statistical dialog management with the facilities that VoiceXML offers, thus introducing statistical methodologies for the development of commercial (and not strictly academic) dialog systems. Our technique employs a statistical model based on neural networks that takes into account the history of the dialog up to the current dialog state in order to predict the next system response [3]. To learn the dialog model we propose the use of dialog simulation techniques. Our approach for acquiring a dialog corpus is based on the interaction of a user simulator and a dialog manager simulator [5]. In addition, the system prompts and the grammars for ASR are implemented in VoiceXML compliant formats, for example, JSGF or SRGS.

A VoiceXML-compliant platform (such as Voxeo Evolution[2]) is used for the creation of Interactive Voice Response (IVR) applications and the provision of telephone access. Static VoiceXML files and grammars can be stored in the voice server. We propose to simplify these files by generating a VoiceXML file for each specific system prompt, as can be observed in the bottom left corner of the figure. Each file contains a reference to a grammar that defines the valid user's inputs for the corresponding system prompt.

The conversational agent selects the next system prompt (i.e. VoiceXML file) by consulting the probabilities assigned by the statistical dialog manager to each system prompt given the current state of the dialog. This module is stored in an external web server and is implemented using a data structure to store the information that is provided by the user in each dialog turn. The result generated by the statistical dialog manager informs the IVR platform about the most probable system prompt to be selected for the current dialog state. The platform just selects the corresponding VoiceXML file and reproduces it to the user.

Our second approach is focused on the development of multimodal conversational agents for mobile devices operating with the Android OS [4]. Our proposal integrates the Google Speech API to include the speech recognition functionality in a multimodal conversational agent. The development of multimodal systems involves user inputs through two or more combined modes, which usually complement spoken interaction by also adding the possibility of textual and tactile inputs provided using physical or virtual keyboards and the screen. In our contribution, we also model the context of the interaction as an additional valuable information source to be considered in the fusion process. We propose the acquisition of external context by means of the use of sensors currently supported

---

[2] http://evolution.voxeo.com/

Fig. 1. Different functionalities of the *MyCineApp* multimodal system

by Android devices. The Android sensor framework (*android.hardware* package) allows to access these sensors and acquire raw sensor data.

The dialog manager of the system is based on the previously described statistical methodology. The visual structure of the user interface (UI) is defined by means of layouts, which are defined by declaring UI elements in XML or instantiating layouts elements at runtime. Finally, we propose the use of the Google TTS API to include the text-to-speech functionality. The *android.speech.tts* package includes the classes and interfaces required to integrate text-to-speech synthesis in an Android application.

3 Demonstration

We have developed different conversational agents using the described approaches. As an example of the application of the first approach we present a conversational agent developed to provide information in Spanish about movies, current billboard, and awards in different festivals. This information has been extracted from the FilmAffinity movie recommendations website[3]. The application is internally divided into three main modules. The first module corresponds to the beginning of the interaction in which the user is welcomed and the system provides detailed instructions about the different functionalities. The second module includes the access to these functionalities, related to information about

---

[3] http://www.filmaffinity.com

movies, festivals and current billboard. The third module includes different libraries developed in PHP to access and parse the information extracted from the filmaffinity website and generate the corresponding system prompts.

As an example of the application of our second approach we present a multimodal system developed for a similar domain, providing information about films and TV programs in Android-based devices. This information is adapted taking into account the specific preferences and suggestions selected by the users. The application is divided into different modules that allow application registration, complete a user profile, access the list of TV programs and the current billboard, or obtain adapted recommendations related to these information sources. Figure 1 shows different screens of the *MyCineApp* multimodal system.

4 Conclusions

In this paper, we propose two techniques for developing conversational agents using well-known standards and operative systems like VoiceXML or Android, and also including a statistical dialog manager automatically learned from a dialog corpus. The main objective of our work is to reduce the gap between academic and industry perspectives and take the best of both methodologies. On the one hand, the effort that is required for the definition of optimal dialog strategies is reduced. On the other, VoiceXML and Android-based implementations makes it possible to benefit from the advantages of using the different devices and platforms that are already available to simplify the development of conversational agents. The paper also describes two systems developed using the described techniques and respectively providing spoken or multimodal access to users' adapted information about movies and TV programs.

Acknowledgements. This work was supported in part by Projects MINECO TEC2012-37832-C02-01, CICYT TEC2011-28626-C02-02, CAM CONTEXTS (S2009/TIC-1485).

References

1. Pieraccini, R.: The Voice in the Machine: Building Computers that Understand Speech. The MIT Press (2012)
2. Corchado, J., Tapia, D., Bajo, J.: A multi-agent architecture for distributed services and applications. Computational Intelligence 24(2), 77–107 (2008)
3. Griol, D., Hurtado, L., Segarra, E., Sanchis, E.: A Statistical Approach to Spoken Dialog Systems Design and Evaluation. Speech Communication 50(8-9), 666–682 (2008)
4. McTear, M., Callejas, Z.: Voice Application Development for Android. Packt Publishing (2013)
5. Griol, D., Carbó, J., Molina, J.: An Automatic Dialog Simulation Technique to Develop and Evaluate Interactive Conversational Agents. Applied Artificial Intelligence 27(9), 759–780 (2013)

Addressing Large Scale and Dynamic Scheduling by Nature Inspired Mechanism

Shaza Hanif, Shahab Ud Din, and Tom Holvoet

Department of Computer Science
KU Leuven

1 Introduction

Scheduling problems are faced in many application domains like manufacturing control, educational timetabling, nurse rostering, and logistics. These problems involve allocation of resources, abide constraints, and often need to optimize against user specified objectives (sometimes multi-objective). Large scale dynamic scheduling (LSDS) problems are a special class of scheduling problems which involves large number of entities (for examples in case of logistics large amount of goods to transport) and environment that can change at runtime (for example breaking of a resource and a new task appearing). The large scale and dynamism, makes LSDS problems even more challenging to address.

According to our interview with a company that provides scheduling solutions across Europe, currently in industry, more than 90% of the logistic solutions are based on centralized combinatorial optimization techniques [1]. However, in future, decentralized solutions may become a necessity for multiple reasons. For instance: 1) In logistics, With the emergence of third party logistics (3PL) [9] and fourth party logistics (4PL) [8], the companies may not want to share all their information with each other. This requires that logistic solutions to be decentralized. 2) Due to large no of participating entities in LSDS problems it will be difficult, if not impossible, to gather the information about (and from) individual entities to a single point and then process this huge information for decision making. This situation makes centralised decision making nearly infeasible.

Decentralized solutions for LSDS problems impose additional set of challenges. These include: 1) Local decisions can hardly lead to globally optimal solutions. As all the entities have only local information about themselves and the environment in their surrounding, making it harder to abide by the problem constraints. 2) Sending and receiving the information from all the participating entities is infeasible in terms of both communication and computation.

Systems in nature like colonies of ants or termites, bee hives and neural system in human mind have common characteristics with LSDS problems. They are large scale, decentralized, and all the participating entities work to achieve a global objective. These participating entities communicate with each other in order to share information. They take decentralized decisions based on this information. Thus, these systems in nature are dealing with similar challenges. These similarities inspired many researchers in the fields of Multi-Agent system (MAS) and Multi-Robots systems (MRS) to devise solutions of LSDS problems based on inspirations of systems in nature [3] commonly referred as bio-inspired and nature inspired systems. Though LSDS face some similar challenges to systems in nature, it is difficult to map solutions from nature directly to computing solutions as ready recipes. Researchers analyse fundamental principles behind natural systems and apply these fundamental principles to the computing solutions.

In this paper, we discuss our experience of applying a nature inspired coordination mechanism in two case studies of LSDS problems. The entities communicate using Delegate MAS coordination mechanism which enables us to build a decentralized software solution. The basic principle of coordination mechanism is that local decision makers are provided with the relevant information, so that they can make effective decisions. We obtained encouraging results on both LSDS problems.

In section 2 we briefly introduce the two case studies namely: pick up and delivery problem (PDP) and Ready-Mix Concrete delivery (RMC) problem. Section 3 discuss the approach and demonstration to address both case studies. A brief discussion and conclusion are described in Section 4.

2 Case Studies

In this section, we briefly introduce the two case studies from LSDS problems.

Case Study 1 – PDP
In a PDP, loads have to be transported from origins to destinations by a set of vehicles. In this case study we consider the 'dynamic pick up and delivery problem with time windows'. It can be described as follows. A new arriving task need to be allocated to a truck that can serve the request. A task is comprised of a pick up and delivery location and a delivery time window. In our problem, dynamism is caused by continually arriving requests. All the customer requests need to be satisfied by delivering the packages without violating time windows. The optimization concern is that the total distance travelled by the trucks needs to be minimized.

Case Study 2 – RMC
Dynamic RMC is a scheduling problem that is sub category of PDP in logistics. A single order typically requires a series of deliveries from multiple trucks. One delivery refers to a round trip of a truck: it loads at a production plant, travels to an order site, unloads and then returns back to a production plant. There are hard constraints while devising truck schedules due to the perishable nature of concrete. For instance: a) the time between the successive deliveries of an order may not exceed 30 minutes. b) Consider a truck is broken down during its delivery to an order, and the construction is already in progress. This introduces a dynamic event. A new truck needs to be scheduled which also has to abide by the constraint of not exceeding the time beyond 30 minutes from the last delivery. Moreover, the optimization objectives for dynamic RMC problem is to minimize: travel time by trucks; concrete wastage; and the delay from required start time of an order.

In next section, we demonstrate how nature inspired mechanisms are used to address the two problems.

3 Nature Inspired Approach and Demonstration

We address these LSDS problems by developing decentralized software for scheduling trucks. They are two MAS simulations, in which agents generate schedules by coordinating with each other. For PDP case study, our solution consists of two types of agents: Truck agents and Package agents. While for dynamic RMC problem the two types of agents are Order agents and Truck agents.

We used nature-inspired Delegate MAS [6] for coordination between agents. It is a decentralized coordination mechanism, inspired from social insects that live in colonies, like ants and termites.

Using Delegate MAS, Agents coordinate via environment: Agents disseminate their information, and later collect the relevant information from the environment [6]. They delegate part of their responsibilities to the Delegate MAS component, which communicates with the environment using light weight agents called ants. While designing the coordination mechanisms, we adhered to the patterns of Delegate MAS [7], and the relevant information is disseminated and collected periodically. Figures 1 and 2 give some insight to simulation and results

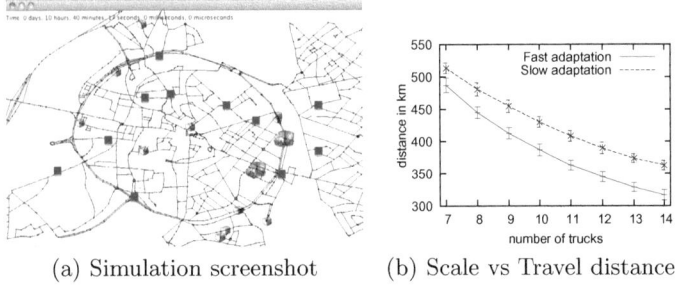

(a) Simulation screenshot (b) Scale vs Travel distance

Fig. 1. Results from case study of PDP. In (a) map of Leuven city is shown, with trucks performing transport. The blue squares show the destination of packages. (b) The distance covered is minimized with adaptation to dynamic events is faster.

of approach. The technical details about the coordination mechanisms to address PDP and RMC can be found in [5] and [4] respectively. These attempts encourage us to investigate new nature inspired approaches for solving LSDS.

4 Discussion

In this paper, we presented two case studies of LSDS problems, that are addressed by nature inspired coordination mechanism. There are two features in our solutions. First, the control is decentralized. Agents make decisions based on their localized view. Second, agents coordinate with each other through the environment, which enables the solution to dynamically adapt to the changing environment.

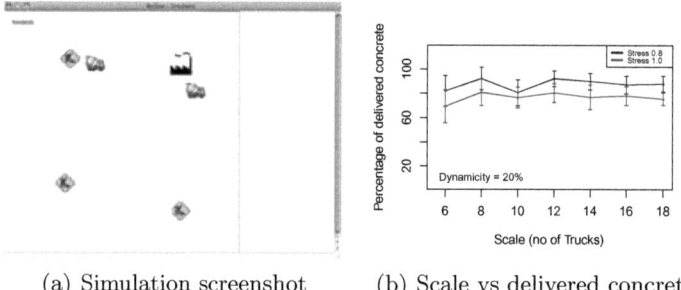

(a) Simulation screenshot (b) Scale vs delivered concrete

Fig. 2. Results from case study of RMC. In (a) the screen shows, two trucks making delivery towards three orders. (b) indicates that in different stress conditions, the coordination mechanism shows consistent performance when scale of problem is increased.

Although countless nature inspired algorithms have been presented in past decades, success of computing solutions is still far from the success of natural systems. One opinion is that since success of systems in nature is credited to natural selection of evolution [2], may be instead of engineering a computing solution, we may need to evolve it. It is also possible to semi-engineer a computing solution, and then let it evolve using evolutionary computing techniques.

References

1. Burke, E.K., Kendall, G.: Search methodologies. Springer (2005)
2. Camazine, S.: Self-organization in biological systems. Princeton University Press (2003)
3. Chiong, R. (ed.): Nature-Inspired Algorithms for Optimisation. SCI, vol. 193. Springer, Heidelberg (2009)
4. Hanif, S., Holvoet, T.: Dynamic scheduling of ready mixed concrete delivery problem using delegate MAS. In: Demazeau, Y., Corchado, J.M., Zambonelli, F., Bajo, J. (eds.) PAAMS 2014. LNCS (LNAI), vol. 8473, pp. 146–158. Springer, Heidelberg (2014)
5. Hanif, S., van Lon, R.R.S., Gui, N., Holvoet, T.: Delegate MAS for large scale and dynamic PDP: A case study. In: Brazier, F.M.T., Nieuwenhuis, K., Pavlin, G., Warnier, M., Badica, C. (eds.) Intelligent Distributed Computing V. SCI, vol. 382, pp. 23–33. Springer, Heidelberg (2011)
6. Holvoet, T., Valckenaers, P.: Exploiting the environment for coordinating agent intentions. In: Weyns, D., Van Dyke Parunak, H., Michel, F. (eds.) E4MAS 2006. LNCS (LNAI), vol. 4389, pp. 51–66. Springer, Heidelberg (2007)
7. Holvoet, T., Weyns, D., Valckenaers, P.: Patterns of delegate MAS. In: Third IEEE International Conference on Self-Adaptive and Self-Organizing Systems, SASO 2009, pp. 1–9. IEEE (2009)
8. Li, X., Liu, W., Lei, L., Zhao, Y., Ren, S.: The design and realization of four party logistics. In: IEEE International Conference on Systems, Man and Cybernetics, vol. 1, pp. 838–842. IEEE (2003)
9. Selviaridis, K., Spring, M.: Third party logistics: a literature review and research agenda. International Journal of Logistics Management 18(1), 125–150 (2007)

Illustrating an Intuitive and Informative Learning Platform for Third Level Education

Olapeju Latifat Ayoola and Eleni Mangina

`olapeju.ayoola@live.com, eleni.mangina@ucd.ie`

Keywords: e-learning, managed learning environment, adaptive personalisation, information filtering, multi-agent system.

1 Introduction

Learning has become more ubiquitous due to the constant growth of the modern technologies. Students are constantly acquiring knowledge statically or on the go via their modern devices and internet. These students need flexible learning time in order to cope with their part-time work and their rapidly declining attention span. For some students, distance proves to be an obstacle to getting the education needed hence distant learning bridges the gap for them. It produces a better way to intuitively educate and seamlessly integrate social learning behaviour in an educational or social learning environment.

Modern universities have adapted to offering unconventional learning services to all type of students, including matured students that have full-time job and undergraduates who hold part-time jobs, via virtual learning environment (VLE) or managed learning environment (MLE), which acts as a repository for courses' content and online support centre. University College Dublin (UCD) transited from its once traditional education system to an increasingly modularized and credit-based educational framework, known as UCD Horizon, which is first of its kind in Ireland. UCD Horizon enables students to take courses from different schools in the university. UCD offers its vast scale of students MLEs, such as Moodle and Blackboard, and internet connection for accessibility of resources available across each distinct school.

Research [1] was carried out to detect the effectiveness of the MLEs UCD provided. It was discovered that students don't use these MLEs intuitively; aside from downloading, submitting assignments and viewing grades which are compulsory, some useful tools such as collaborative tools are not being used. The MLEs are distinctly different hence lack transferrable skills; the only thing that they have in common is basic user information such as the user's full-name. Some students have to use both MLEs for different courses; this is rather daunting because they have to learn new skills to use both MLEs. Moreover, UCD has to pay for cost of maintenance for both MLEs. The research also showed that UCD students are constantly moving with trends hence they are avid mobile users. As of the time of this research, Moodle and Blackboard were not flexible for mobile users; this was because they lacked a mobile interface.

Though recent observation has shown that these MLEs now have a mobile interface and UCD's distant learning students tend to collaborate and socially learn via Moodle but it is not as interactive or seamless as it should be. There is still lack of activities on most of the forums offered for interactive and learning discussion. And full-time students still hardly make use of the collaborative tools. Another problem that still persists with the MLEs is that their interface layout and navigation, though not as bad as it was at the time of the research, is still somewhat complex even for a tech-savvy person.

2   Main Purpose

Over the years the hypothesis for this project has been tweaked several times, due to the constant growth of technologies, in order to develop an intuitive single-supported learning platform for UCD with the hope of embedding learning effortlessly into the UCD's students' lifestyle. The concept of the proposed and developed platform is to infuse intuitive learning environment via fusion of adaptive personalisation, social learning and collaborative learning.

Adaptive personalisation plays a major role in the development of this platform; it is used for design and content delivery. The main purpose of the project is to enhance students' learning experience and embed the learning platform into their lifestyle by enabling them to access not just content they need but to also have access to content they may find useful while they are static or on the go. There was a need to create something efficient, effective yet simple to use and understand, hence Personalised Ubiquitous Learning Platform (PULP) [2] was developed to help UCD cut down on maintenance costs and to help students learn effortlessly anywhere, anytime.

3   Demonstration

Adaptive personalisation technique such as content-based information retrieval (IR) was used to create user models for enhancing search results, while adaptive content delivery and adaptive navigation support were used to present the content intuitively. Key features such as student's academic strength, collected from assignment grades, and student's interest, collected from the student's profile were used to create the user models.

The platform is developed in Php, Java, XHTML, CSS and maintained with Bash shell scripts. A multi-agent system (MAS) that comprises of 4 benevolent agents was built with Java-based software agents middleware known as JADE to create user profiles which are used to enhance students' search results distinctively. The algorithm (*fig. 1.*) the agents used to determine the strength of students take into consideration the modules they registered for when computing all their grades. The agents then create a profile which contains strength and interest in descending order, whereby 1.0 indicates excel, 0.5 indicates pass and 0 indicates fail.

Solr/Lucene, which is an open source enterprise search platform, is used to index PULP's content, such as modules' content and student records, which are stored in the database. Solr/Lucene returns search results for search query, the agents check for any changes in student's details as stored in database and updates profile according. Another algorithm is used to re-order rank, the recommendations are pushed to the top, with a star annotation beside them and they are not relisted again at the bottom.

Algorithm ComputeAcademicStrength

Input: max grade X & student grade Y for assignment A of module M.
Output: the academic strength R of a student S for A of M.

```
    avgMaxGrade = avgGrade(X);
    grade = gradePercentage(X,Y);

    failRange = avgMaxGrade - 11;
    passRange = avgMaxGrade + 9;

    if grade > failRange & grade <= passRange then
R = pass;
    elseif grade < failRange
R = fail;
    elseif grade > passRange
R = excel;
    return R;
```

Fig. 1. The algorithm the MAS uses to determine students' strength and weakness

Information filtering will be used to illustrate PULP below:

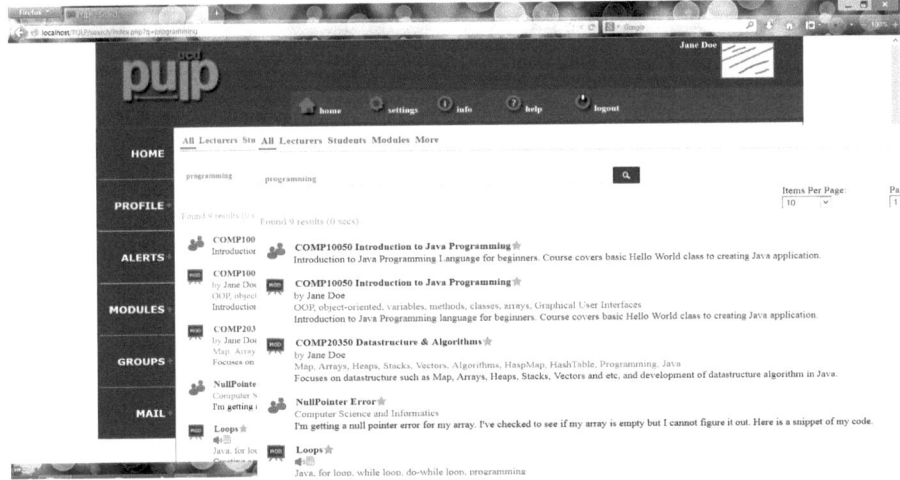

Fig. 2. Recommended search results for a student who takes Java courses and did a search for "programming"

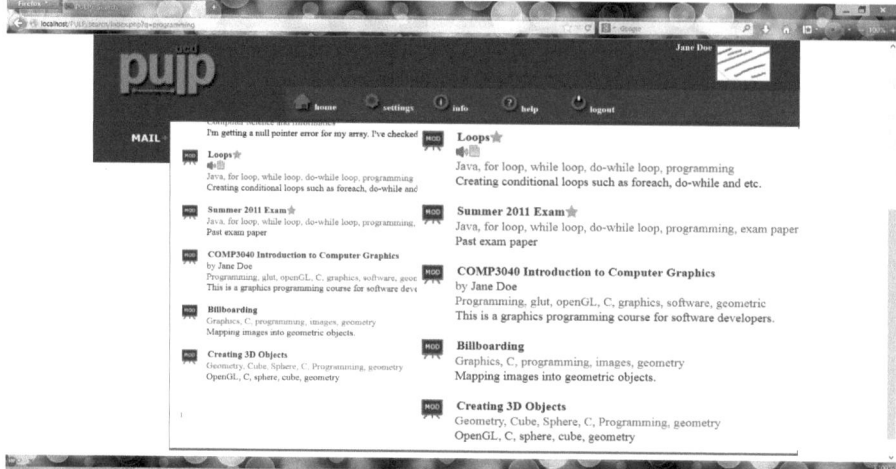

Fig. 3. This is a continuation of Fig. 2. Out of 9 results, the top 6 results are recommended, the last three results are for C programming module. The top result shows that it contains audio and document attachment (with the audio & document icons as annotation).

4 Conclusion

There is a need to offer seamless learning to modern students who are trying to balance their academic and work life. Students need access to intuitive learning platform that enables them to learn on the go or statically while they take advantage of their modern devices and internet connectivity. The internet has made unconventional learning more feasible and affordable. UCD's students need to benefit from the growth of technologies and make use of all the resources such as internet connectivity that are provided for them. PULP is developed as an intuitive and informative learning platform that offers seamless learning and enhances students' learning experience. Furthermore, it will help cut down on cost of maintaining two MLEs.

References

1. Ayoola, O.L., McGovern, E., Mangina, E., Collier, R.: Adaptive e-learning: Harnessing mobile e-learning to enhance the third level academic experience. In: International Conference on Information Communication Technologies in Education (2008)
2. Ayoola, O.L., Mangina, E.: Building an Ubiquitous and Social Learning Environment for Third Level Education. In: The Fourth International Conference on e-Learning (2013)

A Federation Layer for Query Processing over the Web of Linked Data

Xuejin Li[1], Zhendong Niu[1], Chunxia Zhang[2], and Junyue Cao[1]

[1] School of Computer Science, Beijing Institute of Technology
{xuejinli7,junyuecao}@gmail.com, zniu@bit.edu.cn
[2] School of Software, Beijing Institute of Technology
cxzhang@bit.edu.cn

Abstract. Today, the Web of Linked Data has grown considerably. Transparent query access over multiple Linked Data sources is a key challenge for many semantic applications. In this contribution, we present a query federation for executing distributed SPARQL queries on Linked Data. A sample semantic application is used to demonstrate the practicability and efficiency of the presented architecture.

Keywords: Linked Data, Semantic Web, Query Federation.

1 Introduction

In recent years, the World Wide Web has evolved from a global information space of linked documents to one where both documents and data are linked [1]. The Web of Linked Data enables new types of applications which can aggregate data from different data sources and integrate fragmentary information from multiple sources to achieve a more complete view. Answering queries across multiple distributed Linked Data sources is a key challenge for this possibility.

As a reaction to this challenge, researchers have proposed many solutions [2–5]. These approaches can be divided into three main categories: central approach, link traversal based approach and query federation. With the ever-increasing amount of data sources accessible via SPARQL endpoints, federated query processing has attracted more and more attentions [6–8]. We outline two key factors concerning the performance of federated query systems: the accuracy of query decomposition and the efficiency of distributed join execution.

In this demonstration paper we present an architecture for providing integrated access to data sources over the Web of Linked Data. The presented architecture has been implemented in our prototype system - LDMS. The system has the ability of monitoring, managing distributed RDF data sources and allows to retrieve data using SPARQL queries.

In the following we will describe the LDMS system and give a demonstration of its practical applicability in the Semantic application. In section 2 we present our main purpose and give some insights into the framework of LDMS. Next, in section 3 we present the demonstration scenario. Finally, we conclude with some remarks on future work.

2 Main Purpose

LDMS[1] is being developed to provide an efficient solution for virtually integrating Linked Data. Figure 1 shows the framework of an application built on top of LDMS. The application layer uses data retrieved by LDMS to provide users with a complete view. An semantic application which provides information about movies is employed for our demonstration (presented in section 3).

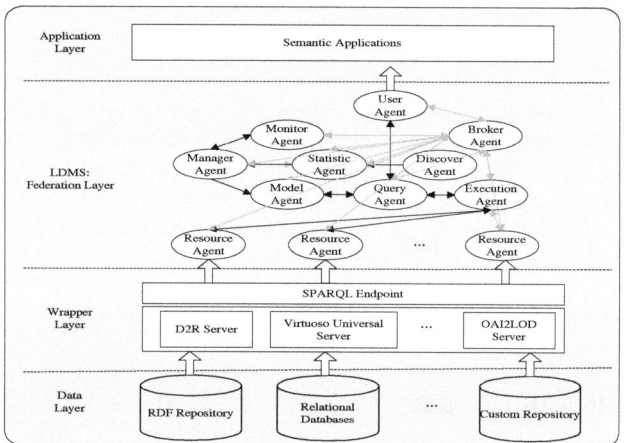

Fig. 1. LDMS System Overview

The federation layer is comprised of a network of cooperating agents communicating by means of the agent communication language ACL. Agents register their network addresses and services in the broker agent. When an agent has accomplished its work or needs help from other agents, it will send a request to the broker agent which routes this request to an appropriate agent or send back an address of the needed agent.

The query federator in LDMS is implemented in java based on Jena API. Clients submit SPARQL queries via user agents. The queries are routed by brokerage agents to specialized agents for data retrieval from remote data sources and integration of intermediate results. This federated query processing is transparent for the user, i.e., it gives the user the impression to query one single RDF graph despite the real data being distributed on the web.

The main technologies used in LDMS are:

1. Query decomposition: Query decomposition affects the performance of query systems in two ways: time performance and result completeness. LDMS uses a SPARQL GRAPH keyword based approach to make the query decomposition to be convenient and accurate.

---

[1] LDMS is only available as Java source code(eclipse project) from the SVN repository: https://svn.code.sf.net/p/semwldms/code/LDMS/trunk

2. Join order: The main goal of join order is to reduce the cost of network transmission. In LDMS, all sub-queries in a query plan are ordered by the number of intermediate results.
3. Group join: To reduce the number of requests and avoid program errors, joins are computed in a group-join which makes a compromise between pipeline join and semi-join.
4. Agent-based architecture: To achieve a flexibility and openness, LDMS adopts the technologies of agent and provides flexible, extensible means to manage data sources.

For evaluations With FedBench[2], LDMS shows a significant improvement of query performance compared to state-of-the-art federated SPARQL query systems, namely SPLENDID and FedX.

3 Demonstration

To illustrate the practicability of LDMS, define a demonstration scenario using the previously presented framework. The sample application is developed to provide information about movies. It integrates data from multiple Linked Data sources for a complete view of movies. The scenario steps from the user's point of view are summarized in the following and illustrated in figure 2.

1. Data source discovery. Discovery Agent in LDMS discovers new data sources by periodically accessing a global data registry institution.
2. Data source management. Management Agent in LDMS provides an interface for system managers to add, update or delete data sources.
3. Query submission. User Agent in LDMS verifies user queries, transfers them to query agent and returns query answers to clients.
4. Query evaluation and result presentation. In LDMS, Query Agent decomposes original queries into some sub-queries and makes query plans. Execution Agent applies its optimizations and interacts with Resource Agents for executing query plans. Then, Query Agent integrates the intermediate results returned by Execution Agent. Finally, User Agent transforms the final result answers to the application layer for presentation.

For the demonstration we simulate a real-world environment using the FedBench benchmark. It includes two subsets of data sources in the Linked Data cloud: Cross Domain and Life Science. FedBench focus on testing and analyzing the performance of federated query processing strategies on semantic data such as those of LDMS. Since LDMS provides a decoupled architecture and improves the query performance compared to existing solutions, it is valuable effort for providing an infrastructure of the development of semantic applications.

---
[2] FedBench project page:http://code.google.com/p/fbench/

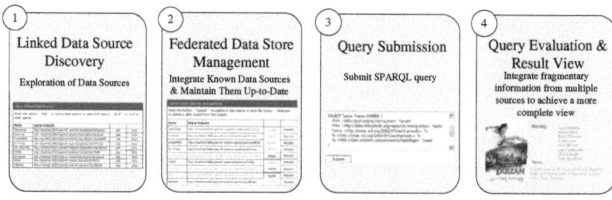

Fig. 2. Illustration of the Demonstration Workflow

4 Conclusions

In this paper we have presented an infrastructure for developing semantic applications. LDMS uses the SPARQL GRAPH based approach to decompose original queries and the group-join approach to improve distributed join operations. Besides, it implements a decoupled architecture which is the key to system scalability and extensibility. The evaluation based on FedBench benchmark indicates a significant improvement about query response time. In the future version, we propose to combine more advanced optimization techniques into LDMS for further improving query performance.

Acknowledgment. This work was supported by the National Natural Science Foundation of China (#61272361, #61370137).

References

1. Bizer, C., Heath, T., Berners-Lee, T.: Linked data-the story so far. International Journal on Semantic Web and Information Systems (IJSWIS) 5(3), 1–22 (2009)
2. Quilitz, B., Leser, U.: Querying distributed RDF data sources with SPARQL. In: Bechhofer, S., Hauswirth, M., Hoffmann, J., Koubarakis, M. (eds.) ESWC 2008. LNCS, vol. 5021, pp. 524–538. Springer, Heidelberg (2008)
3. Hartig, O., Bizer, C., Freytag, J.-C.: Executing SPARQL queries over the web of linked data. In: Bernstein, A., Karger, D.R., Heath, T., Feigenbaum, L., Maynard, D., Motta, E., Thirunarayan, K. (eds.) ISWC 2009. LNCS, vol. 5823, pp. 293–309. Springer, Heidelberg (2009)
4. Ladwig, G., Tran, T.: Linked data query processing strategies. In: Patel-Schneider, P.F., Pan, Y., Hitzler, P., Mika, P., Zhang, L., Pan, J.Z., Horrocks, I., Glimm, B. (eds.) ISWC 2010, Part I. LNCS, vol. 6496, pp. 453–469. Springer, Heidelberg (2010)
5. Langegger, A., Wöß, W., Blöchl, M.: A semantic web middleware for virtual data integration on the web. In: Bechhofer, S., Hauswirth, M., Hoffmann, J., Koubarakis, M. (eds.) ESWC 2008. LNCS, vol. 5021, pp. 493–507. Springer, Heidelberg (2008)
6. Schwarte, A., Haase, P., Hose, K., Schenkel, R., Schmidt, M.: FedX: Optimization techniques for federated query processing on linked data. In: Aroyo, L., Welty, C., Alani, H., Taylor, J., Bernstein, A., Kagal, L., Noy, N., Blomqvist, E. (eds.) ISWC 2011, Part I. LNCS, vol. 7031, pp. 601–616. Springer, Heidelberg (2011)
7. Görlitz, O., Staab, S.: Splendid: Sparql endpoint federation exploiting void descriptions. In: COLD (2011)
8. Stuckenschmidt, H., Vdovjak, R., Houben, G.J., Broekstra, J.: Index structures and algorithms for querying distributed rdf repositories. In: Proceedings of the 13th international conference on World Wide Web, pp. 631–639. ACM (2004)

Market Garden: A Simulation Environment for Research and User Experience in Smart Grids

Bart Liefers[1], Felix N. Claessen[1], Eric Pauwels[1],
Peter A.N. Bosman[1], and Han La Poutré[1,2]

[1] Centrum Wiskunde & Informatica (CWI)
P.O. Box 94079, 1090 GB Amsterdam, The Netherlands
[2] TUDelft, Delft, The Netherlands
{liefers,claessen,pauwels,bosman,hlp}@cwi.nl

Abstract. Market Garden is a scalable research environment and demonstration tool, in which market mechanisms for smart energy systems and the interaction between end users, traders, system operators, and markets can be simulated. Users can create scenarios in a user-friendly editor in which a hierarchical market architecture and a model of the physical grid can be defined. Individual market mechanisms are set up in a modular fashion, which means they can easily be coupled and interchanged. A visualiser in which the results can be explored in a graphical and intuitive way is included, making Market Garden very suitable for user experience and demonstration purposes.

Keywords: Electricity markets, simulation, user experience.

1 Introduction

In electrical power systems, a transition towards a more dynamic, decentralized, and interactive structure takes place. In recent decades, electricity wholesale markets were introduced that facilitate competition among a limited number of large energy suppliers. However, trading energy in the competitive environment of the wholesale market subject to the physical constraints of the transmission network is complex. This has inspired many researchers to develop simulation tools (e.g. AMES[1], EMCAS[2], MASCEM[3]), in order to study market design, bidding strategies, ahead planning, and balancing at the transmission level.

However, due to their focus on wholesale power, these simulation tools lack the link to the retail markets, the end users (producing or consuming energy), and the distribution grid. This link is crucial, because many other innovations occur in and around the distribution grid, like smart houses and electric vehicles. Furthermore, distributed generation (wind, solar, micro-CHP) makes up an increasingly large part of our energy supply. These developments give rise to new challenges and opportunities for techniques that enable the exploitation of the available resources more efficiently. PowerMatcher[4] for example focusses on matching supply and demand by letting end users react to dynamic energy prices. However, this system relies solely on real-time balancing. Ahead planning is important for e.g. generators that face startup time, or electric vehicles that need to be fully charged in time.

Regarding the simulation of smart energy systems, Power TAC[5] is a simulation environment in which the retail market is open to energy trading agents in a competitive setting. It includes a wholesale market and customer models, while the trading agents are created by competing researchers. This ensures the traders are competitive, but the market design in which they act is fixed. This can become restrictive, since it is not yet clear what mechanisms will be needed in the future, and different scenarios may require different mechanisms.

In this paper we present Market Garden[1], a simulation environment for research and user experience in smart grids. Like Power TAC, Market Garden focusses on the link between end users and wholesale trading, and the possibility to test trading strategies in a competitive environment. Important distinctive features of Market Garden are the following. The market mechanisms in Market Garden are modular: A library of basic market mechanisms is included, and developers can easily develop and add new mechanisms. The included mechanisms are flexible, allowing trade on arbitrary time scales rather than within fixed timeslots. The simulation of traded energy is combined and directly related with a model of the physical grid, which allows us to include transmission losses and ancillary services. Furthermore, simulations in Market Garden can be run in a hierarchical and distributed computation environment, ensuring scalability to larger simulations, and allowing it to include possibly millions of nodes.

2 Main Purpose

Market Garden aims to give experience to end users, traders, or e.g. Distribution System Operators (DSOs) in a smart grid environment. Market results, energy prosumption, network flows, and market organisation can all be visualised in an intuitive way. This makes Market Garden excellently suitable for demonstrations.

With Market Garden, we wish to study market design and timing. The time between trading and delivery of electricity can significantly influence the behaviour of traders in a specific market. This is because for most devices the accuracy of predicted energy output increases as we get closer to real time, and traders may face startup costs or opportunity costs. The market mechanisms in Market Garden have parametrizable time schedules (see below for more details), and thus enable the type of timing-based research that we wish to do.

Another concept of interest is the interaction between end users and retail traders. Most end users are too insignificant to influence market prices, and therefore only react to them. However, the prices form based on the equilibrium between supply and demand. So, from the point of view of a market designer the prices are a consequence of the behaviour of the trading parties, while from

---

[1] In [6] an informal introduction for a broad audience to an early version of Market Garden was given.

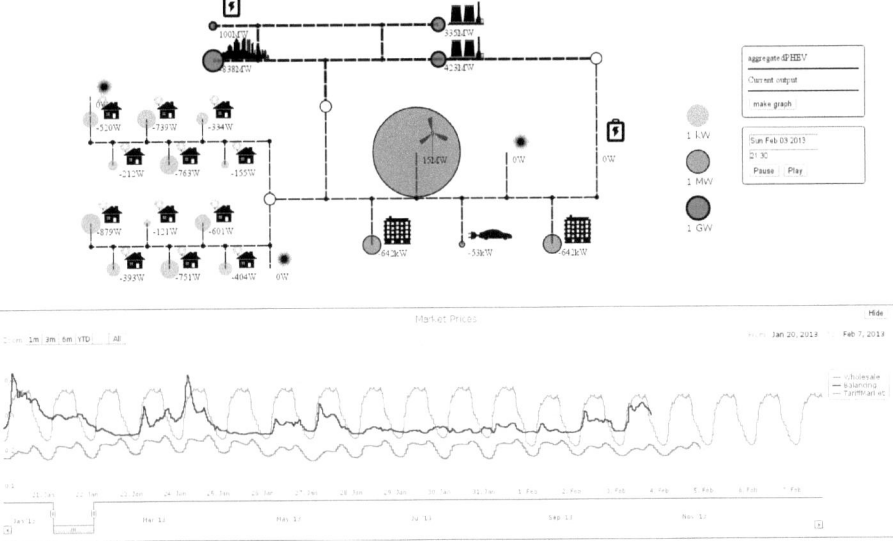

Fig. 1. A screenshot of a part of the visualisation. The green and red circles in the network represent, respectively, energy production and consumption at nodes. The panels at the right provide more detailed information and options. The chart at the bottom depicts the fluctuation of market prices. The green, blue and black lines respectively represent the unit prices of a time-of-use tariff, wholesale, and balancing power.

the point of view of an energy end user the prices define their behaviour. With Market Garden we wish to study this interaction more closely.

3 Demonstration

At the heart of Market Garden is the DSO. The DSO monitors the energy supply and demand throughout the network. The network may contain several points of flexibility (ancillary services such as spinning reserves or batteries). The DSO in Market Garden will issue them according to the current needs of the network, such that the total energy loss due to transmission and distribution is minimized.

Nodes in the network represent sets of energy producing or consuming entities. Energy end users can therefore be represented by nodes. For any given time interval in the past, a node can be asked for its energy prosumption. The DSO can aggregate these values to a supply or demand at a substation. This aggregated value can be used as input for a node, representing a subnetwork, in another simulation that runs simultaneously, but possibly on a different machine. Extensive hierarchies can thus be built, yielding a scalable system.

Within a simulation, multiple wholesale markets (e.g. real-time, intra-day) can be defined, on which futures (binding commitments for energy in future timeslots) can be traded. The markets have parametrizable time schedules, so market open and close horizons, timeslot durations, and repetition intervals can be specified by the user. Retailers interact with end users by offering tariffs that define the energy prices to which the end users can subscribe. Time-of-use tariffs can be defined, where prices vary on arbitrary time scales (e.g. hourly, weekly or monthly). The retailer is responsible for balancing the energy prosumption of its customers, and can trade on the wholesale markets to achieve this. Imbalances that may occur in real time are resolved by the DSO. The costs for this will be assigned to the retailers through the balancing market present in the simulation.

To ease working with Market Garden, user friendly interfaces are included. Network descriptions and market timing can be defined in an editor. A visualiser can be connected to a running simulation, or it can be started from a log of a previously run simulation. For demonstration purposes, the power flow in the network can be animated and the market organisation can be visualised. The user can create charts of energy prosumption, market prices or network flow in an intuitive and interactive way. A screenshot can be seen in Fig.1.

4 Conclusion

We presented Market Garden, a software environment that can provide valuable insights in energy trading in smart energy systems, and can serve as a unique, scalable research environment in this area. With Market Garden, novel market mechanisms can be tested and validated in an interactive and competitive setting, making it excellently suitable for both research and demonstration purposes. Substantial scalability is achieved, because Market Garden can run in a distributed computation setting. Finally, Market Garden includes a user-friendly visualisation. This can help scientists understand which mechanism works best in a given setting, and policy makers in designing laws and regulations that ensure societal benefits.

Acknowledgements. This project was supported by ICT Labs, as part of the European Institute of Innovation & Technology (EIT).

References

1. Li, H., Tesfatsion, L.: Development of Open Source Software for Power Market Research: The AMES Test Bed. Journal of Energy Markets 2(2), 111–128 (2009)
2. Koritarov, V.: Real-world Market Representation with Agents. IEEE Power and Energy Magazine 2(4), 39–46 (2004)
3. Praca, I., Ramos, C., Vale, Z., Cordeiro, M.: MASCEM: A Multiagent System that Simulates Competitive Electricity Markets. IEEE Intelligent Systems 18(6), 54–60 (2003)
4. Kok, J.K., Warmer, C.J., Kamphuis, I.G.: PowerMatcher: Multiagent Control in the Electricity Infrastructure. In: AAMAS 2005: Proceedings of the 4th Int. Joint Conf. on Autonomous Agents and Multiagent Systems, pp. 75–82 (2005)
5. Ketter, W., Collins, J., Reddy, P.: Power TAC: A Competitive Economic Simulation of the Smart Grid. Energy Economics 39, 262–270 (2013)
6. Claessen, F.N., Höning, N., Liefers, B., La Poutré, H., Bosman, P.A.N.: Market Garden: A Scalable Research Environment for Heterogeneous Electricity Markets. ERCIM News 92, 25–26 (2013)

Multi-agent Multi-level Cartographic Generalisation in CartAGen

Adrien Maudet[1], Guillaume Touya[1], Cécile Duchêne[1], and Sébastien Picault[2]

[1] Université Paris Est, IGN, Laboratoire COGIT, Saint-Mandé, France
{adrien.maudet,guillaume.touya,cecile.duchene}@ign.fr
[2] LIFL, Université Lille 1, Villeneuve d'Ascq, France
sebastien.picault@lifl.fr

Abstract. The objective of cartographic generalisation is to simplify geographic data in order to create legible maps when scale decreases. This demonstration presents the implementation of a work in progress, aiming at defining a multi-agent, multi-level solution for generalisation. The demonstration introduces the basics of cartographic generalisation and shows some aspects of the model currently being developed, including parameterisation and detailed execution of some interactions, as well as results.

Keywords: Cartography, Cartographic Generalisation, Multi-Level Modelling, Spatialised Problems, Interaction-Oriented Design, Constraints Solving.

1 Introduction

Generalisation is a process of the cartography domain, aiming at adapting the level of details of geographic objects to a given scale. Different agent-oriented approaches have been used to automate the generalisation process, e.g. [1;2;3;4]. A work in progress [5] aims at enhancing multi-level representation in agent-oriented in order to deal with more complex relation between objects. The proposed model is based on the PADAWAN model [6], initially designed for multi-level simulation, which has been adapted to perform constraint problem solving dedicated to the specific cartographic generalisation application case. In this demonstration, we show an implementation of this model in CartAGen [7], a platform developed and used for research in cartographic generalisation, which is based on the GeOxygen project[1].

2 Main Purpose

Geographic information is stored in vector geographic databases, where objects (e.g. buildings, roads) are stored with theirs geometries (e.g. points, polylines, polygons), and attributes (e.g. nature of a building, administrative status of a road). During the map creation process, these objects are drawn with given symbols, and depending on the map scale the objects may need to be simplified because room to display the same

---

[1] http://oxygene-project.sourceforge.net/

portion of the real world is smaller at a smaller scale. Modifications need to be done in order to fit the visual perception levels of the final user.

Such readability requirements can be expressed through constraints (e.g. buildings must be above a minimum size, symbols have to be sufficiently spaced). In order to satisfy these constraints, objects may be suppressed, moved, or get their geometry modified, using different algorithms.

The orchestration of these operations is a complex process, because, to generalise one object, other objects, with which constraints may be identified (e.g. a building aligned with others buildings, a road parallel to another road), must be taken into account in order to use appropriate algorithms, with appropriate parameters. In order to automate the generalisation process, agent-oriented solutions were proposed, where geographical objects are described as autonomous agents interacting in order to satisfy its constraints and generalise themselves. Depending on the models, two kinds of interactions are considered:

- Hierarchical interactions (e.g. a building and the urban block, i.e. the portion of space bounded by roads, it belongs to).
- Transversal interactions (e.g. a building with a neighbouring building).

We are developing a model, based on the PADAWAN paradigm, in order to represent interactions and levels used for generalisation in a generic way. PADAWAN is interaction oriented, and interactions are assigned to agents in interactions matrices. In our approach, PADAWAN was modified in order to fit the constraint oriented aspect of generalisation. An agent will evaluate its constraints and choose an interaction to execute. More details on the agent behaviour are given in [5].

Fig. 1. Screenshot of CartAGen with data loaded

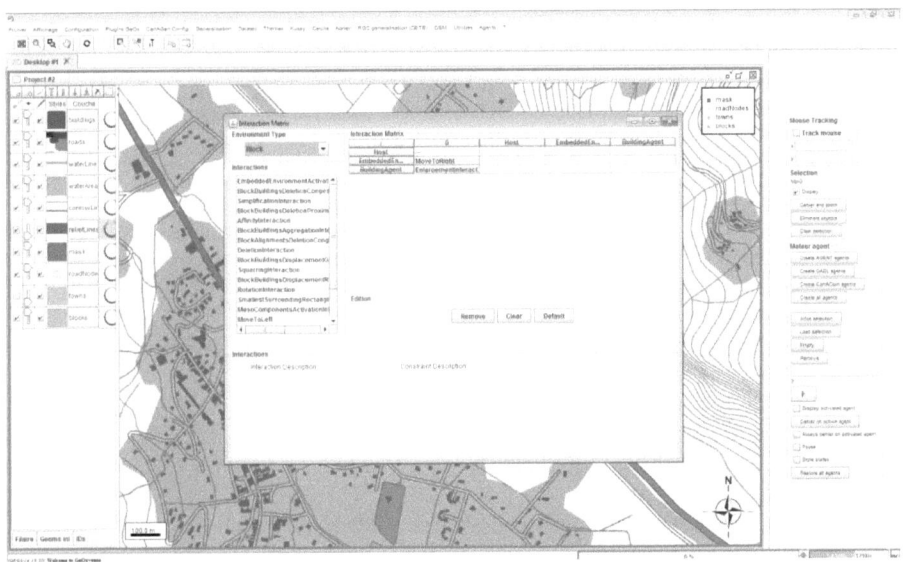

Fig. 2. Screenshot of CartAGen with interactions matrices editor

3 Demonstration

CartAGen is a module of the GeOxygene project, developed in Java at COGIT laboratory. It allows to load, symbolise and display geographical data from various sources, and contains various algorithms to analyse and modify the objects geometries.

In this demonstration, we show the different steps of generalisation using the implementation of our model:

— Loading and symbolising data.
— Creating agents and assign interactions to them in interaction matrices.
— Launching the multi-agent process for a small part of the loaded data.
— Showing the result of generalisation process.

4 Conclusion

This demonstration shows the complexity of the automated cartographic generalisation process. It shows the different steps of a whole generalisation process on a small data set, and a view of some interactions in a detailed way, in order to understand the behaviour of agents. The adapted PADAWAN model is a work in progress, and will be further improved and developed, in order to give solutions for other generalisation issues.

References

1. Baeijs, C., Demazeau, Y., Alvares, L.: SIGMA: Application of Multi-Agent Systems to Cartographic Generalization. In: Perram, J., Van de Velde, W. (eds.) MAAMAW 1996. LNCS, vol. 1038, pp. 163–176. Springer, Heidelberg (1996)
2. Barrault, M., Regnauld, N., Duchêne, C., Haire, K., Baeijs, C., Demazeau, Y., Hardy, P., Mackaness, W., Ruas, A., Weibel, R.: Integrating Multi-agent, Object-oriented, And Algorithmic Techniques For Improved Automated Map Generalization. In: 20th International Cartographic Conference, vol. 3, pp. 2110–2116 (2001)
3. Duchêne, C., Ruas, A., Cambier, C.: The CartACom model: transforming cartographic features into communicating agents for cartographic generalisation. International Journal of Geographic Information Science 26(9), 1533–1562 (2012)
4. Gaffuri, J., Duchêne, C., Ruas, A.: Object-field relationships modelling in an agent-based generalisation model. In: Proceedings of 11th ICA workshop on Generalisation and Multiple Representation, Montpellier, France (2008)
5. Maudet, A., Touya, G., Duchêne, C., Picault, S.: Representation of Interactions in a Multi-Level Multi-Agent Model for Cartography Constraint Solving. In: Demazeau, Y., Corchado, J.M., Zambonelli, F., Bajo, J. (eds.) PAAMS 2014. LNCS (LNAI), vol. 8473, Springer, Heidelberg (2014)
6. Picault, S., Mathieu, P.: An Interaction-Oriented Model for Multi-Scale Simulation. In: 22nd International Joint Conference on Artificial Intelligence (IJCAI/AAAI), Barcelona, Spain, pp. 332–337 (2011)
7. Renard, J., Gaffuri, J., Duchêne, C.: Capitalisation problem in research –example of a new platform for generalisation: CartAGen. In: 12th ICA Workshop on Generalisation and Multiple Representation, Zürich, Switzerland (2010)

An Agent-Based Approach for the Design of the Future European Air Traffic Management System

Martin Molina, Jorge Martin, and Sergio Carrasco

Department of Artificial Intelligence
Technical University of Madrid
Campus de Montegancedo S/N 28660 Madrid, Spain
`martin.molina@upm.es, {scarrasco,jmartin}@fi.upm.es`

Abstract. This paper describes an agent-based approach for the simulation of air traffic management (ATM) in Europe that was designed to help analyze proposals for future ATM systems. This approach is able to represent new collaborative decision processes for flow traffic management, it uses an intermediate level of abstraction (useful for simulations at larger scales), and was designed to be a practical tool (open and reusable) for the development of different ATM studies. It was successfully applied in three studies related to the design of future ATM systems in Europe.

Keywords: Agent-based modeling, agent-based simulation, air traffic management system.

1 Introduction

In recent years, important initiatives have been developed to modernize air traffic management (ATM) systems. For example, the SESAR (Single European Sky ATM Research) program is an ambitious research and development initiative funded by the European Union, Eurocontrol and industry. The ultimate goal of SESAR is to develop a future ATM system for Europe, ensuring the safety and fluidity of air transport over the next thirty years, making flying more environmentally friendly and reducing the costs of air traffic management [4].

This paper summarizes the results of our research work[1] under the CASSIOPEIA project (Complex Adaptive Systems for Optimization of Performance in ATM) that that we developed in the context of the SESAR program. In our approach, we developed a solution to simulate new collaboration strategies of ATM stakeholders in large geographic areas at an intermediate level of abstraction that is between the microscopic and macroscopic level. Our approach was developed as a practical tool that is open and reusable for different ATM problems, and it was applied successfully in three different ATM studies.

---

[1] See more details about our agent-based approach in [3].

2 Main Purpose

The goal of the CASSIOPEIA project project was to propose a modeling approach, using techniques of complex systems and paradigms of computer science, that could provide policy-makers with the means to understand and explore initiatives that affect complex ATM networks, allowing them to test potential concepts, regulations and mechanisms to manage delay propagation, capacity limits, network congestion, and other ATM phenomena. This project was envisioned as a solution to facilitate an understanding of the cause-effect relation between policy decisions in different sectors of aviation and air traffic performance for different scopes and scales of application of regulations.

In general, agent-based approaches have been successfully applied to model ATM systems [1] [2] [5]. However, the design of future ATM systems, as it is defined by the goals of the SESAR programme in Europe, presents new challenges in agent-based modeling and simulation such as: (1) modeling new decision levels in ATM systems (such as strategic decisions related to flow and capacity management with longer temporal horizons), (2) designing new representation methods to simulate at a larger scale (e.g., multinational geographic areas in Europe) taking into account limitations concerning existing data, and (3) creating new practical tools (more easily available to the research community) to support the development of new ATM studies. In the following sections, we summarize our agent-based approach in CASSIOPEIA that we designed that addresses these challenges.

3 The Agent-Based Approach and Applications

The agent-based model in the CASSIOPEIA project includes agents corresponding to different ATM stakeholders. For example, there are agents such as network managers, airlines (with agent subclasses: network airline, cargo airline, low-cost airline, etc.), airports (with information such as geographic location, category, etc.), and aircraft (with information such as model, capacity, CO emissions, weight, etc.). The model also includes objects related to the environment and general decision-making processes such as flight plans, time slots, and geographical sectors. The agent models follow a BDI approach, with beliefs, goals and plans.

This model includes algorithms to simulate collaborative decision-making processes corresponding to future ATM systems. For example, we implemented algorithms that simulate how airlines interact to bid and sell air traffic slots to reschedule flight plans with lower costs. We follow an intermediate level abstraction with a stochastic approach to simulate certain air traffic processes. For example, we follow this approach to simulate how airlines coordinate aircrafts in the presence of delays. The stochastic approach is used to simulate the movement of aircraft between airports, abstracting details about delays [3].

This agent-based approach was used in three different studies in the CASSIOPEIA project: (1) analyze the effects of new environmental regulations (e.g., restrictions of night traffic at certain airports to reduce noise pollution), (2) analyze the effect of capacity constraints considering as a new strategy that airlines can exchange traffic slots, and (3) analyze the effect of new methods of speed adjustment for aircraft based on environmental conditions. For these studies, we used data on air transportation in Europe from several sources. The majority of the data was acquired from ALL-FT+, a dataset collected by the PRISME group from Eurocontrol. Each study included several simulations with different input data corresponding to various scenarios. For example, for the first study, we used data from 79,852 flights, 838 airports and 84 airlines and generated approximately 4,500 interaction messages (during one of the simulations).

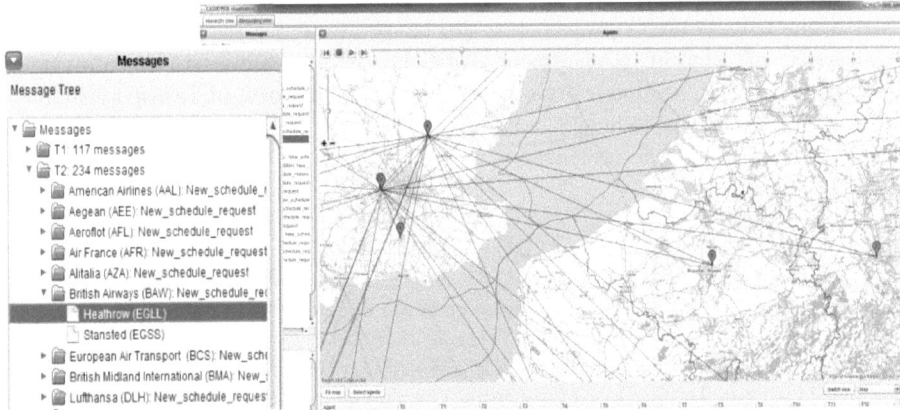

Fig. 1. Visualization tool showing agent interaction messages

The software architecture in the CASSIOPEIA project was designed to be a general tool for use in various ATM studies. Agent models are specified using the XML declarative language, together with algorithms implemented in the Java language for agent plans, with reusable libraries of classes. The software architecture was developed by integrating open software tools (Jadex, MySQL, OpenStreetMaps, etc.) to facilitate reusability at reduced costs. The architecture includes a visualization tool, developed in this project, to visualize complex agent interactions with large numbers of messages. This tool aggregates information using different dimensions (spatial, temporal, types of messages, types of agents, etc.) and presents the information using animations on geographic maps and specific types of hierarchies and tables (Figure 1). The software architecture was reused to develop the agent models for the three studies. We reused 78% of the agent specifications in the XML language, 72% of the Java code and 91% of the database design.

4 Conclusions

The design of future ATM systems, as it is defined by the SESAR program in Europe, presents new challenges for agent-based modeling and simulation. We designed an agent-based approach in the CASSIOPEIA project to address theses challenges with new algorithms for distributed-collaboration decision making and intermediate abstraction levels for simulations using stochastic approaches. Our software architecture in CASSIOPEIA was designed as a general tool and was used in three ATM studies with high percentages of reuse (more than 70%) of the different components. In comparison to previous related studies, we simulated new ATM decision processes, and they were applied to larger areas (with hundreds of airports and longer temporal scales).

Acknowledgements. The research presented in this paper was carried out under the CASSIOPEIA project. This project received financial support from Eurocontrol under the SESAR program (Single European Sky ATM Research). The consortium members of the CASSIOPEIA project were the Innaxis Research Institute, the Technical University of Madrid (Department Artificial Intelligence and Department of Air Transport) and the University of Westminster (Department of Transport Studies). The authors would like to thank a member of our research group, Nataliia Stulova, for the implementation of the visualization tool.

References

1. Agogino, A.K., Tumer, K.: A multiagent approach to managing air traffic flow. Autonomous Agents and Multi-Agent Systems 24(1), 1–25 (2012)
2. Campbell, K., Cooper, W., Greenbaum, D., Wojcik, L.: Modeling Distributed Human Decision-Making in Traffic Flow Management Operations. In: Third USA/Europe Air Traffic Management Research and Development Seminar. The MITRE Corporation, McLean (2000)
3. Molina, M., Carrasco, S., Martin, J.: Agent-Based Modeling and Simulation for the Design of the Future European Air Traffic Management System: The Experience of CASSIOPEIA. In: Corchado, J.M., et al. (eds.) PAAMS 2014 Workshops. CCIS, vol. 430, pp. 22–33. Springer, Heidelberg (2014)
4. Sesar: Single European Sky ATM Research, http://www.sesarju.eu
5. Wolfe, S., Jarvis, P., Enomoto, F., Sierhuis, M., Putten, B., Sheth, K.: A Multi-Agent Simulation of Collaborative Air Traffic Flow Management. In: Bazzan, A., Klugl, F. (eds.) Multi-agent Systems for Traffic and Transportation. IGI Global Publishing (2009)

Multi-robot System for Vacuum Cleaning Domain

Agris Nikitenko, Janis Grundspenkis, Aleksis Liekna, Martins Ekmanis,
Guntis Kulikovskis, and Ilze Andersone

Riga Technical University,
Faculty of Computer Science and Information Technology,
Department of Systems Theory and Design,
1 Kalku Street, Riga, LV 1658, Latvia
{agris.nikitenko,janis.grundspenkis,aleksis.liekna,
martins.ekmanis,guntis.kulikovskis,ilze.andersone}@rtu.lv

Abstract. This demonstration paper presents a prototype multi-robot system of vacuum cleaning robots. System was designed with the aim to join multiple robots in a team able to accomplish tasks that are beyond the capabilities of a single robot.

Keywords: Multi-robot systems, vacuum cleaning.

1 Introduction

Vacuum-cleaning robots are becoming more popular among household users. Such robots are capable of cleaning individual rooms and small offices. Nevertheless, cleaning large indoor areas such as hangars is still a challenge, which had not been addressed by commercial applications yet.. To address this challenge we have developed a multi-robot vacuum-cleaning system. We use existing iRobot Roomba [1] vacuum cleaning robots as robot platforms. We improved them with additional capabilities required for participating in a multi-robot system by attaching a custom-made extension on top of the robot. This extension includes a computational element with an Intel Atom[2] processor, a web-camera for localization purposes, additional bumper sensor and an additional battery. The added computational element provides means to address localization, map building and path planning as well as interaction functionality with team members.

System architecture is partially centralized, where a central server plays the central role by allocating tasks to individual robots and merging individually created robot maps. When a task is assigned to a robot, the task is executed autonomously and the server has no direct control over the low-level actions of the robots.

System operates in the following way. User initiates the task allocation procedure by requesting a cleaning operation using the user interface. This request is then sent to server and it spreads the whole cleaning area into smaller sub-regions called responsibility areas. Each robot is assigned a responsibility area. After receiving such

---

[1] http://www.irobot.com
[2] http://www.intel.com/content/www/us/en/processors/atom/atom-processor.html

an assignment, robot travels to the responsibility area and performs the cleaning operation. After the operation is complete, next unassigned responsibility area is assigned to that robot. The process continues until all areas are properly cleaned.

2 Main Purpose

The main purpose of the developed solution is to join multiple existing robots in a multi-robot system to accomplish tasks that are beyond capabilities of a single robot. Particular task can be defined as area coverage or sweeping task where multiple robots are required to cover a particular area, however we focus on the overall system architecture and implementation not the sweeping algorithms themselves. The following constraints are assumed to be held: a) capabilities of a single robot are not enough to cover the whole area; b) each robot is capable of autonomously covering some part of the area; c) a task can be decomposed into subtasks in such a way that each subtask can be accomplished by a single robot. An example of such a task is cleaning a large area warehouse using vacuum-cleaning robots that are designed to clean a hotel room – no robot is capable of cleaning the whole warehouse in a reasonable time, but the warehouse can be divided into smaller areas each of which can be cleaned by a single robot.

We use iRobot Roomba vacuum cleaners as robot platforms. These robots already have a built-in algorithm for cleaning a designated area. Our objective was to use these robots as a basis and extend their capabilities to produce a multi-robot system. To reach the set objective the following interrelated challenges were addressed:

- *Task Allocation.* To use the built-in cleaning algorithm of the robots, they must each operate in a distinct designated area. This was achieved by splitting the total cleaning area into smaller ones called responsibility areas which are then assigned to individual robots.
- *Localization.* For the robot to be able to travel to assigned responsibility area and perform cleaning afterwards, it is essential for the robot to "know" at least the relative coordinates of itself and the target area. To provide the necessary means of localization, we use a combination of artificial landmarks (glyphs) observable by robot onboard camera and robot odometry (wheel encoders) to estimate robot position and angular direction in the environment. Our approach is based on assumption that the indoor environment is available for landmark use – it means that it is possible to install specially designed landmarks for robot positioning in global coordinates. Details on applied localization techniques are published in [1] and [2].
- *Path Planning.* To travel safely while avoiding obstacles, an obstacle-free plan for the path towards the goal area must be constructed. We use Rapidly-Exploring Random Tree (RRT) algorithm [3] for robot path planning. The aim is to find the shortest path from current position to destination point while avoiding obstacles in the way. A modified version of original RRT algorithm is used as published in [4].
- *Map Building.* To construct an obstacle free-plan, it is essential to know the coordinates of the obstacles, as well as the source and destination positions. This is why a map of the environment is required. Robots build their map using only the factory-installed iRobot Roomba sensors. We do not add any additional sensors motivated by sustaining reasonable cost of the solution. More specifically we use short-range infrared and bumper sensors to detect obstacles in the environment. We start with an

empty map of the environment with (approximately) predefined size. Map is populated with information about obstacles and "free spaces" while robots move in the environment. Refer to [5] for detailed information on applied mapping algorithm.
- *System Architecture.* Organization and management of multi-robot system must be supported by appropriate software architecture. To address this problem a partially decentralized solution is adapted in the following way. An application runs onboard each robot and is responsible for the low-level control of the robot and serves as individual localization and mapping source. A server component is also introduced and serves as a central point of the system. Detailed description of system architecture can be found in [1].
- *Robot Hardware Enhancements.* To cope with challenges previously described in this list, a specialized hardware platform is designed and developed. This platform is attached on top of iRobot Roomba vacuum-cleaning robots. It consists of a computational element with Intel Atom processor, a rechargeable battery to support the computational element, a web camera for glyph recognition used in localization and an additional bumper sensor to compensate extra height of the platform. Only a few screws and a UART cable are necessary to connect the platform to an existing robot – no interference with internal robot design is required.

3 Demonstration

Demonstration consists of 8 minutes long video showing the system in operation, complimented by the interviews of main contributors (see Fig. 1). The interview include complementary information about the used methods, approaches and achieved results as well as outlines the future plans of the team.

Fig. 1. System operation

4 Conclusions

By solving the challenges of task allocation, localization, path planning, map building, system architecture and robot hardware enhancements, a working multi-robot system is produced, successfully joining multiple robots in a unified system capable of completing tasks that are beyond the capabilities of a single robot.

Acknowledgements. This work has been partly supported by ERDF European Regional Development Fund project 2010/0258/2DP/2.1.1.1.0/10/APIA/VIAA/005 Development of Intelligent Multiagent Robotics System Technology.

References

1. Liekna, A., Nikitenko, A.: Architecture and .NET Implementation of Multi-Robot Management System. Applied Computer Systems 14, 59–66 (2013)
2. Nikitenko, A., Liekna, A., Ekmanis, M., Kulikovskis, G., Andersone, I.: Single Robot Localisation Approach for Indoor Robotic Systems through Integration of Odometry and Artificial Landmarks. Applied Computer Systems 14, 50–58 (2013)
3. LaValle, S.M., Kuffner Jr., J.J.: Rapidly-exploring random trees: Progress and prospects. In: Proceedings Workshop on the Algorithmic Foundations of Robotics (2000)
4. Nikitenko, A., Ekmanis, M., Liekna, A.: RRTs Postprocessing for Uncertain Environments. In: Proceedings of the 2013 International Conference on Systems, Control and Informatics (SCI 2013), pp. 171–179 (2013)
5. Andersone, I., Liekna, A., Nikitenko, A.: Mapping Implementation for Multi-robot System with Glyph Localisation. Applied Computer Systems 14, 67–72 (2013)

receteame.com: A Persuasive Social Recommendation System

Javier Palanca, Stella Heras, Vicente Botti, and Vicente Julián

Departamento de Sistemas Informaticos y Computacion
Universitat Politècnica de València
Camino de Vera S/N 46022 Valencia, Spain
{jpalanca,sheras,vbotti,vinglada}@dsic.upv.es

1 Introduction

Over the last few years, the emergence of social networks has changed the main activities performed by users on the Internet, going from a mere search and navigation over stored information to a direct interaction with other users. Users have evolved from being consumers of information to real producers (what is known as the transition from Web 1.0 to Web 2.0). Due to the increasing number of heterogeneous users and information that is generated, their unpredictable behavior and the high dynamism of the network structure, users have to cope with a high degree of uncertainty when choosing who to interact to or what information to consume [1]. In order to deal with this uncertainty, users require tools that help them to make decisions regarding their activities within the network. Recommendation systems [2] [3], which are systems that provide effective recommendations about what action users can take or what information they can consume, can be effective tools for performing theses decision-support tasks.

In this paper, we present a persuasive social recommendation system for recipe recommendation in a social network (called receteame.com). The proposed system allows the recommendation of recipes taking into account aspects like persuasion, similarity, friendship, trust, reputation and user food tastes.

2 Main Purpose: Recommendation in Social Networks

Traditional recommender systems base their recommendations on quantitative measures of similarity between the user's preferences and the current items to recommend (i.e. content-based recommenders [4]), between the user's profile and the profile of other users with similar preferences (i.e. collaborative filtering recommenders [5]) and on combinations of both (i.e. hybrid recommenders [6]). However, [7] has stated the inability of current recommender systems to use the large amount of qualitative data available online to empower recommendations. Usually, recommender systems do not provide an explanation about the reasoning process that has been followed to come up with specific recommendations. Recommendations tend to come directly from the recommendation algorithm that runs the website and not from the acquaintances that a user has in his social network. However, this does not follow current trends on the Web, where discovering is becoming social and recommendations could be expected to come directly from acquaintances in a decentralised way. Moreover, people trust recommendations more when the engine can provide reasons for them [8]. Thus, what is understood as a good recommendation is changing from the one that minimises some error evaluation to the one that really makes people happier.

In addition, online recommender systems suffer from problems inherent to their use in complex social networks, where the number of users and/or items to recommend can be very high. In the case of collaborative filtering, for instance, the process for comparing two users with the aim of extracting their similarity requires that they have qualified the same objects, which can be unreaslistic in large social networks. Another major weakness of online recommender systems is their trustworthiness. In an open network with a large number of users it is impossible to ensure that all views expressed are true opinions of users and there is no tampering with the resulting recommendations. In order to overcome these problems, it is necessary to embed a social layer in current recommender approaches, taking into account aspects such as the generation of arguments that support recommendations, reputation and trust. Therefore, there are a number of open challenges for the development of a new generation of recommender systems [7], such as *exposing underlying assumptions* behind recommendations, *approaching trust and trustworthiness* from the perspective of backing recommendations and *providing rationally compelling arguments* for recommendations. Our work involves a contribution in these areas, presenting a persuasive social recommendation system for recipe recommendation in a social network.

3 Demonstration: receteame.com

receteame.com[1] is a website that uses a persuasive social recommendation system to recommend recipes customized for each user. The system retrieves recipes from the Internet, automatically calculates their nutritional information and dietary restrictions and uses this information to make recommendations. The site runs an intelligent algorithm (based on argumentation techniques and social network analysis) to learn the tastes and needs of each user and recommend fully customized recipes. *receteame.com* is able to learn user preferences from two main sources of information: from the votes that users give to each recipe, and, if the user is registered within Facebook, from the activity of the user and friends, and thus can propose new recipes that the user may like.

Once registered in the system, the user can use the *"Recommend me"* button for obtaining a recommendation that matches the user's taste and dietary restrictions. This action launches the persuasive social recommendation algorithm that implements the main recommendation functionality of the website. The algorithm receives a recipe recommendation query for a specific user, with a footprint that can include parameters describing the user profile (preferences and tastes, dietary restrictions, etc.) and the context of the query (e.g. if the

---

[1] http://www.receteame.com; http://buscador.receteame.com

user is looking for a main course, the number of dinner guests, etc.). With this query and the recipe footprint, the algorithm performs two main searches to select a potential set of recipes to recommend to the user. On the one hand, the algorithm follows a content-based recommendation approach to generate a list of recipes that match the recipe footprint. However, note that the accuracy of recommendations generated by this process completely relies on the amount and accuracy of previous votes that the user made to recipes with similar footprints. Therefore, it is highly influenced by the *cold start problem* (i.e. new users do not have rated recipes) and the drawbacks of applying traditional recommendation approaches on large social networks. To overcome these problems, the algorithm performs an alternative search that follows a social recommendation approach.

On the other hand, the algorithm selects a set of users of the system (the set of friends of the target user and some randomly selected set to avoid the cold start problem when the target user is new on the system and does not have many friends) and spreads the query to obtain recommendations from these users. Each user that has received the query selects a set of recipes that match the original query from his own set of known recipes (those voted by this user). Then, for each user, this part of the algorithm generates an ordered list of recipes to recommend according to three criteria: 1) the preferences of the user that is being asked for recommendations, for instance, taking into account the votes of the user; 2) the preferences of the target user, for instance, taking into account the votes of the target user to a recipe (if any); and 3) previous recommendations. This values calculates the confidence on the recommendation of a recipe according to previous recommendations made between the same pair of users.

With the full set of recommended recipes from other users, the algorithm makes an overall ranking of recipes employing three social criteria parameters: 1) the trust on the user who had recommended a recipe from the point of view of the target user and his friends: this parameter is calculated by using a direct trust evaluation between these two users, and, if any, the trust evaluations of the friends of the target user that are also friends of the user that made the recommendation; 2) the reputation of the user who had recommended a recipe: this is a global parameter calculated by computing the average trust regarding all recommendations made by one user in the network; and 3) the strenght of the friendship between the target user and the user that had recommended the recipe: this parameter is calculated by using several predictive friendship variables [9] and depends on the activity of the target user on the social network where the algorithm operates (e.g. Facebook).

The result of this process is a unique and ordered list of recipes to recommed to the target user. Finally, the algorithm mixes the recommendations that has obtained from both searches, assigning weights to ponderate content-based and social recommendations, and selects the best recommnedation to propose. This process also includes an internal agreement procedure based on argumentation techniques, which allows the algorithm to promote those recommendations that come from users that are able to provide better justifications for them [10].

4 Conclusions

This work presents a persuasive social recommendation system for the recommendation of recipes. The system is embedded in the website *receteame.com* that is active on the Internet and has more than 2.000 registered users and 30.000 recipe views up to date. We are currently working on making the recommendation process faster and increasingly more accurate and on adding new functionalities to the website. For example, allowing users to add recipes or their own versions of recipes that are already on the web. We will also gradually introduce a more comprehensive dietary restrictions to include those diseases and intolerances that are not yet available. *receteame.com* may be able to recommend full menus in the future, such as a weekly menu for a family that takes into account the preferences of all members, or a menu for a dinner with friends where one can cook something with confidence that it will like to all guests.

Acknowledgments. This work was partially supported by MICINN TIN2011-27652-C03-01 and MINECO/FEDER TIN2012-36586-C03-01 projects of the Spanish government.

References

1. van der Aalst, W.M.P., Song, M.: Mining Social Networks: Uncovering Interaction Patterns in Business Processes. In: Desel, J., Pernici, B., Weske, M. (eds.) BPM 2004. LNCS, vol. 3080, pp. 244–260. Springer, Heidelberg (2004)
2. Adomavicius, G., Tuzhilin, A.: Toward the Next Generation of Recommender Systems: A Survey of the State-of-the-Art and Possible Extensions. IEEE Transactions on Knowledge and Data Engineering 17(6), 734–749 (2005)
3. Zhou, X., Xu, Y., Li, Y., Josang, A., Cox, C.: The state-of-the-art in personalized recommender systems for social networking. Artificial Intelligence Review 37(2), 119–132 (2012)
4. Pazzani, M.J., Billsus, D.: Content-Based Recommendation Systems. In: Brusilovsky, P., Kobsa, A., Nejdl, W. (eds.) Adaptive Web 2007. LNCS, vol. 4321, pp. 325–341. Springer, Heidelberg (2007)
5. Ben Schafer, J., Frankowski, D., Herlocker, J., Sen, S.: Collaborative Filtering Recommender Systems. In: Brusilovsky, P., Kobsa, A., Nejdl, W. (eds.) Adaptive Web 2007. LNCS, vol. 4321, pp. 291–324. Springer, Heidelberg (2007)
6. Burke, R.: Hybrid Recommender Systems: Survey and Experiments. User Modeling and User-Adapted Interaction 12(4), 331–370 (2002)
7. Chesñevar, C., Maguitman, A., González, M.: Empowering Recommendation Technologies, pp. 403–422. Springer (2009)
8. Linden, G., Hong, J., Stonebraker, M., Guzdial, M.: Recommendation Algorithms, Online Privacy and More. Communications of the ACM 52(5) (2009)
9. Fogués, R., Such, J., Espinosa, A., García-Fornés, A.: A Tool for Retrieving Meaningful Privacy Information from Social Networks. In: Infrastructures and Tools for Multiagent Systems, ITMAS, Editorial Universitat Politècnica de València, pp. 37–50 (2012)
10. Heras, S., Navarro, M., Botti, V., Julián, V.: Applying Dialogue Games to Manage Recommendation in Social Networks. In: McBurney, P., Rahwan, I., Parsons, S., Maudet, N. (eds.) ArgMAS 2009. LNCS, vol. 6057, pp. 256–272. Springer, Heidelberg (2010)

Automatic Electricity Markets Data Extraction for Realistic Multi-agent Simulations

Ivo F. Pereira[1], Tiago M. Sousa[1], Isabel Praça[1], Ana Freitas[1], Tiago Pinto[1], Zita Vale[1], and Hugo Morais[2]

[1] GECAD – Knowledge Engineering and Decision-Support Research Center, Institute of Engineering – Politechnic of Porto (ISEP/IPP), Porto, Portugal
{ifdsp,tmsbs,icp,1080598,tmp,tmcfp,zav}@isep.ipp.pt
[2] Automation and Control Group Department of Electrical Engineering Technical University of Denmark (DTU) Elektrovej build. 326, DK 2800 Kgs. Lyngby, Denmark
morais@elektro.dtu.dk

1 Introduction

Electricity markets worldwide suffered profound transformations. The privatization of previously nationally owned systems; the deregulation of privately owned systems that were regulated; and the strong interconnection of national systems, are some examples of such transformations [1, 2]. In general, competitive environments, as is the case of electricity markets, require good decision-support tools to assist players in their decisions. Relevant research is being undertaken in this field, namely concerning player modeling and simulation, strategic bidding and decision-support.

The functioning of liberalized markets over the last years provides valuable information most of the times available to the community. Lessons can be learnt from these last years to improve knowledge about markets, to define adequate players' profiles and behaviors, but also to test, validate and improve existing simulation tools, such as MASCEM (Multi-Agent System for Competitive Electricity Markets) [3, 4], making them suitable to represent reality and provide the means for a coherent and realistic analysis of the evolution of the electricity markets sector (or possible alternative pathways for its future).

Nowadays market operators make available to the general public, through their respective websites, numerous data relating to the electricity market and to the power systems [5, 6]. Data is available concerning market proposals, including quantities and prices; accepted and refused proposals and established market prices; proposals details; execution of physical bilateral contracts; statement outages, accumulated by unit type and technology; among others. Automatic tools, able to gather, storage, actualize and organize data from distinct real electricity markets will be a key issue to improve markets simulators and entities' capabilities by extracting knowledge and providing the means to really learn from these last years' experience.

The definition of realistic simulation scenarios, supported by real data, constantly updates as it is made available, as provided by such tools, greatly improves the capability of representing the different intervenient players as independent agents, and analyzing their interactions, and the influence they have on the market operation itself, thus turning multi-agent based simulators into powerful decision support tools.

2   Main Purpose

MASCEM is a multi-agent simulator of competitive electricity markets. The access to real data, its analysis and subsequent knowledge extraction, are the key factors for the definition of scenarios that allow simulations in MASCEM to have a fundamental role in the decision making of market participant players. One of the main contributions of this work is to ensure the access and storage of up-to-date data that is made available by market operators, in order to achieve realistic simulations.

The system's purpose is to allow easy access and constantly updated data concerning electricity markets transactions, which allows the subsequent definition of scenarios that illustrate markets' reality. The application was developed in order to be easily able to do the extraction, processing and automatic file storage of all the relevant data [7].

In order to pursue the system's purpose, we must be aware of the complete data available, since different operators make available different types of information, some of them providing even entities' technical characteristics and localization.

This process implies analyzing different types of files with different updating times. In fact there are ".xls" files, ".txt" files, ".pdf" files, and even other types, such as compressed files, that must be automatically downloaded, analyzed and saved. This implies a profound analysis and effective means of combining data, sometimes correlated data, appearing in different files.

Some requirements for the application are: assuring the treatment of different file types; reliability in storing all the gathered data; actualization of the extracted data whenever it is available. Another relevant issue is the efficiency regarding the treatment of great amounts of files, which, mainly in the initial use of the application may imply an enormous amount of files to assure gathering historic relevant data.

Within the developed automatic tool there are four major steps [7]:

- Download data - the download of several files containing the new data. The download depends on the website from which the data is being extracted, and it is performed accordingly to the data type of each file;
- Parse data - the extraction of the stored data from the downloaded files. The parsing of the data includes the analysis of the data fields of each file, from which the information and its associated value are taken;
- Store data - the storage of collected data in the database. The storage of the parsed data takes into account the necessary connections between different sets of data. This enables the data to be stored appropriately, respecting the interconnectivity and dependencies between all data;
- Mechanism for automatic data updates –Automatic definition of downloads periodicity. The availability timings of each file are analyzed so that the developed tool can process all available data as soon as possible.

Summarily, the system has the purpose of automatically searching for new electricity market data, extracting it from various websites, parsing the information, and storing it in the appropriate database, so that it can be used by MASCEM multi-agent simulator to model realistic scenarios [7]. This tool is also adaptive to the data availability timings; it is capable of dealing with different data formats, and it includes parallel processing capabilities to deal with multiple data sources processing.

3 Demonstration

In order to provide an adequate and useful environment the system provides a friendly user interface, which allows users to control all the extraction, storing, and updating process. Users can also track the information that is being processed at each time.

The interface makes the user aware of the whole process' completion, and allows the cancellation of any file's processing at any moment. Users are also provided with a display notification of errors that may arise during the process regarding the content of the files, or even failure of internet connection.

Fig. 1 presents the system interface during the extraction process, and as can be seen, for each file is shown its corresponding current state: *Downloading*, *Extracting* (only for compressed files), *Parsing*, *Saving* and *Finished* (completion status).

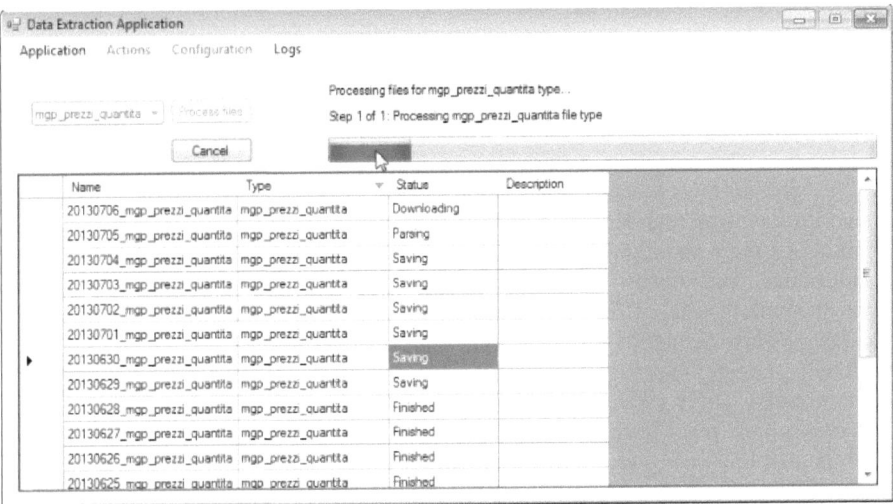

Fig. 1. System interface during the extraction process

The user can select the file type to be processed, or even several ones, in order to verify if there are new files available for download. Otherwise the user can also choose a file type that is being required for the definition of a particular scenario.

This tool includes the capability of managing files using parallel processing, allowing the system to deal with multiple data sources at the same time. The different data files are accessed through a machine learning approach for automatic downloads of new information available on-line. All procedures are secured by a reliability mechanism that prevents from the storage of incomplete or unviable information [7].

More technical aspects related to the performance of the application, such as the parallelism level, scheduling option configuration for each file and type of files supported by the tool and can be configured by the user. The system can be run on different computers, and configure the directory information files (*logger*) and the temporary directory of the files to be processed, saving the final information in the global database contained in the server.

This database is accessed by a scenarios generation mechanism of the MASCEM simulator, which uses the stored data to generate realistic scenarios.

4 Conclusions

This paper presents the development of a tool that provides a database with available information from real electricity markets, ensuring the required updating mechanisms. Some important characteristics of this tool are:

- Capability of collecting, analyzing, processing and storing real electricity markets data available on-line;
- Capability of dealing with different file formats and types, some of them inserted by the user, resulting from information obtained not on-line but based on the possible collaboration with market entities;
- Definition and implementation of database gathering information from different market sources, even including different market types;
- Machine learning approach for automatic definition of downloads periodicity of new information available on-line.

This is a crucial tool to go a step forward in electricity markets simulation, since the integration of this database with a scenarios generation tool, based on knowledge discovery techniques, provides a framework to study real market scenarios allowing simulators improvement and validation.

The possibility of using electricity market simulators capable of providing scenarios based on real data is an enormous asset for the study of electricity markets. Market operators and regulators are able to experiment and test new market rules and mechanisms, and obtain valuable insights regarding the consequences of such changes, both in what affects the market itself, and also in what way it influences the market players. Scenarios based on real data provide players the means for testing different strategic behaviors and analyzing their results. Real market players are able to thoroughly study competitor players' actions, coming to understand how they behave, act and react in different circumstances and contexts, meaning an invaluable tool for adapting their own behaviors to the expected actions from the competitors.

Acknowledgments. This work is supported by FEDER Funds through COMPETE program and by National Funds through FCT under the projects FCOMP-01-0124-FEDER: PEst-OE/EEI/UI0760/2011 and PTDC/SEN-ENR/122174/2010.

References

1. Shahidehpour, M., et al.: Market Operations in Electric Power Systems: Forecasting, Scheduling, and Risk Management, pp. 233–274. Wiley-IEEE Press (2002)
2. Meeus, L., et al.: Development of the Internal Electricity Market in Europe. The Electricity Journal 18(6), 25–35 (2005)
3. Praça, I., et al.: MASCEM: A Multi-Agent System that Simulates Competitive Electricity Markets. IEEE Intelligent Systems 18(6), 54–60 (2003)
4. Vale, Z., et al.: MASCEM - Electricity markets simulation with strategically acting players. IEEE Intelligent Systems 26(2) (2011)
5. Nord Pool – homepage, http://www.nordpoolspot.com (accessed on April 2013)
6. EPEX – European Power Exchange – homepage (April 2013), http://www.epexspot.com
7. Praça, I., et al.: Adaptive Tool for Automatic Data Collection of Real Electricity Markets. In: 1st Workshop on Intelligent Agent Tech, Power Syst. and Energy Markets, IATEM (2012)

Look, Who's Talking: Simulations of Agent Clusters

Kavin Preethi Narasimhan and Graham White

Cognitive Science Research Group
School of Electronic Engineering and Computer Science
Queen Mary University of London, London E1 4NS

Abstract. This paper demonstrates agents forming clusters that are spatially akin to human conversational groups. Demo works based on two different models: Model 1 operates at a global level to organize agents into predominantly circular clusters; whereas Model 2 operates at a local level to organize agents into variably shaped clusters.

Keywords: agent clusters, human conversational groups, social norms.

1 Introduction

Conversational clusters refer to groups of two or more people engaged in face-to-face interaction. People are quite sensitive to the presence of conversational clusters. E.g., if we were to walk in the corridor and find a group of people talking ahead of us, more often than not we'd avoid walking through the group. In unavoidable situations (e.g., due to a narrow corridor), we'd either dip our heads or utter "sorry" as we walk past the group. Such behavioural sensitivities expressed towards conversational clusters is a consequence of their spatio-temporal existence, which is made manifest by the arrangement of interlocutors' bodies in space [4]. This paper presents two different models (Model 1 and Model 2) to simulate agent clusters that are spatially akin to human conversational groups. Models have applications in social behaviour modelling for virtual characters (i.e., in AI) and for reasoning about the process of forming conversational groups (i.e., in Social Science).

2 Motivation

Most of the existing approaches to simulate conversational clusters are an adaptation of the social force model proposed in [2]. Examples include [5], [6] and [7]. The global strategy used in the social force model results in predominantly circular agent clusters. Empirical evidence endorses circle as one possibility (e.g., [4]) but never as the only possible spatial manifestation for conversational clusters. This paper implements a working version of the social force model (i.e., Model 1), and another contrasting model (i.e., Model 2), which adopts a local strategy to simulate agent clusters. The aim is to see if Models 1 & 2 simulate significantly different shapes for agent clusters.

3 Working of the Models: The Demo

Theoretical Underpinnings. According to Hall (1969), there are four distinct zones of space surrounding every individual – intimate, personal, social and public. Among these, he identifies the area just outside the personal zone (about 4 feet from an individual) as being ideal for face-to-face conversations. According to Kendon (1990), assuming that a hypothetical line is drawn extending outwards from the center of an individual's midriff, there is an area of space called the *transactional segment*, which extends upto 45 degrees on either side and reaches up to 4 feet from an individual's body [3]. When engaging in face-to-face conversations, interlocutors tend to overlap their individual transactional segments so as to have complete visual and auditory access to one another. The hypothetical space that arises out of overlapping individual transactional segments is referred to as an o-space [4].

The Simulation Platform. Kendon's (1990) and Deutsch's (1977) representation of humans as blobs with pointed noses motivated us to use a similar representation for agents (see figure 1). Similarly, a virtual equivalent of transactional segments are also defined for agents (see figure 2). Figure 3 shows an instantaneous capture of the simulation window with 25 agents spread across. Of these, agents with transactional segments are the ones that are stopped, while others were in motion at the time of generating the screen capture. Agents and the simulations have been implemented using Processing[1].

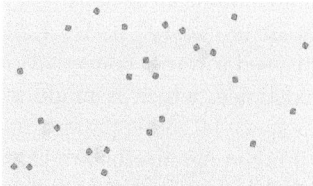

Fig. 1. Blob shaped agent   **Fig. 2.** Agent & its transactional segment   **Fig. 3.** The simulation window

Basic Working. During the simulation, each agent assumes one of the following states: stopped, walking or readjusting. When the simulation begins, each agent starts moving from a random (x,y) position in a random direction pointed to by its nose. This state is referred to as *walking*. At every time step t of the simulation, an agent stores and updates the following information in its state parameter: (i) its (x,y) position; (ii) the direction θ in which it is facing; (iii) a list of neighbours (i.e., other agents within its personal zone); and (iv) the current state (i.e., whether stopped, walking or readjusting). Movement of an agent is realized by updating its (x,y) position over time. An agent stops walking

---
[1] http://www.processing.org

whenever it recognizes other agents within, or on the boundary of, its personal zone. This state is referred to as being *stopped*.

In the stopped state, an agent might re-adjust its spatial stance (position and/or orientation) with respect to its neighbours depending upon Model 1 or Model 2. This state is referred to as *readjusting*. In this state, both Models 1 and 2, operate on a given agent together with its neighbours. However, the difference is that, for Model 1, an agent's neighbours will consist of its neighbours, *their* neighbours, and so on; whereas for Model 2, it will just be an agent's immediate neighbours. Based on the location of self (loc_{self}) and that of its neighbours[2], the collective centroid (C) and the average distance from self to centroid (E_p) are calculated as follows:

$$C = \frac{loc_{self} + \Sigma loc_{neighbours}}{|neighbours| + 1} \qquad (1)$$

$$E_p = \frac{d_{self,C} + \Sigma_{neighbours} d_{neighbour,C}}{|neighbours| + 1} \qquad (2)$$

Model 1: A Globally Driven Model. Model 1 explicitly motivates nearby agents that are stopped to form a circular o-space. Once established, sustaining the circular o-space governs all future changes to interactant agents' position and orientation. To achieve this, Model 1 strives to make $d_{self,C} = E_p$ by moving an appropriate distance towards or away from C. In essence, doing this coerces a collection of nearby agents to maintain an equal distance from their centroid. This eventually leads agents to being organized in a circular arrangement.

Model 2: A Locally Driven Model. Unlike the global strategy used in Model 1, Model 2 motivates self to alter its position and orientation with a view to maximize the overlap of its individual transactional segment with those of its immediate neighbours alone. Agents start off from the same state as in Model 1: stopped and ready to form conversational clusters by readjusting their spatial stance. Then, for each agent in neighbours, the heading of a vector pointing from loc_{self} to $loc_{neighbour}$, is calculated. If this heading is greater than 45 degrees (meaning outside the transactional segment), the excess angle accumulates in a variable called θ_{excess}. Based on the net value of θ_{excess}, a redefined target location is computed as follows:

$$t_{redefined} = \{loc_{self}.x + \cos(\theta_{self} + \theta_{excess}), \\ loc_{self}.y + \sin(\theta_{self} + \theta_{excess})\} \qquad (3)$$

Then, $t_{redefined}$ is divided by the total number of neighbours that lie beyond self's hypothetical transactional segment. Finally, self is motivated to move towards or away from C until $d_{self\text{-}to\text{-}redefined} = 0$.

---

[2] 'Self' denotes the agent which currently acts based on Model 1 or Model 2; 'neighbour' denotes every other agent within self's list of neighbours which differs for Model 1 and Model 2.

Figures 4 and 5 show an instantaneous distribution of agent clusters resulting from the respective models. After a prefixed stopping time, which is the same for both Models 1 & 2, an agent disengages from its neighbours and moves away. The same disengagement mechanism is used for both Models 1 & 2 – a vector pointing away from the locations of its neighbours is used for steering away.

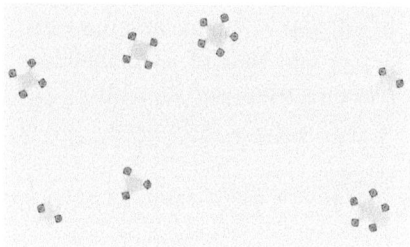
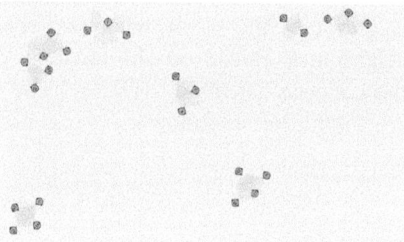

Fig. 4. Clusters resulting from Model 1   **Fig. 5.** Clusters resulting from Model 2

4 Conclusions

The paper introduces two different models to simulate agent clusters akin to human conversational groups. Coercing nearby agents to maintain equal distance from the centroid causes Model 1 to simulate explicitly circular agent clusters. On the other hand, allowing an agent to maximize the overlap of its transactional segment with those of its immediate neighbours, causes Model 2 to simulate agent clusters of different shapes.

References

1. Hall, E.T.: The hidden dimension, p. 119. Anchor Books, New York (1969)
2. Helbing, D., Molnar, P.: Social force model for pedestrian dynamics. Physical Review E 51(5), 4282 (1995)
3. Deutsch, R.D.: Spatial structurings in everyday face-to-face behavior: A neurocybernetic model. Association for the Study of Man-Environment Relations (1977)
4. Kendon, A.: Conducting interaction: Patterns of behavior in focused encounters (1990)
5. Jan, D., Traum, D.R.: Dynamic movement and positioning of embodied agents in multiparty conversations. In: Proceedings of the Workshop on Embodied Language Processing, pp. 59–66. Association for Computational Linguistics (June 2007)
6. Pedica, C., Vilhjálmsson, H.: Social perception and steering for online avatars. In: Prendinger, H., Lester, J.C., Ishizuka, M. (eds.) IVA 2008. LNCS (LNAI), vol. 5208, pp. 104–116. Springer, Heidelberg (2008)
7. Pedica, C., Högni Vilhjálmsson, H.: Spontaneous avatar behavior for human territoriality. Applied Artificial Intelligence 24(6), 575–593 (2010)

Developing Intelligent Virtual Environments Using MAM5 Meta-Model

J.A. Rincon, Carlos Carrascosa, and Emilia Garcia

Universitat Politècnica de València
Departamento de Sistemas Informáticos y Computación (DSIC)
Camino de Vera s/n, Valencia, Spain
{jrincon,carrasco,mgarcia}@dsic.upv.es

1 Introduction

An IVE (Intelligent Virtual Environment) is a virtual environment simulating a physical (or real) world, inhabited by autonomous intelligent entities[2]. Today, this kind of applications are between the most demanded ones, not only as being the key for multi-user games such as *World Of Warcraft*[1] (with more than 7 million of users in 2013)[2] but also for inmersive social networks such as *Second Life*[3] (with 36 million accounts created in its 10 years of history)[4]. It is in the development of these huge IVEs where the need of a quick and easy-to-use modelling toolkit arises.

Besides, Multi-Agent Systems (MAS) could be of interest to give support to these applications as a way to avoid big servers and to have some easy extensibility, scalability and fault tolerance.

This work is based on the MAM5 meta-model [1] which describes a method to design IVEs. MAM5 is based in the A & A meta-model [3] that describes environments for MAS as populated not only by agents, but also for other entities that are called *artifacts*. According to this, an IVE is composed of three important parts: artifacts, agents and physical simulation. Artifacts are the elements in which the environment is modelled. Agents are the IVE intelligent part. The physical simulation is in charge of giving the IVE the look of the real or physical world, allowing to simulate physical fenomena such as gravity or collision detection.

2 Main Purpose

In the last years, there have been different approaches for using MAS as a paradigm for modelling and engineering IVEs, but they have some open issues:

---

[1] http://eu.battle.net/wow
[2] http://www.statista.com/statistics/276601/number-of-world-of-warcraft-subscribers-by-quarter/
[3] http://www.secondlife.com
[4] http://massively.joystiq.com/2013/06/20/second-life-readies-for-10th-anniversary-celebrates-a-million-a/

low generality and then reusability; weak support for handling full open and dynamic environments where objects are dynamically created and destroyed.

As a way to tackle these open issues, and based on the MAM5 meta-model, we have developed the JACALIVE framework. It provides a method to develop this kind of applications along with a supporting platform to execute them. Figure 1 shows the steps that should be followed in order to develop an IVE according to the JACALIVE framework.

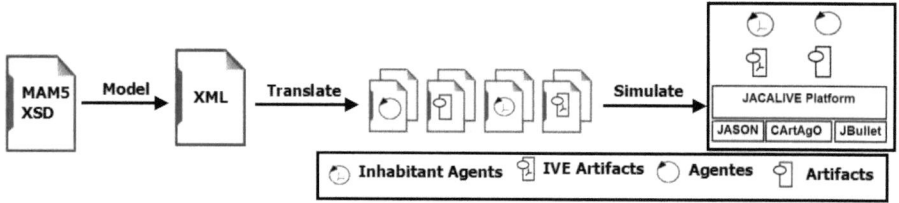

Fig. 1. General Scheme, JACALIVE

1. Model: The first step is to design the IVE. JACALIVE provides an XSD based on MAM5 meta-model. According to it, an IVE can be composed of two different types of workspaces depending on whether they specify the location of its entities (`IVE_Workspaces`) or not (`Workspaces`). It also includes the specification of agents, artifacts and the norms that regulate the physical laws of the IVE Workspaces.
2. Translate: The second step is to automatically generate code templates from design. One file template is generated for each agent and artifact. JACALIVE agents are rational agents based on JASON. The artifacts representing the virtual environment are based on CArtAgO. The developer must complete these templates and then the IVE is ready to be executed.
3. Simulate: Finally the IVE is simulated. As is shown in Figure 1, JACALIVE platform uses JASON, CArtAgO [4] and JBullet[5]. JASON offers support for BDI agents that can reason about their beliefs, desires and intentions. CArtAgO offers support for the creation and management of artifacts. JBullet offers support for physical simulation. JACALIVE platform also includes internal agents (JASON based) to manage the virtual environment.

3 Demonstration

In this section we test the versatility of the JACALIVE framework by means of the development of a case study. The selected case study is an example of modular robotics [5]. A modular robot is a self-configuring system with variable morphology. Robots of this kind are able to adapt their shape to changes in the environment. Specifically, we want to build an IVE able to simulate virtual

---

[5] http://jbullet.advel.cz/

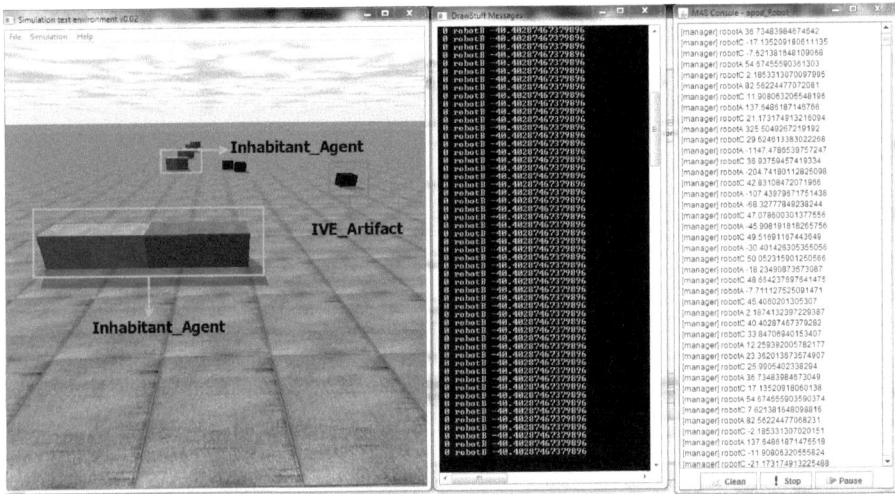

Fig. 2. Modular robotic simulation

modular robots. These robots have the ability to change its shape depending on environment conditions. In the present example, an agent's body is initially formed by two IVE_Artifacts. Following the main steps of the development of this case study are summarized:

1. Model: The design of the case study is formalized using an XML based on the JACALIVE XSD. The main parts of this XML are: (i) An IVE_Workspace called apodoRobot_Workspaces. (ii) Fifteen IVE_Artifacts. One of the attributes of these artifacts is whether they are linkable or not, that is, if they can be joined to other artifacts or not. Three of these artifacts are linkable; two are unlinkable and the other ten form the bodies of the inhabitant agents. (iii) Five Inhabitant_Agent. Each one of them is associated to two of the previously defined IVE artifacts.
2. Translate: From the XML file that represents the design of the system, the JACALIVE framework automatically generates the following files: (i) Fifteen java files representing the IVE artifacts (Ten files representing the agent bodies, three files corresponding to linkable artifacts and two files correspond to unlinkable artifacts). (ii) Six JASON files that correspond to the agents. (iii) A file called jacalive.asl, where the developer programs the communication between agents and artifacts.
3. Simulate: Entities that have been modeled and programmed in the previous steps are simulated. Since JACALIVE physical engine handles the IVE physics simulation, any visualization engine can be used to view the simulation. In this case study the render used is implemented with OpenGL. Figure 2 shows an snapshot of the simulation.

4 Conclusions

In this paper we present a framework for the design and simulation of IVEs. This framework differs from other works in the sense that it integrates the concepts of agents, artifacts and physical simulation. Besides, IVEs developed using the JACALIVE framework can be easily modified thanks to the XML modellation and the automatic code generation.

Following the MAM5 perspective, the modules used to interact with the developed IVEs are uncoupled from the rest of the system. It allows to easily integrate different kinds of modules as needed. For example, it allows to adapt the visualization render to the requirements of the specific IVE we want to simulate.

This work is partially supported by the TIN2012-36586-C03-01, PROMETEOII/2013/019 and the FPI grant AP2013-01276 awarded to Jaime-Andres Rincon.

References

1. Barella, A., Ricci, A., Boissier, O., Carrascosa, C.: MAM5: Multi-Agent Model For Intelligent Virtual Environments. In: 10th European Workshop on Multi-Agent Systems (EUMAS 2012), pp. 16–30 (2012)
2. Luck, M., Aylett, R.: Applying artificial intelligence to virtual reality: Intelligent virtual environments. Applied Artificial Intelligence 14(1), 3–32 (2000)
3. Omicini, A., Ricci, A., Viroli, M.: Artifacts in the A & A meta-model for multi-agent systems. Autonomous Agents and Multi-Agent Systems 17(3), 432–456 (2008)
4. Ricci, A., Viroli, M., Omicini, A.: CArtAgO: A framework for prototyping artifact-based environments in MAS. In: Weyns, D., Parunak, H.V.D., Michel, F. (eds.) E4MAS 2006. LNCS (LNAI), vol. 4389, pp. 67–86. Springer, Heidelberg (2007)
5. Schmickl, T.: How to engineer robotic organisms and swarms? In: Meng, Y., Jin, Y. (eds.) Bio-Inspired Self-Organizing Robotic Systems. SCI, vol. 355, pp. 25–52. Springer, Heidelberg (2011)

Multi-agent Platform for Designing Real Time Adaptive Scheduling Systems

Petr Skobelev[1], Denis Budaev[2], Vladimir Laruhin[2], Evgeny Levin[2], and Igor Mayorov[2]

[1] Institute of the Control of Complex Systems of Russian Academy of Science,
petr.skobelev@gmail.com,
[2] Smart Solutions, Ltd., Russia, Samara
{budaev,vl,levin,imayorov}@smartsolutions-123.ru

Abstract. The multi-agent platform for development of adaptive scheduling systems for real time resource management is considered. The platform provides rapid prototyping of multi-agent systems for real time resource management and helps to reduce man-efforts and time of developments in 2-3 times. The platform was applied for developing multi-agent scheduling systems for managing resources in aircraft jet production, load balancing in computer grid networks and energy production in power-, gas- and heating networks.

Keywords: multi-agent technology, adaptive scheduling, distributed problem-solving, optimization, simulation, real-time.

1 Introduction

Modern enterprise resource management systems are basically characterized by the application of classical methodology and platforms of resource allocation, scheduling and optimization based on methods of linear and mixed programming, different heuristics, genetic algorithms and others [1, 2].

However, the increase in complexity, high uncertainty and dynamics of modern business as well as a number of other challenges of modern real-time economics do not allow efficient use of the traditional combinatorial mathematical and heuristic methods. In this regard, more and more scientists and engineers turn to multi-agent technologies [3,4], that give appropriate solutions based on methods of distributed problem solving with conflicts discovery and finding trade-offs by negotiations in order to achieve the balance of interests (consensus) of all parties involved.

However. in spite of significant progress in developing multi-agent solutions and technology, platforms and tools in last decade the design process for multi-agent adaptive scheduling systems still remains to be very resource- and time-consuming.

We present multi-agent platform for development of adaptive scheduling systems for real time resource management. The platform applied for developing of multi-agent scheduling systems for managing resources in aircraft jet production, load balancing in computer grid networks and energy production in power-, gas- and heating networks.

The first experience confirms that the platform provides rapid prototyping of multi-agent systems for real time resource management and helps to reduce man-efforts and time of developments in 2-3 times.

2 Multi-agent Platform for Developing Adaptive Scheduling Solutions

Multi-agent platform is designed to automate developed methodology and increase quality and efficiency of development process for creating real time resource management systems for application in different problem domains.

The developed multi-agent platform combines functionality of basic adaptive scheduler that can be easily modified for new domain with simulation environment. This is useful for experiments with the different demand and resource network (DRN) models, methods and algorithms.

Functionality of multi-agent platform provides possibility for end-users to specify initial network of resources, form sequence of events manually or automatically or load it from external files, make individual setting for all demands and resources, run simulations with different parameters and visualize process and results of experiments.

Example of one of the screens with user interface of the platform representing results of experiments discussed below is shown in Fig. 1.

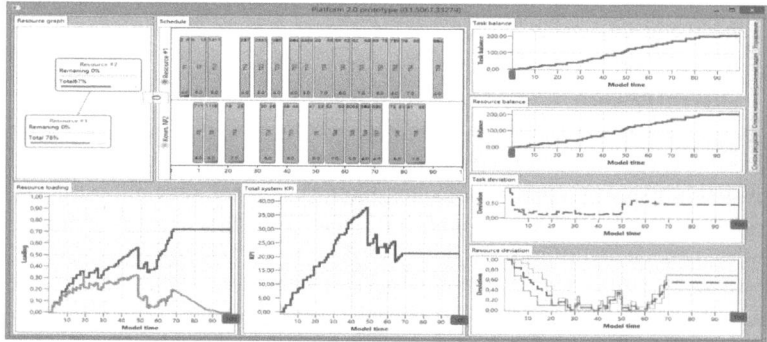

Fig. 1. General view of platform user interface

In Fig. 1 one can find the windows presenting resource network, Gantt chart with the schedule of the resources, orders and resources workload and satisfaction and some others.

As a result of simulation, a number of useful charts and diagrams can be visualized or exported in Excel files for future analysis:

- graph of network loading – shows how busy all resources are loaded;
- Gantt chart – shows allocation of demands to resources in time;
- communication activity diagram – shows how many messages are generated in the platform at any moment of time;

- satisfaction of demand and resources and system as a whole – shows how level of satisfaction is changing during the process of simulations;
- orders execution – shows how good is the execution of orders in time;
- resource utilization – shows how busy are resources at different moment of time;
- log of messages – shows message exchange between the selected agents in text of graphical view;
- log of decision-making – presents the results of decision-making for the selected agent;
- log of financial transactions – shows virtual money transfer between the demand and resource agents.

The architecture of the platform includes the following components: initial scene editor, event generator, event queue for main classes of events, multi-agent world built as virtual market, basic classes of demand and resource agents and negotiation protocols, visual components for editing agents setting and visualization of results, export and import of data, logging and tracking of messages and agent financial transactions and other specific components.

These components can be easily adjusted for new domains and applications.

3 Examples of Experiments

Let us consider the platform operation with an example of demands and resources network. We will assume that there are two servers in computational grid network, that receive the flow of orders with requirement of due date of completion and given financial resources.

This example shows that the system can react to the occurring changes in the plan operatively adjusting the plan to decrease the negative effect of the changes. Activity of agents negotiations changes correspondingly and can be used to observe general state of the system and how it is operating at the moment, how much it is loaded, etc.

In the chart of virtual money balance (account), one can notice the increase of virtual balance of the resources that gain money by selling free slots to the orders.

The chart of deviation of system resource agents shows how system decreases deviation from the ideal even after introducing minor and major disturbances. For example, at the 40th moment of simulation time there was a big disturbance that was managed by the system during about 10 steps of simulation time.

Similar chart for orders agents also shows system ability to adaptation for the changes. System load chart provides general information on changes in loading resources with orders. In charts, one can also observe the changes of the sum of objective function values for system agents. Adaptive reaction to the worsening of the situation can be noticed as the total system target improvement after another round of negotiations.

At the moment platform is already used for rapid prototyping of new multi-agent systems for resource management and was successfully applied for computational networks, project management, production planning, energy production in power-, gas- and heating networks and some other applications [5,6,7,8,9].

The first experience shows that the developed platform allows making the development of the system 3-4 times faster comparing with traditional developments that is especially important for industrial commercial applications.

4 Conclusions

Multi-agent platform allows making a step in implementing the advantages of multi-agent approach to scheduling and optimization of resources in real time.

The further development of the platform supposes using of ontology editor for introducing new problem domains, generalization and advancing of virtual market mechanisms with self-regulation of agents and improving of results visualization.

The experience in platform application shows significant possibilities for increasing the quality and efficiency of development process with the reducing the required labor, delivery time and costs for clients.

References

1. Leung, J.: Handbook of Scheduling: Algorithms, Models and Performance Analysis. Chapman & Hall, CRC Computer and Information Science Series (2004)
2. Voß, S.: Meta-heuristics: The State of the Art. In: Nareyek, A. (ed.) Local Search for Planning and Scheduling. LNCS (LNAI), vol. 2148, pp. 1–23. Springer, Heidelberg (2001)
3. Shoham, Y., Leyton-Brown, K.: Multi-Agent Systems: Algorithmic, Game-Theoretic, and Logical Foundations. Cambridge University Press, New York (2009)
4. Meisels, A.: Distributed Search by Constrained. Springer (2008)
5. Skobelev, P.: Multi-Agent Systems for Real Time Resource Allocation, Scheduling, Optimization and Controlling: Industrial Applications. In: Mařík, V., Vrba, P., Leitão, P. (eds.) HoloMAS 2011. LNCS, vol. 6867, pp. 1–14. Springer, Heidelberg (2011)
6. Madsen, B., Rzevski, G., Skobelev, P., Tsarev, A.: Real-time multi-agent forecasting & replenishment solution for LEGOs branded retail outlets. In: Proc. of 13th ACIS Int. Conf. on Software Engineering, Artificial Intelligence, Networking and Parallel/Distributed Computing (SNPD 2012), Kyoto, Japan, August 8-10, pp. 451–456 (2012)
7. Granichin, O., Skobelev, P., Lada, A., Mayorov, I., Tsarev, A.: Cargo transportation models analysis using multi-agent adaptive real-time truck scheduling system. In: Proc. of the 5th Int. Conf. on Agents and Artificial Intelligence (ICAART 2013), Barcelona, Spain, February 15-18, vol. 2, pp. 244–249. SciTePress, Portugal (2013)
8. Goryachev, A., Kozhevnikov, S., Kolbova, E., Kuznetsov, O., Simonova, E., Skobelev, P., Tsarev, A., Shepilov, Y.: Smart Factory: Intelligent system for workshop resource allocation, scheduling, optimization and controlling in real time. In: Proc. of Int. Conf. "Manufacturing 2012", Macao, China. Advanced Materials Research, vol. 630, pp. 508–513 (2013)
9. Vittikh, V., Larukhin, V., Tsarev, A.: Actors, Holonic Enterprises, Ontologies and Multi-Agent Technology. In: Mařík, V., Martinez Lastra, J.L., Skobelev, P. (eds.) HoloMAS 2013. LNCS, vol. 8062, pp. 13–24. Springer, Heidelberg (2013)

An Agent-Managed Ad-hoc Social Network to Facilitate F2F Networking at PAAMS 2014

Ludo Stellingwerff and Giovanni E. Pazienza

Almende BV,
Westerstraat 50, Rotterdam 3016 DJ,
The Netherlands
{ludo,giovanni}@almende.org

Abstract. The world of social networks could greatly profit from using an approach based on multi-agent systems, in which *personal agents* running on the users' personal devices autonomously access information from different data sources (managed and combined by *context agents*) in order to bring physically together users that may have common interests. In this demonstration, we will present the first example of such a system, which has been specifically created to facilitate networking among PAAMS 2014 participants.

Keywords: Multi-agent systems, Context awareness, Social networks, Android.

1 Introduction

Social networks are one of the fastest developing areas of science. Nevertheless, despite their success, they have raised numerous criticisms especially due to privacy concerns and to the creation of 'virtual' ties in lieu of 'physical' ones. Also, they are generally self-contained (except for some limited links between specific social networks) and they lack of real-time data fusion features (excluding location, which is at times considered).

Our viewpoint is that the world of social networks would greatly profit from the use of an approach based on multi-agent systems, which could help to overcome many of the drawbacks listed above. Each user could have a virtual *personal agent* counterpart which manages part of the user's interactions and communicates autonomously with other virtual *context agents* that handle and combine data from different data sources, such as 'traditional' social networks, physical locations, and personal agendas.

The potential advantages of this approach are multiple: first, the *personal agent* is a proactive entity that can autonomously negotiate with other *personal agents*, for instance sharing information or planning meetings; second, *personal agents* are able to establish communications with several information sources (which may include sensors and cloud data) via other kinds of agents; third, there is little or no need to share data on centrally stored databases, since the *personal agents* have direct access to its user's personal device; fourth, the network can be created and destroyed ad-hoc at any time (for instance, forcing that *personal agents* communicate to each other only if running on devices that are located in the same wi-fi network during a given time window); fifth, all well-known strong points of multi-agent systems – such as scalability and robustness – apply to this system.

Thanks to this approach, the user is now living is a sort of 'augmented reality' environment where s/he has much more information about the people surrounding him or her; also, we have a basic implementation of an 'intelligent amplification' in which human beings and software agents collaborate to reach better performances. It is also important to mention that the social network connects the 'virtual world' with the 'physical world' by encouraging face-to-face meeting thanks to the information available in the cloud. It is important to mention that this demonstration has nothing to do with the well-known concept of agent-based modelling/simulation of social networks: this in neither a model nor a simulation, but real action involving human beings and software agents.

The demo presented at PAAMS 2014 and described in the next two sections is a particular instantiation of this approach, aimed at getting together PAAMS participants with similar scientific interests. Of course, it can be easily extended and tailored to a number of different applications.

2 Main Purpose

The main goal of our demo is presenting an agent-managed ad-hoc social network – called SMAAP – that facilitates face-to-face networking among the participants at PAAMS 2014. In events involving up to a few hundred people, such as PAAMS, it may happen (and it surely happens for larger meetings) that people are missing potential useful connections because they do not know each other.

This is exactly the role of SMAAP: a personal device hosting SMAAP will browse around searching for SMAAP users to whom the device owner may be interested in talking to (for instance, because they have used the same keywords or they have referenced each other in their PAAMS papers) and notify both users when they are close to each other, thus prompting a face-to-face communication. In conclusion, SMAAP will help to start conversations, and hopefully collaborations, that otherwise would have never occurred.

3 Demonstration

The demonstration to be held at PAAMS 2014 will consist of two parts: first, a short presentation including a demo featuring two test devices, which will be brought on stage by the presenter; second, a real-life test running throughout the duration of PAAMS and involving all participants owning an Android device and willing to take part to the experiment.

The main functionality of SMAAP can be summarised as follows: for each user, a personal SMAAP agent autonomously retrieves the user position as well as all the information about the keywords and the references of the PAAMS paper of that user. Then, when the *personal agent* of a user (say User A) finds out that another user (say, User B) to which s/he may be interested in talking to (for instance, somebody s/he has referenced in the PAAMS paper or has used the same keywords) is nearby[1], it prompts a notification message, like the one in Fig. 1(a). Now, user A can take five actions: 1) ignore the message by closing the notification window (the same message will not be displayed again); 2) localize User B in order to chat face-to-face; 3) read the paper of User B at PAAMS (if it exists); 4) check the LinkedIn profile of User B (if it exists); 5) request access to User B contact details, such as the telephone number. In the last case, the User B is notified that the User A has requested access to his/her personal contact details via the notification message shown in Fig. 1(b); such request may be accepted (by pushing the correspondent button) or denied (by closing the notification message). Also, User B has the same options described above to explore the information about User A, that is via LinkedIn, physical localisation, and PAAMS paper.

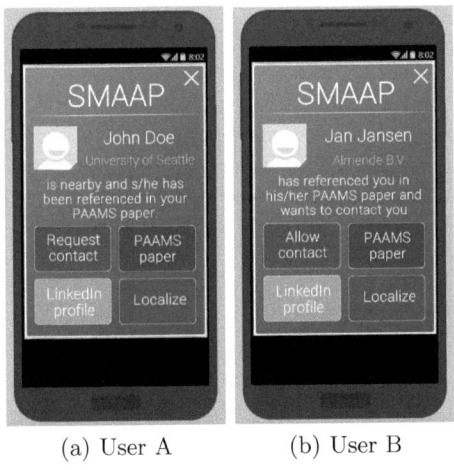

(a) User A (b) User B

Fig. 1. Mock-up of the SMAAP notification screens of User A (who establishes the contact) and User B (who has been contacted)

Besides the notification screen, a user has access to the position and to the list of SMAAP users nearby (see Fig. 2(a) and Fig. 2(b), respectively). Further interaction from these screens will be possible too.

From the technical point of view, SMAAP is an implementation of the Context-Aware Programming Environment (CAPE) [1] and it is built by using the agent platform Eve [2]; both works have been presented at PAAMS 2014. It is important to emphasise that without the novel features offered by CAPE and Eve, implementing a SMAAP-like system would have been difficult, if at all possible.

At the end of May, we will perform a test of SMAAP in an event at the University of Delft involving the students of the CS department. The participants will

---

[1] For this demo, the detection of the proximity among users is achieved by means of four 'beacon' smartphones dislocated throughout the meeting space.

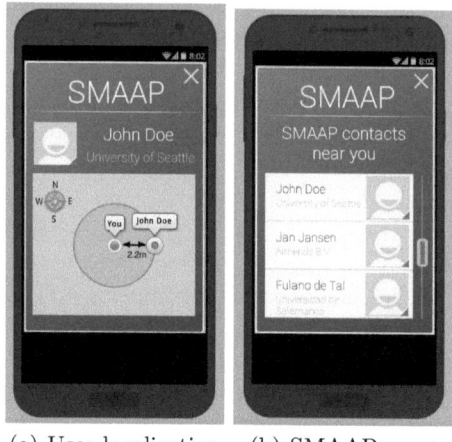

(a) User localization (b) SMAAP users

Fig. 2. Mock-up of the SMAAP screens for the user localisation and the overall list of SMAAP users nearby

be matched on the basis of their scientific interests, which will be autonomously retrieved by SMAAP agents from 'traditional' social networks as well as from university records. A video of this event will be presented at PAAMS 2014 and it will be used to promote the SMAAP system during the conference.

4 Conclusions

This demonstration has concerned an agent-managed ad-hoc social network whose main goal is to facilitate face-to-face meetings among the PAAMS 2014 participants. This system relies on the technical features of the programming environment CAPE and the agent platform Eve, both presented at PAAMS 2014, and it overcomes some of the typical drawbacks of existing social networks. Of course, the scopes and the fields of application of SMAAP can be easily extended beyond this conference, where it has been presented for the first time.

References

1. Stellingwerff, L., Pazienza, G.E.: An agent-based architecture to model and manipulate context knowledge. In: Demazeau, Y., Corchado, J.M., Zambonelli, F., Bajo, J. (eds.) PAAMS 2014. LNCS (LNAI), vol. 8473, Springer, Heidelberg (2014)
2. Stellingwerff, L., de Jong, J., Pazienza, G.E.: Practical applications of the web-based agent platform Eve. In: Demazeau, Y., Corchado, J.M., Zambonelli, F., Bajo, J. (eds.) PAAMS 2014. LNCS (LNAI), vol. 8473, pp. 268–278. Springer, Heidelberg (2014)

Author Index

Ahrndt, Sebastian 1
Albayrak, Sahin 1
Andersone, Ilze 13, 363
Argente, Estefanía 110
Ayoola, Olapeju Latifat 343

Barange, Mukesh 25, 315
Boissier, Olivier 110
Bonnet, Grégory 279
Bosman, Peter A.N. 351
Bosse, Tibor 38
Botti, Vicente 367
Bourdon, François 279
Budaev, Denis 383

Campillo-Sanchez, Pablo 319
Cao, Junyue 347
Carrasco, Sergio 359
Carrascosa, Carlos 379
Chevaillier, Pierre 25, 315
Chevrier, Vincent 207
Choudhury, Bikash 50
Choudhury, Subhrabrata 50
Ciarletta, Laurent 207
Claes, Rutger 62, 74
Claessen, Felix N. 351
Coninx, Kristof 74, 323
Créput, Jean-Charles 171
Crespo, Berta 291

Deconinck, Geert 74
de Jong, Jos 268
De Keukelaere, Camille 25
Delecroix, Fabien 86, 327
Dey, Piyali 50
Din, Shahab Ud 339
Di Napoli, Claudia 98, 331
Di Nocera, Dario 98, 331
Duchêne, Cécile 183, 355
Dutta, Animesh 50

Ebert, Philipp 1
Ekmanis, Martins 363
Esparcia, Sergio 110

Fähndrich, Johannes 1
Fiorino, Humbert 231
Freitas, Ana 371
Fuentes-Fernández, Rubén 291

Garcia, Emilia 379
García-Magariño, Iván 122
Gómez-Sanz, Jorge J. 291, 319
Griol, David 134, 335
Grundspenkis, Janis 363
Gutiérrez, Tomás Navarrete 207

Hanif, Shaza 146, 339
Heras, Stella 367
Holvoet, Tom 62, 74, 146, 323, 339

Jamont, Jean-Paul 159
Julián, Vicente 367

Kabil, Alexandre 25, 315
Koukam, Abderrafiaa 171
Kulikovskis, Guntis 363

La Poutré, Han 351
Laruhin, Vladimir 383
Lauri, Fabrice 171
Leemput, Niels 74
Levin, Evgeny 383
Li, Xuejin 347
Liefers, Bart 351
Liekna, Aleksis 363
Lindgren, Helena 303

Mangina, Eleni 343
Martin, Jorge 359
Maudet, Adrien 183, 355
Mayorov, Igor 383
Métivier, Marc 231
Miguel, Araceli Sanchís de 134, 335
Mogles, Nataliya M. 38
Molina, José Manuel 134, 335
Molina, Martin 359
Morais, Hugo 371
Morge, Maxime 86, 195, 327

Narasimhan, Kavin Preethi 244, 375
Nieves, Juan Carlos 303

Nikitenko, Agris 13, 363
Niu, Zhendong 347

Occello, Michel 159
Ondráček, Jakub 219

Palanca, Javier 367
Pauwels, Eric 351
Pazienza, Giovanni E. 256, 268, 387
Pěchouček, Michal 219
Pellier, Damien 231
Pereira, Ivo F. 371
Picault, Sébastien 183, 355
Piette, Eric 195
Pinto, Tiago 371
Praca, Isabel 371

Raievsky, Clément 159
Rincon, J.A. 379
Rossi, Silvia 98, 331
Routier, Jean-Christophe 86, 327

Skobelev, Petr 383
Sousa, Tiago M. 371
Stellingwerff, Ludo 256, 268, 387

Touya, Guillaume 183, 355
Treur, Jan 38

Vale, Zita 371
Vallée, Thibaut 279
Vandael, Stijn 74
Van den Berghe, Katrien 62
Vaněk, Ondřej 219

White, Graham 244, 375

Xavier, Daniela 291

Yan, Chunli 303

Zhang, Chunxia 347